THE APPROACHING FURY

VOICES OF THE STORM, 1820–1861

BOOKS BY STEPHEN B. OATES

.

The Whirlwind of War: Voices of the Storm, 1861–1865 (1998)

The Approaching Fury: Voices of the Storm,
1820–1861 (1997)

A Woman of Valor: Clara Barton and the Civil War (1994)

Portrait of America (2 vols., 6th edition, 1994)

Biography as History (1991)

William Faulkner, The Man and the Artist:
A Biography (1987)

Biography as High Adventure: Life-Writers
Speak on Their Art (1986)

Abraham Lincoln: The Man Behind the Myths (1984)

Let the Trumpet Sound:
A Life of Martin Luther King, Jr. (1982)

Our Fiery Trial: Abraham Lincoln,
John Brown, and the Civil War Era (1979)

With Malice Toward None:
A Life of Abraham Lincoln (1977)

The Fires of Jubilee: Nat Turner's Fierce Rebellion (1975)

To Purge This Land with Blood:
A Biography of John Brown (1970)

Visions of Glory (1970)

The Republic of Texas (1968)

Rip Ford's Texas (1963)

Confederate Cavalry West of the River (1961)

THE APPROACHING FURY

VOICES OF THE STORM, 1820–1861

STEPHEN B. OATES

HarperPerennial

A Division of HarperCollins*Publishers*

A hardcover edition of this book was published in 1997 by HarperCollins
Publishers.

HarperCollins books may be purchased for educational, business, or sales
promotional use. For information please write: Special Markets Department, HarperCollins Publishers, Inc., 10 East 53rd Street, New York, NY
10022.

First HarperPerennial edition published 1998.

Designed by Interrobang Design Studio

The Library of Congress has catalogued the hardcover edition as follows:

Oates, Stephen B.
    The approaching fury : voices of the storm, 1820–1861 / Stephen B.
Oates. — 1st ed.
        p.   cm.
    Includes bibliographical references and index.
    ISBN 0-06-016784-X
    1. United States—History—1815–1861. 2. United States—
History—1815–1861—Biography. 3. United States—History—Civil
War, 1861–1865—Causes. I. Title.
    E338.025   1997
    973.5—dc20   96-31965

ISBN 0-06-092885-9 (pbk.)

98 99 00 01 02 ❖ 10 9 8 7 6 5 4 3 2 1

To the memory of my father,
STEVEN THEODORE OATES
1905–1990

Events by themselves are unimportant; it is the perception of events that is crucial.

—JOHN FERLING

I think that no one individual can look at truth. It blinds you. You look at it and you see one phase of it. Someone else looks at it and sees a slightly awry phase of it. But taken all together, the truth is in what they saw though nobody saw the truth intact.

—WILLIAM FAULKNER

CONTENTS

THE SPEAKERS

Thomas Jefferson

Henry Clay

Nat Turner

William Lloyd Garrison

John C. Calhoun

Frederick Douglass

Harriet Beecher Stowe

George Fitzhugh

Stephen A. Douglas

Abraham Lincoln

John Brown

Jefferson Davis

Mary Boykin Chesnut

PREFACE

This is the story of the coming of the American Civil War. It is told from the viewpoints of thirteen principal players in the drama, from Thomas Jefferson and Henry Clay in the Missouri crisis of 1820 down to Stephen A. Douglas, Jefferson Davis, and Abraham Lincoln in the final crisis of 1861. A sequel, *The Winds of Civil War: Voices of the Storm, 1861–1865*, will recount the war from the perspectives of some of the same players, plus several new ones, including Mary Livermore, Robert E. Lee, Ulysses S. Grant, William Tecumseh Sherman, and John Wilkes Booth.

The fiction of William Faulkner inspired me to tell the story of the coming of the Civil War from multiple points of view. This technique illustrates the profound truth that the people of the past responded to events and to one another according to their perception of reality, and that their responses shaped the course of succeeding events. Like all people, antebellum Americans acted according to what they *thought* was true. Their perception of events, therefore, played a crucial role in the nation's inexorable drift toward civil war.

I resisted turning this book into a massive tome, bogging the narrative down with too many characters, too many shifting perspectives, and too many tangents into side issues. Determined to tell a taut, lean tale, I limited the number of characters to thirteen and focused on their perceptions of what brought the war on, which were escalating tensions over the complex slavery question and the rival political agendas, racial views, ideologies, and constitutional interpretations which that produced.

At first, I intended to write this book in the traditional third-person voice of the biographer and historian. When I tried to compose, however, I could not get beyond the first page. The trouble, I realized, was the detached third-person voice. It seemed to wring all the life out of my characters and the antebellum era. I decided, therefore, to try something different, something creative, and let my figures speak in the first person. It was a revelation. The technique gives the story a passion and a sense of immediacy and freshness it could not possibly possess had it been told in the third-person voice. With awe and not a little trepidation, I forged ahead with what became a narrative of interconnected dramatic monologues. It fascinated me to discover how the protagonist in one monologue becomes the antagonist in another.

Each speaker takes his or her turn on stage, serving as narrator for critical events in which he or she was the major instigator and participant or eyewitness. In adopting this technique, I was strongly influenced by Robert Altman's films *Nashville* and *Short Cuts,* which employ multiple viewpoints and segue ingeniously from one character to another. My narrative likewise segues back and forth from one historical figure to another, showing how their lives intersected—how they perceived and argued with one another, influenced each other's actions, and shaped the events that led to the Civil War. I also drew inspiration from Hal Holbrook's one-man portrayal of Mark Twain, *Mark Twain Tonight!,* and Julie Harris's staged impersonation of Emily Dickinson, *The Belle of Amherst,* both of which showed me the power and the possibilities of the dramatic monologue.

The Approaching Fury: Voices of the Storm is my impersonation of thirteen central figures in the coming of the Civil War. The metaphor in the title comes from them: one after another, they described the approach of war in terms of a gathering storm, a coming tornado. By necessity, my cast is dominated by white men, for they controlled the country in the antebellum era and were mainly responsible for the coming fury. To write the monologues, I steeped myself in the words of my speakers—their letters, speeches, interviews, reminiscences, and other recorded utterances—and then simulated how, if they were reminiscing aloud, they would describe historical events in which they were the principal players or eyewitnesses. In each case, I found that I had to get into character, much as an actor gets into a role. As much as possible, I used the actual words of my characters—their phrases, even whole sentences. When that was not possible, I simulated their language and rhythms of speech in order to recount developments in which they participated. As my references indicate, the events and themes in the monologues adhere to the actual historical record.

There are many dramatic scenes in my story. Most of these are a matter of the record and are fully documented in my notes. In several instances, however, I amplified the historical record when my speakers seemed to demand it; these occasions are pointed out in my references. An example is the 1857 meeting between John Brown and William Lloyd Garrison in Theodore Parker's house in Boston. The source for this meeting, *William Lloyd Garrison, 1805–1879: The Story of His Life*, written by his sons, tells us only that the two abolitionist adversaries "discussed peace and non-resistance together, Brown quoting the Old Testament against Garrison's citations from the New, and Parker from time to time injecting a bit of Lexington into the controversy, which attracted a small group of interested listeners." As the speaker for this segment of the story, Brown insisted on describing his exchange of views with Garrison. Not to do so, I realized, would be totally out of character for a man of Brown's righteous zeal. Since his and Garrison's beliefs are fully documented in the historical literature and are presented at length elsewhere in my text, I let Brown narrate what they surely said to one another during this momentous confrontation.

In short, in this and several similar instances, I simulated what took place by using facts imaginatively. The technique is not new with me. Allan Nevins, one of the greatest American historians of all time, wove historical data into graphic scenes and simulated dialogue in his widely acclaimed work of nonfiction, *The Emergence of Lincoln.** Like Nevins, I believe that a little fact-based creativity of this sort enhances our appreciation and understanding of the people of history.

A word about my portrayal of Stephen A. Douglas. The Little Giant was a profane man. The newspapers of the time reported that his speeches were punctuated with vulgar expressions and plenty of "Goddamn's," "hell's," and "by God's" that could be clearly heard in the galleries. One can imagine what he was like in private conversation. In re-creating his voice, I honored his character and let him curse with gusto. I do not think this technique violates the truth of history. On the contrary, it gets closer to what the historical Douglas was like than does a rigid adherence to his recorded utterances, which were highly sanitized.

---

*See Nevins, *The Emergence of Lincoln* (2 vols., New York: Charles Scribner's Sons, 1947), 1:151, 261–62, 2:11–20.

My portrayal of Nat Turner also requires an explanation. A couple of people who read the book in manuscript thought that I might have made Nat too erudite. I don't think so. Thanks to his extraordinary intelligence, to his intensive study of the Bible, which he could recite from memory, and to other books he saw in the Big House, and thanks to the influence of old Master Benjamin Turner, Nat was unusually literate, with a remarkable eloquence that earned him a county-wide reputation as a slave preacher. In fact, local blacks and whites alike regarded him as the most intelligent person in Southampton County, and I tried to present him that way.

There are many legitimate ways to write history. Indeed, the great strength of the field is its Renaissance breadth and diversity. By composing this book in the first person, from multiple viewpoints, I hope to suggest a bona fide alternative to the more traditional third-person approaches. This alternative allows us to walk in the footsteps of the people of history, to think their thoughts and feel their feelings, to experience them in all their flawed and glorious humanity. For me, assuming the roles of thirteen other human beings—which required that I show them all an equal degree of empathy—was the most inspiring and edifying adventure of my entire life as a writer. I hope that the first-person approach enables readers to relate directly to my speakers, to empathize with them, understand them, be touched and enlightened by them, without the intrusion of an omniscient, third-person narrator.

PROLOGUE

1. THOMAS JEFFERSON

Monticello, April twenty-second, 1820, in the seventy-seventh year of my life. I have never been so distressed, so full of dread, as I am over the momentous Missouri question. Long ago I ceased to read newspapers or to pay attention to public affairs, because I believed them in the hands of good Republicans and was content to be a passenger on the sloop that carries me ever closer toward the final shore. I am stooped now and lean with age. To threescore and seventeen years add two years of prostrate health, and you have the old, infirm, and nerveless body that I now am. I am unable to write but with pain and unwilling to think without necessity. Last year I suffered three dangerous and protracted illnesses, and my legs are so swollen that I find it difficult to walk. But I am not so infirm that I have to depend on my servants to get me through my daily regimen. I still rise at dawn and dress myself, still light my own fire in the fireplace, and still make my own way into my study in the south end of the mansion, which I am proud to say I designed and built myself. Here, before breakfast, I answer letters with a painful hand and a fearful heart, for the Missouri question, like a haunting nightmare, dominates almost every line I write.

My correspondents kept me informed about the crisis in Congress last year, when the Missouri Territory sought admission as a slave state, which at the time would have given the slaveholding states a one-vote margin over the non-slaveholding states in the Senate and opened the way for the expansion of slavery into the rest of the unorganized Louisiana Purchase region. To the Missouri enabling bill Congressman Tallmadge of New York proposed an amendment that prohibited white settlers from taking any more slaves into Missouri and decreed that all henceforth born there would be freed at age twenty-five. Since another New Yorker, Rufus King, led the fight for restriction in the Senate, I suspected that the amendment was the pernicious design of certain northern interests. Of course the amendment enraged the representatives of the slaveholding states! Congress has no power to free the slaves of a territory; the Federal Government is limited to powers explicitly enumerated in the Constitution, and the power to emancipate is not one of them. That power belongs exclusively to the states. Had I been there, I, too, would have blamed the crisis on Tallmadge and King and demanded that the rights of slaveowners in Missouri be respected and guaranteed.

Both sides threatened dissolution of the Union and civil war. So spoke the wisdom of the current generation of leaders! Yes, a compromise finally emerged, to take effect this year, which averts immediate disunion. I do not object to the first two parts of the compromise, which admit Missouri as a slave state and Maine as a free state, thus maintaining an equal number of slaveholding and nonslaveholding states. But the third part is fraught with danger, for it creates a geographical line across the rest of the Louisiana Purchase Territory, at the latitude of 36 degrees, 30 minutes, with slavery permitted south of the line but prohibited above it.

I am so utterly withdrawn from public affairs that nothing could arouse me but the adoption of a geographical line which on an abstract principle dangerously sectionalizes the country, separating the slaveholding states (the South) from the non-slaveholding states (the North), now and in the future. I wrote my friend John Holmes that this momentous question, like a fire bell in the night, awakened and filled me with terror. It is the death knell of the Union. For the moment it is hushed. But it is a reprieve only, not a final solution. For a geographical line, coinciding with a marked principle, moral and political, once conceived and held up to the angry passions of men, will never be obliterated; and every new irritation will mark it deeper and deeper until it provokes a storm of unrelenting fury.

The Federalists and their moribund party are behind this mischief: despairing of ever reviving the old divisions of Federalist and Anti-Federalist, they have devised a new division of slaveholding and non-slaveholding states, which, while it has a semblance of being moral, is at the same time geographical, and calculated to give the non-slaveholding states the ascendancy. The compromise line prohibits slavery in the far *larger* portion of the Louisiana Purchase Territory, which means that it will produce more non-slaveholding states than slaveholding states. The latter are doomed to become a permanent geographical minority. With the non-slaveholding states, it is but a question of power. With us, a geographical minority, it is *a question of existence*. What troubles me is that the treacherous Federalists seduced many of their old Republican opponents into a coalition with them that backed the compromise and its geographical line. It was a wicked party trick. Real morality is on the side that *opposed* the compromise and its provocative line.

I can say, truthfully, that there is not a man on earth who would sacrifice more than I would to relieve us of slavery, if there were any practicable way to do so. Slavery is a hideous evil, a foul blot on our country. It makes a mockery of our sacred creed, embodied in the Declaration of Independence: We hold these truths to be self-evident, that all men are created equal, that all men are entitled to life, liberty, and the pursuit of happiness. When I wrote those words, I meant *all men*, not just white men. It would not cost me a moment's thought if the slaves could be gradually freed and expatriated outside the United States, along the lines of the plan outlined in my *Notes on the State of Virginia*. Is there an enlightened man who would deem the plan unreasonable? It calls for the state of Virginia to free only those slaves who are born *after* the plan is adopted. Thus slavery would gradually wither away over the span of more than a generation. As for the emancipated blacks, they are first to live with their parents as charges of the state, which is to provide for their education in the arts, the sciences, and the practical aspects of tillage; they are to be freed at a prescribed age—eighteen for females, twenty-one for males—and then colonized outside Virginia so as to avoid having to assimilate into the state a race of black people who are inferior to the Caucasian in color, in beauty, and perhaps in intellectual faculty, especially the ability to reason. This unfortunate difference of color and perhaps of intellect is a powerful obstacle to the emancipation of these people. Many of their advocates, while wishing to free them, are also anxious to preserve the Caucasian's dignity and beauty. Hence the slaves, when freed, are to be removed beyond the reach of mixture.

I well remember the difficulties encountered with my plan back in 1785, when I was in Paris serving as U.S. minister to France. Madison and other men of virtue in Virginia were prepared to offer my plan as an amendment to the slave-code bill adopted by the Virginia General Assembly. But they refrained from doing so after witnessing what happened to petitions for gradual emancipation proffered by the Methodists and Quakers. The petitions "were not thrown under the table," Madison wrote me, "but were treated with all the indignity short of it." In fact, the House of Delegates *unanimously rejected* a bill for general emancipation sponsored by the Quakers. Since the public mind would not yet bear the proposition, Madison and my other friends decided not to propose my plan to the General Assembly. Madison wrote me about their decision, pointing out that my plan was doomed to fail and that an unsuccessful attempt to abolish slavery in Virginia would only rivet the chains of bondage tighter than ever and throw the entire movement backward.

When Jean Nicolas Démeunier called on me in Paris, and asked why the slave bill had been adopted without the clause of emancipation, I told him what Madison had told me. I paced back and forth, gesticulating as I spoke. "What a stupendous, what an incomprehensible machine is man!" I said. "Who can endure toil, famine, stripes, imprisonment or death itself in vindication of his own liberty, and the next moment be deaf to all those motives whose power supported him through his trial, and inflict on his fellow men a bondage, one hour of which is fraught with more misery than ages of the bondage he rose in rebellion to oppose in 'seventy-six. But we must await with patience the workings of an overruling Providence, and hope that Providence is preparing the deliverance of these, our suffering brethren. When the measure of their tears shall be full, when their groans shall have involved heaven itself in darkness, doubtless a God of justice will awaken to their distress, and provide for their liberation by diffusing light and liberality among their oppressors . . . or"—and I trembled when I said this—"a God of justice will liberate the sufferers by His exterminating thunder."

While in Paris, far away from political realities at home, I decided to take a crucial step, to set an example for other Virginians: I would free my own Negroes, all one hundred and eighty of them, and allow them to remain on my estates as tenants. But by 1790, after I returned to America, I realized that this idea was not practicable: I was too much in debt to British creditors to free any of my slaves. Also, my daughter was getting married and needed a dowry; I was obliged to give her twenty-seven of my Negroes, both children and adults, along with a thousand-acre estate in Bedford. Nor did I

proselytize for general emancipation in Virginia. Since public sentiment there had hardened against manumission and since I had been
appointed and confirmed as Washington's Secretary of State, I
deemed it best to leave the removal of slavery to the next generation—to the young men of Virginia, who would have my plan of
gradual emancipation and repatriation to guide them. Yes, I washed
my hands of the matter, contenting myself with the belief that as
time softened and enlightened the attitudes of men, others would be
able to accomplish what I could not.

Six years later, the Virginia House of Delegates rejected a recom-
mendation for gradual emancipation, and I accepted its verdict.
William Loughton Smith of South Carolina summed up the prevailing sentiment when he said that slavery had become "so engrafted
into the policy of the Southern states, that it cannot be eradicated
without tearing up by the roots their happiness, tranquillity, and
prosperity." Slavery is, then, a necessary evil, which cannot be prac-
ticably eradicated. Therein lies our dilemma. We have the wolf by
the ears, and we can neither hold him nor safely let him go. If we
hold on to slavery, the Negroes, I fear, will one day rise up in insurrection, and when that happens God will not be on our side. We
Caucasians will suffer the rage of His exterminating thunder. I do
indeed tremble for Virginia when I remember that God is just. But if
we let the blacks go free, allowing them to roam at will among us, it
would also lead to deadly convulsions. Deep-rooted prejudices entertained by the whites and ten thousand recollections by the blacks of
the injuries they suffered in bondage would prevent the two races
from ever living together in freedom and harmony. The result would
be a race war that would probably never end until one of the races is
annihilated in a tempest of whirling axes and exploding muskets.

What is the solution? I say without equivocation that *diffusion* is
the solution: the uninhibited expansion of slavery, without congressional restriction, across the entire Louisiana Territory and all future
territories. Diffusion would make the slaves individually happier
because it would spread them over a greater surface and among a
greater number of slaveowners. Diffusion would also foster emancipation. At present, the slaves are concentrated in the hands of a rela-
tively few wealthy planters who will never consent to the sacrifice of
their property for the good of society. Diffusion would break up that
concentration and facilitate emancipation by dividing the burden
among a greater number of masters.

By declining to restrict slavery, Congress would avoid the excitement and fear caused by an unconstitutional act of power, that is, an attempt by Congress to regulate the condition of the different descriptions of men composing a state. Only a state can regulate that. Nothing in the Constitution takes that power from the states and gives it to the general government. Once Congress goes beyond the Constitution to arrogate to itself the right to exclude slavery from a territory and thus a future state, its next step, in the hands of the non-slaveholding majority, will likely be to prohibit slavery in the states, thus producing the ultimate sectional crisis.

The Missouri Compromise has thrown me into a state of such profound melancholy that I find it difficult to sleep or to think about anything else. I mope in the parlor and on the portico, oblivious to the majestic panorama of my mountaintop, which affords a splendid view of the Blue Ridge Mountains to the east and Charlottesville, where my University of Virginia is being constructed, a few miles to the north. I fear that it will be up to the University, which I designed, to inculcate sound Republican values in the minds of Virginia's young men and protect them from "anti-Missourism." It is a canker eating the vitals of our national existence.

Yes, I fear for the future of our Union. I have been among the most sanguine in believing that it should be of long duration. I now doubt it much. When I look into the future, I shiver with foreboding, for I see the event of disunion at no great distance, and it is the direct consequence of this Missouri controversy. One day it will burst on us like a tornado.

I regret that I am now to die in the belief that the sacrifice of the generation of 1776, to establish self-government and life, liberty, and the pursuit of happiness in this country, is to be thrown away by the unwise and unworthy passions of our sons. My only consolation is that I live not to weep over it. If our sons would only contemplate the blessings they are throwing away, they would pause before they would perpetrate this act of suicide against themselves, and of treason against the hopes of the world. Alas, I fear the worst: they are to take the fatal leap from the precipice, and the Union is to crash with them on the rocks below.

To spare me from witnessing that, I welcome death. Besides, when all our faculties have left, or are leaving us, one by one—sight, hearing, memory, every avenue of pleasing sensation—and debility and malaise are left in their places, when the friends of our youth are all gone, and a self-destructive generation is risen around us whom we do not know, is death really an evil? I think not.

> *When one by one our ties are torn*
> *And friend from friend is snatched forlorn*
> *When man is left alone to mourn*
> *Oh! then how sweet it is to die. . . .*

PART ONE

STORM WARNINGS

2 . HENRY CLAY

I was Speaker of the House during the Missouri crisis and was shocked by the violent passions it provoked in the new Hall of Representatives, an elegant, domed, semicircular room modeled after a Greek theater. Day after day, men leaped to their feet and threatened disunion and civil war with reckless abandon. Tallmadge of New York, who precipitated the crisis, and Thomas Cobb of Georgia were the worst. They yelled and shook their fists at one another, ignoring me when I pounded my gavel and called for order.

"If you persist, the Union will be dissolved," Cobb said. "You have kindled a fire which a sea of blood can only extinguish."

"If disunion must take place," Tallmadge cried, "let it be so! If civil war must come, I can only say, let it come!"

What a vexed question! I told John Quincy Adams: "Within five years, I fear, the Union will be divided into three distinct confederacies."

Quite frankly, I sympathized with the restrictionists. I told them that I would gladly support a congressional ban against importing any more slaves into a new state if that were constitutional. The trouble was, I pointed out, it *wasn't* constitutional. Under the Constitution, only the people of Missouri had the right to approve or to ban slavery. I beseeched the restrictionists to listen to reason, pointing out that the *unrestricted* expansion of slavery into fertile new lands—the theory of diffusion, which was popular among Jeffersonians at the time—would work to end slavery in this country: it would enhance the well-being of the slaves and ease fears of abolition in those slaveholding states now overcrowded with blacks. In time, with slavery weakening as it spread across the West, free labor would drive down the value of slave labor; unable to compete, slavery would disappear, eliminated by economic growth and a national commitment to freedom. Slavery, I argued, would prove to be a *transient* phenomenon.

But the restrictionists were deaf to reason. So was antirestrictionist John Randolph of Virginia when cooler heads proposed a compromise. "There can be no compromise on this question," Randolph shrieked in his shrill voice. "God has given us Missouri and the devil shall not take it from us." When a northerner quoted the Declaration of Independence, Randolph angrily dismissed it as "a fanfaronade of metaphysical abstractions."

That outburst brought me out of the Speaker's chair. Metaphysical abstractions! My God, man, the Declaration of Independence is the *foundation* of our liberty. It is the *white man's charter of freedom*. It guarantees him the right to better himself, to go as far as his talent and toil will take him. Thanks to the Declaration, no white man is restricted to the condition of his birth; he has the right to rise above it, which is the very essence of our experiment in popular government. I am a prime example of how the system works: a poor, orphaned mill boy from the Virginia slashes, I was free to make myself into a successful planter and statesman—I was a United States Senator by the age of twenty-nine, Speaker of the House by the time I was thirty-three. And one day—I told men this in all candor—I expected to elevate myself to the Presidency and lead America into a golden new age of prosperity and world prominence. I would ask friends and adversaries with a smile: "Is there, frankly, anyone better qualified to be President? I have yet to meet the gentleman who is my superior."

In a desperate attempt to prevent disunion, I threw my support behind a compromise bill passed in the Senate; this was the bill admitting Missouri as a slave state and Maine as a free state and dividing the rest of the Louisiana Purchase into proslavery and antislavery spheres. In the Hall of the House, I went from desk to desk appealing to my colleagues' patriotism. Is compromise not the genius of our people? Is not the Constitution itself based on it? We finally broke the House deadlock over Missouri by resorting to a *coup de main:* we divided the compromise measure into three separate bills and persuaded recalcitrant members of both sides to accept separately what they opposed as a whole.

Thinking the question settled and the Union saved, I resigned as Speaker of the House (but not as a member) and returned home to attend to private matters. When I returned to Washington City, I was stunned to find Congress embroiled in yet *another crisis* over Missouri. As it happened, Missouri had adopted a state constitution that prevented free coloreds from entering its borders. Antislavery northerners leaped on the offending passage as a violation of the privileges and immunities clause of the Federal Constitution and demanded that Missouri delete the restriction or be kept out of the Union. This in turn provoked southerners to renewed threats of secession and war. Unhappy subject! This time, however, my sympathies were with my fellow southerners. It seemed to me that northerners were harassing Missouri unfairly, since few places in the country allowed free coloreds equal privileges and immunities with whites. To make matters worse, my resignation as Speaker left the House rudderless in the currents of the controversy. When nobody else would do so, I took charge and begged, instructed, adjured, supplicated, and exhorted my northern colleagues to have mercy on the white people of Missouri. In the end I won a majority of Congress to my compromise proposal, which allowed Missouri to retain its exclusion clause as long as the legislature pledged itself never to restrict persons who were or might become U.S. citizens. It was, I admit, a bit of political legerdemain, upholding both the supremacy of the Federal Constitution and the Missouri restriction that flouted it. Yet it avoided catastrophe and earned me kudos throughout the country as a compromiser for whom Union is his motto, conciliation his maxim. I told a dinner audience in Washington that the slavery question was now happily settled and that mutual forbearance and mutual toleration would restore concord and harmony to the country.

But to tell the truth, slavery troubled me. Like my mentors, Jefferson and Madison, I am a slaveowner. And like them, I hate the institution and wish it banished from the face of our country. There are men who doubt my sincerity, contending that it is not possible to be an antislavery slaveowner. Yet my critics will find my public utterances consistent in damning bondage as the greatest of human evils and an appalling stain upon the American name. This I learned from George Wythe, a gentleman of the Enlightenment, a signer of the Declaration of Independence, and a mentor of Thomas Jefferson and many other notable Virginians. I fell under Mr. Wythe's spell while working as a young man in the clerk's office in the High Court of Chancery in Richmond. Mr. Wythe, the chancellor, was a childless widower who delighted in molding the character of young men and helping them on to legal and political prominence. He befriended me and often took me to his home, where we spent many an hour in intense conversation in his library. I shall never forget the sight of this bald and brilliant gentleman, unaffected by his crippled hand, denouncing slavery as "a great political and moral evil" and expatiating on the "sacred cause" of gradual emancipation. Soon I found myself echoing his words in animated conversations with my acquaintances.

Under Mr. Wythe's guidance, I became a lawyer and was soon admitted to the Virginia bar. I was then only twenty years of age, a tall, slender, loose-jointed lad with prematurely white hair, glittering gray eyes, and a practiced smile. My mouth, however, was so wide and thin that I could never learn to spit. Already, I admit, I had a fondness for bourbon, cards, snuff, and good-looking women.

In 1797, thinking that the new state of Kentucky offered better opportunities for a young attorney on the rise, I migrated to the bluegrass state owning only the clothes I had on and the horse I was riding. I'll never forget the day I rode into Lexington and headed down the rutted, unpaved main street of this "Athens of the West," situated on a bend in the Kentucky River. I made my way past a train of emigrant wagons from the Wilderness Road and droves of bellowing cattle, with the odor of manure and whiskey pungent on the wind. The plank sidewalks teemed with rowdy men dressed in buckskin and homespun—one offered to share a bottle of whiskey with me over a game of cards, another challenged me to a wrestling match. I was struck by the bombast and gusto, by the *restless aggressiveness,* of the men I met, their temperament being so much like my own. Wonderfully profane, they tossed down glasses of raw whiskey in Lexington's saloons and wallowed in the pleasures of its bawdy houses. I would soon demonstrate that I could gamble, drink, wench, and cuss with any man in town.

Kentucky, of course, was a slave state, and Negroes were everywhere in Lexington; they drifted along like flotsam in a moving sea of whites, their faces devoid of expression. Near the public square, a gang of Negroes was constructing a wooden edifice, singing in that sad, mysterious way of theirs. In a muddy corner of the square stood a pen with a dozen or so slaves in it; they were awaiting auction like cattle. The spectacle disgusted me. It had no place in our system. The square also had a whipping post where "incorrigible or delinquent Negroes" were publicly flogged. As I approached, a male slave was getting a severe whipping for some offense, probably for running away, and his blood-curdling screams had attracted a crowd. *Crack* went the whip across his bare back. *Crack, crack.* Thirty-nine times, I counted. His screams made my skin crawl.

In the days that followed, I set about ingratiating myself with the leading townspeople, many of them transplanted Virginians like me. I even joined a "debating society" that met in a smoky tavern. There I diligently polished my oratory, learning to stress points with a graceful sweep of the arm and a gesture of the snuffbox.

Just turned twenty-one, a member of the Lexington bar for only one month, I also plunged into an incipient abolition movement, aligning myself with a group of outspoken reformers who called for a new state constitution that would provide for general, gradual emancipation, similar to the plan in Jefferson's *Notes on the State of Virginia*. On the platform and in the local newspaper, I beseeched Kentuckians to rid themselves of the curse of slavery: "Can any humane man be happy and contented when he sees near thirty thousand of his fellow beings around him, deprived of all rights which make life desirable, transferred like cattle from the possession of one to another?" Like Jefferson, I pointed out that blacks were not the only victims of bondage. "All America acknowledges the existence of slavery to be an evil, which while it deprives the slave of the best gift of heaven, in the end injures the master too, by laying waste his lands, enabling him to live indolently, and thus contracting all the vices generated by a state of idleness. If it be this enormous evil, the sooner we attempt its destruction the better."

The opponents of emancipation, especially the prominent slaveholders in town, were furious with me. Who the hell was this brash and beardless boy to lecture us! they cried. As it turned out, the vast majority of white Kentuckians objected to emancipation in any form, lest it result in amalgamation, in racial violence and chaos. In 1799 they sent an overwhelming number of anti-emancipation delegates to a state constitutional convention, which went on to draft a new charter that incorporated the proslavery provisions of the old. And so the reform movement went down to defeat in Kentucky, crushing my hopes that my adopted state might lead the way in removing the curse of slavery from our shores.

It was one of the greatest disappointments of my life. Yet I'm a realist. What was the point in crusading for an unpopular cause? I accepted the will of the majority and blended into my Kentucky environment. In the same year Kentucky turned back the gradual-emancipation movement, I bought a slave and married my dear Lucretia, the daughter of Lexington's most prosperous businessman and speculator. I chose my fixed attachment carefully—after all, there is no remedy for an unhappy choice! Lucretia had the qualities I most admired in a woman: she was loyal, amiable, practical, and efficient, and she came from an excellent family. While she managed our home, I built a successful law practice. By age twenty-eight, I'd risen to the top of the legal profession in Kentucky. Before I turned thirty, I'd acquired a plantation near Lexington, named it Ashland, and bought additional slaves to work my fields. Eventually I owned sixty Negroes, a number that ranked me in the middle of the planter class. I soon had a personal empire comprising six hundred acres on the home plantation, a second farm, a house in Lexington, and additional land in Missouri. I was literally *a self-made man,* which is possible only in America. Lucretia and I could be seen at Olympian Springs, a fashionable resort near Lexington, where wealthy planters met for mint juleps, billiards, cards, and the soothing comfort of the medicinal baths.

Of all my possessions, Ashland is my proudest. It is where I feel most alive. I take great delight in showing guests about its immaculate grounds, its tree-lined paths, its fertile fields bristling with corn, hemp, and rye, its rolling bluegrass meadows landscaped with clusters of trees like a park. Here my stock of blooded cattle and horses graze serenely. With such a farm, I am better off than Moses. He died without reaching the Promised Land. I occupy as good a farm as any he would have found there; and mine has been acquired, not by hereditary descent, but by my own labor.

Not that life has been easy for us at Ashland. Lucretia and I have suffered our share of sorrows. In all, she's borne me eleven children, five sons and six daughters, but all our daughters died, our last, Anne, passing on in childbirth at the age of twenty-eight. When the news reached me in Washington, I fainted. It damn near killed me. I couldn't stop weeping for my dear, dear child, she was so entwined around my heart. I wrote Lucretia: "Alas! my dear wife, the great Destroyer has come and taken away from us our dear, dear, only daughter! How inscrutable are the ways of Providence!" It still hurts to remember her death, my bouts of weeping, my poor efforts at consoling Lucretia when I returned home, to find what little comfort I could in the quiet shades of Ashland.

I said that I kept buying slaves, rooting myself ever deeper into a system I abhorred. Let me explain that for me slavery is a *necessary evil.* I need a large labor force to till my lands and the slave market is the only place I can get it. Goddamn it, a man can't operate a plantation and compete in Kentucky without slave labor.

Making the best of a bad system, I've always tried to be kind to my slaves. They would be the first to testify that *I have been* kind to them. I've manumitted several of my Negroes for faithful service. I dislike whipping my people, but I'm not averse to having my overseer apply the lash if one of them is indolent, impudent, or violent. I admit that a few ingrates have run away from Ashland. One troublemaker, Black Lottie, whom Lucretia and I brought to Washington with us, had the Goddamned audacity to file a suit there for her freedom! To forestall further defections, I dealt harshly with that unfaithful wench: I had her jailed while I successfully contested the suit. That broke Black Lottie of any further desire to defy my authority. When another house servant, a mulatto boy, took flight from Lucretia, I offered a $50 reward for his capture. I told Lucretia we'd spoiled the little bastard with too much good treatment.

Do not misunderstand me. Slavery is a *brutal* system, has always been so. The international slave trade, which brought the Africans here in the first place, was the most abominable traffic that ever disgraced the annals of the human race. I've said so again and again. The slavers in the main got their cargo by buying captives from warlike Africans who'd attacked villages to procure them. This shocking commerce tore husbands from their wives, parents from their children, brethren from one another; it herded its victims to the coast and put them aboard cargo ships, where they were branded and fastened in parallel rows in loathsome holes, crowded so closely together that they could scarcely breathe. The goal was to transport the greatest possible number to the New World at the least possible cost. Yet the slavers' greedy indifference to the welfare of their captives often resulted in losses of entire cargoes of human beings, who died from disease, unimaginable suffering, even suicide. How much happier were those who died than were their miserable survivors! While serving in the Senate during Jefferson's second term, I devoted one of my first orations to damning the international slave trade and its unparalleled atrocities. No American was happier and prouder than I was when Congress, following Jefferson's lead, outlawed this infamous commerce in 1808.

The domestic slave trade, however, continued to thrive, with its brutal coffles, rancid jails, and repugnant auctions. When I first emigrated to Kentucky, I condemned the domestic slave trade as barbaric. But in time I saw that the internal slave traders, despicable though they may be as men, were actually performing a service for Kentucky: they acted as scavengers for the public by carrying off the vicious and incorrigible slaves to another country where new characters may be formed with better habits and propensities.

Though I represented Kentucky in Congress, I had an international vision, a dream of the United States as the world's foremost power. After the second British war, with John C. Calhoun, I devised the "American System" to implement that vision. The system called for a tariff to protect America's infant industries, a national bank to stimulate and stabilize the country financially, and internal improvements to promote the general welfare. In the long run, we hoped to unify the country by establishing a mutually supporting and balanced economy of manufacturing, commerce, and agriculture. In this scheme of things, each of the three great sections was to produce what suits it best: the South was to concentrate on staples like cotton and rice, the West on livestock and grain, and the Northeast on manufacturers. Yes, the system was founded on sectional interests, yet the whole—national interest—would bind the sections together in a powerful federation of interdependent economies.

The Missouri crisis threatened that dream, revealing as it did the grim possibility of disunion and a sectional war over slavery. The compromise which averted a blowup in 1820 did not solve the underlying difficulty, and that was what troubled me. I feared that slavery and its concomitant problem—the presence of blacks in a white man's country—would continue to inflame and divide white Americans. It seemed clear to me that both slaves *and* free coloreds had to be removed if the nation was ever to be united under the banners of the American System.

Since the failure of gradual emancipation in Kentucky, I'd continued to hope that the southern states would one day eradicate slavery by gradual emancipation. The problem was how to persuade them to do so, especially in view of what had happened in Kentucky. The more I dwelled on the problem, the more I believed that emancipation had failed there for want of a program of colonization that would ease white fears by resettling the liberated blacks outside the country. The key to emancipation, it seemed to me, was to establish a successful colonization scheme first, as an inducement to the states to act. They might be willing to rid themselves of slavery if they could count on a flourishing colonization operation to siphon off the blacks as they were manumitted.

That is why I co-founded the American Colonization Society, a private, philanthropic organization dedicated to removing the free black population from this country and planting it in Africa. I met with some fifteen other gentlemen in a Washington tavern to discuss the idea, which had been proposed by Mr. Caldwell. We agreed it was a worthy project. Four days before Christmas 1816, we formally established the American Society for Colonizing the Free People of Color of the United States. We met again on New Year's Day and chose little Bushrod Washington, a justice on the Supreme Court, as first president and myself, Andrew Jackson, and ten other well-known southerners as vice-presidents (a few years later, I became the society's third president). Madison, Daniel Webster, Chief Justice John Marshall, and Francis Scott Key were all sponsors; President Monroe gave the organization his blessing, and Jefferson sent a letter of support from his Virginia mountaintop.

In the decade after the Missouri crisis, I campaigned vigorously for colonization and made speeches in Washington and Kentucky in behalf of our society. And while I was gratified by our growth—by 1830 we had almost two hundred auxiliary societies in the slave and free states—and while I was cautiously optimistic about our success—we had now colonized some 1,500 free coloreds in Liberia, which boasted of a working government, schools, and cultivated fields—I was distressed by the criticisms and misconceptions that dogged us wherever we labored. On the platform, I rehearsed my arguments for colonization, urging Americans to hear me well, for the voluntary deportation of free persons of color would lead to the end of slavery and save the country from the horrors of disunion and civil war.

"First," I said, "colonization of free persons of color removes the most vicious, degraded, and contaminated class in America—a national menace—whose wretched condition is the inevitable consequence of liberating members of an inferior race and allowing them to remain among the superior race, with its unconquerable prejudices.

"Second, there is a peculiar, moral fitness in restoring blacks to the land of their fathers. If through such black missionaries Americans could give heathen Africa the blessings of our arts, our civilization and our religion, may we not hope that America will extinguish a great portion of that moral debt which she has contracted to that unfortunate continent?

"Third, colonization removes the great obstacle to emancipation, so often expressed—the lack of a proper disposal of manumitted slaves."

To facilitate our efforts, the society petitioned Congress for Federal grants. But southern congressmen blocked our efforts because they wrongly perceived us as *abolitionists*. They seemed to fear that a congressional appropriation for colonization would lead to a congressional attack against the institution of slavery itself. I assured my southern colleagues that the colonization society did not want the general government to touch slavery as an institution, for the government had no constitutional authority to do that. Only the states where slavery existed had the power to emancipate. Appealing to skeptical slaveowners who misunderstood our purposes, I stressed that the American Colonization Society was *not an abolitionist society;* it entertained no purpose, on its own authority or by its own means, to attempt emancipation partial or general. Our goal was to point the way, to demonstrate to the slave states that colonization was practicable, in hopes that those states would incorporate the society's plan into their own schemes of gradual emancipation. If the southern states would free and transport only the annual increase of blacks within their borders, I argued, the value of slave labor would one day diminish to the point where it would succumb to superior white labor, and the states would thus rid themselves of a universally acknowledged curse.

As we moved through the second decade of our efforts, and I began serving Kentucky in the national Senate, I remained optimistic. Yes, there was intransigence and opposition to us in the slaveholding states. Yet I believed that those states would one day adopt and execute my plan of gradual emancipation and colonization, by cooperative or separate effort.

I warned my fellow slaveowners, however, that we sat atop a powder keg, which could explode at any moment. "When we consider the cruelty of the origin of Negro slavery, its nature, and the character of the free institutions of the whites; when we consider the irresistible progress of public opinion throughout the Americas, where slavery has been abolished in every country save Brazil and the United States, and throughout Europe, where Great Britain now has a great emancipation effort under way; it is impossible not to anticipate frequent insurrections among the blacks in the United States. They are rational beings like ourselves, capable of feeling, of reflection and of judging of what naturally belongs to them as a portion of the human race. By the very condition of the relation which exists between us, we are enemies of each other. The blacks are kept in subjection only by the superior intelligence and superior power of the predominant race. If an insurrection is attempted, what shocking scenes of carnage, rapine, and lawless violence might not be perpetrated before the arrival at the theatre of action of a competent force to quell it! And, after it is put down, what other scenes of military rigor and bloody executions would be necessary to punish the insurgents, and impress their whole race with the influence of a terrible example! All the more reason, then, to free and return that race to its fatherland."

3 · NAT TURNER

I was born on October second, 1800, the property of old Benjamin Turner, who owned a large farm in a remote neighborhood down county from Jerusalem in southeastern Virginia. When I was still a child, my father ran away to the North, leaving me to be raised by my mother and grandmother. Because I was born with bumps and scars on my head and chest, my mother announced that I was destined to become a leader, and she and my grandmother told the other slaves that I was intended for some great purpose. One day a slave gave me a book from the Big House to play with, and to the astonishment of the adults I proceeded to spell out the names and objects in the volume. I don't remember how I learned to read and write; only that I began doing it with ease. This made me a source of wonder among the slaves in the neighborhood.

Old Master Benjamin praised me for having "a superior intelligence" and encouraged me to study the Bible and save my soul for a better day a comin'. Soon I could recite entire Biblical passages from memory, and my mother and grandmother, the other slaves, and Master Benjamin all said that I had too much sense to be raised in bondage, that I would never be of any service to anyone as a slave.

Inspired by the slave preachers I heard, I memorized the Old Testament and grew to manhood with the words of the prophets thundering in my ears. I became a preacher myself and exhorted neighborhood slaves in forest tabernacles, voicing their needs, their hurts and sorrows, as they clapped and called out to me.

Upon the death of Master Benjamin, I became the property of his son, Samuel, a hard man who ordered me to the fields. It was then that the rage began, like a slow-burning fire in the pit of my stomach. I'd expected to be freed like a number of other freed coloreds in the area, and I felt betrayed. Everyone had said I was too intelligent to remain a slave, and yet Master Samuel made me a cotton-patch nigger, putting me under an overseer who kept me in the fields from first sun to last light. When the overseer whipped me one day, I ran away as my father had done, but returned in thirty days with the hand of God at my back. I prayed for guidance and took for my wife a young girl, Cherry, who was also a slave at Master Samuel's place.

The rage grew in me as I grew; it filled my imagination with visions of retaliation. One day, while I struggled behind my mule-drawn plow, I heard a voice in the wind-swept trees; it was the voice of the Spirit calling out to me, "Seek ye the kingdom of Heaven, and all things shall be added to you." I felt a surge of joy, certain that God had ordained me for some great purpose. I told a few of my friends that something extraordinary was soon to happen, something that would allow me to fulfill the great promise made to me.

In 1822 Master Samuel died, and my wife and I were sold to different masters, which forced us to live and sleep apart. We still saw one another from time to time, and she bore my children, but not being able to live with them filled me with sorrow and fueled my rage. Why was it that *white men* could keep their families and *black men* could not? Why was it that *white men* could enslave *black men*, but not the other way around? Why was it that *white men* had the whips and the guns, and *black men* only the hoes? There was nothing in the Bible that ordained such relationships.

My new master, Thomas Moore, had paid $400 for me and vowed to get his "money's worth" from "the new nigger." Under him, my days degenerated into mindless toil: I built the morning fires, hauled water, fed the cows, slopped the hogs, chopped wood, raised and repaired fences, cleared new fields, spread manure, grew and gathered the hay for the stock, stumbled behind a mule-drawn plow, constantly taking orders, not daring to protest my condition (my protests screamed only in my mind) lest Moore prohibit me from ever seeing my family again. I hated the cruel life I was living. Surely this could not be my purpose. Surely God did not intend a man of *my* gifts, *my* intelligence, to toil all my life for nothing and die in misery like a mule. When I read my Bible, which my master let me keep, my eye fell again and again on Scriptural injunctions against human slavery, on Exodus 21:16: "And he that stealeth a man, and selleth him, or if he be found in his hand, he shall surely be put to death." And Deuteronomy 24:7: "If a man be found stealing any of his brethren of the children of Israel, and maketh merchandise of him, or selleth him; then that thief shall die." I dreamed that I was Gideon sent by Jehovah against the Midianites, that I was Moses who broke the chains of the Israelites and led them out of Egypt to the Promised Land.

Seeking an answer to my enslavement, I prayed and fasted, sometimes going for days without food. Angrier than ever, my imagination fired to incandescence by the roar of the prophets on my lips, I began to have visions in the fields and woods southwest of Jerusalem: I saw white spirits and black spirits locked in battle, and the sun darkened, and thunder pealed across the Heavens, and blood flowed in streams, and I heard a voice saying, "Such is your luck, such you are called to see, and let it come rough or smooth, you must surely bear it." I was struck with awe, but what did the voice mean? What must I bear? I prayed for a revelation; and one day while I was plowing, the Spirit called out, "Behold me as I stand in the Heavens." And I looked up and saw forms of men there in a variety of attitudes. And there were lights in the sky to which the children of darkness gave other names than what they really were, for they were the lights of the Savior's hands, stretched forth from east to west, even as they were extended on the cross on Calvary for the redemption of sinners.

I revealed my visions to a handful of fellow field hands. The Savior, I told them, was about to lay down the yoke he had borne for the sins of men, and the great day of judgment was at hand. But for many months nothing else happened. Despite all my visions and revelations, I was still the white man's property, still a thing, a *black* thing, so that freedom—so near in my mind—was in reality more remote than ever. I smoldered with resentment and hatred. Then suddenly, on May twelfth, 1828, there occurred the most epochal vision of all. I heard a loud noise in the Heavens, and the Spirit instantly appeared to me and said the Serpent was loosened, and Christ had laid down the yoke he had borne for the sins of men, and that I should take it on and fight against the Serpent, for the time was fast approaching when the *first* should be last and the *last* should be first. Now it was clear. By signs in the Heavens would Jehovah show me when to commence my great work, whereupon I should arise and prepare myself, and slay my enemies with their own weapons, so that the whites would be on the bottom rail and the *Negroes* would be on the top. But until God gave me the sign to begin, I must keep my lips sealed.

But I was too excited to keep silent. I blurted out to Moore that the slaves ought to be free and would be one day or other. Furious at such rebellious talk from an otherwise good nigger, the man took me to the shed and flogged me. Every stroke of his whip on my back stoked the fire in my belly like a hot wind.

For almost three years, there were no further signs. But word passed from slave to slave that insurrection scares had frightened whites in several Virginia neighborhoods, which convinced me that others were seething with defiance as I was. Meanwhile Moore had died, and I, God's chosen instrument to right the great wrong against my people, became in the white world the legal property of his nine-year-old son, Putnam. In 1829, Joseph Travis, a wheelright, married Moore's widow, Mrs. Sally; he moved to her place and assumed supervision of Moore's slaves until young Putnam came of age. So it was that, twice owned, I sank deeper than ever into the pool of slavery. Fasting and praying, I played the good nigger around Mr. Travis and Mrs. Sally, and I won their greatest confidence. Mr. Travis treated me kindly enough, even allowed me to preach to the slaves on other farms. I took the opportunity, away from white scrutiny, to spread disaffection among my fellow blacks.

Then in February 1831 there was another sign. This time it was an eclipse of the sun, which caused the superstitious of both races to cry out, "Is it the end of the world?" Certain that this was the sign I had been waiting for, I gathered around me four trusted field hands—Hark, Henry, Nelson, and Sam—and told them what I was called to do. We would commence the work of death on July fourth, the white man's Independence Day. But we formed and rejected so many plans that my mind was affected. I was seized with dread, for once the work of death began, who knew how many of both races would die and where it would all end? I fell sick, and Independence Day came and passed.

But in mid-August, the month of jubilee, there was another sign: the sun grew dim until it looked like polished silver. As I watched, transfixed, from the Travis farm, a dark spot passed over the sun like a black hand. This was unmistakable proof that Jehovah wanted me to move. With awakened resolution, I told my confederates that as the black spot passed over the sun, so shall the blacks pass over the earth.

On Sunday night, August twenty-first, we met deep in the forest near the Travis place. There were two new recruits, one of them a powerful, implacable man named Will, who said he would gain his freedom or die in the attempt. In the glare of pine-knot torches, I revealed my plan. We would rise that night, I said, and kill all the white people. The insurrection would be so swift and terrible that the whites would be too panic-stricken to fight back. Until we had sufficient recruits and weapons, we would destroy everybody in our path, including women and children. Did not God say through his prophet Ezekiel, "Slay utterly old and young, both maids, and little children, and women"? I told my lieutenants I had purposely avoided an extensive plot involving many slaves. From the slaves' word of mouth, I knew that Negroes had frequently attempted similar things, but their plans had leaked out. I intended for the insurrection to happen without warning. The march of destruction, I explained, would be the first news of our work, and others would join us as we moved.

We struck first at the Travis homestead; my men slaughtered Mr. Travis, Mrs. Sally, and young Putnam in their beds, using axes to make quick and silent work of it. After we left, someone remembered the Travis baby. Will and Henry returned and killed it in its cradle. So it went through the night, as we took farm after farm by surprise, my men breaking down doors with axes and hacking entire families to death. By dawn we had fifteen recruits, nine on horses, and bore down on Elizabeth Turner's farm, where I had lived until Master Samuel's death. Will broke down the door of the big house with a single blow of his ax. Inside, in the middle of the room, too frightened to move or cry out, stood Elizabeth and a neighbor, Mrs. Newsome. While Will dispatched Elizabeth with his ax, I took Mrs. Newsome's hand and hit her over the head with a light dress sword I was carrying; but the blade was dull and failed to kill her. Will moved me aside and chopped her to death as if he were cutting wood. Then we moved on to Catherine Whitehead's place, where Will shredded her grown son Richard with windmill blows. Before we were done, my men had slain Catherine, three of her daughters, and a grandchild, and I'd beaten Margaret Whitehead to death with a fence rail.

By the time we reached the Barrow Road, we were forty strong and all mounted. I put twenty of my most dependable fighters in front and sent them sweeping forward toward Jerusalem, the county seat. They attacked Levi Waller's homestead in a whirlwind of axes and swords, slashing his wife to death and decapitating his ten children as they ran about screaming in terror. Oh Lord God! I cried. Wilt thou destroy all the residue of Israel in thy pouring out of thy fury upon Jerusalem? By the time we reached the Jerusalem highway, we had sacked some fifteen homesteads and slain about sixty whites. We could see crows and vultures circling overhead where we had been. I'd spared a few homesteads because the poor white inhabitants thought no better of themselves than they did of Negroes.

By now we numbered sixty or seventy men, but several of the new recruits had drunk copiously from brandy stills and were too drunk to ride or fight. I resolved to march at once on nearby Jerusalem, whose church bells were tolling the alarm now—*insurrection, insurrection*. Soon we encountered a column of white men marching toward us behind their mounted leaders, and I cried "Charge! Fire on them!" My men rushed forward yelling and wielding axes, clubs, and gun butts; they knocked two white men down and chased the rest into a cornfield, but the whites, reinforced by a second column from Jerusalem, regrouped and counterattacked, wounding five or six of my best men and routing the others.

With sixteen lieutenants I beat a horseback retreat into the dense forests along the Nottoway River, intending to cross the Cypress Bridge and strike Jerusalem from the rear; but the bridge was crawling with armed whites, and my men grew frightened. What now, Nat? they asked. I led them back to the south and raided several more farms and a plantation, picking up recruits until we numbered forty again; all the whites, however, had fled. We encamped for the night in the woods near the Ridley plantation, but the countryside was swarming with white patrols and baying dogs—we could hear them crashing through the timber. That night an alarm stampeded my new recruits, so that by Tuesday morning we had only twenty men left. I led them to Simon Blunt's plantation to gather more recruits, but the Blunt slaves betrayed us: while old man Blunt and another white man fired volleys of buckshot into our ranks, Blunt's slaves poured out of the kitchen and pitched into us with axes, clubs, and pitchforks, scattering us in all directions.

In the forest beyond Blunt's place, I found Will and a handful of other insurgents, and we headed back toward the Travis neighborhood. But the militia caught us and killed Will and most of the others. I escaped through the dense forests, running so hard I was gasping for air. I could hear white patrols with their howling dogs in the woods behind me. I hid in the forest near the Travis place all night and all Wednesday morning, but when the bloodhounds closed in I fled again.

For two months I circled the woods in the Travis neighborhood, eluding the patrols by concealing myself by day and running by night. I was in rags, a mere scarecrow, when a white man armed with a shotgun captured me near the home place, and turned me over to a patrol at a nearby plantation. They put me in chains and marched me up to Jerusalem, carrying on about how quickly the whites had suppressed the insurrection—old Nat's war, they called it. In a joking manner, they told me that militia and vigilante forces from all over southern Virginia and North Carolina had converged on the county, and that some of them had stormed through the backwoods, butchering scores of niggers, maybe hundreds, in retaliation. One North Carolina company had decapitated fifteen slaves and placed their heads on poles as a warning to all who would undertake such a plot. *God's will be done,* I muttered through clenched teeth. I kept my head high and grinned as the guards steered me past crowds of maddened whites. Men shook their fists at me; women screamed and called me a monster; boys ran up and spit in my face. To satisfy the crowds, my guards removed my rag of a shirt and publicly whipped me. But I never stopped grinning.

In Jerusalem, the guard turned me over to two court justices who interrogated me in the presence of numerous local whites, one of whom made a comment about my eyes having a sinister expression. I wanted to put such fear in their hearts that they and all the other white people would never forget what we had done, would never be free of the fear that somewhere, in some slave quarter, another slave like me was plotting to rise up and take the ax to them.

"No," I said, "I'm not sorry for killing all those white people. I alone conceived the idea of insurrection, which had been evolving in my mind for several years. I am in particular favor with Heaven," I warned them. "God has given me special powers over the weather and the seasons. By praying, I can cause raging thunderstorms or searing droughts. I can also heal disease by the imposition of my hands, and once healed a comrade that way. No, I've not done wrong. And no, I didn't fail. Our names are written in blood across the map of this county, nor will we be the last." When someone remarked how futile my attempt had been, I pointed out how *far* we had gone, to the very gates of Jerusalem itself, against the whites' superior numbers and firepower. And if I could do it all over again, I said, I must necessarily act in the same way.

They put me on trial and sentenced me to hang. "I am not guilty," I told the court, "because I do not feel so."

I'm now in the condemned hole of the county jail, secured with manacles and chains, awaiting my execution. I've told my story to an elderly white man, Thomas R. Gray, who says he intends to publish it as a "confession" for the benefit of the white public. I looked on it as a way of continuing my war, Nat's war: through that "confession," my *words* will strike terror in white people long after I have gone. As I described the killings to Gray, sparing few details, I raised my manacled hands Heavenward. Gray looked at me as if his blood had just frozen in his veins.

4 · WILLIAM LLOYD GARRISON

The Southampton insurrection left me horror-struck. Yet I'd predicted just such a calamity. In the inaugural issue of the *Liberator*, January first, 1831, I warned southern slaveowners what would happen if they did not repent and abolish slavery at once:

> *Woe if it come with storm, and blood, and fire,*
> *When midnight darkness veils the earth and sky!*
> *Woe to the innocent babe—the guilty sire—*
> *Mother and daughter—friends of kindred tie!*
> *Stranger and citizen alike shall die!*
> *Red-handed slaughter his revenge shall feed,*
> *And Havoc yell his ominous death-cry;*
> *And wild Despair in vain for mercy plead—*
> *While Hell itself shall shrink, and sicken at the*
> *deed!*

This was a warning, not an exhortation to violence, for I'm a *non-resistant* abolitionist. I believe in the power and efficacy of moral suasion to win all Americans to immediate, pacific emancipation. In the first issue of the *Liberator*, I cautioned the slaves: "Not by the sword shall your deliverance be; Not by the shedding of your masters' blood; Not by rebellion. . . . *God's time is best!*—nor will it long delay." But blame not Nat Turner and his brethren for taking axes to their masters. The white man-stealers of the South had only themselves to blame. The Southampton affair, I said in the *Liberator*, was but the *first violent gust* of a far worse storm that was coming. "If we would not see our land deluged in blood," I said, "we must instantly burst the shackles of slaves. IMMEDIATE EMANCIPATION alone can save the South and the nation from the vengeance of Heaven and cancel the debt of ages."

How tyranny blinds! The southern press and southern political leaders universally blamed *me* for the insurrection, contending that my words in the *Liberator* had deranged Nat Turner and his brethren and caused them to revolt. The *Free Press* (hypocritical name!) of Tarboro, North Carolina, pointed at "an incendiary paper, the *Liberator*, published in either Boston or Philadelphia by a white man, with the avowed purpose of exciting rebellion in the South." The *Daily National Intelligencer* in Washington called the

Liberator "a diabolical paper, intended by its author to lead to precisely such results as the Southampton Tragedy." The *Intelligencer* denounced me as "the instigator of human butchery," as "a deluded fanatic or mercenary miscreant, a cut throat." Other newspapers portrayed me as a "murdering hound," an "incendiary plotter," an "infamous wretch."

"Ye patriotic hypocrites!" I retorted in the *Liberator;* "ye fustian declaimers for liberty! ye valiant sticklers for equal rights for yourselves! Ye accuse the pacific friends of emancipation of instigating the slaves to revolt. *The slaves need no incentive at our hands.* They will find them in their stripes—in their emaciated bodies—in their ceaseless toil—in their ignorant minds. What more do they need? One word explains what has infuriated the southern slaves. OPPRESSION!"

Aroused by the charges of the southern press, the Georgia legislature offered $5,000 to anyone who would bring William Lloyd Garrison to Georgia for prosecution. Such a monstrous proposition shocked me. "A price upon the head of a citizen of Massachusetts—for what?" I asked in the *Liberator.* "For daring to give his opinion of the moral aspect of slavery! Where is the liberty of the press and of speech? Where the spirit of our fathers? Where the immunities secured to us by our Bill of Rights? Is it treason to maintain the principles of the Declaration of Independence? Must we say that slavery is a sacred and benevolent institution, or be silent? Know this, ye Senatorial Patrons of kidnappers! that we despise your threats as much as we deplore your infatuation. The *Liberator* shall yet live to plead for the perishing slave."

Driven mad by the slaughter in Southampton County, Governor John Floyd of Virginia and Senator Robert Hayne of South Carolina demanded that the Boston authorities silence me. Mayor Otis and the other members of the city government replied that they had never heard of me or the *Liberator!* To find out if I did publish an incendiary paper, Otis sent a couple of policemen to my printing office in Merchants' Hall; they looked contemptuously around the two spare rooms, at the little press and composing stand, the grimy walls and ink-spattered windows, the editorial and mailing table with its piles of newspapers, and the unmade bed on the floor, where my co-publisher, Brother Isaac Knapp, and I alternately catnapped— we might have cleaned the office up had we expected such *important* company. They presented me with a letter from Senator Hayne demanding to know if *I* had sent him the copy of the *Liberator* he had received a few weeks ago? "Well," the policemen said, "did you?" I demanded to know by *what authority* Senator Hayne and the city of Boston *put* such a question?

The policemen reported back to Mayor Otis that I did exist, but that my office was an "obscure hole," that a Negro boy was my only visible employee, and that my supporters were a "few insignificant persons of all colors." Thereupon Mayor Otis assured Floyd and Hayne that this "new fanaticism" would make few "proselytes" among respectable northerners. We would see about that.

In mid-October, while Nat Turner was on trial in Jerusalem, I sent the Washington *Daily National Intelligencer* a letter denying that the *Liberator* was a violent sheet out to foment slave insurrections. On the contrary, I said, "its objects are to save life, not to destroy it; to overthrow—by moral power, by truth and reason—a system which has no redeeming feature, but is full of blood—the blood of innocent men, women and babies—full of adultery and concupiscence—full of blasphemy, darkness and woe—full of rebellion against God, and treason against the universe—full of wounds and bruises and putrefying sores—full of temporal suffering and eternal damnation—full of wrath, and impurity, and ignorance, and brutality, and awful impiety; to make the slave states as happy and prosperous as the free states; to elevate and improve the bodies and souls of millions of our fellow beings, who can never be educated while they remain in servitude; and finally to extract a root of bitterness, which is poisoning the whole nation; to preserve the Union by removing an evil, which, if suffered to grow, must inevitably produce a separation of the states.

"Sirs, the present generation cannot appreciate the purity of my motives or the value of my exertions. I look to posterity for a good reputation. The unborn offspring of those who are now living will reverse the condemnatory decision of my contemporaries. Without presuming to rank myself among them, I do not forget that those reformers who were formerly treated as the 'offscouring of the earth,' are now lauded beyond measure; I do not forget that Christ and his apostles,—harmless, undefiled and prudent as they were,—were buffeted, calumniated and crucified; and therefore my soul is as steady to its pursuit as the needle to the pole. No dangers shall deter me.

"I am for immediate and total abolition. The law of God and the welfare of man require it. This doctrine is at present unpopular in this country; and he who maintains it is ranked among madmen and fanatics. If we would not see our land deluged in blood, we must instantly burst asunder the shackles of the slaves—treat them as rational and injured beings—give them lands to cultivate, and the means of employment—and multiply schools for the instruction of themselves and their children. We shall then have little to fear. Tell me not that an evil is cured by covering it up; that it is dangerous to vindicate the rights of the slaves; that if nothing be said, more will be done; and that no adequate remedy can be found. The reasoning is absurd. If every slaveholder would but reform himself, there would be an end of slavery."

The editors of the *National Intelligencer* refused to print my letter. But of course! They were typical of the doughfaces, the apologists, traitors, and cowards at the North who helped sustain the system of slavery. Still, I believed in 1831 that a mighty change was at work among the people of New England. They were not hostile to the South; they were willing to give advice and money toward the liberation of the slaves; but they felt that they could not remain constitutionally involved in the guilt and danger of slavery. If the bodies and souls of millions of rational beings must be sacrificed as the price of the Union, better, aye far better, that a separation should take place.

"Why so hot my little man?" Ralph Waldo Emerson once asked me, as he and others objected to the severity of my language. Was there not *cause* for severity? I had to melt icebergs of silence around the evil of slavery. I also felt a personal identification with the Negro, as if the iron of slavery had pierced my own soul. While I was a child, my mother first made me aware that slavery was wrong, pointing out that it violated the very spirit of Christianity. After my father left us, never to return, we suffered from searing, slavelike poverty. I can still see myself—a slight, frail lad, small for my age—forced by my mother to go from house to house with a tin pail, begging for scraps from our neighbors' tables. It pains me even now to reflect on those harsh years, when my mother's piety alone got us through. She drilled me constantly on the need for unbending rectitude: *Lloyd,* she lectured me, *shun every appearance of evil for the sake of your soul as well as your body!* I was just seventeen when my mother died, God rest her soul. Then apprenticed to a printer in Newburyport, I discovered the *force* of language and the *power* of the printed word. After my apprenticeship, I became sole owner, editor, and printer of the Newburyport *Free Press;* but the paper failed because my uncompromising views against religious infidelity,

intemperance, licentiousness, warfare, and cigar smoking antagonized too many readers.

Removing to Boston, I fell under the spell of Reverend Lyman
Beecher, my spiritual mentor, who was then crusading for Christian
morals and trying to transform America into a benevolent empire
under Christian leadership. I remember sitting at the back of
Beecher's Hanover Street Church and watching in awe as he strode
to the pulpit, a stocky figure cloaked in flowing robes, and thundered from on high about the need for purity in American life. As
editor of the *National Philanthropist,* I echoed Reverend Beecher's
campaign for purity, for Christian control of parties and politics.

But it was Benjamin Lundy, editor of the *Genius of Universal
Emancipation,* published in Baltimore, who gave me my true cause. I
met him in 1828, in a hotel room in Boston, where he was present-
ing his arguments for gradual emancipation and colonization to a
group of ministers. He was a slight, stooped man with reddish hair
and a burning intensity in his words that held me spellbound. He
was certain, he said, that slaveowners could be persuaded that the
slave system was wrong and that they should free their blacks—but
only if the blacks were to be colonized outside the country. Lundy
had set out with a knapsack on his shoulder to find a place where
the black man could hold his head up; he'd found such a place in
Haiti and thereafter had traveled across the United States trying to
rally support for gradual emancipation and colonization of the freed
Negroes in Haiti. He failed to convert the Boston ministers; but he
converted me. I kept nodding my head in joyous agreement. Though
I was just twenty-two, a shy, pale youth who wore steel-rimmed
spectacles and had a prematurely balding head, Brother Lundy
admired my zeal and rectitude and hired me to serve as co-editor of
his paper.

Before I moved to Baltimore, however, I read two antislavery
pamphlets—one by George Bourne, the other by James Duncan—
that damned slavery in graphic terms and argued that *gradual* abolition of such a "heinous sin" was "moral turpitude." Their arguments for *immediate* emancipation were so persuasive that I thought
they were right and I told Mr. Lundy so when I joined him in Baltimore. I also said that I'd changed my mind about colonization and
now considered it a sinful attempt to stamp blacks with the mark of
inferiority. I was beginning to see that all races of men are equally
God's children, that all are created in the same divine image, and
that all are entitled to the same inalienable rights. Only the *total* and

immediate emancipation of the blacks and their *assimilation* met the demands of Christianity, I said. If Mr. Lundy was afraid that my views would offend his readers, who were primarily southern Quakers, he did not belabor the point.

"Thee may put thy initials to thy articles, and I'll put my initials to mine, and each will bear his own burden," he said.

"Very well," I replied, "and I'll be able to free my soul."

So it was in Baltimore, in slaveowning Maryland, that I freed my soul and began my career as an abolitionist editor, castigating slaveowners as unregenerate sinners and demanding immediate emancipation. Every day I saw unspeakable sights in Baltimore, which was a center of the domestic slave trade. I watched, sad and sickened, as my fellow human beings were sold like stock at the market. For two days I hid a slave who'd been viciously whipped from his neck to his buttocks, and for what crime? For the *crime* of failing to load a wagon fast enough! At night, as I lay in my upstairs room, I could hear in the street outside the crack of whips against human flesh and cries of pain that made me weep in shame and outrage. During the day, I saw droves of manacled blacks herded aboard slave ships bound for ports farther south, and I learned that a quarter of the blacks would die en route. Appalled, I launched a blistering attack against slave traders in the columns of the *Genius of Universal Emancipation.* We were besieged with angry letters, even threats of reprisals. I admitted to Mr. Lundy that I had an impetuous disposition, but argued that delicacy was not to be counseled. Slavery was a *monster,* I said, and must be treated as such.

When I learned that a slave ship belonging to Francis Todd of Newburyport, Massachusetts, was taking a cargo of slaves to New Orleans, I wrote an editorial damning Todd and his captain as highway robbers and murderers who ought to be locked in solitary confinement for life. Todd and the state of Maryland sued me for libel. The court found against me and fined me $50, but I refused to pay— I didn't have the money anyway—and cheerfully went to jail for forty-nine days.

There I confronted a slaveowner who had come to reclaim a slave: "Sir, what right have you to that poor creature?"

"My father left him to me," the slaveholder said.

"Would you keep money your father left you if the money had been stolen?" I asked. The man just looked at me, stupefied. He was even more incredulous when I asserted that I would be willing to have a black man as President.

"How would you like to have a black man marry your daughter?" was his riposte.

"Sir," I said, "I'm not familiar with your practices; but I do know that the South has the largest concentration of mulattos. Allow me to say that it's you *slaveholders* who seem to be attracted to amalgamation."

I was released from jail when Brother Arthur Tappan, a New York merchant who'd been converted to immediate emancipation by my editorials, paid my fine. That was in May of 1830. I told Mr. Lundy good-bye and left for New England, certain that I'd borne up under my adversities like the Alps—unshaken, storm-proof. Opposition, abuse, slander, prejudice, and judicial tyranny—all were like oil to the flame of my zeal. I was disappointed that so few in our land felt an interest in the great cause of emancipation. American slavery was *unequaled* for cruelty—not even antiquity could produce its parallel. And yet it was boastingly proclaimed to the world that this was the land of the free and the asylum of the oppressed! Was liberty ever so degraded? Still, I told my friends not to despair: the time would come, for the mouth of the Lord of Hosts had spoken it, when all oppression would cease.

Resolved to struggle against wind and tide to effect the death of slavery, I repaired to Boston, the birthplace of liberty. Here, within sight of Bunker Hill, at the beginning of 1831, Brother Knapp and I launched the *Liberator,* hurling the paper like a thunderbolt at our complacent countrymen. Through moral suasion, we aimed first to arouse the conscience of the North—until we of the North were purified, it was fruitless for us to cleanse others. Then we would use the North's superior moral power to compel southern slaveowners to reform themselves and free the slaves.

I had learned from the British abolitionist press the shock value of denunciation and rebuke and did not hesitate to brand northern accomplices in the slave system—editors, churchmen, and merchants—as thieves, moral lepers, degraded bullies, blackguards, pimps, and knaves, and southern slaveholders as satanic man-stealers, whoremongers, the greatest of sinners, the fiercest enemies of mankind, and the bitterest foes of God. As I explained to Brother Samuel May: Until the term *slaveholder* sent as deep a feeling of horror to the hearts of those who heard it as did the terms *robber, pirate,* and *murderer,* we must use and multiply epithets in condemning the sins of the slaveholder, who was guilty of "the sum of all villanies."

In the *Liberator* and in my pamphlet *Thoughts on African Colonization,* I declared *moral warfare* against the American Colonization Society and its most ardent champion, Henry Clay of Kentucky. I warned genuine antislavery men that the American Colonization Society, by Clay's own admission, was *no abolitionist organization.* Dedicated to affixing the stamp of inferiority upon Negroes in order to remove them from the country, the colonization society, I said, was malignant, sinful, and inhumane, the foulest conspiracy in the history of the world. Clay's demeaning of free blacks as "notoriously ignorant, degraded and miserable, mentally diseased, broken-spirited, and incapable of self-government" filled me with rage. "'My bowels, my bowels!'" I cried. "'I am pained at my very heart; my heart maketh a noise in me.' Are we pagans, are we savages, are we devils? Could pagans, or savages, or devils exhibit a more implacable spirit than is seen in the extracts of the colonization society?"

I pointed out that Clay contradicted himself in claiming that these same free blacks, under the auspices of the colonization society, would take civilization to pagan Africa. As he put it, "every emigrant to Africa is a missionary, going forth with his credentials in the holy cause of civilization and religion and free institutions." *How,* I asked the colonizers, *was an ignorant, miserable, mentally diseased people supposed to "civilize a pagan continent"?* What nonsensical impudence. This was not the poetry of philanthropy, but the insanity of prejudice. Moreover, by the colonizer's logic that white citizens may conspire to remove black ones, could not tall citizens conspire to remove short ones, and corpulent citizens to remove the lean and the lank [like Mr. Clay himself!], and so on throughout the human race? Finally, I asked, how was the colonizer's *debasement* of free persons of color supposed to win them to his voluntary program?

The plain truth was, the colonization society was a miserable failure. Between 1820 and 1830, the total population of free persons of color in the United States grew from 233,635 to 319,889. Yet, as of 1832, the colonization society had persuaded only 1,857 free blacks to move to Liberia. Thus the vast majority of free blacks in this country rejected the society's efforts. I knew how much they *detested* the society because I fraternized with free persons of color, visited their homes and shared their meals; they also made up most of the *Liberator*'s subscribers; it was *their* paper and it reflected *their* views. No matter how badly they were treated in this country, facing universal prejudice and discrimination against them because of their color, America was their home, too; they had roots and family here, and they were *not leaving*.

The American Colonization Society had also failed miserably in the other half of its mission: it had not persuaded a single slaveholding state, not even Virginia or Kentucky, to abolish its peculiar institution. In the aftermath of Nat Turner's insurrection, the Virginia legislature debated and then rejected a plan of gradual emancipation and colonization on the grounds that the latter was too expensive and difficult to carry out and that emancipation without colonization was unthinkable. Virginia then revised its slave codes, shackling its blacks to the system of slavery more fiercely than ever. If Virginia, stricken by a slave revolt, would not embrace Clay's program of gradual emancipation and colonization, then no slave state would ever do so. Yet Clay went on trumpeting colonization as a panacea that would somehow solve the slavery problem, somehow save the country from disintegration. What could we expect? It was morally impossible for a slaveholder to reason correctly on the subject of slavery.

Our program of immediate emancipation and assimilation, I maintained, was the only panacea, the only Christian solution, to an unbearable problem. Despite what my detractors said, I did have a program. "By immediate emancipation," I explained, "we do *not* mean that the slaves should be turned loose upon the country to roam as vagabonds; that they should be instantly given all political rights and privileges; or that they should be expelled from America, their native land, as a price and condition of their liberation. We mean that the power invested in all slaveholders should instantly cease, that the slaves should receive the protection of the law, that they should be placed under benevolent and disinterested supervision, which shall secure to them the right to obtain secular and religious knowledge; and that they should be employed as free workers, fairly compensated for their labor and protected in their earnings. We contend that laws against miscegenation should be repealed, for the free mixing of colors is part of God's design. The freed people, we believe, will make good citizens; they will not be idle, but industrious; they will not rush through the country firing dwellings and murdering inhabitants; for freedom is all they ask."

I was proud of our initial successes. My verbal assault against the colonizers routed their leaders, whose deathlike silence proved that my charges could not be answered. What I said forced antislavery men to take sides, and most sided with the cause of immediate emancipation, thus ending whatever antislavery usefulness the colonization society might claim. Indeed, within four years of the launching of the *Liberator,* I saw my principles embraced by thousands of the best men in the nation. In December 1833, in New York City, we formed the American Anti-Slavery Society, the first national abolitionist organization in this country. I drafted its Declaration of Sentiments, which asserted that ours was a moral crusade to remove slavery instantly by moral law and political action, and that those laws then in force, admitting the right of slavery, were therefore, under God, utterly null and void, being an audacious usurpation of the Divine Prerogative, a daring infringement on the law of nature, a base overthrow of the very foundations of the social compact, and a presumptuous transgression of all the holy commandments.

We were determined to redeem the soul of America. We were determined to win as many friends as possible, to assist in the deliverance of my poor fettered, guiltless countrymen from bondage. Toward that end, the national society sent out agents to arouse local communities and organize local societies. By 1840, we had some two thousand societies and two hundred thousand members. Across the free states, we published newspapers, handed out abolitionist tracts, and circulated thousands of abolitionist petitions; our voices rang out from hundreds of platforms. The circulation of the *Liberator* itself rose to three thousand. "Where now is the American Colonization Society?" I asked in the *Liberator.* "Struggling in the agonies of dissolution! Look, now, at that powerful association, the American Anti-Slavery Society! Look at the flood of our publications sweeping through the land."

We also flooded the slave states with our literature, mailing nearly two million abolitionist documents there in one three-year span. But the man-stealers in Dixie reacted in predictable fashion: in Charleston a so-called citizens committee broke into the post office, carried off packages of abolitionist society publications, and put them to the torch. Across the South postmasters refused to deliver our publications, and vigilance committees seized and burned them, incinerating our words in bonfires of tyranny. Every slave state outlawed abolitionist societies and abolitionist literature. Southern legislatures sent northern legislatures ringing demands that our societies and publishers be *silenced.* But we would *not* be silenced. In 1835–1836, we flooded Congress with abolitionist petitions, and I published the debates about them in the *Liberator.* Senator John C. Calhoun of South Carolina leveled murderous charges against us, crying that the abolitionist attack was all-out war against the South and that the petitions should not even be *received.* This prompted

Representative John Quincy Adams of Massachusetts to rise in eloquent defense of the sacred right of American citizens to petition their government. But in an act of high-handed despotism, the House adopted the "gag rule," or "Pinckney gag," proposed by Representative Henry L. Pinckney of South Carolina, which automatically tabled abolitionist petitions, and the Senate also voted to receive and then table them. Such "gag" rules meant that *neither house* would ever act upon our petitions. This was a baleful portent glaring ominously in our moral sky. The adoption of the gag rules made me doubt that slavery could ever be abolished by political action, the Federal Government being so completely dominated and polluted by the Slave Power.

Rebuffed in Washington, we also ran into a wall of conservative resistance at the North. As I had privately feared, a majority of Americans did not want to face the moral issue of slavery and branded us as irresponsible agitators who were upsetting the "harmony" of the country! They feared, too, that emancipation would unleash hordes of southern blacks to invade the North. A storm of anti-abolitionist and anti-Negro violence broke across the land. Crowds shrieking racial epithets hurled bricks through the windows of our meeting houses, pelted our speakers with rotten eggs and stones, and broke up our gatherings. They called themselves "men of property and standing," but in reality they were black-hearted thugs and head-hunting vigilantes. In New York City, their mobs not only routed the meeting of the American Anti-Slavery Society, but sacked Brother Lewis Tappan's home and wrecked a Negro school, three Negro churches, and twenty Negro homes. In Cincinnati, a mob destroyed the printing office of abolitionist editor James G. Birney, flung his press into the Ohio River, and smashed up the black section of town. "And what has brought our country to the verge of ruin," I asked in the *Liberator*. "THE ACCURSED SYSTEM OF SLAVERY! To sustain that system, there is a general willingness to destroy LIBERTY OF SPEECH and of the PRESS, and to mob or murder all who oppose it. In the popular fury against the advocates of a bleeding humanity, every principle of justice, every axiom of liberty, every feeling of humanity is derided and violated with fatal success."

The more opposition we met, the more determined I became to redeem the soul of this slave-cursed land. Yet as devoted as I was to the cause, I admit that the crusading editor of the *Liberator* was lonely in his personal affairs, that he needed female companionship.

Yes, I'd once told myself that a wife and a family would be burden-some, would distract me and weaken my strength. But in reality it was *loneliness* that was enervating my strength. I'd met someone I cared for in Providence, but I was so lacking in confidence that it was ten months before I could muster the nerve to write her. Her name was Helen Benson, and she was the twenty-two-year-old daughter of an old-time antislavery man, who was a friend of Ben-jamin Lundy. The girl had a sweet disposition and the loveliest face I'd ever seen, with high cheekbones, a full mouth, dark brown hair, and large, sparkling eyes. Oh, those eyes! I could not get them out of my mind. With my first letter, we began a tentative courtship, car-ried on mostly by mail. Finally I wrote her: "Neither years nor the conflicts of life have indurated my heart—I weep as easily as a babe, am as sensitive as a flower, and as aerial as a bird. To you, is offered the whole heart of Yours, with increasing esteem." When I next saw her, I wanted to tell her how I felt, but my heart was timorous and my tongue was tied. After we parted, she wrote me that she was sure I loved her and that she opened her whole heart to me as well. "Oh! generous, confiding, excellent girl!" I replied. "Do you then recipro-cate my *love?* Yes, my fears are dispelled—my hopes are con-firmed—and I can shed delicious tears of joy!" From that moment on, she was my sweet Helen, my chosen one, my kindest best, my Flower of Friendship, my charming conqueror. "Dear Helen," I wrote her, "am I not a strange compound? In battling with a whole nation, I am as impetuous, as daring, and as unconquerable as a lion; but in your presence, I am as timid and gentle, and submissive as a dove." We were wedded on September fourth, 1834, and began our married life in a rented house in Roxbury we called "Freedom's Cottage."

Not long after our wedding, the great English abolitionist George Thompson came to New England by my invitation. The English abolitionist movement had recently won a resounding vic-tory, having persuaded Parliament to abolish slavery in the British colonies by a gradual program. Eager to help us in our work, the gentle, thoughtful Thompson undertook a speaking tour that pro-voked unprecedented fury and abuse from the so-called *gentlemen* of property and standing. In August of 'thirty-five, in Boston's Faneuil Hall, an obstreperous crowd of them accused us and "foreign" agents like Brother Thompson of trying to "scatter among our Southern friends firebrands, arrows, and death." The next day I retorted that Faneuil Hall, known as the Cradle of Liberty, should now be called the Coffin of Liberty because proslavery apologists had turned it into an Augean stable of filth and degradation. When Helen and I awoke the next morning, a gallows made of maple beams stood menacingly in front of our house.

Yes, my life was in danger; I even had a vision of a howling rabble lynching me on the Boston Common. My showdown with Boston's proslavery bullies came on October twenty-first, 1835, when George Thompson was scheduled to address the Boston Female Anti-Slavery Society on the third floor of Anti-Slavery Hall. While noisy intruders disrupted the ladies' meeting inside, a mob of a thousand white men coalesced in the street outside and started shouting, "Thompson! Thompson!" The mayor and a group of constables soon arrived to restore order; the mayor told the ladies to go home and assured the rioters that Thompson was not there and would not appear. At that they screamed, "Garrison is there! Garrison! Garrison! We must have Garrison! *Lynch* him!" They were in a perfect frenzy. I hid in a storage loft upstairs, but several ruffians broke through the door and found me behind a pile of boards. I barely had time to remove my spectacles before they dragged me to an open window—I was certain they were going to throw me out. But someone placed a ladder against the side of the building and ordered me to come down. I bowed at the blurred sea of faces below and then climbed down to the street as they hooted and jeered. The rioters put a rope around my waist and ripping the clothes from my body pulled me through the streets in my underclothing. I was certain they would hang me, yet I felt perfectly calm, for to me it was a blessed privilege to suffer in the cause of Christ. Death for me did not present one repulsive feature.

The mayor and his posse, however, rescued me from the clutches of my would-be murderers. Charging *me* with disturbing the peace, the mayor had me locked up in the city jail. He assured me that this was indispensable to my personal safety. Before being released, I wrote the following inscription on the wall of my cell: "Wm. Lloyd Garrison was put into this jail on Wednesday afternoon, October 21, 1835, to save him from the violence of a 'respectable and influential' mob, who sought to destroy him for preaching the abominable and dangerous doctrine, that 'all men are created equal,' and that all oppression is odious in the sight of God."

Fearful for Helen's safety, I moved her to Brooklyn, Connecticut, where she gave birth to our first child and where we lived for a couple of years before we thought it safe to return to Boston. In the meantime, our movement had acquired a new and eloquent voice, the golden voice of Brother Wendell Phillips. This tall, slender young attorney and wealthy patrician joined our cause after he saw the mob drag me through the streets of Boston. We had need of his eloquence and energy, because the political and religious forces of the land were now arrayed against us. Initially I had expected support from the clergy—how could Christian ministers not hate slavery and demand its extinction? But alas! the vast majority of America's clergymen proved to be hostile to our cause. The Baptist Board of Foreign Missions rejected emancipation; the Baptist Church and Old School Presbyterians showed no interest in addressing it; and the General Conference of the Methodist Church voted to prohibit any discussion of slavery whatever.

"O, the rottenness of Christendom!" I wrote Brother May. "I am forced to believe, that, as it respects the greater portion of professing Christians in this land, Christ has died in vain." The orthodox churches, I argued, were "disgraces to Christianity, heathenish, filled with apologies for sin and sinners of the worst sort, predominantly corrupt and servile, connivers with slaveholders." The religion preached and practiced in this country was "an oath-taking, war-making, man-enslaving religion," and I wanted nothing more to do with it. Inspired by the perfectionism of John Humphrey Noyes, I advocated a "Come Outer" stance, urging my fellow abolitionists to renounce all churches and all governments because they were corrupt and sinful to the core; all had to be dashed to pieces before society could be perfected and the Kingdom of God on Earth could begin.

Some abolitionists, however, failed to see the light and refused to follow the path of true righteousness; they favored a softer line on the churches and advocated political action in the form of an abolition party, a liberty party. But this I categorically rejected. Abolition, I said, was a *moral* not a *political* contest. Because slaveholders and their northern allies dominated all levels of American government and controlled both the Whig and the Democratic parties, slavery could never be removed by political action. Only moral force could abolish it and save our unhappy, guilty, oppressive country. But others, principally the New Yorkers, disagreed, and we took to squabbling among ourselves. Such internal dissension pained me deeply, and it grew worse. When I proposed that female abolitionists have an equal voice in our national society, that they be allowed to speak and vote and sit on our executive committee (they could not yet do any of these), the political-action men vehemently objected. Yet I refused to back down on "the woman question"—to me it was a matter of principle that a society which *battled* oppression on the basis of color must not *practice* oppression on the basis of sex. Led by Arthur Tappan, three hundred dissident political men defected and formed their own abolitionist organization with their own newspaper. I regretted their defection, yet it did leave the American Anti-Slavery Society in the hands of the unswerving and incorruptible adherents of pure abolitionism, the no-government, anti-clerical men and women who followed me.

Meanwhile the forces of reaction, branding *us* as the outlaws, *us* as the incendiaries, surged on against us in riot after riot. In 1837, in Alton, Illinois, a proslavery mob murdered abolitionist editor Elijah Lovejoy and hurled his printing press into the Mississippi River. We were still a long way from redeeming the soul of America! I intoned in the *Liberator:* "Whatever scenes of violence might transpire in the slaveholding states, we did not anticipate that, in order to uphold southern slavery, the free states would voluntarily trample under foot all order, law and government, or brand the advocates of universal liberty as incendiaries and outlaws. It did not occur to us, that nearly every religious sect, and every political party, would rally on the side of the oppressor. The whole land has been thoroughly proved, by a series of tests, to be diseased beyond the power of recovery. In the solemn language of another—'The violence of mobs—the protector and apologists in Church and State, are but the tremendous convulsions, the fearful delirium, the dying throes of an expiring nation.'"

5 · JOHN C. CALHOUN

These abolitionist fanatics will yet destroy the Union. By agitating our slaves and attacking our character and domestic institutions, they are committed to our total destruction. We of the South know that slick-tongued abolitionist agents instigated the Vesey insurrection plot, which rocked Charleston in 'twenty-two, and the Southampton outbreak a decade later. We also perceive the abolitionist menace behind Clay's American Colonization Society. We believe none of Clay's denials of abolitionist intent—does he not proclaim slavery a *wrong* and a *curse?* As Vice-President and then Senator from South Carolina and as the South's premier spokesman, I led the congressional fight that blocked the society's petition for Federal funds. I exposed it for what it was: an entering wedge for Federal emancipation or a means of provoking the slaves to revolt.

During the decade of Vesey and Turner, the South also suffered from economic dangers, as northern protectionist interests seized control of Congress and shackled us with the tariff of 1824 and the tariff of abominations four years later. The tariffs had a ruinous effect on the southern economy: in Charleston alone imports fell by fifty percent, and I and nine-tenths of the other planters were forced to operate at a loss. The best way to guard the minority South from the tyranny of the northern majority, I maintained, was through the magnificent superstructure of state rights, which is guaranteed by the residual powers clause of the Tenth Amendment to the Constitution. In the *South Carolina Exposition and Protest* and in my subsequent Fort Hill Address, I argued that through the Constitution the sovereign states had delegated specific powers to Congress; that each state could determine when Congress exceeded those powers; and that each state could veto, or nullify, and refuse to enforce, any act of Congress found to be in violation of its delegated authority. In 1832, the state of South Carolina adopted my argument when in convention assembled it nullified both the tariff of abominations and the so-called compromise tariff of 'thirty-two.

But the other southern states failed to see the wisdom of my argument and declined to stand with South Carolina behind the bulwark of nullification. The South thus missed the opportunity to establish a powerful shield with which to protect itself from all forms of majority tyranny. I was profoundly dismayed when President Jackson—King Andrew!—threatened to hurl an army of fifty thousand troops into South Carolina, and Congress passed a Force Act empowering the President to uphold the tariff in South Carolina by coercive means. I protested bitterly that the use of Federal force against a sovereign state was repugnant to the genius of our system and destructive of its very existence.

To ward off a devastating civil war in South Carolina, however, I not only supported Clay's compromise tariff of 1833 (which gradually reduced duties to permissible levels), but persuaded the nullification convention to accept the new tariff and repeal its nullification ordinance. I warned my fellow southerners, however, that the use of unrestrained Federal power embodied in the Force Act was certain to rouse the dormant spirit of abolitionism, which would try to harness that power to destroy our *domestic institution.* "It requires no stretch of the imagination," I said in the Senate, "to see the danger which must one day come, if not diligently watched."

Just two years later, the abolitionist danger was upon us, as well-organized northern agitators attempted to fill our mails with their incendiary literature and petitioned Congress itself to abolish slavery in the District of Columbia, plunging Senate and House alike into rancorous debates on how to treat such petitions. The abusive language in them enraged me. One from Ohio accused the South of "dealing in human flesh" and claimed that all Christian nations had branded such traffic as piracy. Worse still, the petition pronounced slavery a "sin" because it "violated the laws of God and man" and "corrupted the public morals." The petition spoke of us slaveholders as *pirates* and *butchers.* Strange language! We could not permit the men we represented to be thus insulted.

In January of 1836, I moved that Congress refuse even to receive the petitions of these fanatics, because receiving them would open the door to petitions calling for *the abolition of slavery everywhere in the land.* I urged my fellow southerners to be *obstinate* in their resistance, even to the extent of disunion, if that should be necessary to arrest this new evil. But I trusted that it would be checked far short of such an extremity, that the South could yet effect a change of sentiment in the North in reference to our doctrines.

There followed weeks of debate and maneuver on my motion. Most Senators rejected emancipation in the District of Columbia, but contended that, since Congress had jurisdiction over slavery there, it ought at least to receive the petitions. I argued that it was dangerous even to *discuss* the subject. "Every man knows that there exists a body of men in the Northern States who are ready to second any insurrectionary movement of the blacks," I said, fixing my eyes on my northern colleagues; "and that these men would be on the alert to turn these discussions to their advantage." I was furious when Senator William King of Alabama, a man devoid of insight, disagreed with my motion; he urged the Senate to receive the petitions and then simply disapprove of them. This, he thought, would uphold the right of petition *and* the rights of the states. I objected to such idiotic thinking. Did King not understand where it would lead him? Was he prepared to receive petitions urging the abolition of slavery in U.S. naval yards and arsenals? Did he not understand the need for southern unity on this momentous question? If we yielded a single inch, we were gone.

This abolitionist attack was *war,* all-out *war.* "It is a war of religious and political fanaticism," I told the Senate, "mingled, on the part of the leaders, with ambition and the love of notoriety, and waged, not against our lives, but our character. The object is to humble and debase us in our own estimation, and that of the world in general; to blast our reputation, while they overthrow our domestic institutions." How to stop them? "There is but one way: we must meet the enemy on the frontier, on the question of receiving the petitions; we must secure that important pass—it is our Thermopylae."

I spoke rapidly, my eyes searching and probing my colleagues as I looked around the chamber. Congress, I warned, was about to take the first step that would control all its subsequent movements. If it received such petitions and established the monstrous, impious principle that it was obliged to do so, if it assumed permanent jurisdiction over the subject of abolition, whenever and in whatever manner the abolitionists might ask, the consequences would be disastrous. "Such a course," I said, "would destroy the confidence of the people of the slaveholding states in this government. We love and cherish the Union; we remember with the kindest feelings our common origin, with pride our common achievements, and fondly anticipate the common greatness and glory that seem to await us." But all that was nothing compared to this abolitionist threat. "It is to us a vital question. It involves not only our liberty, but, what is greater, if to freemen any thing can be, existence itself."

As I feared, the Senate voted down my motion and adopted the expedient of receiving and then tabling these incendiary petitions. That vote was a fatal stab to the rights of southerners and pregnant with evil foreboding.

In the summer of 1836, I returned home to Fort Hill, my plantation in the Carolina upcountry, with its towering cedars and fields of cotton, corn, wheat, oats, potatoes, and rice that rolled southward to the Seneca River. I was tired, extremely tired. I felt and looked older than my fifty-four years. When I gazed into a mirror, I saw a figure tall, gaunt, and stooped, with unruly gray hair and sunken, glittering eyes.

I could find little rest at Fort Hill, however, for my crops were the worst I had ever had. Because of my long absences in Washington City, I had to rely upon my brother-in-law and son-in-law to manage the place and oversee my seventy slaves, who lived in "the quarters," a stone building that stands just past the barn, about an eighth of a mile from the Big House. I am of course a kind and just master, but I do not shrink from ordering thirty lashes well laid on as punishment for a slave who runs away or manifests impudence or rebelliousness. Indulged niggers, after all, make the worst slaves.

I have given slavery a great deal of thought and regard its essentially racial nature as a practical question. The device by which an alien, savage race has been fitted into our social order, slavery is primarily designed to regulate relations between the races. With us, the two great divisions of society are not the rich and the poor, but the black and the white.

As the summer wore on, I devoted myself to repairs of the mansion. It is a T-shaped, two-story white frame dwelling, situated on a hilltop, with a Greek pediment and portico in front and high-columned verandahs on both sides. But Floride, my wife of twenty-five years, a small woman with dark hair and dark eyes, displayed her apoplectic tendency and hectored me so much with her suspicious, fault-finding temper that I took refuge in the master's office at the rear of the house. Perhaps the death of three of our children in infancy left Floride irreparably scarred. Upon deaf ears had fallen my argument, when our little daughter passed on, that death was the lot of humanity; that almost all parents had suffered equal calamity; that Providence might have intended it in kindness to her and ourselves, as no one can say what, had she lived, would have been her condition; and that above all we had the consolation to know that she was far more happy in Heaven than she could be here with us.

I could not get the abolitionists off my mind. I warned my neighbors that those demagogues had ample funds, complete organization, and an energetic press, and that the young, the thoughtless, and the enthusiastic would naively swallow their poison. The abolitionists had to be defeated at the pass of Thermopylae by a united South, confident in the justice of its cause and the moral rightness of its institutions. To counter the abolitionist attack, I devised a defense of slavery aimed at assuaging southern fears and self-doubts and winning the opinion of the civilized world.

In February of 1837, back in Washington City, I prepared a major address on the abolitionist danger. When I rose to speak in the semicircular Senate chamber, my fellow senators sat attentively at their mahogany desks, some of them leaning forward in their armchairs, others taking notes. The galleries above them were full of spectators.

"See what the abolitionist petitions say about us!" I cried, my words tumbling out in a rush. "The peculiar institution of the South, on which the very existence of the slaveholding states depends, is pronounced to be sinful and odious, in the sight of God and man; and this with a systematic design of rendering us hateful in the eyes of the world, with a view to a general crusade against us and our institutions. I do not belong to the school which holds that such aggression is to be met by concession. Mine is the opposite creed, which teaches that encroachments must be met at the beginning, at the frontier, with a fixed determination of maintaining our position at every hazard."

The abolitionists' first step, I admonished my fellow southerners, was to persuade Congress to receive their petitions. The next step was to get them referred to committee. If the South yielded, we would proceed step by step to the final consummation of the object of these petitions, which was *the abolition of slavery in the several states by congressional law*. True, this incendiary spirit had not yet won over Congress or the intelligent and business portion of the North. But if it was not swiftly checked, it would spread and work upwards until it gained political control of the North and brought the two great sections of the Union into fatal conflict.

Be assured, I cautioned the South, that emancipation itself would not satisfy these fanatics—that gained, the next step would be to raise the Negroes to a social and political equality with the whites; and that being effected, we would soon find the present condition of the two races reversed. *They* would be the masters and *we* the slaves.

"However sound the great body of the non-slaveholding States are at present," I said, "in the course of a few years they will be succeeded by those who will have been taught to hate the people and institutions of nearly one half of this Union, with a hatred more deadly than one hostile nation ever entertained toward another. By the necessary course of events, if left to themselves, we must become, finally, two peoples.

"Abolition and the Union cannot co-exist. As the friend of the Union, I openly proclaim it. We of the South will not surrender our institutions. To maintain the existing relations between the two races, inhabiting that section of the Union, is indispensable to the peace and happiness of both. It cannot be subverted without drenching the country in blood, and extirpating one or the other of the races. Be it good or bad, it has grown up with our society and institutions, and is so interwoven with them, that to destroy it would be to destroy us as a people.

"But let me not be understood as admitting even by implication that the existing relations between the two races in the slaveholding states is an evil—far otherwise." From Africa, I pointed out, the black race came among us in a low, degraded, and savage condition and grew up in a few generations under the fostering care of our institutions to its present comparatively civilized condition. "But I take a higher ground," I said. "I hold that in the present state of civilization, where two races of different origin, and distinguished by color, and other physical differences, as well as intellectual, are brought together, the relation now existing in the slaveholding states between the two, is, instead of an evil, *a good—a positive good.*" It was *good* for the master race and *good* for blacks and *indispensable* to the happiness of both.

We of the South, I concluded, must *defend ourselves,* for no one else would do it for us. "Surrounded as the slaveholding states are with such imminent perils, I rejoice to think that our means of defense are ample, if we shall prove to have the intelligence and spirit to see and apply them before it is too late. All we want is *concert,* to lay aside all party differences, and unite with zeal and energy in repelling approaching dangers. Let there be concert of action, and we shall find ample means of security without resorting to secession or disunion."

Alas, there was not yet concert of action, for many southerners, including many in the Senate, did not share my sense of danger. Some of them worried that strident speeches would antagonize the North and stimulate the growth of abolitionism there.

In my rooms, speaking to myself, I planned my next move with great care. With King Andrew gone now and Van Buren of New York in the White House, I concluded that the best way to block abolitionist thrusts in Congress was for southerners to gain control of the Democrats, the country's majority party (after the nullification crisis, I had left the party and allied with Clay and other Jackson opponents to form the Whig coalition). I supported the Democratic Van Buren administration in establishing an Independent Treasury, which was intended to divorce the government from the banking interests. In return, with abolitionist petitions piling up on congressional tables, the Democratic party embraced all my major views on slavery. In December of 1837, Senate Democrats approved a series of resolutions, proposed and defended by me, that put the Senate on record as opposing any interference with slavery anywhere in the country. Passed by large majorities in the Senate, the resolutions asserted that a state was sovereign over its domestic institutions, that the Federal Government was bound to protect such institutions, that abolitionism was subversive of the Constitution and destructive to the Union, and that the citizens of one state had no right to intermeddle with the domestic institutions of another. The next year, in a long address issued to the nation, the Democratic members of Congress affirmed that Congress had no power over slavery in the states and no authority to abolish it in the District of Columbia as a means of hurting slavery in the states. In 1840, the national Democratic platform asserted similar principles, and I and other influential southern defectors formally rejoined the party. That same year, the House embraced my position on dealing with abolitionist petitions, by voting outright against receiving them.

Because of my triumphs, the abolitionist press took to calling me "the malevolent genius of the Slave Power." It was a title I wore with honor.

6. CLAY

From the period of the Missouri controversy, the public mind was kept in a state of feverish excitement on the subject of slavery. It was the one issue that disturbed the nation's tranquillity, the one subject that was ever regarded with the deepest anxiety by all who were sincerely desirous of the permanency of the Union. Still, I believed it possible to quiet the sections, to unite them under the flag of my American System, until this new agitation began in the thirties, this onslaught of the northern abolitionists. I thought them rash and impolitic, the way they inundated Congress with their provocative petitions (which I nevertheless voted to refer to an appropriate Senate committee) and damned all slaveholders in the vilest, most incendiary language I've ever read. When abolitionist John Greenleaf Whittier exhorted me to join their ranks, I replied that I deeply regretted that the abolitionists had started agitating for immediate emancipation, that this was highly injurious to the slave himself, to the master, and to the harmony of the Union, and that the abolitionists were unwarrantably meddling with a southern institution that was none of their Goddamned concern. I said repeatedly that there could never be emancipation in any form without colonization, and I defended our colonization society and its unmixed humanity and benevolence from the bitter denunciations of Garrison and his crowd. I pointed out to my southern brethren that the friends of colonization could not be abolitionists since the real abolitionists hated us and attacked us at every turn.

What also troubled me was the *southern reaction* to the abolitionist attack, the extravagant opinions coming out of southern mouths that slavery was a blessing, that it ought to exist in every well-organized society, and that it was indispensable for the preservation of liberty! Southerners were blowing out the moral lights with this new defense of slavery, this calling it "a good, a positive good," as Calhoun did on the floor of the Senate, with his eyes blazing defiance and his mane of white hair standing straight up as he pointed a bony finger at our northern colleagues. I emphatically disagreed with Calhoun and all those who espoused slavery as a positive good, because such a view was indefensible, unintelligible, and brought reproach upon us from the civilized world.

"*I consider slavery as a curse,*" I told the Senate, "a curse to the master, a wrong, a grievous wrong to the slave. In the abstract it is ALL WRONG; and no possible contingency can make it right."

That got me damned by both houses, as proslavery men called me an abolitionist and abolitionist papers accused me of having "no conscience," of being "hypocritical" and "malignant" and "an ultra in my slave notions." The abolitionists even said I was more dangerous than Calhoun because I came disguised in the cloak of philanthropy! And of course the abolitionists brought up the subject of my slaveowning, which in their view disqualified me from being a true friend of liberty. Thus was vilified a man who had ever regarded slavery as a curse, a great evil, that ought to be gradually removed.

The abolitionist attack set the cause of emancipation back fifty years. Because of the intense public excitement caused by the abolitionist agitation, any proposition looking even to remote emancipation was out of the question. In fact, when the issue of gradual emancipation came up in Kentucky during the legislative session of 'thirty-seven and 'thirty-eight, white people were so alarmed by the northern abolition crusade that they voted the proposition down by a margin of four to one. Certain that the time was not right for gradual emancipation in my adopted state, I myself felt constrained to take immediate, bold, and decided ground against it.

When Calhoun introduced his resolutions on slavery, obliging the Senate to record its opposition to any intermeddling with it, I voted for most of them, not from any confidence I had in their heal-

ing virtues, but as abstract propositions. I did not think that petitions calling for the abolition of slavery in the District of Columbia
constituted a "direct and dangerous attack upon the institution of
slavery in the states," as Calhoun charged. Hell, there was about as
much chance of Congress's abolishing slavery in Washington as
there was of its abolishing the Christian religion.

There was a great difference between Calhoun and myself on
how best to protect the just rights of the states. He went for strong
language, menacing tones, irritating measures, and mean-spirited
attacks on the Declaration of Independence itself, the white man's
charter of liberty. I went for temperate, but firm language, conciliation, and for obeying the injunction of the Constitution in respect to
the right of petition. Taken together, Calhoun's resolutions, I feared,
would strengthen the abolition issue in the free states and cause further rift between the sections. Worse still were Calhoun's threats of
disunion if the country did not accept his views. "We slaveholders
allow ourselves to speak too frequently, and with too much levity, of
a separation of this Union," I said in the Senate. "I cannot believe
that it is prudent or wise to be so often alluding to it. We ought not
to be perpetually exclaiming wolf, wolf, wolf."

But I could understand the intense anxiety of my fellow slaveholders, particularly when the abolitionists invaded politics, when
they formed the Liberty party and promoted antislavery men for
state and national offices. I was horrified by this new element. I had
run for the Presidency in 'thirty-two, and had lost to Jackson in
what to me was a bitter personal defeat. In 'thirty-six, the Jacksoni-
ans had seemed so powerful that I had not even offered myself as a
candidate, which put Jackson's chosen successor, the sneaky Van
Buren, in the White House. But I had hopes of victory in the next
presidential canvass—until the introduction of this new element of
abolition into our elections. In 'thirty-eight, the Whigs suffered
reversals in the state elections, especially in Ohio, where the political
abolitionists went against Whig candidates virtually to a man. I perceived at once the danger to my own presidential aspirations.
Indeed, I received a letter from abolitionist James Birney declaring
that the abolitionists would view the election of any slaveholder to
the Presidency as "a great calamity to the country." Political abolitionism, I wrote a Kentucky friend, caused me the deepest solicitude.
"The danger is that the contagion may spread until it reaches all the
free states; and if it ever comes to be acted on as a rule among them,
to proscribe slaveholders, they have the numbers to enforce it. My

own position, touching slavery, at the present time, is singular enough. The abolitionists are denouncing me as a slaveholder, and slaveholders as an abolitionist, while they both unite on Mr. Van Buren."

Convinced that I had to make a choice in order to survive politically, I sided with my fellow slaveholders. I did so in my major address on the abolitionists, given in the Senate in February of 'thirty-nine. Word had gone out that "Prince Hal" was going to speak, and the galleries were overflowing with gentlemen and brightly dressed ladies who had come to enjoy the show. Dressed for the occasion in tailored broadcloth, glittering shirt front, high white collar, and black cravat, I bowed to the ladies and then strode to the front of the chamber, where the President of the Senate sat on an elevated platform flanked by ornate marble columns. The circular apertures of the overhead dome admitted shafts of light which fell across the floor as I spoke.

I made a careful distinction between those who, like myself, opposed slavery but also opposed any disturbance of the peace and tranquillity of the Union, and the real ultra-abolitionists who were resolved to persevere in the pursuit of their object at all hazards, and the consequences be damned. Pointing my snuffbox, I took aim at the dangerous program they advocated. "They proclaim that *color* is nothing; that the organic and characteristic differences between the two races ought to be entirely overlooked and disregarded. They would teach us to eradicate all the repugnances of our nature, and to take to our bosoms and our boards, the black man as we do the white, on the same footing of equal social condition. They promote intermarriage and amalgamation, an unnatural and revolting admixture alike offensive to God and man."

The consequences of immediate emancipation, I warned with a sweep of my arm, would be calamitous. It would cause an influx of blacks to the North, where they would compete with the industrious and laborious white classes, lowering their wages, augmenting their hardships, contaminating them by a mixing of the black element. Immediate emancipation—and here I agreed with Calhoun—would be followed by a desperate struggle for immediate ascendancy of the black race over the white race, by instantaneous collisions between the two races that would break out into a race war that would end in the extermination or subjugation of the one race or the other.

Where were the abolitionists leading us? "With them," I said, "the rights of property are nothing; the deficiency of the powers of the general government are nothing; the acknowledged and incontestable powers of the states are nothing. A single idea has taken possession of their minds, and onward they pursue it with reckless disregard for the Union. They began by professing to use persuasive means in appealing to the humanity and enlightening the understanding of the slaveholding portion of the Union. But impatient with the slow effects of the power of persuasion, they now propose to substitute the powers of the ballot-box; and he must be blind who does not perceive that the inevitable tendency of their proceedings is to invoke the more potent powers of the bayonet and to set one section against another.

"If they succeed in that, it will be attended by all the violent prejudices, embittered passions, and implacable animosities, which ever degraded or deformed human nature. The most valuable elements of union—mutual kindness, the feelings of sympathy, the fraternal bonds—which now happily unite us, will be extinguished forever. One section will stand in menacing and hostile array against the other. The collision of opinion will be quickly followed by the clash of arms in civil war. And what then? The abolitionists themselves will shrink back in dismay and horror at the contemplation of desolated fields, conflagrated cities, murdered inhabitants, and the overthrow of the fairest fabric of human government that ever rose to animate the hopes of civilized man. And there will be no glory in such a war. Whoever wins will have achieved a conquest without laurels, a suicidal conquest; a conquest of brothers over brothers.

"I do not speak as a friend of slavery. The searcher of all hearts knows that every pulse of mine beats high and strong in the cause of civil liberty. But I prefer the liberty of my own race to that of any other race. The liberty of the descendants of Africa in the United States is incompatible with the safety and liberty of the European descendants. Slavery forms an exception—an exception resulting from stern and inexorable necessity—to the general liberty of the United States. The liberty of the black race can only be established by violating the powers of the states and subverting the Union. And beneath the ruins of the Union would be buried, sooner or later, the liberty of both races."

When I finished, Calhoun jumped to the floor and declared my speech "the finishing stroke" to the abolitionists and their invasion of American politics. Alas, it proved a premature benediction, since the Liberty party ran Birney for President in the election of 1840. I lost the Whig party nomination to William Henry Harrison, the "war hero," who went on to win the Presidency that year. It pained me deeply that the party I had built should prefer Harrison, a political tyro, to a veteran statesman who was trying to pacify and unite the country. I felt cheated of an office for which I was far better qualified than any of those who had occupied it since Monroe. I felt even more cheated when Harrison died and John Tyler of Virginia, contemptuously known as "His Accidency" and committed to strict construction and other obsolete ideas, succeeded to the Presidency and proceeded to veto my efforts to recharter the national bank and raise the tariff. I was so disillusioned that I resigned from the Senate, announced my retirement from politics, and went home to Ashland.

The Whig party, however, was nothing without me. State party leaders, North and South, acknowledged that I was the only Whig who had a chance to win the Presidency in 'forty-four. The national convention, need I say, nominated me by acclamation. When the Democrats chose James Polk, a slaveholder from Tennessee and a political nonentity on the national stage, I felt certain that my time for the Presidency had come. But my chances took a turn for the worst when the Democrats endorsed the annexation of slaveholding Texas, a quarrelsome issue we had hoped to keep out of the contest. I had gone on record as opposing Texas annexation, on the grounds that it would bring on a war with Mexico. What this country needed, I maintained, was union, peace, and patience. The Democrats, however, advocated Texas annexation with aggressive appeals to national pride, claiming that America had a God-given right to acquire Texas and Oregon and to rule the continent. Then for good measure, they attacked me as a duelist, a rake, and an abolitionist who opposed Texas annexation because I wanted to free the blacks! The last accusation not only eroded my support in the South; it also aroused the zealots of the Liberty party. Afraid that antislavery voters might go for me, they attacked Henry Clay as a "man-stealer" under the control of the Slave Power. Thus did unscrupulous fanatics on both sides gang up on me!

In a desperate bid for southern support, I made a public statement—the so-called Alabama letters—that I had no personal objection to annexation, indeed would *like* to have Texas, slavery and all, if it could be done with honor and without war with Mexico. That statement, alas, cost me pivotal New York state, where antislavery Whigs went for Birney, the Liberty party candidate, and threw the state and the election itself to Polk. Had I won but a third of the New York vote, I would have gone to the White House. As it was, I lost the election by only 38,000 popular votes out of a total of 2,700,000 cast in all the states. I had never witnessed such God-damned *mad*ness. By combining against me, an avowed opponent of slavery, Liberty men and antislavery northern Whigs had elected a *proslavery Democrat*, whose victory led to the annexation of slave-holding Texas and a war with Mexico to expand slave territory to the Pacific.

Embittered by this, the most painful defeat of my entire political life, I declared myself forever off the public stage.

7. CALHOUN

I was at Fort Hill, in March of 1844, when I received a letter from President Tyler offering me the post of Secretary of State, made vacant by the death of Abel P. Upshur in a ship explosion on the Potomac. I accepted the position because the country had reached a crisis over Texas and British designs there, and the Administration had need of me to accomplish the great end of annexation. Upshur had written me about England's treacherous plot to abolitionize Texas by offering it a loan, without interest, if it would free its slaves. This alarming news confirmed information I had received from a variety of sources. There could be no doubt that the English were determined to abolish slavery throughout the American continent—that the present attempt upon Texas was the beginning of England's operations against the United States. It was worse than childish to suppose that England meditated this great movement simply from an impulse of philanthropy. I could find no other motive on her part than a desire to create markets for her surplus manufacturing.

Her scenario of conquest was to work like this. If she succeeded in abolitionizing Texas, it would pose a direct threat to Louisiana and Arkansas, whose slaves would find an asylum in Texas. Since the American government would do nothing to help the slaveholder, he would be forced to take the matter into his own hands. He would reclaim his escaped slaves by force, and this would lead to war. The northern states would not aid in such a war, waged for such a cause, and this would cause a separation of the Union. In this state of things, England would not be idle; she would be working to bring such a separation about. The English, in sum, were on a crusade to abolish slavery as a means to weaken and then destroy the United States. I was convinced that the annexation of Texas was indispensable for the very survival of the South and the nation.

When I took office on April first, secret negotiations were already under way between Texas and the United States on the subject of annexation. I found on Upshur's desk a copy of a letter written by Lord Aberdeen, outgoing British foreign minister, which confirmed my worst suspicions about British intentions in Texas. Aberdeen contended, disingenuously, that his government had no desire to acquire Texas or to interfere in its internal affairs. Then he contradicted himself by asserting that Great Britain hoped to accomplish "the general abolition of slavery throughout the world," including the Republic of Texas. He even admitted that Great Britain was trying to induce Mexico to recognize Texas independence if Texas could be persuaded to emancipate her slaves. This was incriminating evidence of Britain's ulterior designs.

Convinced that our great cause of slavery must be brought out fully and favorably to the world, I wrote Richard Pakenham, the new British foreign minister, a frank letter. "So long as Great Britain confines her policy to the abolition of slavery in her own possessions and colonies in this hemisphere," I said, "no country has a right to complain. But when she goes beyond, and avows it as her settled policy, and the object of her constant exertions, to abolish it throughout the world, she makes it the duty of all other countries, whose safety and prosperity are endangered by British policy, to adopt such measures as they deem necessary for their protection." It was with still deeper concern, I said, that the United States regarded the avowal of Lord Aberdeen of the desire of Great Britain to see slavery abolished in Texas. An abolitionist Texas, I pointed out, would be immeasurably dangerous to the prosperity and safety of this Union. Accordingly, the United States intended to annex Texas in order to protect their slave property from Britain's world abolition movement.

The experience of more than half a century, I informed Pakenham, convinced me that it would be neither humane nor wise to abolish slavery. The census of 1840 and other records showed that, in all instances in which the northern states had abolished slavery, the condition of the African, instead of being improved, had become worse. The free Africans had invariably sunk into vice and pauperism, accompanied by the bodily and mental inflictions incident to that condition—deafness, blindness, insanity, and idiocy to a degree without example. But in the states that retained the ancient relation between the races, the Africans had improved greatly in every respect—in number, comfort, intelligence, and morals. In short, the Negro was far healthier and happier within the civilizing constraints of bondage. "The abolition of slavery," I warned Pakenham and his government, "would (if it did not destroy the inferior race by conflicts, to which it would lead) reduce it to the extremes of vice and wretchedness."

By the time I wrote that letter, Texas and the United States had already agreed to a treaty of annexation. Aberdeen's letter and my response to Pakenham accompanied the treaty to the Senate. There were rumbles of protest from northerners about my linking a defense of slavery to annexation. But I was determined to commit the general government and the nation itself to the protection of our peculiar institution. When Van Buren and Clay (in an act of treason against his section) published letters opposing annexation, the Texas treaty went down to defeat in the Senate. But the election of Polk in November of 1844 was a popular mandate for annexation, and it rallied Democrats in Congress behind the outgoing Tyler Administration. By a straight party vote, Congress approved a joint resolution to annex Texas, and I persuaded Tyler to make the offer to our sister slaveholding republic on the last day of his Presidency.

I had succeeded, by a bold, unhesitating course, in securing annexation, and I expected the incoming Polk administration to retain me as Secretary of State. But to the regret of almost the entire country, with no small censure on the Administration, I was not asked to remain; and I decided to retire from politics and concentrate on my treatises on government, which I had begun in 1843. Now sixty-three, I was in poor health, having suffered a severe attack of congestive fever that left my lungs permanently impaired and my voice scratchy and weak. I feared that I had not many years left.

From the ramparts of Fort Hill, I advanced a new theory of government to replace the theory of nullification. By now, the very idea of democracy filled me with loathing. It meant rule by the absolute numerical majority, to which I was utterly opposed and the prevalence of which would destroy our confederate system and destroy the South. I now believed that our liberty could only be safeguarded under a system of *concurrent* majorities. This would check the tyranny of the North's popular majority of similar interests, which begot the centralism and abolitionism that threaten the South's slave-based minority. In my treatises, I maintained that the instrument to ensure concurrent majorities and reestablish sectional equilibrium was a dual executive, one elected by the North and one by the South, and each with a veto power.

In my speeches and writings, I mounted an ideological counterattack against the subversive doctrines of the Declaration of Independence, which sanctions revolution and chaos. It was this most dangerous of all political error, I pointed out, that had given birth to abolitionism, to the deep and dangerous agitation which now threatened to engulf our political institutions. Therefore the sentiments in the Declaration had to be discredited and destroyed. They are nothing, I contended, but glittering generalities and self-evident lies. A good example is its assertion that all men are born free and created equal. This is an illogical absurdity. *Men* are not born; *infants* are born and they are not born free. They are incapable of freedom, being destitute alike of the capacity to think and act, without which there is no freedom. They are also subject to the dictates of parents, society, and state. Nor is it less false to hold that men are born "equal." They are not so in any sense. The whole idea of equality is sentimental rubbish. *Inequality* and *slavery* are the achievements of human progress. There never has yet existed a wealthy and civilized society, from that of ancient Greece to our own, in which one portion of the community did not, in point of fact, live on the labor of the other.

Let me make my position clear: I care nothing about slavery, it is entirely a secondary question with me. In three hundred years' time there will not be a nigger on the face of the globe. As the Indian is now retreating before our civilization, so the nigger will gradually be eliminated and his place taken by a higher and more intelligent race; it is only a question of time. I advocate slavery in the South because it is a guarantee of stability and the supremacy of the white race.

8. GARRISON

I rejoiced in the insane tirades in defense of slavery that poured forth from Calhoun and his perverted kindred. I told Brother Quincy in 1845 that the enemy had never dreaded or hated us more than at the present time, and that it was the greatest sign we had of our efficiency. Yet this was a trying period for us all. The annexation of slaveholding Texas took place that year, and it was a crime unsurpassed in the annals of human depravity. It was effected by the man-stealers, Calhoun and Tyler, and the proslavery Democratic party, whose unparalleled hypocrisy and Heaven-daring profligacy cannot adequately be described by any of the languages of the globe. Annexation was proof that the Slave Power now held an omnipotent mastery over this nation, proof that it was engaged in a murderous plot to augment slave territory and multiply its victims. I read Calhoun's letter to the British minister Pakenham—a copy of it appeared in the *New York Evening Post*. That letter, written by the South's proud and merciless tyrant, *admitted* the Slave Power conspiracy.

The Slave Power's mastery over the nation was made possible by the accursed Constitution, which established and guaranteed slavery as an institution. Robert Toombs, the man-stealer from Georgia, said as much on the floor of Congress. "We have a right to call on you to give your blood to maintain the slaves of the South in bondage," he told us of the North. "Gentlemen, deceive not yourselves; you cannot deceive others. This is a pro-slavery government. Slavery is stamped on its heart—the Constitution." By 1843, I saw that the slaveholders were right: the Constitution *was* a proslavery document. "The compact which exists between the North and the South," I told the Massachusetts Anti-Slavery Society, "is 'a covenant with death, and an agreement with hell'—involving both parties in atrocious criminality; and should be immediately annulled." I gave the *Liberator* a new slogan, "NO UNION WITH SLAVEHOLDERS," which the following year was adopted by the American Anti-Slavery society. It abjured all loyal abolitionists "to withdraw from this compact" and "by a moral and peaceful revolution to effect its overthrow" as provided for in the Declaration of Independence. I told loyal abolitionists to circulate a declaration of "DISUNION FROM SLAVEHOLDERS" across the North. Hold mass meetings, I cried, assemble in conventions, nail your banners to the mast!

This of course brought cries of protest from the Liberty party men: *This is not our position*. Of course it was not their position. They had abandoned abolitionism by choosing to work within a wickedly corrupt, proslavery, blood-cemented political system which was an insult to the world. Well, I said, let the Liberty men howl all they wanted. Ours were the voices of true abolitionism, for we functioned *outside* the proslavery Constitution and the hellish government it created. From its inception, the Liberty party was morally bankrupt. I must confess to a certain ironic joy when Whigs and Democrats alike—all tools of the Slave Power—accused the Liberty party of advocating disunion. As one opposition paper said, "It is now almost universally admitted that the abolitionists are traitors, wicked hypocritical villains, *as a body*." Such words were music to my ears! By 1847, the Liberty party was moribund.

There were cynics who demanded to know how disunion would help the slaves and claimed that we were in fact abandoning them. Not so, I replied; the separation of the free states would help the slaves by giving the deathblow to the entire slave system. The slave republic would have to face the appalling fact that it would have three million enemies in its midst, smarting from numberless wrongs and outrages, with no possibility of help from the North to put down insurrections. Moreover, the slave republic would have on its northern borders a free-state republic that would stand as a powerful beacon to the slaves. How could the South prevent the escape of an indefinite number of them to the northern republic, which would have no constitutional obligation to return them? The border slave states, losing the largest number, would find themselves so unstable that each state would be compelled to emancipate all the slaves on its soil. The same necessity would be imposed upon the states next in geographical position; and this would lead to a general and peaceful abolition through the entire South.

But ultimately disunion was with me a question of abstract morality—of obedience to the "higher law" of God. My position was a moral one. The Union was founded at the expense of the slave population of the land. I could not swear to uphold it. They who asked me to do so, asked me to do an immoral act—to stain my conscience—to sin against God. How could I do this?

At this time, I had a new disciple, Frederick Douglass, who admirably espoused my disunion arguments. This tall, handsome black man, with his shock of hair and brilliant dark eyes, had joined our movement after escaping from slavery in Maryland. Later Douglass would turn against me and the cause of true abolitionism, would sell out to our bitterest enemies, the Liberty men, to satisfy his own selfish ambition. But in our early years together he was a devout Garrisonian and an impressive speaker as the representative of his enslaved brethren and sisters. When doubters questioned his story, saying that he was too eloquent to have been a slave, Brother Douglass wrote a narrative of his life that was so bold and forthright that Wendell Phillips urged him to burn it lest the slave catchers apprehend him and drag him back into slavery. The narrative, however, was published, with a preface by me and a letter of introduction by Brother Phillips. As a precaution, Douglass went to England for two years. I joined him there in the summer of 1846, and we often shared the platform in addressing English antislavery audiences. When our English friends raised the money with which to purchase Douglass's freedom, I gladly contributed my mite to the purchase fund. Alas, some of our abolitionist associates at home protested the purchase, arguing that it recognized the right to traffic in human beings. I retorted that it recognized no such thing. It was never wrong to ransom one held in cruel bondage, and we had simply paid a ransom to set our brother free.

When we returned home, the Slave Power had forced the country into war against inoffensive Mexico for the sole object of expanding slave territory and multiplying slave states. The Mexican War was the most atheistical and impious conflict ever recorded on the gory pages of history. I prayed for success to the injured Mexicans and overwhelming defeat to the American troops. The Constitution, I said in the *Liberator*, making ample provision as it did for a navy and an army, and giving Congress authority at any moment to declare war, was an evil instrument, to be regarded with abhorrence by all good men. The Union, erected as it was on the prostrated bodies of three million slaves, deserved to be held in eternal execration and dashed to pieces like a potter's vessel.

While the United States raped and plundered Mexico, Brother Douglass and I toured Pennsylvania and Ohio seeking converts to immediate abolition and disunion. Douglass created a sensation with his commanding presence, mellifluous voice, exquisite talent for mimicry, and a gift for sarcasm that matched my own. For me, listening to him was like hearing myself, so perfectly did he present my arguments.

"I look with pleasure upon the movements of Mr. Calhoun and his party," Douglass told one Pennsylvania audience. "The slaveholders are now marshaling their hosts for the propagation and extension of the institution. Abolitionists, on the other hand, are marshaling their forces not only against its propagation and extension, but against its very existence. I like to gaze upon these two contending armies, for I believe it will hasten the dissolution of the present *unholy* Union, which has been justly stigmatized as 'a covenant with death, an agreement with hell.' I welcome the bolt, either from the North or the South, which shall shatter this Union; for under this Union lie the prostrate forms of three million with whom I am identified."

The venomous spirit of the Slave Power, however, was abroad in Pennsylvania, for we encountered hostile crowds almost everywhere we went. The worst was in Harrisburg. When Douglass tried to address a public meeting in that city—the first "nigger" to do so—a mob of surly whites broke out the windows of the meeting house with firecrackers and brickbats and hurled rotten eggs at Douglass as he stood at a desk. The eggs spattered the desk and the wall behind him. One struck my head and dripped down my coat—the stench was perfectly nauseating—and a large stone hit Brother Douglass in the back. All the while our attackers yelled "Out with the Goddamned nigger!"

"Our mission to Harrisburg is ended," I told Douglass, and we got out, gladly.

We rode the cars to Chambersburg and there planned to take a stagecoach over the Alleghanies to Pittsburgh. But, to our serious regret, we found that Douglass's ticket, which he had purchased at Harrisburg, enabled him to go directly through on the afternoon stage, while I had to wait for the evening one. Proceeding alone, Brother Douglass had a hard time of it. Every time his stage stopped at an inn, the proprietor refused to let him sit at the eating table, and for two days and nights he scarcely tasted a morsel of food. When I rejoined him and learned about his ordeal, I was furious. O, what brutality! I lamented that most white northerners cared about nothing so much as despising and proscribing the colored race. We had indeed a long way to go before we converted the North to freedom and brotherhood! Resolving to proceed come what might, we spoke in Pittsburgh and other towns and then set out across eastern Ohio. After addressing two meetings in dark, drizzly weather, I fell ill with a bilious fever and a swollen tongue. My brain was terribly oppressed and highly inflamed; I was indescribably wretched, a crushed man. While I lay in bed in Cleveland, helpless as an infant,

Douglass went on alone. Not once while I convalesced did he write a single line to me to inquire about my health.

While still in bed, I read in a Cleveland paper that Douglass had elected to establish a black newspaper in Rochester, New York, to be called the *North Star*. I felt betrayed. Douglass had mentioned such a project in Boston, shortly after our return from England, but I and other friends had dissuaded him from pursuing it. The *Liberator* was the black man's newspaper, after all, and it did not need any more competition. From my sick bed, I wrote Helen that Brother Douglass had not once on our tour opened his lips to me on the subject, nor asked my advice in any particular whatever. Such conduct grieved me to the heart. I thought Douglass's behavior was impulsive, inconsiderate, and highly inconsistent with his decision in Boston.

The first issue of the *North Star* appeared in early December of 1847, after I had returned home, fully recovered. While I gave the paper a reluctant public endorsement, I was happy to see Douglass attacking Henry Clay in the inaugural issue. Douglass wrote: "Sir: your recent speech on the subject of slavery serves up one of the most helpless, illogical, and cowardly apologies for the wrong of slavery I have ever read. For fifty years of your life you have been a slaveowner. You are at this moment the robber of nearly fifty human beings, of their liberty, compelling them to live in ignorance. Let me ask if you think that God will hold you guiltless in the great day of account, if you die with the blood of these fifty slaves clinging to your garments?" It was a brilliant rapier thrust into the heart of Clay's hypocrisy, but it belonged in the *Liberator*, not in a rival newspaper.

In February 1848, the Mexican War ended in victory for the Slave Power, which stole the entire Southwest from Mexico for the purpose of mutilating the bodies and souls of millions. The Lord God in His wisdom and mystery had not answered my prayers for an American defeat. With the Slave Power in command of our nation and our fate, the future looked grim indeed for the great abolitionist cause.

9 · CALHOUN

I opposed the war with Mexico. I thought Polk needlessly provoked it, and I broke with him, the Democratic party, and the South
itself over his bellicose course. I had come out of retirement in late
1845 because of the diplomatic crisis over Oregon and Texas and
because of continued abolitionist agitation. Reelected to the Senate
by the near unanimous vote of the South Carolina legislature, I led
the peace coalition in Congress that steered the country away from
war with England over the Oregon boundary: we persuaded a blus-
tering Polk and the Senate to drop American claims to all of Oregon
in favor of the English offer to extend the forty-ninth parallel to the
Pacific.

That left the difficulties with Mexico. I sided with the Whig
opposition against war with that country, because I feared that war's
inevitable centralizing tendencies would favor the majority section
against the South, allowing the North more power than ever to tyr-
annize us and threaten our domestic institutions. I also feared that
war would undo the Oregon settlement and invite abolitionist England to intervene on the side of Mexico. English intervention, I
feared, would lead to catastrophic consequences: a defection of the
North from us, a humiliating defeat followed by a massive influx of
cheap English manufacturers into what remained of the country,
which would then fall victim to panic, disorder, and disintegration. I
shuddered to contemplate it.

When Mexico refused to sell New Mexico and California to the
United States, Polk resolved to seize that territory by war and sent
Taylor's army into the disputed Texas border country to provoke an
incident. "It cannot be so!" I said when I learned of the move. "It is
impossible!" I remember calling on Polk in the White House and trying to reason with him to adopt a pacific course with Mexico. As I
explained the disastrous consequences of a war with Mexico, Polk
said not a word, his dull gray eyes averting my stare. He was a stiff,
lean, grimacing little man with long gray hair combed straight back
behind his ears. Nothing I said penetrated his stubborn silence, and I
left certain that we would soon be at war.

Upon learning that Mexican troops had attacked Taylor's force,
Polk demanded of Congress an immediate declaration of war. I was
virtually the only southerner in Congress who abstained when
Congress voted for war. That I did so caused cries of protest to be

raised against me in the South, even in South Carolina. How, southern men demanded, could I be *for* the annexation of Texas and
against the war with Mexico, which was certain to result in the
acquisition of Mexican territory? I was *not* against the seizure of
New Mexico and California, since both places had American settlers. What I objected to was the cry of some members of the war
party that *all Mexico* should be taken by us. What a fearful idea! It
meant the American race would have to ingest a population filled
with Indians and mixed bloods. Ours was a government of the white
man. Were we to associate with ourselves, as equals, companions,
and fellow citizens, the Indians and the mixed races of that
benighted republic? Mexico, I warned, was forbidden fruit. The
penalty of eating it would be to subject our institutions to certain
death. It would lead to *racial amalgamation* and *more agitation
against slavery*, since the Mexican ruling class (no doubt encouraged
by the English) was abolitionist to the core.

My stand against the war weakened me with the Democratic
party and the unthinking portion of the community. My position
was to wait quietly for a good opportunity, and the subsiding of the
existing excitement, and then put myself right before the country
and the world.

The war had hardly begun when the Wilmot Proviso threatened
to alter forever the equilibrium of power between the fourteen slaveholding states and the fourteen non-slaveholding states and to inau-
gurate revolution, anarchy, and civil war. Proposed in August 1846
by an obscure Democratic congressman from Pennsylvania, the Proviso would prohibit slavery in all territories won from Mexico. It
passed in the northern-dominated House; but in the Senate, our bastion of defense against the encroachments of abolitionism, we were
able to get the Proviso tabled. I apprehended at once that behind the
Wilmot Proviso was a united northern majority conspiring to annihilate us. Though comprising just five percent of the northern population, the abolitionists had turned the non-slaveholding states against
us with their unceasing agitation; every portion of that section now
entertained views and feelings more or less hostile to slavery.
Because both of the great political parties at the North were equal in
size, the abolitionists held the balance of power between them; they
could determine the outcome of elections, and politicians of both
parties sought their votes and promoted their cause. The result was
the Wilmot Proviso, a scheme which aimed to monopolize the powers of the general government, to obtain sole possession of its territo-

ries, and ultimately to attack our domestic institution. There was no mistaking the signs of the times! Already we were in a minority in the House, in the electoral college, and in every department of the general government. Only in the national Senate did we have an equality. Once we were excluded from the territories, we would be at the complete mercy of the non-slaveholding states. There was ample room in the territories we then possessed and those we would likely acquire from Mexico for up to fourteen more free states. The North would then have *twenty-eight states*—double our number! Both houses of Congress, the Presidency, and the courts would all be lost to us. The inevitable result would be a Federal attack against slavery in the states. Thus would the bitter fruit of the Mexican War cause the death of our institutions!

Frustrated by our victory in the Senate, the Wilmot men next struck on the Oregon question: they introduced in the House a bill organizing the Oregon Territory and prohibiting slavery in that far northwestern country by extending the Northwest Ordinance of 1787, which had excluded slavery from the Old Northwest Territory around the Great Lakes. I knew that slavery would likely never take root in the northern reaches of Oregon, but I wanted to establish a bulwark for our defense in the territory south of it acquired from Mexico. At my urging, therefore, Congressman Armistead Burt offered an amendment to the Oregon bill which extended the Missouri Compromise line to the Pacific. If adopted, this would have permitted slavery to exist in the territory won from Mexico which lay south of the Missouri line of 36 degrees, 30 minutes, but would have excluded it in Oregon, which lay north of the line. I had always considered the Missouri Compromise a great error and highly injurious to the South, because it surrendered those high principles of the Constitution upon which I thought we ought to stand. Like Jefferson, I objected to any compromise line on slavery. But, in order to preserve the peace of the country as we fought Mexico, I was willing to acquiesce in a continuation of the Missouri Compromise line to the Pacific. The northern majority in the House, however, treated the Burt amendment with arrogant contempt and not only sent it down to defeat, but approved the Wilmot Proviso itself a second time! So much, then, for my effort at compromise. I would not make that mistake again.

The only effective means of protecting ourselves, I concluded, was to match the unity of the North with an even more steadfast unity of the slaveholding states. If we men of the South were to remain in the Union, we had to throw off old party allegiances and unite in an *all-southern party* committed to resisting the Wilmot Proviso and the abolitionist agitation which had produced it, and to preserving and expanding slavery for our survival. To counter Wilmot and establish a platform for a new sectional party, I proposed a set of resolutions in the Senate—Thomas Hart Benton of Missouri, an Administration man, snidely called them the Calhoun Proviso. My resolutions demanded equal rights for the South in the territories. They advanced the idea of state proprietorship—that the territories were the joint and common property of the sovereign states, that the general government, as a creation of the states, held the national lands in trust for them, and that southern settlers migrating to the new regions took with them the laws of their home states, which protected slavery. Congress had no authority to deny them that right. I warned my fellow southerners: *there could be no compromise on the territorial issue.* A compromise was but an act of Congress. It could be overruled at any time. It gave the South no security. I saw our way in the Constitution. It was stable. It was a rock. On it we could stand. On it we could meet the North's aggression on our rights and honor. On it we, not our enemies, could control the territories and the Union.

"Hear me well," I told the citizens and representatives of the non-slaveholding states. "I am proud to be from the South. There are my family and connections; there I drew my first breath, there are all my hopes. I am a southern man and slaveholder—a kind and merciful one, I trust—and none the worse for being a slaveholder. I say I would rather meet any extremity upon earth than give up one inch of our equality—one inch of what belongs to us as members of this great republic."

Alas! many of my fellow southerners did not comprehend the danger I saw, did not understand the extent of the forces arrayed against us in the North, with the specter of world abolitionism lurking behind it, and sometimes *in* it, as English abolitionists crossed the Atlantic to speak at northern abolitionist meetings and help plot our destruction. To my dismay, Polk and the southern Administration men in Congress promoted their favorite compromise on the Oregon and Mexican territory questions: the extension of the Missouri Compromise line to the Pacific. As hard as we tried, as passionately as we pleaded, I and my followers failed to win them to our side, and the Calhoun resolutions never came up for a vote.

The Mexican War had ended with the territories of New Mexico and California ceded to us, but with Congress deadlocked over the question of slavery there and over the Oregon territorial bill. Passions were running at white heat. Senator John Hale, a corpulent, black-haired abolitionist from New Hampshire, spoke to us with studied contempt. I turned my back on him; I would as soon argue with a maniac from bedlam as with that fanatic. Senator Henry S. Foote, a small, pugnacious Mississippian, invited Hale to visit Mississippi so that the citizens of that sovereign state could justly hang him. Senator Benton of Missouri, an Administration man, insulted Andrew Butler of South Carolina so egregiously that Butler challenged him to a duel. Fortunately, it never came off. I warned southern men that we would *never* present a united front to the North if we kept fighting among ourselves.

In June of 1848, the Oregon territorial bill came up again. During the debates, Jefferson Davis, the other Mississippi Senator and a Mexican War hero, emerged as an invaluable disciple. I liked this tall young planter, with his military bearing and bright gray eyes. I had met him and his congenial young wife in Memphis not long after he returned from Mexico with a wound in his foot, which forced him to get about on crutches. Now, on the floor of the Senate, he repeated my positive-good defense of slavery and rehearsed my arguments for southern rights in the territories. "Here upon the threshold we must resist," Davis's voice rang out, "or forever abandon the claim to equality of right, and consent to be a marked caste, doomed, in the progress of national growth, to be dwarfed into helplessness and political dependence."

In late June, I gave my major address on the Oregon bill and the entire territorial question. Standing on the Senate floor, staring at my colleagues and the crowded galleries above, I argued that Congress had no authority to prohibit slavery in the territories, that such a prohibition violated the property-rights clause of the Fifth Amendment to the Constitution. Consequently, the Northwest Ordinance of 1787, which had excluded slavery in the Old Northwest before the adoption of the Constitution, had no binding force; it could apply nowhere else without violating the Constitution. As for the Missouri Compromise, the line forced on us by the northern majority was plainly unconstitutional. True, I said, the compromise had been moved by one of the South's distinguished citizens, Henry Clay; but it was equally so, that it had been carried by the almost united vote of the North against the almost united vote of the South, and had been imposed on the latter by superior numbers. The South had never given her sanction to it, nor assented to the power it asserted, the power of Congress to exclude slavery in the national lands.

In the present crisis, the advocates of that compromise, and of the Wilmot Proviso, liked to hold up the great name of Jefferson, claiming they were acting in his name. This was palpable nonsense! Jefferson had *opposed* the Missouri Compromise and its odious line. To demonstrate that point, I had the Senate secretary read Jefferson's letter to John Holmes of April 22, 1820. As Jefferson's words filled the Senate sanctuary, the galleries fell silent.

> *This momentous question, like a fire-bell in the night, awakened and filled me with terror. I consider it at once as the knell of the Union. It is hushed, indeed, for the moment. But this is a reprieve only, not the final sentence. A geographical line, coinciding with a marked principle, moral and political, once conceived, and held up to the angry passions of men, will never be obliterated; and every new irritation will mark it deeper and deeper.*

Mark his prophetic warning! I cried. Mark his profound reasoning! Twenty-eight years had passed since these remarkable words were penned, and there was not a thought in that letter which time had not thus far verified, and would, I feared, continue to verify, until his prophecy was fulfilled. If the Union did perish, I said, a future historian would explain it with a chapter on the Northwest Ordinance, another on the Missouri Compromise, and a third on the present agitation, and he would trace the root cause to the pernicious proposition of the Declaration of Independence that "all men are born free and equal," for it was that proposition which inspired the earlier bans on slavery and the Wilmot attack.

I warned the South: Are you prepared to be stripped of your dignity of equals among equals, and be deprived of your equality of rights in this Federal partnership of states? The time was at hand when the South must rise up and bravely defend herself, or sink down into base and acknowledged inferiority. How could the question be settled? It could be finally and permanently adjusted but one way, I said, and that was on the high principles of equal rights in the territories for both sections. If the North and the South could not stand together on that broad and solid foundation, there was none other on which they could stand.

In the end, we lost the battle over Oregon because Benton and Houston of Texas deserted us. In a final vote on the Oregon bill in August, the northern Senators, joined by Benton and Houston, carried the day. The passage of the Oregon bill, with its prohibition of slavery, was a flagrant assertion of power by the majority section. "The great strife between the North and South has reached a new level," I said bitterly. "The North is determined to convert all the southern population into slaves; and I will never consent to let that happen. The North and the South are now completely separated."

The final battle for the Mexican Cession—and the future control of the Union—remained to be fought.

10. CLAY

The war with Mexico sickened me. What a waste of human life. What a waste of our treasury. A war between two neighboring republics was intolerable. But a terrible fever had gripped our land: our newspapers and politicians screamed for a war of conquest; our young men heard in it the bugle call to glory. Go where you would, and the talk was war, war against Mexico, war to avenge the abuse and injury Mexico had dealt us, war to prove the superiority of the Anglo-Saxon bayonet, war to conquer the continent for *our* race and *our* institutions. I had foretold the madness and now lamented its very existence. It would *never* have occurred had *I* been President.

Nothing troubled me so deeply as the decision of my third son, Henry Jr., to enlist in the Second Kentucky Volunteers, bound for Mexico. I bade him farewell at Ashland in a tearful embrace. Henry was my beloved favorite son, on whose shoulders rested all my hopes. So many of my other sons had been disappointing to Lucretia and me: poor Thomas, with his swollen face and dull eyes, had early shown the effects of a dissipated life. Poor Theodore, unable to control his violent passions, had gone insane and had to be confined to a lunatic asylum for a time; poor John was also afflicted with mental aberrations and had to pass a month in an asylum. But things were different with Henry: he had graduated from West Point, had become a lawyer, and had married a lovely girl, Julia. They had given me cherished grandchildren, one of whom, our little Martha, had died in infancy. Then Julia herself died of a terrible hemorrhage two weeks after giving birth to Thomas Julian. Her death almost killed Henry, who sobbed uncontrollably, saying that the temple of his happiness had been shattered. I consoled the boy, sympathized with him, felt his sorrow as if it were my own. We took in his two children while Henry remained in Louisville trying to repair his broken life. When he bid unsuccessfully for political office, I begged him to come home to Ashland and join me in some business that might benefit us both. That had not happened, and now he was off to war, and I could not control a sense of foreboding. Our family had suffered so many sad afflictions that I found it impossible not to fear another.

I spent the winter in New Orleans, where news from the army left me in anxious suspense. Evidently Taylor had done some hard fighting with heavy losses. Henry was with Taylor's army, and I worried constantly about his safety. April found me back at Ashland with Lucretia. It was such a beautiful spring—I can still recall the bright sunshine beaming all around on my buildings and meadows. Then one day, as we were eating dinner in the dining room, James, my second youngest, entered with grief depicted in his countenance. "It's Henry," James said, and he handed me a letter. It reported that our beloved Henry was dead, killed at Buena Vista by Mexican bayonets. The news shattered the temple of *my* happiness beyond repair. I could not stop weeping. Oh God! I cried. How inscrutable are thy dispensations! The hurt in my heart was so deep that only God could ever heal it. Later, an officer sent us a lock of Henry's hair. I affixed it to a breast pin and wore it over my heart.

Henry's death intensified my hatred for the war, and in November of 'forty-seven, on a dark and gloomy day in Lexington, I gave my first speech against it. I blamed Polk for starting the conflict with his lies and treachery, demanded his impeachment, insisted that the fighting stop, and objected to any acquisition of territory from Mexico for the purpose of propagating slavery. I knew that the speech would offend southern Whigs, for the war was most popular in the slave states, but my stand against slavery had already cost me dearly there. I hoped that my speech would win me support in the North among the so-called conscience Whigs who opposed the war.

In January of 'forty-eight, I addressed the American Colonization Society in Washington City. The dwindling success of our repatriation efforts disappointed me, and I appealed to the country to support our attempts to colonize the Negro. I emphasized the broad and incontestable fact that the two races could not, on equal terms, live together in harmony in the same community. Where in this country, I asked, did the black man enjoy an equality with his white neighbor in political rights? In one word: nowhere. As to social rights, they were out of the question. In no city, town, or hamlet throughout the entire land was the black man regarded as on an equal footing with us. Better, then, to send him back to his native Africa.

The war ended while I was in Washington. God knows how many lads like my Henry had died on Mexico's bloody ground. Nothing could ever justify the loss of life and the betrayal of honor in that war. The end of hostilities made me grieve anew for Henry, who would never be coming home to us.

On my way back to Kentucky, I was dumbfounded to discover how beloved I had become with the people. As I approached Pittsburgh by steamboat on the Monongahela River, one of the most brilliant scenes opened on me that I ever beheld. A beautiful wire bridge, gracefully spanning the river, was crowded with people. A bend in the river, from the waters' edge back to the summit, was also full of people. With cannon booming and flags flying, the entire multitude was cheering *me,* calling *my* name. As the boat, filled with passengers and resounding with music, moved down the river, similar scenes greeted me at every town and village we passed, huge crowds smiling and cheering me amidst the incessant roar of cannon. They called me the Sage of Ashland.

With such popular support, I dared hope in private that I might win the Presidency in 'forty-eight, should the Whig convention nominate me when it met in Philadelphia in June. But that was not to be. General Zachary Taylor, the so-called hero of Buena Vista, enjoyed a groundswell of popular support that took me completely by surprise. The destiny of this Republic, I complained, ought not to reside with a military man with no known political opinions. But the Whig convention thought otherwise and went for Taylor on the fourth ballot. Even some of the Kentucky delegation endorsed Taylor. I felt betrayed. How could the Whigs nominate a man so wholly inept, so vacillating and unstable? It was, I feared, the end of the great Whig party. Looking back on it, I think that the vexed slavery question cost me the nomination. My public opposition to slavery and the Mexican War had already alienated southern Whigs, and the fact that I lived in a slave state hurt me among northern Whigs. It was 1844 all over again. By rejecting me, the northerners had helped nominate a Louisiana slaveholder who was far more deeply imbued with the doctrines of slavery than I ever was or ever would be.

Already in poor health, I came down sick and spent much of November in bed. When Taylor won the election that month, I could not conceal my bitterness and frustration. I was sure I would have won had I been the Whig nominee. Now the fate of the Republic lay in the hands of an incompetent *military* chief at a time when it most needed an experienced statesman at the helm. For the Republic faced a grave new danger now: the proper adjustment of the momentous question which grew out of the acquisition of New Mexico and California from Mexico—the question of slavery there. As I reflected on the question, I thought that northerners were overly concerned, since the plantation-slavery system could not possibly survive in the arid Southwest. Still, the slave states ought to be magnanimous and assent to the prohibition of slavery in the Mexican Cession. If they resisted restriction, I warned, it would lead to the formation of a sectional northern party, which would sooner or later take permanent and exclusive possession of the government.

In mid-February of 'forty-nine, I learned that the Kentucky legislature had elected me once again to the national Senate. I decided to accept the election and "unretire" myself, in the hope that I could help resolve the vexed new question involving the territories. While awaiting the opening of Congress, I lent my voice once again to the cause of gradual emancipation in Kentucky. A convention was scheduled to meet in the fall to amend the state constitution, and the friends of gradual emancipation thought that an open letter from me might induce the convention to adopt an emancipation amendment. I had no hope of success, but believed it my duty to speak out for a cause that was dear to my heart. In an open letter to a Kentucky friend, which was widely published in the newspapers, I reiterated all my old arguments for gradual emancipation and colonization— that slavery was a great *evil,* that it was a wasteful, inefficient labor system which retarded the state's economic development, and that colonization of all the blacks freed in Kentucky was absolutely indispensable for the peace and harmony of both races. I also challenged the racial argument of many of my fellow slaveholders that Africans deserved enslavement because of their alleged intellectual inferiority to the white race. Beware, I warned. Such an argument would prove that any white nation which had made greater advances in civilization, knowledge, and wisdom than another white nation, would have a right to reduce the latter to a state of bondage. Nay, further, if the principle of subjugation, founded upon intellectual superiority, be true, and be applicable to races and to nations, what was to prevent its being applied to individuals? In that case, the wisest man in the world would have a right to make slaves of all the rest of mankind! The only possible justification for slavery's existence, I said, was grim necessity and the dispensations of Providence. The solution to the sectional problem was not disunion (unhappy word!); it was a program that would gradually *remove* the cause of the problem from our soil, a program, say, that freed and colonized all slaves born after 1855 or 1860 when they reached twenty-five years of age.

My letter brought cries of outrage from many Kentuckians and other southerners, who damned me as an abolitionist, a traitor to my region and my race. At the same time, the abolitionists raised their usual hue and cry against me. I'd expected my letter to bring odium upon me from both sides. Still, I'm glad it was published. I owed it to the cause, to myself, and to posterity.

In the end, Kentucky rejected my appeal. Not a single pro-emancipation delegate was elected to the state constitutional convention. In fact, the new Kentucky constitution drawn up there forbade the legislature to remove slavery. It was painfully evident that the state would never in my lifetime relinquish that institution, would never in my lifetime lead the country in removing the curse from our shores. I assured myself, though, that slavery would *ultimately* be extinguished, at a time when there was a great increase in our white population and a great diminution in the value of slave labor.

11. GARRISON

I knew from the newspapers that Clay had lost a son at Buena Vista and that it caused him great suffering. Such, I believed, was God's punishment for Clay's slaveholding and his complicity in the Slave Power conspiracy to extend slave territory. Still, as a father, I could commiserate with him, for it was a difficult time for my family, too. In the spring of 1848, the dreaded lung fever swept through our house, prostrating Helen, myself, and our five children with high fever and wracking coughs. The disease killed our dear little Lizzy— our first child to die—and we mourned her in our sickbeds. That summer I took the water cure in Northampton, in western Massachusetts; I found myself submerged at intervals, from dawn to bedtime, in inky water that reminded me of the black vomit. I was also subjected to sprays, douches, and other "internal applications" and to a severely restricted diet—no coffee, no tea, no butter, no milk save for a spoonful or two of cream, no meat except a lean slice by special permission, no hot bread, no warm dish of any kind; I subsisted on cereal, cold bread, and all the water I wanted. A part of the time I was in the woods where I shouted at the top of my weakened lungs, which was good exercise for them.

In October, after I returned to Boston in improved health, Helen presented me with another son, with black hair, dark eyes, "cheeks like thumping red potatoes," and weighing ten-and-a-half pounds; we named him Francis Jackson after my dear friend and benefactor. "Heigh-ho!" I rejoiced. "The *boys* have it, out of all proportion over the girls—five to one! Should they 'all live to grow up,' the *Garrisons* will be strongly *manned*." But in April 1849 sorrow fell upon us again: six-year-old Charles, the most robust and beautifully developed of all our children, fell ill with what I was certain was rheumatic fever. He looked very much flushed in the face, complained of feeling sick at the stomach, vomited occasionally, and had pain in his limbs. At the advice of a friend, who offered his wife to help, I decided not to go for a physician and instead to give Charley a medicated vapor bath to sweat the poison from his body. We procured the necessary chair and apparatus, and in the evening my friend's wife kindly came to give the bath. While he was in the chair, some fifteen or twenty minutes, he became perfectly frantic, his screams were appalling, he begged most piteously to be released. No other person was in the room except the lady and myself. She tried to soothe him, and I appealed to his little manhood in the best way I could, thinking he was nervously affected, and urging him to bear it all with fortitude, as he would be helped by the operation. But when we took him from the bath, we found that the poor boy had been horribly scalded, especially where he had sat down, the skin being entirely destroyed on one side. He was delirious for four days. Then with a gentle sigh and a smile at his mother, dear Charles passed on. His mother, always so uncomplaining, did not blame me, but in all candor I felt pangs of guilt, fearful that the death of my robust, intelligent boy, who had seemed born to take a century upon his shoulders without stooping, was my fault, that he was defrauded of his life through unskillful treatment. We had yet five children remaining to us, but the death of Charles left a void in our hearts that nothing could ever fill. I tried to console myself with the thought that Charles was now with our darling Lizzy. How glorious was the thought of immortality! How glorious were the visions of eternity! "O Death, where is thy sting? O Grave, where is thy victory?"

In the same spring that our Charles died, I read in the press a public letter from Henry Clay again urging gradual emancipation in Kentucky and colonization of the free blacks. It was a perfectly loathsome letter, remorseless in purpose, cruel in spirit, delusive in expectation, sophistical in reasoning, and tyrannous in principle. Lest any true antislavery men be won over by his arguments, I wrote the man-stealer an open letter in the *Liberator*, which exposed *his* role in the Slave Power conspiracy.

To Henry Clay: Truly you are a pitiable object; the sands of your life are nearly run out; years are pressing heavily upon you; yet no sign of repentance do you give for the countless wrongs and outrages you have inflicted, or caused to be inflicted, on an unoffending weak and helpless race. You have been an awful curse to them, to your country, to the world. You have long stood at the head of as cruel a conspiracy against God and man as was ever contrived—a conspiracy expressly designed and adapted to give vigor and safety to the soul-crushing system of slavery, and ample indulgence to slave-holders to continue in their iniquitous course. As the author of the Missouri Compromise, you have done more than any other to lengthen the cords and strengthen the stakes of oppression. If Mexico has been wantonly invaded, her towns and cities devastated, her people slain by thousands, and the immense territories of New Mexico and California coerced from her, for the purpose of extending the dominion of the Slave Power, the criminality is eminently yours, for the same reason. The self-complacency, therefore, which you exhibit, in speaking of the "extravagant opinions" of those "who believe that slavery is a blessing," would excite in us ludicrous emotions, could we restrain our indignation in view of such profligate inconsistency. For one, sir, I am constrained to regard John C. Calhoun as a more honest, trust-worthy and harmless man than yourself, even on this question of slavery. It is true, he openly advocates slavery for all time—you only for a limited period; but, in practice, you are as bad as he is, for you hold a large number of your fellow-creatures as bona fide property; while you are more to be feared, and can do incomparably greater mischief, by your double-dealing and hypocrisy.

You say that "a vast majority of the people of the United States deplore the necessity of the continuance of slavery in any of the States." This assertion is not true: "a vast majority of the people" really care nothing about it: they are agreed in nothing so well as in despising and proscribing the colored race, whether bond or free. Sir, slavery is "the sum of all villainies"—it is pollution, concubinage, adultery—it is theft, robbery, kidnapping—it is ignorance, degradation, suffering, injustice—it is the exaltation of a master above all that is called God. This you know; and yet you dare to affirm that its continuance is a matter of "necessity!" Ah! this is ever "the tyrant's plea," and you are a tyrant. . . . Yours, for immediate emancipation without expatriation, WM. LLOYD GARRISON.

To think that such a noble spirit aspired to sit in the White House. Brother Douglass had the best thing to say about that. With exquisite sarcasm, he told our antislavery society: "I want to say a word about the Colonization Society, of which Henry Clay is President. He is *President* of nothing else."

12. CALHOUN

In December of 1848, the abolitionists in the House—the so-called conscience Whigs—launched a carefully plotted political offensive whose ultimate objective was to destroy us. First they reported a bill organizing a free territorial government in California on the basis of the Wilmot Proviso. Next they moved that a bill be reported abolishing the slave trade in the District of Columbia, and the House approved the resolution. Then they dropped a bombshell. An obscure Whig from Illinois rose at the back of the Hall of Representatives and announced in a shrill voice that he intended to offer a bill *abolishing slavery itself in the District of Columbia*! I had never heard of this tall, ungainly Illinoisan, Lincoln I think his name was, but I knew that he and his cronies were aiming for a Federal strike against slavery in the states. I had long warned that the abolitionist agitation, commencing with the petition campaign of 1835, would lead to a congressional attack against slavery in the District, whose real purpose was to clear the way for a *bill abolishing slavery in the South itself*. Now that congressional attack was upon us.

Eighty-eight southern Democrats and Whigs met in caucus to determine a course of action to defend our southern homeland. Benton and Houston, of course, were absent. Most of those in attendance agreed with me that the South must stand united, and they chose me to draft an address to the southern people.

On the night of January fifteenth, 1849, we reconvened in a lamp-lit Senate chamber, and I read my "Address to the Southern People," which recounted the long history of northern aggressions and encroachments on our rights by which the free states planned to encircle, invade, and annihilate the slave South. I cited the hostile legislation—the so-called personal liberty laws—enacted by certain northern states to obstruct the apprehension of fugitives. I cited the secret combinations which were believed to exist in many of the northern states whose object was to entice, decoy, entrap, inveigle, and seduce slaves to escape from their owners, and to pass secretly and rapidly, by means organized for the purpose, into Canada, beyond the reach of masters and the Federal fugitive slave law of 1793.

But worse of all, I said, was the incessant abolitionist agitation. To unite the North in fixed hostility to slavery in the South, societies and newspapers were everywhere established, debating clubs opened, lecturers employed, pamphlets and other publications disseminated, pictures and petitions thrown at Congress regardless of truth or decency. At the same time, the abolitionists deployed emissaries and circulated incendiary publications in the South to excite discontent among the slaves. This agitation had augmented over the years until it now loomed aggressive and dangerous to the rights of the South and subversive of the ends for which the Constitution was established, among which was to ensure domestic tranquillity.

For almost thirty years now, the North had also agitated to restrict the spread of slavery so as to alter the equality of states. This agitation first appeared in the Missouri Compromise and the disquieting debates that accompanied it, which, with the effects that followed, did so much to alienate the South and the North and to endanger our political institutions. With the introduction of the Wilmot Proviso, the North repudiated the Missouri Compromise and formed a conspiracy to keep slavery out of the territories altogether. This was blatantly unconstitutional, for the Federal Government had no more authority to restrict slavery than it had to abolish it. It had no power to legislate on slavery whatever, and certainly no power to prohibit us from migrating with our property into the territories.

The northern agitation against slavery, I pointed out, had culminated in the abolition bills currently before Congress. These bills, indeed the entire northern conspiracy of restriction and encirclement, had but one objective: to prostrate the white race by destroying the existing relation between the free and servile races in the southern states. It would begin with emancipation, to be effected through the agency of the Federal Government once it was controlled by the dominant power of the northern states. Impelled by fanaticism and love of power, the northern majority would not stop with emancipation. Another step would be taken—to raise the blacks to a political and social equality with their former owners, by giving them the right to vote and hold political office. The blacks would then become the principal recipients of Federal offices and patronage in the South, and would, in consequence, be raised above the whites there in the political and social scale. We would, in a word, change conditions with them—a degradation greater than had ever yet fallen to the lot of a free and enlightened people, and one from which we could not escape except by fleeing our homes and abandoning our country to the former slaves, leaving it the permanent abode of disorder, anarchy, poverty, misery, and wretchedness.

What could the southern people do to prevent this? "We are of the opinion," I said, "that the first and indispensable step, without which nothing can be done, and with which every thing may be, is to be united among yourselves. The want of union and concert has brought the South, the Union, and our system of government to their present perilous condition. If you become united, and prove yourselves in earnest, the North will be brought to a pause and to a calculation of consequences. If this does not happen, nothing will remain to you but to stand up immovably in defense of your rights—your property, prosperity, equality, liberty, and safety."

Finished reading, I sat down in the flickering light and awaited the response of my colleagues. Most of the Democrats approved the address; but Robert Toombs, speaking for the Whigs, said its tone was too "bullying" and "threatening." Six feet tall, with uncombed long black hair, arched brows, and a goatee on his chin, Toombs argued for party loyalty and assured his fellow Whigs that President-elect Taylor would "make everything right." In the end, the southern Whigs deserted us. Of the forty-eight southerners who signed the

Address, only one was a Whig. This emboldened Toombs to gloat that the Whigs had foiled "Calhoun's miserable attempt to form a southern party." A few days after the caucus, I collapsed on the Senate floor and had to be helped to my quarters. Distraught and ill with a terrible congestion in the lungs and bouts of coughing, I told my friends that I had nothing to live for.

Still, there were a few encouraging signs. Perhaps unnerved by the fury of our opposition, the congressman from Illinois never offered an abolition bill for the District of Columbia. And southerners of both parties were strong enough to prevent Congress from considering any of the abolitionist bills during the current session. With both houses deeply divided on the territorial issue, Congress failed to provide either California or New Mexico with a territorial government, and adjourned in deadlock early in the morning of March fourth, 1849, a Sunday. The next day, Zachary Taylor, a Louisiana slaveholder (albeit a Whig), was inaugurated as President. Privately I thought him better for the South than the Yankee Democrat he had defeated, Lewis Cass of Michigan. As things now stood, I said, the prospect was that before four years had elapsed, the Union would be divided into two great hostile sectional parties.

I returned home to recuperate my health and contemplate the future. Conditions at Fort Hill, however, were not good. I was so deeply in debt that I had to secure a loan of $5,000 at once, with another $13,000 or so to follow, to meet the demands of my plantation and slaves, who now numbered eighty. On the advice of my son, a physician, I submitted to the "water cure" as a reasonable alternative to the medicinal brandy toddies I'd been drinking, which I detested. While I lay in bed, my body servants removed my clothes, wrapped me in a damp sheet, covered me with eight or nine blankets, and left me to perspire for an hour and a half. This was followed by a warm bath and a rubdown. The process was soothing and pleasant. I felt well enough, in the privacy of my office, to finish the final draft of my "Disquisition on Government" in which I laid out my argument for concurrent majorities. I also made excellent progress on my "Discourse on the Constitution and Government of the United States," which contained my proposal for a dual Presidency.

While thus engaged I learned that California had adopted a constitution prohibiting slavery and would seek admission into the Union as a free state. There were reports that New Mexico, too, would soon be ready for admission as a free state. This was a

calamitous development for the South, the next stage in the abolitionist conspiracy to seize the territories and take over the Federal
Government. Two new free states would upset the equilibrium of
slaveholding and non-slaveholding states, which now stood at fifteen
apiece, and permanently alter the balance of power between the sections. I vowed to sunder the Union before I would let that occur. At
my instigation, Mississippi issued a call for an all-southern convention to meet in Nashville, Tennessee, in the summer of 1850. This
convention would be poised to take the slave states out of the Union
if California and New Mexico were admitted as free states.

By now, my health had taken another turn for the worse: I was
so sick and enfeebled that I could barely get about. My neighbors
begged me not to return to Washington City for the winter session
of Congress. They left unsaid what I already sensed, that I was dying
of the lung sickness. But duty to the South, duty to the survival of
the white race and Christian civilization itself, would not let me
remain at Fort Hill. Who else had the strength of resolve to rally the
South against northern tyranny? Who else could lead the South out
of the Union if our rights were not preserved?

In December, wrapped in flannels, I left for Washington City for
what could well be the last congressional session before the breakup
of these United States.

13 · CLAY

Back in Washington that December of 'forty-nine, I took rooms
in the National Hotel—a parlor and an adjoining bedroom—and
received old friends over brandy and cigars. Although I was in poor
health, suffering from a bad cold and a persistent cough, I made the
requisite social rounds. I attended a White House dinner and spoke
briefly with President Taylor, who was short and heavy-set, with
deep wrinkles in his face and a slovenly way of speaking: he mispro-
nounced words, slurred, stammered, and stuttered as if language
were foreign to him. I had little faith that this mere *military* man
could provide effective executive leadership in the new crisis imperil-
ing the nation.

When I visited the empty Senate chamber after an absence of
more than seven years, I was overwhelmed with emotion. I loved

this sedate sanctuary, with its ornamented dome, crimson and gold carpets, fluted drapes, and columns of variegated marble and gilt iron. I gazed for a long moment at Rembrandt Peale's portrait of Washington, which hung on the east wall, just above the Vice-President's desk. The light shining through the windows on the east wall and the apertures of the dome gave the chamber a cathedral appearance. Despite our vortex of difficulties, it was good to be back.

The crisis over California and New Mexico dominated conversation in the congressional corridors. No one, I told my friends, could be more opposed than I was to the extension of slavery into these new territories. It was my contention that slavery was excluded from them by Mexican law, which had abolished slavery and which had carried over when the United States assumed control. I hoped that Congress could resolve the problem in a spirit of mutual and friendly forbearance.

That, clearly, was not going to occur. When Congress went into session, I had never seen either house so bitterly divided, not even in 1820. The House was in such an uproar that it required *sixty-three* ballots to elect a Speaker, Howell Cobb of Georgia. During the stormy House debates, Toombs of Georgia, whom I'd thought a Union man and a patriot, took Calhoun's side and flung down the gauntlet before his northern colleagues: "I do not hesitate to avow before this House and the country, and in the presence of the living God, that if by your legislation you seek to drive us from the territories of California and New Mexico and to abolish slavery in this District, I am for disunion."

"Sir," retorted an Illinois Whig, "we do not believe the Union *can ever be dissolved*. We will not be intimidated by threats of violence."

"The South," Toombs cried, "is prepared to teach the North that she is in earnest. If any bill is passed by this Congress abolishing slavery in the District of Columbia, or incorporating the Wilmot Proviso in any form, I will introduce a resolution in this House declaring that this Union be dissolved."

In the Senate, where my return was greeted with a resounding ovation, Jefferson Davis of Mississippi echoed Toombs's threat. As erect and sharp-edged as a bayonet, Davis seethed with defiance. "If northerners think it proper to sow the seeds of disunion," he warned, "and to inflame the passions and prejudices of their section whilst they drive the other by every possible provocation to the point of civil war, then all I have to say is, that the representatives of the South are prepared to meet the issue here and now."

Calhoun, in a gracious gesture from an old rival, strode across the aisle to welcome me back. He said it was the "common opinion" that the South would not remain in the Union unless her equality and security within it were guaranteed. I suspected that his hand had orchestrated the call for the Nashville convention, the very thought of which filled me with foreboding. Calhoun was coughing worse than I was and looked sick and terribly emaciated, his cheeks sunken, his hair almost totally white, his cavernous eyes burning feverishly.

The feeling for disunion among the intemperate southern politicians was stronger than I'd supposed it could be. But I was determined to find a way of conciliating the two sides and averting disaster. *I* was the Great Pacificator, was I not? I had saved the Union twice before, in 1820 and 1833, and I would do it again somehow. Frail and weak myself and coughing constantly, I hurried from house to house, speaking to leaders of both sides, appealing to their reason and patriotism. But Congress was so divided along sectional lines that I despaired of ever finding an acceptable compromise on the infernal territorial problem and the other vexed questions over slavery. At one extreme stood the northern party—the conscience Whigs, antislavery northern Democrats, and the new Free-Soil splinter group—who were adamant in demanding the admission of California as a free state and the imposition of the Wilmot Proviso in the other territorial governments. Many of that party also demanded the abolition of the slave trade in the District of Columbia. Some like Joshua Giddings, a tall, robust Ohioan with curly blond hair, also wanted slavery itself abolished there. At the other extreme stood the southern party—Calhoun and the southern Democrats and many southern Whigs—who strenuously opposed the Wilmot Proviso, insisting on an implied constitutional right to take slave property into the national lands and threatening disunion if that right was denied. When Mason of Virginia proposed a new fugitive slave law, the two sides argued like men representing two hostile countries on the verge of war.

There were two compromise positions on the territorial issue: one called for the extension of the Missouri Compromise line; the other touted popular or "squatter" sovereignty, which would leave it up to the settlers of each territory whether to have slavery or not. The two positions, however, had the support of almost nobody beyond their immediate sponsors. Calhoun, for his part, declared himself unalterably opposed to any compromise on the slavery question. He dismissed popular sovereignty with a wave of his hand, calling it "the greatest of all absurdities," since it divided the sovereignty over a territory between the initial settlers there and the United States. "How can sovereignty—the ultimate and supreme power of a state—be divided?" he demanded, speaking in that staccato style of his. When I stated that in my opinion Mexican law precluded slavery in the Mexican Cession, he looked upon me as if I had taken leave of my senses. "The sovereignty and authority of Mexico in the territory acquired by the United States," he said flatly, "became extinct the moment the peace treaty between them was ratified."

Before returning to the Whig side of the Senate chamber, I spoke with Jefferson Davis of Mississippi, who said that the only compromise he would accept was the extension of the Missouri Compromise line. This was the one point on which he differed from Calhoun.

"Congressional non-action is better for you," I said. "If you vote to extend the Missouri line, you vote for Congress to legislate upon slavery, and legislate for its restriction north of the line without any guarantees for its admission south of the line. Yes, it's been said that the poor soil and arid climate of the Southwest precludes the existence of slavery there anyway, but we can't help that. Who can you reproach but nature and nature's God?"

As we talked, Davis remarked that "our northern enemies" came in various guises—as abolitionists, non-extensionists, Liberty men, Free-Soilers, "conscience" Whigs—but from the South's view they were all one family, differing somewhat in their mode of attack, but not at all in the final purpose of it, which was to destroy the peculiar institution. "We have to meet the evil, this geographical party, which startled Jefferson like a fire bell in the night," Davis said. "We have surrendered too much to these fanatics and demagogues already. Sir, there will be no more surrendering."

Thus was the Mexican Cession poisoning us! *Damn* that misguided war with Mexico and its malignant fruit! I feared that there was no hope of settling the territorial question and that disunion and civil war were upon us. Still, I refused to give up. Working virtually without sleep, I began developing an all-encompassing compromise plan to pull us back from the brink.

The President meanwhile devised his own plan of settlement, which he revealed in a special message that was read to Congress on a cold, rain-swept day in January of 1850. Taylor's plan provided for the admission of both California and New Mexico, presumably as free states, without offering southerners anything in return. The President advised Congress to do nothing, *nothing at all*, until California and New Mexico formally applied for statehood.

Calhoun and his followers were furious. "This *Executive* Proviso," Calhoun said derisively, "is worse than the Wilmot Proviso. What Wilmot proposes to effect directly and openly, Taylor proposes to effect indirectly and covertly. By God, we won't stand for it."

Had Taylor acted out of sheer ignorance or sheer obstinacy? I did not for a moment believe, as some northerners did, that this bungling *military* chief had placed his idea of national welfare above his loyalty to the South and his slaveholding class. It enraged me that he would blindly pursue his own plan instead of joining with Congress to work out some broad and comprehensive scheme of healing, one that would settle all the questions that agitated the sections. More than ever now, it was up to me to do the healing.

That night, sick though I was with a cold, I took my carriage through the rain to see Senator Webster of Massachusetts, my great Whig rival for the Presidency, with whom I had spoken little in the last eight years. I called at his house without an appointment and told him that in this hour of peril we must put our personal animosities aside. I then outlined my compromise plan and asked for his support. He listened with his massive head cocked to one side, his puffy red face without expression, his black, brooding, deep-set eyes staring at me as I spoke. "I approve the substance of what you propose," he said finally. "It is great and highly patriotic. You can count on me to support it." I thanked him and hurried home in the rain.

In late January, I introduced in the Senate eight separate resolutions designed to settle all current disputes over the slavery question. The first resolution admitted California as a free state. The second organized the territories of New Mexico and Utah without congressional conditions on slavery (I assumed that Mexican law, which had abolished it, would continue in both territories). The third and fourth resolutions dealt with Texas: one assumed the Texas preannexation debt, the other adjusted the disputed Texas–New Mexico border. The fifth resolution declared the abolition of slavery in the District "inexpedient." But the sixth resolution did abolish the slave trade there. The seventh resolution, aimed at mollifying southerners, provided for a stringent new fugitive slave law. This measure would override attempts by certain northern states, through the enactment of personal liberty laws, to impede the capture of runaways. A final resolution, also aimed at southerners, rejected congressional authority over the internal slave trade.

At one point in my speech, I held up a precious relic I had recently received—it was a fragment taken from the coffin of George Washington. Holding it aloft, I said: "The venerated father of the country is warning us from Mount Vernon. Do not destroy his handiwork!"

But few in Congress were in the mood for compromise. In the Senate and House alike, the ultras of both sections savaged my proposals and rehearsed old grievances. Calhoun was absent from the Senate, confined to his quarters with pneumonia, but his acolytes, Davis and Mason, greeted my resolutions with open contempt. "What," Davis demanded, "does the South get out of this plan? The South gets nothing while the North gets everything." One Virginia hotspur not only denounced my "sneaking compromises" but dubbed me the "prince of charlatans and traitors." The Calhounites threatened disunion if my measures were approved. Northerners were just as intransigent. Giddings predicted that my plan would "fall stillborn." William Seward of New York, who had a beaked nose like a buzzard's, dismissed my entire effort as "magnificent humbug."

Undaunted, I announced that I would defend my resolutions in a major address in early February. When the day came, I was so sick that a fellow Kentuckian had to help me up the steps of the Capitol. We found the Senate chamber crowded with spectators who had come to hear the Sage of Ashland. They filled the galleries, jammed the aisles, and overflowed into the corridors, the rotunda, and even the congressional library. As my friend and I made our way through the crowd, I paused to kiss the pretty girls, as is my wont. They blushed and giggled delightfully, unembarrassed that the gentleman kissing them was almost seventy-three, with sunken cheeks, graying hair, and a bald spot on top of his head.

When it came time for me to speak, I stood with an effort and looked around the chamber at my colleagues. "Never, on any former occasion," I said, "have I risen under feelings of such deep solicitude, to address an assembly so oppressed, so appalled, so anxious." Speaking more than four hours all told, I defended my compromise measures point by point, stressing that they required neither side to surrender any great principle. I asked my scowling southern brethren, how could California be denied admission to the Union? Did not Californians have the incontestable right to declare theirs a free state? What principle did that surrender, for the North or the South? Had not men of the South conceded that the people of a territory, at the time of statehood, could rule on the slavery issue? That was all that Californians had done.

Then I addressed my northern colleagues. For the sake of peace, I said, let the northern states stop promoting the Wilmot Proviso. There was no need for a Federal law prohibiting slavery in California and New Mexico. It was already banned there by Mexican law and by the great law of nature. "What do you Free-Soilers want?" I asked. "You want that there shall be no slavery introduced into the territories acquired from Mexico. Well, haven't you got it in California already, if admitted as a state? Haven't you also got it in New Mexico, in all human probability? What more do you want? You've got what is worth a thousand Wilmot Provisos. You've got nature on your side."

As for slavery in the District of Columbia, I conceded that Congress had the power to abolish the institution there, but argued that it ought to remain on the grounds of necessity, grim necessity. The *slave trade,* however, was a different matter altogether. I agreed with northern men that it was a national disgrace to see long trains of slaves passing daily down Pennsylvania Avenue from the Capitol to the executive mansion. The trade could be abolished without injuring the slaveholding states. "Outlaw the slave trade in the District and adopt my other measures," I said, "and I venture to predict that, instead of the distractions and anxieties which now prevail, we will have peace and quiet for the next thirty years."

Then I took up the new fugitive slave bill, which faced considerable northern opposition. The fugitive slave clause in the Constitution, I maintained, obligated every citizen and every state official in the country to help southern slaveowners retrieve their runaways. In *Prigg v. Pennsylvania*, I pointed out, the U.S. Supreme Court had declared it unconstitutional for a state to interfere with the retrieval of fugitives. True, in that same decision, the court had also exempted state officials from having to enforce the 1793 fugitive slave law. Well, I said, I disagreed with the court on that point, but no matter. If the Federal Government alone was responsible for enforcing the fugitive slave clause of the Constitution, then a powerful, coercive new Federal measure was all the more mandatory. "I will go with the furthest Senator from the South," I said, "to impose the heaviest sanctions upon the recovery of fugitive slaves, and the restoration of them to their owners."

But, I said, I stood *against* those southerners who kept clamoring for disunion. No state or states had the right to secede. Such a course would lead to rival confederacies and a war of extermination, the consequences of which would be the emergence of a tyrant who would crush the liberties of both the dissevered portions of this Union. "Sir," I said, facing the President of the Senate, "we may search the pages of history, and none so furious, so bloody, so implacable, so exterminating, from the wars of Greece down—none, none of them raged with such violence as will that war which shall follow that disastrous event—if that event ever happens—of dissolution."

I begged my congressional colleagues, I begged my countrymen North and South, to pause at the edge of the precipice, before they took the fearful and disastrous leap into the yawning abyss below, which would lead to certain and irretrievable destruction. If the Union were dissolved, I fervently prayed that I might not be alive to behold the sad and heartrending spectacle.

One after another, Davis and the other southerners leaped to their feet to object. They accused me of turning on my native region, of selling out to the North. I retorted that my plan offered equal and impartial justice to both sections. "I consider us all as one family, all as friends, all as brethren," I said. "I consider us all as united in one common destiny; and those efforts which I shall continue to employ will be to keep us together as one family, in concord and harmony; and above all, to avoid that direful day when one part of the Union could speak of the other as an enemy. I know no South, no North, no East, no West. My allegiance is to the Union and to my own state." Then I addressed Davis and the other Calhoun men. "If gentlemen suppose they can exact from me an allegiance to some future confederacy of the South, I declare here, on this floor, that I owe *no allegiance* to it." Day after day, southern hotspurs continued to rend the air with grating and doleful threats of dissolution, treason, and war.

I did win some support. Cass of Michigan, Stephen A. Douglas of Illinois, and of course Daniel Webster were with me. Houston of Texas, dressed in a Mexican sombrero, a panther-skin coat, and a fiery red vest, also declared in favor of compromise. It warmed my heart to hear him say in his drawl, "I wish no epitaph to be written to tell that I survived the ruin of this glorious Union." But beyond these gentlemen, my resolutions ran into insurmountable opposition. President Taylor, in a display of mule-headed defiance, refused to endorse any plan but his own. Northern Free-Soil advocates remained adamantly opposed to my plan, as did the Calhounites, who had begun a House filibuster against the admission of California. I heard that Calhoun, although sick and probably dying, was preparing a major rebuttal to my plan. What else could one expect? This one-time nationalist had surrendered himself to a bitter, uncompromising sectionalism.

"We are still in the woods here, on the slavery question," I wrote my son James, "and I don't know when we shall get out of them. All other business is superseded or suspended. I do not absolutely despair of settlement on the basis of my resolutions." I did not *absolutely* despair, but I did despair pretty badly. Because in certain moments when I peered into the future, I could see scenes of civil war—sacked cities, desolated fields, smoking ruins, streams of American blood shed by American arms. And it sickened my soul.

14. CALHOUN

Sick with pneumonia and confined to my quarters, I missed Clay's speech in defense of his compromise proposals. I was anxious lest a single southerner be duped by his palliatives. There could be *no compromise* with the North, not now, not ever. If we yielded a single inch on any of the slavery questions, we would lose everything. Afflicted with a wracking cough, I prepared a formal address to be given in the Senate on March fourth. I knew that it might well be the last speech I would ever give.

Alas, when March fourth came, I was too sick to deliver the speech. James M. Mason, a manly, clean-shaven Virginian who called himself "Jeems," offered to read it in my stead. Just past noon that day, I entered the Senate chamber on the arm of my friend, General James Hamilton of South Carolina, and took my seat with Davis and my Deep South supporters gathered around. Clay and Webster, in a gesture of courtesy, crossed the aisle to welcome me back. As I slumped in my seat with my black cloak wrapped around me, Senator Mason began reading my script, and my words swept the Senate sanctuary.

"I have, Senators, believed from the first that the agitation of the subject of slavery would, if not prevented by some timely and effective measure, end in disunion. The agitation has been permitted to proceed, with almost no attempt to resist it, until it has reached a point when it can no longer be disguised or denied that the Union is in danger.

"What has led to the current crisis? The long-continued agitation of the slavery question on the part of the North, and the many aggressions which they have made on the rights of the South. The Northwest Ordinance, the Missouri Compromise, the Wilmot Proviso, and the new Executive Proviso of General Taylor, which arrogantly usurp the sovereignty of the states over the territories, all had or have but one purpose: to give the North absolute control over the Federal Government, with a view to the final abolition of slavery in the southern states.

"It is a great mistake to suppose that disunion can be effected at a single blow. The cords which bind these states together in one common Union, are far too numerous and powerful for that. Disunion must be the work of time. It is only through a long process, and successively, that the cords of Union can be snapped, until the whole fabric falls asunder. That long process is now well under way: the spiritual and ecclesiastical cords have already snapped with the split of the Methodist, Presbyterian, and Baptist churches over slavery; and the political cords are now breaking as well.

"How can the Union be saved? Not by the plan proposed by the distinguished Senator from Kentucky, which has been so ably replied to by others. The plan of the Administration cannot save the Union, because it fails to satisfy the slaveholding states that they can, consistently with safety and honor, remain in the Union. The Administration's plan is but a modification of the Wilmot Proviso, and both are dangerous wounds to the Constitution.

"How, then, can the Union be saved? There is but one way, and that is for the North to consent to remanding California to territorial status, to concede the South an equal right in the acquired territory, and to do her duty by causing the stipulations relative to fugitive slaves to be faithfully fulfilled—to cease agitating the slave question, and to provide for the insertion of a provision in the Constitution, by an amendment, which will restore to the South, in substance, the power she possessed of protecting herself, before the equilibrium between the sections was destroyed by the action of this government. At all events, the responsibility of saving the Union rests on the North, not on the South.

"If you, who represent the stronger section, cannot agree to settle our differences on the broad principle of justice and duty, say so; and let the states we both represent agree to separate and part in peace. If you are unwilling that we should depart in peace, tell us so, and we shall know what to do, when you reduce the question to submission or resistance."

I was vague about the constitutional amendment that would allow the South to protect herself. After I was dead, southerners who read my treatises on government and the Constitution would know what to demand in such an amendment: either a dual executive or a state veto.

The next day, to my anger and dismay, "Hangman" Foote of Mississippi, once my ardent supporter, betrayed us. Arguing that there was no need for a constitutional amendment to protect the slaveholding states, this tempestuous little traitor defected to Clay and the compromisers. On March seventh, Webster, too, spoke in favor of Clay's compromise plan. He damned the abolitionists and the Wilmot Proviso, for which I was grateful. But when he declared that secession and disunion were impossible, I interjected, "No sir! The Union *can* be broken." I warned Webster, Hangman Foote, Clay, and all the Wilmot men that nothing short of the terms I proposed could settle the crisis. A few days later, the abolitionist Seward delivered a demented speech about how there was a higher law above the Constitution—God's law—which excluded slavery from the territories. Such were the delusions of Yankee fanaticism.

In private, I told Mason that I believed the Union was doomed regardless of what happened. "I am satisfied in my judgment that even if the questions now agitating Congress are settled to the satisfaction and the concurrence of the southern states, it will not avert the catastrophe. I fix its probable occurrence within twelve years or three presidential terms. You and others your age will probably live to see it; I shall not. The mode by which it will be is not so clear; it may be brought about in a manner that none now foresee. But the probability is, it will explode in a presidential election."

15 . CLAY

Calhoun died on March thirty-first, and it made me painfully aware of my own mortality. He, Webster, and I had served so long together that they called us The Great Triumvirate. My memories of Calhoun stretched back to the first "War Congress" almost forty years ago, when he had been "a star bright and brilliant." I won't forget his flashing eyes and his oratory, that torrent of clear, concise, compact logic, which always won our admiration even if it did not sway us or contribute to our understanding. Calhoun's death removed a powerful obstacle to compromise, to be sure, but that gave me no personal satisfaction. In my eulogy the next day, I paid Calhoun my final respects. "I was his senior in years," I said, "in nothing else. Mr. Speaker, he is gone. He is now a character in history."

Since proposing my compromise resolutions, I had caucused day after day with pro-Union men, northern and southern, Whig and Democrat, trying to find a way out of the deadlock. As chairman of the Senate Committee on Territories, young Douglas of Illinois proved an invaluable ally. A short man with stubby legs and a gigantic head like Webster's, Douglas worked hard to bring northern Democrats around to our side.

In May, I tried a new approach, first proposed by Senator Foote. I offered all my resolutions in a single omnibus bill. That approach had worked during the Missouri crisis in 1820; perhaps it would again. I pleaded for my colleagues, North and South, to stop all the mutual threats and recriminations and vote for the broad and comprehensive scheme of healing embodied in the omnibus bill. "I go for honorable compromise whenever it can be made," I said. "Life itself is but a compromise between death and life, the struggle continuing throughout our whole existence, until the great Destroyer finally triumphs. All legislation, all government, all society, is formed upon the principle of mutual concession, politeness, comity, courtesy; upon these everything is based."

But the new bill provoked still more raucous debates. Jefferson Davis, who took Calhoun's place as leader of the opposition, tried to derail the measure by proposing an amendment asserting that the Constitution guaranteed slavery in New Mexico and Utah. "I repeat what I have said before," I told Davis, "that I *cannot* vote to convert a territory already free into a slave territory." Taylor also sought to obstruct my efforts by waging war, open war, undisguised war against us. As if all this were not bad enough, there were reports of imminent civil war between New Mexico and Texas over their disputed border! The madness was out of control.

The only good news came from Nashville, where the all-southern convention met, made noisy fulminations in favor of southern rights, and adjourned without action. Then on July ninth—I won't forget that day either—General Taylor died of cholera morbus, caused, apparently, by the consumption of huge amounts of raw fruit and vegetables, washed down with ice water, after he had returned from a Fourth of July celebration at the unfinished Washington monument. Quite frankly, I could not conceal my jubilation. Taylor's death seemed like divine intervention to ensure our success. Now we had a pro-compromise man in the White House, Millard Fillmore. A little shorter than I am, with white hair, a pink complexion, and merry blue eyes, the new chief had the build of an outdoorsman. My relations with him were intimate and confidential. He not only came to me for advice, but appointed Webster as his Secretary of State.

At our urging, Fillmore formed a coalition with us to get the omnibus bill through Congress. But it was not to be, as Davis and the southern disunionists, the northern conscience Whigs and Free-Soilers, and the Taylor men joined in a malignant alliance against us. The bill sank in a vortex of acrimonious speeches, amendments, and shouts to adjourn from its combined opponents. My whole heart was bound up with the omnibus bill. When it went down to defeat, I rose from my desk and without a word walked out of the Senate chamber.

At Douglas's suggestion, we reverted to the original strategy of pushing the bills individually, hoping thereby to unite the friends of compromise instead of its enemies. But exhausted, worn down by sickness, and coughing worse than ever, I lacked the strength and the will to carry the program through. I left for Newport, Rhode Island, to rest and recuperate on the seashore. I did some seabathing, and the cool water and invigorating air made me feel a little better.

I had left the execution of the measure-by-measure strategy in the competent hands of young Douglas, the Little Giant of Illinois Democrats. In a remarkable display of legislative skill and maneuvering, Douglas won the support of Democrats in both houses and guided the measures one by one into law. When I returned to Washington in late August, the slave-trade bill was the only one not yet enacted; I gave it my personal guidance and saw it through. I was grateful that Douglas called the bills collectively "Mr. Clay's compromise."

I pronounced it "the reunion of this Union" and with Webster attended a victory celebration, where we drank toasts of champagne and whiskey to the salvation of the country. President Fillmore rightly declared the Compromise of 1850 "a final settlement" of all sectional disputes. The slave trade, with its obnoxious slave depot and trains of manacled blacks, was gone from Washington City, and the status of slavery in every territory was now decided. It was banned in Oregon, in the unorganized northern section of the old Louisiana Purchase Territory, and, I assumed, in New Mexico and Utah by Mexican law. When pro-Union, pro-compromise candidates swept to victory in the southern state elections, I was confident that we had averted disunion and civil war.

The new fugitive slave law, I believe, kept the South in the Union in 'fifty and 'fifty-one. Not only does it deny fugitives trial by jury and the right to testify; it also imposes a fine and imprisonment upon any citizen found guilty of preventing a fugitive's arrest. The law is enforced by specially appointed Federal commissioners, who receive five dollars for each acquittal and ten dollars for each conviction, since a conviction requires more paperwork.

Yes, since the passage of the compromise, the abolitionists and free coloreds of the North have howled in protest and viciously assailed me, and twice in Boston there has been a failure to execute the law, which shocks and astounds me. There is also a rumor that some "poor little dwarfish insane man" here in Washington City has threatened to "murder Mr. Clay." But such people belong to the lunatic fringe. The vast majority of Americans, North and South, support our handiwork, the great compromise that pulled the nation back from the brink.

It is now sometime in the spring of 1852, and I am lying in bed in a dark room of the National Hotel, too sick to go home to Ashland, too sick even to walk across the room. My physicians are guarded about my condition, but I know it is near my time. Unable to sleep, wracked by fits of coughing, I lie here afloat on a sea of memories. Thomas, my youngest, is here to help me through. I wish Lucretia could come. God bless and preserve you, my dear wife. I'm not afraid of death, no, I've no fear of the Great Destroyer, for soon I'll be with Henry, Anne, little Martha, and all the others. When Frank Blair came by for a visit and urged me not to despair, I told him: "Sir, there is no such word in my vocabulary."

My last will and testament stands as my personal benediction to the vexed slavery question: it provides for the gradual liberation and colonization of all children born after January first, 1850, to the thirty-five slaves I now hold.

God save the Union.

PART TWO

CROSSWINDS

16. FREDERICK DOUGLASS

The fugitive slave law plunged Negroes of the North into the bitterest anguish. That horrible, hell-black enactment embodied the Virginia principle that every person of color was a slave until proved otherwise. How could any of us be safe now? Afraid that they would be arrested and dragged to the South in chains, thousands of black folk abandoned their homes and fled to Canada, beyond the reach of the Federal Government and the two-legged bloodhounds operating under its auspices.

Other men of color—and I was one of them—advocated *resistance* to the new law. "If any pale-faced wretch enters my house to enforce this law on me or mine," cried Robert Purvis of Philadelphia, "I'll take his life, I'll shed his blood." That was my sentiment exactly. I told my Rochester neighbors that nothing short of *physical* resistance would render the colored people of the North safe from the enormities which must result from an execution of this vile law. The only sure way to make it a dead letter, I said, was to make a half a dozen or more dead kidnappers. Resistance was not only wise and just; it was *divine*. What had the sage of the Old Dominion said about the possibility of a war between the victims of the slave system and their oppressors? "God has no attribute that could take sides with the oppressor in such a contest. I tremble for my country when I reflect that God is just, and that his justice cannot sleep forever." Such was the warning voice of Thomas Jefferson! And every day's experience since its utterance until the passage of this infernal law confirmed its wisdom and commended its truth.

The fugitive slave law was further manifestation of the slaveholders' control over the Union. Though a mere fraction of the American people and a minority even in the South, this small knot of tyrants dominated both major parties and possessed indisputable power in the councils of the nation. Every great northern man had to bow to the knee of this mysterious power. Whence came this power? It derived from the unity of all southerners around one all-absorbing and all-commanding interest, which was the maintenance, prosperity, and propagation of slavery. They talked about their "domestic institutions" and their "southern rights," but slavery was the only thing meant by these euphonious terms.

With the fugitive slave law, however, the tyrants pushed the North too far. The sage of Concord, Ralph Waldo Emerson, said that the new law made "slave catchers of us all," and he vowed not to obey it. Brother Garrison claimed that it converted more northerners to abolition than had any event since the murder of Elijah Lovejoy. Abolitionists Wendell Phillips and Thomas Wentworth Higginson, heretofore disciples of Garrison, agreed with me that forceful, even armed, resistance was an act of conscience.

Brother Garrison, however, vehemently disapproved of such action and clung stubbornly to the now outmoded doctrine of nonresistance. "Many persons glory in their hostility to this immoral law," Garrison argued. "But evil as it is, opposition to it is no proof in itself of antislavery fidelity. That law is merely incidental to slavery, and there is no merit in opposition which extends no further than to its provisions. Our warfare is not against slave-hunting alone, but against the existence of slavery." That was easy for Garrison to say: he was not black. The slave catchers were not after him and his wife and children. But they *were* after mine. Many white abolitionists, I am glad to say, did not agree with him, and the venerable Garrison was thrust into the background as we rushed to the barricades to resist the fugitive slave law.

Garrison professed to be profoundly disappointed in me. Of all his disciples, he said, he had thought me the most dedicated to Garrisonian dogma. And for a long time I was. When I first came to Massachusetts, after stealing myself from slavery in Maryland, I became a subscriber to Garrison's *Liberator*. It was my meat and drink. It set my soul on fire. Garrison's denunciations of slaveholders, his passionate cries for brotherhood, his colorful denunciations of church and clergy, all left me entranced. I had never felt such joy. I *loved* this paper and its editor.

I could also vouch for the accuracy with which it exposed the brutalities of the slave system. I had witnessed them firsthand during my boyhood days on the Lloyd plantation on Maryland's Eastern Shore. The son of Harriet Bailey, a slave, and an unknown white man, I was the legal property of Captain Aaron Anthony, Lloyd's chief lieutenant. I saw slaves brutally whipped. I was there when the cruel overseer, Mr. Sevier, tied Nelly to a tree and flogged her for the crime of "impudence." I was there when Old Master himself thrashed fifteen-year-old Hester for the crime of seeing a boy her own age. I had fallen asleep in the storage closet, only to be awakened by Hester's piercing screams. As I peered through a crack in the door, I could see the back of Old Master as he beat her with a heavy sticklike whip, three feet in length, consisting of dried ox-hide strips bound together and tapering to a point; with this weapon he lashed her naked back, again and again, as hard as he could, until he collapsed from exhaustion. The whipping of young Hester, I later told antislavery audiences, vividly illustrates the absolute power the slavery system conferred on one human being over another, which was the root of its evil.

I, too, felt the bite of the slavemaster's lash upon my back. I, too, knew hunger and cold. I, too, suffered the painful realization that I was a *thing*, a piece of property, *a slave for life* because I was *black*. When Old Master died, I, too, was lined up with other slaves and livestock on evaluation day—horses and men, cattle and women, pigs and children, all holding the same rank in the scale of social existence, and all subjected to the same narrow inspection, to ascertain their value. At this moment, I saw more clearly than ever the brutalizing effects of slavery upon both slave and slaveholder.

Yet I was more fortunate than most. Made the property of Thomas Auld, who sent me to Baltimore to live with his brother Hugh and Hugh's wife, Sophia, I enjoyed liberties beyond the dreams of plantation slaves. Miss Sophia was a kind woman who said to me: "Look up. Don't be afraid." I did look up and tried not to be afraid. She read to me from the Bible and taught me the alphabet and the spelling of short words.

But Mr. Auld put an end to that. "If you teach that nigger how to read," he said, "there'll be no keeping him. It'll make him forever unfit to be a slave. He'll want to know how to write, and that accomplished, he'll be running away with himself."

His proscriptions against the forbidden only heightened my desire to acquire it. Put to work in Auld's shipyard, I learned how to read and write on my own. And he was right: I dreamed of stealing myself and escaping to the North. When I heard white schoolboys talking about their rhetoric book, *The Columbian Orator*, I purchased a copy with fifty cents I had earned from blackening boots. The book was a revelation. It opened up a whole new world to me, the world of language and oratory. I read with a pounding heart Daniel O'Connell's electrifying speech for Catholic emancipation, which contained intoxicating words like *liberty*, *hatred of tyranny*, *freedom*. I learned that words were power! Words could set men free! I dreamed that some day *I* would be free, that some day *I* would deliver orations like O'Connell's.

When I was thirteen or so, I befriended Father Lawson, a pious free man of color who became my spiritual father. When I complained bitterly because I was a slave for life, Father Lawson consoled me. "The Lord can make you free, my dear. If you want liberty, ask the Lord for it, in faith, and he will give it to you." Father Lawson assured me that the Lord had great work for me to do and that I must prepare for it. He made me feel better for a while. But the older I became, the more I longed to go wherever I liked, to work for whomever I pleased. *I wanted to own myself.* In my frustration, I often thought about Nat Turner, whom I had read about in the newspapers. Would I end up like that prodigious figure, striking back at the system with a black fist? Fully grown at fifteen, over six feet in height and muscular, I had a lot of old Nat in me: I was angry and defiant; I was known as "a bad nigger." Returned to Thomas Auld, my legal owner, I refused to call him "master" and called him "Captain" instead. Once when he accused me of stealing a lamp, I hotly denied it. For that, the captain beat me with a cart whip.

Unable to control "the bad nigger," Auld finally hired me out to Edward Covey, who had a reputation for taming difficult slaves—the blacks called him a "nigger-breaker." He beat me repeatedly with switches that cut into my skin, raising welts as big as my index finger and leaving scars I carry to this day. I was so brutalized that I identified with the oxen: they were property; so was I. They were to be broken, so was I. With Covey's whip constantly upon my back, I struggled in his field with other slaves. From first sun to last light we human cattle moved, wielding our clumsy hoes; hurried by no hope of reward, no sense of gratitude, no prospect of bettering our condition; nothing save the dread and terror of Covey's whip. After six months with him, I was crushed in body, soul, and spirit. A voice cried out in my mind, O why was I born a man, of whom to make a brute! I am left in the hottest hell of unending slavery. O God, save me! God, deliver me! Let me be free! Is there any God? Why am I a slave? I will run away. I have only one life to lose. I had as well be killed running as die standing. I ran back to Thomas Auld and begged him for mercy, begged him to take me away from Covey. But Auld sent me back to him with a harsh warning not to run away again. I had now hit bottom; I could not go any lower. When Covey came at me the next day, I felt something come awake in me—a fighting madness rising from some inner depth. In an explosion of pent-up rage, my arms flew out and my hands seized Covey by the throat, I wrestled him around the barnyard, parried his blows, yelled that I would not be whipped any more. When Covey tried to reach for a stick, I took him by the collar and hurled him face forward into a pile of fresh dung. That took the fight out of him. Unable to persuade another slave to help him beat me ("My master hired me here to work, not to help you whip Frederick," was the slave's insurrectionary reply), Covey finally gave up the struggle. The man never, as far as I know, said a word about the fight to anybody. For me, it was the turning point of my life. It revived my crushed self-respect. It taught me that a man without force is without the essential dignity of humanity. I told myself that no matter how long I remained a slave in form, I would never again be a slave in fact.

That revelation was the beginning of my march to freedom. When Thomas Auld reclaimed me, I resolved to run away to the North when the right opportunity presented itself. Thomas considered selling me, for I was still a troublesome slave, then changed his mind and sent me back to his brother Hugh in Baltimore, who apprenticed me as a ship's caulker. Unknowingly, he helped prepare me for freedom. Once I escaped, I would have a skilled trade with which to support myself. I also joined a secret black debating group called the East Baltimore Mental Improvement Society. I was nineteen years of age now and my confidence was soaring. In one debate, I vowed that some day I would be a United States Senator! Why not dream? Nothing seemed impossible to me now. During our secret meetings, I met quiet, steady Anna Murray, a free black housekeeper, and we planned to marry after I made my escape; she would join me in New York City. In 1838, disguised as a black sailor with freedom papers borrowed from a colored friend, I boarded the train and rode north to my freedom and my destiny.

Anna and I exchanged wedding vows in the home of a new friend, David Ruggles, a leader of the New York Vigilance Committee who did everything he could to help runaways. He was a whole-souled black man, fully imbued with a love of his afflicted and haunted people. I took a new surname, Douglass, after a character in Sir Walter Scott's *Lady of the Lake*. We moved on to New Bedford, Massachusetts, where I hoped to find employment as a ship's caulker. But no one would hire me because white laborers would not work with a colored man; it was my first introduction to northern colorphobia. Wherever Anna and I went, it seemed, white mouths were constantly telling us: "We don't allow niggers here!" They told us that when we tried to attend the lyceum, a revival, an eating house, a public exhibit: "We don't allow *niggers* here." When I tried to take a seat in the omnibus, they told me: "We don't allow *niggers* here." For three years, we worked at whatever we could find: Anna hired on as a domestic servant for a white family, and I chopped wood, shoveled coal, drove a coach, swept chimneys, and waited on tables.

It was in New Bedford that I discovered the *Liberator*, which set my soul all on fire; and here that I first heard Brother Garrison speak on abolition. With his inner fire, his uncompromising principles, his harsh language, he seemed to be uttering the spontaneous feeling of my own heart. I introduced myself to him and Brother William C. Coffin. They took a special interest in me when I confided in them that I was an escaped slave. At their invitation, I told my story to an abolitionist convention the following day. Twenty-three years old, just three years up from slavery, I stammered and hesitated a good deal. But Garrison liked what he heard.

"Have we been listening to a thing, a piece of property, or to a man?" he asked the group.

"A man! A man!" they shouted in reply.

Afterward, no doubt at Garrison's suggestion, the general agent for the Massachusetts Anti-Slavery Society, John A. Collins, took me aside. "Why don't you join us as an agent?" he asked. "You would be an invaluable asset to the cause. Just tell your story; it would be a wonderful answer to the proslavery apologists, who claim that the slaves are happy and that the system is benign."

Thus began my career as an agent of the Massachusetts Anti-Slavery Society and an unwavering disciple of Brother Garrison. I told my story to mostly white audiences, exposing the evil of slavery from a personal view, often eliciting bursts of laughter when I mimicked how a slaveholding clergyman exhorted the slaves to obey their masters. Imitating him, I looked impudently up at an imaginary slave's gallery, where sat the poor colored drivers and the rest. "Oh, receive into your souls these words of the only apostle," I said, with my hands extended. "Servants, be *obedient* to your masters. Oh! if you wish to be happy in eternity, you must be *obedient* to your masters; *their* interest is *yours*. God, don't you see, made *one* portion of men to do the working, and *another* to do the thinking. How *good* God is! Isn't he *good*? Now, *you* have no trouble or anxiety. But ah! you can't imagine how perplexing it is to be your masters and mistresses to have so much *thinking* to do in your behalf! You cannot appreciate your blessings; you don't know how happy a thing it is for you, that you were born of that portion of the human family which has the *working*, instead of the *thinking*, to do! Oh! how grateful and obedient you ought to be to your masters! How beautiful are the arrangements of Providence! Look at your hard, horny hands. See how nicely they are adapted to the labor you have to perform! Look at our *delicate* fingers, so exactly fitted for *our* station, and see how manifest it is that God designed *us* to be his thinkers, and *you* the workers. Oh! the *wisdom* of God."

On a hundred platforms, I championed moral suasion and non-resistance, damned the churches, proclaimed the Constitution a proslavery document, advocated disunion, denounced the North's complicity in the slave system, assailed the colonization society, and castigated southern leaders like Calhoun in uncompromising Garrisonian terms. "Mr. John C. Calhoun," I said on one occasion, with all the sarcasm I could muster, "is regarded in the United States as a real democrat. And yet, sir, that very man stands upon the floor of the Senate, and actually boasts that he is a robber! that he is an owner of slaves in the southern states. The audacity of such men is astounding. I scarcely know what to say in America, when I hear men deliberately get up and assert a right to property in my limbs—my very body and soul; that they have a right to ME! that I am in their hands, 'a chattel personal,' 'a thing' to be bought and sold! a slave! a marketable commodity! I do not know what to think of Mr. John C. Calhoun when he vehemently declaims for liberty, and asserts that any attempt to abridge the rights of the southern people should be met with the sternest resistance on all hands, deliberately stands forth at the head of the Democracy of that country and talks of his right to property in me; and not only in my body, but in the bodies and souls of hundreds of thousands of others in the United States."

Wherever I went, of course, I was doomed by an inveterate prejudice against color to insult and outrage on every hand. I was called "nigger Douglass" and was spit at, jeered, and jostled at every turn. I was denied the privileges and courtesies common to others in the use of the most humble means of conveyance—shut out from the cabins on steamboats—refused admission to respectable hotels—caricatured, scorned, scoffed, mocked, and maltreated with impunity by anyone with a white skin. When I boarded a train, the white conductors always made me sit in the filthy boxcars reserved for "coloreds." Once Wendell Phillips, a fellow Garrisonian, stepped off the regular coach and walked with me back to the wretched boxcar. "Douglass," he said, "if you cannot ride with me, I can ride with you." Phillips and Garrison often went hungry rather than dine in an eating house that refused to serve me.

Finally, I'd had enough. I refused to make any more concessions to the spirit of slavery and prejudice. I *resisted*. When I boarded a train now, I seated myself in the regular coach and refused to remove myself to the boxcar. Sometimes the conductor and break-man would beat me. Once, on a train from Lynn bound for New-buryport, I thought to argue with the conductor when he ordered me out of the regular coach. "I paid for a first-class ticket," I said. "Besides, I am but half a Negro, betwixt and between, as they say." The conductor invited six "fellows of the baser sort" to eject me from my seat. They seized me by the head, neck, and shoulders, but could not budge me because I had wound myself around the seat. Finally they yanked me out, and I tore away two or three of the sur-rounding seats and did the car no service in other respects. After that, I told my fellow blacks that we must never submit to acts of discrimination. *No man can make you inferior unless you let him.*

At abolitionist meetings, there were those who doubted that I had ever been a slave. "How," they demanded, "can a man only six years out of bondage, who has never gone to school a day in his life, speak with such eloquence—with such precision of language and power of thought?" To silence the skeptics, I wrote the *Narrative of the Life of Frederick Douglass*, which recounts my experiences as a slave in Maryland. Because that book revealed my identity, my friends were afraid the slave catchers would find me and drag me back into bondage.

Fearing for my life and my liberty, I left Anna and our children in Lynn and spent two years in Great Britain. Thank heaven for that respite! There I was treated as a man. I wrote Brother Garrison: "I gaze around in vain for one who will question my equal humanity, claim me as his slave, or offer me an insult. I employ a cab—I am seated beside white people—I reach the hotel—I enter the same door—I am shown into the same parlor—I dine at the same table—and no one is offended. No delicate nose grows deformed in my presence. I find no difficulty here in obtaining admission into any place of worship, instruction, or amusement, on equal terms with people as white as any I ever saw in the United States. I meet nothing to remind me of my complexion. I find myself regarded and treated at every turn with the kindness and deference paid to white people. When I go to church, I am met by no upturned nose and scornful lip to tell me, "*We don't allow niggers in here!*"

When word came from America that Hugh Auld, who now had title to me, had threatened to retrieve his escaped slave "cost what it may" and put him back in the cotton fields, my British friends begged me to stay in England; they even raised $500 with which to bring over Anna and the children, and promised to furnish us a comfortable house. But I declined their generous offer. No matter how hypocritical and slave-cursed America was, my mission, I realized, was there; my destiny lay with my black brothers and sisters in bondage. I must struggle with them for that emancipation which would yet be achieved by the power of truth and principle.

Before I returned home, Anna Richardson and her sister-in-law Ellen handed me the sweetest gift of all: my bill of sale and manumission. They had purchased my freedom from Hugh Auld for about $1,250 in American currency, and the papers had been filed at Baltimore Chattel Records Office. As of 10 A.M., December twelfth, 1846, I was a free man. At long last, *I now owned myself*. When word of the sale reached my American friends, however, some of them expressed dismay, even outrage, contending that the purchase recognized the "right to traffic in human beings." I wrote the *Liberator* that my critics were misguided. They confused the crime of buying men into slavery with the meritorious act of buying men out of slavery. As for rights, I told a London audience, I had as much right to sell Hugh Auld as he had to sell me. If anybody in the audience wanted to buy Auld, I said, just give the word. There was polite chuckling all around, but nobody offered to buy him.

In my farewell address to my British friends, I said that the people of the United States were the boldest in their pretensions to freedom and the loudest in their profession of love of liberty; yet no nation upon the face of the globe could exhibit a statute book so full of all that was cruel, malicious, and infernal, as the American code of laws. Every page was red with the blood of the American slave.

I was determined to confront American prejudice and hypocrisy on my own terms, with my own words, in my own independent newspaper. When I reached Lynn by train and approached my home, my two bright-eyed boys, Lewis and Frederick, Jr., came running and dancing with joy to meet me. I took one in my arm and the other in my hand, and hastened inside to see my dear Anna, who was not well—she seldom enjoyed good health—but was exceedingly glad to have me once more at home.

In late 1847, I established my own paper, the *North Star*, in Rochester, New York, and moved Anna and the children there. Brother Garrison, of course, was annoyed that I should desire my own paper. He and Brother Phillips were certain that I would be financially ruined since black-owned papers had been attempted before and all had failed. "The land is full of the wreck of such experiments," Garrison warned. Why is it that white people are always telling black people what is good for them? I was determined to produce a successful paper that encouraged the growth of an industrious, thrifty, educated free colored population; that was the best possible refutation of slavery and of the colonization arguments of Henry Clay.

But with only seven hundred subscribers and with almost no help from the Garrisonians, I had a difficult time keeping the *North Star* afloat. I raised funds through lectures but even that was not enough; at one point I had to mortgage my house to pay the paper's expenses. What hurt the most was the indifference of the free colored population—only one of five subscribers was black. It troubled me deeply that blacks did not realize the importance of such a paper to the progress and elevation of our race.

In 1848, my dear English friend, Miss Julia Griffiths, came to Rochester to help me make the *North Star* solvent. Anna, who was with our fifth child, did not object when I moved Miss Julia into our house (we could not afford to rent rooms for her elsewhere). There were whites in Rochester who were offended by the spectacle of a white woman living in Fred Douglass's house. But I ignored them. And well I did, for Miss Julia proved the savior of the *North Star*. In one year, she put the paper on sound financial footing: she sent out pleas for funds, organized fairs, and raised the circulation to four thousand; she even paid off the mortgage to our home. How could I ever repay her? Literate, well-educated, and attractive, she was a splendid conversationalist. Since Anna could neither read nor write, Miss Julia became my intellectual companion. She helped me improve my writing. In the evenings, while Anna rocked quietly, or tended wordlessly to her sewing, Miss Julia would read to me from the English classics. In all ways she was my faithful friend.

In the *North Star*, I continued to tow the Garrison line on non-resistance, moral suasion, and disunion. I continued to assail Henry Clay—"yours, sir, is the most helpless, illogical, and cowardly apologies for the wrong of slavery that I have ever read"—and to denounce colonization—"shame upon the guilty wretches that dare propose, and all that countenance such a proposition. We live here—have lived here—have a right to live here, and mean to live here." If Clay wanted to colonize anybody, I argued, *let him colonize himself and his fellow slaveholders*.

But the truth was, I had for some time privately doubted Garrison's conviction that moral suasion and non-resistance were the sole solutions to slavery. I became even more skeptical after I met John Brown in late 1847. Several prominent men of color had mentioned his name to me as a passionate hater of slavery, always speaking of him in a whisper. Desirous of meeting Brown, I called on him at his home in Springfield, Massachusetts. He was about fifty years in age, under six feet high, less than 150 pounds in weight, with large, callused hands, and coarse, slightly gray hair that grew low on his forehead. His eyes were bluish-gray, and in conversation they were full of light and fire. We shared a simple meal with his wife and children, after which he brought up the slavery question. With glaring eyes, he declared that slavery was "a state of war" and that the slaves had a right to gain their freedom "any way they could." He said that he had "a plan" and unfolded a map of the United States on the kitchen table.

"These mountains," he said, running a gnarled finger along the Alleghenies, "are the basis of my plan. God has given the strength of the hills to freedom. My plan is to take about twenty-five armed men and send them down to the fields to induce the slaves to join them, and then to run them off to the North. The object is to destroy the value of slave property by rendering it insecure." He paused, staring at me. "I am not averse to the shedding of blood," he said. "Guns in the hands of black men will give them a sense of their manhood. No people can have self-respect, or be respected, who won't fight for their freedom."

Looking at the map, I said: "The southerners will use bloodhounds to hunt you out of the mountains."

"They might attempt that," Brown said, "but the chances are, we'll whip them and when we've whipped one squad, they'll be careful how they pursue."

I conceded that his plan had much to commend it and finally bade him good-bye. I wrote in the *North Star* that Brown, though a white gentleman, was in sympathy a black man and as deeply interested in our cause as though his own soul had been pierced with the iron of slavery. Brown's contention that slavery was "a state of war" impressed me profoundly, so much so that my own utterances became more and more tinged by the color of this man's strong impressions. In an 1849 editorial, I argued that slaveholders had forfeited their right to live, and if the slave should put every one of them to the sword tomorrow, who would dare pronounce the penalty disproportionate to the crime? A few months later, addressing the American Anti-Slavery Society, I stunned Garrison and his followers by declaring that the slaves had a moral right to strike back and that I would welcome the news of a slave insurrection. This appeared to align me with Henry Highland Garnet, the fiery preacher of Troy, New York, who had exhorted the slaves to rebel. "Brethren, arise, arise!" he'd cried. "Strike for your lives and liberties. Now is the day and the hour. Let every slave throughout the land do this, and the days of slavery are numbered. Let your motto be resistance! *resistance*! RESISTANCE! No oppressed people have ever secured their liberty without resistance."

But the truth was, I shuddered at the horrors of insurrection, even though the entire white South deserved to be put to the knife. Ambivalent about bloodshed as a solution to our problems, groping for a workable method to remove a nightmarish and complex institution, I still called myself a Garrisonian abolitionist. But the passage of the fugitive slave law caused me and many other abolitionists to cast aside non-resistance once and for all. Black resistance groups sprang up in Chicago, New York, and Boston. Resistant abolitionists in Boston liberated the fugitive Shadrach from a Federal marshal and helped him flee to Canada. A similar group rescued a fugitive slave in Syracuse. In Springfield, Massachusetts, my friend John Brown organized forty-four colored men into a mutual-defense league and urged them to kill any southerner or Federal officer who tried to apprehend them.

I agreed with Brown. "Every colored man in the country," I told a Pittsburgh audience, "should sleep with his revolver under his head, loaded and ready for use. Fugitives, on their arrival in any northern city, should be immediately provided with arms, and taught that it is no harm to shoot any man who would rob them of their liberty." I argued in the *North Star* that nothing short of resistance on the part of colored men could wipe out the prevailing mood that we were an inferior race. "Every slave-hunter who meets a bloody death in his infernal business," I said, "is an argument in favor of the manhood of our race."

Garrison, of course, viewed me as a traitor to the "true" abolitionist cause because I'd had the audacity to disagree with him. In 1851, breaking from him completely, I declared myself a *political* abolitionist like my dear friend and benefactor, the warm, gregarious Gerrit Smith. This great landowner and reformer of Peterboro, New York, had generously advanced me funds to help keep my paper afloat. My removal to Rochester had brought me into steady contact with Brother Smith, William Goodell, and Samuel Ringgold Ward, all political abolitionists, who posed to me iron-linked arguments in support of the position that the Constitution, legally construed, was an *antislavery* instrument. I had never studied the Constitution. When I escaped from slavery and joined the Garrisonians, I knew nothing of law and constitutions; I had never had an hour of schooling in my life. Now, at Smith's urging, I made a careful study of the Constitution and the just and proper rules of legal interpretation. I noted that the words *slave* and *slavery* were nowhere mentioned in the document. I concluded that Smith and his friends were right, that the Constitution, which was inaugurated (in the words of its noble Preamble) to "form a more perfect union, establish justice, insure domestic tranquillity, provide for the common defense, promote the general welfare, and secure the blessings of liberty," could not well have been designed at the same time to maintain and perpetuate a system of rapine and murder like slavery, especially as not one word can be found in the Constitution to authorize such a belief. I believed that the Constitution was our warrant for the abolition of slavery in every state of the Union. I therefore ceased to proclaim disunion and joined ranks with the Liberty men to effect abolition by political action.

At the 1851 convention of the American Anti-Slavery Society, I made my new creed publicly known. Brother Garrison was furious. "There is roguery somewhere," he exclaimed, meaning that I had sold myself to his "*deadliest* enemies," the political abolitionists. I'll never forget Garrison's insulting remark. But that was only the beginning. When I insisted that my change of position was a matter of principle and demanded to know why I was being treated as an alien, Garrison and the whole Garrisonian crowd, including Wendell Phillips, declared me guilty of rank opportunism, of abandoning true abolitionist principles because the political abolitionists had offered me support and money. They accused me of "avarice, faithlessness, treachery, ingratitude." Brother Phillips, once my good friend, told a female abolitionist that "Douglass is completely estranged from us."

Such criticism hurt. To make matters worse, there were new financial problems with the paper. And there were "home trials," too, as Miss Julia described Anna's unhappiness. I had spells of almost unbearable anxiety. I fell ill with what Miss Julia thought was inflammatory rheumatism. At one point, I was laid up with an ulcerated throat, which Miss Julia attributed in part to my anxiety over the paper. I told her I was afraid of going crazy. Alarmed, she seldom left my side; she sang my favorite hymns and read aloud to "tranquilize" me.

By 1852, we Liberty men were trying hard to keep alive what remained of the party. The most practical solution, we decided, was a merger with the new Free-Soil party, whose platform called for the exclusion of slavery from the territories. Despite the anti-black attitudes of many Free-Soilers, I endorsed the party and its presidential candidate, John P. Hale, who ran against the "compromise" of 1850 and its fugitive slave provision, which was championed by the Democratic candidate, Franklin Pierce. When Gerrit Smith announced for Congress as a Free-Soil candidate, I campaigned hard for him, attending eighteen meetings in twelve New York towns in one month alone. But we were a long way from winning the soul and the conscience of white America: Pierce, a northern "dough-face" under the sway of the Slave Power, easily won the Presidency in November. When I learned that Smith had won his congressional race, however, I wrote him that the cup of my joy was full.

By then, my feud with Garrison had become ugly and personal. I had rejected his "Come-Outer" stance toward the churches because I thought it wiser to cooperate with antislavery groups within the churches than to damn them all to eternity. In my editorials I accused the Garrisonians of religious infidelity, of glorying in their disbelief of the Bible. That elicited cries of outrage from the entire Garrisonian phalanx, which pronounced *me* an ally of "the whole proslavery press and pulpit in the United States." Garrison himself published my editorials in the *Liberator*'s "Refuge of Oppression," a column reserved for proslavery outrages and diatribes.

Worst of all, Garrison brought up my relationship with Miss Julia, who by now had moved out of our home to a place of her own. "For several years past," Garrison wrote in the *Liberator*, "he [Douglass] has had one of the worst advisers in his printing-office, whose influence over him has not only caused much unhappiness in his own household, but perniciously biased his own judgment; who, active, futile, mischievous, has never had any sympathy with the American Anti-Slavery Society." Thus did Brother Garrison descend into the gutter. Miss Julia and I were furious. We helped Anna pen a note to Garrison denying that "the presence of a certain person in the office of Frederick Douglass causes unhappiness in his family." Garrison published the note, with the meretricious remark that it was "evasive in its language," as our charge "had reference to the past and not to the present." Stung to the core, I devoted an entire issue of my paper, now called *Frederick Douglass' Paper*, to the Garrisonian attack against me, which had arisen mainly because I had dared to differ with the imperious Garrison. For this, I said, he had invaded my household and violated the sacredness of my home. My family relations, I argued, involved considerations wholly foreign to the present controversy. A man's wife and children should be spared the mortification involved in a public discussion of matters entirely private.

It was bad enough that Garrison had invaded my private affairs. In his attempts to slur me, he had also managed to insult my race, claiming that the abolitionist cause had "transcended the ability of the sufferers from American slavery and prejudice, as a class, to keep pace with it, or to perceive what are its demands, or to understand the philosophy of its operations." Henry Clay could hardly have made a more bigoted statement.

"The colored people," I replied, "ought to feel profoundly grateful for this magnificent compliment (which does not emanate from a colonizationist) to their high, moral worth, and breadth of comprehension so generously bestowed by William Lloyd Garrison!" Thus did the *great champion* of Negro rights concede all that was claimed respecting Negro inferiority by the bitterest despisers of our race.

It was a bad time for the abolitionist cause. The movement was bitterly and hopelessly divided. The Free-Soil party was dying for lack of voter support outside Massachusetts and upstate New York. The Mormon government in Utah Territory had legalized slavery (New Mexico Territory would do the same in a few years). The Slave Power continued its stranglehold upon our national existence. In Boston, Anthony Burns, a black man who had escaped from slavery in Richmond, left the store where he worked, only to be seized by deputy Federal marshals and locked up in the courthouse, where he was to be tried by a Federal commissioner under the fugitive slave law. Determined to save him from a hellish fate, the Boston Vigilance Committee broke into the courthouse with axes and a battering ram, but fifty special guards armed with guns and sabers dispersed the would-be liberators. In the melee, a deputy marshal (a Boston truckman in civilian life) was killed. In my paper, I challenged those who called the killing of this man a crime. "It was glorious for Americans to drench the soil, and crimson the sea with blood, to escape the payment of a three-penny tax upon tea; but it is a crime to shoot down a monster in defense of the liberty of a black man and to save him from a bondage 'one hour of which (in the language of Jefferson) is worse than ages of that which our fathers rose in rebellion to oppose.'" Alas for poor, defenseless Burns. Found guilty of being a fugitive and ordered back into bondage, Burns left Boston under the escort of a small army of Federal deputies and United States soldiers, who flung him into the bowels of a ship bound for Virginia. Thus was the law enforced in this Christian, liberty-loving land.

17. HARRIET BEECHER STOWE

I was on my way from Cincinnati to Brunswick, Maine, with our three older children, when I heard people on our steamboat talking about the new fugitive slave bill being debated in Congress. When we stopped in Boston to visit brother Edward, who was pastor of Salem Church, the new bill was the main topic of conversation. Edward was an abolitionist, and the measure made him furious. "It declares open season on all Negroes in the North," he said. "Without benefit of jury or judge, any black can be hauled back into slavery on the word of anybody who claims to be an owner or to represent an owner." By the time I reached Brunswick, my soul was on fire with indignation at this new violence about to be inflicted by the Slave Power on the innocent and defenseless. But what could a mere woman do? Eight months with child, with three children in tow and loaded down with a cargo of trunks, I felt powerless to help the poor souls.

With my head dizzy from the whirl of railroads and steamboats, I led the way to our new home, situated on Federal Street near the Bowdoin campus. It was a dreary, damp, spacious old house, whose every window afforded a view of the pine woods. My husband, Calvin, had accepted a position on the faculty at the college, after having served as Professor of Biblical Literature for almost seventeen years at Lane Seminary in Cincinnati. I'd elected to come ahead with the older children and prepare the house for Calvin's arrival. We unpacked our trunks and opened windows to rid the house of the dampness and musty odors from its being shut up. I wondered how we would ever furnish such a large place. Quite frankly, I surprised myself by my own ingenuity: I converted barrels into chairs and packing-boxes into sofas, fashioned cisterns (the house was water-less) out of hogsheads that had to be dismantled and set up again in the cellar, and persuaded the landlords to install a kitchen sink.

In early July 1850, Calvin arrived with our two youngest, Henry Ellis and Eliza. A week later our seventh and last child, Charles Edward, was born. He was as much like our first Charley as one mold of clay could be to another. Our first Charley had died of the cholera in his eighteenth month, had caught the disease during an epidemic in Cincinnati, had gone into convulsions and died. I was inconsolable. There was no sorrow like my sorrow. I could never love another child as I did Charley—he was my "summer child." I could not open his little drawer of clothes without feeling an arrow of pain through my heart. Is there a peculiar love given us for those that God takes from us—Is there not something brighter and better around them than around those who live—Why else in so many households is there a tradition of one brighter more beautiful more promising child than all the rest, who was laid low early in life?

At Charley's dying bed and at his grave I learned what a poor slave mother must feel when her child was torn away from her. I was thinking the same thing—this is how a slave mother must feel after losing her child—when on the eve of my departure for Maine I sorted through Charley's clothes in his little drawer. There were cir-cumstances about his death of such peculiar bitterness, of what seemed almost cruel suffering, that I felt I could never be consoled, unless the crushing of my own heart might enable me to work out some great good to others.

Next day, waiting with the children and our heavy trunks at the steamboat landing, I saw a posted handbill offering "$1200 to 1250 DOLLARS FOR NEGROES." I was glad we were leaving this city, situated across the Ohio from slaveholding Kentucky. In distant Maine, my family would be spared the sight of posters offering money for slaves or rewards for runaways.

But the passage of the fugitive slave law brought Maine itself within reach of the Slave Power. The *National Era* and other anti-slavery papers reported how slave snatchers would seize blacks in northern communities and drag them weeping and screaming back into slavery. Boston friends wrote me about the terror and despair felt among industrious, worthy colored people in that city. I even heard of families breaking up and fleeing to Canada. It filled me with grief—shame—mortification—an almost total inability to believe my eyes and senses—that half the professed Christians of

America and most of her political and social leaders were down on their knees before this cruel enactment. According to Edward, Boston ministers generally *favored* the bill; others were indifferent. How could men of the cloth support such a cruel wrong? How could they be apathetic? It was incredible—amazing—mournful. I wished that my father Lyman Beecher would come to Boston and preach on the fugitive slave law as he had once preached on the slave trade, with Mrs. Judge Reeves crying in one pew and I in another. Would to God that I could *do* something to help the colored people. Tears dropped on my pillow when I thought of the wrongs and sorrows of those oppressed ones.

A letter came from Isabella, Edward's wife. "Hattie," she wrote, "if I could use a pen as you can, I would write something that would make this whole nation feel what an accursed thing slavery is."

I stood with the letter crumpled in my fist and said, "I *will* write something. I will if I live." I had long dreamed of writing something important, something that would make a difference. Now God had given me the opportunity. I informed Calvin, who was spending the winter term at Andover Seminary in Massachusetts, that I was projecting a sketch for the *National Era* about the capabilities of liberated blacks to take care of themselves. I hired a governess to help me with the older children, and worked on my story while the baby slept.

It was a bitterly cold winter. The snow piled up in the streets, and the wind rocked the house and howled at the eaves. The cold was so intense that the children kept begging to get up from table at mealtime to warm their feet and fingers. Our airtight stoves heated all but the floor, leaving our feet chilled to the bone. If I sat by the open fire in the parlor, my back froze; if I sat in my bedroom and tried to write, my head ached and my feet were cold. When I had a headache and felt sick, there was not a place in the house where I could lie down and take a nap without being disturbed. Overhead was the schoolroom, next door was the dining room, where the twins practiced the piano two hours a day. Searching for a comfortable place to write, I finally settled on the parlor. Here, before an open fire, I composed on Great-Grandfather Ward's drop-leaf table, shutting out the music of the piano next door and the noise of the children's school above.

By January 1851 my sketch was leading to something else, something more direct. I realized that what I really wanted to write about was the sufferings of actual slaves. As a woman, a mother, and a

Christian, I felt called to speak for the oppressed who could not speak for themselves. My brother Henry Ward Beecher came up from his Brooklyn pulpit to visit us, and I decided to confide in him what I was attempting. A blizzard had struck Brunswick, and the wind was churning up snow in the streets and tearing at the branches of the trees surrounding our house. After the children were in bed, Henry and I sat before a fire with the wind howling outside, and we talked in earnest about the fugitive slave law.

"My heart," I said, "is burning itself out in indignation and anguish at the blindness, the obtuseness, of otherwise good people on so simple a point of morality as this terrible law. What can we do as testimony against it?"

"I intend to fight the battle in New York," Henry said, his protuberant eyes fixed on mine. "My church will stand by me in resisting the tyrannies of southern slaveholders."

"I, too, have begun to do something," I said. "I have begun a story, trying to set forth the sufferings and wrongs of the slaves."

He rose, gesturing dramatically. "Do it, Hattie. Finish it, and I will scatter it like leaves on the wind."

But the story resisted me; it lay on the table in vague, inchoate fragments. Though I prayed to God for strength, I was almost paralyzed with self-doubts. I was just a little bit of a woman, not quite forty, about as thin and dry as a pinch of snuff; never very much to look at in my best days, with no accomplishments beyond bearing children and publishing a little book of New England sketches. Who was *I* to write about so terrible an evil? Who was *I* to speak for the poor slaves, *I* to awaken America to their cries? I felt so *inadequate*. Some days I had fits of depression as bad as the black spells I used to get back in Cincinnati, when I gave birth to six children in twelve years and felt overwhelmed with domestic responsibilities. Oh, those were trying days! I can still see myself in our rented faculty house on the Lane campus, a frail mite of a thing toiling endlessly in the nursery and kitchen. With babies crying all the time and requiring my constant attention, I was nothing but a home-bound drudge with no time for thoughts, reflections, and sentiments. I loved my babies more than anything, but sometimes I was so sick of feeding them all that I never wanted to eat again.

I got so little help from Calvin, my balding, roly-poly rabbi, an otherwise dear and gentle soul, but absentminded and preoccupied with his books and teaching. He was so often away raising funds for the seminary that neighbors called me "Widow Stowe." Because the seminary was in dire straits and could not pay Calvin his full salary, we sank into poverty. To make ends meet, we took in boarders—eight of them eventually, plus Anna, my factotum. I had to manage the house, collect the rent, deal with complaints, do the daily marketing, supervise the meals, run the nursery. When we fell short of money for a new carpet or mattress, I would tell my faithful Anna, who shared all my joys and sorrows, "Now, if you will keep the babies and attend to the things in the house for one day, I'll write a piece, and then we'll be out of this scrape." So I became a part-time author. I say it in all candor, though: had it not been for Anna, a noble-hearted English girl who clave to me as Ruth did to Naomi, I would never have survived the grind of housework and childbearing. As it was, I suffered from excruciating headaches, blinding pain in my eyes, and bouts of weakness that could immobilize me for months. Sometimes all I could do was sit at a window and cry.

I felt like such a *failure,* so incompetent as a mother and teacher of my children, so worthless as a wife. I longed to have Calvin's freedom outside the home, to be a man in his place, to be the son my father Lyman Beecher the famous minister had always wanted me to be. Had I been a Beecher male, maybe I would have become an abolitionist, like my brothers. I would certainly have stood with Mr. Birney, the abolitionist editor, against the mob that wrecked his printing office and hurled his press into the Ohio River. I did write a letter to a Cincinnati newspaper denouncing mob rule and defending freedom of speech, but since a proper woman did not speak out on such things, I signed the letter with a male pseudonym.

The abolitionists who came to Cincinnati aroused my conscience; but it was the stories I heard that stirred my heart in sympathy with the slaves. While attending an assembly of Protestant churches in Ripley, Ohio, I listened, transfixed, as our amiable young host, the Reverend John Rankin, revealed that he was a "stationmaster" on the Underground Railroad and that he often hid runaways in his house, which sat on a high bluff above the Ohio River. That was why he kept the lantern burning in the window throughout the night—as a beacon for the fugitives. "That reminds me of a story," he said, and he proceeded to tell us about a young slave named Eliza Harris, who had escaped from Kentucky with her infant son. With slave catchers and baying hounds in pursuit, she held her child tightly and crossed the half-frozen Ohio River by leaping over ice floes running in its waters. A sympathetic white man helped her and the child to Rankin's house, where the Reverend fed and sheltered them and then sent them on to the next "station." A few weeks later, her husband George also escaped on the Underground Railroad, found Eliza and their child, and took them to Canada, beyond the reach of the slave catchers.

What a thrilling story! I kept *seeing* Eliza's harrowing escape across the ice floes in the river, kept *seeing* the sympathetic white agents who helped her and her husband escape. By assisting runaways, the agents willingly broke the law and often paid the consequences. When I asked for more information about them, the Reverend Rankin told us about Levi and Catharine Coffin, the famous Quaker couple, who assisted so many runaways—some two thousand, according to Reverend Rankin—that Levi became known as the "president" of the Underground Railroad. Another agent was John Van Sandt of Springdale, who would drive his wagon down to Cincinnati, unload his produce, pick up fugitives hiding there, and carry them back to his farm for food and shelter before sending them on to the next station.

Calvin and I were so inspired by their example that we started sheltering fugitives ourselves. The first was a young black girl I'd hired, who claimed to be legally free. One day she told me the truth: she was a fugitive from Kentucky, and her master was in Cincinnati hunting for her. "Oh, Miss Harriet," she cried, "will you save me?" I told Calvin, "We must get her away from here," and I fetched brother Henry to help. Armed with pistols, they escorted her on a daring night ride to the safety of Van Sandt's farm. More than once after that we gave refuge to frightened fugitives escaping on the Underground Railroad, which I may say ran through our barn.

Sometime after we helped the slave girl escape, I acquired a copy of *American Slavery As It Is: Testimony of a Thousand Witnesses*. Compiled by the abolitionist Theodore Dwight Weld, it was a compendium of southern newspaper clippings, legal documents, and eyewitness accounts that documented the evils of slavery. It told of families broken up, of whippings, beatings, brandings, and gunshot wounds; of the iron collars, chains, and fetters used for torture. It told of slaves roasted and flogged, of slaves burned alive; one slave was chopped piecemeal and burnt. The screams of the suffering leaped off the pages. One story in particular wrenched my Christian heart: it was about a pious slave whose master flogged him to death because he had refused to deny his Christ. How could southern society, any society, sanction such crimes!

My brother Charles told me similarly lurid tales about life in

Louisiana, where he worked for several years as a collecting clerk for a mercantile house. He saw plantations with amazingly fertile soil but unhealthy climates. The soil was so rich, the planters said, that it was more economical to work their "niggers" to death and buy new slaves than to care for them when they were diseased. One planter Charles met had a hard, callused fist. "He made me feel of his fist," Charles said. "It was like a blacksmith's hammer. 'I got that from knocking down niggers,' the planter said."

Several black women I hired as domestic servants were liberated slaves, and they corroborated the truth of such accounts. Working with them in the kitchen, I encouraged them to tell their stories. Eliza Buck, our cook, a fat, gentle, easy, loving woman with a sweet voice and refined manner, had lived through the whole sad story of a Virginia-raised slave's life. Her original owners, a kind family, had raised her to be a slave nurse and seamstress, but the family became "embarrassed" and had to sell Eliza "down river" to a plantation in Louisiana. She told me how she was suddenly forced into a carriage and driven away while her little mistress screamed from a window. She described scenes on the Louisiana plantation, telling how she would steal out to the slave quarters at night to minister to "poor slaves, who had been mangled and lacerated by the whip." Then she was sold again—to a Kentucky man, her last master, who became the father of her children. When I realized the real nature of the connection, Eliza apologized. "You know, Mrs. Stowe, slave women cannot help themselves."

I felt so *sorry* for her. She was such a faithful friend and servant, I wanted to make amends somehow. Because Cincinnati had no schools for blacks, I enrolled Eliza's two pretty quadroon daughters and other young blacks in the school I ran at home for my own children. I shall never forget one of the little black girls; she was one of the brightest and most amusing children in the school. When she stopped attending, I went to her mother, who wrung her hands in anguish. Her daughter, she said, was still a slave, the legal property of an estate in Kentucky; a slave catcher had seized and returned her there. The mother showed me a letter from that despicable man: it demanded $200 for the daughter, otherwise she would be sold on the auction block. The sum for the little one's ransom was made up by subscription in our neighborhood, but the incident left a deep mark on my mind as to the practical workings of the institution of slavery. I learned that separating mothers from their children occurred regularly in the southern slave trade and that the mother's agonies were no more regarded than those of a cow when her calf is separated from her.

It was indeed a monstrous system that could sanction such atrocities and implicate otherwise kind and decent whites in its crimes. I wept that such a system could enjoy the protection of our national government and our Constitution. What could enlightened people do to end such evil? Should they join the abolitionists? All of my older brothers had gone over to them, and young Henry Ward would soon follow. Like them, I read the *Liberator* and gloried in Mr. Garrison's impassioned sermons on nonviolent moral suasion as the only true means to abolish slavery. Yes, that did seem right. As a nation, we must undergo a moral regeneration, North and South together, then we must free the slaves and invite them into our schools and churches. But until slavery ended, it seemed to me that fugitive blacks must leave the country for their own safety. They must go to Canada, as Eliza and George Harris did, or perhaps to the colony in Liberia, which was so well championed by Senator Clay.

I did not, however, become an abolitionist except in sympathy. My duty was to my children and my husband. Besides, I disagreed with some of the abolitionists' tactics, especially their blasphemous assaults on the churches, which made them most unfashionable in Cincinnati and neighboring regions. Like all who assert pure abstract right as applied to human affairs, they were regarded as a species of moral monomaniacs, who, in the consideration of one class of interests and wrongs, had lost sight of all proportion and all good judgment. Both in church and in state, they were looked upon as "those that troubled Israel."

I also believed, as I wrote in an 1845 piece in the *Evangelist*, that the great error of the controversy was that it assailed *persons* rather than the system. The slave *system* concentrated more wrong than any other then existing, and yet those who lived under and in it might be enlightened, generous, and amenable to reason. If the system alone were attacked, such minds would be the first to perceive its evils and to turn against it; but if the system were attacked through individuals, in the manner of the abolitionists, then self-love, wounded pride, and a thousand natural feelings would be at once enlisted for its preservation. Was this not behind the shrill defenses of slavery offered by Senator Calhoun and other southern leaders?

Still, I agreed with Mr. Garrison that slavery was an egregious sin against God and that it was a Christian's duty to resist it. But how did a wisp of nerve like me, burdened with the responsibilities of caring for my husband, raising my children, and running my home, become involved? "No one," I told Calvin, "can have the system of slavery brought before him without an irrepressible desire to *do* something, but what is there to be done?"

As I sat in my parlor in Maine, remembering those years in Cincinnati, I thought: "I have known a great many slaves, have had them in my family, have known their history and feelings, have seen how alike their hearts beat to any other throbbing heart. Above all, what a woman feels deepest of all, I have seen the strength of their instinctive and domestic attachments in which as a race they excel even the Anglo-Saxon." *That*, I thought, *that* was what I must write about, in the context of the cruelties of the slave system and its offense to God.

But where to begin such a story? Who were to be the central characters? On Communion Sunday, as I sat at the communion table in Brunswick's First Parish Church, a vision began playing before my eyes that left me in tears. I saw an old slave clad in rags, a gentle, Christian man like the slave I had read about in *American Slavery As It Is*. A cruel white man, a man with a hardened fist, was flogging the old slave. Now the cruel master ordered two other slaves to finish the task. As they laid on the whips, the old black man prayed for God to forgive them.

After church, I rushed home in a trance and wrote down what I had seen. Since Calvin was away, I read the sketch to my ten- and twelve-year-old sons. They wept, too, and one cried, "Oh! mamma, slavery is the most cursed thing in the world!" I named the old slave Uncle Tom and his evil tormentor Simon Legree. Having recorded the climax of my story, I then commenced at the beginning, introducing Eliza and George Harris and a younger Uncle Tom and his wife Chloe, who lived on the Shelby plantation in Kentucky.

I envisioned a series of three or four sketches and arranged to serialize them in the *National Era*, published in Washington City by Gamaliel Bailey; he agreed to pay me $300 for the three or four weekly installments. My object, I told him, would be to hold up slavery and the Negro character, which I'd had ample opportunities for studying, in the most graphic manner possible, through a series of word pictures. I decided at once that there would be no male pseudonym for "Uncle Tom's Cabin; or, Life Among the Lowly," as I titled my story. I would write it under my full name, Harriet Beecher Stowe.

From page one, the story was not so much written as *imposed* upon me. It seemed to have a life and will of its own, swelling into forty installments, a full-fledged book, as scenes, incidents, conversations—a living world—rushed upon me with a vividness and importunity that would not be denied. The book insisted upon getting itself into being, and I had no choice but to follow where it led me. I wrote during every spare moment I had—at the kitchen table, in the bedroom, in the candle-lit parlor at night when the children were in bed. My sister Catharine arrived in August and took charge of the house with her usual gusto and cheer, freeing me from domestic duties. Even so, I feared my health would fail me; I prayed earnestly that God would help me till I got through.

As my pen swept through the chapters, I drew constantly from my Ohio experiences, from my personal observations and all the stories I'd heard. I thank God that He gave me a retentive memory! I do believe that God sent me to Ohio so that I could acquire the knowledge needed to write my book. What my memory could not provide, of course, published sources could.

The slave trader Haley comes from my personal knowledge of this class of trader, the kidnapper, the Negro-whipper, like the despicable man who kidnapped my schoolchild and demanded a $200 ransom from her anguished mother. The fictional Eliza and George Harris are modeled after their actual counterparts and are so light-skinned that they can pass for whites, which is what enables them to escape. To fill out George's character, I drew from Frederick Douglass's wonderfully descriptive narrative of his life. Like Douglass, George is highly intelligent, teaches himself to read and write, and becomes a skilled slave, which shows the workings of a determined mind through all the squalid misery, degradation, and oppression of slavery.

John Van Trompe, who helps Eliza escape with her little boy, Harry, is a fictional version of John Van Sandt. Rachel and Simeon Halliday, the kindly Quakers who also assist Eliza, come from real Quakers Levi and Catharine Coffin. Mary Bird, who chastises her otherwise kindly husband for his amoral stand on fugitives, embodies much of me, for she, too, lost a beloved summer child. When Eliza relates that two of her own children died before Harry was born, Mrs. Bird sorts through the drawer of her dead child—exactly as I did with Charley's drawer in Cincinnati—and gives the dead child's clothes to Eliza for little Harry. Aunt Chloe and Cassy, slave women of great moral strength, both derive from Eliza Buck, my

Cincinnati cook and trusted friend. The violence done to slave families and Negro women in my story is based on Eliza Buck's experiences and those of other former slaves I knew.

As I wrote, I turned again and again to *American Slavery As It Is*, which furnished all the details I needed about brutal whippings, &c., and which I kept close by at all times, even under my pillow as I slept. I hoped that female readers, especially Christian mothers, would sympathize with Eliza, Aunt Chloe, and Cassy, and, like Mrs. Bird, exert moral pressure on their practical-minded husbands to *do* something to help the oppressed ones.

My southern white characters and their worlds also derive from actual sources. Uncle Tom's first owners, the kindly Shelbys, are modeled on the refined Virginia family who first owned Eliza Buck and then sold her down river to Louisiana. I also drew on a trip I made to Kentucky, where I conversed with several pious ladies, and upon the statements of a venerable friend, born and educated a slaveholder, who used the very words I attributed to Mrs. Shelby: "I never thought it was right to hold slaves." I borrowed from Charles's descriptions of plantation life in Louisiana and from an able paper about the practical operations of a cotton plantation written by its owner.

As for Augustine St. Clare, I met such men during my visit to Kentucky. He represents that class of men in the South who could not and would not be deluded by any of the shams and sophistry wherewith slavery had been defended. I drew his character with enthusiasm and with hope that such men, to whom God had given the power to perceive and the heart to feel the unutterable wrong and injustice of slavery, would not remain silent and inactive. St. Clare's cousin, Miss Ophelia, personifies the prejudice of caste and color prevailing in the North. I patterned the death of saintly Little Eva after the death of my little Charley in Cincinnati. Little Eva's passing was like a death in my own family—it affected me so deeply that I could not write a word for two weeks afterward. Then I realized what had only been a hope after my Charley's death: the crushing of my own heart was now enabling me to do great good for others, by writing *Uncle Tom's Cabin*.

The character of Uncle Tom I designed from an actual slave in Kentucky, a worthy, excellent soul and a devoted Christian, whose wife, a free woman, worked for me for a time. When he would come to visit her, she would beg him to run away; but he would refuse because "Master *trusts* me, and I cannot." To enrich Uncle Tom's character, I borrowed from the memoirs of former slave Josiah Henson, who had been so severely beaten by a white overseer in Maryland that it had crippled his arms. When Henson's mean, drunken master decided to sell him, he escaped to Canada with his wife and children. There he educated himself and became a preacher. He was so pious that he forgave his former masters and even prayed for their salvation.

Like Father Henson—like my own dear departed mother, Roxana Ward Beecher—Uncle Tom is the *perfect* Christian, a person of towering moral strength. Like our Saviour, he turns his other cheek, he sacrifices himself for others, he prays for the souls of his masters and evil tormentors. In his triumphant final scene, dying from the brutal beatings of Legree and Sambo and Quimbo, he forgives Legree—"Ye poor miserable critter!"—and converts the two blacks to Christ. His martyred soul will be reunited with God in Paradise.

The mighty feelings that drove my composition had increased in intensity until with the death of Uncle Tom it seemed as if the whole vital force had left. A sense of profound discouragement came over me. Would anybody read this tale? Would anybody listen to its cries? I had my answer when Mr. Bailey reported an enthusiastic response to the serialization. Thus reassured, I pushed on to the end of the story, when George Harris, in a bitter farewell to America and his white father's race, decides to relocate his family in Africa and help forge a black Christian nation of his own.

In the last chapter, I appealed directly to the generous, noble-minded men and women of the South to admit that there were woes and evils in the slave system. I appealed, too, to the men and women of the North, to the ship captains and sailors, the merchants and clerks, and especially to the mothers: do not say we have nothing to do with slavery! We have defended, encouraged, and participated in the slave system, and are more guilty for it, before God, than southerners are. What can we of the North do? We can have sympathy for the slaves and pray for them. Let our churches receive these poor sufferers in the spirit of Christ. Let us (as Mr. Garrison urged in the *Liberator*) receive them to the educating advantages of Christian republican society and schools, until they have attained somewhat of a moral and intellectual maturity. Then—and here I borrowed the plan of Senator Clay—let us assist them in their passage to Africa, where, as he said, they can put in practice the lessons learned in America. In Africa, the Negro race would no longer be despised and trodden down, but would exhibit the highest form of the peculiarly

Christian life. As I said in Chapter Fifteen: Perhaps, as God chastens whom He loves, He has chosen poor Africa in "the furnace of affliction" for a special purpose: to make her the highest and noblest in that Kingdom He will set up, when every other kingdom has been tried and failed; for then the first shall be last, and the last shall be first.

When I finished *Uncle Tom's Cabin*, in the late winter of 1852, I felt as if I had written some of it almost with my heart's blood. I then set about revising the story for publication in book form while it was still running in the *National Era*. What had I created? First of all, *Uncle Tom's Cabin* is a mosaic of facts—no, it is fiction *truer* than fact. It exposes readers to a *living reality*. It depicts the oppressed ones as real people who suffered terribly from the loss of their loved ones and from the cruelties meted out to them, and who longed for freedom just as whites did.

Equally important—and I can't say this enough—my story indicted the *system* of slavery, not the southern people. I believed there was an antislavery sentiment in the South which, if judiciously appealed to, was the most hopeful agent—the only hopeful one in fact—for the relief of this evil. I hoped to arouse that sentiment, by portraying my southern characters as decent people trapped in a vicious system. As St. Clare says, "The *thing* itself is the essence of all abuse." As for the villain Simon Legree, I took pains to make him a transplanted New Englander, thus stressing how much slavery contaminated anyone it touched, regardless of sectional allegiance.

Yes, I took a risk in writing such a story. What if the country rebuked me? What if my father disapproved—came flying through the door, crying, "Hattie! This is not the proper subject for a lady to write about!" But I felt I had to speak out, because as a woman and a mother I was oppressed and brokenhearted with the sorrow and injustice I saw, because as a Christian I felt the dishonor of Christianity, and because as a lover of my country, I trembled in the coming day of wrath, when God would punish North and South alike for this terrible offense.

I was quite unprepared for the success of *Uncle Tom's Cabin*. When on March twentieth, 1852, John Punchard Jewett of Boston published a two-volume book version, we were worried that the initial printing of 5,000 copies would never be sold. To our surprise, 3,000 copies were sold the first day, the balance on the next! Additional printings of 45,000 copies were gone in two months. The public appetite for the book—"Tom mania," they called it—seemed insatiable. Every mail brought scores of letters from admiring readers—I despaired of ever answering them all. By March 1853 total sales in this country had reached 305,000 copies and were still climbing. Yes, Calvin and I enjoyed the money the book brought in—some $60,000 in the first year and a half alone. We would never be poor again. Every book I wrote after that commanded a large audience, seldom selling fewer than 100,000 copies.

Uncle Tom's Cabin also appeared in Great Britain in a score of pirated editions, but I received only $500 from the hundreds of thousands of copies sold there. Nevertheless, I was gratified by the British enthusiasm for my story. I was told that Queen Victoria wept when she read it. The statesman Lord Palmerston, who had not read fiction for thirty years, was reported to have read *Uncle Tom's Cabin* three times.

I was utterly incredulous of all that was said about *Uncle Tom's Cabin*. It passed me like a dream. I could only see that when a Higher Being had a purpose to be accomplished, He could make even "a grain of mustard seed" like me the means. When I look back on *Uncle Tom's Cabin*, I am certain that God wrote it. I was but the instrument in His hand.

In the summer of 1852 we moved to Andover, Massachusetts, where Calvin had joined the faculty of the Andover Theological Seminary as Professor of Sacred Literature. We installed ourselves in a renovated stone house, a former coffin shop, which we called "The Cabin," and employed a cook, a housekeeper, and a governess for the smaller children. Because Calvin remained preoccupied with his books and his teaching, I made the family decisions and earned and invested our money. Still, I needed my old rabbi. "It's not fame nor praise that contents me," I told him. "I long to hear you say how much you love me."

We had so *many* visitors that first year, but the two most distinguished were Frederick Douglass and William Lloyd Garrison, both of whom had had so much influence on me. I actually invited Mr. Douglass to call on us—I wanted to meet him and also ask his advice. We were soon to leave for England, where I expected to collect a substantial sum of money from the sales of my book. I intended to use that money for the permanent improvement of free blacks in America and hoped that Mr. Douglass would like my idea and agree to help.

When he stepped into our hallway, I was quite impressed. He was tall and handsome, with a shock of curly hair, dark sensitive eyes, and a clear, musical voice that was so pleasant to listen to.

"We couldn't feel more at home," he said as we seated ourselves in the parlor. "You who have walked with lighted candle through the darkest and most obscure corners of the slave's soul, and have unfolded the secrets of the slave's lacerated heart, couldn't be a stranger to us; nor could we make ourselves a stranger to you." He was such a nice man, I felt my face flush. "*Uncle Tom's Cabin* is the *master book* of the nineteenth century," he said, adding to my embarrassment. "The word in it is addressed to the soul of universal humanity. *God bless you for that word*!"

"You inspired me, Mr. Douglass," I said. "Your *Narrative* gave me such invaluable insights into slavery. It's *I* who thank *you* for *your* word." He had the most beautiful smile and the loveliest white teeth I'd ever seen on a man.

Our discussion turned to what might be done to help the free colored people of the country. I suggested that an industrial school for blacks might be a good idea. Mr. Douglass wholeheartedly agreed, saying that a purely educational institution did not meet the needs of free blacks in the North. Since they were barred from all lucrative employment, they needed money most of all. "Their poverty keeps them ignorant and their ignorance keeps them degraded," he said. "We need more to learn how to make a good living than to learn Latin and Greek."

We parted in the warm spirit of commitment and friendship. But as I collected so little money in England from *Uncle Tom's Cabin*, I could not pursue the idea of a Negro industrial college. Black and white abolitionists objected to the idea of a racially exclusive school anyway, and the project died for lack of support.

My abolitionist mentor, William Lloyd Garrison, called at the Cabin in the same month that Mr. Douglass did. Quite honestly, I had great trepidation about meeting the master of vituperation, the notorious wolf of all wolves in the abolitionist movement. I was afraid he would devour me. My, how I was surprised! Neatly dressed and wearing wire-rimmed spectacles, he was polite and mild-mannered, as dignified as a scholar. As we sat together, he displayed a remarkable tact at conversation, which I pointed out to him.

"The principal difference between you and some others," I said, "is that they are wolves in sheep's clothing and you are a sheep in wolf's clothing. Pardon the simile."

He too extolled *Uncle Tom's Cabin*. "I repeat what I said in the *Liberator*, Mrs. Stowe. The vivid narrative made my nerves tremble and my heart grow liquid as water. The story awakens the strongest compassion for the oppressed and the utmost hatred of the system which grinds them to dust." He said he was particularly impressed with Uncle Tom. "He's sketched with great power and rare religious perception—he triumphantly exemplifies the nature, tendency, and results of Christian non-resistance." The idea that Uncle Tom might be a Garrisonian abolitionist had not occurred to me. "No insult, no outrage, no suffering," Mr. Garrison said, "could ruffle the Christ-like meekness of his spirit, or shake the steadfastness of his faith." The only objection Mr. Garrison had was to my sentiments respecting African colonization, which he said he "regretted."

I thanked him for his praise and said I was attentive to his criticism. "But I, too, have an objection," I said. "I've read the *Liberator* constantly, and I like its frankness, fearlessness, truthfulness, and independence. But some of your positions I consider erroneous, hurtful to liberty and the progress of humanity. What bothers me most of all, Mr. Garrison, are the hasty assertions, appeals to passion and prejudice, with which you sometimes deal with the Christian church. I fear you might take poor Uncle Tom's Bible away from him, and give him nothing in its place. To tell the truth, I sometimes worry that you aren't even a Christian. *Are* you a Christian, Mr. Garrison?"

"Oh, I'm most definitely a Christian," he said. "What I abhor are the proslavery attitudes of far too many clergymen in this country. "

"I've followed the action of the churches on slavery with humiliation and bitter sorrow," I said, "but I've not given up hope. I believe there is life there yet. With God's help, we must appeal to the very soul of the church."

During my interviews with Mr. Garrison and Mr. Douglass, I became aware of their harsh dislike for one another. The rift between them troubled me so much that I tried to negotiate a reconciliation. I spoke with Mr. Douglass about the matter and then wrote Mr. Garrison that Mr. Douglass did not appear to have any deep bitterness toward him, nor did he hold any views that could not be defended. I told Mr. Garrison that he'd been unjustly severe on Mr. Douglass, that I regretted the antipathy expressed by both sides, and that the abolitionist movement had plenty of room for both of their positions and views. But my appeals were in vain. Mr.

Garrison persisted in viewing Mr. Douglass as a traitor to the cause of true abolitionism.

When I first met the two gentlemen, I was writing a sequel to my novel called *The Key to Uncle Tom's Cabin*. This was my response to the outrage with which southern slaveholders had greeted my book. They sent me so many violent and hateful letters—one contained a black human ear! It just made us sick. I learned that the authorities in Dixie had seized and burned the book because they believed its "incendiary propaganda" would drive the slaves mad and cause them to rebel. In pamphlets, editorials, reviews, and letters sent to me, southern writers called me a "fanatical" and "wicked" Yankee woman contriving to promote sectional hatred. *Uncle Tom's Cabin*, they said, slandered the South from the first word to the last. Their "niggers" were *happy,* they insisted, because slavery was a benevolent institution, "the best in the world." "Uncle Tom's Cabin," thundered one review, "is a fiction throughout; a fiction in form, a fiction in its facts, a fiction in its morals. Fiction is its form and falsehood is its end." As Mr. Garrison said, all the defenders of slavery were letting him alone now and abusing me. They were indeed! To "correct" my "lies," several proslavery women authored "anti-Tom" novels that purported to tell the truth about life in Dixie: they claimed that the slaves were not only wonderfully happy but far better off than were northern free workers. One could not help but wonder, as the New York *Independent* did: if slavery was really so benign and the slaves really so contented, why did southerners not sell their own children to the slave traders?

I could not *understand* the South's savage response to my story. I was so hurt—mortified—*angry*. I had tried so hard to portray southern whites sympathetically and to appeal to their basic goodness. Well, I would not let them call my novel a lie. I decided to publish a book of sources—this was *The Key to Uncle Tom's Cabin*—that proved the accuracy and truth of my novel. The *Key* describes all the historical materials (personal observations, eyewitness accounts, &c.) used to prepare *Uncle Tom's Cabin*. It also contains additional sources—court records, state slave codes, legal decisions, reprints of slave trials, and the testimony of southerners themselves—which corroborate my thesis about the cruelties of slavery as a system.

My research left me exhausted and depressed. "The slave system is worse than I supposed or dreamed," I wrote an English friend. "Much as I thought I knew before, I had not begun to measure the depth of the abyss. I suffer exquisitely in writing these things. This horror, this nightmare abomination! can it be in my country? It lies like lead on my heart, it shadows my life with sorrow; the more so that I feel, as for my own brothers, for the South, and am pained by every horror I am obliged to write, as one who is forced by some awful oath to disclose in court some family disgrace. Many times I have thought that I must die, and yet I pray to God that I may live to see something done."

18. George Fitzhugh

Nothing proved the dissolution and demoralization of antebellum Free Society more than the emergence of women there who assumed a masculine character and bestirred themselves with cant about their "rights." It was unnatural and offensive. So long as woman is nervous, fickle, capricious, delicate, diffident, and dependent, man will worship and adore her. Her weakness is her strength, and her true art is to cultivate and improve that weakness. Woman naturally shrinks from public gaze, and from the struggle and competition of life. She has but one right, and that is the right of protection. The right to protection involves the obligation to obey. If she be obedient, she is in little danger of maltreatment. But if she insists upon a public role as her right, is coarse and masculine, man will loathe and despise her, and end by abusing her.

So it was with Mrs. Stowe: we loathed and despised her because she lusted for the public gaze and preached abolition. Nothing was more unnatural and despicable than a woman preaching abolition in a fat novel whose picture of our society was so deranged, so incredible, so far removed from the truth, that only someone demented could have produced it. Mrs. Stowe's "liberation" from her nursery and kitchen had plainly driven her mad. Like her character Aunt Chloe, Mrs. Stowe was a she-man who continually bored and elbowed us with her twisted virtues. Northern women like her were the deformed offspring of the obnoxious doctrines of liberty and equality and one more proof of the unnatural tendencies of Free Society.

You ask, who am I? I am a resident of Port Royal, in the Northern Neck of Virginia, with an illustrious ancestry that includes a Tory gentleman, William Fitzhugh, who had strong ties to the

British court. When I wedded Mary Metcalf Brockenbrough in 1829, we settled in the Brockenbrough family mansion, which sat on the banks of the Rappahannock River near Port Royal. Here I acquired slaves, sired nine children by Mary, took long walks, dabbled at a law practice, conducted research on my ancestors, and studied by day and by night (I am an incurable insomniac) abolitionist papers like the *Liberator* and the New York *Tribune* and conservative English journals like the *Edinburgh Review, Westminster Review, Blackwood's Magazine*, and the *North British Review*. I read with relish the writings of Thomas Carlyle, the celebrated English man of letters, who damned the French Revolution and the revolutions that swept Europe in 1848–1849, when "everywhere immeasurable Democracy rose monstrous, loud, blatant, inarticulate as the voice of chaos." Democracy, said Carlyle, was "anarchy plus a street constable." It was anarchy plus the guillotine and the death of the ruling classes! "Liberty," the "rights of capital," "private enterprise"—the favorite shibboleths of abolitionists and laissez-faire economists—were the foe of order and stability. Liberate the human spirit, Carlyle warned, and it inevitably loosens "a sudden outburst of revolutionary rage" that destroys everything in its path.

By 1850, I had discovered my real vocation—the writing of polemics in defense of our Slave Society, the most stable and serene way of life yet contrived by man. In the nocturnal privacy of my writing chamber, with bats flapping at the eaves and crevices of the old mansion, I offered battle to Free Society, to abolitionism, Jeffersonian liberalism, the Mammonism of industrialism, and all the other putrid "isms" that sprang from the Age of Enlightenment, which ended once and for all the halcyon days of feudalism. In a pamphlet entitled *Slavery Justified*, included as an appendix to my first book, *Sociology for the South*, published in 1854, I stated my thesis thusly: "First—That liberty and equality, with their concomitant free competition, begot a war in society that is as destructive to its weaker members as the custom of exposing the deformed and crippled children. Secondly—that slavery protects the weaker members of society just as do the relations of parent, guardian and husband, and is as necessary, as natural, and almost as universal as those relations."

Only the North of the United States and France had fully embraced Free Society, or capitalism, attempting a social organization predicated on "universal liberty and equality of rights," or free competition. England had only tried this in her commercial and manufacturing cities. And the experiment in all three cases had failed miserably. I had conclusive proof that liberty and equality had not conduced to enhance the comfort or the happiness of the people in those countries. Look at the discontent of the masses there, as evidenced by the Socialists, Communists, and a thousand other agrarian sects. Look at the disastrous rise in crime and pauperism, which was commensurate with the advance of liberty and equality in those countries. Look at their labor strikes for higher wages and their daily revolutionary outbreaks, all of which proved that the poor understood that their condition was far worse under the new than under the old order of things.

Yes, I said, Free Society was an abject failure, because it encouraged a war of wits, fostered a destructive attitude of every man for himself, enabled and impelled the stronger race to oppress and exterminate the weaker. Liberty and equality, in short, threw the whole weight of society on its weakest members. Look at what happened to the situation of woman when she was thrown into the war of competition, and had to support herself by her daily wages. For the same or equally valuable services she got not half the pay that man did, simply because the modesty of her sex prevented her from resorting to all the arts and means of competition which men employ. He who would emancipate woman, unless he could make her as coarse and strong in mind and body as man, would be her worst enemy; her subservience to and dependence on man was necessary to her very existence. She was not a soldier fitted to enlist in the war of free competition. Now look at Slave Society. We did not set children and women free because they were not capable of taking care of themselves, not equal to the constant struggle of society. To set them free would be to give the lamb to the wolf to take care of. Society would quickly devour them.

In Free Society, I said, the vulgar landlords, capitalists, and employers had the liberties and lives of the people more completely in their hands than had the kings, barons, and gentlemen of former times; and they hated and oppressed the people as cordially as the people despised them. They were vulgar parvenus. Self-interest made the employer and free laborer enemies. The one preferred to pay low wages, the other needed high wages. War, constant war, was the result, in which the operative perished, but was not vanquished. He was hydra-headed, and when he died two took his place.

There was but one remedy for this evil, so inherent in Free Society, and that was to identify the interests of the weak and the strong, the poor and the rich. Domestic slavery did this far better than any other institution. Look at Greece and Rome, at Egypt and Judea, at all other distinguished states of antiquity, and what do you find? It was to domestic slavery that they were indebted for their great prosperity and high civilization. As for feudalism, it only answered the purpose in so far as it retained the features of slavery, which made it a stable arrangement. Certainly the feudal barons were more generous and hospitable and less tyrannical than the petty landholders of modern times.

"Oh Equality," I wrote, "where are thy monuments? Echo answers where! Echo deep, deep, from the bowels of the earth, where women and children drag out their lives in darkness, harnessed like horses to heavy cars loaded with ore. Or perhaps it is an echo from some grand, gloomy, and monotonous factory, where pallid children work fourteen hours a day, and go home at night to sleep in damp cellars. It may be too, this cellar contains aged parents too old to work and cast off by their employer to die. Great railroads and mighty steamships too, thou mayest boast, but still the operatives who constructed them were beings destined to poverty and neglect. Not a vestige of art canst thou boast, free society; not a ray of genius illumines thy handiwork. The sordid spirit of Mammon presides over all, and from all proceeds the sighs and groans of the oppressed."

Now, I said, compare the lot of the worker in Free Society to that of the southern slave. A wild sect of French Communists proposed that all property be held in common and profits be divided according to each man's wants. Now this was precisely the system of domestic slavery with us. We provided for each slave, in old age and in infancy, in sickness and in health, not according to his labor, but according to his wants. The master's wants were more costly and refined, and he therefore got a larger share of the profits. A southern farm was the beau ideal of Communism; it was a joint concern, in which the slave consumed more than the master of the coarse products, and was far happier, because although the concern might fail, he was always sure of a support; he was only transferred to another master to participate in the profits of another concern; he married when he pleased, because he knew he would have to work no more with a family than without one; and whether he lived or died, that family would be taken care of; he exhibited all the pride of ownership and was as happy as a human being could be. There was no rivalry, no competition to get employment among slaves, as among free laborers. Nor was there a war between master and slave. The master's interest prevented his reducing the slave's allowance or wages in infancy or sickness, for he might lose the slave by so doing. His feeling for his slaves never permitted him to stint them in old age. The slaves were all well fed, well clad, had plenty of fuel, and were happy. They had no dread of the future—no fear of want. A state of dependence was the only condition in which reciprocal affection could exist among human beings—the only situation in which the war of competition ceased, and peace, amity, and goodwill arose.

This dependency, in turn, elevated the slaveholder, allowing him full exercise of his affections. His whole life was spent in providing for the minutest wants of others, in taking care of them in sickness and in health. Hence he was the least selfish of men. He was generous, affectionate, brave, and eloquent; he was superior to the northerner in everything but the art of thrift. Nature compelled master and slave to be friends; nature made employers and free laborers enemies. In slavery, moreover, women did little hard work and were protected from the despotism of their husbands by their genteel masters.

You see how wrong Mrs. Stowe was? At the slaveholding South all was peace, quiet, plenty, and contentment. We had no Simon Legrees, no disillusioned St. Clares, no suffering Uncle Toms, no frightened Elizas. All were figments of a deranged imagination vomited up by Free Society. We had no mobs, no trade unions, no strikes for higher wages, no armed resistance to the law, but little jealousy of the rich by the poor. We had but few in our jails, and fewer in our poorhouses. We were wholly exempt from the torrent of pauperism, crime, agrarianism, and infidelity which Europe was pouring from her jails and almshouses on the already crowded North.

Until the 1830s, I wrote, our great error was to imitate northern habits, customs, and institutions. Our circumstances were so opposite to theirs, that whatever suited them was almost sure not to suit us. Until that time, in truth, we distrusted our social system. We thought slavery morally wrong, we thought it would not last, we thought it unprofitable. But when the abolitionists assailed us, we looked more closely into our circumstances; we became satisfied that slavery was morally right, that it would continue ever to exist, that it was as profitable as it was humane. Thus began our self-confidence, our self-reliance. From that time our improvement was rapid. Now we could safely say that we were the happiest, most contented and prosperous people on earth.

Our only problem—and I addressed this in a separate essay included in *Sociology for the South*—was the free black population. Free Negroes were an intolerable nuisance that blighted every neighborhood in which they lived, North and South. They were thieves from necessity, for nature had made them so improvident they could not in health provide for sickness, in youth for old age, nor in summer for winter. A free Negro! Why, the very term seemed an absurdity. The Negro's was not human freedom, but the wild and vicious license of the fox, the wolf, or the hawk. Free Negroes corrupted our slaves and made them less contented with their situation. The competition of free Negroes was also injurious to our white laboring citizens. To maintain order, the Negro must always occupy a situation subordinate to the white man. North and South, every deviation from this policy led to violence, in which the blacks were the sufferers. The solution was to re-consign the free Negro to slavery, the only condition for which the Negro was suited.

The people of the South, I said in *Sociology for the South*, must wake up to the revolutionary tumult, uproar, and crime of Free Society, and resist its encroachments. But to resist the evil we must first inform ourselves about its origins. How did Free Society come about? With the Renaissance and Reformation, a new, malignant spirit of individualism broke down medieval authority and its monopolistic forms and benevolent serfdom. This malignant new spirit, in turn, spawned Adam Smith's *The Wealth of Nations*, published in 1776, which promoted the heretical notion that individual well-being and social and national wealth and prosperity would be best promoted by each man's eagerly pursuing his own selfish welfare unfettered and unrestricted by legal regulations or governmental prohibitions. This philosophy of laissez-faire and free trade, which seized the North, was false and rotten to the core, for it was that philosophy which created an exploitive system that fostered ruthless competition at the expense of the weak.

To protect her people from the new order, I said, Virginia must free herself from the centers of trade, with their noxious concepts of free enterprise and competition, and make herself self-sufficient by rigorous government participation in the state's economic growth. We must learn from history to prize and guard state rights. We must, as far as was consistent with the Constitution, make each slave state independent of the rest of the world. We must restore primogeniture and entail, which Jefferson destroyed. We need not fear the mad dog cry of hereditary aristocracy; a man with an entailed estate of five hundred acres, and a coat of arms to boot, would not be a very dangerous character. We had the things, exclusive hereditary privileges and aristocracy, amongst us, in their utmost intensity; let us not be frightened by the name.

We must, I said, stand before the world as enlightened reactionaries, family based, proudly aristocratic, fiercely anti-capitalist. We must do battle against Lockean liberalism and the entire Age of Enlightenment, which begot individualism and laissez-faire economics in the first place. We must combat the doctrines of natural liberty, human equality, and the social contract as taught by Locke and the American sages of 1776. Under the spell of Locke and the Enlightenment, Jefferson and other misguided patriots ruined the splendid political edifice they erected by espousing dangerous abstractions—the crazy notions of liberty and equality they wrote into the Declaration of Independence and the Virginia Bill of Rights. No wonder the abolitionists loved to quote the Declaration of Independence! Its precepts are wholly at war with slavery and equally at war with all government, all subordination, all order. It is full of mendacity and error. Consider its verbose, newborn, false, and unmeaning preamble. Men are not born physically, morally, or intellectually equal. Some are born large, strong, and healthy, others weak, small, and sickly—some are naturally amiable, others prone to all kinds of wickedness—some grave, others timid. Their natural inequalities beget inequalities of rights. The weak in mind or body require guidance, support, and protection; they must obey and work for those who protect and guide them—they have a natural right to guardians, committees, teachers, or masters. Nature has made them slaves; all that law and government can do, is to regulate, modify, and mitigate their slavery.

Nor are men born entitled to equal rights. It is far nearer the truth to say that "some are born with saddles on their backs and others booted and spurred to ride them" and that the riding does them good. No institutions can prevent the few from acquiring rule and ascendancy over the many. There is, finally, no such thing as inalienable rights. Life and liberty are not inalienable; they have been sold in all countries, and in all ages, and must be sold so long as human nature lasts. Jefferson, in sum, was the architect of ruin, the inaugurator of anarchy. As his Declaration of Independence stands, it deserves the appropriate epithets which Major Lee somewhere applies to the thought of Mr. Jefferson, it is "exuberantly false, and aborescently fallacious."

I argued that we must stand before the world as the Negro's best friend, rejecting the racial doctrine "Types of Mankind," advanced by Nott, Gliddon, Gobineau, and others to "prove" that Negroes are inferior brutes. In *Sociology for the South,* I said I abhorred that doctrine because it encouraged and incited brutal masters to treat Negroes not as weak, ignorant, and dependent brethren, but as wicked beasts, without the pale of humanity. The southerner was the Negro's *only* friend. Let no intermeddling abolitionist, no refined philosophy, dissolve that friendship.

After *Sociology for the South* was published, I accepted an invitation to debate abolitionist Wendell Phillips before the lyceum of New Haven, Connecticut, in a lecture series begun by Emerson. The hall was full and included several Yale professors. The topic of my talk was "The Failure of Free Society," and it ranged from a condemnation of Jeffersonian liberalism to the natural origin of slavery. Moncure Conway said about my lecture: "Fitzhugh's method of proving Free Society a failure was by theories and speculations which had got into crevices and under the eaves of his brain, like the bats in the rickety old mansion, situated on the fag-end of a once noble estate, in which he resided." Clever words, but Conway did not disprove my theories, nor did Wendell Phillips; in fact, he refused to answer me. His own lecture—a tirade against church and state, law and religion—was flat treason and blasphemy. Still, I am an affable gentleman, and if I may say so unflappable in the presence of the enemy; and I smiled throughout the lecture. I thought Phillips the most eloquent and graceful speaker I had ever heard, liked him as a man, and got along well with him and other abolitionists, to whom I listened carefully and always with a smile, although I disagreed with them on virtually every point.

On the morning after my lecture, Samuel Foote took me on a carriage ride; he turned out to be Mrs. Stowe's favorite uncle. A gruff Yankee and former sea captain, Foote told me sarcastically: "I'll show you how Free Society has failed!" He drove me through New Haven's best neighborhoods, pointing out homes and cottages that would have been "marvels of elegance in Virginia." Foote claimed that mechanics and even day laborers owned some of these mansions. He claimed that the city had no slums, that even the poorest classes resided in comfortable homes, and that free labor, without government assistance, had created a prosperous, stable community there. I did not believe a word of it. Foote was not showing me the real North—you could read about that North, its crimes and upheavals, in its newspapers.

During my stay in New Haven, I shared my insights into the failure of Free Society with everyone I encountered, with strangers at hotels and fellow passengers on public conveyances. None of them, of course, agreed with me: half were atheists; the rest were anti-church, anti-law millenarians. You can't argue with such men. The city's abolitionists, however, entertained me well enough and sent me off with pamphlets, speeches, and books, which I perused on the trip home. I discovered that in attempting to prove Free Society a failure in my lecture at New Haven, I was "but carrying coals to Newcastle." The Liberty party had discovered that failure long before I did, and was as intent on subverting and reconstructing Free Society at home as on abolishing slavery with us.

My trip to the North reinforced my conviction that Free Society had produced a vampire capitalist class whose competitive ideals and practices were little better than moral cannibalism. This was the thesis of my second book, *Cannibals All; or, Slaves Without Masters*. I told the northern employer: "You, sir, with the command over labor which your capital gives you, are a slaveowner—a master, without the obligations of a master. They who work for you, who create your income, are slaves, without the rights of slaves. Slaves without a master! Why are there more millionaires in the North than in the South? Because of Free Society's superior techniques of human exploitation. Northern masters live in ten times the luxury and show that southern masters do, yet free laborers have not a thousandth part of the rights and liberties of Negro slaves. The Negroes of the South are, in fact, the happiest, and, in some sense, the freest people in the world." I argued that slavery was the natural and normal condition of the laboring man, white *and* black, and that slavery for both was right and necessary.

The publication of *Cannibals All!* established my reputation in the South. "Mr. George Fitzhugh," said *De Bow's Review*, "is one of the boldest and most daring thinkers of the age. He grapples with things as they are in reality." Because my unsigned articles appeared in a number of publications, in *De Bow's Review*, the *Southern Literary Messenger*, the Richmond *Examiner*, even the New York *Day Book*, many northerners believed that I had won the entire South to my views, that I had become *the* voice of Slave Society. It was not an inaccurate conclusion, for "Fitzhughisms" were appearing widely in the southern press and on the lips of prominent political leaders. Here are a few examples:

The Charleston *Mercury*: "Slavery is the natural and normal condition of the laboring man, whether white or black. Master and slave is a relation in society as necessary as that of parent and child, and the northern states will yet have to introduce it."

The New Orleans *Delta*: "Modern Free Society, as at present organized, is radically wrong and rotten. It is self-destroying and can never exist happily and normally until it is qualified by the introduction of some principle equivalent in effect to the institution of southern negro slavery."

The Muscogee (Alabama) *Herald*: "*Free* Society! We sicken of the name. What is it but a conglomeration of *greasy mechanics, filthy operatives, small-fisted farmers*, and moon-struck theorists?"

James M. Mason of Virginia (to the Senate of the United States): "It is now almost universally believed, in the South, that slavery is ennobling to both races, white and black. Free Society has failed; and that which is not free must be substituted."

Increasingly I believed that Free Society and Slave Society could not coexist in the same country. I was not yet in favor of secession and disunion, because I believed that we would yet convert the people of the North to our system. "Free Society," I wrote in the Richmond *Examiner*, "is an impracticable form of society; it is everywhere starving, demoralizing, and insurrectionary. Two opposite and conflicting forms of society cannot, among civilized men, coexist and endure. The one must give way and cease to exist, the other become universal. If Free Society be unnatural, immoral, unchristian, it must fall, and give way to Slave Society—a social system old as the world, universal as man."

I began a correspondence with William Lloyd Garrison, the king of the socialist, infidel, woman's-rights, and abolition party of the North. "We live in a dangerous crisis," I told him, "and every patriot and philanthropist should set aside all false delicacy in the earnest pursuit of truth. I believe slavery natural, necessary, indispensable. You think it inexpedient, immoral, and criminal. Neither of us should withhold any facts that would enable the public to form correct opinions."

Garrison published my letter in the *Liberator*, with the remark that *Sociology for the South* was "a shallow, impudent, and thoroughly satanic work" and that its author was "evidently a moral lunatic." He also devoted considerable attention in his paper to *Cannibals All!*, quoting long passages to show the extremes to which "this cool audacious defender of the soul-crushing, blood-reeking system of slavery" would go in defense of "the cradle-plunderers and slave-drivers at the South." He went on: "Mr. Fitzhugh is the Don Quixote of Slavedom—only still more demented than his 'illustrious predecessor.'" I did not object to Garrison's intended slur. I cherished Cervantes's book, which showed that only a "mad" Don Quixote was sane enough to care about and defend the old values. "Mr. Fitzhugh," Garrison continued, "sees in freedom a terrific monster which is devouring its millions, and valiantly essays to drive it from the earth. If he is not playing the part of a dissembler, he is certainly crack-brained, and deserves pity rather than ridicule or censure." Such revilement proved that my writings had touched a nerve in the great anarch of the North. Why did Garrison denounce government as "usurpation, imposture, demagoguism, swindling, and tyranny," as "intrinsically inhuman, selfish, clannish, and opposed to a recognition of the brotherhood of man"? Because Garrison *recognized* the exploitive nature of Free Society.

I wrote him that the abolitionists were on the wrong side of history, that public opinion, realizing that Free Society was an historical aberration, was about to decide in favor of slavery as the most stable and natural system in the world. The abolitionists, however, were trying to forestall that decision through Federal legislation. Failing that, they intended to plunge the nation into a civil and fratricidal war.

I had tried hard to reach them, to convince them of the disastrous and cruel failure of the North's little experiment in Free Society, to ask why they had Bloomer's and Women's Rights men, strong-minded women (like Mrs. Stowe), Mormons, anti-renters, "vote myself a farm" men, Millerites, Spiritual Rappers, Shakers, Widow Wakemanites, Agrarians, Grahamites, and a thousand other superstitious and infidel "isms," and why western Europe was now starving and had been fighting and starving for seventy years, if my critique of Free Society was not true? "Should you not, therefore," I asked the abolitionists, "abolish your form of society and adopt ours?"

But all my entreaties were in vain. Instead of listening to reason, they intensified their barbaric crusade against us, and finally I had had enough. "For thirty years," I told my fellow slaveowners, "the South has been a field on which abolitionists, foreign and domestic, have carried on offensive warfare. Let us now, in turn, act on the offensive, transfer the seat of war, and invade the enemy's territory."

PART THREE

THE APPROACHING FURY

19. STEPHEN A. DOUGLAS

When, in January of 'fifty-four, I introduced the revised Kansas-Nebraska bill with an explicit repeal of the Missouri Compromise line, my enemies put out the so-called "Appeal of Independent Democrats in Congress to the People of the United States," which was widely published in the press. This craven document accused my bill of violating "a sacred pledge," of being "part and parcel of an atrocious plot" to transform the northern portion of the old Louisiana Purchase "into a dreary region of despotism, inhabited by masters and slaves." It charged me with conspiring to cover the whole land with "the blight of slavery." It called me a "servile demagogue" who had sold himself to the Slave Power in his lust for the Presidency!

The authors were *not Democrats*. They were abolitionists, Free-Soilers, and northern Whigs hell-bent on smearing me and dividing the great Democratic party. Their ringleader was Chase of Ohio, a black-hearted abolitionist who speaks with a lisp and has the face of a baby with premature wrinkles. The Goddamned coward was afraid to hand me the "Appeal" in person—I got my copy in the mail from Ohio. When I read it, I was empurpled with rage. How dare those sons of bitches impugn the honor of the Little Giant! How dare they call the Little Giant a liar and a fraud! I wanted to strangle that prissy Chase with my bare hands. I crumpled the Appeal and flung it to the floor.

"I'm *not* proslavery," I told the son of a friend, as I paced back and forth in my parlor, smoking a cigar. "I think it's a curse beyond computation to both white and black. But the only way to destroy slavery is with the sword, and once the sword is drawn no one will be able to see the end." I lit another cigar. "The integrity of the Union is worth more to humanity than the whole nigger race."

My Nebraska bill violated no sacred pledge, was part of no "atrocious plot" to expand slavery and put me in the White House. It simply organized the northern section of the Louisiana Purchase into the new territories of Kansas and Nebraska. There was no controversy in that—all who believed in America's manifest destiny could applaud that. Yes, the bill repealed the Missouri Compromise line, which had prohibited slavery in the region in question. In place of that line, the bill established popular sovereignty, which embodies the great principle of self-government, which allows the citizens of each new territory to vote on whether to permit slavery or exclude it. I ask you, what could be a fairer, more American, more democratic formula for dealing with the Goddamned slavery question than that? Was self-government not the fundamental principle upon which our Republic and its institutions were founded?

Do not believe the lies of my abolitionist enemies. Stephen A. Douglas did not hope to cover the land with "the blight of slavery." Stephen A. Douglas intended to open the western territories to *freedom*, by leaving the people there perfectly free to do as they pleased. To know who I am is to appreciate the purity of my motives. I am a western man from the great state of Illinois; I believe in the supremacy of the white race and the God-given right of the United States to rule this continent. I cannot remember when I did not think so. I was born and raised in Vermont and studied law in Canandaigua, New York. In 'thirty-three, at the age of twenty, I set out by stage to seek my fortunes in the West. In Cleveland, I almost died of bilious fever—the doctors told me I should prepare myself for my "final dissolution." Bah! Nothing can keep Stephen A. Douglas down! Four months later I was upright and on the move again. I went to Illinois, the paradise of the world, with its regular, rolling landscape of timber and prairie interspersed in just proportions. I taught school in Winchester and then settled in Jacksonville, where I established a law practice and took up politics as a defender of Andy Jackson and his war against that powerful monster of the aristocracy, the United States Bank.

As legislator, state's attorney, and judge on the state supreme court, *I* built the Democratic party in Illinois, *I* was its generalissimo. A well-organized, disciplined Democratic party, I argued, allowed the friends of democracy to *act together* against the Federalist-Whig party of privilege, to embody and give effect to the popular will, to maintain the people's ascendancy and unite their efforts, to perpetuate those genuine principles of democracy which make government responsive and obedient to the people, to their pleasure and desires.

Nobody then or since could match me at political oratory. In the heat of debate, I like to rip off my cravat, fling my waistcoat open, and, voice thundering, pitch into an opponent with shaking fists and stamping feet, exposing him for the enemy of the people that he is. That is why they call me the Little Giant, the slayer of political pretenders, of villainous liars and pusillanimous scoundrels.

It was in 'forty-four, during my first term in the national House, that I initially wrote and introduced a bill to organize the northern section of the Louisiana Purchase into a single territory, Nebraska, whose name revived the euphonious aboriginal word. The bill was "part and parcel" of my larger plan for settling the West, for stretching the American empire to the Pacific and connecting the two oceans with a mighty railroad. A bad policy, begun years before, had collected the various Indian tribes in the different states and planted them permanently in the Nebraska country, on the western borders of Arkansas, Missouri, and Iowa. This permanent Indian barrier said to Christianity, Democracy, and Civilization, "thus far mayest thou go, and *no* farther." Bah! I said to that. How were we to develop, cherish, and protect our immense interests and possessions on the Pacific, with a vast wilderness fifteen hundred miles in breadth standing in the way—a wilderness filled with hostile savages and cutting off all direct communication? The Indian barrier, I said, had to be removed. The tide of emigration and civilization had to be permitted to roll onward until it rushed through the passes of the mountains, spread over the plains, and mingled with the waters of the Pacific. Continuous lines of settlements with civil, political, and religious institutions all under the protection of law, were imperiously demanded by the best national considerations.

No man, moreover, could keep up with the spirit of the age who traveled on anything slower than the locomotive and failed to receive intelligence by the lightning speed of the telegraph. We needed to organize the Nebraska Territory so that railroads and telegraphs could be constructed across it to connect the Atlantic to the Pacific. The removal of the Indian barrier and the extension of the laws of the United States in the form of territorial governments were the first steps toward the accomplishment of these objectives.

But the question of slavery in the Mexican Cession derailed my Nebraska bill, diverting public attention from the importance of our unorganized old territory and concentrating the hopes and anxieties of all upon our new possessions. During the divisive debates over slavery in the Mexican Cession, I voted against the Wilmot Proviso because I've always believed it the right of each state and each territory to decide the slavery question for itself. Nevertheless, to reconcile the Wilmot men and the Calhounites, I proposed that the Missouri Compromise line be extended to the Pacific. Though I doubted the wisdom of that line, I adhered faithfully to it and advocated its extension across the Mexican Cession, because I thought it a useful expedient to resolve the controversy.

My proposal, however, was voted down by northerners with Free-Soil proclivities. The defeat of the extension of the Missouri line led me to champion a new formula for dealing with slavery in the Mexican Cession and all future territories. That formula, first advocated in the Senate by Daniel S. Dickinson of New York and embraced by myself and Lewis Cass of Michigan, was popular sovereignty. The Compromise of 1850, for which I was largely responsible, embodied the new formula: in the place of a geographical line separating free and slave territory, the people of the territories would be allowed to do as they thought proper on the slavery question. The new formula took the question *out* of Congress, where it did nothing but stir up violent agitation that threatened our national stability, and gave it back to the people of a territory where it belonged. I didn't care a damn whether they voted slavery up or down, so long as Congress stayed out of the matter.

In short, the 1850 Compromise superseded the 1820 Compromise. The principle of territorial self-government replaced the geographical line. I ought to know, Goddamn it, I was the chairman of the Senate Committee on Territories; I wrote most of the bills and supported and defended all the measures of the 1850 Compromise. Yes, I called it Mr. Clay's compromise, but I will tell you this: if his name had not been associated with it, I would have gotten the bills passed long before. The Taylor administration was jealous of Clay and hated him, and some Democrats were weak enough to fear that the success of the compromise would make him President. But let it always be said of old Hal that he fought a glorious and patriotic battle. No man was ever governed by higher and purer motives.

During the height of the 1850 controversy, a Whig paper in Illinois published a scurrilous article, "Hon. S.A. Douglas the Owner of Slaves." It was a bald and blatant lie, gotten up by the Whigs and abolitionists to discredit me in the eyes of northern voters. It was true that my wife, Martha Denny Martin, owned about 150 niggers and a cotton plantation in Mississippi, which she inherited from her father after he passed on. The old man had offered the estate and the niggers to me as Martha's dowry, but I refused to accept them because a plantation and slaves, in my name, would have been a political liability. The fact of my refusal was stated in Mr. Martin's will, but I did not make it public as the public had no fucking business with my private affairs. When the Whig paper published its story, however, I prepared an anonymous statement in the third person, to be used by the Democratic press back home, stating that the plantation and the Negroes were not Senator Douglas's property; they belonged by Mississippi law to *Mrs. Douglas* as her separate and exclusive estate. It may be true that I managed the estate and slaves for her—I was her husband, wasn't I?—and that a certain percentage of our income came from her plantation. That was none of the public's damned concern.

In January of 'fifty-three, my dear wife of just six years died in childbirth; our baby girl died a month later. It was a crushing bereavement which left me in great despair. I frequented smoky taverns and oyster saloons. I tried to drown my sorrow in brandy. Finally I went abroad, to London, Saint Petersburg, the Crimea, and returned to Washington feeling much improved and ready again to promote my western program as the undisputed leader of the Senate.

The Compromise of 1850, which gave peace and quiet to the country, was ratified by both the Democratic and the Whig national conventions in 'fifty-two. With the new compromise firmly in place, I pushed again for the organization of the Nebraska Territory. A new Nebraska bill, employing the popular sovereignty doctrine, was written by myself, at my house, with no man present, in December of 'fifty-three. Surely, I thought, the necessity and importance of the measure were manifest to the whole country. As far as the slavery question was concerned, I trusted that everyone would be willing to sanction and affirm the principle of congressional non-intervention and local self-government established by the compromise measures of 1850.

My friends and fellow Democrats of the F Street Mess—so called because they lived together on F Street—helped me work out legislative strategy. They were the most powerful southerners in the Senate: florid-faced, hot-tempered David R. Atchison of Missouri; white-haired Andrew Butler of South Carolina; blunt and clean-shaven James M. Mason of Virginia; and stolid, disheveled R. M. T. Hunter, also of Virginia.

In January of 'fifty-four, I reported my Nebraska bill from the Committee on Territories. At this juncture, to avoid controversy, my bill did not even refer to the Missouri Compromise; it simply stated that "all questions pertaining to slavery in the territories, and in the new States to be formed therefrom, are to be left to the people residing therein, through their appropriate representatives." The Compromise of 1850, I explained in my report, had already repudiated the Missouri Compromise when the slave states were excluded from that part of California lying below the Missouri line, that is, the latitude of 36 degrees, 30 minutes. Now the Nebraska bill, by indirectly repudiating the Missouri Compromise above that line, put the saddle on the other horse.

Predictably, the abolitionists leaped to the floor in protest. "*Th*enator Douglas," cried a lisping Chase, "hath out-*th*outhernized the *Th*outh!" Then Archibald Dixon of Kentucky, the Whig who took Clay's seat in the Senate, a hard-faced lawyer and planter, offered an amendment that caught me by surprise. Not only did the amendment explicitly disavow the Missouri Compromise; it also acknowledged the *right* of citizens to *hold slaves* in Nebraska and any other territory.

Appalled, furious, I charged to Dixon's desk. "I can't accept this! This *legislates* slavery into the territories. It violates the very principle of popular sovereignty, of letting the people decide."

But the Senators of the F Street Mess and Philip Phillips of Alabama agreed with Dixon. The error in my bill, they said, was that it did not explicitly repeal the Missouri Compromise line. Therefore that line remained in force. Without the appeal, my bill was a "delusion" and would never get the support of the South.

I went back to Dixon. "By God, sir, you're right. I'll incorporate your amendment in my bill, the part repealing the Missouri line. But I know it'll raise a hell of a storm."

At my urging, Philip Phillips drafted an amendment declaring the Missouri Compromise "inoperative, void and of no force and effect." Phillips said: "We do not believe that slavery can go into the cold northern clime of Nebraska. But we want the *theoretical right* to take it there."

I said, let them have that barren right, if it meant southern support for Nebraska. As revised by me, the bill now stated that the Missouri Compromise was "superseded" by the 1850 Compromise and was therefore (to use Phillips's word) "inoperative." I also made another change in the bill, providing for *two* new territories, Kansas (lying due west of Missouri) and Nebraska (lying due west of Iowa). All of the Missouri and Iowa delegations wanted this modification, and I saw no harm in giving it to them.

Now to get the support of the Pierce Administration. The explicit repeal of the Missouri line was potentially dangerous—I was unwilling to proceed without the President's backing. But time was of the essence. It was now Sunday, January twenty-second. The bill was scheduled to come up in the Senate the next morning. The problem was, the President had a firm policy against conducting business on the Sabbath. With Atchison, Mason, Phillips, and Hunter, I called on Jefferson Davis, the Secretary of War, who was a personal friend of the President and the coldest, stiffest man I ever met. We stated our purpose and asked him to gain us an interview with Pierce that same Sunday.

At first Davis thought the repeal was a bad idea. The election of Frank Pierce of New Hampshire, he said, was a tacit understanding by both sections that the Compromise of 1850 was the final settlement of the slavery question. But when he heard our reasons for the repeal, Davis came around to our view. "It sounds like a step in the right direction," he said, and left to set up the interview with Pierce.

The President greeted us coolly in the White House Library. Pale and thin, with a knot of hair hanging over one side of his forehead, Frank Pierce usually bubbled with affability. His aloofness this Sunday had but one source: his Cabinet had met with him the day before and most of them had voiced their opposition to the revised Nebraska bill. With great care, then, I made our case for direct repeal. The southern Senators joined in. Jefferson Davis, the only Cabinet member present, said he agreed with us. We had Pierce surrounded.

Unable to resist such a powerful array of Senators and the logic of our arguments, Pierce capitulated. "You're right," he said. "The Compromise of 1850 did indeed supersede the Missouri Compromise."

"And made it inoperative," I said.

"Yes, that, too," he said.

"I want that in writing," I said. He hesitated for a moment, then wrote it down.

On Monday, I reported my revised bill to the Senate, pointing out that it had the support of the Administration; and the next day Chase and his abolitionist cronies put out their rabble-rousing "Appeal to the People," which accused me of a criminal betrayal of my trust, of committing an atrocious plot against the cause of free government. I replied to those maggoty scoundrels on January thirtieth, with most of the House of Representatives present, the galleries packed, and the press section filled with correspondents for the national papers. Shaking with anger, I refuted Chase's charge that the repeal of the Missouri Compromise was "a falsification of the truth of history." *I* ought to know the truth, Goddamn it. *I* made the history Chase and his fellow abolitionists accused me of falsifying. It was *they* who falsified history, I cried, *they* who had raised this political tornado. As I explained what the Committee on Territories had done, Chase tried to interrupt, but I refused to yield the floor to that squeaking bastard. I pointed out that it was worse than folly to think that slavery could exist in either Kansas or Nebraska. As Webster and others had pointed out, the laws of nature (climate, soil) banned the institution of slavery there, so that the Missouri line had never been necessary. I said, "I do not like, I never did like, the system of legislation on our part, by which a geographical line, in violation of the laws of nature, and climate, and soil, and of the laws of God, should be run to establish institutions for a people." Now, thanks to the Compromise of 1850, that line had been abandoned and the great principle of self-government, which allowed the people to determine for themselves which institutions they wanted to have, had been established in its place. I had, I said in closing, a higher and a more solemn obligation to that great fundamental principle of democracy and free institutions which lies at the basis of our creed than I ever did to a provocative geographical line that should never have existed.

The bill raised a hell of a Goddamned storm all right, with a trio of abolitionist Senators—Chase and Wade of Ohio and Sumner of Massachusetts—providing most of the opposition, which was obstreperous. As I expected, Chase accused *me* of renewing the "strife and controversy" that now divided Congress. Sumner, a nauseating Anglophile who wore tailored coats, checkered trousers, and English gaiters, blathered on about how my bill reversed the original policy of the government and made slavery *national* instead of sectional. He demanded that the "sacred" Missouri line be restored, and that "*freedom,* not slavery, be made national." The arrogant prick spoke in a Boston accent that always irritated the hell out of me. Not surprisingly, William H. Seward of New York, a little fart of a Whig with a scrawny neck, beaked nose, and shaggy eyebrows, joined the malcontents. "The slavery agitation you deprecate so much," he said, "is an eternal struggle between conservatism and progress, between truth and error, between right and wrong." The disgusting Sumner jumped up and pronounced it the greatest speech of Seward's life.

I expected flatulent protests from all of them. But there were southerners who opposed us, too. John Bell of Tennessee, a Whig, did so to the bitter end. Old Frank Blair of Maryland believed that shit about a Slave Power plot. "The whole work of Kansas-Nebraska," he said, "was done by the southern plotters." The renegade Houston whined: "If no new slave states can come from the two new territories, why repeal the Missouri Compromise? I, as the most extreme southern Senator upon this floor, do not desire it. I repudiate it. I reject it. Maintain the Missouri Compromise! Do not stir up agitation! Give us peace!" What else could you expect of him? Houston was a fucking drunk.

There was a troublesome point in the debates when Toombs of Georgia voiced an interpretation of popular sovereignty that differed from mine and Cass's. A six footer with long, uncombed black hair, brilliant white teeth, and a little goatee on his chin, Toombs argued that the people of a territory could not vote on slavery until that territory was ready for statehood. Lewis Cass, somber and soldierly, rose to reply. "Sir," he told Toombs, "you're wrong. The Nebraska bill gives full legislative power to these territories over all questions of human concern, including slavery, unless restrained by the Constitution." At that, Clayton of Delaware jumped to his feet. If the territories could legislate against slavery, he cried, then the principle of non-intervention had been abandoned! Other southerners told me that they, too, were apprehensive about any interpretation of popular sovereignty that allowed the territories to vote on slavery. But, like Clayton, they promised to support the bill because they wanted the repeal of the Missouri line.

I made a final change in the bill when Chase offered a snide challenge. "If you wish to break up the time-honored Missouri Compromise," he said, "do it openly—do it boldly." I obliged the Goddamned bastard. The revised section on the Missouri Compromise now declared it "*void*" as well as "inoperative" and "superseded."

As the debates drew to a close, I treated the galleries to the kind of oratory for which I was famous: I went after the abolitionist Senators with what one newspaper described as "a perfect torrent of invective, argument, satire and ridicule." If, as the opposition New York *Tribune* reported, my manner was "sneering" and "vulgar," if my "harangue" was punctuated by "God damns" and "by Gods," the abolitionists deserved it. Besides, the people in the galleries loved my performance, clapping and hooting at almost every word.

The truth is, I passed the Kansas-Nebraska bill myself. I had the authority of a dictator throughout the whole controversy in both houses. The speeches were nothing. What counted was the marshaling and directing of men, at which I had no equal in this Republic. Working both houses with ceaseless energy and vigilance, I made the Kansas-Nebraska bill a test of Democratic party loyalty. "The only way to avoid a division of the party," I told fellow Democrats, "is to sustain our principles. The Administration is with us and will stand by this bill at all hazards. The principle of this bill forms the test of parties: you have a choice of standing with me and the Democracy or with Seward and the abolitionists."

In the end, the Kansas-Nebraska bill passed both houses by the overwhelming approval of the Democratic majority. Houston and Bell were the only southern Senators who opposed it. When, on May thirtieth, the President signed the measure into law, the great principle of self-government ruled in the territories.

Seward gave a bitter valedictory in behalf of the abolitionists. "Come on, then, gentlemen of the slave states; since there is no escaping your challenge, I accept it in behalf of the cause of freedom. We will engage in competition for the virgin soil of Kansas, and God give the victory to the side that is stronger in numbers as it is in right."

"I accept your challenge," I cried. "Raise your black flag; call up your forces; preach your war on the Constitution, as you have threatened it here. We will be ready to meet all your allied forces."

I speak frankly, though: I did not anticipate the popular outcry against the Nebraska Act in the North, did not anticipate the mass protest rallies and the bitter newspaper attacks. When I made a train trip through the East, I was *booed* at Trenton, *jeered* in New York City, *hissed at* in Philadelphia. I glared back in defiance, yet the hostile crowds disturbed me. There was trouble at home, too. Twenty-five clergymen sent me the proceedings of an anti-Nebraska meeting in Chicago, which condemned the repeal of the Missouri Compromise as "a great moral wrong, a violation of God's will, and an infringement of His holy law." I fired off a furious twenty-one-page rebuttal. To make matters worse, Democrats and Democratic papers in central and northern Illinois were reported to be defecting to the enemy. This was serious. It could mean trouble for the party in the upcoming congressional and legislative elections. We could lose a seat in the national Senate, since James Shields, the other Senator from Illinois, was up for reelection in the legislature. Determined to pull the party together, I set out for Illinois by train, only to encounter angry crowds along the entire route. "Judas!" they screamed at me. "Traitor Arnold!" I could have traveled from Boston to Chicago by the light of my burning effigy. All along the Western Reserve of Ohio I saw my effigy upon every tree we passed.

20. GARRISON

The Kansas-Nebraska Act was further proof that the party demagogues who controlled the Federal Government were the tools and
vassals of the Slave Power. Those who begot this foul measure did so
against the laws of God and the rights of universal man—in subver-
sion of plighted faith, in utter disregard of the scorn of the world,
and for a purpose as diabolical as can be conceived of or consummated here on earth. That purpose—now the ultimate goal of the
Slave Power plot—was the *nationalization* of slavery. The first step
in the conspiracy was to suppress all abolitionist dissent. The second
was to repeal the Missouri Compromise and extend slavery into the
territories. The next was to expand it into the free states, into New
York and New England, into New Jersey and Pennsylvania, into
Ohio, Indiana, and Illinois, into Wisconsin, Minnesota, and Iowa,
until the entire North was part of the Slave Power. And all this, as
Brother Henry Blackwell warned, was but "a prelude to the annexation of Cuba, and the dismemberment of Mexico; and finally the
revival of the international slave trade."

Brother Phillips was right: "The future seems to unfold a vast
slave empire united with Brazil, and darkening the whole west."

I told all true abolitionists: "Now, more than ever, we must
make every northern man see and confess that our boasted Union is
a snare, a curse, and a degrading vassalage to the Slave Power, that
there is no Union for freedom to be dissolved, but one to be created.
We must stand together, we of the North, and resolve: 'That the
American Union is the supremacy of the Bowie knife, the revolver,
the slave-driver's lash, and lynch law, over freedom of speech, of the
press, of conscience, of locomotion, in more than one half of the
nation; and that the debasement of the nation and of the entire
North to the wretched Slave Power, as evidenced by this new outrage, is to be resisted, denounced, and repudiated by every lover of
liberty, until the utter overthrow of the proslavery Union shall be
consummated.'"

I was glad to see that Brother Douglass, however disloyal, self-
serving, petulant, and egotistical he might be, had sense enough to
stop attacking me and lash out instead at Stephen A. Douglas for his
"falsehood, treachery, and tyranny" in producing this monstrous
measure and its equally monstrous "principle" of popular
sovereignty. "The sovereign right," said Douglass, "to make slaves

of their fellow-men if they choose is the only sovereignty that Douglas's bill secured. Where did the bill get this right, which it so generously gave away? Did it get it from Douglas? I would like to know where he got that right—Who gave to him the right to make slaves of other men?"

Bravo, Douglass. But such sentiments were uttered in the *wrong place*—on the political stump in Illinois—and for the *wrong purpose*—the election of anti-Nebraska men to public office. The only true course, I kept telling him in the *Liberator*, was non-resistance, non-political action, and disunion.

I was also glad to see Mrs. Stowe make her "APPEAL TO THE WOMEN OF THE FREE STATES OF AMERICA" in the New York *Independent*, which repeated my dire warning that the Slave Power intended to legalize slavery everywhere. "Four years hence," she told her female readers, "there may be slave depots in New York." She went on: "Women of the free states, the question is not Shall we remonstrate with slavery on its own soil, but Are we willing to receive slavery into the free states and territories of this Union? Shall the whole power of these United States go into the hands of slavery? Shall every state in the Union be thrown open to slavery? This is the fearful crisis at which we stand." Amen to *that*, I said. "And now," she asked, "is there anything that the women of a country can do? Woman can use her influence for the right. She can gather signatures on congressional petitions; spread information throughout her neighborhood; employ lecturers to put the subject before the people; circulate speeches of her congressmen that touch on slavery; and above all make it a matter of constant prayer. . . . For the sake, then, of our dear children, for the sake of our common country, for the sake of outraged and struggling liberty throughout the world, let every woman of America now do her duty."

I thought: *Well said, Mrs. Stowe! If only the women of America will heed you.*

She also warned what I had been warning for more than twenty years: "We who are Christians, and believe in the sure word of prophecy, know that fearful convulsions and overturnings are predicted before the coming of Him who is to rule the earth in righteousness. . . . We are on the eve of a conflict that will try men's souls, and strain to the utmost the bonds of brotherly union that bind this nation together."

While I called on abolitionists to rally the North to disunion, I confessed, in private conversations with Brother May and others, that the Kansas-Nebraska Act filled me with despair. The government and the nation had now fallen completely into the grip of the Slave Power. "We are beaten," Brother Phillips said flatly. "There is no hope." Brother May kept arguing that non-resistance was outmoded now, that the Garrisonians would have to adopt *resistance* to the government, *resistance* to the fugitive slave law, *resistance* to the expansion of slavery, if we were ever to terminate the iron rule of the Slave Power on this continent. "Maybe you're right," I said. "Certainly I would not be unhappy if the slaves rose in insurrection." But I was not yet ready to abandon the rest of that nonviolent creed which to now had been my life's blood.

Vowing to do something dramatic to protest the laws of this slave-cursed country, I journeyed to Framingham for the annual Fourth of July celebration of the Massachusetts Anti-Slavery Society. Some three thousands of us gathered in a picnic grove near a lake. Our platform was decorated with two white flags bearing the respective inscriptions *Kansas* and *Nebraska*. Above the platform a United States flag, draped in black, hung upside down. There was music and refreshments, and some people went sailing on the lake. Then I brought the meeting to order. Brother Phillips, Lucy Stone, and several others gave speeches, and then it was my turn.

"The history of mankind," I began, "is a record of the saddest mistakes, the wildest aberrations, the most melancholy inconsistencies, the bloodiest crimes. In this country, the worst inconsistency is the discrepancy between the ideals of the Declaration of Independence and the practice of slaveholding. I regret that Americans, in submitting to the Slave Power, have degenerated in regard to reverence for the cause of liberty and the Higher Law of God." I paused. The audience waited. Somebody coughed. "I must now do something as testimony of my own soul to what I feel about the proslavery laws of this country." I lit a candle, picked up a document from a table beside me, and said: "This is a copy of the fugitive slave law. Behold!" I touched the candle flame to the paper and held it overhead, intoning, "And let all the people say, Amen!"

"Amen!" replied several in the crowd.

When the fugitive slave law had burned up, I picked up another paper. "This is a copy of Judge Loring's decision that sent Anthony Burns back into slavery. Behold!" I applied the flame to that decision as well. "And let all the people say, Amen!"

"Amen!"

I picked up a third document. "This is a copy of the Federal

Constitution, the source and parent of all other atrocities. Behold!" I set the Constitution afire and held it between a thumb and finger as it burned, its charred remains fluttering to the platform. Then I ground the ashes beneath my foot. "So perish all compromises with tyranny! And let the people say, Amen!"

"Amen!"

Of the episode, the *Daily Commonwealth* reported: "The burning of the Slave Act and Loring's decision was received with decided approbation; but the burning of the Constitution was witnessed with disgust and indignation by a large number of those who were assembled, some of whom vented their feelings by hisses and outcries."

"I burnt a PRO-Slavery Constitution," I said in the *Liberator*, "and therefore was faithful to the slave in so doing." My only regret was that I did not burn a copy of the Kansas-Nebraska Act and an effigy of Stephen A. Douglas while I was at it.

21 . ABRAHAM LINCOLN

I was attending court in Urbana when the papers reported that Pierce had signed the Kansas-Nebraska Act into law. I was thunderstruck and stunned. The Missouri Compromise line was gone! A vast northern domain once preserved for freedom was now open to a proslavery invasion. This, I told my friends, violated the very intentions of the founding fathers and changed the entire course of the Republic as far as slavery was concerned. Those old-time men had taken steps to ensure the ultimate extinction of slavery, by hemming it in where it already existed and prohibiting its spread. But now, under the pretext of squatter sovereignty, Judge Douglas and the Democratic party had opened "a great highway for the onward march of slavery," so that it would grow and expand until it became permanent. Then the Republic would never remove the contradiction of slavery in a nation originally dedicated to the inalienable rights of man.

Like Henry Clay, my beau ideal of a statesman, I thought slavery a great evil that ought never to have existed in this country. I hated the institution, had always hated it. I hated it because it violated the sacred principles of the Declaration of Independence: that all men are born equal and are entitled to life, liberty, and the pursuit of happiness. I hated it because it tarnished our experiment in popular government, which stands as a beacon of hope for the oppressed and a model for the liberal party throughout the world. I hated it because I had *seen* something of its evils. In 'forty-one, on board a steamboat on the Ohio River, I saw a coffle of ten or twelve slaves, shackled together with irons, on their way down river, probably to some cruel cotton plantation in the Deep South. That sight was a continual torment to me; and I saw something like it every time I touched a slave border. Slavery, I said, had the power of making me miserable.

Yet I was not an abolitionist. The abolitionist label would kill a political career in Illinois, but this wasn't the only reason I avoided that group. The abolitionists were too extreme and too loud to suit me. They never learned the old true maxim that a drop of honey catches more flies than a gallon of gall. My feelings and judgments ever led me to oppose those like William Lloyd Garrison who would shiver into fragments the Union of these states; tear to tatters its venerated Constitution; and even burn the last copy of the Bible, rather than that slavery could continue a single hour. Their inflexible bombast only provoked an increasing number of southern men to go to the opposite extreme—that of ridiculing the Declaration of Independence, the sheet anchor of American republicanism, for the sake of perpetuating slavery. The first American of any note to do this was John C. Calhoun, whose denunciation of the equality doctrine sounded strange in America! The like was not heard in the fresher days of the Republic.

Like Clay—like the founding fathers—I accepted slavery as a necessity *where it already existed*. Evil though it was, it could not be at once eradicated in the southern states, without producing a greater evil to the cause of human liberty itself. Besides, the Constitution did not give the Federal Government in peace time the power to abolish slavery in the southern states—only they could do that. But the Constitution *did* grant the national government jurisdiction over slavery in the territories. Therefore I opposed the *extension* of slavery; I wanted it kept *out of the territories* by force of Federal law. During my one term in Congress—from 'forty-seven to 'forty-nine—I voted for the Wilmot Proviso or the idea behind it at least forty times. I kept reassuring myself that slavery had to grow in order to survive. Contain it, as the founders had done, and it was doomed to die by the gradual erosion of time. When it did die out, I believed—as Clay believed—that the liberated blacks ought to be voluntarily colonized in Africa. If a future generation succeeded in freeing our land from the dangerous presence of slavery; and, at the same time, in restoring a captive people to their long-lost fatherland, with bright prospects for the future; and this so gradually that neither races nor individuals should have suffered by the change, it would indeed be a glorious consummation.

But under the new territorial policy, none of that was possible. Under the new policy, southerners were free to drag manacled blacks into Kansas and Nebraska and all future territories, and the spectacle on the Ohio River that continually tormented me would be repeated on the broad prairies and mountains of the frontier and wherever else the nation spread. Slavery would take root there by littles, so that by the time settlers formed territorial governments slavery would already have a foothold; it would become one of their "domestic institutions" and would be impossible to remove.

Aroused as I'd never been before, I took to the political hustings against Judge Douglas and the great wrong and injustice of his Kansas-Nebraska Act. Scores of other anti-Nebraska men were out campaigning, too, hoping to defeat pro-Nebraska Democrats in the congressional and legislative elections in November. Some of us were anti-Nebraska Whigs, others were anti-Nebraska Democrats, still others were Free-Soil men and "fusion" men. Local anti-Nebraska groups in Wisconsin and Michigan, and one here in Illinois, even adopted the name Republican. Whatever we called ourselves, we shared a common purpose: to repeal the insidious Nebraska doctrine and return the Republic to the sacred ground of the founding fathers.

Judge Douglas hurried back to Illinois to defend himself, and well he might: the repeal of the Missouri Compromise had provoked a mighty roar of protest across the North. When the Judge attempted to speak in Chicago, a hostile crowd booed and yelled so loudly that he couldn't finish his speech. What followed was pure Douglas: he shouted and shook his fists at the crowd, then tried to stare them into silence. When that failed, he stormed off with a defiant gesture. Then he set off across Illinois, promising to whip the "unholy alliance" of Whigs, renegade Democrats, abolitionists, "nigger-lovers," and "disgruntled office-seekers" who, he claimed, were trying to destroy him. He vowed to force defecting Democrats to embrace popular sovereignty and return to the fold or "suffer the Goddamned consequences."

I was astounded to hear him claim: "The Kansas-Nebraska Act

will not extend slavery and was not designed to extend it." I answered Douglas by using an illustration: "Lincoln owns a fine meadow containing beautiful springs of water, and it is well fenced. John Calhoun agreed with Abraham (originally owning the land in common) that the meadow should be Lincoln's, and the agreement was consummated and was regarded by both as sacred. In the course of time, however, John Calhoun became owner of an extensive herd of cattle. But with the prairie grass drying up and no convenient water to be had, Calhoun looks with a longing eye on Lincoln's meadow, then tears down the fences, and exposes it to the ravages of his starving and famished cattle. 'You rascal,' says Lincoln, 'what do you do this for?' 'Oh,' replies Calhoun, 'everything is right. I've taken down your fence; but nothing more. It's my true intent and meaning not to drive my cattle into your meadow, nor to exclude them from it, but to leave them perfectly free to form their own notions of the feed, and to direct their movements in their own way!' Now was not the man who committed this outrage both a knave and a fool—a knave in removing the restrictive fence, which he'd solemnly pledged himself to sustain—and a fool in supposing that there could be one man found in the country to believe that he had not pulled down the fence for the purpose of opening the meadow for his cattle?"

I caught up with Judge Douglas in Bloomington and followed him down to Springfield, where he spoke in the great hall of representatives while I paced back and forth in the lobby, anxious to answer him. His voice was hoarse and strained from speech-making, but I caught the gist of his arguments, which I'd heard before: the Compromise of 1850 had superseded and voided the Missouri Compromise and substituted the "sacred" principle of self-government in place of the Missouri line . . . the Judge had faithfully applied that principle to Kansas and Nebraska . . . slavery was prohibited there anyway, by the great laws of nature. When he was done, I stood on the stairway landing and shouted: "I'll answer Judge Douglas here! Tomorrow!"

I'd worked hard on my speech, writing it out with great care as to logic and historical accuracy. The speech was "all afire," as my law partner Herndon might say, with the anger and alarm I felt over this new territorial policy. Many of the points had been argued by others—Chase in particular—but the whole reflected my deepest convictions and laid out most of the arguments I would use against Judge Douglas for the next few years. Later I gave the same address at Peoria—hence it's often called the "Peoria Speech."

When I rose to speak in Springfield, on the fourth of October, the great hall of representatives was overflowing with people and was stifling hot. Looking out over that sea of faces, I began by telling a few stories—"Lincolnisms," according to the opposition papers—with sweat soaking my hair and streaming down my face. Picture a homely looking man, dressed in trousers and shirt sleeves, whose parts are somewhat out of kilter: his head too small for his height of six feet, four inches, nearly; his chest too narrow and thin in contrast to his long arms and legs, his huge hands and feet; with a swarthy complexion, a scrawny neck with a prominent Adam's apple, a mole on the right check, big ears, and coarse, unruly black hair which (according to Herndon) "lies floating where the fingers or the wind left it." Picture that fellow and you have a pretty good picture of me.

I picked up my speech and began to read in a voice often described as shrill, high-pitched. To stress a point, I stooped down and then rose up sharply and extended both arms high overhead, as if to get God's help.

I wished, I said, to *make* and to *keep* the distinction between the *existing* institution, and the *extension* of it, so broad, and so clear, that no honest man could misunderstand me. The founders of the nation tolerated the *existing* institution as a necessity, hiding the thing in the Constitution without direct reference to it, just as an afflicted man hides away a wen or a cancer, which he dares not cut out at once, lest he bleed to death. At the same time, I said, these old-time men expected slavery to perish someday—another reason why the words *slave* and *slavery* do not appear in the Constitution— and they sought to hedge and hem it into the narrowest limits of necessity. Why else had they excluded slavery from the old Northwest Territory—why else had they outlawed the international slave trade—if they had not expected it to disappear?

After the country acquired the Louisiana Purchase, the Missouri Compromise—a sacred compact, agreed to by both sections—saved the entire northern portion for freedom. But the Missouri line, I pointed out, applied solely to the Louisiana Purchase; it was not intended as a universal principle to be constantly extended. Therefore, when the Mexican Cession was added to the national domain, we Wilmot men voted against extending the Missouri line to the Pacific, because, by implication, it gave up the southern part of the Mexican Cession to slavery, while we were bent on having it *all* free. Yet we desired to keep the old line, then thirty years old. We saw retaining it where it already existed and stretching it to the Pacific as two entirely separate issues. Certainly we did not, as Judge Douglas now maintained, repudiate the Missouri line by voting against extending it. To argue this, I said, was no less absurd than to say that because I refused to build an addition to my house, I thereby decided to destroy the existing house!

When, by Judge Douglas's hand, the Missouri line was repealed, it took us by surprise, I said; it astounded us, and we reeled and fell in utter confusion. But we rose each fighting, grasping whatever he could first reach—a scythe—a pitchfork—a chopping ax, or a butcher's cleaver—because that act was an egregious wrong. It was wrong in its direct effect, letting slavery into Kansas and Nebraska—and wrong in its prospective principle, allowing it to spread to every other part of the wide world, where men could be found inclined to take it.

"This *declared* indifference," I said, "but as I must think, covert *real* zeal for the spread of slavery, I can not but hate. I hate it because of the monstrous injustice of slavery itself. I hate it because it deprives our republican example of its just influence in the world—enables the enemies of free institutions, with plausibility, to taunt us as hypocrites—causes the real friends of freedom to doubt our sincerity, and especially because it forces so many really good men among us into an open war with the very fundamental principles of civil liberty—criticizing the Declaration of Independence, and insisting that there is no right principle of action but *self-interest*.

"Yet I have no prejudices against the southern people. They are just what we would be in their situation. When they tell us they are no more responsible for the origin of slavery than we are, I acknowledge the fact. When it's said that the institution exists; and that it's very difficult to get rid of it, in any satisfactory way, I can understand and appreciate the saying. I surely will not blame them for not doing what I should not know how to do myself. If all earthly power were given me, I should not know what to do, as to the existing institution. My first impulse would be to free all the slaves and send them to Liberia—to their own native land. But a moment's reflection would convince me, that whatever of high hope there might be in this in the long run, its sudden execution is impossible. It does seem to me that systems of gradual emancipation might be adopted; but for their tardiness in this, I will not judge our brethren in the South."

When they reminded us of their constitutional rights, I acknowledged them fully and fairly. I granted them the fugitive slave law, degrading though it was to the free states, because the Constitution requires that people "held to Service or Labor in one State" must be sent back if they escaped. Thus, I said, we were under legal obligation to catch and return their runaway slaves to them—a sort of dirty, disagreeable job, which I believed, as a general rule, the slaveholders would not perform for one another. Then again, in the control of the government, the slave states had greatly the advantage of us. The three-fifths clause in the Constitution granted them disproportionate political power and was manifestly unfair to us. This principle, in the aggregate, gave the slave states, in the current Congress, twenty additional representatives—being seven more than the whole majority by which they passed the Nebraska bill. Still, I conceded them that disproportionate power so long as it was our constitutional obligation. But I would not grant them the right to *augment* such power by making new slave states out of the territories.

Whether slavery should go into Nebraska, or other new territories, I said, was not a matter of exclusive concern to the people who went there. The *whole nation* was interested that the best use should be made of these territories. We of the North wanted them for the homes of free white people, not of slaves, which was what the Missouri Compromise guaranteed us. But Judge Douglas argued that the Compromise of 1850 voided the Missouri Compromise and established popular sovereignty as the new principle for determining the status of slavery in the territories. The 1850 Compromise did no such thing. It applied *solely* to New Mexico and Utah, and no place else. At no time, I said, did the public ever demand that the Missouri line be eradicated and replaced with popular sovereignty. Nor was I confident—to touch on one of Douglas's inferior arguments—that the soil and climate of the West would exclude slavery "*in any event.*" This, I warned, was a *palliation*, a *lullaby*. Delaware, Maryland, Virginia, Kentucky, and Missouri are all north of the Missouri line, and the climate and soil in those states had not kept slavery out.

Judge Douglas went on to argue that popular sovereignty was "sacred" because it applied to the slavery question the sacred right of self-government. "The doctrine of self-government," I said, "is right—absolutely and eternally right. But it has no just application as here applied. If the Negro is a man, is it not a total destruction of self-government to say that he shall not govern *himself*? When the white man governs himself that is self-government; but when he governs himself, and also governs *another* man, that is *more* than self-government—that is despotism. If the Negro is a *man*, why then my ancient faith teaches me that 'all men are created equal' and that there can be no moral right in connection with one man's making a slave of another." But, I said, where bondage already existed, we must, of necessity, manage as we best could.

What was the solution? I asked. We must restore the Missouri Compromise line and reaffirm the Declaration. We thereby restored the national faith, the national confidence, the national feeling of brotherhood. But, I warned, if we followed Judge Douglas and allowed popular sovereignty to rule in the territories, violence would break out in Kansas, where northern emigrants and proslavery Missourians were already gathering. Because what was involved there was the struggle between slavery and freedom. Slavery, I said, is founded in the selfishness of man's nature, and opposition to it in his love of justice. The principles are *eternally* antagonistic, and when brought together, as they were in Kansas, they led inevitably to shocks, throes, and convulsions. And once blood was shed in Kansas, I said, would this not be the real knell of the Union?

Yes, I said, the Nebraska doctrine was fraught with evil, but what I particularly loathed was the new position it gave slavery in our body politic. At the birth of the nation, the founders were hostile to the principle of slavery and tolerated it only as a necessity. But now it was to be transformed into a "sacred right." Now, through the Nebraska doctrine, we were giving up the old faith for the new and were placing slavery on the high road to extension and perpetuity. We began by declaring that all men are created equal; but from that beginning we had now run down to the other declaration, that for *some* men to enslave *others* was a "sacred right of self-government." But let nobody be deceived, I said: the spirit of Nebraska and the spirit of 'seventy-six were utter antagonisms. Yet the spirit of Nebraska was rapidly taking over.

"Fellow Countrymen," I pleaded, "Americans south, as well as north, shall we make no effort to arrest this? Already the liberal party throughout the world express the apprehension 'that the one retrograde institution in America is undermining the principles of progress, and fatally violating the noblest political system the world ever saw.'

"Our republican robe is soiled, and trailed in the dust. Let us turn and wash it white, in the spirit, if not the blood, of the Revolution. Let us turn slavery from its claims of 'moral right,' back upon its existing legal rights, and its arguments of 'necessity.' Let us return it to the position our fathers gave it; and there let it rest in peace. Let us re-adopt the Declaration of Independence, and with it, the practices, and policy, which harmonize with it. Let North and South—let all Americans—let all lovers of liberty everywhere—join in the great and good work. If we do this, we shall not only have saved the Union, but we shall have so saved it, as to make, and to keep it, forever worthy of saving."

When I finished, I was pretty wrung out, having spoken for more than two hours. Judge Douglas then took the floor in rebuttal and repeated his stock arguments in defense of the Nebraska doctrine, all the while swinging his arms, clenching his fists, and stomping his feet. I'd come to know those gestures well in our twenty-year rivalry.

When, in the November election, anti-Nebraska men won control of the legislature, I announced my candidacy for the national Senate. James Shields was up for reelection in the legislature, and I wanted his seat in order to contest the Nebraska doctrine on a national stage, as Henry Clay would have done had he been alive. I wrote my political friends that it would be very foolish, and very false, for me to deny that I would be pleased with an election to that honorable body, and I urged anti-Nebraska men in the legislature to make a mark for me.

The trouble was, Lyman Trumbull, an anti-Nebraska Democrat, was also a candidate. I feared that anti-Nebraska Democrats would never vote for me, a Whig, and I was right: they didn't. On election day—that was in February of 'fifty-five—I was on top through the first few ballots, with Shields second and Trumbull last. I was so close to being Senator Lincoln I could taste it. Trumbull's supporters, however, refused to throw their votes to me. When the regular Democrats dropped Shields and peddled a fellow named Matteson who was popular even among Whigs, I wound up on the bottom and Matteson rose to near victory. To prevent his election and a triumph for Judge Douglas and squatter sovereignty, I released my support to Trumbull, who then won the election. I admit, I was badly disappointed. I would have to wait three years hence, when Judge Douglas was again up for reelection, before I could make another run for the Senate. Still, it was a great consolation to see the regular Democrats worse whipped than I was.

The great question now was: should we anti-Nebraska men abandon our old political affiliations and form a new coalition party? An abortive attempt had already been made to establish a Republican party in Illinois; the organizers pressed me to join, but I refused because I still regarded myself as a Whig. Still, as a Whig, an American, and a national man, I was ready to fuse with anybody who stood right on the Nebraska question.

A letter came from my old friend, Joshua Speed, now a farmer in Kentucky, asking where I stood politically. We'd lived together in Springfield back in the thirties, before either of us had married. He said that our views probably differed now. While he thought slavery might be wrong in the abstract, he would rather dissolve the Union than give up the right to own slaves. I wrote him back: Who was asking him to give up his right to own slaves? Very certainly *I* was not. I confessed that I hated to see the poor creatures hunted down, and caught, and carried back to their stripes and unrewarded toils; but I bit my lip and kept quiet. I told him: "You ought to appreciate how I and the great body of northern people crucify our feelings in maintaining our loyalty to the Constitution and the Union when it comes to slavery in the southern states. I plainly see you and I would differ about the Nebraska law. I look upon that enactment not as a *law*, but as *violence* from the beginning. It was conceived in violence, passed in violence, is maintained in violence, and is being executed in violence." I should have added what the papers reported: that proslavery Missourians were vowing to exterminate every "Goddamned abolitionist" who came to Kansas, which the Missourians seemed to regard as their territory by some sort of divine right.

As to where I stood politically, I said I was still a Whig, though some men said that there were no Whigs and that Lincoln was an abolitionist. One thing I knew for certain: I was not a Know-Nothing, not a member of their American party, which wanted to exclude foreigners and Catholics from America, claiming her solely for native-born white Protestants. "How could I be a Know-Nothing?" I asked. "How can anyone who abhors the oppression of Negroes be in favor of degrading classes of white people? Our progress in degeneracy appears to me to be pretty rapid. As a nation, we began by declaring that '*all men are created equal*.' We now practically read it 'all men are created equal, *except Negroes*.' When the Know-Nothings get control, it will read 'all men are created equal, except Negroes, *and foreigners, and Catholics*.' When it comes to this I should prefer emigrating to some country where they make no pretense of loving liberty—to Russia, for instance, where despotism can be taken pure, and without the base alloy of hypocracy."

That same year, 'fifty-five, an unsigned article in the Richmond *Examiner* forcibly caught my attention. "Social forms so widely differing as those of domestic slavery, and (attempted) universal liberty cannot long co-exist in the Great Republic of Christendom," the article stated. "They cannot be equally adapted to the wants and interests of society. The one form or the other must be very wrong. The war between the two systems rages everywhere; and will continue to rage till the one conquers and the other is exterminated." A subsequent article in the *Examiner* restated the theme: "Two opposite and conflicting forms of society cannot, among civilized men, coexist and endure. The one must give way and cease to exist, the other become universal."

Just as disturbing were the writings of George Fitzhugh of Virginia, who not only waged a pernicious ideological war against the Declaration of Independence, but advocated the enslavement of *white* workers as well as Negroes. The clamor for white slavery seemed to be in all the papers I read from the Deep South. "Free society!" shrieked one Alabama paper. "We sicken of the name! What is it but a conglomeration of *greasy mechanics, filthy operatives, small-fisted farmers,* and moon-struck theorists? This is your free society which the northern hordes are endeavoring to extend to Kansas."

The sentiments pouring forth from Dixie made me despair that slavery could ever be removed from this country by peaceful means. I wrote a friend that our political problem now was: "Can we, as a nation, continue together permanently—forever—half slave and half free?" The problem, I said, was too mighty for me to answer. But over time, in spare moments away from legal work, I did write out counter arguments to proslavery advocates like Fitzhugh, sometimes addressing them as though they were sitting in my Springfield law office.

First: "If *slavery* is not wrong, *nothing* is wrong."

Second: "The right to the fruit of our labor is self-evident, made so plain by our good Father in heaven, that all *feel* and *understand* it, even down to brutes and creeping insects. The ant, who has toiled and dragged a crumb to his nest, will furiously defend the fruit of his labor, against whatever robber assails him. So plain, that the most dumb and stupid slave that ever toiled for a master, does constantly *know* that he is wronged. So plain that no one, high or low, ever does mistake it, except in a plainly *selfish* way; for although volume upon volume is written to prove slavery a very good thing, we never hear of the man who wishes to take the good of it, *by being a slave himself*."

The third argument elaborated on a point in Henry Clay's public letter of 'forty-nine, urging gradual emancipation in Kentucky. "If A. can prove, however conclusively, that he may, of right, enslave B.," I wrote, "why may not B. snatch the argument, and prove equally, that he may enslave A.?

"You say A. is white, and B. is black. It is *color*, then; the lighter, having the right to enslave the darker? Take care. By this rule, you are to be a slave to the first man you meet, with a fairer skin than your own.

"You do not mean *color* exactly?—You mean the whites are *intellectually* the superiors of the blacks, and, therefore have the right to enslave them? Take care again. By this rule, you are to be a slave to the first man you meet, with an intellect superior to your own.

"But, say you, it is a question of *interest*; and, if you can make it your *interest*, you have the right to enslave another. Very well. And if he can make it his interest, he has the right to enslave you."

Fourth: "The extension of slavery is a sectional question—that is to say, it is a question in its nature calculated to divide the American people geographically. Who is to *blame* for that? *who* can help it? Either side *can* help it; but how? Simply by *yielding* to the other side. There is no other way. In the whole range of possibility, there is no other way. Then which side shall yield? To this again, there can be but one answer—the side which is in the *wrong*." And the side of *slavery* was in the wrong. "Do those who refuse to stand with us really think that by right surrendering to wrong, the hopes of our Constitution, our Union, and our liberties, could be bettered?"

By 'fifty-six it was clear to me and most other anti-Nebraska men that our Union and our liberties could only be saved through a new coalition party, a Republican party, which would unite all the disparate anti-Nebraska elements. The Whig party, in which I'd toiled all my political life, was hopelessly divided over the slavery question and was disintegrating. As a consequence, anti-Nebraska Whigs now joined with anti-Nebraska Democrats and Free-Soilers and formally launched the new Republican party on Washington's birthday, in Pittsburgh. The party planned to run a full slate of national and state candidates in the 1856 presidential election.

I was anxious to join the Republicans and help shape the party according to the principles I'd elucidated at Springfield and Peoria. Accordingly, I was on hand at Bloomington, in central Illinois, in late May, when anti-Nebraska Whigs and anti-Nebraska Democrats, Free-Soilers, and abolitionists came together from all across the state to establish the Republican party of Illinois. On the first evening, the delegates thronged the street in front of the Pike House, yelling for speeches. My friend Leonard Swett gave a rousing talk from the balcony of the Pike House. So did Congressman Long John Wentworth of Chicago—an original character who stood six feet six, and wore an old straw hat and untied shoes. Wentworth accused Douglas of wanting to extend slavery in order "to make his own two hundred Negroes down South more valuable." Standing on the balcony, I made a few comments myself, mainly about the atrocities in Kansas. Since the territory had been thrown open to settlement, Missouri Border Ruffians had repeatedly crossed into Kansas, threatening and murdering free-state settlers and voting illegally in territorial elections. As a result, the free-state majority found themselves saddled with a "bogus" proslavery legislature and a spate of "bogus" laws, including slave codes and sedition measures which made it a crime even to criticize slavery.

"A man can't think, dream or breathe of a free state there," I said, "but what he's kicked, cuffed, shot down and hung." I had a lot more to say about the slavery question, I said, but was saving it for the convention the next day.

I'd hoped to play an important role in organizing the state party. But Orville Browning of Quincy, a powerful Whig who was my superior in every aspect except in height and homeliness, took charge of the proceedings and chose fifteen or twenty leaders of the various political groups to meet with him in his hotel room that night. I was not invited. Evidently my loss in the Senate vote last year had depreciated my political currency.

The next morning, the Chicago papers, which had just reached Bloomington, reported "NEW OUTRAGES IN KANSAS." A column of Border Ruffians had attacked the free-state town of Lawrence, wrecking printing presses, pillaging homes, and destroying the free-state hotel with cannon fire. At the same time, back in Washington, in the hallowed chamber of the Senate, Congressman Preston Brooks of South Carolina had almost caned Senator Sumner of Massachusetts to death for delivering a "Crime Against Kansas" speech a few days before. Throughout the day, telegrams reached us with additional details about "Bleeding Kansas." One rumor had it that the free-state governor had been arrested and was being held in chains on the prairie for want of a jail to put him in!

The news about Bleeding Kansas and the beating of Sumner inflamed every one of us. We felt an even greater urgency to organize our new party and save our embattled country from Pierce, Douglas, and the Democrats. Convening in Major's Hall that same morning, the convention nominated a full slate of Republican candidates for state offices and chose sixty-two delegates and alternates to represent Illinois at the first national Republican convention, to convene in Philadelphia. I was glad to be selected as one of the delegates, at least.

Several prominent men gave speeches that day. Browning, in his suave, robust fashion, talked about how Henry Clay would've been with us were he alive. Big, broad-shouldered Owen Lovejoy, brother of the murdered abolitionist editor and often identified as an abolitionist himself, said that his principles were in opposition to the *extension* of slavery—that this was as far as his abolitionism took him. As he spoke, he kept bringing his right hand down hard as if to pound his outstretched left hand, only to stop short of hitting it. A young abolitionist by the name of Emery made a passionate plea in favor of armed intervention in Bleeding Kansas. That kind of talk always alarmed me. I was itching to say my piece before the convention, to steer the new party away from extremists and set it up in the right direction, upon the right principles.

But nobody asked me to say a word. When it was time to adjourn, I sat at the back of the hall, feeling like the boy who'd stumped his toe—I was too big to cry and too badly hurt to laugh. Suddenly, though, some fellows up front called on Lincoln to make a few closing remarks, and pretty soon the whole convention was calling my name. Since I had a reputation as a yarn-spinner, they probably wanted me to crack jokes and make them laugh, now that the convention's serious work was done. I had no intention of cracking jokes.

I unwound myself and said: "I believe I will just say a few words from here."

"No, no," they shouted, "take the platform."

I strode to the platform and spoke without a prepared script, saying pretty much the same thing I had at Springfield and Peoria, but with a good deal more force, I think, in light of the recent proslavery atrocities in Kansas and the caning of Senator Sumner. I spoke against young Emery, who'd talked about "invading Kansas with Sharps rifles." I said: "No, my friends. Physical rebellions and bloody resistance would only hurt the free-state cause in Kansas and the cause of freedom in general. The way to right a wrong is through political action and moral influence. I'll tell you what we'll do. We'll wait until the presidential election in November. Then we'll shoot *paper ballots* at them."

I described the pressing reasons for the Republican movement, said we had to stand together as one man in the great moral fight against slavery extension. But, I cautioned, we must take care to stand right. Let us stand *with* the abolitionists and *against* the Nebraska men in opposing the extension of slavery. But let us stand *against* the abolitionists in upholding the Constitution and the fugitive slave law. In both cases, I said, we avoided dangerous extremes. In both cases, we occupied a *national* ground and held the country level and steady.

About halfway through my speech, I became aware that the audience, more than a thousand strong, was unusually quiet during my pauses—there was hardly a cough—and that the reporters had stopped writing; some had even laid their pencils down. Nobody seemed disappointed that I wasn't telling jokes. In my conclusion, I denied that the anti-Nebraska movement wanted to break up the Union, as some charged. Then, standing on my tiptoes and raising my arms overhead, I warned the slave states: "We do not intend to dissolve this Union, and we don't intend to let *you* dissolve it."

At that, the entire assemblage jumped up, clapping and cheering in near delirium. No crowd had ever reacted to one of my speeches quite like that. They were throwing their hats into the air and rushing to the platform to seize my hand. "Electrifying," one fellow said. "You had us all the way! We were leaning forward or rising as you did."

"Lincoln," said Dr. Browne of Springfield, "I swear, grandeur and fire and light flashed from your head as you spoke! There are no anti-Nebraska Democrats here today, no Whigs or Free-Soilers or abolitionists. You've harmonized us into one body. We're all Republicans according to the definition you've given us."

But the euphoria of that day evaporated with the latest reports from Kansas: a massacre on Pottawatomie Creek, five proslavery men hacked to death with swords, and they blamed it on an abolitionist named Brown. In retaliation, proslavery columns were burning and pillaging free-state settlements. Civil war raged on the Kansas prairie, just as I'd predicted would happen under squatter sovereignty, and nobody knew how far it would spread. Was this the start of the great storm so long predicted? we wondered. Was it the knell of the Union?

22. JOHN BROWN

I rode into Kansas Territory in eighteen and fifty-five in a one-horse wagon filled with revolvers, rifles, powder, and two-edged artillery broadswords. I expected war to break out between the free-state forces and the Border Ruffians, and I was ready to buckle on my armor and give battle. Five of my grown sons had already come to Kansas to settle; I did not go there to settle, but because of the difficulties. John Jr. had written me that "hundreds of thousands of proslavery men, desperate men armed to the teeth with revolvers, Bowie knives, rifles, and cannon are massing along the Kansas-Missouri border to fasten slavery on this glorious land. Father, you must come at once and bring us weapons—plenty of guns and knives. The storm every day thickens, its near approach is hourly more clearly seen by all. Now is the time to help in the cause, because the great drama will open here, when will be presented the great struggle in arms, of Freedom and Despotism in America."

In John Jr.'s words I heard the thundering voice of Jehovah exhorting me to slaughter the Border Ruffians as He'd called Gideon to slay the Midianites. Yes, my greatest or principal object—*eternal war against slavery*—was to be carried out in Kansas Territory. Praise be to God! I was a scarred old man, guilty of many sins before God, but I saw now that all my previous trials were but God's way of preparing me for His purpose on the battleground of Kansas. For fifty-five years I'd smarted under the rod of Providence—I'd had many difficulties and reversals, as a tanner, a speculator, a shepherd, a wool merchant, and my first wife and nine of my twenty children had died. But I praised God! because such sore afflictions taught me how utterly dependent I am on the one, true God and made me believe completely in God's justice, His mercy, and the divine purpose of His plans. Early on, I knew that God had put me in this world, which is not man's true home, to see if I was worthy of joining him in Paradise; I often had a strong and steady desire to die so that I could be united with Him. I tried hard to combat my haughty obstinate temper and vanity; because the one attribute men should have above all others is humility before God. What can so properly become poor dependent, sinning, and self-condemned mortals like us, as humility? We must *fear God*, remembering always that Jehovah brings famine and pestilence to those who do not "fear the Lord thy God" and fail to "serve Him and swear by His name." For "the fear of God," as the Preacher says in the last chapter of Ecclesiastes, "is the whole duty of man."

Fear of God. That is why I hate slavery—because I *fear* God, because I *fear* His wrath and justice. The Scriptures teach us that slavery is *a great sin against God.* It is the *sum of all villainies.* It is *a rotten whore* of an institution; and the foul and wicked men who perpetuate it, who violate an entire race of victims with the whip in one hand and the Bible in the other, blasphemously quoting Scripture to justify their fiendish acts, are destined for a special corner of Hell. *By your acts shall ye be judged.*

I was a mere boy when God first showed me the evils of slavery and made me a most determined abolitionist. I'd driven my father's cattle to Michigan Territory to sell—this was during the second war with England. At an inn I met a slave boy near my own age who was badly clothed and poorly fed. Before my eyes, his master beat him with iron shovels, and his screams resound in my ears to this day. I felt the blows of those shovels as if *I* were being beaten, as if *I* were that poor, bleeding boy, without a father or a mother, and it filled me with rage. I swore then and there, *Eternal war against slavery.* I repeated that vow when I read the *Liberator* in my father's house in Ohio and sickened at the horrors it described—the countless daily cruelties and violence inflicted on Negroes. "We hear their screams, O Lord, and tremble at thy wrath!"

I could not tolerate the indifference of the North to such wickedness. The doughfaced statesmen there—the Whigs and Democrats—loved to be bribed, and browbeaten, and fooled, and cheated by the slaveocrats, and thought themselves highly honored if they were allowed to lick up southern spit. I could not tolerate the docility of so many Negroes of the North, who sought the favor of white men by tamely submitting to every species of indignity, contempt, and wrong instead of nobly resisting their brutal aggressions from principle.

My own rage grew with every new aggression of the southern slaveocrats. When they murdered the abolitionist editor, Elijah Lovejoy, in eighteen and thirty-seven, I rose in the back of a memorial meeting in Ohio and swore an oath: "Here, before God, in the presence of these witnesses, from this time, I consecrate my life to the destruction of slavery." While living in Springfield, Massachusetts, where I sorted and sold wool for growers, I secretly planned *offensive* warfare against the Slave Power, by raising a company of God-fearing men, whites and Negroes, to run slaves off to the North through the Alleghenies. My purpose was to destroy slave property by making it insecure. I confided my plan in the great black man and abolitionist, Frederick Douglass, who called at my house to meet me.

"I don't intend to cause a slave insurrection," I told him. "That would defeat my object. But I'm not averse to shedding blood, because using guns will give black men a sense of their manhood."

"Maybe that won't be necessary," Douglass said. "Maybe we can still convert the slaveholders."

"No, no," I cried, "that can never be; I know their proud hearts. They'll never give up their slaves until they feel a big stick about their heads." I added: "I have no fear of being killed. I have no better use for my life than to lay it down in the cause of the slave."

When the hellish fugitive slave act was passed, I exhorted my black friends to fight back with guns if the slave catchers came after them. I organized forty-four black men and women of Springfield into a mutual defense league called the Branch of the United States League of Gileadites, based on the story of Gideon in the Book of Judges. "Remember Hebrews 9:22," I told them. "'And almost all things are by the law purged with blood; and without shedding of blood is no remission.'"

Yes, I preached violent resistance to slave catchers, Federal marshals, and all the fiends clothed in human form who used the churches, the courts, and the national government to perpetuate slavery. But hatred was not the only thing I felt. I had *love* and *respect* for black people, who were my brothers and sisters under God the Father. I addressed them as "Mr." and "Mrs.," not as "Uncle" and "Auntie," and I prayed and shared my table with them. I dreamed for years of setting up a school for Negro children, but never had the money for it. After my wool business in Springfield failed, I moved my second wife, Mary, and my younger children to a black community at North Elba, on Gerrit Smith's land in the Adirondacks, where I hoped to teach the poor despised Africans how to farm and better themselves. As in Springfield, I exhorted my black neighbors to resist the fugitive slave law *by any means*, and I made my family swear to shield our Negro friends even if that meant imprisonment and death. And I continued to plot my slave-running operation in the Alleghenies, awaiting a sign from God when *He* wanted me to commence meddling with slavery directly. "In all thy ways acknowledge Him and He shall direct thy paths."

But the sign, when it came, directed me to battle Satan's legions in another part of the field. When John Jr. wrote me that the great showdown between freedom and despotism in America would take place in Kansas, I heard the voice of Jehovah calling me to save Kansas for freedom and the right. Yes, that was my destiny; that was what had been ordained for me throughout eternity. Electrified, I left Mary at North Elba and headed west to Ohio, where I raised rifles, revolvers, and heavy broadswords for the free-state cause. Then in the fall I headed west with Oliver, my seventeen-year-old, and Henry Thompson, my young son-in-law, intending to meddle directly with the peculiar institution in Kansas.

When we rode up to my sons' claims on North Middle Creek, near the California Road and Pottawatomie Creek in eastern Kansas, most of the families were sick with the ague; all were shivering in the cold winds, with no shelter, nor any crop of hay, corn, beans, or potatoes secured for the winter. I took charge at once and started putting the claims in order.

That night, around the campfire, John Jr. talked about the condition of affairs. "After we got here, the Missouri Border Ruffians voted illegally in our territorial election, which produced a bogus proslavery legislature. That was the first outrage. Then the legislature enacted a series of bogus laws. That was the next outrage. Father, those laws *legalize* slavery in Kansas and provide severe punishment for anybody who says that slavery does not exist in the territory, or denies a man's right to own slaves, or circulates abolitionist literature, or helps runaways. My brothers and I—and other free-state men— have repeatedly violated these laws. Let them come after us if they dare! We intend to establish a rival government and write a free-state constitution. In fact, an election to choose delegates is scheduled in a few days."

On election day, we turned out powerfully armed in case the dreadful Border Ruffians interfered again. But no enemy appeared, and we returned to Brown's Station to finish putting up cabins despite cutting cold winds and storms. I spent Thanksgiving in the nearby town of Osawatomie, visiting my preacher brother-in-law, Sam Adair.

"I'm impressed," I told him, "with the idea that God has raised me up on purpose to break the jaws of the wicked."

While I was at Osawatomie, the Border Ruffians again invaded the territory and gathered along the Wakarusa River to burn Lawrence, the chief free-state settlement. I hurried back to Brown's Station. "Come on, boys," I said, "we've got God's work to do." I loaded our weapons in the wagon and with four of my sons walked the thirty-five miles to Lawrence to help in its defense. I told the free-state leaders, Robinson and Lane, that we ought to sneak up on the Missourians during the night and slaughter them in their sleep. But the two men chose instead to work out a peace treaty with the proslavery governor, by taking advantage of his fear of the result of an engagement, together with some resort on their part to Yankee ingenuity and a most horrible supply of brandy, with which they got him quite elated. The invaders soon left, but not before they had committed certain robberies and acts of violence against the defenseless inhabitants, including the murder of an unarmed man.

Even so, the signs appeared to favor us. The free-state men met at Topeka and drafted a free-state constitution, which was ratified in December. They also set elections for a free-state governor and legislature, which came off in January, eighteen and fifty-six, with John Jr. being chosen as one of the delegates. "What now remains for the free-state men of Kansas to do," I rejoiced, "is to *hold* the ground they now possess, and *Kansas is free*."

With the onset of winter, we barricaded ourselves in our cabins at Brown's Station. There were almost constant snowstorms for six weeks. Fierce winds drove the snow across the prairie in violent, swirling gusts; and the temperature plunged to twenty-nine below zero. I'd never seen such weather, not even in the Adirondacks.

Over the winter there were signs that a wicked conspiracy was still afoot to fasten slavery on the virgin soil of Kansas, a conspiracy that involved the Pierce Administration as well as the bogus legislature and the Border Ruffians. First, travelers who braved the storms brought us word of *new* and *shocking* outrages at Leavenworth: bitter fighting had broken out during an election, and two free-state men were wounded and one proslavery man was killed. In retaliation, a gang of bogus men murdered a free-state settler, also named Brown, by hacking him with knives and a hatchet; they flung his mutilated body at his cabin door, in front of his hysterical wife. Meanwhile all the free-state people fled to Lawrence, which place was again threatened with attack. "If that takes place," I wrote Mary, "we may soon again be called upon to 'buckle on our Armor,' which by the help of God we will do."

We also heard reports that Franklin Pierce had declared the Topeka government "revolutionary" and that he meant to crush the free-state men of Kansas with government troops. "He will have his hands full if he tries that," I said. "For once I have no desire to have the Slave Power cease its acts of aggression." I quoted Deuteronomy:

"Their foot shall slide in due time." As the wind howled outside, I heard a constant ringing in my ears: it was the despairing cry of millions whose woes only God knew. *Bless God, O my soul, for He hears.*

When the snows melted, Federal troops turned up in the Pottawatomie vicinity, for the alleged purpose of removing intruders from certain Indian lands. I wrote antislavery Congressman Joshua R. Giddings that their real object was to enforce the *hellish* enactments of the bogus legislature, which we Browns had repeatedly violated. I was certain that the next move of the Administration and its proslavery masters would be to make Pottawatomie citizens submit to those infernal enactments or to assume "treasonable grounds" by shooting the soldiers. "I ask in the name of Almighty God; I ask in the name of our venerated forefathers; I ask in the name of all that good or true men ever hold dear; will Congress suffer us to be driven to such 'dire extremities'? *Will anything be done?*"

Giddings replied that Pierce would not dare use Federal troops "to shoot the citizens of Kansas." Which meant that nothing was to be done—our friends in the East had cast us off. When word came that the bogus territorial government would indeed enforce its laws and make us pay taxes to support it, free-state settlers called a meeting in Osawatomie. I went there with several of my sons.

"We have no choice but to submit," one man said. "They have Federal troops behind them, for God's sake!"

I took the floor. "I'm an abolitionist. Hear me! I would rather see the Union *drenched in blood* than pay taxes to the proslavery government. I swear to you, I'll *kill* any officer, any soldier, any *man* who tries to make me obey the bogus laws."

With rumors of war in the wind, thirty or forty free-staters formed the Pottawatomie Rifles and chose John Jr. captain. They should have elected me to lead them: *I* was the senior Brown; I could fight the proslavery Philistines better than anybody in the Pottawatomie area. Irritated as I was, I heartily agreed when John Jr. declared that we ought to carry the war to the enemy. "The war cry heard on our plains," he said, "will not only reverberate across the hemp and tobacco fields of Missouri but through the swamps and plantations of the sunny South. If the first act in the drama of insane despotism is to be performed here, you may look elsewhere for the theater of other acts."

In April the proslavery court convened at Dutch Henry's Tavern, the proslavery headquarters on Pottawatomie Creek, just to the southeast of us. I was certain it was the first appearance of the machinery for crushing us out. John Jr. called out his Pottawatomie Rifles, and they remonstrated against the court on a nearby parade ground. I myself took a free-state ultimatum inside the tavern and handed it to the bogus judge. *If you try to enforce the bogus laws,* it warned, *you do so at your peril.* The ultimatum had its desired effect when the court moved on without ordering the arrest of a single free-state man.

With spring came more rumors that "a distant storm" was gathering, that any day now a proslavery army of Border Ruffians and Kansas Law and Order men would sweep across the prairies, exterminating every free-state settler in Kansas Territory. Some bogus men on Pottawatomie Creek added weight to the rumors. Allen Wilkinson, Dutch Henry and William Sherman, Allen Doyle and his boys, all members of the proslavery Law and Order party, made repeated threats "to shoot and exterminate" all the free-state men. Dutch Henry and his brother liked to bully free-state men who came to their tavern; Henry boasted that he would rather kill an old free-state man named Baldwin than kill a rattlesnake. James Hanway, of our side, said that Wilkinson was a particularly violent, abusive man, and that he had vowed to kill and burn us out. His wife—"a fine woman," Hanway said—urged him to be more quiet, but he told her to shut up and kept making threats.

In early May, a company of armed Georgians turned up on the Pottawatomie—the vanguard, I was certain, of the proslavery army bent on exterminating us. To find out their plans, my son Salmon and I disguised ourselves as government surveyors and pretended to run a line through the enemy camp. We heard them say they planned to "annihilate those damned Browns" and "to stand by the proslavery court until every Goddamned abolitionist was in Hell."

John Jr. put the Pottawatomie Rifles on alert. "Will you join us, Father?" he asked.

"I take orders from nobody," I said.

I organized Henry Thompson and my other sons—Owen, Oliver, Salmon, and Frederick, all made strong from hard, honest labor, and all obedient to me—into a little company to ourselves. It was time to make "the wicked cease from troubling." It was time for war.

We did not have long to wait. On May twenty-first, a horseman thundered through the neighborhood with news from Lawrence. "A proslavery army has concentrated outside of town," he cried, "and they've got cannon! Their leader is David Atchison; he vows to exterminate all 'the freedom shriekers.' Send help at once!" Too excited to wait for reinforcements from Osawatomie, the Pottawatomie Rifles and our little company set out across the prairie for Lawrence. My boys and I brought all our guns, revolvers, and Bowie knives, plus those double-edged artillery broadswords. I was surprised to see my son Jason marching with the Rifles: sad-eyed and sensitive, he lacked guts and usually backed away from a fight; all he could talk about was planting orchards. I suppose he was aroused by the threats of war and extermination like the rest of us.

The next morning, just before daybreak, we ran into another messenger from Lawrence. "The free-state leaders have decided not to fight," he reported. "The Border Ruffians are now sacking and burning the town. The Free State hotel is on fire. They've robbed people, destroyed printing presses, and looted stores."

"Those *cowards*!" I cried. I was *furious* that the free-state leaders had not resisted. We sent a runner back to get the Osawatomie volunteers and started for burning Lawrence. But we hadn't gone far when another messenger rode up. "The crisis is over," he said. "Federal troops are in town, and the Missourians are leaving. You all had best go home. Lawrence is short of food, and anyway nothing can be done now."

This latest intelligence threw the Pottawatomie Rifles into confusion as to what to do. "March on!" I insisted. "We can't turn back now." But James Hanway carried a vote to encamp and await the reinforcements from Osawatomie. "You cowards!" I said. "You're letting the Philistines escape. I would rather be ground into dust than passively submit to proslavery atrocities."

"We're going to wait, Father," John Jr. said, and he led his men off to make camp.

In a frenzy of rage and frustration, I turned back to our troubles on the Pottawatomie. It was up to me—it was up to me and my little company—to avenge the sack of Lawrence, the threats of annihilation, the murder of innocent men. Yes, it was time to fight fire with fire, to strike terror in the hearts of the proslavery enemy. I would deliver a blow against the slave hounds on the Pottawatomie who'd aided and abetted the Missourians and vowed to kill and burn out our suffering people. *The blow would be so brutal, so shocking, that it would create a restraining fear.* Calling my company around me, I said we were going to deliver a radical retaliatory measure against our enemies on the Pottawatomie. "It will involve some killing," I said.

It was dark now; we would rest and move at first light. I lay awake all night, my mind roaring with Scripture. *The Lord God is a man of war: the Lord is his name. He is mighty and terrible. Thy right hand is become glorious in power. Thy right hand, O Lord, hath dashed in pieces the enemy! I put on righteousness and it clothed me: I break the jaws of the wicked and pluck the spoil out of his teeth.*

The next morning I told Hanway: "It was well that you made the motion to make camp yesterday—it was a providential circumstance. I'm glad you did it."

That same morning a fourth messenger arrived from Lawrence, bringing the news that Charles Sumner had been brutally beaten in the U.S. Senate, and they said Brooks of South Carolina had done it. My boys and I went "crazy—*crazy*," to quote Salmon. It seemed to be the final, decisive blow.

I called the Rifles together and said: "Something must be done to show these barbarians that we, too, have rights. I need volunteers for a secret mission." A huge Austrian named Weiner stepped forward, saying he'd had abusive run-ins with the Doyles and Shermans and wanted to settle the score.

John Jr. came up to me. "Father, I object to any of the men leaving. We're getting up here near the enemy and may need them."

"To do *what*?" I demanded. "You're too cowardly to fight." I was indignant that a son of mine should question my authority. We argued bitterly. But not even my "Tut, tut!" and fierce-eyed stare, which had once silenced him in an instant, could sway him now. I stomped off, with Weiner following. John Jr. called out: "Father, be careful. Please don't do anything rash."

I sought out James Townsley, who had the only wagon and team in camp. "You left a wife and children on the Pottawatomie," I said. "We expect trouble there. Will you take us back?" He agreed to do it. Returning to our camp, I had the boys hone our artillery broadswords to razor-sharp edges.

Eyeing those swords, Hanway came up. "What are you going to do?" he asked.

"Regulate matters on the creek," I said.

"Well," he said, "I hope you'll act with caution."

"Caution, caution, sir," I said. "I am eternally *tired* of hearing that word. It is nothing but the word of cowardice. I'll show those Missouri barbarians and the weaklings in Lawrence: here's one free-state man who's *not afraid* to fight. I've taken all the Ruffian outrages I can stand."

We started back toward the Pottawatomie—Weiner on his horse, the rest in Townsley's wagon, eight of us all told, constituting the Army of the North. All day Saturday we hid in a stand of timber near the creek, going over my plan. We would pick off the men prominent in enforcing Border Ruffian laws and threatening our annihilation: the Doyles, Shermans, Wilkinson, maybe others. "It is better," I said, "that a score of bad men should die than that one man who came here to make Kansas a free state should be driven out."

A damp wind was blowing when we set out, after dark, heading first for the Doyle cabin. As we approached it, two savage bulldogs barked furiously at us. Townsley and Frederick cut one down with their cutlasses and drove the other into the timber. I knocked on Doyle's door. "Yes," said a man's voice. "Who is it?" I asked the way to Wilkinson's. "I'll tell you," he said. When he opened the door, we barged inside brandishing pistols and knives.

"We are the Army of the North," I told old man Doyle. "You're our prisoners. Surrender your guns."

Mrs. Doyle screamed at her husband: "I *told* you what you were going to get for the course you've been taking."

"Hush, Mother, hush," he said.

I told Doyle and his three sons to come with us. Mrs. Doyle broke into tears and begged me to spare her youngest boy. Feeling pity for her, I motioned to my men: leave the youngest. Then we took Doyle and his two oldest, William and Drury, out into the night.

About a hundred yards from the cabin, Owen and Salmon fell on the Doyles with broadswords. They staggered backward, trying to shield themselves from the chopping blows. When the work was done, I walked up to old man Doyle, who was dead from a stab in the chest, and shot him in the forehead with a revolver, to make certain work of it. William lay dead nearby, with his head and his side cut open. Drury lay about a hundred yards farther on, with his arms and fingers cut off, his head slashed open, and a hole in his chest.

Later somebody said: "You should have let the two Doyle boys go. They were slavers, but they were young, just boys."

"Nits grow to lice," I said.

We made our way to Wilkinson's cabin on Mosquito Creek and roused him with a loud knock on his door. I asked if he was opposed to the free-state party. "I am," he said through the barred door. "Then you're our prisoner," I said. "Open the door or we'll break it down." He opened the door and we marched inside, seizing him and confiscating a gun and a powder flask.

His wife said she was sick with the measles and begged us to spare her husband. "At least let me get somebody to stay with her," Wilkinson said. "I'll be here in the morning if you still want me. I'm a proud man. I won't run." I pushed him outside in his stocking feet. Three of my men attacked him with swords, slashing his head and side open and slitting his throat. They left his body in some dead brush.

It was after midnight, Sunday, when we reached the cabin of James Harris, a juror on the proslavery court. We broke through the door and roused the inhabitants, including two visitors, at sword point. "We are the Northern army," I said. "It's useless to resist." I recognized one of the visitors: William Sherman. Where was Dutch Henry? I demanded of Harris. "Out on the plains looking for lost cattle," Harris said. I was bitterly disappointed that Dutch Henry would get away this night. I spared Harris and the second visitor because I believed them when they said they had never assisted the proslavery party and had never harmed or threatened free-state settlers. We didn't bother interrogating William Sherman—we knew he was guilty. We led him down to Pottawatomie Creek. There, at my order, Weiner and Thompson hacked him to death with their cutlasses and flung his body into the creek. While my men washed their swords in the Pottawatomie, I looked down at Sherman's mangled body. His head was split open and some of his brains were seeping out into the water.

On the way back to camp, I was transfixed. The proslavery Philistines had murdered five or six free-state men in the great struggle for the soul of Kansas. Now we had got five of them. *God alone is my judge. His will be done.*

They hunted us into the summer—gangs of Ruffians and Law and Order men armed with warrants for our arrest from a bogus judge. They hunted us like wolves or coyotes, wanting us dead or alive, it made no difference. "War! War!" thundered the bogus press. And "War! War!" is what Satan's legions brought to Bleeding Kansas, plundering and burning Brown's Station and other free-state settlements all the way from Osawatomie to Topeka.

My men and I escaped into the brush, but we heard that the Ruffians had captured John Jr., Jason, and several other free-state men, all under indictment for "treasonably" resisting the bogus laws, and had turned them over to Federal troops. John Jr. had tried to hide, but owing to excessive fatigue, anxiety, and constant loss of sleep, he'd become quite insane and in that condition had given up. Later we learned that the Federal troops, blaming him for the affair on the Pottawatomie, tied him to a tent pole and beat him with rifle butts. Then John Jr., Jason, and five others were *chained two and two like a gang of slaves* and driven on foot, dragging their chains after them, the whole distance to Tecumseh. A Federal commissioner released Jason and four others, but John Jr. was indicted for treason and imprisoned.

By then, new recruits had joined my company and we rode out to meet the Philistines who were plundering and punishing our people. Wearing a soiled straw hat and well-armed, I rode at the head of my column like a Biblical warrior of old. I liked what the New York *Tribune* correspondent said about me: "Captain John Brown is a strange, resolute, repulsive, iron-willed, inexorable old man whom the Missourians both hate and fear." And why not? It was God's war we waged in Bleeding Kansas—an eye for an eye and a tooth for a tooth. In retaliation for Ruffian atrocities, we burned and pillaged proslavery settlements, confiscating horses and equipment for the continuation of the struggle. *For thou shalt eat the spoil of thine enemies, which the Lord thy God hath given thee.*

I trusted that God who had not given us over to the will of our enemies would keep and deliver us. In early June He delivered into our hands a force of Ruffians, who were encamped at Black Jack Springs like the Midianites at the Wall of Harod. As Gideon slew the host and drove them across the Jordan, I slew and captured the Ruffians, in what was the first regular battle fought between free-state and proslavery men in Kansas. "May God gird our loins and hold our right hands," I wrote Mary, "and to Him may we give the glory."

We heard that scores of Federal troops were on the ground to enforce the bogus laws and scatter the free-state men, who were out in considerable force to resist the roving columns of Ruffians. A day or two after Black Jack, a company of Federal troops discovered our camp and compelled my company to surrender our prisoners and our horses and weapons. The Ruffians did not go a few miles before they began to rob and injure free-state settlers again. Allowing them to do that was in keeping with the cruel and unjust course of the Pierce administration and the army throughout this whole Kansas difficulty. For reasons I cannot explain, the Federals did not arrest us, but simply ordered us to disperse. Being only a handful, we were obliged to submit.

After that, like David of old, we had our dwelling with the serpents of the rocks and wild beasts of the wilderness; being obliged to hide away from our enemies, who were out looking for us in even greater force. We fell sick with the ague and lay in camp shaking from its wasting fevers. We were nearly destitute of food, clothing, and money. But we were not disheartened. We trusted that God would *still* keep and deliver us. We felt assured that He who sees not as men see, did not lay the guilt of innocent blood to our charge.

As we lay in hiding on the prairie, voices spoke to me in the whispering of the wind. The voices were from far away—from Virginia and Louisiana. "If we're forced to leave Kansas," I told a couple of my men, "we might start South, to Louisiana, and get up a Negro insurrection, thereby compelling the slavers to let go their grip on Kansas." But I was uncertain what to do. At night, I scanned the Heavens, searching for a sign from God. *What is it You wish me to do?*

In late August, I was fixing breakfast with twelve or fifteen recruits, and mulling over our next move, when a messenger ran into camp yelling that the Border Ruffians had attacked Osawatomie and killed my son Frederick and another free-stater. "Men, *come on*!" I cried. We raced to Osawatomie, where Frederick, my poor boy, lay in the dirt with a proslavery bullet through his heart. The town's defenders were confused and frightened. "Form a line in the trees there!" I said. No sooner had we reached the trees than the Missourians wheeled off the road and charged down the hill, firing their guns as they came at us. They dismounted and brought a cannon into action, blasting the timber around us with volleys of grapeshot. The fighting was hot and bitter, but they bested us on account of superior numbers and scattered us across the Marais des Cygnes.

I escaped into the timber above Osawatomie with my son Jason. As we looked for a ford to cross the Marais des Cygnes, Jason pointed toward town: a column of smoke was rising over the trees. The Missourians were burning Osawatomie! We could hear their shouts and gunfire as they rode through the settlement looting cabins and herding off cattle. They murdered my Frederick and now this! "God sees it," I said, trembling with grief and rage. "I have only a short time to live—only one death to die, and I will die fighting for this cause. There will be no more peace in this land until slavery is done for. I'll give them something else to do than to extend slave territory. I'll carry this war into Africa."

Hiding in the brush near Lawrence, we heard that Governor John W. Geary, head of the so-called peace party, had brought a force of cavalry out to end the "fratricidal strife" in eastern Kansas and drive the Missourians out of the territory. When word came that Geary intended to arrest me, I left Kansas with three of my sons— Jason, Owen, and John Jr., who'd been released from prison. Trembling from the ague, I lay on a bed inside the wagon as it bounced along rutted roads, heading for New York State and New England. This was in the autumn of eighteen and fifty-six. I was hardly aware of the journey, for I had visions of God-fearing men, men who respected themselves, fighting in mountain passes and ravines for the liberation of the slaves. Yes, I told myself, God was calling me to a greater destiny now. He'd chosen the Kansas civil war and the killing of Frederick to show me what must be done to avenge the crimes of this "slave-cursed" land.

What was it the Prophet said? "That it might be fulfilled which was spoken of the Lord by the prophet saying, 'Out of Egypt have I called My son.'"

23. DOUGLAS

At first, I blamed all the Kansas troubles on the Massachusetts Emigrant Aid Society, a vast moneyed corporation which sent armed settlers out to the territory for the purpose of *provoking* a God-damned civil war. With armed northerners pouring into Kansas, I argued, Atchison's Missourians were forced to enter the territory to preserve law and order. Yes, irregularities had occurred in elections, but they were justified because of the northern invasion. In the Senate, over the bleatings of Sumner and other Black Republicans, I declared the proslavery legislature to be the legitimate government of Kansas and condemned the defiant free-state revolutionists, who engaged in treason, violence, fraud, and rebellion against that government.

When foreign elements from the North plunged Kansas into civil war in 'fifty-six, I lamented a resort to physical force as a substitute for truth and reason in the decision of public questions. If both sides,

I argued, would lay down their arms and embrace the great principle of popular sovereignty, which allowed the bona fide residents of a territory to decide the slavery issue, it would end the slavery controversy in Congress and between the sections. It would put an end to political agitators whose hopes of position and promotion depended upon their capacity to disturb the peace. The slavery controversy, I said, would cease to be a national one—would dwindle into a mere local question, and would affect only those residents of a state or territory who had the exclusive right to control it.

But Sumner and the Black Republicans, Goddamn them, did all they could to keep the controversy alive in Congress. In May of 'fifty-six, Sumner gave the most violent and abusive speech I have ever heard, the so-called "Crime Against Kansas." I tell you, he had that speech written, printed, committed to memory, and practiced it every night before the glass with a nigger boy to hold the candle and watch the gestures. It annoyed the boarders in the neighboring rooms until they were forced to quit the house. I can still hear Sumner describing the "crime against Kansas" in his arrogant Boston accent. "It is the rape of a virgin territory," he said, "compelling it to the hateful embrace of slavery; and it may be clearly traced to a depraved longing for a new slave state, the hideous offspring of such a crime, in the hope of adding to the power of slavery in the national government." He damned the intruding Missourians as "hirelings, picked from the drunken spew and vomit of an uneasy civilization, who renewed the incredible atrocities of the assassins and thugs." He resorted to bitter personal tirades against me and several southerners, particularly Senator Butler of South Carolina. Butler's "shameful imbecility from slavery," Sumner said, made him incapable of speaking truthfully or coherently. "He has chosen a mistress"—slavery—"to whom he has made his vows, and who, though ugly to others and polluted in the sight of the world, is always lovely to him." So much for the distinguished and courteous Butler! As for Stephen A. Douglas, Sumner said: "He is the squire of slavery, its very Sancho Panza, ready to do all its humiliating offices. He is one of these mad spirits who would endanger and degrade the Republic, while they betray all the cherished sentiments of the fathers and the spirit of the Constitution, in order to give new spread to slavery."

As he spoke, I leaned over to a colleague and said: "That damn fool will get himself killed by some other damn fool." The bastard went on and on, for two days! When he finally sat down, I took the floor barely able to control my rage. "The libels, the gross insults, which we have heard today, were written with cool, deliberate malignity," I said. "The Senator spit them forth upon men who differ with him—for that is their only offense." Why, I asked, had Sumner abused certain individuals by name and two-thirds of the Senate collectively? It was, I said, to turn the Senate into a Goddamned bear garden.

Sumner retorted that I was "intemperate" and "vulgar" and even accused me of improperly modeling myself after a "noisome, squat, and nameless animal," meaning a monkey. I recognized the comparison, I shouted, but I would never imitate the Senator from Massachusetts in that Goddamned capacity.

Two days later, I was talking with several men in the reception room when a messenger ran in crying that Preston Brooks, the South Carolina congressman, was beating Sumner with a cane in the Senate chamber. I rose involuntarily to my feet, thinking that I should go to the Senate at once and help put an end to the affray. But it occurred to me, in an instant, that my relations with Sumner were such that if I went into the chamber, my motives would be misconstrued. So I sat down again. Besides, I thought the contentious son of a bitch deserved to be taught a lesson. According to the papers, Brooks told Sumner: "You've libeled my state and slandered my white-haired old relative, Senator Butler, and I've come to punish you for it." He then struck Sumner a dozen blows on the head with the cane, knocking him down between two desks. Sumner lay there whimpering, "I'm *most* dead! Oh, I'm *most* dead!" Only a Goddamned Anglophile from Boston would talk like that. No, he wasn't dead, just badly beaten. Complaining that his "brain and whole nervous system" were "*most* jangled," he left for Boston and later went to London, where he belonged. The Black Republicans, of course, made much of his empty chair as a symbol of southern "barbarism."

They also made much of "the crime against Kansas" in the presidential canvass of 'fifty-six. Blaming the civil war there on me, Pierce, and the "Slave Power," they nominated abolitionist John Charles Frémont for President, on a divisive platform that defied the Constitution by demanding Federal prohibition of slavery in the territories. The platform revealed to the world the warmongering, abolitionist tendencies of the allied army of *isms* that made up the new party. How to roll back the Black Republican menace and save the country? The best course was to nominate and elect the Little Giant to the Presidency. I was the most capable national man in America and the powerful and undisputed leader of the northern wing of the great majority party. But to avoid dividing the party, I refrained from being an *open* candidate. The circumstances connected with the Kansas-Nebraska struggle, I told one and all, would render the triumph of the cause of popular sovereignty my perfect and complete vindication. "To that end, all my energies are directed," I said. "I ask no other reward, seek no higher victory."

When the Democratic convention gathered in Cincinnati, I instructed my campaign manager, William A. Richardson: "Let no personal considerations disturb the harmony of the party or endanger the triumph of our principles." But I'll tell you plainly: I wanted the nomination more than I'd ever wanted anything in my life. On the first ballot, James Buchanan of Pennsylvania was first, Pierce was second, and I was third. In subsequent ballots, Pierce fell out of the running. The convention, however, was soon deadlocked between Buchanan and me in that order. The voting was so close that had Massachusetts cast five votes for me instead of two, I would have won. It was the defection of the Northwest to Buchanan, who was unconnected with the Kansas troubles, that hurt me the most. "There was a deep undercurrent of feeling in your favor running through the entire convention," one of my supporters reported to me, "and had it not been for the eternal cry of 'availability,' 'safe man,' 'prudent politic statesman,' 'can carry the doubtful Northern States,' and all such stuff, about Buchanan, I firmly believe that you would have received the nomination."

When it became evident that an embittered state of feeling was being engendered at the convention, I had my name withdrawn for the sake of party harmony, which gave the nomination to Buchanan. I was bitterly disappointed that I'd lost to a party hack and a lackey of southerners like James Slidell of Louisiana, a royal shit if there ever was one. Yes, I was mollified to some extent by the platform, which held that congressional non-intervention with slavery in the states, the territories, and the District of Columbia was "the only sound and safe solution of the 'slavery question.'" By implication, I contended, the platform had endorsed the great principle of popular sovereignty and thus had vindicated my position on slavery in the territories.

Hurt though I was by Buchanan's nomination, I embraced the party ticket and campaigned furiously against wind and tide in Illinois. The Black Republicans, of course, held strident rallies and vowed to "exterminate" the northern doughfaces and dismantle the "heinous" Slave Power. We exposed them for what they were: a *sec-*

tional abolitionist party out to destroy the Constitution, free the niggers, and elevate them to a political and social equality with the white man—in short, to foment revolution. The Know-Nothings were in the race, too, running former President Millard Fillmore as their candidate and drawing support (which we encouraged) from former Whigs who could not stomach Frémont. But the contest was mainly between us—the constitutional, law-abiding, Union-loving men—and the radical Frémonters, who disturbed southern leaders and newspapers sufficiently that many threatened disunion if the Black Republicans won the government.

During the canvass, the enemy press and some of our own papers demanded to know which interpretation of popular sovereignty the Democrats endorsed—mine or the South's? I did not want to be drawn into a debate over an ambiguity that might divide our party. But I did not want to lose the critical Free-Soil vote either. To Illinoisans, I carefully repeated what I'd said before: a territory's bona fide voters could determine which institutions they desired at any time during the territorial stage; they did not (as southerners maintained) have to wait until the moment of statehood. My interpretation was widely popular among northern Democrats. Geary, the governor of Kansas, also endorsed it.

In November, Buchanan won the White House by carrying all but one of the slave states and the four states of the lower North, plus California. Thanks to my efforts and those of my followers, he'd won the crucial state of Illinois. I couldn't help but feel bitter that I was not elected in his place. Had I been, the disastrous course of the next four years would have been avoided. On the other hand, I rejoiced because the election was a great victory for my territorial policy. The people had resoundingly endorsed the wisdom and propriety of the Kansas-Nebraska Act. As a consequence, I expected to have a major voice in shaping the Cabinet and the policies of the new Administration.

Meanwhile I had some personal business to attend to. I'd been courting a tall and beautiful young Washington socialite, Adele Cutts, of a prominent Maryland family. Not yet twenty-one (to my forty-three), she was, to quote a friend, "beautiful as a pearl, sunny-tempered, unselfish, warm-hearted, unaffected, sincere." I worried that a lovely creature like her would never marry a widower with two sons who was twice her age; but I was determined to have her, and I wooed that girl with all the magnetic powers I possess. When I put the question to her, she smiled radiantly and said, "Of course!"

On Thanksgiving day, in the home of her family, I took my darling Adele to be my wife.

She proved a great asset to me personally and politically. Not only was she a splendid stepmother to my sons, whom she placed in a Catholic school; she also got me away from saloons, cut down on my cigar smoking, saw to my wardrobe, and made our mansion on the hill a popular center of Washington society. Before the Little Giant knew it, Mrs. Douglas had transformed the fireball of the Democratic party into a real gentleman.

In February of 'fifty-seven, Buchanan came to Washington to consult about his Cabinet. I had a full and free conversation with him at his own request. At sixty-five, he was tall and heavy-set, with a mop of white hair and a pronounced crease between his eyebrows. When being spoken to, he has an oddly deferential way of tucking in his chin and cocking his head forward and to the side, as if he's in complete agreement with you. For me, it was hard to believe that this unmarried, indecisive old bastard was now to guide the country.

I told him that the Northwest deserved two Cabinet posts and that I wanted a share of the patronage in my section. "I ask nothing for myself," I said. "I want only a fair share for my friends. I want the bold true men who fought the battle to be sustained."

Tilting his head forward, as if in apology, Buchanan changed the subject. "A sense of duty alone induced me to accept the nomination," he said. "They tell me my name will still the agitated waters and restore public harmony—by banishing sectionalism and removing all fears of disunion." He made it clear, though, that his sympathies were southern. "A storm of abolition against the South has been gathering for almost a quarter of a century. Now it's produced the Frémont sectional party and brought on a crisis that seriously endangers the country. The battle for the Union must be fought by the Democrats of the free states—*after* we heartily adopt the principles of the South on the subject of slavery."

I glared at him. There was no mistaking his import: he meant that northern Democrats must subscribe to the *southern* interpretation of popular sovereignty—that slavery must remain an open question until a territory was ready for statehood. When I protested, Buchanan tilted his head again and muttered: "Well, it's of no practical importance, is it? It really is a judicial question, best left to the Supreme Court."

I saw, then and there, that I was an outsider. My advice was not coveted nor my wishes and opinions regarded. When Buchanan announced his Cabinet, four of his six secretaries were southerners. All my recommendations had been snubbed. As I feared, the patronage in the Northwest had been decided before the nomination, without any discussion with me or consideration for my followers. When I learned that a bitter enemy of mine, Jesse Bright of Indiana, was one of Buchanan's closest advisers, I exploded. Bright was a Goddamned *pimp*. A stooge of Slidell and the other southerners who had Buchanan's ear. By God, I said, if it was war they wanted, it was war they would get: I would show no quarter. I told Slidell so with a shaking fist. Let the fucking bastard report *that* back to Buchanan.

In his Inaugural Address, Buchanan observed that a "difference of opinion" had arisen as to when the people of a territory could decide the slavery question for themselves. Then he repeated what he'd told me—it was a judicial question, which was now pending in a case before the United States Supreme Court, and it would be "speedily and finally settled" by that tribunal. But it was his "individual opinion," he said, that the southern version of popular sovereignty was correct.

Two days later, the Supreme Court handed down the Dred Scott decision. Led by the Chief Justice, Roger Taney of Maryland, the robed justices filed into the little Supreme Court room in the basement of the Capitol. Taney was almost eighty, so bent and emaciated that he struggled to walk. Though he was reported to have freed his own slaves, he remained dedicated to southern slave society. Before an overflowing crowd, he proceeded to read the majority opinion in a high, faltering voice, his bony fingers trembling. I heartily agreed with the first part of the decision: Negroes at the time the Republic was formed had no rights a white man respected. They were excluded from the Declaration of Independence and the Constitution, and therefore could not be citizens of the United States. I also heartily agreed with half of the second part of the decision: the Federal Government had no authority to exclude slavery from the territories, as any such exclusion was a violation of the property-rights clause of the Fifth Amendment to the Constitution. The Missouri Compromise, as a consequence, was unconstitutional. Thus did the court vindicate my entire course in nullifying that measure. And thus, to my great pleasure, did the high court destroy the very platform of the Black Republican party.

It was the next part of the decision that frankly troubled me: "if Congress cannot exclude slavery—if it is beyond the powers conferred on the Federal Government—it will be admitted, we presume, that it could not authorize a Territorial Government to exercise them. It could confer no power on any local Government, established by its authority, to violate the provisions of the Constitution."

With those unhappy words, the court tried to nullify my interpretation of popular sovereignty, to negate everything I'd been saying about territorial autonomy, about the right of the people of a territory to determine their own domestic institutions. I'd staked my political career on the principle of popular sovereignty as I defined and defended it. Now the proslavery court had moved to outlaw my position on that principle, siding with Buchanan and his southern advisers in what was plainly an attempt to hurt me politically.

The news from Kansas was troubling, too. In February, the proslavery legislature had authorized an elected convention to meet at Lecompton in September and draft a constitution making Kansas a slave state. Governor Geary, however, had vetoed the bill authorizing the convention, on the grounds that no provision had been made to submit the constitution to the people of Kansas for their ratification. The legislature had defiantly and recklessly overridden his veto. When the outgoing Pierce severely criticized Geary for his stand against the proslavery party, Geary resigned in protest on the very day Buchanan was inaugurated.

The Lecompton convention disturbed me. I could not stand idly by and allow the proslavery minority to devise a constitution that did not represent the will of the people! I could never champion popular sovereignty again, anywhere. Besides, I'd changed my mind about the northern settlers in Kansas. I'd received reports from serious men, men I respected, that the northern majority genuinely opposed the proslavery legislature and its "obnoxious" laws, which had been forced upon them by fraud and violence. The settlers from the North and West, according to my correspondents, were not fanatical abolitionists and hirelings, as I'd earlier supposed, but were "earnest men" who sought "a home mainly for the purpose of bettering their condition." Convinced that all this was true, I warned my southern colleagues that Kansas must inevitably be a *free* state.

As chairman of the Senate Committee on Territories, I resolved to take the lead in dealing with Kansas. I would see to it that Congress repudiated the proslavery legislature and took control of the entire state-making process, thereby ensuring that a state constitution would be drafted by a truly representative convention and then submitted to the people. "It's the right thing to do," said my colleague, Senator Charles E. Stuart of Michigan. "It's also the only way to save what is left of the Democratic party in the Northwest. Either we succeed or it's our political burial. I've seen several men from our section, and they all say that the excitement is increasing both in amount and intensity in reaction to Buchanan's inaugural and the Dred Scott decision."

We received an unexpected ally when Buchanan appointed Robert J. Walker of Mississippi as the new governor of Kansas. I was surprised and elated: Walker was a personal friend of mine and a capable man who'd served with distinction as a U.S. Senator and Polk's Secretary of the Treasury. Though small of stature, Walker possessed a nervous, magnetic, soft-spoken charm. He agreed with me that Kansas would ultimately be free, if the majority of bona fide residents were allowed to decide the matter for themselves. When first offered the post, however, Walker was reluctant to accept. The proslavery minority was reckless and determined, he pointed out; the free-state majority was no less resolved. The territory could explode again into civil war.

I told him: "You've got to go. I feel intensely about this. The whole success of popular sovereignty in Kansas depends on your consenting to go. I beg you to do it."

He did go—on the condition that Buchanan support him in seeing to it that bona fide Kansas residents were allowed to choose their domestic institutions without interference by the Missourians. Any state constitution, Walker insisted, must be drafted by a truly representative body and submitted in its entirety to the people. To my surprise, given his pro-southern leanings, Buchanan agreed to Walker's conditions "unequivocally."

After Congress adjourned, I headed home to reassure anxious Illinois Democrats about the territorial question in light of Dred Scott. I'd found a way to reconcile popular sovereignty with the Dred Scott decision, by reviving an argument I'd made earlier. I unveiled that argument in June of 'fifty-seven, before a large crowd in the Illinois statehouse in Springfield. I spoke impromptu about the entire territorial question and a concomitant issue, the Mormon uprising in Utah. To thunderous applause, I not only approved the sending of troops to Utah, but demanded that Congress rescind Utah's territorial status and punish the rebels—in short, "apply the knife and cut out this loathsome, disgusting ulcer."

Then I turned to the Dred Scott decision, which, I admitted, initially troubled me. Yes, the court had guaranteed the right of masters to their slaves in the territories. But that right, I said, necessarily remained a barren and worthless right unless sustained, protected, and enforced by appropriate police regulations and local protective legislation, prescribing adequate remedies for the violation of that right. These regulations and remedies must necessarily depend entirely upon the will and wishes of the people of the territory in question. If they wanted slavery, they would pass the requisite police measures and slave codes. If they didn't want slavery, they would refuse to enact such laws. *Hence*, I said, *the great principle of popular sovereignty and self-government was sustained and firmly established by the authority of the Dred Scott decision.*

Lincoln and other Black Republicans were in the audience, and I gave them hell for their dangerous racial doctrines. I was, I said, in perfect agreement with the main proposition in the Dred Scott decision: that "a Negro descended from slave parents is not and cannot be a citizen of the United States." But the Republicans, I cried, were in open revolt against that proposition; they called it "cruel, inhuman, and infamous" and insisted that the Negro was included in the Declaration of Independence. How wrong they were! The signers of the Declaration of Independence, I said, referred to the *white race* alone, and not to the African, when they declared men to have been created free and equal. The history of the revolutionary era, I pointed out, clearly showed that Negroes were regarded as an inferior race, who in all ages, and in every part of the globe, and in the most favorable circumstances, had shown themselves *incapable* of self-government. But what did the Black Republicans say? They demanded *equality* and *amalgamation* with Africans, heedless of that great natural law which demonstrates that amalgamation between superior and inferior races reduces the superior race to the lower level of the inferior one.

Yet, I said, it did not follow that, because the Negro race was incapable of governing itself, therefore Negroes should become slaves and be treated as such. The safe rule was *popular sovereignty*: the African race should be allowed to exercise all the rights and privileges they are capable of enjoying consistent with the welfare of the community in which they reside. Under our form of government, the people of each state and territory must be allowed to determine for themselves the nature and extent of those privileges.

I was Goddamned proud of that speech. I'd successfully squared popular sovereignty with the Dred Scott decision, and judging by the enthusiastic response from fellow Democrats and the party press, I'd rallied Illinois and the Northwest back to the great principle of self-government in the territories. "As a Democratic Presidential aspirant," said the New York *Herald*, "Mr. Douglas is now without a rival in the great Northwest." If my Kansas policy succeeded, I told my aides, I was certain to be reelected to the Senate in 'fifty-eight. Then the Presidency would truly be within my reach.

24. LINCOLN

When Douglas finished his speech in the statehouse, several fellows in the audience called for a reply. I went forward and said I would speak in the same place, two weeks from now, on June twenty-sixth. "*It will be an answer*," cried my law partner, Herndon. We Republicans were deeply disturbed by the sinister concatenation of events from the repeal of the Missouri Compromise to the Dred Scott decision. That ruling sent us reeling; it destroyed the very premise of our party and, in net effect, legalized slavery in all the territories. And now Judge Douglas had used that decision to charge us once again with desiring *racial amalgamation*; he'd made a mangled ruin of the Declaration of Independence and had shifted his ground regarding popular sovereignty, making it vaguer than ever, so as to hide that *real zeal* of his for spreading and perpetuating slavery.

He deserved a rebuttal all right, but not an abusive, threatening rebuttal—we heard too much of that kind of talk. We Republicans, I maintained, must appeal calmly and judiciously to the man of reason. We must convince him that slavery was a vast *moral wrong* and ought to be *restricted*. We must convince him that the Republican party was dedicated to preserving the central idea of the Republic— that all men are created equal and deserve an equal chance to rise— whereas the Democrats wanted to discard that idea and replace it with the principle that slavery was *right* and ought to be *extended*. We Republicans must forget our own differences, unite, and go forward together in the cause of free soil, free labor, and free men, upon which the destiny of all men everywhere depends.

In spare moments away from my law practice, I went to the library of the Illinois Supreme Court and studied the nine separate opinions of the Dred Scott decision and the reaction to it. The judges, I noted, had voted along party as well as sectional lines. Six Democratic judges, five from the slave South, were in the majority, with the seventh Democratic judge concurring. The two non-Democrats, Curtis of Massachusetts (a Whig) and McLean of Ohio (a Republican), dissented. The majority had rendered the decision after ruling that the court had no jurisdiction in the case. Clearly, the Democratic judges had used the judicial power to decide a *political* question.

Southerners, of course, applauded the ruling and declared it the law of the land. But a tornado of indignation swept across the Free-Soil North. The Republican and abolitionist press damned the decision as "infamous," "unjust," and "inhumane." So, I was glad to see, did the legislatures of Maine, Vermont, Massachusetts, Connecticut, and Rhode Island. The New York legislature not only excoriated the court, but made it a law that slavery could never exist in that state in any form, for any period; slaves brought there, even in transit, would be set free immediately and their owners subject to imprisonment. Republicans, on the national and state level, spoke as one man against "this wicked and false judgment." Herndon, his black, cavernous eyes on fire, told me that the court had "ruined itself" and that people were "stunned" and were "ready to flee or fight."

The Democratic papers condemned the Republican attacks against the court and accused the Republican party of trying to provoke revolution and anarchy. Douglas himself charged that the Republicans were trying to destroy "our whole republican system of government" by preaching "violent resistance to the highest judicial tribunal on earth." This line of attack, I noted, had to be met and defeated.

Busy with court and other legal matters during the day, I had to write my speech at home in the evenings. This concerned my wife, Mary, who worried that I worked too hard. "Now, Mother," I teased. "If I don't work hard, you won't have the money to make those shopping trips of yours." She was still as plump and handsome as when she was a girl, with a round-moon face, long lashes, intelligent blue eyes, and a slow smile that created dimples in her cheeks. When we married, *I* was a poor nobody, whereas *she* was the daughter of a prominent Kentucky family, the lordly Todds, who never liked me much. I was lucky, I reckon, that a girl of such a *refined* family would have me.

"I don't shop *nearly* as much as I'd like," she said in a teasing voice of her own. "I wish I could go to Europe; they have such excellent shops in London and Paris." She sighed. "But I guess poverty is my position." She added: "I'm determined my next husband shall be *rich*."

"That I'm a railroad lawyer doesn't count, I guess."

She worked her expressive little mouth into a smile, indicating that it counted plenty. In a good year, I earned $5,000 from my practice, enough to let us live comfortably. We had a well-furnished, two-story frame house on the corner of Eighth and Jackson streets in Springfield, money in the bank, and investments in real estate, mortgages, insurance policies, and interest-bearing notes.

Mary and I made a pretty good match. We had the same mind about raising our three boys—neither of us ever took a whip or a hand to them. She liked me to tease and dote on her and call her "my Molly" or "my little woman." When she went abed with a spell of the headache, I doctored her myself, wiping her forehead with a wet cloth. "You're *everything* to me," she said, "lover-husband-father, *all*." In return, she was fiercely loyal to me, affectionate, sensitive to my moods, and unfailingly supportive.

Of course, Mary and I had our differences. She liked to entertain more than I did and once invited five hundred guests to our house, which I considered a little excessive. Owing to a rainstorm, however, only three hundred showed up. She could also get the wildcat in her sometimes, especially after I'd been away riding the circuit, which I did twice a year, three months at a stretch. Then she would yell to beat all hell. Still, I could hardly blame her for being cranky, since I left her to manage the house and the boys with only the maid to help. What got Mary most riled was when a pretty young woman flirted with me at a party or a Republican picnic. It didn't bother me, though.

On my side, I had the habit of drawing into myself—the hypo, I called it—which I know isn't easy to live with. Once, I recollect, a spell came on while I was pulling one of the little boys in a wagon. When we went over an uneven plank sidewalk, the little fellow fell out. I was so absorbed I didn't know it and trudged on with my head bent forward, pulling the empty wagon around the neighborhood. Mary really got after me that time. God knows what the neighbors thought.

She found some of my other habits equally annoying. I like to answer the door myself, often with my boots off. I also like to lie on my back in the hallway, with my head against an upside-down chair, and read newspapers aloud, so as to bring two senses into play at the same time. Coming from the highfalutin Todds, she viewed such behavior as "unsophisticated."

"You knew I was unsophisticated when you married me," I said.

"*You're* not unsophisticated, just some of your habits," she said. "On the whole, you're more sophisticated than any man I know, a lot more so than Stephen Douglas. You know I've always bragged about how you tower over him intellectually, just as you do physically."

"He's an ambitious fellow," I said. "But so am I." I thought over the years since I'd first met him in Vandalia, back in 'thirty-four. We were both young then; he a trifle younger than I. Even then we were both ambitious. "With Douglas," I said, "the race of ambition has been a splendid success. His name fills the nation; it's not unknown in foreign lands. With *me*, the race of ambition has been a failure—a flat failure."

"You're not a *failure*," Mary said.

"I don't hold a political office—haven't had one in eight years. Oh, sure, I've got a successful law practice, and I've contributed my mite to the Republican cause in Illinois. But in politics, compared to Douglas, I'm a failure."

"I think you're going to be President of the United States some day. I've always told you that."

"I'll settle for Douglas's seat in the national Senate," I said. The Presidency for me was too far-fetched to contemplate. Besides, I had little interest at that time in a tedious administrative office. I had my eye on the Senate, where Clay had rendered his great service.

After dinner, I would retire into the parlor to work on my speech, the only political speech I gave in 'fifty-seven. I'd spent so much time campaigning the year before that I'd neglected my law practice. As I toiled at my desk, Mary kept the little fellows, Willie and Tad, from interrupting me until they went to bed. She didn't complain when I came to bed long past midnight.

On Sunday afternoons I liked to putter around the law office, on the second floor of a brick building across the square from the courthouse. To give Mary time to herself, I brought Willie and Tad along. Thirteen-year-old Robert, our oldest, was in school, I believe. Lying on the couch, with my legs spread across a couple of chairs, I read legal papers aloud to myself. Giggling with delight, the boys crawled over me and otherwise entertained themselves. They pulled all the books down from the shelves, banged the points of pens against the stove, turned the inkstands over, tossed pencils into the spittoon, scattered letters about the floor and danced on them. I suppose I should have disciplined the little fellows—Herndon would glower when he saw the wrecked pens and the ink stains—but I didn't have the heart to do it.

On June twenty-sixth, after a day in court, I was ready to answer Judge Douglas. By appealing to principles, I hoped to shape the Republican position on the Supreme Court and the Dred Scott decision, the Declaration of Independence, and the Negro. I hoped to refute once and for all the allegation that we were trying to stir up revolution and that we desired a mixing of the races. This last lethal charge had cost us Illinois and the rest of the lower North in the 'fifty-six presidential contest, which in turn lost us the election. We had to dispel that charge if we were to carry the lower North and win the government in 1860. We had to dispel that charge if I was going to defeat Douglas here in Illinois.

At a little past 8:30 that evening, I carried an armload of legal volumes into the great hall of representatives and read my address to a mostly Republican crowd. I began with Utah. If the Mormons were in rebellion, I said, they ought to be coerced to obedience, as Douglas advocated. The Republicans could fall in on that without taking back anything they had said. But, I pointed out, it would be a considerable backing down by Judge Douglas from his much vaunted doctrine of self-government for the territories. This was only additional proof of what was plain from the beginning, that that doctrine was a mere deceitful pretense for the benefit of slavery.

As to the Dred Scott decision, I affirmed the Republican position of obedience to and respect for the judicial department. We thought its decisions on constitutional questions, when fully settled, should be the general policy of the country, subject to be disturbed only by a constitutional amendment. More than this would be revolution. But, I went on, we thought the Dred Scott decision was erroneous. The court that made it had often overruled its own decisions, and we would do what we could to have it overrule this decision. We offered no *resistance* to it.

The decision was wrong, I said, because it was based in part on assumed historical facts which were not true. For instance, Chief Justice Taney went to great lengths in arguing that Negroes were not part of the people who made, or for whom was made, the Declaration of Independence or the Constitution. But Judge Curtis of Massachusetts, in his dissent, demonstrated that in five of the original thirteen states—in Massachusetts, New Hampshire, New York, New Jersey, and North Carolina—free Negroes had been voters and, in proportion to their numbers, had the same part in making the Constitution that the white people had. I quoted Curtis: "These colored persons were not only included in the body of 'the people of the United States,' by whom the Constitution was ordained and established; but in at least five of the states they had the power to act, and, doubtless, did act, by their suffrages, upon the question of its adoption."

I also pointed out that the black man had steadily *lost* what he'd once enjoyed in the days of the Revolution. In two states—New Jersey and North Carolina—he'd had the right to vote taken away, and in another—New York—that right had been greatly abridged. In the days of the Revolution, masters could, at their own pleasure, emancipate their slaves; but since then, so many legal restraints had been made upon emancipation as to amount almost to prohibition. In Revolutionary days, the spread of the black man's bondage to new territories was prohibited; but now, Congress decided that it *could not* continue that prohibition, and the Supreme Court decided that it *could not* if it wanted to. In Revolutionary days, our Declaration of Independence was held sacred by all, and thought to include all; but now, to aid in making the bondage of the Negro universal and eternal, it was assailed and sneered at, and misconstrued, and hawked at, and torn, until, if its framers could rise from their graves, they would not at all recognize it.

I was swinging my arms now and moving up and down and sideways for emphasis. All the powers of earth, I said, now seemed rapidly combining against the Negro. Mammon was after him; ambition followed, and philosophy followed, and the theology of the day was fast joining the cry. They had him in his prison house; they had searched his person and left no prying instrument with him. One after another they had closed the heavy iron doors upon him, and now they had him, as it were, bolted in with a lock of a hundred keys, which could never be unlocked without the concurrence of every key; the keys in the hands of a hundred different men, and they scattered to a hundred different and distant places; and they stood musing as to what invention, in all the dominions of mind and matter, could be produced to make the impossibility of his escape more complete than it was.

Taney, I said, admitted that the language of the Declaration was broad enough to include the whole human family, but he and Judge Douglas argued that the authors of that instrument had not intended to include Negroes, by the fact that they had not, at once, actually placed them on an equality with the whites. Now this grave argument, I said, came to just nothing at all, by the other fact that the authors had not, at once or ever afterward, actually placed *all white people* on an equality with one another. What, I asked, had the authors of that notable instrument meant by the statement, "all men are created equal"? They intended to include *all men*, I said, but they did not intend to declare all men equal in *all respects*. They did not mean to say that all were equal in color, size, intellect, moral developments, or social capacity. They defined, with tolerable distinctness, in what respects they did consider all men created equal—equal in "certain inalienable rights, among which are life, liberty, and the pursuit of happiness." This they said, and this they meant. They did not mean to assert the obvious *untruth*, that all were then actually enjoying that equality, nor yet, that they were about to confer such a boon. They meant to declare the *right*, so that the *enforcement* of it might follow as fast as circumstances should permit. They meant to set up a standard maxim for free society, which should be familiar to all, and revered by all, constantly looked to, constantly labored for, and even though never perfectly attained, constantly approximated, and thereby constantly spreading and deepening its influence, and augmenting the happiness and value of life to all people of all colors everywhere.

None of this meant, however, that the Republicans favored amalgamation. There was, I admitted, a natural disgust in the minds of nearly all white people, to the idea of an indiscriminate amalgamation of the white and black races. Judge Douglas, I said, evidently based his chief hope upon the chances of being able to appropriate that disgust to himself. According to him, the Republicans contended that the Declaration included all men, black as well as white, because they wanted to vote, and eat, and sleep, and marry with Negroes. "Now," I said, "I *protest* against that counterfeit logic which concludes that, because I do not want a black woman for a *slave*, I must necessarily want her for a *wife*. I need not have her for either, I can just leave her alone. In some respects she certainly is not my equal; but in her natural right to eat the bread she earns with her own hands without asking leave of any one else, she is my equal, and the equal of all others."

Judge Douglas, I said, declared himself especially horrified at the thought of the mixing of blood by the white and black races: agreed for once—a thousand times agreed. There were white men enough to marry all the white women, and black men enough to marry all the black women; and so let them be married. If Judge Douglas could show that his policy was better adapted to prevent amalgamation than ours, we would adopt his. Let us see. Of the 405,751 mulattos in the United States in 1850, I pointed out, 348,874 of them resided in the slave states. These statistics demonstrated that slavery itself, which brought white masters and female slaves together, was the greatest source of amalgamation. By demanding that slavery be excluded from the territories, that the two races be kept separated where they were not already together, Republicans were trying to *curtail* amalgamation, not bring it about.

The separation of the races, I said, if ever effected at all, had to be effected by colonization—voluntary colonization. Yet no political party, as such, was now doing anything directly for colonization. The enterprise was a difficult one, I admitted, but "where there is a will there is a way," and a hearty will was what colonization needed the most. Will, I said, sprang from the two elements of moral sense and self-interest. Let us be brought to believe it was morally right, and, at the same time, favorable to, or, at least, not against, our interest, to transfer the African to his native clime, and we would find a way to do it. After all, I said, the children of Israel, to such number as to include four hundred thousand fighting men, went out of Egyptian bondage in a body.

This brought me, in conclusion, to one of the fundamental differences between the Republican and the Democratic parties. "The Republicans," I said, "inculcate that the Negro is a man; that his bondage is cruelly wrong, and that the field of his oppression ought not to be enlarged. The Democrats deny his manhood; deny, or dwarf to insignificance, the wrong of his bondage; so far as possible, crush all sympathy for him, and cultivate and excite hatred and disgust against him; compliment themselves as Union-savers for doing so; and call the indefinite outspreading of his bondage 'a sacred right of self-government.'"

As I expected, Springfield's Democratic paper accused me of arguing for "negro equality" and reported that all "right thinking men" thought my speech "contemptible." But the *Illinois State Journal*, the Republican paper in town, declared my speech "overwhelming, unbeatable." Some Republicans, however, thought I was too gentle with Douglas—they wanted a harangue. And they got one a few days later when blond and bespectacled Lyman Trumbull, who was skilled at thrust-and-cut oratory, spoke in Springfield against the Dred Scott decision. To thunderous applause, the Senator damned it as the "odious and infamous opinion of a slave-driving court" and demanded that it be "revolutionized." That kind of rhetoric I thought we ought to avoid; we did not want the Democrats accusing us of fomenting revolution. Herndon agreed. "You hit the right tone against Douglas," he said. "You were gentlemanly, strong, and conclusive, while Douglas was a rabble-rousing dog."

I had struck the first blow in my uphill struggle for Judge Douglas's Senate seat, which would be decided in 'fifty-eight. I had not addressed his new interpretation of popular sovereignty as an alleged free-soil device—all that mumbo jumbo about police measures and the like. I would have plenty to say about that later, in light of sinister new developments involving Kansas and the Buchanan administration.

25 . BROWN

To accomplish the great mission Jehovah had designed for me, I needed men and money, a lot of money. Crisscrossing the North, I spoke guardedly to groups of abolitionists and Free-Soilers about my struggles in Kansas, but collected only a trifle of the funds I needed to put my secret plan into action. I didn't reveal my real objective, but I hinted at it in an angry encounter I had with William Lloyd Garrison, in Reverend Theodore Parker's house in Boston.

"Non-resistance," Garrison argued, "is the only course for all true abolitionists. Our movement was baptized in the spirit of peace. If it capitulates to violence, in Kansas or anywhere else, it will lose its moral power."

"Don't give me your milk-and-water pacifism," I cried. "All I hear from you and your followers is talk! talk! talk! *Talk* won't free the slaves. We need *action*."

"Moral suasion, Mr. Brown, *is* action; it's the power of truth and righteousness prevailing over wickedness."

"Moral suasion is a failure," I said, "a flat failure. You've preached it for almost thirty years, yet slavery is more entrenched in this country than when you began. Every peaceful solution has failed. The gradual-emancipation movement got nowhere. The Liberty party movement disappeared after a few years. Now we have the Republicans, but they're hopelessly wishy-washy on the issue. All they advocate is *restriction*. By their own admission, it may take a hundred years for slavery to die out by that method. That is no solution. And neither is moral suasion or any other peaceful approach."

We were surrounded by Garrison's friends. "We're for peaceful *disunion*," one piped up. "No union with slaveowners."

"That may ease your conscience," I snapped, "but it won't help the poor slave."

A minister broke in. "We must give peace a chance, Captain Brown."

"Don't talk to me of peace," I said. "How can we have peace when the Supreme Court wages war against black people? How can we have peace when the President of the United States sides with the proslavery legions in Kansas? How can we have peace when the President, the Supreme Court, the Congress, the Republican and the Democratic parties, and the Constitution, all acknowledge the right of white men to own Negroes, to reduce *human beings* to *property*?"

I glared at them. "Don't talk to *me* of peace when slavery throughout its entire existence in this country has been a most barbarous, unprovoked, and unjustifiable *war* of one portion of its citizens upon another portion. Don't talk to me of peace when four million of our fellow human beings face perpetual imprisonment and hopeless servitude or absolute extermination, in utter disregard and violation of those eternal and self-evident truths set forth in our Declaration of Independence."

"What you say is true," said Garrison. "But it doesn't justify violence and war—"

"I think Captain Brown is right," interrupted Reverend Parker, a balding man with thick glasses and a white beard. "We need to interject a bit of Lexington into the controversy."

"We've reached the point," I said, "where nothing but *war* can get rid of slavery in this guilty nation. It's better that a whole generation of men, women, and children should pass away by a violent death than that slavery should continue to exist." I meant that literally, *every word of it*.

While in Boston, I called on young Frank Sanborn, a Concord schoolteacher and secretary of the Massachusetts Kansas Committee, which had furnished guns and money for the free-state cause in the territory. Sanborn stared at me, wide-eyed, when I told him who I was and said I needed the committee's backing to continue battling Satan's legions in Kansas. He couldn't *believe* that Osawatomie

Brown, the hero of 'fifty-six, was standing in front of him. "Captain Brown," he said finally, "it would be an honor to help you." He in turn persuaded Dr. Samuel Gridley Howe, George Luther Stearns, and the other committee members to furnish me with guns and money for the defense of Kansas. I had no intention, of course, of using the money and weapons in Kansas. When the right time came, I would tell the committee where I really intended to strike.

I then went to Worcester and enlisted the help of Thomas Wentworth Higginson, a tall, fiery Unitarian minister who'd led the resistance group that had tried to free the fugitive, Anthony Burns, from the Boston courthouse. "I'm a *disunion* abolitionist, Mr. Brown," he said. "The disease of slavery is too deep for cure without amputation." When I hinted that I was plotting a union-splitting operation on the Missouri border, he became quite excited and promised to help me raise money and guns.

Later, in a drugstore in Collinsville, Connecticut, I met Charles Blair, a forge-master for the Collins Company, which manufactured edged tools. I showed Blair a Bowie knife I'd captured in Kansas.

"If I had a lot of these blades fastened to poles about six feet long, they would make good weapons for our free-state settlers to keep in their cabins," I said. "You're a forge-master. You can make good edge tools. What would you charge to make five hundred or a thousand of these pikes?"

"Well," he said. "I could probably make you five hundred at a dollar and a quarter apiece, or a thousand at a dollar apiece."

"I want them made," I said. I signed a contract for 950 pikes, each with a ten-inch, double-edged steel blade, and gave Blair a down payment of $500 with a promise of $450 more when the pikes were delivered.

"I appreciate the business," Collins said, "but I'm puzzled about something. Why would settlers skilled in the use of firearms want pikes? And why would you come to me when a blacksmith in Iowa or Kansas could make them just as well?"

"Just see to the work," I said and left.

In New York, I engaged an English adventurer named Hugh Forbes to train a guerrilla company I intended to raise. About forty-five years of age, he'd fought with Garibaldi in the Italian Revolution of eighteen and forty-eight and had authored a two-volume manual on military tactics. He agreed to serve in my company for $100 a month, but made it clear that he wasn't interested in merely saving Kansas for free white people.

"Don't worry," I told him. "My plans call for something far greater than defensive operations in the territory. What I have in mind will result in the emancipation of the slaves."

We met later in Tabor, Iowa, and I revealed for the first time what my plan entailed. If Federal troops were sent against me, I told Forbes, my New England partisans would call a northern convention and overthrow the proslavery Buchanan administration. An obstinate, self-styled expert on military matters, Forbes disputed that contention and countered with his own plan. But I waved him off. *I* was the commander of this operation; I'd been perfecting *my* plan for many years, and it was ordained by God through all time and eternity. "God," I said, "has made me His special angel of death to the slaveholders." Forbes started to say something, but my fierce-eyed stare and tut! tut! silenced him. That night, by lantern light, I pored over maps of the southern states and made a list of towns containing Federal forts or arsenals from Florida to Texas.

Using the alias Nelson Hawkins, I returned to Kansas Territory and set about raising recruits for my guerrilla company. In November of 'fifty-seven, I rendezvoused with the first of them, all committed abolitionists and all veterans of the Kansas civil war, on the prairie northeast of Topeka. A cold wind howled out of the night as I piled wood on the campfire and spoke of the trials ahead. Sitting closest to me was John E. Cook, a fresh-faced, blue-eyed boy of twenty-seven who loved to talk about himself. Next to Cook sat Aaron D. Stevens, a tall, muscular young man with dark, brooding eyes. I valued him because he could use a saber with deadly skill and wouldn't hesitate to slaughter the Philistines. He'd once thundered at a Kansas sheriff: "We're in the right and will resist the universe." Next to Stevens was young John Henry Kagi, my most trusted lieutenant, an Ohio schoolteacher and passionate idealist who hated slavery as I did. He'd once been arrested and jailed four months for the crime of advocating the free-state cause in Kansas. In a scuffle in Tecumseh, he'd shot and killed a man from Alabama who'd tried to murder him with a bludgeon.

"Captain Brown," Kagi said in a tone of deep respect, "we're proud to serve with you. But we were wondering what specific plans you've made to continue the war against the Slave Power. We know you've got other recruits. Where is it you want us to fight?"

"Kansas is quiet now," I said, "and anyway it's too cold to do much campaigning out here. So we're going to Ohio to drill. My sons and a few others will go with us." I handed Cook a draft for

$82.68. "Get that cashed in Lawrence tomorrow," I said. "We'll meet again at Tabor in Iowa. Then I'll tell you what we're going to do. If you want hard fighting, you'll get plenty of it."

At Tabor, nine recruits gathered around me. They were furious about the latest news from Kansas: the proslavery politicians were now pushing to make the territory a slave state.

"Forget Kansas," I said. "Our destination is Virginia."

26. DOUGLAS

I was at home in Chicago when news of the great swindle in Kansas came out in the papers. That was in November of 'fifty-seven. Without the consent of Congress, a convention of mostly proslavery delegates met at Lecompton, the territorial capital, and drafted a proslavery constitution that would make Kansas a slave state. In reckless violation of the Kansas-Nebraska Act and the expressed wishes of President Buchanan, the bastards made no provision for submitting the full document to the people of Kansas for their endorsement or rejection. Instead the convention set a special election for December twenty-first, at which time the people were to vote only on the question, "The constitution with slavery" or "The constitution without slavery." If the voters chose the last question, a provision was to be added stating that "slavery would no longer exist in the state of Kansas except that the right of property in slaves now in this territory shall in no measure be interfered with." What kind of fucking hocus-pocus was this? I had to rub my eyes to make sure of what I was reading. This seemed to mean that either way the people voted, slavery would exist in Kansas and it would be a slave state.

The convention also created a provisional government in place of the territorial government, thus ousting my friend Governor Walker and all the other Federal territorial officers. This was a Goddamned outrage! The convention had no legal power to create a provisional government; it only had the authority, derived from the territorial legislature, to collect, ascertain, and embody the will of the people of the territory upon the subject of admission into the Union, and to send the same as a memorial to Congress. What the hell was going on out there?

I found out when Walker passed through Chicago on his way to see Buchanan. He was even madder than I was. "What's going on out there is a Goddamned crime," he said. "John Calhoun, the president of the convention, told me that the decision for no submission of the constitution came *directly from the President*."

"But Buchanan gave you his word that the constitution would be submitted in its entirety," I said.

"Calhoun claimed the President changed his mind," Walker said. "I told Calhoun the vote they'd arranged was a vile fraud. I would denounce the damn thing whether the administration sustains it or not."

"That lying son of a bitch," I said of Buchanan. "I might have known he would surrender to his southern advisers and Cabinet secretaries. This is the work of Cobb, Thompson, Floyd, and especially Slidell, that slimy bastard."

"The free-staters are going to boycott the election of December twenty-first," Walker said, "and I don't blame them. Steve, that constitution represents scarcely one-tenth of the people of Kansas. If the free-state majority is coerced into accepting a slave-state constitution, I'm afraid it will provoke another civil war out there, and it will spread throughout the nation."

After Walker left for Washington, I pondered my course of action with a coterie of close aides. We all agreed that I had to defy the Lecompton swindle come what may. There was a damned good political reason to do so: the admission of Kansas as a slave state would destroy the Democratic party in Illinois and me with it. "Remember, the *only* fight of 1858 will be here," one aide said, in reference to my bid for reelection to the Senate. But, for me, defiance was a matter of principle, not politics. "We must," I said, "stand firmly by the principle of the Kansas organic act and the Cincinnati platform, which guarantees the right of the people of each state and territory to form and regulate their own institutions in their own way." As chairman of the Senate Committee on Territories, I would see to it that Congress required *full* submission of the Lecompton constitution to the people of Kansas in a fair election. If they rejected it, they must be authorized to assemble a new convention that would devise another constitution for statehood. *Whatever constitution was adopted,* I said, *must express the will of the majority in Kansas.* If I did not demand that, I could never champion popular sovereignty again. The South, of course, would never forgive me for what I was about to do. Not that I wanted their Goddamned forgiveness. As far as I was concerned, the South could go to hell.

In mid-November, Buchanan's mouthpiece, the *Washington Union*, served up an editorial endorsement of the Lecompton constitution. This left no doubt about where the old bastard stood. "Can you believe his Goddamned arrogance?" I told a friend. "I run the Committee on Territories. He should have consulted me before approving the Lecompton fraud. He'll pay for that. By God, sir, I made Mr. James Buchanan, and by God, sir, I'll unmake him." In late November, accompanied by Adele, who was with child, I left for the capital in a growing rage.

As soon as we reached Washington, I went straight to the White House. The Lecompton constitution, I told Buchanan bluntly, was a blatant fraud on the people of Kansas and the process of democracy, and I warned him not to recommend acceptance of it. With his head tilted forward in that bizarre habit of his, he said that he intended to endorse the constitution in his message to Congress.

"If you do," I thundered, "I'll denounce it the moment it's read."

His face turned red with anger. "I'll make Lecompton a party test," he said. "I expect every Democratic Senator to support it."

"I will not, sir!"

He rose, cutting the interview off. "Mr. Douglas, I want you to remember that no Democrat has ever yet differed from an Administration of his own party without being crushed." He added: "Beware the fate of Tallmadge and Rives when they opposed General Jackson."

"Mr. President," I said, "I want you to remember that General Jackson is *dead*." I turned and stormed out of the White House.

"The battle will soon begin," I wrote Douglas men in Illinois. "We will nail our colors to the mast and defend the right of the people to govern themselves against all assaults from all quarters. The Indiana Senators, Bright and Fitch, are pledged to the Lecompton fraud, but we can succeed without them."

Congress convened on December seventh in the midst of noisy construction. The old Capitol was undergoing a renovation, and stacks of bricks, stones, and timber lay about the grounds. Workmen had dismantled the old wooden and brick dome and were constructing a new iron dome by means of scaffolding, a derrick, and two steam engines, whose roar often drowned out speakers in the old legislative chambers. Scores of other workmen were adding north and south wings, which contained larger and more modern House and Senate chambers respectively. The new Senate chamber still had a ways to go, but the new Hall of Representatives was almost ready for occupancy. It had a magnificent ornamented ceiling, three hundred desks set up in a semicircle, and impressive galleries for 1,200 spectators. The doorways and panels, however, were too gaudy to suit some people. Benjamin French, former commissioner of public buildings, complained that the interior was more suitable for a lager beer saloon, or a steamboat cabin, than a legislative hall.

The day after Congress convened, the President's message was read to both houses in an atmosphere fraught with tension. The part dealing with Kansas made me puke. The President said he approved the work of the Lecompton convention because it adhered to "the great principle of popular sovereignty" embodied in the Kansas-Nebraska Act, which, he said, merely required submission of the slavery question, not of the entire constitution. He insisted that his instructions to Walker had not meant full submission of the constitution, even though they may have sounded like that; his instructions meant only "that the people of Kansas should furnish to Congress the evidence required by the organic act, whether for or against slavery." My jaw fell open in a silent scream. That lying scoundrel! His instructions to Walker had been Goddamned explicit about full submission. His message stopped short of urging Congress to accept the Lecompton constitution and admit Kansas as a slave state. But that sure as hell was the implication.

I replied to Buchanan the next day, speaking to packed galleries and a full assemblage of the press. The President's remarks about the Kansas-Nebraska Act were in error, I said, and that error lay at the foundation of his entire argument about the Lecompton constitution. The Kansas-Nebraska Act, I reminded the President, required that the people of the Kansas Territory determine *all* their domestic institutions, not just slavery. The law therefore required the *full* submission to them of any constitution intended for statehood. I ought to know—I wrote the Goddamned law. As for Buchanan's instructions, Governor Walker had gone to Kansas and proclaimed, in his inaugural and in speeches at Topeka and elsewhere, that it was the distinct understanding, not only of himself, but of those higher in power than himself—meaning the President and his Cabinet—that the constitution was to be submitted to the people for their free acceptance or rejection, and that the President would use all the power at his command to defeat its acceptance by Congress, if it were not thus submitted to the vote of the people.

The election arranged by the Lecompton convention, I said, was a vile system of trickery and jugglery by which all men in favor of the constitution could vote for it, but all men against it could not vote at all. This was as fair an election as was Napoleon's when he was chosen First Consul. "If you vote for Napoleon," he said, "all is well; vote against him and you are to be instantly shot." So it was in the election for the Lecompton constitution: all men who voted against it would be shot. Now why, I asked the Senate, was the Kansas election arranged this way? I'd interrogated a number of gentlemen who framed the constitution and a larger number who were their friends, and I received the same answer from every one of them. They said that if they allowed a negative vote, the constitution would be rejected by an overwhelming free-state majority, and hence those fellows would not be allowed to vote at all.

I glared at the "Buchaneers"—our name for the Buchanan men—on my side of the Senate chamber. "Is that the mode in which I am called upon to carry out the principle of self-government and popular sovereignty in the territories—to force a constitution on the people against their will?" I did not care about the right or wrong of that document, I said. "If Kansas wants a slave-state constitution, she has a right to it; if she wants a free-state constitution, she has a right to it. It is none of my business which way the slavery clause is decided. I care not whether it is voted down or voted up." But I took it for granted that it would be voted down, since the facts proved undeniably that an overwhelming majority of the people of Kansas wanted a free state.

My proposal to Congress was this: "Ignore Lecompton, ignore the free-state Topeka government, treat both those party movements as irregular and void; pass a fair enabling bill for Kansas statehood, have a fair election on its constitution, and you will have peace in the Democratic party, and peace throughout the country. But if this constitution is to be forced down our throats, in a submission process that's a mockery and insult, I'll resist it to the last. I'll stand on the great principle of popular sovereignty and follow it wherever its logical consequences may take me."

The galleries exploded in cheers and wild applause. That brought Mason of Virginia, a Buchaneer, to his feet. "I move that the galleries be cleared!" he cried. "The offenders against the peace and decorum of the Senate must be expelled." Save for Mason, the Democratic side of the Senate was silent. The Republicans, however, were clapping in delight. "I've never seen a slave insurrection before," said Bluff Ben Wade of Ohio. I started to say something to that snide bastard, but checked myself. My fight this time was not with the Black Republicans; it was with the southern Senators and northern lackeys of the Administration.

As I expected, Buchanan's footmen in the Senate—Bigler, Bright, Fitch, and Green—rushed to the attack. They accused me of trying to divide and destroy the party; they contended that there was no reason why Kansas should not be admitted at once on the basis of the Lecompton constitution.

"You do," I said, "and it will lead directly to civil war!" I warned the anti-Lecompton Democrats of the North that the President intended to put the knife to the throat of every man who dared to think for himself on this question and carry out his principles in good faith. "God forbid," I said "that I should ever surrender *my* right to differ from a President of the United States for my own choice. I'm not the *tool* of any President."

Support for me poured in from across the North. The governor of Minnesota wrote that "999 out of every thousand voters in our party, except the office-holders under the present Administration, are with you." So were Ohio's Democrats. So were New England's. In Illinois, every Democratic paper declared in favor of my battle against Lecompton. My aides, going over my Illinois mail, told me I must never "falter, hesitate, or back down one inch." I had no God-damned intention of doing so.

Before Christmas, I met with several influential Republican congressmen in my mansion on Minnesota Row. Schuyler Colfax was their spokesman. Nicknamed "Smiler" because he wore a constant grin, he was a young-looking fellow with blue eyes and light-brown hair. He and his colleagues, quite frankly, were in awe of my break with the Administration and eager to form an alliance with me to block the admission of Kansas as a slave state. I said I was angry at some Republicans who insisted that the Lecompton outrage was the direct result of my Kansas-Nebraska Act, and that I should have foreseen it and all the other troubles in Kansas when I repealed the Missouri Compromise line. What stupid Goddamned reasoning! Still, I was ready to put aside our differences for the sake of a common cause. As my Republican visitors smoked cigars and sipped brandy with me, I said I was surprised at the opposition to the simple demand for justice I'd made for the people of Kansas. "But I'm going to stand my ground inflexibly," I said. "I intend to uphold the principle of popular sovereignty even if it drives me to private life. I know what the Administration will do: they'll say that Kansas must come in at once and try to rush Lecompton through. If they succeed, all is lost. Our strategy is clear: we must delay a vote as long as possible. We'll probably lose in the Senate, where I count thirty-seven pro-Lecompton men to twenty-five or so on our side. But I think we can defeat Lecompton in the House, where there's a lot of disaffection and wavering among the Democrats and the fourteen Know-Nothings. But I need time to win them over.

"This fight goes deeper than Kansas," I said. "I have reports that Jefferson Davis and other southern ultras are ready for disunion and are looking for an opportunity to break up the nation. If Lecompton goes down to defeat, that might be their opportunity. To stop them, we might need to form a grand Constitutional Union party. We want to put the disunionists in their real light before the country. When the break comes, they'll be in the position of insurgents. Then the army and the power of the nation will be against them."

Smiler Colfax said: "I think I speak for my Republican colleagues. We're with you a hundred percent against Lecompton. But I won't promise you Republican support for your reelection to the Senate next year or for the Presidency in 1860."

"You're right," I said. "Forget what I said about a grand Union party. I ask no support except in the present contest. Tomorrow I'll consult with your man in the House, Nathan Banks, and work out a program of battle."

That I did. On December eighteenth, I introduced a Kansas enabling bill which authorized a new constitutional convention and complete submission, and Banks introduced a similar bill in the House, which was now in its new hall in the Capitol's north wing. With that, the temporary alliance of the Little Giant and the congressional Republicans went to war to save the great principle of popular sovereignty in Kansas. Horace Greeley's New York *Tribune*, the chief Republican organ, and other Republican papers in the East gushed with praise for the Little Giant, and it was bruited about that he was soon to be "baptised" a Republican. I would never join the Black Republican party, whose radical racial doctrines were repugnant to me, but I loved to see the Administration men in Congress squirm from our combined assaults. According to the *Washington Union*, we were driving Buchanan crazy. Whenever the subject of Kansas came up, he broke into an incoherent tirade against the Little Giant.

After the Christmas recess, the Administration unleashed its heavy horsemen: Davis, Slidell, Hunter, Toombs, and Hammond, all southerners. They damned me as a traitor and demanded that I be stripped of my chairmanship of the Committee on Territories and read out of the Democratic party. Let the fucking bastards threaten, proscribe, and do their worst, I told my followers; it would not cause any honest man to falter. If my course divided the Democratic party, it would not be my fault. We were engaged in a great struggle for principle, I said, and we would defy the Administration to the bitter end.

The news from Kansas strengthened our resolve. In the election of December twenty-first, the one called by the Lecompton convention, the question, "the constitution with slavery," was approved by more than six thousand votes because the vast majority of free-staters boycotted the canvass, just as we expected. On January fourth, 1858, the Free-Soilers held their own canvass on the Lecompton constitution. That election was authorized by the newly elected free-state legislature, which Acting Governor Frederick P. Stanton had convened in an attempt to mollify the angry free-state majority. In the free-state election, the Lecompton constitution was overwhelmingly defeated by more than ten thousand votes. As I told the Senate, the two elections, taken together, meant that the people of Kansas rejected the Lecompton constitution by nearly two to one. This established conclusively that this counterfeit document did not embody the popular will of Kansas.

Buchanan, of course, accepted the first election as the valid one and sent over a special message demanding the immediate admission of Kansas as the sixteenth slave state on the basis of the Lecompton constitution. Kansas, he maintained, was "at this moment as much a slave state as Georgia or South Carolina." The Administration men then brought forth a Kansas bill embodying the President's proposal, and it plunged Congress into violent debates. Jefferson Davis declared that a stranger entering the Senate might have supposed that "here stood the representatives of belligerent states preparing to make war upon each other."

Davis I despised; he had a cold, arrogant air about him, a haughty certitude that on every issue he was right. He was touchy, hotheaded, ready in a second to defend his honor. I enjoyed goading the petulant prick. "Sir," I said, fixing my eyes on Davis, "see how certain of my southern friends have deserted me. *I* will set the conditions upon which they are to be let back into the Democratic party." Davis leaped to his feet, beat his chest, and shouted incoherently.

Several times in the debates, he lost control of himself and charged an antagonist as if to run him through with an imaginary saber.

As I predicted, Davis and his cronies threatened disunion if "noble" old Buchanan's "high-minded" wishes about Kansas were not obeyed. James Hammond of South Carolina, a short, fat planter who owned four hundred slaves, gave an obnoxious speech about the supremacy of the South with its world monopoly on cotton. "Cotton is king," he cried with quivering jowls. "Without firing a gun, without drawing a sword, when they make war on us we can bring the whole world to our feet by refusing to sell our cotton." He claimed that the South could equip and maintain a larger army than any power on earth and declared himself prepared "to have a final and conclusive settlement instantly" with the *inferior* North.

The Republicans, led by Seward, Wilson, Trumbull, and Fessenden, advanced a conspiracy theory that rankled the hell out of me. They argued that Lecompton was the penultimate stage of a "sinister design" on Kansas that had begun in 'fifty-four: that it started with the repeal of the Missouri Compromise line, which allowed slavery into Kansas under the pretext of territorial self-government; that the next step was the Dred Scott decision, which denied the authority of the people of Kansas to exclude slavery; that the complaint now was that slavery was being forced on them by deceit and trickery; and that the next step would be a Supreme Court ruling that a state could not prohibit slavery.

I wasn't part of any Goddamned conspiracy! No sir, my motives were pure. But there was *no* denying that certain southern extremists were promoting just such a final step as the Republicans feared. In November of the previous year, Buchanan's paper, the *Washington Union*, had argued that the emancipation acts of New York, New England, Pennsylvania, and New Jersey were outrages upon the right of property and were violations of the Constitution of the United States. The proposition was advanced that a southern man had a right to move from South Carolina, with his niggers, into Illinois, to settle there and hold them there as slaves, in defiance of the constitution and laws of Illinois. I saw right there that a fatal blow was being struck at the sovereignty of the states of this Union, a death-blow to states' rights, subversive of the Democratic party and its longtime principles. I felt bound, as a Senator from the free and sovereign state of Illinois, to repudiate and rebuke this doctrine, and I did so in the Senate debates.

But most of the time, while others debated, I worked the floors

of both houses, marshaling and directing men against the Administration and its Kansas bill. In mid-February, however, a crisis at
home called me away from the great battle. Adele had a miscarriage
and almost died; I was constantly at her bedside for several days,
and off and on for a couple of weeks, until she was out of danger. I
returned to the Senate for a crucial night session, when the majority
tried to force the Kansas bill through to a quick vote. But our side
was determined and resolute and compelled them to give up at 6:30
in the morning.

With that, Buchanan used the patronage ruthlessly against anti-
Lecompton Democrats in an effort to drive them back into line. We
stalled a vote for more than a month of furious debate and maneuver, but finally relented to superior numbers. In the final debate in
the Senate, I spoke for three hours despite a lingering illness.
"Reverse the case," I told the opposition. "Suppose Kansas Free-
Soilers were in the minority. Would southern men, if a convention of
Free-Soilers made a constitution, and allowed you to vote for it, but
not against it, and then attempted to force that constitution on a
slaveholding majority against their will, would you southern men
submit to such an outrage?" Hammond, of course, denied that there
was any such outrage. The next day, the Senate approved the
Lecompton bill by a vote of thirty-three to twenty-five. Some Republicans, to my chagrin, observed that it was almost exactly four years
ago that the Kansas-Nebraska bill had been enacted.

The debates roared on in the House, where there were long and
bitter night sessions and a lot of drinking. When Republican
Galusha A. Grow crossed over to the Democratic side, Keitt of
South Carolina exploded: "Go back to your side of the House, you
Black Republican puppy!" When Grow said he would go where he
damn well pleased, they started shoving one another, and Grow
punched Keitt to the floor. This provoked a thirty-minute melee in
which, according to the *New York Weekly Tribune*, "fifty middle-
aged and elderly gentlemen pitched into each other, most of them
incapable, from want of wind and muscle, of doing each other serious harm."

My forces in the House fought a brilliant delaying action while I
worked to win over wavering Democrats. When we introduced a
substitute bill, Buchanan called a dozen congressmen to the White
House and exhorted them not to forsake the Administration. He was
cursing and in tears. He had reason to be: on April first, a coalition
of ninety-two Republicans, twenty-two anti-Lecompton Democrats,

and six Know-Nothings sent Lecompton down to defeat by passing the substitute bill. This bill provided for a popular vote on the Lecompton constitution and for a new convention if the people rejected that document, as they surely would.

"The agony is over," cried one of my aides, "and thank God the right has triumphed. Poor Old Buck!" Poor Old Buck had just had his face rubbed in shit. By our "indomitable courage," as another aide put it, we'd whipped this "powerful and proscriptive" Administration and forced the Black Republicans to support a substitute measure which fully embodied the great principles of the Kansas-Nebraska Act.

27. JEFFERSON DAVIS

I was desperately ill throughout the month of March and missed the final debates and the vote on the Lecompton bill in the Senate. My illness began with a severe cold, which brought on laryngitis and a terrible neuralgia which paralyzed the entire left side of my face and inflamed my left eye so badly that it was ready to burst. Unable to tolerate the slightest light, I lay in a dark room, blindfolded and speechless, for four weeks. "You could only communicate your thoughts by feeling for the slate and writing them," says my wife Varina. "Don't you remember Dr. Hayes of Philadelphia, the great specialist? He came to help our family physician attend to you. They prescribed doses of atropine and applied leeches . . . I couldn't look at them. Oh, Jeffy, you were hurting so badly; only I knew how much. Your rigid self-control kept most of it hidden. When Doctor Hayes asked you why the eye hadn't burst, you wrote on the slate, 'My wife saved it.'"

Among my regular visitors was Senator Seward, the Republican leader, who kept me apprised of developments in Congress. As I lay in bed with the blindfold over my eyes, he would tell me what "your man" did or "our man" did in the debates on Lecompton. The little fellow amazed me; he was my mortal enemy, a Black Republican, yet he was as congenial and friendly as if he were a fellow southerner. He joked and told stories, and laughed hysterically at them, unconcerned, or unaware, that I did not concur in his humor and lay there, frowning.

One day, when I was able to speak again, the subject of slavery came up. I asked Seward: "Sir, how can you make your piteous appeals for the Negro in the Senate? After being a schoolmaster in Georgia, you surely don't believe the things you say."

"No," he said, "I don't, but my appeals have a potent effect at the North."

"But, Mr. Seward, do you never speak from conviction?"

"Nev-er," he said with a chuckle.

I was shocked. Raising my blindfolded head from the pillow, I whispered intently: "As God is my judge, I never speak from any other motive."

I could never figure him out. "Mr. Seward has a problematical character, full of contradictions," Varina said. "He can be so sympathetic with people when they're suffering, yet truth means nothing to him unless it serves an end. You know what he told me the other day? 'Political strife is a state of war, and in war all stratagems are fair.'" That troubled me profoundly. I could never trust a man who believed that. When I recovered, I intended to keep an eye on that unprincipled New Yorker.

I don't remember who brought me the news that the Lecompton bill had been defeated in the House and that a substitute bill had been carried by the evil coalition of Douglas Democrats and Black Republicans. I detested Douglas even more than any of the Black Republicans; he was double dissembler, a Judas to the Administration and the Democratic party and a fake friend of the Republicans to boot; he had allied with them not from any principle—the man had no principle—but to win back his loss of support at the North in his unrelenting greed to be President. God forbid that that moral midget should win the White House! As the Administration's principal spokesman in the Senate, I intended to see Douglas drummed out of the Democratic party and destroyed.

A visitor, probably a southern colleague, told me that President Buchanan had threatened to veto the House's substitute bill, but had now decided on a compromise. "To save face," said my visitor. "It's called the English bill. It offers Kansas voters a choice: if they approve the Lecompton constitution immediately, the territory gets an enormous Federal land grant, some four million acres, and other benefits. The Republicans are calling it a bribe. Douglas apparently went for it at first, but then changed his mind, and now damns it as 'congressional intervention with a bounty.' The Administration is pulling out all the stops on this one. I heard they've spent almost

$40,000 to win over wavering Democrats. The vote is going to be close, too close to call."

At that time, I had complete confidence in Mr. Buchanan, thought him a noble old patriot whose Roman firmness and integrity of purpose could not be questioned. Whatever he did in the present crisis was for the good of the country and the Democratic party. On the day of the scheduled vote for the English bill, I was determined to be there and had myself literally carried into the Senate, only to see (with one eye) the vote postponed until the next day, April thirtieth. I returned that day, on my feet, upright, with one arm around Varina's shoulders and the other around my physician's, and cast my yea for the English bill and President Buchanan. When the measure passed both houses by a narrow vote, I declared it a triumph for the Administration and a vindication of southern rights and principles regarding the territories.

Yes, the people of Kansas ended up voting down the land grant offer—and with it the Lecompton constitution and immediate statehood on that basis—by some outrageous margin. Still, it was a victory on principle for us, inasmuch as the vote on slavery had occurred *at the moment of statehood*, according to the southern position. At this point, Kansas was neither a slave state nor a free state. Indeed, I thought the decision that Kansas not become a state at this time was fortunate and wise; the people of Kansas lacked the essential characteristics of a community, not to mention the requisite population and resources necessary to bear the expense of government.

When Congress adjourned in mid-June, Douglas returned to Illinois, where, according to Seward, he faced a strong Republican challenge for his Senate seat. I desired to go home, too, but my physicians insisted that the journey back to Mississippi was too great for me and that I needed complete rest, so Varina and I planned to spend the summer in Maine with the children.

I missed Brierfield, our plantation. It was located some thirty miles down river from Vicksburg, on a peninsula in the Mississippi River called Davis Bend. Our mansion had balancing wings, each with a verandah. When I was home, I liked to rise early and ride over my cotton lands, tilled by more than seventy slaves. As I rode by, they always greeted me affectionately, "Hello, Marse Davis!" And well they should. A kind, humane master, I provided my people with neat cabins, held wakes and wedding feasts for them, brought a dentist down from Vicksburg periodically to look at their teeth, established a slave hospital and a day nursery for the small children of mothers who worked in the fields, and allowed the blacks to settle disputes in their own courts.

The abolitionists, howling at us from afar, could not see how well treated our slaves were. They called slavery a sin. By what standard did they measure it? Not by the Constitution, which recognized property in slaves. Not by the Bible; that justifies it. Not by Christianity; for servitude was the only agency through which Christianity reached the Negro race. Not by a comparison of the slave's lot to that of the free black in the North: the one well provided for in all his physical wants and steadily improving in his moral condition; the other miserable, impoverished, loathsome from the deformity and disease which follow after penury and vice. Negroes were not fit for freedom because they were unable to care for themselves. As the descendants of Ham, the graceless son of Noah, they carried God's curse on Ham and so were slaves by divine decree. How, then, could slavery be a sin? It was, in fact, a moral, a social, and a political blessing.

The best overseer I ever had was a black man, an *unusual* black man. James Pemberton was his name. He died of pneumonia after the Mexican War, and I never found a white overseer who was his equal as a manager of slaves. My white overseers, one after another, complained that the field hands were so lazy that only the whip could make them work. I forbade the use of the whip under any circumstances. I wanted my people to be healthy and happy, even if that meant smaller crops.

Varina, of course, took the side of the overseers. "The slaves *do* malinger, Jeffy. They'll do anything to get out of work. A whipping now and then is necessary." When a slave complained of feeling sick, Varina would march out to the quarters with a quart bottle of castor oil in one hand and a jar of quinine powder in the other, whereupon the slave would experience an astonishing recovery and head for the cotton fields, with Varina standing victoriously in the doorway.

I well remember the day I first met Varina—it was at a Christmas party in 1843, at my brother Joseph's mansion on Davis Bend. I was still suffering from the loss of my first wife, Sarah Taylor Davis, daughter of General Zachary Taylor, who would become President in 1848. She had died in my arms, of malaria, while singing a strange, eerie song, "Fairy Bells." When I met Varina, she was just seventeen—eighteen years my junior—and was highstrung and temperamental. But she had a fine mind and was quite pretty, if a little tall, with large dark eyes, full lips, and lustrous black hair. From the first, I was quite fond of her and during our courtship wrote her endearments in French: "Adieu, au revoir, ma chère, très chère, plus chère Varina. Dieu te bénisse." She said she found me "most agreeable," with "a peculiarly sweet voice" and "a winning manner" of asserting myself. "You're the kind of person," she said, "who would rescue a girl from a mad dog at any risk, then insist on a stoical indifference to the fright afterward." We were married in 1845, at my sister Anna's plantation home in Louisiana, the very place where Sarah had died.

Though Varina and I had a strong union, there was a strain between us in our early days together, in part due to her being childless for seven years, a condition we both regretted, since a proper southern wife was expected to be with child within a year of marriage. It was 1852 when "Winnie" gave birth to our first child, Samuel, but we lost him just two years later, when he took sick and died. I was inconsolable. Varina says that I could not bear the sound of a child's cry in the street, that it almost drove me mad. "You also suffered greatly from a nervous cough and painful depressions," she says. "For months, you walked half the night, and worked fiercely all day." However, the birth of our daughter, Margaret Howell, in 1855, did much to restore my balance of mind.

In the early years of our marriage, Varina's most frequent complaint was that I was "incorrigibly" opinionated. "You have a way of taking for granted," she said, "that everyone agrees with you when you state an opinion, which offends me."

"I take it for granted that you agree with me," I said, "because my opinion is based on careful thought and accords with the facts."

"Come on, Jeff. You resent it when someone disagrees with you. You always ascribe it to the perversity of your opponent."

"It *is* his perversity!"

"You are *never* wrong, then?"

It was a useless argument. I find it difficult to believe that anyone would differ with me after I have explained the reasons on which my position is based. But I do have one infirmity of which I am ashamed. When I am aroused in a matter, I lose control of my feelings and become personal.

When the Mexican War broke out, I told Varina I intended to volunteer in the army. I was a West Point graduate. I had served in the Black Hawk War, had spent seven years at frontier posts. The army needed a man of my military experience at the war front. But Varina made a terrible scene: she begged me not to leave her and wept and carried on as if my death on the field of battle was a foregone conclusion. I am indeed a stoical man who tries not to show anger; but that day it showed. In the end, though, I was the one who gave in and agreed to stay. But when the First Mississippi Regiment elected me colonel, I told Varina that I had to go, it was my *duty* to go. She finally relented, saying she supposed she could bear it. "But God only knows how bitter it is to me," she added.

So I went off to Mexico at the head of the "Mississippi Rifles." During the battle of Buena Vista, already shot in the foot, with the bone of my heel shattered and the wound bleeding profusely, I directed the repulse of a Mexican cavalry charge. Returning home on crutches, I found myself celebrated as "the hero of Buena Vista"—President Polk even offered me a brigadier general's commission. I declined it in favor of an interim appointment to the national Senate, where I could look after Mississippi's interests and defend her constitutional rights. Pale and emaciated ("from the nervous pain consequent upon his wound," Varina explained), I entered the Senate chamber hobbling on crutches. The smallest misstep still caused me pain. Inspired by John C. Calhoun, who was my mentor and political idol, I joined in the battle against the abolitionists, the Wilmot Proviso, the admission of California, against the whole catalogue of injustices which disturbed the tranquillity of our people and the perpetuity of our constitutional Union.

After Mr. Calhoun passed on, I inherited his mantle as chief spokesman and watchdog for the minority South. Like him, I opposed the Compromise of 1850 because it was injurious to the interests of the slave states. In fact, I resigned from the Senate to run for the Mississippi governorship against Hangman Foote, one of the southern traitors—another was Clay—who helped the abolitionists in Congress get the compromise measures through. A runt with a huge, bald head, Foote had organized a new Union Democratic party which supported the compromise; I was the candidate of the regular Mississippi Democrats who opposed it. Throughout the campaign, Foote accused me of being a disunionist. "I'm *no* disunionist," I cried. I was tempted to respond to Foote with a monosyllabic answer which was not fit to be used in public, but which was the only reply that ought to be made to so foul an assailant.

"My heart beats for the welfare of the Union," I said in the campaign, "yet the Union is not so dear to me as Mississippi. If I have to choose between secession or political and social degradation for Mississippi and the South, I will choose secession." I believed that we of the South ought to assert our right to secede for the public record. The *assertion* of a right, I pointed out, was no evidence of an intention to *use* it.

I lost the election to Foote by only 999 votes. It was all the more humiliating because Foote kept boasting that he was "the vanquisher of Jefferson Davis," the "would-be" successor to John C. Calhoun. Foote was a changeling, a mere demagogue, as full of intrigue and selfishness as he was destitute of truth and principle. In short, he was a southern Douglas. Twice I came close to fighting a duel with Hangman and dispatching him to the nether regions.

I showed him I was not "vanquished." I became Frank Pierce's Secretary of War and left an outstanding record. I succeeded in getting the regular army increased by four full regiments, including a new regiment of cavalry under Colonel Albert Sidney Johnston, my very great friend and the best soldier in the country, and Lieutenant Colonel Robert E. Lee. I also dispatched a commission of officers, among them Lieutenant George B. McClellan, to observe the Crimean War; and I introduced camels in the desert Southwest as an experiment in military transportation. After Frank Pierce's term ended, I returned to the national Senate to stand again as a sentinel on the watchtower, ready to sound the note of alarm whenever the rights of Mississippi and the South should be invaded or their honor assailed, and prepared to go as far as the farthest in their defense and vindication.

True, I initially supported the Kansas-Nebraska Act because I favored the repeal of the Missouri Compromise line. But I never trusted that shyster Douglas or his "squatter" sovereignty idea. It was too ambiguous, lending itself to sinister Free-Soil interpretation, which robbed southerners of the full measure of our rights. Douglas was quite incorrect in contending that a decision on slavery could be made once a territorial government began operating. This would allow the majority section to send hordes of armed invaders into a territory, as they did in Kansas, and proceed to vote us out by sheer numbers. Douglas's interpretation of territorial self-government bestowed upon a territory a sovereignty it did not possess. Sovereignty belonged exclusively to the states and to the national government as a creature of the states; it could not be transferred by the national government to the territories. As Mr. Calhoun taught us, the territories were the common property of the Union of sovereign states; within those territories, southerners and northerners had equal rights as joint owners. Each of us had the right to go into the territories with whatever property was recognized by the Constitution of the United States, and slavery was so recognized. Congress had no power to limit or abridge that right; was bound, instead, to see that it was fully enjoyed. The Supreme Court, in the Dred Scott decision, upheld that position because it was the correct one. The inhabitants of a territory had the right to decide the question of slavery only when they were ready, as a people, to form a state government, and no power upon earth had the right to decide it before that time.

One of my supporters rightly maintained that Douglas's version of squatter sovereignty was more subversive of the South than the Republican doctrine of slave restriction because it invited the slaveholder "to come into the territories, to be unceremoniously kicked out again." I once cornered Douglas in the Senate and asked him where the people of a territory derived the power to exclude slavery. "The power comes from God!" he said.

From God! he said. So much for a government of law! So much for abiding by the Constitution! Douglas cared nothing for either: his sole concern was his own ambition. He shifted with the political winds—aha! the majority of the North was now Free Soil; therefore he was for Free Soil, assuring the northern majority that they could kick slaveholders out of the territories through the *great* principle of squatter sovereignty. Humbug! All he really cared about—I'll say it again—was regaining the support of the majority section so that he could win the Presidency. That was why he formed that perverted alliance with the Black Republicans and sought to split the Democratic party, the last undivided national organization in the country, into northern and southern wings. Now you see why I considered him a dangerous man.

You ask, why did we argue the right to take slaves into Kansas and the other western territories? Was that not a barren, theoretical right? I believed that slave labor could be adapted to the gold and silver mines and the cattle ranches of the Southwest—the Spaniards had employed Indian slaves in such enterprises in their conquest of Mexico. I was all for buying Cuba and annexing Mexico and other tropical regions where our slave-based agriculture could thrive; manufacturing had an equal right to go there, too, of course. The point is, we needed to extend slavery because of the war that was being made against our institutions; because of the want of security which resulted from the action of our bitter foes in the northern states. This I told the Senate during the heat of debate over Lecompton. "You have made it a political war," I warned the North. "*We* are on the defensive. How *far* are you to push us?"

The Black Republicans, of course, were trying to push us to the brink. Having incorporated the lunatic abolitionists and given them a political outlet, they were our avowed and implacable enemies. They had begun as a faction and grown to the colossal proportions of a sectional party which was now plotting our ruin. They intended to encircle us with free territories and free states in a heinous effort to strangle us into submission. They were determined to turn the North against us and precipitate a war of sections so that they could free the Negroes and put them on top of the whites in the South.

In June of 'fifty-eight, we had further proof of their bellicose purpose from Illinois: on the very day Congress adjourned, Lincoln, the Black Republican candidate for Douglas's Senate seat, gave a violent abolitionist speech before a convention of pestilent Republican zealots. Lincoln declared that this country could not remain half slave and half free, and called for a war of extermination against the South and its domestic institutions. With the dark cloud of fanaticism looming over the land, you can understand why I called myself a pretty good secessionist.

28. LINCOLN

The rumpus among the Democrats over the Lecompton constitution was an intriguing development, but I wrote Trumbull that the Republicans should stand clear of it. In our view the President and Douglas were both wrong, although Buchanan was a little more wrong than the Little Giant, and Republicans should not espouse the cause of either. But my advice didn't carry much weight in the East: Horace Greeley's New York *Tribune,* the most powerful Republican paper in the country, began heaping praise on Douglas for his "courageous" stand against Lecompton and the Buchanan administration. The *Tribune* even endorsed Douglas for reelection and urged Illinois Republicans to support him.

I tell you, I was offended. "What does the New York *Tribune* mean by its constant eulogizing, and admiring, and magnifying of

Douglas?" I wrote Trumbull. "Does it, in this, speak the sentiments of the Republicans at Washington? Have they concluded that the Republican cause, generally, can be best promoted by sacrificing us here in Illinois?"

The thing left me pretty depressed. "I don't think Greeley is doing me right," I told Herndon. "I'm a true Republican. I've been tested in the hottest part of the antislavery fight, and yet I find him taking up Douglas, a dodger—once a tool of the South, now its alleged enemy—and pushing him to the front. Greeley forgets that when he does that he pulls me down at the same time. I'm afraid his attitude will damage me with Sumner, Seward, Wilson, and other friends in the East."

"Mr. Lincoln," Herndon said, "you've been promised the Republican nomination for the Senate, and Greeley is not going to cheat you out of it. We're our own masters out here." Herndon sent Sumner a salty warning: "We don't want to be huckstered off in the political alleys or on corrupt corners by pimps of legislation without our consent."

Early in 'fifty-eight Herndon went east to talk with Greeley and other Republicans. Herndon reported back: "Greeley evidently wants Douglas sustained and sent back to the Senate. He did not say so in so many words, but I know it from the spirit and drift of his conversation. He talked bitterly—somewhat so—against the Republican papers in Illinois, and said they were fools. I asked him this question, 'Greeley, do you want to see our party triumph, or do you want Douglas to ride to power through the North, which he's so much abused and betrayed?' and to which he replied, 'Let the future alone; it will all come right. Douglas is a brave man. Forget the past and sustain the *righteous*.' Good God, Douglas is *righteous*, eh! Greeley asked me this question, 'You will sustain Douglas in Illinois, won't you?' and to which I said '*No, never*!' By the bye, Greeley told me this, 'The Republican standard is too high; we want something practical.' In other words, he wants to lower the platform to let Douglas on it."

"Not if I can help it," I said.

I warned Illinois Republicans that Douglas had not changed, that he was still the same old *Little* Giant. There remained all the difference there ever was between him and the Republicans—we insisting that Congress *shall*, and he insisting that Congress *shall not*, keep slavery out of the territories. Did he now express any wish that Kansas, or any other place, should be free? I asked. Nothing like it.

He said in the Senate that he cared not whether slavery was voted *down* or voted *up*. His whole effort was devoted to clearing the ring, and giving slavery and freedom an equal fight. In short, he considered slavery just as good as freedom. "We Republicans must not hook on to Douglas's kite," I told party members in Illinois. "We must avoid strange and new combinations, must maintain our Republican identity and defend our Republican principles. Douglas is not your man for the Senate. *Lincoln is your man—Lincoln, a pure Republican.*"

To my relief, Trumbull reported from Washington that he and the Illinois delegation had no intention of abandoning me. Norman Judd, chairman of the Republican State Central Committee, announced that he would resign if the party supported Douglas. Governor Bissell and nearly all the other state party leaders also stuck by me. "The Republicans of Illinois," declared Dr. Charles Ray, senior editor of the Chicago *Tribune*, "are unanimous for Lincoln and will not swerve from that purpose." Party leaders scheduled a state convention to meet in Springfield on the sixteenth of June, and ninety-five Republican counties named Lincoln as their "first, last, and only choice" for the Senate. I felt reassured by that show of unity, which the Chicago *Tribune* attributed to the "outside meddling."

The Illinois Democrats held their convention in April, with the Douglas forces in firm control, and endorsed the Cincinnati platform. That tipped the Judge's hand: he had no intention of compromising his own doctrines and forming an alliance with eastern Republicans. Since every Republican in the country regarded popular sovereignty as an abomination, that pretty much ended the flirtation with the Little Giant. When a group of rival Buchaneer Democrats held their own convention and plotted to oppose Douglas in the campaign, I was in high spirits. "If we don't win," I said, "it will be our own fault."

On June sixteenth, flag-draped trains whistled into Springfield from all over the state, disgorging scores of Republican delegates. They gathered in the great hall of the statehouse and unanimously nominated Lincoln for the national Senate "as the successor of Stephen A. Douglas." It was unprecedented—the first time a convention had ever chosen a senatorial candidate, to be voted on in the legislature after the fall elections. It was hot that day, near suffocating inside the packed hall, yet a heady optimism pervaded the convention. "Illinois is going to have *two* Republican Senators," they said.

I was scheduled to speak that evening about my greatest concern as a Republican and an American in this difficult time. The signs indicated that our enemies were plotting something far more ominous than extending slavery into the western territories. That was just the first step in the plan. The abolitionists, Garrison and that crowd, had been warning us for a long time that something evil was afoot, and we were slow—I was slow—to come around to that view. But now I had no doubt about it. Consider this. In December of 'fifty-seven, the *Washington Union*, Buchanan's official paper, declared that the free states had no constitutional authority to prohibit slavery within their borders. It didn't matter that Toombs of Georgia announced that no southerner wanted to extend slavery into the North. Who could believe Toombs when the Richmond *Examiner* contended that slavery and freedom could not "co-exist" in this country, and that "the one must give way and cease to exist, the other become universal"? Who could believe Toombs when George Fitzhugh advocated the eradication of free labor and the enslavement of all workers, white and black alike? Who could believe Toombs when the sentiment in favor of white slavery now prevailed in the newspapers of Virginia and the Deep South? Who could believe Toombs when Hammond of South Carolina stood in the Senate and proclaimed that every civilization was built on the mudsills of society; that the South had them in the form of inferior Negro slaves who were well cared for and were "happy, content, unaspiring" in that capacity; that the North's "whole class of hireling manual laborers and 'operatives'" were "essentially slaves," but were worse off than the Negro slave because they were "hired by the day, not cared for, and scantily compensated"? Hammond's implication seemed pretty damn plain. *Our* white workers should be enslaved like *his* Negroes.

I was not the only Republican to see a definite pattern, a design, in southern defenses of slavery and recent political events. Trumbull, Seward, Fessenden, and Chase all saw it, too. The logical procession of sinister events—Douglas's repeal of the Missouri line, Taney's Dred Scott decision, Buchanan's Kansas policy—pointed to a southern conspiracy to *nationalize* slavery. We Republicans had to make the entire North see what was going on, lest we wake up one day to find that our Republic had become a *slave house*.

And so I told the Illinois Republican convention—and the country beyond—that June night: "We are now far into the *fifth* year, since a policy was initiated, with the *avowed* object, and *confident* promise, of putting an end to slavery agitation. Under the operation of that policy, that agitation has not only *not ceased*, but has *constantly augmented*. In *my* opinion, it *will* not cease until a *crisis* shall have been reached, and passed. 'A house divided against itself cannot stand.' I believe this government cannot endure, permanently half *slave* and half *free*. I do not expect the Union to be *dissolved*—I do not expect the house to *fall*—but I *do* expect it will cease to be divided. Either the *opponents* of slavery will arrest the further spread of it, and place it where the public mind shall rest in the belief that it is in course of ultimate extinction; or its *advocates* will push it forward, till it shall become alike lawful in *all* the States, *old* as well as *new—North* as well as *South*."

Had we no tendency to the latter condition? I warned. Let anyone who doubted it carefully contemplate that now almost complete legal combination—piece of *machinery* so to speak—compounded of the Nebraska doctrine and the Dred Scott decision. If we studied the history of the machinery's construction, we could see the evidence of design, of concert of action. First, I said, there was Judge Douglas's Kansas-Nebraska Act, which opened all the national territories to slavery, and was the first point gained. This was justified by the argument of squatter sovereignty, of the sacred right of self-government, which was perverted to mean just this: that if any *one* man chose to enslave *another*, no *third* man should be allowed to object.

Second, as the Nebraska bill passed through Congress, the Dred Scott case worked its way through the U.S. circuit court in Missouri, and both came to a decision in May of 'fifty-four. Next was Buchanan's inaugural, in which he announced that the U.S. Supreme Court was about to render a decision and that the people must abide by it. In a few days came the Dred Scott decision, which the author of the Nebraska bill endorsed in Springfield, vehemently denouncing all opposition to it. At length a squabble sprang up between the President and the author of the Nebraska bill on the *mere* question of *fact*, whether the Lecompton constitution was or was not, in any just sense, made by the people of Kansas; and in that squabble the author of the Nebraska bill declared that all he wanted was a fair vote for the people, and that he cared not whether slavery be voted *down* or voted *up*.

The several points of the Dred Scott decision, I said, in connection with Senator Douglas's "care not" policy, constituted the piece of machinery in its *present* state of advancement. This was the third point gained. The main working parts of the machinery were, first, that Negroes could not be citizens of the United States; and, second, that neither Congress nor a territorial legislature could exclude slavery from any national territory. The last point was made in order that individual men could fill up the territories with slaves and thus enhance the chances of *permanency* to the institution through all the future. Auxiliary to all this, and working hand in hand with it, the Nebraska doctrine, or what was left of it, and the "don't care" policy were calculated to educate and mold *northern* public opinion to not *care* whether slavery was voted *down* or voted *up*. This, I said, showed exactly where we now were, and partially whither we were tending.

We could not, I admitted, absolutely know that all these exact adaptations were the result of preconcert. But when we saw a lot of framed timbers gathered at different times by different workmen— by Stephen, Franklin, Roger, and James, in reference to Douglas, Pierce, Taney, and Buchanan—and when we saw these timbers joined together to make the frame of a house or a mill, all the tenons and mortises fitting exactly, and all the lengths and proportions of the different pieces exactly adapted to their respective places, we found it impossible to not believe that Stephen and Franklin and Roger and James all understood one another from the beginning and all worked upon a common *plan* or *draft* drawn up before the first lick was struck.

By leaving it an open question as to the constitutional authority of the states to prohibit slavery, I said, the workmen left a nice little niche for the final timber. This was to be *another* Supreme Court decision, declaring that the Constitution did not permit a *state* to exclude slavery from its limits. This could especially be expected, I warned, if the "don't care" doctrine should gain upon the public mind sufficiently to give promise that such a decision could be maintained when made. We would lie down pleasantly dreaming that Missourians were on the verge of making theirs a free state; and we would wake up to the *reality*, instead, that the Supreme Court had made *Illinois* a *slave state*.

To meet and overthrow the conspiracy, I said, was the work now before us. There were those who whispered that Senator Douglas was the aptest instrument with which to effect that object. They reminded us that he was a *very great man* and that the largest of us were very small ones. Let this be granted. But "a *living dog* is better than a *dead lion*." Judge Douglas, if not a dead lion for this work, was at least a *caged* and *toothless* one. "How can he oppose the advances of slavery?" I asked. "He don't *care* anything about it. His avowed *mission is impressing* the 'public heart' to *care* nothing about it. Clearly he is not *now* with us—he does not *pretend* to be—he does not *promise* to *ever* be. Our cause, then, must be intrusted to and conducted by its own undoubted friends—those whose hands are free, whose hearts are in the work—who *do care* for the result. In 1856 the Republicans mustered over thirteen hundred thousand strong, under the single impulse of resistance to a common danger. Of *strange, discordant,* and even *hostile* elements, we gathered from the four winds, and formed and fought the battle through, under the constant hot fire of a disciplined, proud, and pampered enemy. Did we brave all *then,* to *falter* now?—*now*—when that same enemy is wavering, dissevered and belligerent? The result is not doubtful. We shall not fail—if we stand firm, we shall not fail."

29. BROWN

"It's too late to settle the slave question through politics, conventions, or any other peaceful means," I said. It was late winter, and I was pacing back and forth in Gerrit Smith's mansion in Peterboro, New York, with Smith and young Franklin Sanborn listening intently. "There's no recourse left to the black man," I said, "but in God and a massive slave uprising in which the blood of slaveholders will be spilled. This is a terrible thing, but slavery is a terrible wrong, the same as murder, and the unrepentant southerners deserve to be violently punished for their sins."

I stopped and stared at my two friends. "God has raised me to deliver the slaves from Egypt," I said. "It's *His* will that I invade Virginia, the queen of the slave states, and provoke a massive slave rebellion with a guerrilla army I'm now raising. From Virginia we'll sweep southward through the southern mountains in a whirlwind of bullets and bayonets, pikes and axes. The balance of the slave states will nearly conquer themselves, there being such a large number of Negroes in them. To prevent anarchy, I intend to establish a provisional government in the territory we conquer. I've drafted a constitution for such a government." I showed them the document. "As you can see, it provides for a commander-in-chief of the army, a president and vice-president, a supreme court, and a one-house congress."

I told them: "Even if the insurrection fails, it will cause such convulsions that the North and the South cannot remain together in the Union. Southerners will see a northern conspiracy behind it, just as they did behind Nat Turner's slave revolt, and will demand retribution. I believe that even a failed insurrection will cause such a violent quake that the entire temple will come crashing down, and slavery with it. I should then have effected a mighty conquest, like the last victory of Samson."

"It's an amazing proposition," young Sanborn said. "But I've got to admit I have some doubts. The plot is . . . sounds . . . well, rather fantastic. Desperate in character, inadequately planned. And what will the result be for certain?"

"Only through insurrection and war," I said, "can this slave-cursed Republic be restored to the principles of the Declaration of Independence. I for one am ready to die to bring that about."

"Noble sentiments, Captain Brown," he said, "but—"

I interrupted him. "If *God* be for us, who can be against us?" He looked blankly at me. "All right," I said. "I'll carry on without you if you've got no faith in me."

"You leave us only the alternatives of betrayal, desertion, or support," he complained. Smith, a tall, stout man with deteriorating health, just shook his head. Later that afternoon, they went for a walk in the snowy hills to talk my proposition over. I was certain they would come around. Both had made public pronouncements in favor of war—that was why I'd come to them for support. Sanborn had said: "If this country is to have a war over slavery, the forces of freedom will need men like John Brown." And Smith had told a Syracuse paper: "I have opposed the bloody abolition of slavery. But now, when it begins to march its conquering bands into the free states, I and ten thousand other peace men are not only ready to have it repulsed with violence, but pursued even unto death, with violence."

When they returned from their walk, Smith came up to me, rubbing his prominent forehead with his hand. He was nervous and agitated, as always. "We cannot give you up to die alone," he said. "We *will* support you. I'll raise all the money I can for you, and Frank here will lay the case before your friends in Massachusetts—Reverend Parker, Dr. Howe, George Stearns, and Reverend Higginson. I can see no other way."

"Praise God!" I said. "When you look at the ample field I labor in and the rich harvest the entire world will reap from it, you'll be glad you were in on it. I've only had this one opportunity in a life of nearly sixty years, and I may never have another. God has honored but a very small part of mankind with any possible chance for such mighty and soul-satisfying rewards. My friends, I expect nothing but to endure hardship. But I assure you, it *will be* a mighty conquest."

Young Sanborn communicated the enterprise to my Massachusetts friends; and in March I met with all five of them in a Boston hotel: Higginson, the tall, stiff-backed, belligerent clergyman from Worcester; Parker, the coughing, blood-and-thunder Unitarian who'd sided with me in my argument with Garrison; Stearns, the long-bearded merchant who always wore a soft hat and liked to give money to benevolent causes; Sanborn, the ardent, smooth-faced young schoolteacher and secretary of the Massachusetts Kansas Committee; and Dr. Howe, the colorful man of causes who'd fought in the Greek revolution against Turkey. I repeated what I'd told Sanborn and Smith: that I was an instrument in God's hands to invade the South and destroy its wicked institution by the sword. "If the insurrection can hold its ground for a few days," I said, "the whole country from the Potomac to Savannah will be ablaze."

They all liked the proposal. Higginson, tugging at his thick mustache, pointed out that he'd long advocated disunion to get rid of the slavery curse and had predicted that a revolution was coming. Parker said that my plan accorded with his belief in violent resistance, and bearded Dr. Howe, his eyes flashing, reminded us that he'd long called for "some move of actual force" against the Slave Power. As they talked, they showed even greater enthusiasm for my alternative objective—the bringing on of a sectional Armageddon in which slavery would be destroyed. So I stressed that objective.

"Even if the insurrection attempt fails," I said, "it will shake this country to its foundations, divide North and South beyond hope of compromise, and bring on war, gentlemen, a maelstrom of violence in which slavery itself will perish. To atone for the crime of slavery, this entire generation of men, women, and children may well be swept away"

"Yes, yes," Parker said. "You're quite right. Only civil war can settle this matter. I've said so for years." The others nodded in solemn agreement. Ah! these brave reformers *liked* the idea of the United States passing through the ordeal of civil war, of an unrepentant South in flames, in order that the slavery curse might be removed at last. With Smith, they formed a Secret Committee of Six to raise $1,000 for the "experiment" and to serve as my "advisers."

I wanted their *money*; not their advice—I took advice from nobody.

I then traveled across the East talking to black leaders. I'd already confided in my friend, Frederick Douglass, and he'd given me $50 and a list of militant Negroes to contact. The first I saw was Dr. James N. Gloucester of Brooklyn. He liked my plan. "I hope all blacks will join you in holy energy and combat against the *all damnable foe*," he said. In Philadelphia, in the house of Stephen Smith, a Negro lawyer, I described my plan to a group of blacks that included Smith; William Still, one of the great conductors of the Underground Railroad; and one-legged Henry Highland Garnet, the eloquent orator and preacher who'd once exhorted the slaves to revolt.

"Mr. Garnet," I asked, "what do you think of the plan?"

"Sir, the time has not yet come for the success of such a movement."

I disagreed. "The *Liberator* and the black paper, *The Ram's Horn,* both report great slave unrest. When I strike, the bees will swarm. You'll see."

I hastened up to Syracuse to see my black friend, Reverend Jermain W. Loguen, a vigilance committee leader who'd escaped from slavery in Tennessee. He thundered against the fugitive slave law: "I don't respect it, don't fear it, and won't obey it!" When he heard me out, he declared himself ready to fight the man-stealers and agreed to recruit other blacks who would "go to war." *Praise be to God*! I cried. I expected Loguen, Douglass, Still, and Smith to raise a Negro army for the coming revolution.

Loguen took me to St. Catherines, Canada, a haven for escaped slaves, where I sought out Harriet Tubman. She was called "Black Moses" because she'd stolen into the land of Egypt eight times and delivered sixty slaves to freedom. The man-stealers hated Black Moses—Higginson said there was a $12,000 reward for her in Maryland, "and she will probably be burned alive if she is caught." Tall and powerfully built, she was the most of a man naturally I ever met. She had sharp, brilliant eyes and a deep voice, and carried scars on her neck, head, and back from her own days under the lash in Maryland.

"There's a war comin', Mr. Brown," she said. "They can say 'peace' all they like, but I know it's goin' to be war."

"Then you'll like what I've come to tell you," I said, and I confided my plan in full. She hooked on her whole team at once, promising to do "missionary work" for me among the thousand fugitives in St. Catherines, and then join me in the South when I gave the signal.

"There is abundant material, and of the right quality, in this quarter, beyond all doubt," I told my son John Jr. I issued a call for black leaders to meet me in a secret convention at Chatham, Canada, about forty miles above Detroit, where I would complete my preparations. Then I would strike.

Our secret convention took place in the spring of 'fifty-eight, in the engine house of a black fire-fighting company. In addition to my twelve recruits, thirty-six Negro delegates showed up. I was greatly disappointed that Douglass and Loguen were not there. Of the Negro delegates, the most promising for my purposes was free-born Martin Delany, an editor and abolitionist orator who had studied medicine at Harvard, worked with Douglass on the *North Star*, and now championed colonization for American Negroes, on the grounds that America was too Negrophobic for blacks to live there in the freedom they deserved. He was a proud, articulate, baldish man with a trimmed mustache and piercing black eyes.

"Captain Brown," Delany said. "Would you state your objectives?"

I rose and faced the convention. "For twenty or thirty years it has been my greatest and principal object to liberate the slaves. Gradually a plan formed in my mind for mountain warfare in the South. To prepare myself, I studied the Spartacus gladiator revolt against the Romans, Toussaint-Louverture's slave war on Santo Domingo in the seventeen nineties, and Nat Turner's revolt in Virginia. I consider Nat Turner a great American hero, greater than George Washington. As I studied these uprisings, a plan of action emerged spontaneously in my mind. I went to Kansas to gain a footing for the furtherance of this matter, and from then on I've devoted my whole being, mental, moral, and physical, all that I have and am to the extinction of slavery. I'm convinced that southern slaves are ripe for rebellion. At the first sign of a leader, they'll immediately rise all over the southern states. Gentlemen, *I* am that leader. My company—twelve of them are standing beside me now—will invade Virginia, in the region of the Blue Ridge mountains, and march into Tennessee and northern Alabama, where the slaves will swarm to us. We'll then wage war upon the plantations on the plains west and east of the mountains, which will serve as our base of operations."

"But what if troops are brought against you?" asked one of the delegates.

I waved the question away. "A small force trained in guerrilla warfare can easily defend those Thermopylae ravines against southern militia and the U.S. Army. I expect thousands of free Negroes in the northern states to join me once the invasion begins."

I then read the constitution that would create the new provisional government once the slaves were freed, with me as commander-in-chief and my most trusted recruit, John Henry Kagi, as secretary of war. The preamble of my constitution declared *war* against slavery because slavery was a perpetual *state of war* against black people. After considerable debate over the constitution, Delany and the other delegates approved and signed it unanimously. Some of the blacks then joined me in singing, *Go down, Moses, way down in Egypt land. Tell ole Pharaoh, to let my people go.*

I felt the presence of Jehovah. Truly the days of vengeance were at hand. *For I am the Lord thy God. I will punish this land for its evil, and the wicked for their iniquity. I will put an end to the pride of the arrogant, and lay low the haughtiness of the ruthless. I will send upon them the sword. The destroyer is on his way. Shall I not visit for these* things? *saith the Lord; shall not my soul be avenged on such a nation as this*? Yes, I cried, Lord God, yes. *I* am your destroyer, *I* am your sword of vengeance. *I* will make the whole land desolate and lay waste to the cities until not an inhabitant is left.

But just as I was ready to move, God in His inscrutable wisdom placed thorns in my path. Loguen reported that Negroes who would go to war did not have the money "to get there with," and he'd decided to "let them all rest for the present." I was also nailed down for want of funds—so far the Six had sent me only about $600, and the money had melted away in expenses. Meanwhile Hugh Forbes, the flighty drillmaster I'd enlisted for my flock of sheep, defected, went to Washington, and told what he knew about the conspiracy to several Republican politicians. The Secret Six were scandalized. "Wilson as well as Hale and Seward, and God knows how many more, have heard about the plot," wailed Dr. Howe. Of the Six, only the fighting Higginson wanted to go ahead. In a perfect panic, the other five voted to send me back to Kansas until things cooled off. They offered me an additional $2,000 or $3,000 as an inducement. Complaining bitterly about their cowardice, I stored my "tools" in a secret hideaway in Ohio and returned to the territory under a new alias, "Shubel Morgan."

In Lawrence that summer, free-state men were talking about the defeat of the Lecompton constitution and praising Douglas for breaking with the wicked Administration over the Lecompton swindle. Douglas was no hero! I cried. He was a monster, a vicious slave-owner himself, a ranting hypocrite with the blood of the innocent on his hands! But I really cared nothing about politics in this foul and loathsome country. We were way beyond politics! I was impatient and frustrated to get on with my great work, my mission. I felt like an avenging angel whose wings were nailed to the ground. But not for long! I kept hearing Jehovah calling me to Virginia, calling me to break the jaws of the wicked. In the Whitney House in Lawrence, I told the New York *Tribune* correspondent: "We have reached a point where nothing but war can settle the question. Don't let the present lull deceive you. It's a treacherous lull before the storm. We're on the eve of one of the greatest wars in history, and I for one am not going to sheathe my sword until the war is over."

30. DOUGLAS

I was still in Washington when Lincoln was nominated to be my Republican opponent and made his "house divided" speech, which was published in the New York *Tribune* under the headline, "Republican principles." That speech was a dangerous call for civil war, and I intended to make the most of it when I returned to Illinois. I had it on good authority that Greeley and other eastern Republicans were furious at the Illinois leaders because they had refused to endorse the Little Giant. But I speak frankly: I didn't give a Goddamn what the state Republican organization did. However, I did expect to pick up support from rank-and-file Republicans who considered Lincoln too radical, and who applauded my stand against the Lecompton monstrosity.

Don't get me wrong: I respected Lincoln as a campaigner. "I'll have my hands full," I told a fellow Democrat. "He's the strong man of the party—full of wit, facts, dates—and the best stump speaker, with his droll ways and dry jokes, in the West. He's as honest as he is shrewd, and if I beat him my victory will be hardly won."

Lincoln may have been honest, but his party was not above forming an unscrupulous alliance with the Buchaneer Democrats in Illinois. Buchanan, the vindictive shit, had set up a rival organization there and was pouring money into it. He was also putting pressure

on the state's Democratic papers to turn against me and was ruthlessly purging Douglas officeholders in Illinois. But I didn't lose sleep
because the Buchaneers and the Black Republicans had joined forces
against me. I vowed to whip the Goddamned bastards in the hardest
and fiercest campaign they would ever see.

On the day Adele and I left for Illinois, Buchanan sent an emis-
sary to the depot to negotiate a reconciliation with me, on the condition that I show "repentance" and support the English bill unequivocally. That craven measure—congressional interference with a bribe,
I called it—was anathema to me, and I had no intention of endorsing
it or showing repentance. The *Washington Union*, however, tem-
porarily suspended its editorial crusade against me, probably to see
if I would come around.

On the train ride back to Illinois, I was gratified by the huge
crowds that greeted us at every stop. Party officials came to my car
and thanked me effusively for my battle against the Lecompton-
Buchanan swindle. When we reached Illinois, the people turned out
to cheer us in some of the largest and most frenzied demonstrations
of affection I have ever seen. So spoke the people! It was an expression of their devotion to that great principle of self-government to
which I had devoted my life, and which had been so violently abused
by Buchanan and his gang. It was also proof that the battle against
Lecompton had restored my popularity with the Illinois voters.

A reception committee of four hundred Chicago Democrats had
met us at Michigan City, Indiana, and escorted us around the lake to
Chicago, which we reached early on a warm July evening. It was the
greatest homecoming of my career. When we pulled into the depot, a
battery fired a 150-gun salute. Colorful streamers, banners, and flags
draped every building in sight. A six-horse carriage took Adele and me
to the Tremont House for an official welcome by a crowd estimated at
thirty thousand. Across the street hung a huge transparency that read:
"WELCOME TO STEPHEN A. DOUGLAS, THE DEFENDER OF
POPULAR SOVEREIGNTY." The people applauded and shouted my
name in near delirium as we entered the hotel and made our way to
the balcony, where I intended to answer Lincoln's "house divided"
speech and also send a message to Buchanan that I remained defiant
and unrepentant.

Told that Lincoln was in the crowd, I invited him to join me on
the balcony. And he did so, taking a seat just inside the window
behind me. I noticed that his nomination for Senator had not
improved his dress: he wore a dusty stovepipe hat and a loose-fitting

black suit; his trousers were so short they revealed the tops of his rusty boots.

I spoke without notes. Having gone without sleep for forty-eight hours, I was tired, and my voice, which was usually clear, deep, and strong, sounded hoarse. But the crowd got into my extemporaneous remarks, interrupting me again and again with thunderous applause and shouts of "Yes," "Yes," "That's right!" "Hit him again!"

I told them that the victory over Lecompton vindicated popular sovereignty and made it triumphant in the land, and I thanked congressional Republicans for coming up manfully and sustaining that principle. Why had I opposed the Lecompton fraud? Solely because it violated the great principle of self-government. The *right* or *wrong* of the constitution, I said, had nothing to do with it. That document was not the act and deed of the people of Kansas, did not embody their will; they were averse to it; and hence I denied the right of Congress to force it upon them. I denied the right of Congress to force a slaveholding state or a free state upon an unwilling people. The great principle, I said, is the right of every community to decide for itself whether a thing is right or wrong, whether it would be good or evil for them. It was no answer to this argument, I said for Lincoln's benefit, to say that slavery was an evil and hence should not be tolerated. You must allow the people to decide that for themselves.

As for Lincoln, I said I took great pleasure in having known, personally and intimately, for about a quarter of a century, that worthy gentleman who had been nominated for my place; I regarded him as a kind, amiable, and intelligent gentleman, a good citizen, and an honorable opponent, and whatever issue I had with him was based on principle, not personalities.

I ignored his preposterous charge of "conspiracy" and focused on the two distinct propositions laid down in his nomination speech. His first and main proposition, to use his own language, Scripture quotation and all, was that "A House divided against itself cannot stand." In that passage, I said, he advocated a war of sections, a war of the North against the South, of the free states against the slave states—a war of extermination—to be continued relentlessly until the one or the other was subdued and all the states had either become free or become slave.

I took bold, unqualified issue with him upon that principle. I asserted that it was neither desirable nor possible that there should be uniformity in the local institutions and domestic regulations of the different states. The framers of our government, I pointed out, never contemplated uniformity in its internal concerns. The fathers of the Revolution and the sages who made the Constitution well understood that the laws and domestic institutions which would suit the granite hills of New Hampshire would be totally unfit for the rice plantations of South Carolina; they well understood that the great differences in a republic as large as ours required different local and domestic regulations in each locality, adapted to the wants and interests of each separate state, and for that reason it was provided in the Federal Constitution that the states should remain sovereign and supreme within their own limits in regard to all that was local and internal and domestic.

Lincoln, I said, had totally misapprehended the great principles upon which our government rested. His insistence on uniformity in local and domestic affairs would be destructive of state rights and state sovereignty, of personal liberty and freedom. Uniformity, I reminded my listeners, was the parent of despotism. It would convert these thirty-two sovereign, independent states into one consolidated empire, with the uniformity of despotism reigning triumphantly throughout the length and the breadth of the land.

The other proposition in Lincoln's speech, I said, constituted a crusade against the Supreme Court on account of the Dred Scott decision. I took direct and distinct issue with him for making war on the court. The right and the province of expounding the Constitution, and construing the law, is vested in the highest tribunal in the country, and its decision must be obeyed until it has been reversed by an equally high authority. Unlike Lincoln, I respected and obeyed the decisions of that august tribunal.

The second reason Lincoln objected to the Dred Scott decision, I said, was because it denied Negroes the right to be citizens of the United States. He claimed this was wrong. He thought the Negro ought to have the rights of citizenship. Well, I took issue with him on that. I was not for Negro citizenship, I said. In my opinion this government of ours was founded on the white basis. It was made by the white man, for the white man, to be administered by white men. (There was great cheering at this.)

Over a crescendo of shouts and applause, I cried in a strained voice: "Thus you see, my fellow-citizens, that the issues between Mr. Lincoln and myself are direct, unequivocal, and irreconcilable. He goes for uniformity in our domestic institutions, for a war of sections, until one or the other shall be subdued. I go for the great principle of the Kansas-Nebraska Act, the right of the people to decide for themselves." The applause was so frenzied and deafening that I had to stop speaking. Probably thinking I was done, somebody exploded a chain of fireworks. Rockets shot into the sky. A band struck up "Yankee Doodle." When it finished, I quieted the throng long enough to complete my remarks. "Lincoln goes for Negro citizenship and equality with the white man. I am opposed to Negro equality. I want to preserve not only the purity of the blood, but the purity of the government from any mixture or amalgamation with inferior races." The crowd roared its approval.

In closing, I said that the Republican leaders had formed an unholy, unnatural alliance with the Buchaneer Democrats and that I intended to fight that allied army wherever I met it. "These men," I cried, "who are trying to divide the Democratic party for the purpose of electing a Republican Senator in my place, are just as much the agents, the tools, the supporters of Mr. Lincoln as if they were avowed Republicans. I shall deal with these allied forces just as the Russians dealt with the allies at Sebastopol. The Russians, when they fired a broadside, did not stop to inquire whether it hit a Frenchman, an Englishman, or a Turk"—the audience roared with laughter—"nor will I stop to inquire whether my blows hit the Republican leaders or their allies."

As I sat down, exhausted, the multitude clapped and chanted: "Douglas! Douglas!" "More! More!" At one street corner, a display of fireworks went off, spelling with blazing letters: "POPULAR SOVEREIGNTY."

It was, I felt, a successful start to a grueling, four-month campaign. As I expected, the *Washington Union* now resumed its bitter editorial attack against me. John Heiss, editor of the *Washington States*, wrote me that Buchanan had personally ordered the articles drumming me out of the party. "He hates you in the most bitter and unrelenting manner," Heiss said. The President even sent out that slimy turd Slidell to sow disaffection in Chicago and help orchestrate the Buchaneer campaign against me. Attorney General Black let it be known that my reelection would "do more injury to the Democratic cause than an abolitionist would have it in his power to do."

Black and Buchanan could go to hell. I told my aides to strap on their Goddamned armor. We were going to *war*.

31 · LINCOLN

The Judge took nothing by his speech in Chicago. In fact, his rampant endorsement of the Dred Scott decision drove back those few Republicans who were favorably inclined toward him. His tactic now was to make it appear that he was having a triumphal entry into and march through the country; but it was all as bombastic and hollow as Napoleon's bulletins sent back from his campaign in Russia.

The Judge's reception at the Tremont House was large and boisterous, but not as large as the Democratic press claimed: the number of people was more like twelve thousand, not thirty thousand. After Douglas left the balcony, Republicans in the audience cried "Lincoln!" "Lincoln!" "Lincoln!" with such gusto that I really believe we could have voted Douglas down in that very crowd.

I answered Judge Douglas the following night, speaking from the same balcony, before a Republican throng that was nearly as large as his and five times as enthusiastic. First, I denied that we had formed an alliance with the Buchanan Democrats, denied that our party had compromised its principles. Second, I denied that I was in favor of making war by the North upon the South for the extinction of slavery. "If you'll read that passage over," I said, referring to the "house divided" segment of my nomination speech, "you'll find that I did not say I was in favor of anything. I only said what I expected would take place. I made a prediction only—it may have been a foolish one perhaps. I did not even say that I desired that slavery should be put in the course of ultimate extinction. I *do* say so now, however." There was a burst of applause, shouts, and laughter.

Judge Douglas, I said, gave himself credit for defeating the Lecompton constitution. Who really defeated it? "He furnished himself," I said, "and if you suppose he controlled the other Senate Democrats that went with him, he furnished *three* votes, while the Republicans furnished *twenty*. In the House of Representatives he and his friends furnished some twenty votes, and the Republicans furnished *ninety odd*. Now *who* was it that did the work?" The audience roared back, "*the Republicans*," and cheered wildly.

I was not, I went on, unaware that this government had endured eighty-two years, half slave and half free. I believed it had so endured because, until the introduction of the Nebraska bill, the public mind rested in the belief that slavery was in the course of ultimate extinction. That brought cries of "Good!" "Good!" and loud applause. I went on: "I've always *hated slavery*, I think as much as any abolitionist. I've always hated it, but I've always been quiet about it until this new era began with the introduction of the Nebraska bill." What I wanted—what the Republicans wanted—was to place slavery *back* on the course of ultimate extinction, where those old-time men, the founders of this government, had originally placed it.

This did *not* mean that I desired uniformity of institutions or a general consolidation of all the local institutions of the various states. How on earth, I asked, could any man draw such an inference from anything I had said? "I've said, very many times, in Judge Douglas's hearing, that no man believed more than I did in the principle of self-government. I believe each individual is naturally entitled to do as he pleases with himself and the fruit of his labor, so far as it in no wise interferes with any other man's rights—that each community, as a state, has a right to do exactly as it pleases with all the concerns within that state that interfere with the rights of no other state. I've said, as an illustration, that I do not believe in the right of Illinois to interfere with the cranberry laws of Indiana, the oyster laws of Virginia, or the liquor laws of Maine."

Slavery, however, was not "an exceedingly little thing" on a level with such laws. It was not, as Douglas would have us believe, something having no moral question to it, something equal to the question of whether a man shall pasture his land with cattle, or plant it with tobacco. Slavery, I said, involved keeping one-sixth of the population of the whole nation in a state of oppression and tyranny unequaled in the world; and a great portion of the American people looked upon it, not as a *little* thing, but as *a vast moral evil* that ought to be restricted and ultimately vanquished.

I took up Douglas's most vicious tactic against us Republicans: his repeated charges of our inclination to marry with and hug Negroes, his declarations of Black Republicanism. The Judge, I said, regaled us with the terrible enormities that take place by the mixture of races; that the inferior bears the superior down. "Why, Judge," I said, "if we don't let them get together in the territories they won't mix there."

The Judge, I said, argued that the idea of equality in the Declaration did not include Negroes. How was that? Did it not declare that all men are equal upon principle? "If we make exceptions to this old Declaration of Independence," I said, "where will it stop? If one man says it doesn't mean a Negro, another can say it doesn't mean some other man. If we can't give freedom to every creature, let it be as nearly reached as it can. If we can't give freedom to every creature, let us do nothing that will impose slavery upon any other creature."

I closed with an appeal: "Let us discard all this quibbling about this man and the other man—this race and that race and the other race being inferior, and therefore they must be placed in an inferior position. Let us discard all these things, and unite as one people throughout this land, until we shall once more stand up declaring that all men are created equal. . . . I leave you, hoping that the lamp of liberty will burn in your bosoms until there shall no longer be doubt of the truth of that old standard."

Gusts of applause and cheers rose from that fiercely responsive crowd. Their candidate, crowed the Chicago *Press and Tribune*, had "knocked Douglas higher than a kite." The Douglas papers, of course, contended that it was the *Republican* nominee who had been kayoed. One thing was certain: Douglas and I had caught the attention of the East. The *New York Times* declared that "Illinois is from this time forward, until the senatorial question shall be decided, the most interesting political battle-ground in the Union."

I remained in Chicago for several days, planning strategy with members of the Republican State Central Committee and studying maps of the state. We conceded southern Illinois—Little Egypt, where men took their Democratic politics as straight as they took their whiskey—to Judge Douglas. We had a pretty solid claim on northern Illinois, whose settlers had come mostly from the Northeast. The question mark—the area that would decide the outcome—was central Illinois, whose inhabitants had southern and northern backgrounds. We all agreed that I and an army of surrogate speakers would concentrate our energies in Sangamon, Macon, Coles, and adjacent counties of central Illinois. We also agreed that I should ride Douglas's coattails, speaking in the same towns that he did. The committee cautioned me, above all, not to let Douglas put me on the defensive.

In mid-July, Douglas set out for Bloomington and Springfield on the Illinois Central with an army of reporters. I had gone home to Springfield for a day and intercepted the Judge in Bloomington on the evening of the sixteenth. He spoke in the public square, giving pretty much a repetition of his Chicago talk with one added point: he reiterated the doctrine of "unfriendly legislation" for the benefit of Free-Soil Illinois. This was the dubious doctrine, first propounded by the Judge in the wake of the Dred Scott decision, that the people of a territory could drive slavery out by withholding the police measures and slave codes necessary for it to exist. There were cries for Lincoln to speak, but I declined. "This meeting was called by the friends of Judge Douglas," I said from the platform, "and it would be improper for me to address it."

The next day, the Judge's entourage moved on to nearby Atlanta. Douglas rode in luxury in his own private car, attended by his pretty young wife and a retinue of aides, stenographers, and party bigwigs. The car belonged to George B. McClellan, vice-president of the Illinois Central and a stout Douglas supporter. A flatcar on the train held a brass cannon named "Popular Sovereignty." When the train neared a prairie town, a couple of young Douglas supporters would fire the damned thing off, announcing the arrival of his imperial majesty.

I rode on the same train as the great man, traveling by myself in a public coach, my old carpetbag sitting in my lap as the Illinois prairie slid backward in the windows of the coach. I didn't complain that Judge Douglas was richer and more famous than I and enjoyed luxuries commensurate with his fame. Not that I'm unambitious. I've never professed an indifference to the honors of official station; and were I to do so, I should only make myself ridiculous. But in 'fifty-eight the triumph of the Republican cause was more important to me than personal success. "*We* have to fight this battle upon principle, and principle alone," I maintained. As the train rocked southward, trailing a plume of black smoke, I turned an idea around in my head. It was that the higher object of this contest—the ultimate extinction of slavery—might not be completely attained within the term of my natural life.

I heard the Judge address a Democratic meeting in Atlanta, then followed him down to Springfield, where he was scheduled to speak in the afternoon at a grove north of town. It had rained heavily, ruining the elaborate decorations, but there was a big turnout for Douglas despite the mud. Republicans circulated in the grove, giving out handbills announcing that I would answer Douglas the following night in the statehouse. The Democrats griped about our strategy, charging that Lincoln followed after Douglas because he couldn't get up his own crowds.

I left the train and headed into town, striding across a steaming field with the tail of my coat flying in the wind. I had to write my own speech and consequently didn't hear what Douglas said. But I read it in the papers next day. For the first time, he addressed the conspiracy charge, denying that he'd ever entered into "political intrigues for partisan purposes." He also rode the color issue for all it was worth, arguing once again that Lincoln lusted for Negro equality. I hated that kind of demagoguery, but it was damned effective because it threw me on the defensive in my own speech the following night.

I hurried back to Chicago to confer with the Republican State Central Committee and other party leaders. Despite the criticism that I was riding on Douglas's back, the committee urged me to stick with the Judge and hit him hard. "Be more aggressive," they kept telling me. "Put *him* on the defensive." We came up with a good idea how I could do that: by confronting Douglas in open debate before the same audiences. Committee Chairman Judd took the offer to Douglas, who was back in Chicago. We asked for fifty official debates around the state. Frankly, I doubted that Douglas would take the bait. He had nothing to gain by it and everything to lose.

To my surprise, he accepted. His pride and competitive instinct, I suppose, got the better of his judgment. But he set the rules, stipulating that we meet only seven times—in the convention towns of each congressional district—and that he would have four openings and rebuttals to my three. My friends complained bitterly. "The little dodger shirks and backs out except for a few places *he* selects," they said. "And he gets to talk more than you do. It's damned unfair." Maybe so, but it was better than my following him around the state, hanging on to his coattails. This way we would stand as equals. I sent Douglas a letter accepting his terms.

A number of Republicans wanted me to nail Douglas to the wall on the contradiction between popular sovereignty and the Dred Scott decision. If he replied with the unfriendly legislation argument, they contended, he would trap himself since the South would not accept this "mere barren right." I appreciated the point, but stressed that Douglas cared nothing about the South—he knew he was already dead there. He only leaned southward now to keep the Buchanan party from growing in Illinois. It would be hard work, I said, to get him directly to the point whether a territorial legislature had or had not the power to exclude slavery. But if we succeeded in getting him there, he would be compelled to say that it possessed no such power, in light of the Dred Scott decision. Then he would instantly take the ground he'd taken at Bloomington: that slavery could not actually exist in the territories, unless the people desired it and gave it protective legislation. If this offended the South, I said, he would let it offend them, as at all events he meant to hold on to his chances in Illinois.

There was a better way, I believed, to trap Douglas and hurt him in Free-Soil Illinois. During the debates on the Nebraska bill, Chase had offered an amendment expressly authorizing the people of a territory to exclude slavery. Douglas, we discovered, voted *against the amendment,* which went down to defeat. This revealed Douglas's true position: he *favored* slavery in the territories. He was *part* of the conspiracy, the original combination, to make slavery national and universal. I meant to hit Douglas with the Chase amendment in our first debate, which was scheduled for August twenty-first, at Ottawa.

32. DOUGLAS

When Judd brought me the offer to debate Lincoln, I was furious at the Goddamned bastards for holding off until my speaking schedule was filled with commitments. "Between you and me," I told my aides, "I don't want to go into this debate. The whole country knows me and has me measured. Lincoln, compared to me, is unknown, and if he gets the best of this debate—and I want to say he's the ablest man the Republicans have got—I'll lose everything. Should I win I gain but little."

But I'd never turned down a challenge in my life. I told myself I could beat Lincoln in open debate even if it did put a strain on my schedule. Goddamn it, I was the Little Giant of the Democratic party! Had I not dueled with the leading men of the country in the national Senate? Was I not, as even the Republicans conceded, "the very embodiment of force, combativeness, and staying power"? So I accepted Lincoln's offer and never gave it a moment's doubt. Hell, I plunged into the campaign like a human tornado. In four months, I not only debated Lincoln seven times, but gave a total of 130 speeches and traveled more than 5,200 miles by railroad, carriage, and steamboat. I defy you to name any man who ever campaigned harder to get his principles before the people.

Before the first debate at Ottawa, Lyman Trumbull came back

from Washington and gave a rabble-rousing speech at Chicago in which he accused me of violating my own principle of popular sovereignty. Before a roaring crowd of Black Republican fanatics, Trumbull claimed that the Toombs enabling bill of 'fifty-six had provided for a popular vote on any constitution framed in the new Kansas Territory, and that I had voted against the measure, which was defeated. See, he cried, this was Judge Douglas's true position, not his subsequent and "deceitful" opposition to Lecompton. "It was the most damnable effrontery that man ever put on," Trumbull cried, "to concoct a scheme to defraud and cheat a people of their right, and then claim credit for it."

Such reckless slander enraged me. "Trumbull is a Goddamned liar!" I said at Beardstown. "The miserable, craven-hearted wretch, he would rather have both ears cut off than use that language in my presence, where I could call him to account." And Lincoln, too, was a Goddamned liar, a coward, a wretch, and a sneak, because he persisted in accusing me of complicity in some fantastic conspiracy to nationalize slavery.

I would show these Black Republicans. I would throw the conspiracy charge back in their Goddamned faces. I vaguely recalled some radical platform adopted by the Illinois Republicans back in 'fifty-four. I wrote Charley Lamphier, editor of the *Illinois State Register*, asking him to search his files for evidence of such a meeting. Back came his answer: yes, there had been a convention of abolitionists and radical Republicans that year, in Springfield. Lamphier furnished me with the resolutions adopted by that meeting, which became the basis of Lincoln's and Trumbull's Republican party. The resolutions were political dynamite. I intended to explode them in Lincoln's face in our first debate, at Ottawa.

Ottawa was located seventy miles southwest of Chicago and was considered to be a Republican stronghold—the county had gone for Frémont in 'fifty-six. Even so, I was impressed with the reception I received. On the day of the debate, August twenty-first, an elegant four-horse carriage, provided by the Douglas reception committee, carried me into Ottawa to the cheers of a flag-waving multitude. In the center of town, two twelve-pound brass cannon announced my arrival with thunderous salutes. In celebration of the occasion, flags, banners, and streamers fluttered at every corner. Bands played, military units paraded noisily, and peddlers hawked their wares, adding to the general hubbub. Thousands of people came streaming in from the surrounding counties by foot, horseback, covered wagon, hay cart, and carriage. They stirred up so much dust that it swirled through the streets and avenues in thick clouds that obscured the sun. By debate time, some twelve thousand people, undaunted by the sweltering heat, encircled a lumber platform in the public square, where Lincoln and I were to speak. Several times, the surge of people nearly forced us and the reporters off the platform.

During the introductions, I glanced over at Lincoln. He looked nervous as hell. He had reason to be. Dressed in a manner befitting a United States Senator and presidential candidate, I wore a ruffled shirt, a well-cut, carefully brushed blue coat with shiny buttons, light trousers, and polished shoes, plus a wide-brimmed white felt hat. Lincoln, by contrast, had on the same frayed suit and battered stovepipe hat he'd worn at Chicago. His coat sleeves and baggy trousers were too short for his long limbs. Compared to me, he looked like a Goddamned hick.

Facing that great sea of faces, I opened the debate with an all-out attack. In 1854, I said, Mr. Abraham Lincoln and Mr. Lyman Trumbull entered into an arrangement, one with the other, and each with his respective friends, to dissolve the old Whig party and to dissolve the old Democratic party in Illinois, and to connect the members of both into an abolition party under the name and disguise of the Republican party. Lincoln's job was to abolitionize the old Whig party all over the state and transfer them over to radical abolitionists Giddings, Chase, and the nigger Fred Douglass. Trumbull's job was to do the same with the Democrats. In pursuance of their arrangement, the parties met at Springfield, in October of 'fifty-four, and adopted an extremist platform for their new Republican party. That platform pledged the new party of Lincoln and Trumbull to the following purposes, and I quoted: "to restore Nebraska and Kansas to the position of free territories; to repeal and entirely abrogate the fugitive slave law; to restrict slavery to those states in which it exists; to prohibit the admission of any more slave states; to abolish slavery in the District of Columbia; and to exclude slavery from the territories." Now, gentlemen, I cried, your Black Republicans cheered every one of those propositions.

Then I hit Lincoln with a series of aggressive questions. "I desire to know whether Mr. Lincoln today stands, as he did in 'fifty-four, in favor of the unconditional repeal of the fugitive slave law; against the admission of any more slave states, even if the people want them; against the admission of a new state with such a constitution as the people of that state may see fit to make. I want to know whether he stands today, as he did in 'fifty-four, pledged to the abolition of slavery in the District of Columbia; to the prohibition of the domestic slave trade; and to the prohibition of slavery in the territories. I want his answer to these questions. I ask him to answer them in order that when I trot him down to lower Egypt I may put the same questions to him." If he answered in the affirmative down there, of course, the people would hoot him off the Goddamned platform.

Next I pointed out that *I* was on the side of the founding fathers, not Lincoln. He claimed that this government could not endure permanently divided into free and slave states, and that the framers of our government felt the same way. He was wrong. Washington, Jefferson, Franklin, Madison, Hamilton, and the great men of that day made this government divided into free and slave states, and left each state perfectly free to do as it pleased on the subject of slavery. Why could this country not exist permanently divided into free and slave states? Why could it not remain on the same basis as our fathers made it? I warned that this new house-divided doctrine preached by Lincoln and his party would dissolve the Union if it succeeded. They were trying to array all the northern states in one body against the South, to excite a sectional war between the free and slave states, in order that the one or the other may be driven to the wall.

Then I assailed Lincoln where he was most vulnerable in Illinois: his beliefs about nigger equality. The vast majority of Illinoisans held niggers in contempt, thought them an inferior race, and were horrified by the very idea of nigger citizenship and equality. I intended to crucify Lincoln on the nigger equality issue. "Mr. Lincoln," I said, "following the example and lead of all the little abolition orators, reads from the Declaration of Independence, that all men are created equal, and then asks how can you deprive a Negro of that equality which God and the Declaration of Independence award to him? He and the abolitionists maintain that Negro equality is guaranteed by the laws of God, and that it is asserted in the Declaration. I don't question Mr. Lincoln's conscientious belief that the Negro was made his equal, and hence is his brother"—there was much laughter at that—"but for my own part, I don't regard the Negro as my equal, and positively deny that he's my brother or any kin to me whatever. Mr. Lincoln, however, holds that the Negro was born his equal and yours, and that he was endowed with equality by the Almighty. Now, I do not believe that the Almighty ever intended the Negro to be the equal of the white man."

"Never, never!" the crowd chanted.

"For thousands of years the Negro has been a race upon the earth, and during all that time, in all latitudes and climates, wherever he's wandered or been taken, he's been inferior to the race which he's met there. He belongs to an inferior race, and must always occupy an inferior position."

"Good," "That's so," voices cried.

Now I did not, I said, hold that because the Negro was the inferior of the white man, that therefore he ought to be a slave. That was a matter for each community to decide. In Illinois, we provided that he not be a slave, and we also provided that he not be a citizen; we protected him in his civil rights, in his life, his person, and his property, but deprived him of all political rights whatsoever, and refused to put him on an equality with white men. I liked and endorsed that arrangement because it was the principle of popular sovereignty at work. I held that Illinois had a right to abolish and prohibit slavery, and I also held that Kentucky had the same right to continue and protect slavery.

I turned the platform over to Lincoln, who stepped to the front in his pigeon-toed, flat-footed gait. He appeared to be dazed and confused as he fumbled with his papers. Lamphier thought that Lincoln had expected a *defensive* speech from me and had shaped his own as a response to that. He was completely unprepared for what I gave him: "a fire in front, rear and on both flanks."

Thrown on the defensive, he denied that he and Trumbull had formed an alliance to sell out and abolitionize the Whig and Democratic parties. To prove what he believed at the time, he took out his spectacles—"I'm not a young man," he apologized to the crowd— and proceeded to read long, boring extracts from his Peoria address of 'fifty-four, which, of course, did not disprove my charge. He did grant southerners legislation for reclaiming their runaways and did admit that he would leave slavery alone where it already existed, but otherwise he would not, *dared* not, answer the questions I had put to him.

Lincoln looked stiff, unsure of himself. His voice had a nervous edge to it, making it higher pitched than usual. As he spoke, he gestured awkwardly, swinging his long arms this way and that. To stress a point, he bent down with a jerk and then thrust himself straight up to his tiptoes. Now and then, when he glanced my way, his little gray eyes flashed with anger.

I had to chuckle when he attempted to explain away his views on niggers. It was a pleasure to see him squirm before that white audience. "I have no purpose," he said shrilly, "to introduce political and social equality between the white and the black races. There's a physical difference between the two, which in my judgment will probably forever forbid their living together upon the footing of perfect equality, and inasmuch as it becomes a necessity that there must be a difference, I, as well as Judge Douglas, am in favor of the race to which I belong, having the superior position." I glowed with satisfaction. I had made *him* agree with *me*.

But then he turned about and stuck his foot in his own trap, by spouting the exact radical abolitionist doctrine I had charged him with embracing in 'fifty-four. "But I hold that notwithstanding all this, there's no reason in the world why the Negro is not entitled to all the natural rights enumerated in the Declaration of Independence. In the right to eat the bread which his own hand earns, the Negro is my equal and the equal of Judge Douglas, and the equal of every living man." I looked out over the huge audience; few were applauding Lincoln for espousing such extremist views.

About twenty minutes into his speech, Lincoln turned to the timekeeper and asked how much time he had left. "An hour and ten minutes," said the timekeeper. "He's *rattled*," my Democratic host whispered into my ear. I nodded in agreement. Lamely Lincoln tried to take the offensive, dredging up once again the argument that I was part of a conspiracy to perpetuate and nationalize slavery. "I know the Judge is a *great* man, while I am only a *small* man"—finally, a truthful remark!—"but *I feel that I have got him* on the conspiracy. Does his broad answer denying all knowledge, information, or belief, disturb the fact? It can only show that he was used by conspirators, and was not a leader of them. I don't say that I know such a conspiracy to exist, but I believe it." That statement had us all laughing. He had no *evidence* of such a conspiracy, yet he *believed* it existed! What Goddamned nonsense! Nobody in Illinois was going to buy that! At some point in his speech, talking about niggers, he said that "anything that argues me into his idea of perfect social and political equality with the Negro, is but a specious and fantastic arrangement of words, by which a man can prove a horse chestnut to be a chestnut horse." But it was Lincoln, on this conspiracy business, who was trying to prove a horse chestnut to be a chestnut horse.

He closed with a new charge involving yet another amendment to the Kansas-Nebraska bill. These Black Republicans and their amendments! I just shook my head. Chase, Lincoln announced, had offered an amendment "under which the people of the territory, through their proper representatives, might, if they saw fit, prohibit the existence of slavery therein." Lincoln looked up at the crowd, then proceeded to read while bobbing up and down and sidewise. "And now I state as a fact, to be taken back if there's any mistake about it, that Judge Douglas and those acting with him, voted that amendment down." I scribbled a reply to that. Lincoln then charged that we Democrats had voted the amendment down to create a niche for the Dred Scott decision, which, of course, was part of the conspiracy in *his mind* to nationalize slavery.

During my rebuttal, Lincoln repeatedly tried to interrupt me, which showed how desperate he was. His denial of a conspiracy to abolitionize the Whigs and Democrats, I said, was a miserable quibble. As for his own conspiracy charge, I proved it to be historically false and a lie. At the time of the Kansas-Nebraska Act, I pointed out, Buchanan was in London as the American minister to Britain. How, then, could he have been part of any conspiracy in this country? Moreover, the Dred Scott case was not even on the court docket at the time of the Kansas-Nebraska Act, so how could the judges of the court have been part of the fanciful plot in Lincoln's imagination? Lincoln's charge, I said, was an unpardonable presumption, without fact and without truth, and showed that he lacked integrity.

Finally, I answered his newest charge. "Mr. Lincoln wants to know why I voted against Chase's amendment to the Nebraska bill. I'll tell him. In the first place, the bill already conferred all the power which Congress had, by giving the people the whole power over the subject. Chase offered a proviso that they might abolish slavery, which by implication would convey the idea that they could prohibit but not introduce that institution. General Cass asked him to modify this amendment, so as to provide that the people might either prohibit or introduce slavery, and thus make it fair and equal. Chase refused to so modify his proviso, and then General Cass and all the rest of us voted it down." There was furious cheering as I sat down. Lincoln's face looked ashen.

I left for the waiting train with a group of happy supporters. Glancing back, I saw Lincoln still sitting on the platform with his knees trembling. "The poor bastard is too frightened to walk," I said. "Must have been my notice that I was going to take him down to Egypt." Glancing back again, I saw that his supporters had to *carry* him from the platform, hoisting his gangly frame over their shoulders. He was grabbing so desperately at their heads that his trousers crawled up to his knees, exposing his underwear.

A couple of weeks later, in a speech at Joliet, I described that hilarious scene, and added that after being carried from the platform, Lincoln laid up seven days consulting with his political physicians—the leaders of the abolition party—and concluded that he could not evade the questions I had put to him at Ottawa.

33. LINCOLN

At Ottawa, I admit, Douglas's demagoguery had me flustered. He demonstrated again that he was one of the most dangerous and ruthless competitors in the country. "I'm glad to know I'm yet alive," I told a friend the next day. Uncertain how to proceed in the next debate, which was scheduled for Freeport, in late August, I wrote Peck of the Republican State Central Committee: "Douglas is propounding questions to me, which perhaps it is not quite safe to wholly disregard. I have my view of the mode to dispose of them, but I also want yours and Judd's. See Judd, you and he keep the matter to yourselves, and meet me at Freeport without fail."

In between the first and second debates, I spoke at Galesburg, Augusta, Macomb, and Amboy. At some point, Joe Medill, a smooth-faced young Irishman who edited the Chicago *Press and Tribune,* caught up with me. He brought advice from Judd, Peck, and other Republicans, who, in response to my letter, had held a strategy meeting in Chicago. "We all agree," Medill said, "the main goal is to discredit Douglas in Free-Soil Illinois. We think you should put a few ugly questions to him, such as 'What becomes of your vaunted popular sovereignty in the territories since the Dred Scott decision? Do you care if slavery is voted up or down?'" Medill added: "You need to pitch into him, be saucy and dogmatical . . . in other words give him *hell.*"

Acting on that advice, I worked up an aggressive strategy for Freeport and subsequent debates. I would pound Judge Douglas with my own interrogatories, endeavoring to put *him* on the defensive by exposing all his vague, contradictory, and inconsistent stands on slavery in the territories. I would demonstrate what I had been saying all along—that popular sovereignty was political fiction, a *lullaby* designed to put northerners to sleep and clear the way for the extension and nationalization of slavery.

When I reached Freeport, a pro-Republican town near the Wisconsin border, some five thousand supporters greeted my train and proceeded to shout themselves hoarse. It was wet, cold, and overcast, but the inclement weather did not dampen the ardor of the crowd. By debate time, some fifteen thousand people were gathered in a grove in back of the Brewster House, around a lumber platform set up for the speakers and reporters.

Escorted by a hurrahing procession and a spirited band, I rode to the debate site in a Conestoga wagon drawn by six white horses. Flags, banners, and mottoes were waving in all directions. A Democratic banner and a Republican banner argued with each other. One proclaimed: "No Nigger Equality." The other answered: "All Men Are Created Equal." Douglas, seeing my plain people's wagon, spurned the luxurious six-horse carriage provided by the Douglas committee, and walked to the site on foot. But that plebeian effort fooled nobody. The Judge was dressed in his "plantation outfit"— white felt hat, dark blue coat, and shiny black boots—which befitted the owner of a Mississippi plantation and more than 140 slaves.

I opened the debate by answering the interrogatories put to me at Ottawa. No, I was *not* in favor of the unconditional repeal of the fugitive slave law. No, I was *not* pledged to the prohibition of the interstate slave trade, or to the abolition of slavery in the District of Columbia, though I would be exceedingly glad to see Congress eradicate slavery there, on the condition that it should be gradual, that it should be on a vote of the majority of qualified voters in the District, and that compensation should be made to the unwilling owners. Yes, I was impliedly pledged to a belief in the *right* and *duty* of Congress to prohibit slavery in all the national territories. As to the admission of more slave states, this was a complex point, and I struggled, not very successfully, to make my position plain. "I state to you very frankly," I said, "that I would be exceedingly sorry ever to be put in a position of having to pass upon that question. I should be exceedingly glad to know that there would never be another slave state admitted into the Union"—there was applause at that—"but I must add, that if slavery shall be kept out of the territories during the territorial existence of any one given territory, and then the people shall, having a fair chance and a clear field, when they come to adopt a constitution, do such an extraordinary thing as to adopt a *slave* constitution, uninfluenced by the actual presence of the institution among them, I see no alternative but to admit their territory into the Union as a state."

Then I asked my own interrogatories, calculated to hurt Douglas in Free-Soil Illinois:

"Can the people of a United States territory, in any lawful way, against the wish of any citizen of the United States, exclude slavery from its limits prior to the formation of a state constitution?

"If the Supreme Court of the United States shall decide that states cannot exclude slavery from their limits, are you in favor of acquiescing in, adopting, and following such a decision as a rule of political action?

"Are you in favor of acquiring additional territory, in disregard of how such acquisition may affect the nation on the slavery question?"

I then addressed the so-called Republican resolutions of 'fifty-four, which inspired Douglas's fanciful conspiracy theory. I did not, I said, recognize any responsibility for those resolutions on my part. Besides, despite the Judge's claim, no such resolutions had ever been passed at any convention held in Springfield. In other words, he had made a mistake. I paused to let that point sink in.

I closed with my contention that, in the introduction of the Nebraska bill in Congress, there was a conspiracy to make slavery perpetual and national. The behavior of Douglas and those who acted with him on the Chase amendment, I repeated, lent credence to that charge. For men who intended that the people of the territory should have the right to exclude slavery absolutely and unconditionally, the voting down of Chase's amendment was wholly inexplicable. It was a puzzle—a riddle. But for men who looked forward to the Dred Scott decision, the voting down of that amendment would be rational and intelligible. "I tell the Judge, then, that it will be vastly more satisfactory to the country for him to give some other plausible, intelligible reason *why* it was voted down than to stand upon his dignity and call people liars. In my opinion the men who voted Chase down left room thereby for this Dred Scott decision, which goes far to make slavery national throughout the United States."

When Douglas rose to reply, an infernal brass cannon, set up behind the speaker's stand and manned by his supporters, went off with an ear-splitting blast which made everybody jump. With that introduction, the Emperor Douglas worked his big, combative face into a scowl and proceeded with a typical Douglas performance. As

he spoke, he stamped his feet and clenched his fists, frowned menacingly, and threw his huge head around with an air of angry and
arrogant superiority. His voice, usually a booming baritone, sometimes came out a harsh bark. He was glad, he said, that he'd succeeded in getting me to answer his questions and define my position.
Then he addressed my questions. In what became known as "the
Freeport doctrine," he argued that, yes, the people of a territory
could "by lawful means" exclude slavery before it became a state.
They could do it by the principle of "unfriendly legislation," by
which, vague as always, he meant *no legislation at all.* Lincoln, he
said angrily, had heard him argue that principle all over Illinois in
1854, '55, and '56, and he had "no excuse for pretending to be in
doubt as to my position on that question."

As to my question about the Supreme Court's outlawing slavery
in the states, he denied that any such thing was possible. "It would
be an act of moral treason that no man on the bench could ever
descend to," he said.

That sneering remark, I noted, hardly answered the question. If
Congress and the territories could not prohibit slavery because it
violated the Fifth Amendment, how, then, could the states get away
with violating the same Amendment? Let me put it another way. The
court had ruled that the right of property in a slave was distinctly
and expressly affirmed in the Constitution. Therefore, since the Constitution is the supreme law of the land, it follows that no state law
or state constitution can destroy the right of property in slaves. In all
the debates, I could never get Douglas to address that point. He
would swell himself up and say: "All of us who stand by the decision
of the court are its friends, all you fellows who dare question it in
any way are its enemies." The truth was, the Judge was *afraid* to
address the dangerous implications of the Dred Scott decision, which
he had so loudly endorsed.

When he took up my third question, he tried to turn it back on
me. "The Black Republican creed," he said with a jerk of his massive
head, "lays it down expressly, that under no circumstances shall we
acquire any more territory unless slavery is first prohibited in the
country. I ask Mr. Lincoln whether he's in favor of that proposition." Glowering, he addressed me: "*Are* you opposed to the acquisition of any more territory, under any circumstances, unless slavery
is prohibited in it?" Then back to the audience: "My position is
clear: whenever it becomes necessary, in our growth and progress to
acquire more territory, that I'm in favor of it, without reference to

the question of slavery, and when we've acquired it, I'll leave the people free to do as they please, either to make it slave or free territory."

Leaping to his conspiracy theory, the Judge admitted that perhaps he'd made an error as to the spot where the Republican resolutions of 'fifty-four had been adopted. The correct spot, he said, was Rockford, in August of 'fifty-four. "But I was not," he said, "and am not, in error as to the fact of their forming the basis of the creed of the Republican party when that party was first organized." He went on at length with his tiresome argument that Lincoln and Trumbull had tried to "abolitionize" the old parties.

The Judge caused the most fireworks when he turned to his favorite line of attack against "you Black Republicans." "White! White!" the crowd yelled. "I have reason to recollect," the Judge said, "that some people in this country think that Fred Douglass, the Negro, is a very good man. The last time I came here to make a speech, while talking from the stand to you people of Freeport, as I'm doing today, I saw a carriage and a beautiful young lady was sitting on the box seat, while Fred Douglass and her mother reclined inside, and the owner of the carriage acted as driver."

There was confusion in the crowd, shouts of *"Right!"* and "What of it?"

"All I have to say of it is this, that if you Black Republicans think that the Negro ought to be on a social equality with your wives and daughters, and ride in a carriage with your wife, whilst you drive the team, you have a perfect right to do so." There were hisses and cries of *"white! white!"* "Those of you," Douglas said, "who believe that the Negro is your equal and ought to be on an equality with you socially, politically, and legally, have a right to entertain those opinions, and of course will vote for Mr. Lincoln."

It was a shocking and repulsive harangue. Negro equality was *not* the issue between me and Judge Douglas. The *moral wrong* of slavery in a country with the Declaration of Independence—and the *need* to place that wrong back on the road to extinction—*that* was the central issue in this contest. Yet Douglas kept evading that issue and turning the debates back on the humbug of Black Republicanism and Negro equality. At one point in his Freeport speech, Douglas spat out the words, "you Black Republicans," so defiantly that the crowd screamed "white men! white men!" and raised such a clamor that Douglas couldn't go on. "When Lincoln spoke," the Judge raged, "there was not a Democrat vulgar and blackguard enough to interrupt him." He glared at the crowd. "I've *seen* your mobs and *defy* your wrath."

In my rejoinder, I asked Douglas why he kept harping on the 1854 resolutions. The plain truth was this: at the introduction of the Nebraska policy, we believed there was a new era being introduced in the history of the Republic, which tended to the spread and perpetuation of slavery; but in our opposition to that measure we didn't agree with one another in everything. We at last met together in 'fifty-six from all parts of the state—this was at Bloomington—and we there agreed upon a common platform for the entire state of Illinois. That platform called for the *restriction* of slavery, not the other things enumerated in the resolutions of 'fifty-four that Douglas obsessively quoted.

I lamented that the Judge persisted in belaboring the "abolition tendencies" of my speeches. "I've so often tried to answer what he's always saying on that melancholy theme, that I almost turn with disgust from the discussion. But I repeat: I do not believe this government *can* endure permanently half slave and half free."

The Republican press applauded my new aggressiveness. "This has been a grand day for Lincoln and a glorious one for the Republican cause," trumpeted the *State Journal,* a Republican paper. Judge Douglas "was completely wiped out and annihilated. To use his own choice vernacular, he was thoroughly 'trotted through.' Lincoln brought him to his milk in a most triumphant manner."

I was not at all sure. I hadn't dispelled Douglas's ugly accusations about Negro equality. The Democrats had killed us with the color argument in the 'fifty-six election, and Douglas was trying to kill me with it now. Unless I could persuade the state's all-white electorate that he was wrong, that the Republican party was *not* for Negro citizenship and Negro political rights and was not an abolitionist party, we were going to lose the contest, and lose it badly.

But the place to do it was not Jonesboro, the site of our next debate. Jonesboro was a little village near Cairo in far southern Illinois, where Negrophobia and proslavery sentiment ran deep. The debate would draw few people who cared a damn what I believed. The place to refute the Negro equality charge was Charleston, in politically uncertain central Illinois, where the audience would be far larger and where we had to pick up support from old-line Whigs. I would answer the Negro question there.

Meantime, on the train southward, I wrote down a mode of attack for Jonesboro and subsequent speeches. I focused on Douglas's "Freeport doctrine" as yet *one more* inconsistency, *one more* example of his shifting of ground, on the territorial issue. "The Judge," I wrote, "began by telling us that the people of a territory could vote to keep slavery out. But when asked if this could be done before statehood, he deemed this 'a question to be decided by the Supreme Court.' He did not stop then to tell us that whatever the Supreme Court decided, the people could by withholding necessary 'police regulations' keep it out. Well, the court then decided the question, ruling that the people of a territory could not prohibit slavery at all. At that, Douglas *shifted his ground* and told us that the people of a territory could still ban slavery through 'unfriendly legislation.' But I hold that the proposition that slavery cannot enter a new country without police regulations is historically false. The history of this country shows that the institution of slavery was originally planted upon this continent without any police regulations. Likewise, slavery had plenty of vigor to plant itself in the territories without protective measures. It takes not only law but the *enforcement* of law to keep it out."

I drafted a new interrogatory which followed up on the Judge's Freeport doctrine: "If the slaveholding citizens of a United States territory should need and demand congressional legislation for the protection of their slave property in such a territory, would you, as a member of Congress, vote for or against such legislation?" I was exceedingly interested to see how the Judge would answer that.

34. DOUGLAS

By now the hellhounds were snarling at my heels in packs. Trumbull, Lovejoy, and Herndon attacked me from one direction; the prissy Chase came over from Ohio and charged from another, only he barked with a lisp. And the Buchaneers, in alliance with the Republicans, howled and bit at my back. They invaded my meetings and held noisy rallies at which they damned and vilified me. "How can you buck them all?" asked my friends. "Because I'm the Little Giant!" I said.

I had reason to be in high spirits. I had the firm backing of the state party machine and nearly all the Democratic papers; I was picking up significant support from old-line Whigs who refused to join the Black Republicans; and I was getting help from outside the state, too. Democratic conventions in Massachusetts, New York, and Ohio had endorsed my stand against Buchanan and the Lecompton fraud, and moderate southerners like Crittenden of Kentucky and Vice-President Breckinridge gave their unqualified public support in favor of my reelection.

The Douglas express roared south for Jonesboro. My wife, with her slim figure and regal face, helped me entertain reporters and Democrats in my private car, courtesy of George McClellan of the Illinois Central. Some of my aides acted like old hens, warning me that my "amusements"—brandy and whiskey—might impair me for the debate the next day. But, hell, I was indestructible. I could drink and smoke cigars all night and the next day argue down a *dozen* Black Republicans and nigger-loving abolitionists on the same God-damned platform.

Jonesboro was Douglas country. The thousand or so people who attended the debate were so hostile to Lincoln that he did not dare wave the Declaration of Independence and argue for nigger equality down there. In fact, I noted, he carefully avoided *any mention* of the Declaration and the radical racial doctrines he'd been preaching up north, at Chicago, Ottawa, and Freeport. He tried to peg me with inconsistency on slavery in the territories, arguing that I could not at the same time endorse the Dred Scott decision and espouse the doctrine of unfriendly legislation. Lincoln also produced another interrogatory: if the slaveholders in a territory called for congressional legislation to protect their property in slaves, would I vote for such a measure if I were in Congress.

I thought it was a stupid question. Congressional non-interference, I pointed out, was a fundamental article of the Democratic creed. Lincoln could have found an answer to his question by consulting the Cincinnati platform. I then explained that Dred Scott and unfriendly legislation were not at all inconsistent or contradictory. If the high court recognized the right of a man to take slaves into the territories, I said, it remained a barren, worthless, useless right unless the territorial governments enacted local protective legislation. "Hence I assert that under the Dred Scott decision, you cannot maintain slavery a day in a territory where there is an unwilling people and unfriendly legislation. It is a practical question," I said to Lincoln, "if the people of a territory want slavery they will have it, and if they do not want it you cannot force it on them."

During the debate, Lincoln declared himself nonplussed by my recent speech at Joliet, in which I stated that he had to be carried off the platform after the Ottawa encounter. "How can the Judge say that about me?" Lincoln whined. "I can explain it in no other way than by believing the Judge is crazy. There was not a word of truth in it."

"Didn't they carry you off?" I asked.

"*There*," Lincoln cried; "that question illustrates the character of this man Douglas, exactly. He smiles now and says, 'Didn't they carry you off?' But he says then, 'He *had* to be carried off,' and he said it to convince the country that he had so completely broken me down by his speech that I had to be carried away. Now he seeks to dodge it, and asks, didn't they carry you off? Yes, they did. But Judge Douglas, why didn't you tell the truth?"

He had me laughing now. Was he suggesting that he'd been carried off in *triumph*? What a Goddamn joke!

But Lincoln could not let it go. "Did the Judge talk of trotting me down to Egypt to scare me to death?" he asked. "Why, I know these people better than he does. I was raised just a little east of here. I'm a part of these people." I shook my head, whispering, *Please, Lincoln, spare us this.* "The Judge," Lincoln persisted, "has set about seriously trying to make the impression that when we meet at different places I'm literally in his clutches—that I'm a poor, helpless, decrepit mouse, and that I can do nothing at all." He said he didn't *want* to call me a liar but didn't know what *else* to call me.

I could not believe it. Lincoln had left himself exposed from his asshole to his Adam's apple, and in my rejoinder I gave him the ax. "I *did* say at Joliet in a playful manner that Lincoln failed to answer when I put my questions to him at Ottawa, and that he trembled and had to be carried off the stand, and required seven days to get up his reply. That he did not walk off from that stand he will not deny. That when the crowd went away from the stand with me, a few persons carried him home on their shoulders and laid him down, he will admit." The audience was laughing and shouting, "go on! go on!" "I wish to say to you that whenever I degrade *my* friends and *myself* by allowing *them* to carry *me* on *their* backs through public streets when I am able to walk, I am *willing to be deemed crazy.*" The audience whooped and shouted, while Lincoln, according to a reporter, "chewed his nails in a rage in a back corner."

The next day, the Douglas train, bursting with supporters and firing its cannon, headed north for Charleston. "I trust that Mr. Lincoln will deem himself answered on his interrogatories," I said to my aides and guests. "He racked his brain so much in devising his four questions that he exhausted himself, and hasn't enough strength to invent the others. As soon as he's able to hold a council with his advisers, the abolitionist Lovejoy and the nigger Douglass, he'll probably frame and propound other questions, and exhaust himself again, the poor, helpless decrepit mouse."

The crowded car howled with laughter.

35 · LINCOLN

As we approached Charleston, a boisterous, banner-waving cavalcade met and escorted us into town, kicking up so much dust that it got into my eyes and mouth. I was amused to see a sign depicting Douglas perilously astride two galloping horses, one labeled "Popular Sovereignty" and the other "Dred Scott." One giant, flower-covered wagon carried thirty-two good-looking young ladies, each holding a flag inscribed with the name of a state. Over their heads a banner proclaimed: "Westward thy star of Empire takes its way, Thy Girls Link-on to Lincoln, Their Mothers were for Clay." That slogan, of course, had a political purpose. Charleston, in central Illinois, had a lot of unconverted Whigs whose votes we desperately needed. But linking me to the greatest Whig of his day was not just for political ends. I truly was Henry Clay's disciple, owing most of my political principles to him.

In the Charleston debate, facing from twelve to fifteen thousand folk, I led right off with the Negro question—the first time I had done so. I spoke at some length, carefully endorsing existing Illinois law against allowing blacks to vote, hold public office, or sit on juries. My aim was to put the combustible Negro issue to rest and shake off the ruinous abolitionist label once and for all, so that we could focus on the real differences between Judge Douglas and myself.

"I am not now," I said, "nor ever have been in favor of bringing about in any way the social and political equality of the white and black races. I am not nor ever have been in favor of making voters or jurors of Negroes, nor of qualifying them to hold office, nor to intermarry with white people; and I will say in addition to this that there is a physical difference between the white and black races which I believe will forever forbid the two races living together on terms of social and political equality. And inasmuch as they can't so live, while they do remain together there must be the position of superior and inferior, and I as much as any other man am in favor of having the superior position assigned to the white race. Yet I don't perceive that because the white man is to have the superior position, the Negro should be denied everything. I don't understand that because I do not want a Negro woman for a slave, I must necessarily want her for a wife. I can just leave her alone."

Since that elicited cheers and laughter, I tried to inject a little humor into what was, for me, a distasteful if necessary argument. "I've never had the least apprehension that I or my friends would marry Negroes if there was no law to keep them from it, but as Judge Douglas and his friends seem to be in great apprehension that they might, if there were no law to keep them from it"—there were roars of laughter—"I give him the most solemn pledge that I will, to the very last, stand by the law of this state, which forbids the marrying of white people with Negroes."

I devoted the rest of my time to Trumbull's Chicago speech, and the charge therein that Douglas in 'fifty-six had voted against an amendment providing for popular submission of whatever state constitution was framed in Kansas. This vote, Trumbull believed, showed that Douglas was part of the original conspiracy to force slavery on Kansas and to clear the way for the Dred Scott decision. I told the crowd and Judge Douglas that I had examined all of Trumbull's evidence and I thought the charge was true: Douglas *had* voted against submission, *had* violated his own popular sovereignty principle, *had* been part of a proslavery conspiracy. Douglas had responded to Trumbull's charge by calling him a liar, but in all the years I had known Lyman Trumbull, I said, I had never known him to fail of his word or tell a falsehood, large or small.

In his reply, Douglas spent much of his time damning me for repeating Trumbull's charge. The pronounced, horizontal wrinkle between the Judge's eyes grew deeper and more menacing. "I thought that I was running against Abraham Lincoln," he cried, "that he claimed to be my opponent, had challenged me to a discussion of the public questions of the day with him, but it turns out that his only hope is to ride into office on Trumbull's back, who will carry him by falsehood." The Judge went into a long, rambling, and deceitful defense of his conduct regarding the amendment in question, but he never convinced me that he hadn't voted against it.

Then, typically, he jumped back to the Negro question, which was safer ground for him. On that point, he accused me of being a hypocrite, a chameleon. In the northern part of the state, he charged, Lincoln waved the Declaration of Independence and argued that its equality idea included Negroes. But down here, Lincoln claimed to be against social and political equality for Negroes. "These Republicans!" the Judge cried. "Their principles in the north are jet black, in the center they're in color a decent mulatto, and in lower Egypt they're almost white." That elicited a lot of laughter. I laughed, too, despite myself. The Judge added with an arrogant toss of his head: "Let me recall to Mr. Lincoln the Scriptural quotation which he's applied to the Federal Government, that a house divided against itself cannot stand."

In my rejoinder, I denied Douglas's charge of inconsistency in my speeches at Ottawa and Freeport in the north and at Jonesboro in the south. "I call upon every fair-minded man to take these speeches and read them," I said, "*and I dare him to point out any difference between my printed speeches north and south.*"

Back on the train, heading northwest for Galesburg, I found myself arguing with Douglas on slips of paper. "But there is a larger issue than the mere question of whether the spread of Negro slavery shall or shall not be prohibited by Congress. That larger issue is stated by the Richmond *Enquirer*, a Buchanan paper in the South, in the language I now read." I had in hand a clipping from that paper. The equality of men, it said, was "a self-evident lie." I resumed writing: "That argument is also stated by the New York *Daybook*, a Buchanan paper in the North. In support of the Nebraska bill, on its first discussion in the Senate, Senator Pettit of Indiana declared the equality of men, as asserted in our Declaration of Independence, to be a 'self-evident lie.' In his numerous speeches now being made in Illinois, Senator Douglas regularly argues against the doctrine of the equality of men; and while he does not draw the conclusion that the superiors ought to enslave the inferiors, he evidently wishes his hearers to draw that conclusion. He shirks the responsibility of pulling the house down, but he digs under it that it may fall of its own weight. Now, it is impossible not to see that these newspapers and Senators are laboring at a common object, and in so doing are truly representing the controlling sentiment of their party."

It was impossible, I believed, not to see that this "common object" was to subvert, in the public mind, and in practical administration, our old and only standard of free government, that "all men are created equal," and to substitute for it a different standard, which *denied* the equality of men, which asserted the *natural, moral, and religious right* of one class to enslave another. *That* was the monstrous proslavery conspiracy of which Judge Douglas, either willingly or ignorantly, was a part.

My fears leaped to the distant horizon. What were they after in the long run—ultimately? Once they nationalized slavery (by a second Dred Scott decision) and overthrew the Declaration of Independence (by destroying it in the public mind), America would become a despotism based on class rule and human servitude. The northern free-labor system and the right to rise would be destroyed, the blessings of the Revolution obliterated, our noble experiment in popular government vanquished from the earth. Mankind would tumble backward into antiquity; kings, emperors, and hereditary lords would rule again, and the masses would be enslaved, toiling in the endless night of servitude, without reward and without hope. Was this not Mr. George Fitzhugh's dream? Were his views not gaining ascendancy in the South?

Somehow I had to make Illinois voters see what was going on. I had to make them understand that their own charter of freedom— the Declaration of Independence—was being undermined. I had to make them see that denying the Negro the right to rise *endangered that right for everyone else*. I had to make them comprehend Judge Douglas's complicity in the assault on equality, the central idea of our Republic, and what that assault was leading to.

And so at Galesburg, facing twenty thousand people in a freezing October wind, I argued that the entire record of the world, from the date of the Declaration of Independence up to within three years ago, may be searched in vain for one single statement, from one single man, that the Negro was *not* included in the Declaration of Independence. I defied Douglas to show that he ever said so, that Washington ever said so, that any President ever said so. What brought on the present affirmation that the Negro *was* excluded from the Declaration? The necessities of the present policy of the Democratic party, in regard to slavery, had to invent that affirmation. I reminded Judge Douglas and the audience that while Mr. Jefferson was the owner of slaves, when he spoke of this very subject, he used the language that he "trembled for his country when he remembered that God is just." Judge Douglas said he went for acquiring additional territory— Cuba, for instance—regardless of whether it had slavery or not. I warned the audience—I warned the nation—that this slavery question was the *only one* that had ever endangered our republican institutions; the *only one* that had ever threatened the Union; the *only one* that had ever disturbed us in such a way as to make us fear for the perpetuity of our own liberty. And so we should not, I said, be acquiring additional territory without considering how it may affect us in regard to this, the only endangering element to our liberties and national greatness.

In the sixth debate at Quincy, I attacked Douglas's latest species of humbuggery about "squatter" sovereignty—the unfriendly legislation idea. "He has at last invented this sort of *do nothing* sovereignty," I said, "that the people may exclude slavery by a sort of sovereignty that is exercised by *doing nothing at all*." I reached for a metaphor to describe it. "Has it not got down as thin as the homeopathic soup that was made by boiling the shadow of a pigeon that had starved to death?"

36. DOUGLAS

By the Charleston debate, Lincoln was so Goddamned desperate that he devoted almost his entire opening hour to Trumbull's preposterous charge that I'd voted against popular sovereignty for Kansas in 'fifty-six. I tell you, there was a conspiracy to carry this election for the Black Republicans by slander and not by fair means—they could not win it by fair means. An examination of the record, I said, showed that Trumbull's claim—that the Toombs bill originally contained a clause requiring the constitution to be submitted to the people of Kansas—was a Goddamned lie. I produced documentation to prove that the bill required only a submission of the land grant; there was no clause in the bill requiring a submission of the constitution. I showed that Stephen A. Douglas had offered an amendment recognizing the right of the people of Kansas to order just such elections as they saw proper. Trumbull, I said, *deliberately falsified* the record in order to make that charge against me. He waited until I became engaged in the 'fifty-eight canvass, and finding that I was showing up Lincoln's abolitionism and nigger equality doctrines, that I was driving Lincoln to the wall, and that white men would not support his rank abolitionism, Trumbull came back from the East and trumped up a system of charges against me, hoping that

I would be compelled to waste my time refuting them. That was the goal of that Goddamned liar. And Lincoln was a man of bad character for retailing that lie. And the reason he did, I told the Charleston crowd, was to conceal from this vast audience the *real questions* which divided the two great parties.

Lincoln defied me to show that his speeches in the north and in the south were not alike and not in entire harmony with each other. At the next debate, in Galesburg, I obliged the Goddamned bastard. I read from his Chicago speech, in which he expressly declared that the Negro ought to be included in the Declaration, and then begged his listeners: "let us discard all this quibbling about this man and the other man—this race and that race and the other race being inferior"—and let us "unite as one people throughout this land, until we shall once more stand up declaring that all men are created equal." Then I quoted his remarks at Charleston in which, in immense contrast to his Chicago doctrine, he denied that he had ever been "in favor of bringing about in any way the social and political equality of the white and black races." There it was—from his own mouth. In northern Illinois, I said, he advocated as bold and radical an abolitionism as Giddings, Lovejoy, or Garrison ever enunciated. But when you got Lincoln down south, he claimed to be an old-line Whig, the disciple of Henry Clay, and had nothing whatever to do with abolitionism or nigger citizenship and equality.

I glared at Lincoln in triumph.

By the seventh and final debate, down at Alton in southwestern Illinois, I had given so many open-air speeches, in blistering summer heat, in torrential downpours, and then the cold winds of fall, that my usually stentorian voice had almost played out. I was so hoarse it hurt to talk. To make matters worse, Buchanan Democrats invaded the Alton debate and heckled me repeatedly as I rasped out my summation. I attacked the Buchaneers as a contemptible crew who were traitorously working with the Black Republicans to break up the great Democratic party. I had a few choice words for the Administration, too, pointing out that it had offered to grant me a political pardon if I would only vote for the English bill. I rejected the benefits of that pardon, I said, for the reason that I'd been right in the course I'd pursued, and hence did not require any forgiveness. There was no safety or success for our party, I warned Buchanan and his southern henchmen, unless we stuck to our principles. I chose not to depart from principle on the Lecompton question, and I never intended to do it on that or any other question.

I devoted most of my remarks, however, to Lincoln's major positions, pointing out again what I believed to be the radical errors contained in them. First, in regard to his doctrine that this government was in violation of the law of God, which says that a house divided against itself cannot stand, I repudiated it as a slander upon the immortal framers of our Constitution. I asserted that in my opinion this government could endure *forever* divided into free and slave states, as our fathers made it, each state having the right to prohibit, abolish, or sustain slavery just as it pleased.

Second, I condemned Lincoln for defying the Supreme Court and the Dred Scott decision. He made war on that court solely because it denied niggers the right of citizenship and controverted his proposition that the Declaration included the niggers. To me, Lincoln's proposition was a monstrous heresy. Unlike him, I said, I never intended to waver one hair's breadth in my convictions, either in the north or the south of Illinois. I held that when the time arrived that I could not proclaim my political creed in the same terms not only in the northern but the southern part of Illinois, not only in the northern but the southern states, and wherever the American flag waved over American soil, that then there must be something wrong with that creed.

There was never a time, I said, when it was as important for the Democratic party, for all *national* men, to rally and stand together as it was today. We needed to stand together as we Democrats had stood with Clay to effect the Compromise of 1850 and save the Union when it was then imperiled. We must stand together today against the abolitionist sectional party and not allow it to agitate this country, to array North against South, and convert us into enemies instead of friends, merely that a few ambitious men might ride into power on a sectional hobby. I appealed to the South: "Your safety and ours depend upon *both of us* acting in good faith, and living up to that great principle which asserts the right of every people to form and regulate their domestic institutions to suit themselves, subject only to the Constitution of the United States." I said: if all patriotic Americans, North and South, adhered to that great principle, if we stood by the Constitution as our fathers made it, obeyed the laws as they were passed, and sustained the decisions of the Supreme Court and the constituted authorities, we would have peace. There would never be a sectional war.

37 · LINCOLN

Alton was the town in southwestern Illinois, near the Mississippi, where the Missouri mob murdered abolitionist Elijah Lovejoy back in 'thirty-seven. On the day of the debate there, a beautiful October day, people from nearby St. Louis came over on steamboats to attend the festivities. As residents of a slave state, they would not like what I had to say. Neither would the citizens of Alton, who had strong sympathies by birth, education, and sentiment with the South.

Judge Douglas and I came in on the same steamboat from Quincy. His statuesque young wife was still with him. He looked bloated and sick—from consuming too much liquor, rumor had it—and his voice was ragged and hoarse. But he still strutted about like a king, gesturing adamantly with a cigar in his hand, that retinue of secretaries and hangers-on always at his beck and call. The Republican press enjoyed ridiculing him as the runt with the giant head. They said he walked like a duck and foamed at the mouth, dribbling "the saliva of incipient madness."

The Democratic papers also got in their licks against me. They said I looked like a scarecrow with "a face of grotesque ugliness," that I talked like Uriah Heep, and that I was so afraid of Douglas that I sat on the platform with my knees "knocked together" and my teeth chattering. One paper—the Chicago *Times*, I believe it was—compared me to Titus Oates, the English impostor, pointing out that we both had the low forehead of the baboon.

When I got to the hotel in Alton, Mary and Bob, our oldest, were waiting for me. It was the first time Mary had attended a debate, and I was glad to see her. I'd been campaigning alone for three months, speaking at one crowded, dust-choked town after another, enduring the endless bedlam—the raucous crowds, the booming cannon, the marching cadets, the loud bands, the torchlit parades, and the packed hotels, whose beds were never long enough for me. Well, it was good to have family with me in Alton. Mary was still sure I was going to be Senator *and* President of the United States.

That afternoon, the Judge and I spoke on a platform at the new town hall, before a crowd of only five thousand at best. He led off, summing up his case against me in a voice that was often no more than a croak. Then it was my turn.

I tried to state precisely, and clearly, and persuasively, the *real issue* in the controversy between myself and Judge Douglas. "On the point of my wanting to make war between the free and the slave states," I said, "there has been no issue between us. So, too, when he assumes that I'm in favor of introducing a perfect social and political equality between the white and black races. These are *false issues*, upon which Judge Douglas has tried to force the controversy. The real issue in this controversy—the one pressing upon every mind—is the sentiment on the part of one class that looks upon the institution of *slavery* as a *wrong*. That is the sentiment of the Republican party: treating it as a wrong and limiting its spread.

"Has anything ever threatened the existence of this Union save and except this very institution of slavery?" I asked. "What is it that we hold most dear amongst us? Our own *liberty* and *prosperity*. What has ever threatened our liberty and prosperity save and except this institution of slavery? If this is true, how do you propose to improve the condition of things by *enlarging* slavery—by spreading it out and making it bigger? You may have a wen or a cancer upon your person and not be able to cut it out lest you bleed to death; but surely it's no way to cure it, to *engraft* it and *spread* it over your whole body.

"This, then, is the *real issue*." I was warming to my subject now, throwing my arms up with fists clenched and sweeping the air. "You may turn over everything in the Democratic policy from beginning to end, whether in the shape it takes on the statute book, in the shape it takes in the Dred Scott decision, in the shape it takes in conversation or the shape it takes in short maxim-like arguments—it everywhere carefully excludes the idea that there is *anything wrong with slavery*.

"*That*'s the real issue," I said. "That's the issue that will continue in this country when these poor tongues of Judge Douglas and myself are silent. It's the *eternal struggle* between these two principles—*right* and *wrong*—throughout the world. They're the two principles that have stood face-to-face from the beginning of time; and will ever continue to struggle. The one is the common right of humanity and the other the divine right of kings. It's the same principle in whatever shape it develops itself. It's the same spirit that says, 'You work and toil and earn bread, and I'll eat it.'" Even the Alton crowd clapped at that. "No matter in what shape it comes," I continued, "whether from the mouth of a king who seeks to bestride the people of his own nation and live by the fruit of their labor, or from one race of men as an apology for enslaving another, it's the same tyrannical principle." As I said that, I rose angrily up on my tiptoes.

Judge Douglas, I said, *looked to no end of slavery*. This pointed out to the people where the struggle really was. Willingly or unwillingly, purposely or without purpose, I said, Judge Douglas had been the most prominent instrument in changing the policy of the framers of the government—who intended that slavery should end one day—and placing it where he openly confessed he had no desire there should *ever* be an end of it. But, I said, if today the Missouri Compromise line were restored and slavery were once more put on the ground of "toleration by necessity" where it existed and put on the course of ultimate extinction, then I would agree that Douglas should stay in office and Lincoln remain out of office as long as either should live. With slavery once again on a course of extinction, there would be *no war, no violence*.

After Alton, the Judge and I campaigned separately. I was tired enough by then that I was speechifying pretty much by rote. The last days of the canvass were a whirlwind; I spoke at Naples, Meredosia, Mount Sterling, Rushville, Carthage, Dallas City, Macomb, Petersburg—the towns went by in a blur of faces and noise and color. There were rumors, which worried me, that the Democrats would introduce into the doubtful districts numbers of fraudulent voters—Irish laborers, for instance, who had been imported to work on railroads. If we could head off the fraudulent votes, I felt confident we were going to carry the day.

Election day, November second, came in rainy and cold. I voted early, then spent the evening with friends at the telegraph office. It all came down to how many Lincoln men or Douglas men were elected to the legislature, which would then meet to choose one of us as Senator. When the election returns were final, the Lincoln men won a plurality of the votes—125,000, to 121,000 for the Douglas Democrats and 5,000 for the Buchaneers. I could take some solace that more people went for me and the principles of Republicanism than for the Little Giant and his don't-care, do-nothing sovereignty. But the selection of Senator depended on the contest for legislative seats, and there the Democrats beat us 46 to 41. With the eight Democratic holdovers in the legislature, the Democrats outnumbered us there 54 to 46. No Democrat—not even a Buchaneer—would vote for a Republican, so I lost the election by that score.

The Democrats in town put on quite a celebration. They fired off cannon and danced in the streets, chanting and shouting: "Glory to God and the Democratic party." Douglas sent a message: "Let the voice of the people rule."

On our side, friends offered me condolences. "Nobody blames you" . . . "You made a noble canvass" . . . "No man could have done more" . . . "It's Greeley's fault and Seward's—their courting of Douglas gave him Free-Soil respect he didn't deserve." Still, the depression of defeat weighed me down pretty bad. I had given the best speeches I was capable of writing, talked as earnestly as I was capable of talking, and in the end it wasn't enough. Once again, I felt like the boy who stubbed his toe—too damned badly hurt to laugh and too damned proud to cry.

I tried to console myself with this thought: the contest gave me a hearing on the great and durable questions of the age, which I could have had in no other way. I tried to tell myself that I'd made some marks which would tell for the cause of liberty long after I was gone.

To my friends and supporters, I said: "While I now sink from view and shall be forgotten, the fight must go on. The question is not half settled. New splits and divisions will soon be upon our adversaries, another explosion will come. Douglas had the ingenuity to be supported as the best means both to *break down* and to *uphold* the slave interest. No ingenuity can keep those antagonistic elements in harmony long."

38. DAVIS

When I read Douglas's speech in his final debate with Lincoln, I was furious. That lying scoundrel! He claimed that *my* view of slavery in the territories accorded with *his*. To support that claim, he quoted from a speech I allegedly made at Bangor, while I and my family where spending the summer in Maine. When I returned to Mississippi, I assured my constituents that I had not capitulated to the hated new Douglas version of popular sovereignty. In the first place, I pointed out, I had never given a speech at Bangor. I spoke at Portland and Boston. In the second place, Douglas misquoted my remarks. What I said at Portland and Boston about slavery in the territories bore no similarity *whatever* to Douglas's new Freeport doctrine, that is, the distinct assertion of the power of territorial legislation to exclude slavery by inaction. This power, I told my fellow Mississippians, I *vehemently* and *consistently* denied. *All* property, I said, requires protection from the society in which it is held. This necessity does not confer a right to destroy, but rather creates *an obligation to protect.*

Douglas's Freeport doctrine was anathema to all true southern men. It was, to quote Senator Alfred Iverson of Georgia, "delusive, deceptive, and fatal." As far as we were concerned, there was no difference whatever between the so-called principle of unfriendly legislation and the Republican demand for congressional prohibition. How to counter and destroy the pernicious Freeport doctrine within the Democratic party—that was the question now before the true men of the South.

I was certain that Douglas had propounded the Freeport doctrine to strengthen his political reputation by catering to the Free-Soil prejudice of the majority section. His goal, of course, was to win the Democratic nomination and the Presidency in 1860. On that aspiration I set my heel with scorn and indignation. I intended to use all my power to block the nomination of that dangerous, grog-drinking demagogue, and to secure a *proslavery* candidate and *proslavery* platform at the 1860 Democratic convention, scheduled for Charleston. I was not myself a candidate for the Democratic nomination, although, as Calhoun's successor, I was the logical choice among men of the South.

Douglas, of course, was not our only concern that fall of 'fifty-eight. The Black Republicans alarmed us by their show of strength in the northern state elections. The abolitionist party not only swept New England but registered shocking victories in the state races of Indiana, Ohio, Pennsylvania, and New York, which were once Buchanan strongholds. The Republicans and anti-Lecompton Democrats also won a total of eighteen northern congressional seats, a veritable disaster for the Administration. The abolitionists and their allies would control the next House of Representatives and would, I was certain, try to promote legislation injurious to the South.

To make matters worse, Seward gave a hostile speech at Rochester, New York, which echoed Lincoln's "house divided" speech. Seward declared the labor systems of the North and the South to be eternally incompatible and on a collision course. "Shall I tell you what this collision means?" he asked. "It's an *irrepressible conflict* between opposing and enduring forces, and it means that the United States must and will, sooner or later, become either entirely a slaveholding nation, or entirely a free-labor nation."

When Seward spoke, the Black Republican Party spoke: slavery was ultimately, by Federal action, to be vanquished in all the southern states. In Jackson, addressing the Mississippi legislature, I deemed Seward a dangerously powerful man, the mastermind of the abolition party now seeking to destroy us, and I contended that Mississippi should leave the Union if a Republican won the Presidency in 1860. Separation from the Union by the state of Mississippi was the last remedy, I said, the final alternative. In the language of the venerated Calhoun, I considered the disruption of the Union as a great, though not the greatest, calamity. However, I said, my recent sojourn in New England convinced me that we still had powerful friends in the North. If a northern army should be assembled to march for the subjugation of the South, they would first have a battle to fight at home.

In late November, I left Brierfield for Washington City with Varina and the children. In a farewell speech at Vicksburg, I told Mississippi that if an abolitionist were elected President in 1860, I would be in favor of seizing the city of Washington, declaring the government at an end, and maintaining our rights and honor, even though blood should flow in torrents throughout the land. I myself would rather appeal to the *God of battles* at once than to live in disgrace under an abolitionist government.

In Washington, Douglas was the chief topic of conversation among southern Democrats. "How can any true state rights southern man maintain that Douglas should be retained as the exponent of the Democratic party?" asked frail, asthmatic Clement Clay of Alabama. "During the last session, he antagonized nearly all Democrats in the Senate on the Kansas issue, and he still opposes them upon a vital question—the rights of the South in the territories—as he demonstrated in his debates with Lincoln."

The President himself was furious with Douglas for proclaiming the Freeport doctrine. It was the last straw. The President declared the Little Giant "no longer a Democrat" and directed the Administration men in the Senate to oust him as chairman of the Committee on Territories and drive him and his cohorts from the party. I was to lead the attack, with the assistance of Slidell of Louisiana, a consummate "wire-puller" with a florid face and long, thinning white hair through which the crown of his head shone like a polished cherry.

We struck before Douglas had even arrived in town (he was reported to be on his way east by way of New Orleans and Cuba): at a caucus of Senate Democrats, we booted him off the Committee on Territories by a vote of seventeen to seven, and replaced him with

Green of Missouri. The Douglas Democrats cursed bitterly, and Toombs of Georgia stomped out in protest. But we had temporized with Douglas long enough. We would not tolerate his new squatter sovereignty doctrine. Those who did not adhere to the proslavery policy of the Administration did not belong in the Democratic party.

A gloating Seward told a correspondent for the New York *Tribune* that the removal of Douglas "was the best illustration that could possibly be given that there was an irrepressible conflict between freedom and slavery. The action against Douglas indicated a settled determination to tolerate no diversity of opinion upon any measure which the South demanded."

Let the Republicans gloat all they wished. We of the minority section were determined to secure our constitutional rights in the territories as our price for remaining in the Union. But to secure those rights, we needed a remedy for Douglas's Freeport doctrine. Albert Gallatin Brown, my fellow Mississippi Senator, offered a suggestion. Sporting a gold-headed cane, he was an animated dandy with prodigious side whiskers and a profusion of dark wavy hair. "Why not," he said, "invoke congressional intervention to protect slavery in the territories? True, until now, we've always advocated non-intervention. And true, there is little territory left to be settled, and therefore no advantage to be derived from such a code at this time. Still, despite all that, a congressional slave code would be an exciting and potent weapon to use against the Freeport doctrine. It would also provide ironclad protection for our property in whatever new slave territory we annex—Cuba, Mexico, or Central America. If the North rejects our demand, I would regard it as grounds for disunion."

I viewed Brown with suspicion. I feared he might be maneuvering to gain control of the Mississippi Democrats—might even be coveting the 1860 Democratic nomination for himself. I also questioned the wisdom of a congressional slave code for the territories lest it prove to be ineffectual. "We've gained several positions within a few years," I argued, "and we should take care to fortify our possession of them. As the smaller of the three contending armies, it behooves us carefully to reconnoiter the ground before we advance to occupy it."

But most of the other southern Senate leaders favored the idea of a congressional slave code, and I went along with them. While awaiting the opportune moment to demand such a code, we also devised a corollary strategy—the acquisition of new slave territory south of the United States. Unless we found the means for slavery to expand, we knew it would indeed perish one day. We therefore sought a $30 million appropriation for the President, so that he could begin negotiations for the purchase of Cuba from Spain. I also advocated the acquisition of Central America by a system of colonization and annexation. When a northern Senator accused us of desiring to seize "the whole tropical belt of the Western Hemisphere," Toombs cried, "It's true; the *whole* of it."

On the fourth of January, 1859, the Senate enjoyed a brief respite from the fierce sectional debates when it formally moved to its new chamber in the Capitol's south wing, turning over its old chamber to the Supreme Court. As chairman of the Senate Committee on Public Buildings, I'd had an important hand in the Capitol's renovations; I was proud of the impressive marble wings and new iron dome, which was still under construction, with a triangular scaffolding and a derrick protruding up from the rotunda. The new Senate chamber featured gas lighting and artificial ventilation, which pumped in warm air in the winter and cool air in the summer. The ceiling consisted of a mass of fresco and gilding, marble ornaments and sculptured cornices, and panels of ornamental glass, which in the daytime cast the luxurious chamber in well-diffused light. Rosewood desks and new leather armchairs, which gave off a pleasant aroma, were arranged on the carpeted floor in four semicircular rows, all facing the elevated platform where the Vice-President sat. The galleries, which rose above him and to his left and right, could seat almost a thousand spectators.

When Douglas finally took his seat in the Senate, early in 1859, we greeted him with studied contempt. To our astonishment, he never complained in the Senate about his removal from the Committee on Territories, but swaggered about the chamber with typical Douglas arrogance, as if nothing had happened. He and Slidell, however, almost came to blows when Slidell called Douglas a "calumniator." Claiming that southerners were plotting to kill him, "the King of Thugs"—Slidell's name for Douglas—hired a Kentucky sharpshooter to act as his bodyguard.

In late February, we launched our demand for a Federal slave code for the territories. Gallatin Brown led off the debate for our side. "The Supreme Court," he said, "in the celebrated Dred Scott case, declared that slaveholders had the same right to carry their slave property to the territories, that any other citizen from any other state had to carry any other kind of property. The venerable Chief Justice declared, further, that the whole duty of this government toward slave property was to protect it—to protect it after we arrived in a territory. We are entitled to *adequate* protection, *sufficient* protection. The mere naked Constitution does not afford that kind of protection which the nature of slave property requires. The Supreme Court has decided that we have the right to call upon somebody to give us that protection, and to make it adequate. Now, sir, upon whom am I to call? According to the doctrine of congressional non-intervention, our first call is upon the territorial legislature. But if the territorial legislature refuses, then what am I to do? Am I to abandon my rights, rights guaranteed by the Constitution, by the Constitution as expounded by the Supreme Court? No, sir, when the territorial legislature refuses protection for my slave property, as the Senator from Illinois claims it has the authority to do, I mean to come to Congress for a remedy. I mean to remind you, Senators, that the territorial legislature is *your* creature—*you* breathed it into existence—and yet your creature is not obeying the Constitution, is denying me rights guaranteed by the sacred charter of our liberties as expounded by the highest judicial tribunal in the land. I mean to come to you and ask you, Senators, to grant me the protection of my slave property through congressional legislation. That is the remedy I mean to seek. And in view of the approaching presidential contest, I'm curious to know what response I am to have to my request. What will be your response, Senators from the North? I've said, and say again, that when our constitutional rights are denied us, we *ought* to retire from the Union. True manhood requires it. Why should we remain in it?"

Douglas took the floor on his fat little legs, gesticulating with a fist. "I never would vote for a slave code in the territories by Congress," he snorted; "and I've yet to learn that there is a man in a free state of this Union who would. I agree that a southern citizen has the right to take his slaves into a territory. But once he's there, his slave property is on an equal footing with other property, and dependent upon the same system of legislation, for protection, as other property. I leave all kinds of property, groceries, horses, mules—and slaves—to the local law for protection. I will *not* exert the power of Congress to interfere with that local law with reference to slave property, or any other kind of property."

He glowered at me and the other southern Administration men. "I know that some gentlemen do not like the doctrine of non-intervention as well as they once did," he said. "It's now becoming fashionable to talk sneeringly of '*your* doctrine of non-intervention.'

Sir, that doctrine has been a fundamental article in the Democratic creed for years. It's been repeated over and over again in every national Democratic platform. And the Nebraska bill was predicated on that idea. Let me warn you, gentlemen, that the Democratic party of the North holds that if the people of a territory want slavery, they'll have it; and if they do not want it, it shall not be forced upon them by an act of Congress. If you repudiate non-intervention, and form a slave code by an act of Congress, you must step off the Democratic platform. We will let you depart in peace, as you no longer belong to us."

I leaped to my feet. "If in the progress of our history," I cried, "we have reached the point where it is necessary to part, as the Senator from Illinois says, or to adopt a creed like the one he announces, I wish him God-speed and a pleasant journey. No, sir; not the breadth of one hair would I follow the Senator on the path he announces."

Then I went after squatter sovereignty and the Freeport doctrine. "I've heard many a siren's song on this doctrine of non-intervention," I said; "it's a thing shadowy and fleeting, changing its color as often as the chameleon, which never meant anything fairly unless it was that Congress would not attempt to legislate on a subject over which it has no control; that it would not attempt to establish slavery anywhere nor to prohibit it anywhere; and such was the language of the compromise measures of 1850, when this doctrine was inaugurated. Since then, it's been woven into a *delusive gauze* thrown over the public mind, and presented as an obligation of the Democratic party to stand still. It's been used to withhold from an American citizen the protection of his property he has a right to claim; to surrender the power of Congress; to *do nothing*. If the theory of the Senator from Illinois be correct, and if Congress has no power to legislate in any regard upon the subject of slavery, how did Congress pass the fugitive slave law?"

Green of Missouri interrupted. "Will the Senator permit me to give him a little information I've just received?"

"Certainly."

"The legislature of Kansas," Green reported, "has passed a law, declaring that from and after the passage of the act, slavery shall cease to exist in Kansas."

The news did not surprise me—we had been expecting it. "It's the obligation of the United States to protect its citizens in their constitutional rights," I said in response. "If it be shown that those constitutional rights are violated by the inhabitants of a territory, or anybody else, it's the duty of Congress to *interpose*, to *make that protection adequate*."

I turned to Douglas. "Never," I said, "will I consent to abandon a constitutional right at the mere bidding of popular prejudice."

Douglas got the floor. "I'm assailed, first on one side, and then upon the other," he said, "as if it's something extraordinary that I should hold the same opinions now that I so fully expressed in the great contests of 1850 and in 1854 and in 1856. I do not think there is anything extraordinary in that. Possibly something might have occurred requiring a modification of opinion." There! I whispered to a southern colleague; an admission that he *had* altered his doctrine. "I have no such pride of consistency," he went on, "as would prevent me from modifying my opinions when convinced of an error; but upon this subject of congressional intervention I think I'm right. I don't believe the peace of the Union can be maintained on any other principle than popular sovereignty."

How *dare* he say that. His damnable principle, which was constantly changing, changing with latitude and longitude, changing with events and expediency, and now changing into the doctrine of territorial *inaction* and *irresponsibility*—that accursed principle was wrecking the Democratic party. I fairly shouted at Douglas that he was full of *heresy* and would not get Mississippi's vote.

"The time will come when you'll seek quarter," he said.

"I *scorn* your quarter," I hissed.

Mason of Virginia scorned it too. "You promised us a fish," he told Douglas, "and you've given us a serpent. When we supported the Kansas-Nebraska Act, we thought you'd given us a substantial right, but it turns out you've given us nothing but an evanescent shadow and delusion."

Other Democrats joined in the fray. For four hours, the southern Democracy battled the northern Democracy whilst most of the Republicans looked on, smirking with delight. "We've had exhibited today," exclaimed Trumbull, "the miserable fruits of the unfortunate Kansas-Nebraska bill and its ambiguous popular sovereignty doctrine—the spectacle of its own friends fighting among themselves!"

One Senator moaned that the debate presaged "a thorough breakup and dissolution of the Democratic party." I lamented that. "If the Democratic party," I told the Senate, "is to be wrecked by petty controversies in relation to African labor; if a few Africans, brought into the United States, where they've been advanced in comfort and civilization and knowledge, are to constitute the element which will divide the Democratic party and peril the vast hopes, not only of our own country, but of all mankind, I trust it will be remembered that a few of us, at least, have stood by the old landmarks of those who framed the Constitution and gave us our liberty. When these landmarks shall become an unpopular doctrine, when men are to lose the great states of the North by announcing them, I wish it to be understood that my vote will only go to a candidate who's *willing* to lose them. I sorrow to hear it said, that upon a question like this, the Democratic party must be divided. I regret it, not merely for the fate of that party, but for the fate of my country."

With a toss of his head, Douglas flung down a challenge: "Why not offer your principle of congressional intervention now, in the form of a bill annulling all antislavery territorial enactments? The Senator from Missouri tells us that the Territory of Kansas has passed an act abolishing and prohibiting slavery. Why not propose a congressional bill repealing that law? If you intend to introduce your doctrine, now is the time." But with both the Republicans and the Douglas Democrats arrayed against us, such a measure was doomed to fail; and so we held back, content with having asserted the right. We had, however, put the northern Democrats on notice: if the party platform in 1860 did not endorse our principles, the slave states would bolt the Democratic convention and choose a candidate who upheld the South's constitutional rights.

The session was hopelessly deadlocked along sectional lines. The northerners sent our $30 million bill down to defeat, and the southern bloc killed all of Douglas's cherished projects—especially his homestead bill, which would give away free homesteads in the West. We saw this for what it was—a Yankee device to populate the territories with free labor and strengthen the Free-Soil encirclement of the minority section.

After Congress adjourned, I left Varina in our cramped little house on G Street—she was with child and near her time—and returned to my neglected plantation in Mississippi. April brought heavy rains to the state, which caused the Mississippi River to rise until it broke through a levee and flooded the plantations at Davis Bend. From the porch of Brierfield, I gazed out over a vast lake which covered our fields and gardens. On top of that depressing contingency, the news from Varina gave me uncontrollable anxiety. She had given birth to a baby boy without apparent complication, only to become seriously ill. I settled my affairs and hastened back to Washington, where I found that Varina was not *physically* ill at all. She was distraught about the baby's name! It was my wish that, if the child was a boy, his name should be Joseph, in honor of my older brother; he had been a father to me after our real father had passed on when I was sixteen. But Varina thought Joseph overbearing and unjust in his dealings with her. She wept for five days, saying she *hated* the name and *hated* Joseph.

"Of course," she said, "you've got a perfect right to name the child. But I can't participate in paying Joseph the highest compliment in a woman's power to give."

My wishes, however, prevailed. *Joseph* remained the child's name.

On June third, I celebrated my fifty-first birthday. The ravages of disease, of facial neuralgia and eye trouble, had aged me beyond my years: I was gray-haired and haggard, with drawn cheeks and thin, bony, bloodless hands. My eyes were sunk deep in their sockets. My left eye was again causing me great pain, brought on by a buildup of fluid beneath the cornea; sometimes I feared the pain would drive me mad. In Washington I finally consented to surgery on the swollen eye lest it ulcerate: to release the fluid buildup, the physician inserted a scalpel into the cornea. But there was little that medicine could do for me, and I ultimately lost the sight in that eye.

Once I was able to get about, I took Varina and the children to Maryland for a cool and healthy retreat. We returned to Mississippi in late June, in time for me to address the Mississippi Democratic convention in Jackson. I found a rapidly increasing feeling in the state in favor of reopening the African slave trade. That question promised to be a prominent one in the approaching presidential canvass. I also found that Gallatin Brown's friends were seriously working to make *him* the nominee at Charleston, and that his big trump in the South was his antagonism to Douglas. Of course, that was *my* trump too.

"We are now nearing a crossroads," I told my friends in Jackson. "One road leads to the destruction of our Union, the other to peace and prosperity. Which road will the country take in 1860? The founding fathers feared the convulsions which the election of a President would produce. The second generation doubted that apprehension. But to our generation, the apprehension may come to pass, because we've witnessed the organization of a fanatical sectional party seeking the possession of the government to execute a hostile policy toward us. If they win the government, we can expect an abolitionist filibuster army to invade our sovereign territory—to liberate our Negroes at gunpoint, and slaughter our women and children, and burn our plantations and towns. That is really what they mean by an irrepressible conflict."

39 . BROWN

Over the winter I struck a blow for God and freedom that resounded across the land: my little army invaded Missouri and liberated eleven slaves and several horses from two enemy homesteads, nearly provoking another civil war along the Kansas-Missouri border. "By this act," I told the world, "I have forcibly restored eleven human beings to their natural and inalienable rights." We escorted the blacks to the Canadian border and freedom, then hurried down to Cleveland where I auctioned the horses off. In a fund-raising lecture attended by reporters, I described the success of the slave-running expedition and pointed out, proudly, that the President had put a price of $250 on my head. I retaliated by putting a price of $2.50 on the *rotten* head of Buchanan.

It was all a diversion to keep my name linked to Kansas in the public prints. In the spring of 'fifty-nine, suffering from the ague and a terrible gathering in my head, I journeyed back to Boston and warned the Secret Six that it was time for war, there would be no more postponements. I now wore a long white beard befitting God's chosen instrument to free the slaves. We all agreed that within the next two months I would raise the mill.

My first objective was to seize the store of guns in the Federal armory at Harpers Ferry, a mountain town in northern Virginia where the Potomac and Shenandoah rivers met. With an advance agent, John E. Cook, already in town, I rented an old two-story farmhouse about seven miles away on the Maryland side of the Potomac; I gave my name as "Smith" and told neighbors I was a cattle buyer from New York. Several recruits came with me, and others trickled in over the summer. They were all principled men, men who respected themselves. High-minded young Kagi and powerful Aaron Stevens were my best recruits; they whiled away the hours reading

Paine's *Age of Reason* and yellowed copies of the *Baltimore Sun*. Sometimes Stevens gave lessons in warfare to the Coppoc brothers, Quakers from Springdale, Iowa, and the other recruits. Three of my sons were among them: dark young Oliver, his eyes fierce like mine; quiet, steady Owen, who would follow me anywhere; and handsome young Watson, who had left a young wife and a newborn child in the Adirondacks, and sometimes woke me at night calling out to them. The oldest raider, Dangerfield Newby, intended to free his wife and six children from a plantation in Virginia. He carried in his pocket a worn letter from her: "Oh dear Dangerfield, come this fall without fail, money or no money. I want to see you so much: that is the one bright hope I have before me."

As I pored over my maps of the South, drawing crosses on counties with heavy slave concentrations, the men studied war and tried to keep occupied. But the cramped quarters and fear of discovery frayed everybody's nerves. I knew that if we did not attack soon, the men would break under the strain. But I couldn't move without an army. Where were all the blacks? Where were Tubman and Loguen? Delany and Douglass? I sent out a flurry of letters exhorting the blacks that it was time to "make the bees swarm" and to come in all haste. A black delegate at the Chatham convention sent a note that he wasn't coming and that he was disgusted with himself "and the whole Negro set, G— D– 'em."

At my urging, Douglass met me for a consultation at an old stone quarry in Chambersburg, Pennsylvania. With his shock of thick hair, piercing, anguished eyes, and "organ-like voice," Douglass was the most imposing man I had ever seen. With him was a tall, muscled fugitive named Shields Green; I had met and liked him when I stayed with Douglass back in eighteen and 'fifty-eight. For the first time, I revealed to Douglass my plan to attack the Harpers Ferry arsenal. I intended to confiscate all the government weapons, I said, take hostages, and then strike south across the mountains.

Douglass looked shocked; his handsome face was contorted in a frown. "If you attack Federal property," he protested, "it'll array the whole country against you. Old friend, listen to me. You're going into a perfect steel-trap. Once in you'll never get out alive. How can you rest on a reed so weak and broken? Virginia will blow you and your hostages sky-high."

"God is my guard and shield," I said. "I trust *all* to Him—*He* alone will determine the outcome. Come with me, Douglass. I'll defend you with my life. I want you for a special purpose. When I strike, the bees will swarm, and I need you to help hive them."

But Douglass shook his head. No, he said, he would not go with me this time. Then he turned to Shields Green and asked what he was going to do. Green stared at me, then at Douglass, and then said: "I b'leve I'll go wid de old man."

I was glad to have Green, but Douglass's defection disturbed me. Back in the cramped farmhouse, I wrote notes about the "duty of all persons in regard to this *matter*" and the "criminality of neglect in this *matter*" and sent out another flurry of letters. I prayed to God for guidance. *Jehovah*! *All powerful Director and Father, tell me what to do. There are only a handful of us; so few to start a war. Please, O Lord, give me a sign.*

He gave me the first sign when a brave young Negro, Osborn P. Anderson, arrived from Canada. Jehovah spoke through him saying, "I'm ready for war." Three more late recruits, one carrying $600 in gold, were an unmistakable sign that He wanted me to move with the men I had. Deep down I thought we would probably fail at the Ferry, would probably die. But I believed that all we had to do was make the attempt, and Jehovah would do the rest: the Heavens would turn black, and thunder would rend the sky, and a mighty storm would uproot this guilty land, washing its sins away with blood. With God's help, I, John Brown, *would* effect a mighty conquest even though it *was* like the last victory of Samson.

On Sunday, October sixteenth, I gathered up my little army—sixteen whites and five Negroes—and said: "We have only one life to live, and once to die; and if we lose our lives it'll do more for the cause than our lives would be worth in any other way." I stored in a carpetbag my constitution, my well-marked maps of the South, and letters that incriminated the Secret Six, Douglass, Delany, and several prominent Republicans, and left the bag in a trunk inside the farmhouse, where it could easily be found. I was the stone God cast into the black pool of slavery, and I wanted the ripples to spread over as much of the North as possible, forcing everybody to take sides.

It was time. "Men," I said, "get on your arms; we'll proceed to the Ferry." Leaving Owen and two others as a rear guard, I climbed into a wagon loaded with guns and pikes and led the men two by two into a damp moonless night.

When the town lights came into view, I motioned to two raiders to fall out and cut the telegraph lines. Then I flung my little army across the covered bridge that led to Harpers Ferry, deploying Newby, Oliver, and others to guard the Potomac and Shenandoah bridges. Except for a few figures strolling the streets, the town was quiet. My men crept through the shadows of Potomac Street, past the well-lit Wager House—a combination railroad station and hotel—and took the watchman at the government works by surprise, pinning him against the gate with their muskets. In the glare of torches, I told him: "I'm here in the name of Jehovah. I came from Kansas and intend to free all the Negroes in this state. If the citizens interfere with me I must burn the town and have blood."

My men secured the government buildings and confiscated the weapons inside them. Meanwhile Kagi and two of the blacks seized Hall's Rifle Works above the armory on Shenandoah Street. By now Owen should have moved the pikes to the schoolhouse near the Potomac where the slaves were to report. My advance agent, Cook, had assured me that they would come forth by the hundreds, once word of the invasion spread among the area's farms and plantations.

Around midnight a detachment of raiders brought three white hostages into the armory yard, plus twelve liberated male slaves and several confiscated weapons. One hostage was Colonel Lewis Washington, a great-grandnephew of George Washington. I told Colonel Washington: "I wanted you particularly for the moral effect it would give our cause having a man of your name as a prisoner." I armed the slaves with pikes and told them to guard the prisoners. Among the weapons was a magnificent sword given to the first President by Frederick the Great. I strapped it on, thinking it a fitting symbol for the war that had begun this night.

Sometime that night, the Baltimore & Ohio train steamed into town from the west. There were gunshots; voices rang out in alarm. My sentinels at the bridges were shooting at the train! I didn't want that—it would arouse the town. I sent one of the Negroes to tell my sentinels to let the train go on. When it finally moved out, heading across the Potomac bridge, Kagi sent back word by a messenger: "He wants to know why you let the train leave. It'll spread the alarm to Monocacy, and the telegraph will alert the entire countryside. Kagi wants to move out now, into the mountains."

"Tell Kagi to stand firm," I said.

Suddenly a church bell started tolling somewhere in town. They were spreading the alarm! The bell tolled on and on—*insurrection, insurrection*—tolling into the dawn. I scanned the overcast Heavens, whispering: "Lord, what do I do?" No word yet from Owen. I told myself we had to wait for him and the slaves—could be as many as 1,500. Then, if it is God's will, we will vacate the town.

About eight o'clock that morning, some of the armory employees arrived for work, heedless of the tolling bell. We took them prisoner and put them with our other hostages in the fire-engine house near the front gate. I sent to the Wager House for breakfast for everyone. Back came hot coffee and biscuits. I ate none of the food, fearful that the cooks had poisoned it.

There was more gunfire, armed men in the streets, *militia*. Another message came from Kagi begging me to order an evacuation; saying we could still fight our way across the bridge. "Tell Kagi to *stand firm*," I said. It was my settled policy not to do anything when I did not know what to do. A good course was sure to be safe in the hands of Jehovah.

Bullets were flying all about us now. I could see figures erecting blockades beyond the armory gate and firing at us, and more armed men were pouring from the bridge leading to Maryland. In all the gunfire, Oliver and another sentinel made it back to the armory, but Dangerfield Newby wasn't with them.

"They got him—a sniper's bullet," said Oliver, out of breath.

"He died for a good cause," I said, and remembered the letter from his wife.

The speed with which the countryside mobilized took me by surprise. "What we going to do, Captain?" asked Osborn Anderson. "They got us surrounded. Can't fight our way out now." Squinting, I peered up at the sky, then at the commotion in the streets. Can't wait for Owen and the slaves, I thought. Must negotiate for a cease-fire, offer to release the hostages if the militia will let us go free. I sent a raider, Will Thompson, out under a truce flag, but the scoundrels seized him and took him off at gunpoint. Ordering the remaining raiders to take cover in the little fire-engine house, I sent my son, Watson, and Aaron Stevens under a second white flag. But the mob gunned them both down. *Those miserable swine*. Watson managed to crawl back to the engine house, where he doubled up in agony at my feet. "Be brave, be a man," I told him, and took up a position in the partly open door.

By late afternoon, crowds of drunken men milled about in the streets, firing at us and screaming obscenities. They threatened to commit vile atrocities on the Negroes with us. Kneeling beside me, Edwin Coppoc, one of the Quaker brothers, drew a bead on somebody: he fired, missed, fired again. "I got him," he said. From the shouts of outrage from our enemies, we learned that Coppoc had killed the mayor. In a moment we saw them drag Will Thompson kicking and screaming toward the Potomac. In a minute we heard a revolver shot. An eye for an eye, I thought bitterly.

There was also gunfire in the direction of Hall's Rifle Works. Then suddenly the firing stopped. No more messages came from Kagi. My noble secretary of war, gone. *The judgments of the Lord are true and righteous.* I turned around in the doorway: militia had just invaded the armory yard from the rear, cutting off our last route of retreat. As night fell, more reinforcements arrived. Rifle fire and drunken cries rang out in the drizzly darkness.

Inside the engine house, it was pitch dark and painfully cold as I took stock. Only four uninjured raiders left, and eleven prisoners. Most of the liberated blacks had disappeared. One raider lay on the floor, dead. My son Oliver had also been shot, and he and Watson lay side by side, both choking and crying in pain. Exhausted from the fighting and lack of sleep, I paced back and forth, trying to think what to do, Washington's sword swinging at my side. I paused, listening to the clank of arms outside, then started pacing again. Oliver kept begging me to put him out of his agony and shoot him. I turned on him. "If you must die, die like a man." Then I spun around to face the prisoners. "Gentlemen, if you knew of my past history you would not blame me for being here. I went to Kansas a peaceable man, and the proslavery people hunted me down like a wolf. I lost one of my sons there." I stood trembling, then called to Oliver. There was no answer. "I guess he's dead," I said, and started pacing again.

When dawn spread through the high windows, we took our places at gun holes we had dug out of the walls, and peered outside. Federal troops had arrived during the night and were deployed in the street, the first column armed with sledgehammers, the second with bayonets, while hundreds of spectators, white and black, looked on. The doors of the engine house were barricaded and loopholed, but I knew they couldn't withstand sledgehammers. I knew that this was it, the end for us.

"Men," I called out, "sell your lives as dearly as you can."

But the soldiers did not attack. Instead a tall, bearded trooper approached under a flag of truce. I opened the door slightly and aimed my rifle at his head. "I'm Lieutenant Jeb Stuart," he said. "I bear a note from Colonel Robert E. Lee." Stuart started reading the note. "Colonel Lee, United States Army, commanding the troops sent by the President of the United States to suppress the insurrection at this place, demands the surrender of the persons in the armory buildings." I looked over the trooper's head and saw a tall, slender man in civilian clothes, standing on an elevation perhaps forty feet away. I guessed that was Lee. "Colonel Lee represents to them," Stuart continued, "that it is impossible for them to escape; that the armory is surrounded on all sides by troops; and that if he is compelled to take them by force he cannot answer for their safety."

"I reject the terms," I said. "I want reassurances that my men and my hostages can leave."

"Colonel Lee will not change his terms," Stuart said. Some of the hostages begged him to go back and speak to Lee. Another cried: "Never mind us, fire!" Suddenly, the trooper jumped back and waved his hat three times, and the storming party rushed forward. I slammed the door and we opened fire on them through the gun holes and cracks in the building, but it was no use. The troops battered down one of the doors with a heavy ladder and swarmed inside. Colonel Washington pointed at me and said: "This is Osawatomie." A sword-wielding officer leaped forward and struck me with such a savage thrust of his weapon that it lifted me almost off the floor. Then he beat me with the hilt of the sword until I slipped into blackness. . . .

When I came to, I could not believe I was alive. I was lying on the grass outside the engine house, cut and bleeding badly about the upper part of my body, but there was no wound in my stomach where the blade had struck. The officer who had tried to kill me was cursing his bad luck. "The blade must've hit his belt buckle. Damned dress sword—I got the wrong one in my haste to leave the barracks. If I'd had my battle sword, I would have disemboweled him." Colonel Lee bent over to look at my wounds and then called for a physician.

With a lynch mob screaming for my head, they carried me into the paymaster's office of the armory and put me under guard. But I was hardly aware of all the commotion. I knew that Jehovah had saved my life, had placed His hand between me and that sword point so that it could not penetrate my flesh. The realization filled me with awe. *Oh, Lord, You've saved me for the greater objective. Your will be done!*

That afternoon, while I lay on a pile of old bedding, Governor Wise of Virginia and a crowd of officers, U.S. congressmen, and reporters interrogated me for a full three hours. This was the first evidence I had of the national attention the raid had generated. In my exalted state, I made the most of it.

"How can you possibly justify your acts?" asked one interrogator.

"I pity the poor in bondage that have none to help them," I sang out; "that is why I'm here; not to gratify any personal animosity, revenge or vindictive spirit. It's my sympathy with the oppressed and the wronged, that are as good as you and as precious in the sight of God." Then I spoke to the entire gathering. "I wish to say, furthermore, that you had better—all you people of the South—prepare yourselves for a settlement of that question that must come up for settlement sooner than you're prepared for it. You may dispose of me very easily; I'm nearly disposed of now; but this question is still to be settled—this Negro question I mean—the end of that is not yet."

They put me on trial in nearby Charles Town and sentenced me to hang for "crimes" against the state of Virginia. There was a miserable attempt by some so-called friends to save my life, by petitioning the governor to declare me insane and commit me to an asylum. I rejected that ploy with contempt. *I* was not the insane one in this drama. The *slaveholders* were the madmen. So was every northern traitor who licked up their spit. But Jehovah acted through Governor Wise, who pronounced me not only "perfectly sane," but "cool, collected, and indomitable," and he refused to commute the sentence.

"Let them hang me," I said. "I'm worth inconceivably more to *hang* than for any other purpose." I assured my friends and supporters in the North that Virginia could not hang my soul, that I went joyfully to the gallows in behalf of millions who had no rights. To hasten the final showdown, I warned the South that others in the North would do as I'd done, that there would be *no rest* until slavery was overthrown.

My jailer, a kind, friendly man named Avis, told me that the authorities had found my carpetbag of papers at the Kennedy farmhouse, and that most of my immediate backers had reportedly fled the country. "You've caused a hell of a ruckus," Avis said. "The town is full of troops. The entire state on alert. They say you're an agent of the Black Republican party—the vanguard of a mighty abolitionist army being assembled in the North to destroy us. They say the irrepressible conflict is at hand, and we should fight it out to the bitter end." I could have wept for joy. The apocalypse must *surely* be coming—I could see it in my mind: *a nation in flames*, with Jehovah thundering His wrath over it all.

The signs all pointed to His approaching fury. Night after night, haystacks and barns blazed beyond my barred window, lighting up the Heavens with a flickering glare. I could hear great commotion outside—the clank of soldiers in the streets, and fearful cries on the wind. Mr. Avis said they blamed the fires on northern agents and distracted slaves. But I knew it was the work of Jehovah.

It's now December second—the day of my hanging, the day the gallows becomes my cross. I'm approaching those gallows while sitting on my coffin in the bed of a military wagon. O dear God, my eyes see the *glory* in *every step* of the *divine journey* that brought me here, to stand on *that* platform, in *that* field, before *all those* soldiers of Virginia. Thank you, Father, for allowing an old man like me such mighty and soul-satisfying rewards. I'm ready to join thee now in Paradise.

> *Sweet is Thy work, my God, my King.*
> *I'll praise my Maker with my breath.*
> *O, happy is the man who hears.*
> *Why should we start, and fear to die.*
> *With song and honors sounding loud.*
> *Ah, lovely appearance of death.*

They can put the halter around my neck, pull the hood over my head. Hanging me won't save them from God's wrath! I warned them, I warned the entire country: I, John Brown, am now quite *certain* that the crimes of this guilty land will *never* be purged away, but with blood.

40. DOUGLASS

I was lecturing in Philadelphia when I learned that Brown had been captured at Harpers Ferry and that letters found in his possession implicated me, Gerrit Smith, Frank Sanborn, Samuel Gridley Howe, Martin Delany, and several others. I was stunned: the old man had actually gone through with it. I had hoped against hope that he would not attack that Federal arsenal and get himself trapped and killed. But he would not listen to me, and now his rash act imperiled all of us who were his friends. When the New York *Herald* reported that a hundred southerners had offered rewards for my head and those of Smith, Giddings, and "other abolitionists and Republicans," I hurried home to Rochester in alarm. There I heard that the New York governor would turn me over to the Virginia authorities when they moved to extradite me.

"Virginia will make a spectacle of you, Fred," my friends warned. "You're the most famous black man in America. They'll put you through a humiliating public trial and then hang you before the world as an example. You're not safe in Rochester. You must get out of the country."

Just as we feared, the Virginia authorities charged me with "murder, robbery, and inciting to servile insurrection," and Governor Wise asked President Buchanan for Federal assistance in apprehending me. When I learned that Federal marshals were on their way to arrest me, I fled to Canada as Howe, Sanborn, Stearns, and other friends of Brown had done. Then I took a ship to England where I would be safe, far beyond the reach of the proslavery American government.

Harpers Ferry filled me with a tempest of mixed emotions. John Brown was my friend, the bravest man I ever met, and he had sacrificed his life for us. A part of me wanted to be with my friend, to march to the gallows by his side, to lay down my life with his for the imbruted and whip-scarred slaves. But what good would I do the abolitionist cause at the end of a hangman's noose? *Words* were my weapons in the war against slavery, and I could best wield them by steering *clear* of the hangman's rope.

In a letter to the Rochester *Democrat and American*, I tried to explain my actions to my fellow abolitionists and my countrymen. I had always been more distinguished for running than for fighting, I said, in reference to my flight from slavery in Maryland. Tried by the Harpers Ferry insurrection test, I admitted, I was most miserably deficient in courage. But I thought the attack on the United States arsenal was reckless and wild, and my field of labor for the abolition of slavery did not extend to such an operation. I was, however, ever ready to write, speak, publish, organize, combine, and even to conspire against slavery, when there was a reasonable hope for success. I had no apology, I added, for keeping out of the way of those "gentlemanly" United States marshals. A government recognizing the validity of the Dred Scott decision was not likely to have any very charitable feelings toward a black man like me.

Brown's attack on Harpers Ferry may have been rash, but his idea of destroying slavery by violence was right. Like my friend, I no longer had any hope of freeing the slaves by peaceful means, and I said so in an editorial sent to my newspaper. "Capt. Brown," I wrote, "has struck the bottom line of the philosophy which underlies the abolition movement. He has attacked slavery with the weapons precisely adapted to bring it to the death. Moral considerations have long since been exhausted upon slaveholders. It is in vain to reason with them. One might as well hunt bears with ethics as to 'pluck the spoiled out of the hand of the oppressor' by the mere force of moral law. Slavery is a system of brute force. It must be met with its own weapons. *Capt. Brown has initiated a new mode of carrying on the crusade of freedom*, and his blow has sent dread and terror throughout the entire ranks of the piratical army of slavery. His daring deed has cost him his life, but the blow he has struck, will, in the end, prove to be worth its mighty cost. Like Samson, he has laid his hands upon the pillars of this great national temple of cruelty and blood and as he falls, that temple will speedily crumble to its final doom, burying its denizens in its ruins."

I was astounded to learn that *Garrison* had come around to our view. The champion of non-resistance himself now saw the necessity of "wielding carnal weapons" against despotism. "It is God's method of dealing retribution upon the head of the tyrant," he told a John Brown prayer meeting in Boston. Yes, yes, even Brother Garrison had it right now. The only penetrable point of a tyrant is the *fear of death*. And John Brown had struck his penetrable point—one could hear the wail of the slaveholders clear across the Atlantic. The outcry they made, as to the danger of having their *throats cut* by abolitionists and slaves, was because they deserved to *have them cut*. The efforts of John Brown and his brave associates had done more to upset the logic and shake the security of slavery than all other efforts in that direction for twenty years.

41 · DAVIS

As the facts became known, I was certain that a conspiracy lay behind the Harpers Ferry invasion which extended across the entire North and implicated leading Republicans. I believed that it reached into England too; that money was contributed there as well as in the North; that the English drillmaster who had defected from Brown was a military leader sent from England to participate, first, in the Kansas trouble and then in the raid upon Virginia. It was foretold in England long before this treasonable act occurred that insurrection among the slaves of the South was bound to happen. The Harpers Ferry attack made us realize the extent to which the South was a lonely slaveholding outpost, surrounded by abolitionist enemies and sitting atop a powder keg.

When I reached Washington in early December of 1859, I found my southern colleagues as furious and indignant about Harpers Ferry as I was. John Brown had just been hanged, but that hardly appeased us. In an ugly mood, a group of us called at the White House to confer with the President.

"Brown was lawless, fanatical, and mad," Buchanan said, "but he obviously didn't act alone. When they captured him, he had two hundred pistols, two hundred Sharp's carbines, and almost a thousand pikes."

"From his northern backers," we said in unison.

Buchanan nodded in agreement. "There is much sympathy for him in the North. On the day of his execution, bells were tolled in many cities, cannon fired, and prayers offered up for him as if he were a martyr. He was placed in the same category with Paul and Silas, and churches were draped in mourning! Ralph Waldo Emerson reportedly said he made the gallows as glorious as the cross."

Said James Mason, a blunt, high-minded old Virginian: "Mr. President, all Virginians are offended by the indecent expressions of sympathy for Brown in the North. The man committed violent crimes; innocent people were killed. His object was to provoke a *slave revolt*, rampant rapine and murder. Yankees who approve of such acts are inhuman."

Said Clement Clay of Alabama: "The Black Republicans are the real culprits behind the Harpers Ferry attack. Four years ago, I said that the natural and necessary result of the antislavery teachings of the Republican party was civil strife and bloodshed, and that it would occur if that party prevailed in the North. My prediction has proved prophetic."

"I made the same prophetic prediction," I said.

Gallatin Brown of Mississippi spoke up, gesturing with his gold-headed cane. "The New York *Tribune* day after day holds up Brown as a martyr to 'the sacred cause of liberty.' I'll put it to the Black Republicans in Congress: why don't you rebuke your newspapers and your public speakers, who openly express sympathy with this criminal? Tell your editors, tell your Greeleys and Sewards, that their course is treasonable."

Buchanan said: "The Richmond newspapers report that Seward subscribed money to Brown, and was a conspirator. A notice in one paper offered $50,000 for Seward's head. God knows how many other Republicans in Congress are implicated." He looked at me.

"We intend to investigate Mr. Seward and all other Republican suspects," I said. "One thing is beyond question: Brown's invasion was the violent offspring of Republican dogma—of the party's 'irrepressible conflict' and 'house divided' doctrines and its platform. By advocating war on our domestic institutions, their leaders inspired that madman to attack us."

"I think their *leaders* plotted the attack," said Senator Alfred Iverson of Georgia, a stern little lawyer with thick jowls. "It's the intention of the Republicans as a party—it's their settled design—to break down the institution of slavery by fair means or foul means; and if they cannot accomplish it in one way, they'll try it in another. Have y'all seen this?"

He showed us a recent Republican circular, which created a sensation in that crowded White House chamber. Signed by sixty-eight Republican congressmen, by Greeley of the New York *Tribune,* and by other influential party members, the circular endorsed *The Impending Crisis,* written by a crazy southern ex-patriot named Hinton R. Helper.

"In his book," Iverson said, "Helper proposes to destroy slavery by exciting the 'poor whites' to revolution against the slaveholders. At the same time, he calculates on inciting the niggers in all the southern states to rise against their masters, burn their property, and cut their throats. The Black Republicans have recklessly distributed a hundred thousand copies of his incendiary tract across the free states. One of the endorsers is John Sherman of Ohio, the *very man* they intend to put forth as Speaker of the House. The party that can sanction such a man for such an office undoubtedly had a hand in Brown's mad act."

"Harpers Ferry," I said, "is the first genuine act of civil war, of one section invading the other. This government cannot continue as a shield to permit one portion of the country to make war upon another. The Federal government must take steps to protect us in our constitutional rights of person and property, or face the consequences."

"Virginia has already taken steps to protect itself," Mason said. "The militia is on alert across the state; 50,000 guns have been distributed."

"South Carolina is also on alert," said Senator James Chesnut.

"So is Mississippi," said Gallatin Brown, and other voices chimed in: "And Georgia." "Alabama, too." "And Tennessee." "And North Carolina." "And Texas."

"United," I said, "let us give the Republicans and the North an ultimatum. We will not tolerate invasion or outside provocation of any sort intended to excite our slaves." I turned to Buchanan. "I trust, sir, that we have your support for a Senate investigation of Harpers Ferry?"

"You do indeed," the President said. "You should investigate Stephen A. Douglas and his supporters while you're at it. An Administration paper in Ohio reports that Brown's carpetbag contained a letter from Douglas. It seems that he contributed a thousand dollars to the old felon's cause." Buchanan fairly bristled with hatred for Douglas. He would have liked nothing better than to crucify that drunken lout on the cross of Harpers Ferry.

"I can't believe he was involved," said Iverson. "Douglas may be a lot of things, but he isn't crazy. He owns slaves and a plantation himself—in Mississippi. Why would he contribute money for a projected slave revolt? I acquit him and the northern Democracy of complicity in Brown's raid. Our quarrel with them is over the question of territorial rights."

I agreed with Iverson. "The pressing matter right now is the Harpers Ferry invasion," I said. "We'll take care of Douglas after we get an investigation of the Black Republicans under way."

As soon as Congress convened, we demanded that the Senate set up an investigating committee; and it plunged the chamber into a furious ten-day debate. The Black Republicans, of course, tried to sidetrack the proposed investigation by amendment and evasion. They spoke out of both sides of their mouths, denying any complicity in Brown's raid, and yet expressing sympathy for the old lunatic's "high ideals." They even accused *us* of being the aggressors.

James Chesnut, a tall, slender young gentleman I had chosen as my protégé, took the floor. "Sir, when did we ever try to subvert any of your institutions?" he asked the Black Republicans. "It's *you* who've cast firebrands among *us*, you who've carried the war to our border; you who seek to shut us out from the common domain. You accuse us of agitation. Gentlemen, the responsibility is with *you*, not with us. I quote from a speech of Mr. Seward, the flag-bearer of your party, in the Senate chamber in March of 1858: 'Free labor has at last apprehended its rights, its interests, its power, and its destiny,' he said, 'and is organizing itself to assume the government of the Republic. It will henceforth meet you boldly and resolutely here; it will meet you everywhere, in the territories or out of them, wherever you may go to extend slavery. It's driven you back in California and in Kansas; it will invade you soon'—Mark the language: '*It will invade you soon.*' What a wonderful similarity of sentiment and purpose with the recent outbreak in Virginia!

"Well, sir, the thing must stop! Our present condition of affairs throws wide open all the portals for our invasion and destruction. It's for you to shut them, or with the help of Heaven we must shut them ourselves. Call it treason, gentlemen, and make the best of it; but I tell you that unless these things cease, we will sunder the Union, pull it to pieces, column, base, and tower, before we'll submit to be crushed."

Sandy-haired Lyman Trumbull replied for the Republicans. "The outbreak at Harpers Ferry," he said, "has arisen *not* from the teachings and the acts of the Republican party, or any of its leaders, or anybody in its ranks, but from the teachings of the party with which the Senator from South Carolina is himself associated. The *Democratic party*, by upholding the proslavery sacking of a Federal arsenal in Missouri, by sending Federal troops into Kansas to arrest and imprison free-state men on trumped-up charges of treason, set an example to the country which engendered the spirit that maddened Brown."

Several Democrats cried out in protest, but Trumbull ignored them. "The North intends no encroachment upon the South," he said. "It's because of the misrepresentation of the objects and views of that party that the prejudices of the South have been excited against it—and chiefly by the misrepresentations which have been made by this so-called Democratic party in the North. They choose to call every person that doesn't unite with them an abolitionist."

These remarks were aimed at Douglas. I looked around to see if he was in the chamber; he was not. He was said to be "indis-posed"—drunk probably—and missed the entire debate on Harpers Ferry.

"Sir, we're *not* abolitionists," Trumbull was saying. "We're *restrictionists*. I quote from our party platform: 'Resolved: That with our republican fathers, we hold it to be a self-evident truth that all men are endowed with the inalienable right to life, liberty, and the pursuit of happiness. Resolved: That we deny the authority of Congress, of a Territorial Legislature, of any individual or associa-tion of individuals, to give legal existence to slavery in any Territory. Resolved: That the Constitution confers upon Congress sovereign power over the Territories, and that it is both the right and the imperative duty of Congress to prohibit in the Territories those twin relics of barbarism, polygamy and slavery.' This is what we believe. We don't advocate meddling with slavery where it already exists."

There were cries of anger and disbelief from our side. Clement Clay, trembling with contempt, rose and faced the Black Republi-cans. A tall man with a trim beard, he was sick with asthma and wheezed painfully as he indicted our foe: "When you teach your constituents that slavery is a crime against man and a sin in the eyes of Heaven, and has no guarantee in the Federal Constitution, how can you expect men to respect our rights or to refrain from acts of violence against us? The principles you profess, the sentiments you avow, the very platform read in our hearing, bind you to exert every means within your power to abolish slavery, not only within exclu-sive Federal jurisdiction, but within the states in which it exists. Your hatred for us and for our institutions is manifest in every word of your platform which was jeeringly read by the Senator from Illi-nois, in which you denounce slavery, in the same breath with polygamy, as 'barbaric,' as a sin and a crime. Furthermore, your platform declares that the *Negra* is entitled to liberty and equality with the white man in social and political rights. This is the root of the evil. This makes a chasm between the North and the South so deep and wide that it can never be filled up or bridged over." He paused for effect. "You show your hatred of us in other ways, too. For twenty-five years, our Negras have been stolen or robbed from us, either by individuals or by organized bands of predatory north-ern invaders."

Henry Wilson of Massachusetts jumped to his feet. Rotund and red-faced, he answered Clay in his slurring, stammering style. "Sir, we *are indeed* opposed to slavery. We believe slavery to be a wrong.

We believe slavery to be an evil—moral, social, and physical. But we do *not* preach ill will or unkindness toward you or any portion of the people of our common country."

"Your party," Clay retorted, "is solemnly pledged by your platform, and by the speeches of Senator Seward and other Republican leaders, to maintain and carry out in the administration of this government, when you get the power, measures which intend to revolutionize our society, to desolate our fields, to deluge our land in blood. *I tell you, sir, it's impossible for us to live under a government administered by your party.*"

Benjamin Wade of Ohio now took the floor for the Republicans. Blunt and irascible, known as "Bluff Ben" for his readiness to duel with slaveholders, he had iron-gray hair, beady black eyes, and a square, beardless face. "We're compelled," he said, "to listen by the hour to speeches filled with denunciations of our party, telling us that the Union is to be dissolved if the people elect as President an honorable man of our party, holding to principles precisely such as the old fathers of the government held. I say to you gentlemen of the other side, these are very harsh doctrines to preach in our ears. I tell you, when you talk so coolly about dissolving this Union, do you know the difficulties you'll have to wade through before that end can be consummated? Do you believe that you can rend all this asunder without a struggle? We're bound in the same ship; we're married forever, for better or for worse."

That last remark made me gag. The Black Republicans were married to their precious *Negroes*, not to us! Wade's blather about the founding fathers added to my indignation. I was sick and tired of hearing it. The *Black Republicans* were not on the side of the framers. *We* were. *We* southern-rights Democrats were the ones who sought to preserve the government as our fathers formed it, and to maintain the sacred principles they established: the sovereignty of the states over their domestic institutions and the joint ownership of the territories. The real disunionists were those of the North who undertook to *sap* the foundations upon which the government stood, not those who sought to preserve them.

On December fifteenth, the Senate voted to establish an investigating committee, with Mason as chairman and myself as chief inquisitor, to find out if any "subversive organizations"—in other words, any Black Republicans—were involved in Brown's crimes. Meeting some forty times, we sifted through myriad reports and conducted interviews with Wilson, Joshua Giddings, John A.

Andrew of Massachusetts, and other Republicans; and with two of Brown's confessed backers, Howe and Stearns.

While we deliberated, Seward returned to the Senate after a visit abroad. I shall never forget his dramatic entry into the chamber. Conspicuous for his beaked nose and scraggly neck, which gave him a birdlike appearance, he rollicked down the aisle in an awkward swagger, his absurdly long coattails flying in his wake. Finding his seat, he took a pinch of snuff, sneezed violently, then dabbed his beak with a yellow silk handkerchief as he asked another Senator for a cigar. I noticed that my southern colleagues were scowling at Seward: they hated this higher-law, irrepressible-conflict Republican, all the more so because he was likely to be the Republican nominee for President.

Although he had issued a public statement disclaiming any connection with John Brown, my committee summoned him for interrogation anyway—more about that in a moment. On the floor of the Senate, he gave what he termed a "conciliatory" speech, in which he observed that "the earth seems to be heaving under our feet, and the pillars of the noble fabric that protects us to be trembling before our eyes." But the tumult would soon subside, he said, as such seasonable agitation always did, and we would find the earth as firm as before. Attempting to appease us southerners, he condemned Brown's raid as "an act of sedition and treason" and assured us that his party meant the South no harm. But he contradicted that very assurance by asserting that the Republicans intended to save the territories, "by constitutional and lawful means, from being homes for slavery and polygamy."

What an infamous blackguard! How dare he compare our institutions to polygamy! His entire speech was a lie, I tell you. Henry Wilson was far more honest about the Black Republican program. "We meant to arrest the extension of slavery, and rescue the government from the grasp of the Slave Power," he told the Senate. "We'll blot out slavery in the national capital. We'll surround the slave states with a cordon of free states. We'll then appeal to the hearts and consciences of men, and in a few years we'll give liberty to the millions in bondage." There it was: the Black Republicans' prescription for our total destruction. You can appreciate why we hated them and viewed them as our deadliest foes.

Both houses of Congress were in a violent mood that winter. In the House, the Republicans had indeed put John Sherman forward as Speaker, which precipitated a fierce party struggle that deadlocked the House for two months before a coalition speaker could be chosen. The floor rang with furious harangues and threats from both sides of the aisle. Murder was in the air. Armed men prowled the lobbies, brandishing revolvers. Almost every member of Congress reportedly carried weapons. "The only men who don't have a revolver and a knife are those who have two revolvers," observed Hammond of South Carolina.

Given the tense state of affairs, our committee was forced to interrogate witnesses with extreme caution, lest we precipitate a war in Congress between Black Republicans and angry southerners. Finally, after months of work, I made the majority report to the Senate. In it, I denounced the Republicans for their reckless "higher law" doctrines and chastised the Massachusetts Kansas Committee for carelessly entrusting guns and money to Brown. But Brown was so secretive that no one, not even his immediate followers, appeared to have known fully of his plans. Nor, in the evidence brought before us, could we find proof of direct Republican collusion with Brown. We concluded that Harpers Ferry was "simply the act of lawless ruffians under the sanction of no public or political authority, against which Congress has no power to legislate."

That was our official report. Privately, we of the South remained convinced that Brown was sustained by an extensive combination at the North and that he was inspired by Republican party doctrine if not by individual Republicans. The raid reinforced our conviction that the Republicans, if they won the upcoming presidential election, would themselves do violence against us and our domestic institutions. As a consequence, Harpers Ferry united the South as had no other previous event. We stood forth as one man and cried: "if a Black Republican is elected President, let the Union be dissolved."

If the Black Republicans were our worst foes, Douglas and his northern, popular sovereignty Democrats were a close second. The presidential election year, 1860, dawned with the Democratic party—the last remaining national institution—hopelessly divided along sectional lines. Because the northern Democrats were the majority, there was no chance that I would get the Democratic nomination at Charleston. I knew, in any case, that a radical advocate of southern rights like myself would attract few votes in the North. To win in November, the party needed a nominee who would appeal to both sections. In my judgment, former President Frank Pierce of

New Hampshire best fulfilled that condition. He was fitted for the emergency we faced by his ability, courage, broad statesmanship, and patriotism.

But Douglas was determined to win the nomination on a popular sovereignty platform, and we southern-rights men were equally determined to stop him. In a recent article in *Harper's Magazine*, Douglas had apparently tried to redefine popular sovereignty in such a way as to make that confusing and nefarious "principle" somehow more acceptable to the South and thus gain our support. Without it, he knew he could not win the White House. But the *Harper's* article, if you could penetrate its dense growth of unintelligible language, succeeded only in making popular sovereignty more elusive, shadowy, and provocative than ever.

"He now asserts the doctrine," as Iverson put it, "that the people of a territory are clothed with the attributes and can exercise all the powers of a *sovereign state*; they can do anything which a sovereign state can do under the Constitution, which means they can regulate and control all their internal polity, subject to the supervision of no Federal court whatever. Heretofore Douglas has always conceded that a territory is under the supervision of the Supreme Court. But not now. Such is the extraordinary position and monstrous doctrine of this new school of northern Democratic politicians! What chance would we of the South ever have under this doctrine to obtain or control another foot of territorial soil? This new version of popular sovereignty, or congressional non-intervention, or unfriendly legislation—or whatever the hell Douglas calls it—is as effectual a bar against the admission of slavery as the Wilmot Proviso or any other congressional prohibition. We'll have *none* of it."

When Douglas finally assumed his seat in the Senate, he acted as if he were the Pope entering the Vatican. He waddled pretentiously down the aisle on his duck legs, holding out his hand to colleagues as he went. He stopped by Gallatin Brown and me.

"Senator Davis," he said. "I'm surprised to see you standing. You look like a Goddamned corpse."

"The potentate returns," I said, glowering. "Overweight and pulpy-faced, but apparently sober—for a change."

Douglas scowled and waddled on to his desk. In his first speech of the session, he took our position respecting John Brown. "I have no hesitation," he said, "in expressing my firm and deliberate conviction that the Harpers Ferry crime was the natural, logical, inevitable result of the doctrines and teachings of the Republican party." It was the only point we agreed upon, for Douglas proved to be as uncompromising as ever in his advocacy of congressional non-intervention in the territories.

Speaking for the southern-rights men, Gallatin Brown warned Douglas: "The South will demand at Charleston a platform explicitly declaring that slave property is entitled in the territories to the same protection that is given to every other species of property, and failing to get it she'll bolt from the convention."

Brown and I both offered resolutions which, in effect, demanded a Federal slave code for the territories if the territorial legislatures refused to protect slave property. My resolutions, in addition, asserted that only when a territory became a state could its citizens reach a decision about slavery; that open and covert attacks against slavery, or any form of intermeddling with it, by one or more states, or combination of citizens, tended to destroy the Union; and that northern personal liberty laws, which were aimed at nullifying the fugitive slave law, were hostile in character, subversive of the Constitution, and revolutionary in effect.

These resolutions, which had the support of the President, were approved by a caucus of Senate Democrats over Douglas's bitter objections. A declaration of southern principles, they put the northern Democrats on notice: these were the requirements for a party platform acceptable to the South. We knew, of course, that Douglas would never embrace a platform calling for a Federal slave code in the territories. Our goal was to block his nomination and force the party to choose a pro-southern candidate—either Pierce, R. M. T. Hunter of Virginia, or John Breckinridge of Kentucky—on a southern-rights platform. We intended, in short, to continue ruling the Democratic party, or see it disintegrate. We would never submit to the rule of that grog-drinking demagogue from Illinois.

42 . DOUGLAS

I loathed Davis for trying to shape a party platform in the Senate. The platform was the job of a national convention, not a God-damned Senate caucus. But it would take more than a bunch of fucking resolutions to stop me at Charleston. I had the most efficient and far-reaching political machine ever put together for a presidential contest. A large and competent staff manned my headquarters at the National Hotel in Washington, mailing out thousands of copies of a popular campaign biography of the Little Giant and serving free whiskey to throngs of editors, politicians, diplomats, and other visitors. Pro-Douglas clubs and organizations were busy throughout the North, and significant support was materializing in the South itself. Pierre Soulé of Louisiana, John Forsyth of Alabama, Alex Stephens of Georgia—all were behind my candidacy. Forsyth, editor of the Mobile *Register*, wrote me: "You are stronger, a thousand times, with the southern people, than superficial currents set in motion by politicians would indicate."

Custom required that presidential candidates refrain from actively seeking a presidential nomination. I broke with tradition and electioneered furiously for the nomination because I considered myself the only candidate who could save the nation in this hour of peril. The fate of the Republic—the fate of the great Democratic party—was on my shoulders. Yes, I was financially strapped, my health was bad, and I was tired—tired of fighting a two-front war against the Black Republicans and the Administration Democrats. But that didn't slow down the Little Giant! I liked what the New York *Tribune* correspondent said: "Douglas may be seen in the Senate lobbies, in the hotels, and on the sidewalks, talking earnestly with his friends, and by look, word and gesture, stimulating them to action. Probably no other candidate for a presidential nomination ever played his hand so openly and boldly."

When most of the northern state conventions affirmed popular sovereignty and pledged their delegates to me, I was confident that I would win the nomination. I was the front-runner; nobody else was even close. Thus far, my adversaries had not been able to unite on a single candidate. They seemed not to heed the old maxim that "you can't beat *somebody* with nobody."

"I don't intend to make peace with my enemies," I told one and all, "nor to concede one iota of principle. I'll repudiate the platform if it contains a Federal slave-code plank. I'll accept the nomination only if the convention endorses the Cincinnati platform, with its popular sovereignty plank, which was agreed to by all sides in 'fifty-six and which remains the fundamental principle of our party."

In April, on the eve of the convention, I met with a group of trusted advisers to plan strategy. Chief among them was my floor manager, Richard Richardson of Illinois, a coarse, capable man with a huge nose and a harsh voice. The key to victory at Charleston, we agreed, was to have strong floor leaders who worked constantly on the state delegations, promising Federal appointments and trading concessions, until they had the two-thirds majority necessary for the nomination.

In mid-April, Richardson and his team set off for Charleston—"the last place on God's earth where a national convention should have been held," one Douglas man said. Since Congress was still in session, I stayed in Washington, maintaining daily telegraphic contact with the Douglas convention headquarters in Charleston's Hibernia Hall. The Douglas men reported that the slimy Slidell was in town with the little Administration turds, Bright and Bigler, doing their Goddamndest to undermine me at the behest of the Big Turd in the White House.

The convention convened on April twenty-third, and I awaited reports at the National Hotel or at my home. Both were crowded with friends and well-wishers, and I tried not to show the anxiety I felt. I'd never been so close to the nomination and the Presidency and I wanted nothing to go wrong. Don't think me immodest when I say that nobody had worked harder and deserved the White House more than I did.

As we had anticipated, the showdown with the southern-rights forces took place on the platform committee, seventeen of whose thirty-three members were anti-Douglas men. After a fractious, five-day debate, the majority reported in favor of a slave-code plank like the one Davis had proposed in the Senate. The minority report endorsed the Cincinnati platform and popular sovereignty. Speaking for the minority report, Henry B. Payne of Ohio accused the southerners of demanding a theoretical right. Why throw away the party and the nation for a mere abstraction? he demanded. "We're committed to popular sovereignty, and we'll never recede from it without personal dishonor, *never, never, never*, so help us God."

The secessionist William Lowndes Yancey, I learned later, gave a fire-eating speech in favor of the majority report. The hot-tempered Alabamian lumped "the Squatter Sovereignty" men with Republicans and abolitionists, declaring that "all represented the common sentiment that slavery is wrong." He told the northern Democrats: "We're in a position to ask you to yield. You must pronounce slavery a positive good. *Ours* are the institutions which are at stake; *ours* is the property that has been invaded and is to be destroyed; *ours* is the honor at stake."

George E. Pugh of Ohio answered angrily: "Gentlemen of the South, you mistake us—you mistake us—we won't do it!"

The telegrams from Richardson assured me that Yancey's fulminating was just the southern way of letting off pent-up steam. "You'll get the nomination," he said. "There might be a little eruption, the bolt of a couple of slave states; Alabama and Mississippi offer the only real opposition. The rest will stick." George Sanders of New York, I learned, wired Buchanan that I was going to get the nomination and that the President ought to offer me his support. It made me laugh with pleasure. "Sanders sent the wire collect," I told a couple of my aides. "And it was a hell of a long wire. I'll bet Old Shit Face had a fit."

For the next two days, the news from Charleston was inconclusive, as the convention haggled furiously over the platform. Finally, on the thirtieth, came the wire I was waiting for: the minority report endorsing popular sovereignty had carried the day by a vote of 165 to 138. Now there seemed nothing to block my nomination. But that night came a shocking telegram from Richardson. Eight lower South states had bolted the convention. The streets of Charleston were teeming with anti-Douglas men, a band was playing, and Yancey was proclaiming the start of "a new revolution."

I was alarmed. This I had not expected, not after Richardson's reassuring telegrams. What to do now? Without the lower South delegations, nobody could win the two-thirds vote necessary for nomination. I sent word to Richardson: demand that the rules be changed, that nomination requires *two-thirds of the delegates present at the convention.* At Douglas headquarters in the National Hotel, we awaited the outcome in a state of terrible anxiety. There was a lot of drinking. I paced back and forth, smoking one cigar after another. I felt sick and feverish. There was a tightness in my chest.

Finally, a telegram came from Richardson. When the Douglas men demanded the change in rules, the rest of the southern delegates threatened to bolt. At that, the president of the convention, Caleb Cushing, a Buchaneer from Massachusetts, overruled our motion. "That son of a bitch!" I cried. I knew then it was hopeless. The convention went through the motions of balloting. After the fifty-seventh ballot, I had a majority of those present, but lacked the two-thirds vote of all delegates required for nomination. Unable to choose a candidate, the convention adjourned on May third. The delegates, however, did agree to reassemble six weeks later, in Baltimore.

I couldn't conceal the pain I felt. "The fucking bastards," I said of the southern seceders. "With them it's rule or ruin. Hate, spite, and jealousy govern the hour. So it's down to this with them: the expansion of slavery or the destruction of the party, and probably disunion. God help our country." We drank and cursed the southerners through the night.

When I returned to the Senate next morning, I was beside myself. "Those Goddamned bloodhounds are after my life," I told my colleagues. "But I'm not going to withdraw. I'm not going to compromise my principles. This controversy has just begun!" I could not keep my mind on the Senate business that day. I fidgeted in my chair, gnashed my teeth, clasped and unclasped my hands, drummed my fingers on the arms of the chair.

"Douglas, are you all right?" someone asked. "You look like you're trying to bite a pin in two."

Richardson and the other Douglas men arrived from Richmond and met with me in a war counsel at the National Hotel. My men were furious, exasperated, and bitter; some were in tears. "The southerners are crazy," they said. "They've repudiated the only platform that will win in the North. What a collection of traitors. The abolitionists are right. They're beyond redemption. They can all go to hell."

"The next President will be nominated by the Republicans at Chicago," one man said.

"That'll be Seward," another said, and everyone groaned.

"Or Chase," another said. "He's got a lot of support in the Northwest."

"Chase!" I said. "Not that prissy bastard. He's *worse* than Seward."

Richardson said in his harsh, rasping voice: "The dark horse, I hear, is Lincoln, from the strong showing he gave you in 'fifty-eight. You made his a national name, Steve. But the odds are long against his nomination."

"Seward as president," an aide said. "What a Goddamned *catastrophe* that would be."

Richardson said: "Alex Stephens fears that within a year we'll be in a war, and the bloodiest in history. I hope to God he's wrong."

"Men," I said, "the hope of the country hangs on the convention when it reassembles in Baltimore." I turned to Richardson. "What are my chances for nomination there?"

"Good, I think, if the seceded delegations are not seated. Your supporters in Alabama, Louisiana, and Georgia are going to get up new delegations pledged to you. The outcome will depend on which lower South delegations are admitted to the convention. Our job will be to keep the seceders out."

"See to it," I said.

"One more thing," Richardson said. "We hear that Davis and the southerners are going to bring up the Davis resolutions in the Senate. They want to lure you into a debate in order to embarrass you."

"I think you should give the infernal scoundrels the devil," one aide said.

"No, *no*," Richardson said. "They want to goad you and make you pitch into them, so they can trap you on the territorial question. Their goal is to block your nomination by getting the Davis resolutions adopted at Baltimore. The best course is for you to remain quiet, not compromise your dignity, and let us work on the convention."

"That won't be easy for me," I said. "All Davis has to do is open his Goddamned mouth and I want to castrate the bastard. But I'll do my best not to be drawn into debate."

When we were alone, Richardson asked: "How do you feel? You look terrible."

"My throat is sore," I said, "and the old bronchial trouble is back. But don't worry about me. I've got the best doctors in town." I added: "It hasn't been easy at home, you know. Our newborn daughter died last week. Adele still hasn't completely recovered from childbirth. I stay with her as much as I can."

"Sorry to hear that, Steve. Well, try not to worry about the convention. We'll do everything we can."

A few days later, just as Richardson warned, Davis brought his resolutions before the Senate for formal debate. He looked sicker than I did. He was little more than a skeleton, with his gray eyes sunk deep in their sockets, his thin lips drawn and trembling, his complexion a ghostly white, his bony hands nervous as hell.

"Mr. President," he said. "I direct your attention to the resolution on the territories. We claim protection for our property there, first, because it is our right; secondly, because it is the duty of the general government." He paused, fumbling with his papers. "Two of my resolutions concern the security of our property from invasion. Last fall, an overt act was committed by men who were sustained by arms and money, raised by extensive combination among the non-slaveholding states, to carry treasonable war against the state of Virginia because she held Africans in bondage. And yet we are asked, if a party hostile to our institutions shall gain possession of the government, that we shall stand quietly by, and wait for an overt act. Wait for an overt act! Is not a declaration of war an overt act?"

When he said that, he glared at me as well as at the Republicans. Like Yancey, Davis evidently considered the northern Democrats to be in league with the Black Republicans. "A party hostile to our institutions" meant *us* as much as the Republicans. I couldn't help but squirm in my seat.

"Sir," Davis said, "this great temple of ours is tottering on its pillars. What, I ask, can be a higher or nobler duty for the Senate to perform than to rush to the pillars and uphold them before they fall and crush us? That is why we seek the approval of these resolutions: to keep the temple from falling. But if the sad fate should be ours to destroy our government, the historian who shall attempt philosophically to examine the question will, after he has put on his microscopic glasses and discovered it, be compelled to cry out: veritably, the unseen insect in the course of time destroys the mighty oak."

Did that son of a bitch just call me an insect? I asked my colleague at the next desk. Unable to restrain myself, I cried out: "I'll respond to the Senator's arraignment tomorrow."

"The champion of squatter sovereignty speaks," Davis said, fixing his one good eye on me. "Sir, I'll grant no quarter to squatter sovereignty."

"I say to you, sir, that it will remain for the *victor* to grant quarter or to grant mercy. I ask none from you."

"The doctrine of squatter sovereignty," Davis said with a smirk, "is a doctrine which the Senator must expect me to arraign, and on which he must expect me to give no quarter, whether I am the victor or the conquered. Nor can I believe that a single individual has a right to appropriate to himself a doctrine *he* did not originate, which was founded by another."

"I never pretended to originate the Goddamned doctrine," I said. "If one man is not the peculiar guardian of it, *it's very evident that one man is the object of attack because of it.*"

I knew I shouldn't have let the bastard needle me into debate. But now that I had committed myself, I resolved to hit him with a full-scale attack. In mid-May, I took the floor for a major address, only to quit after an hour or so because my throat hurt so badly I could barely speak. But I returned the next day with awakened resolve to shut Davis up once and for all, regardless of how bad I felt. At my request, Senator Pugh read extracts from party resolutions and the speeches of Cass, Buchanan, Pierce, and even Yancey himself, to show that the whole of the Democratic party had been pledged to congressional non-intervention since 'forty-eight, and especially since the Compromise of 1850. I quoted from my own speeches to demonstrate that I had been consistent in my commitment to that principle ever since.

I accused Davis of trying to make a party platform in the Senate. "Senators are not chosen for that purpose," I said. "Under our political system, party platforms are made by national conventions. A convention of our party gave us a platform, the Cincinnati platform, which I have stood on firmly and faithfully. It was the only authoritative exposition of the Democratic faith until the Charleston convention met. That convention affirmed the Cincinnati platform. Because of the so-called Freeport doctrine, which reiterated the Cincinnati platform, I was once called a heretic and removed from the chairmanship of the Committee of Territories. Well, I'm no longer a heretic. I'm no longer an outlaw from the Democratic party. The Charleston convention upheld me and repudiated this new test, contained in the Senate resolutions of the Senator from Mississippi. So far as the platform is concerned, I am sustained by the party. The question now is, whether my friend from Mississippi will acquiesce in the decisions of his party, as he did in 'fifty-six, or is he going to leave the party, bolt its nominations, break it up, because the party has concluded not to change from its position of 'fifty-six?"

I was scowling now and shaking my fist. "The advocates of the Davis platform are just as dangerous to the safety of the country as the Republicans are. The advocates of the Davis platform are for congressional non-interference so long as the people want slavery, so long as they will provide by law for its introduction and protection; but the moment the people say they don't want it and won't have it, then Congress must intervene and force the institution on an unwilling people. The Republican party is also for non-intervention so long as the people of a territory prohibit slavery; but whenever the people of a territory say they want it, then the Republicans are for intervening and for depriving them of it. There is *no difference* in principle between intervention North and intervention South. Sir, let this doctrine become the rallying point of the two sections, and you'll find a southern intervention party for slavery, and a northern intervention party against slavery; and then will come the 'irrepressible conflict,' which we've heard so much about."

It was the duty of every Democrat, I argued, to acquiesce in the decision of the majority. The party could not be preserved by allowing a minority to overrule and dictate to the majority. The party could not be preserved by abandoning its fundamental creed. We must remain a unit, I said, so that the party could present an invincible and irresistible front to the Republican-abolition phalanx at the North. "So certain as you abandon non-intervention and substitute intervention, just so certain you yield a power into their hands which will sweep the Democratic party from the face of the globe."

When I slumped to my chair, exhausted, Davis rose to reply. "What right does the Senator have to dictate to us?" he asked. "As a single adherent of the party, how can he stand up against the resolutions pending in the Senate, against the whole of the Democratic body of his associates? He must be outside of the party; he must be wandering in the dark regions by himself."

He paused for effect. "As far as the territorial question is concerned," he said, "the Supreme Court has decided the question. We have the right to go into the territories with our slave property. Why does the Senator not acknowledge our right? Why does he not recognize that the case has been closed by the Court? Instead, he persists in arguing non-intervention, a shadowy, insubstantial doctrine, which has its application according to the circumstances of the case. It seems to have a constantly varying application. It's this confusion of ideas, it's this confounding of terms, this changing of language, out of which a large portion of the dispute arises."

This was apparently an allusion to my recent *Harper's* article, "The Dividing Line Between Federal and Local Authority: Popular Sovereignty in the Territories," in which I argued that the Constitution placed the territories on the same level as the states in the matter of regulating their internal affairs, and that this principle had been recognized by the founders of the Republic. In an effort to appease hostile southerners like Davis, I tried to clarify the Freeport doctrine of unfriendly legislation, stressing that territorial legislatures could "control" slavery like any other form of property. But like the Black Republicans, the southern-rights men deliberately misconstrued my arguments, accusing me of shifting my ground, of changing my language, of modifying the very meaning of the principle. The truth was, my article was consistent with all I had ever said about popular sovereignty. Whether it was called popular sovereignty, or the Freeport doctrine, or congressional non-interference, the principle meant that each local community had the right to "control" or "regulate" or "legislate upon" all its domestic institutions, to uphold or abolish them as that community saw fit.

As he spoke, Davis stooped to personal insults. He referred to my "swelling manner," my "egregious vanity," my "self-laudation." He claimed that he *loved* the Democratic party and accused me of trying to force a platform on the South it would never accept.

"I'll answer the Senator," I said. "He claims he loves his party; but he loves it only when the party agrees with him. He has a penchant for pernicious abstractions. He's following a mere phantom in trying to get a recognition of the right of Congress to intervene for the protection of slavery in the territories, when the people don't want it."

"I say we have a constitutional right to try," Davis shouted.

"We have the right to do a great many foolish things, a great many silly things," I said; "but I hold that the path of duty and wisdom is to quit quarreling over these abstruse theories and to stand by the compact of non-intervention, which alone promises peace, fraternity, and perpetuity to the Union and our cherished institutions."

I left the Senate that day with my throat and lungs on fire, and went home to bed. A messenger came with a warning from my friend, Washington McLean of the Cincinnati *Enquirer*: "Davis, Toombs, and company intend to blackguard you. For God's sake don't imperil interests dear to you, your friends, and the country when you have nothing to gain, but everything to lose. Leave Washington with your wife and visit some springs."

"Tell him I'm too sick to do anything that imperils our interests," I said to the messenger.

An aide brought word from Chicago, where the Republicans were holding their national convention.

"Seward's been nominated," I said.

"No, they chose the dark horse, Lincoln."

"Lincoln!" I said. "Who would've thought it? Well, it'll be a devil of a fight. They've nominated a very able man."

43 · LINCOLN

My friend, Jesse W. Fell of Bloomington, first suggested that I could be a strong candidate for the Republican nomination. It was not long after the Senate contest of 'fifty-eight. I was in Bloomington on legal business and ran into Fell as I was leaving the courthouse. "Got something to talk over with you," he said, and took me by the arm to his brother's law office over the bank. We sat down by the window as twilight was spreading through town.

Fell was Bloomington's first lawyer and secretary of the Republican State Central Committee. He had short hair, a smooth, angular face, and sad eyes. "Lincoln," he said, "I've been in the East as far as Boston, in all the New England states except Maine, in New York, New Jersey, Pennsylvania, Ohio, Michigan, and Indiana; and everywhere I hear you talked about. I've often been asked, 'Who is this man Lincoln, of your state, now running against Douglas?' I told them we had two giants in Illinois instead of one; that Douglas was the little one and you were the big one. Seriously, Lincoln, since Douglas is so widely known, you're getting a national reputation *through him*. Your speeches have been pretty extensively published in the East. Discriminating people there consider you quite a match for Douglas in debate. I've got the decided impression that if your popular history and efforts on the slavery question were brought before the people generally, you could be a formidable candidate for the Presidency."

I disagreed. "There's no use in talking of me for the Presidency when we have men the caliber of Seward and Chase. They're prominently associated with party principles. Everybody knows them. Hardly anyone outside of Illinois knows me. Besides, isn't the nomination due men like Seward and Chase who've endured personal abuse and bitter opposition to bring the party to its present stature? I think so."

"Yes, Seward and Chase have given great service to the party," Fell said. "But the truth is, they've made long records and given radical speeches which would seriously damage them if they were nominated. We were defeated on the issue of radicalism in 1856, and will be again in 1860, unless we get a great many new votes in the North from the old conservative parties, the former Whigs especially. The men of those parties won't vote for Seward or Chase. What the Republican party needs in 1860 is a man of popular origin, of acknowledged ability, committed against slavery aggressions, who has no national record to defend and no radicalism of an offensive character. Your contest with Douglas has demonstrated your ability and your devotion to freedom; you have no embarrassing record. If we can get the facts of your life before the people, depend on it, there's a chance for you.

"Here's what I'd like to do," he went on. "I want to get up a newspaper article telling the people who you are and what you've done, and publish it in my home state of Pennsylvania, so that it can be circulated there and in other states. I know your public life; but I don't know much about your private history, especially your early life. I want you to write it out for me. Will you do it?"

"Fell," I said, "I admit the force of much that you say. I admit that I'm ambitious and would like to be President. But let's be realistic. The Presidency just isn't in store for me. Besides, there's nothing in my early history that would interest you or anybody else. As my friend Judge Davis says, 'It won't pay.' Good night." I wrapped a wool shawl around my shoulders and left.

To be honest, I did not think I was fit for the Presidency and said so to others who pressed me to run. I had no administrative experience and little patience for the tedious chores of executive administration, particularly of the patronage. What I wanted—and had a realistic chance of winning—was Judge Douglas's Senate seat in 'sixty-four. The Senate was where I could best serve the party and the cause—where I could utilize my humble talent for oratory and do battle against the proslavery forces, against Judge Douglas and his party.

With my sights on the Senate, I embarked on an arduous speaking and letter-writing campaign in 'fifty-nine, determined that nobody would ever again call me an unknown. I told Republican groups that we must never forget the larger question before us in these difficult days: this whole matter of the right or wrong of slavery in this Union. The Republican principle, I said, is the profound central truth that slavery is *wrong* and ought to be dealt with as a wrong.

It's incredibly ironic, I said, that we Republicans—supposedly the descendants of the Federalists—are trying to save the ideals of Jefferson from total overthrow in this nation; while the Democrats— who do descend from Jefferson—now condemn his principles as "self-evident lies" and "glittering generalities," as applying only to "superior races."

Such expressions convinced me that the Democratic party, ruled by the iron hand of the Slave Power, was allied to the reactionary forces of the world bent on destroying the liberal parties and free government everywhere. Taking their cue from reactionary parties in Europe, the Democrats were attempting to subvert the principles of free government and restore class, caste, and legitimacy. They were the vanguard—the miners and sappers—of returning despotism. And we had to repulse them or they would subjugate us. I warned the Democrats: "This is a world of compensations. He who would *be* no slave must consent to *have* no slave. Those who deny freedom to others deserve it not for themselves."

I tried to refute the argument of Fitzhugh and Hammond, that southern slave labor was superior to the "wage slavery" of the North, and that Negro slaves were better off than our hired workers. Apparently Fitzhugh and his ilk thought that our laborers were fatally fixed in that position for life. But how little they knew! That was the basic error in southern thought from which flowed all their other mistaken attitudes. It's the *genius* of the free-labor system that there *is* no permanent class of hired workers. Northerners are free to move up, progress, better themselves. Look at me: *I* was a hired laborer myself, working for twelve dollars a month. Yet the system allowed me the right to improve myself, to rise above my humble origins and become a self-made man. In the free-labor system, the hired laborer of yesterday labors on his own account today; and will hire others to labor for him tomorrow. In a speech in Wisconsin, I used a story to describe the process. "The prudent, penniless beginner in the world leaves home with his capital—two strong hands and a willingness to work—and chooses his employer and mode of labor. His employer pays him a fair day's wages for a fair day's work, he saves frugally for a couple of years, buys land on his own hook or goes into business for himself, marries, has sons and daughters, and in time has enough capital to hire another beginner. And this free-labor system, this progress by which the poor, honest, industrious, and resolute man raises himself, is the great principle we Republicans intend to take into the territories, which belong to us, which are God-given for that purpose. For the free-labor system opens the way for all—gives hope to all, and energy, and progress, and improvement of condition to all. Those who remain as workers—and many do—cannot fault the system for their condition. They remain that way either because they have dependent natures, or as a result of improvidence, folly, or misfortune. For the doors are always open for them to rise. The hope for self-improvement is always there."

This was why we Republicans hated slavery—because pure slavery had no hope. It was a *fixed condition* which prevented Negroes from eating the bread their own hands earned. It denied them the right to rise and threatened that right for everyone else. "I want *every man* to have a chance," I said, "and I believe a black man is entitled to it; a chance to better his condition, so that he might look forward and hope to be a hired laborer this year and the next, work for himself afterward, and finally hire men to work for him. That is the true system!"

But that system was in peril if the Democrats retained control of the government. Of them all, I considered Judge Douglas the most dangerous enemy of liberty, because the most insidious one. His blatant electioneering for the Democratic nomination proved that. Like a skillful gambler, he played for all his chances to get it. When the party bosses, the Buchanan Democrats, laid down a territorial slave code as the new test of party loyalty, Douglas opposed it just as he fought them on Lecompton, and presented himself to the North as a great hero. The logic of his position on Dred Scott—he endorsed it categorically—dictated that he *favor* a congressional slave code for the territories. But he never let the logic of principle displace the logic of success, and success required that he pitch himself to the North by defying the proslavery rulers of the party. He couldn't win the nomination without retaining his northern support. The Judge's dilemma was that he couldn't win the nomination without the support of the South either.

To remedy the latter problem, the Judge dropped a bombshell: his "manifesto" on popular sovereignty in *Harper's Magazine*. That article made me pretty damned mad, I tell you. Citing alleged historical "facts," the Judge argued that the founders of the Republic had established popular sovereignty—or congressional non-intervention—as the standard formula for dealing with slavery in the territories. This was historical nonsense. My research disclosed that the founders had voted again and again to let Congress regulate slavery in the territories. Of the thirty-nine men who signed the Constitution, two of them voted for the 1787 ordinance banning slavery in the old Northwest and sixteen approved, and Washington signed into law, a congressional act which implemented the ordinance. Two of the original fathers voted for congressional control of slavery in the Louisiana Territory; and two subsequently voted for the congressional measures known as the Missouri Compromise, which prohibited slavery from half of the Louisiana Territory. In short, twenty-one of the thirty-nine original founders voted at one time or another to exclude slavery from the territories.

From historical error, Douglas went on to moral obtuseness, once again treating the monstrous wrong of slavery as one of those little, unimportant, trivial matters, on a par with onions and potatoes. Then he completely abandoned the Freeport doctrine of unfriendly legislation and insisted that the people of a territory could merely "control" slavery as other property.

Douglas's new position demonstrated yet again that he never let principle get in the way of ambition. The doctrine of "controlling legislation" was an infamous concession to the proslavery forces, a naked attempt to gain southern support so that he could win the Democratic nomination. When Douglas came out to Ohio to defend his new ground, I went after him, intending to speak where he spoke and alert the country to the danger posed by his newest doctrine. "Strike straight from the shoulders," Medill urged me, "hit above and *below* the belt, and kick like thunder."

That I intended to do. At Columbus, addressing a boisterous crowd from the steps of the statehouse, I warned that popular sovereignty, in its many guises, was the miner and sapper for the movement to nationalize slavery and the most imminent danger we Republicans faced. Douglas's entire course in defense of that so-called principle, I said, was a succession of muddled and inconsistent stands, which proved it to be a sham, a deception, designed to clear the way for the spread of slavery. When the Court handed down the Dred Scott decision, Douglas hailed it as "right" and demanded that everyone abide by it. That argument got him in trouble in the Free-Soil North, so he devised the Freeport doctrine—the idea of unfriendly legislation—which contradicted the court's ruling. When you cleared away all the trash and words and chaff from that doctrine, you found that Douglas was propounding a naked and impudent absurdity—*no less than that a thing may be lawfully driven away from where it has a lawful right to be.*

Well, I said, that argument got him in trouble in the South. So he switched his ground again and promulgated his latest doctrine—that the Dred Scott decision did not carry slavery into the territories beyond the power of the people there *to control it as other property.* He no longer argued that slavery could be driven out. Now it could only be controlled as other property. What did this mean, I asked, except that the Negro was to be taken into the territories and used and abused as property? Please, what did proslavery men want more than this?

I then hurried down to Cincinnati, where Douglas had damned Seward's "irrepressible conflict" and my "house divided" speeches as incendiary attempts to get up civil war against the South. When I appeared on a hotel balcony on a September night, the square below was filled with people and torchbearing marchers who had escorted me there. Giant bonfires crackled and roared, and fireworks shot across the sky.

To rebut Judge Douglas's recent accusations, I spoke to Kentuckians across the Ohio River, as though they were in the audience. I think slavery is wrong, morally, and politically, I said. I want to block its spread and desire that it should gradually terminate in the whole Union. But you Kentuckians differ radically with me upon this proposition. You believe that slavery is a good thing; that slavery is right; that it ought to be extended and perpetuated in this Union. Therefore you should nominate Douglas for President, who is more wisely for you than you are for yourselves. But count on this: we Republicans are going to stand by our guns and beat you in a fair election. Yet we won't hurt you. We'll treat you as Washington, Jefferson, and Madison treated you: We'll leave slavery alone where it already exists among you. We mean to remember that you're as good as we are; that there is no difference between us other than the difference of circumstances. We mean to recognize and bear in mind always that you have as good hearts in your bosoms as other people, or as we claim to have, and treat you accordingly. We mean to marry your girls when we have a chance—the white ones I mean (the audience laughed at that)—and I have the honor to inform you that I once did have a chance that way.

You've repeatedly threatened to break up the Union if a Republican wins the presidency in 1860, I said. How will that help you? If you secede, you'll no longer enjoy the protection of the Constitution, and we'll no longer be forced to return your fugitive slaves. What will you do—build a wall between us? Make war on us? You are brave and gallant, but man for man, you're not better than we are, and there are not so many of you as there are of us. Because you're inferior in numbers, you'll make nothing by attempting to master us.

But all my entreaties were in vain. Nobody in the South was listening to me or any other Republican. From one end of the slave states to the other, politicians and newspapers persisted in calling us warmongering abolitionists. Then in October of 'fifty-nine old John

Brown raided Harpers Ferry and split the country worse than ever. It disturbed me when southerners blamed Harpers Ferry on the Republicans, when they claimed that it was the "logical" outgrowth of Republican doctrine, when they accused us of plotting to destroy their cherished "institutions" by the sword. How they reached that conclusion is beyond me. Not one of us had ever advocated an invasion of southern territory. On the contrary, we had consistently pledged to *leave slavery alone there*.

As for Brown, I thought he might be mad. But reading about his life in the newspapers, I realized that he was a man of great courage and rare unselfishness, whose hatred of slavery was genuine. It was slavery, I thought, that had caused the Harpers Ferry outbreak. Even so, I could not approve of Brown's action. No reasonable man could ever condone violence and crime. It did not escape my notice where Brown had begun his career in violence. It was in the Kansas civil war, in all the strife and bloodshed that had plagued that territory for five convulsive years. And the cause of the civil war there, of course, was Douglas's Kansas-Nebraska Act and its pernicious popular sovereignty doctrine.

They hanged old Brown while I was stumping the Kansas Territory in a lashing wintry wind. On the day after Brown's execution, I told a crowd at Leavenworth that hanging the old man was just. Even though he agreed with us in thinking slavery wrong, that could not excuse violence, bloodshed, and treason. But I warned southerners: "If constitutionally we elect a President, and therefore you undertake to destroy the Union, it'll be our duty to deal with you as old John Brown has been dealt with."

Over the winter, many Illinois papers mentioned me as a favorite son for the Republican nomination. Norman Judd, chairman of the Republican State Central Committee and a member of the Republican National Committee, also thought my chances were on the rise. A railroad lawyer with an imposing beard and a confident air, Judd reminded me of a Russian czar. "I'll tell you what's the key to victory in 1860," he said. "It's the populous states of the lower North—New Jersey, Pennsylvania, Ohio, Indiana, and Illinois. They went for Buchanan in 'fifty-six and gave him the victory over Frémont. To win in 1860, we have to carry these doubtful states. I don't think Seward or Chase can do it because of their reputations as radicals. But I think you can, because you were born in Kentucky and live in Illinois."

"Maybe so," I said. "But I'd rather have a full term in the Senate than the Presidency."

Nevertheless, I left all options open, prepared to be placed anywhere that would most likely help to advance our cause. I finally got around to writing a terse biographical sketch for sad-eyed Jesse Fell, who made it the basis for a newspaper article published in Pennsylvania—one of the key states in the upcoming election—and widely copied in the Republican press.

There wasn't much in my sketch, I told Fell, for the reason that there wasn't much of me. But the plain truth is, I was embarrassed about my origins and never liked to talk about them. I stressed the Pennsylvania and Quaker ancestry of my paternal grandfather, admitted that my own father grew up literally without education, and told how the Lincoln family migrated from Kentucky to Indiana, where my mother died when I was ten. I grew up in Indiana, went to school a little, learned only to read, write, and cipher to the rule of three, advanced this store of education under the pressure of necessity, and did farmwork till I was twenty-two, by which time we had migrated to Illinois. There I ran for the legislature, became a lawyer, and served a single term in the national House of Representatives. After that, I returned to my law practice and began losing interest in politics when the repeal of the Missouri Compromise aroused me again. What I had done since was pretty well known. "If any personal description is thought desirable," I concluded, "it may be said that I am, in height, six feet, four inches, nearly; lean in flesh, weighing, on an average, one hundred and eighty pounds; dark complexion, with coarse black hair, and grey eyes. No other marks or brands recollected."

In January of 'sixty, Judd and my friends of the old Eighth Judicial Circuit met with me in a secret caucus in Springfield and officially launched a Lincoln for President movement. At a recent meeting of the Republican National Committee in New York, Judd had pulled off something of a coup: he'd persuaded the committee to hold the national convention in Chicago on the grounds that it was a neutral site since Illinois had no clear presidential contender. I still thought my chances for the nomination were next to naught. But whatever national office I sought, I had to have the united support of the state party organization, and there lay the rub. Some Illinois Republicans thought I was too radical and inexperienced for the Presidency. Senator Trumbull, one of the state's most influential Republicans, frankly went for Judge McLean. In the state at large, there was sympathy for Bates of Missouri in southern Illinois, some for Seward and Chase in the north.

Here was my dilemma: unless the Illinois convention delegates gave me a first-ballot endorsement, my chances for any national office would be seriously jeopardized, because people would doubt my standing at home. I wrote Judd: "I am not in a position where it would hurt to lose the presidential nomination. But I am in a position where it would hurt me not to have the support of the Illinois delegates. Can you not help me a little in your end of the vineyard?" Judd had a close association with the Chicago *Press and Tribune*, the most powerful Republican paper in the state, which at that time was leaning toward Chase. A week after I wrote to Judd, however, the paper announced for me, declaring Lincoln to be the first choice of all Illinois Republicans.

In February, encouraged by that kind of backing, I took the trains to New York City, where I had a crucial speaking engagement at Henry Ward Beecher's Plymouth Church. The state of New York, of course, was a Seward stronghold, and I agreed to speak in Plymouth Church only if I could give a political address, to which my sponsors agreed. Anxious about appearing before an audience of cultured New Yorkers, I spent more time on that speech than on any other I'd ever written. When I arrived in the city, however, I learned that a "young" men's political organization, which opposed the Seward-Weed political machine and hoped to block Seward's nomination, had assumed sponsorship of my visit and had arranged for me to speak at Cooper Union in Manhattan. This forced me to spend most of the day revising my speech for a secular crowd.

When it was time to go, I put on a new black suit I'd bought in Springfield for $100. But the thing turned out to be a bad fit. When I raised an arm to stress a point, the collar had an alarming way of flying up. To make matters worse, a snowstorm had struck New York, and snow swirled through the streets as I made my way to Cooper Union. I was surprised—intimidated—to find that fifteen hundred eastern Republicans had braved the storm to hear "the Westerner." The great New York jurist David Dudley Field escorted me to the platform, and dapper William Cullen Bryant, the famous poet—"America's Wordsworth," they called him—and the editor-in-chief of the New York *Evening Post*, had "the honor" of introducing me. As I began speaking, I was so nervous my hands were shaking. I was sure the audience was comparing me to the neatly dressed Mr. Bryant. It was damned embarrassing that my collar flew up every time I made a gesture.

This speech, I knew, was my test by fire as an aspirant for

national office. I had to show eastern Republicans that I could elucidate the moral principles and goals of Republicanism clearly and persuasively. First, I refuted Judge Douglas's argument that the founders of the Republic had established the principle of nonintervention. Then I spoke to southerners, though I doubted they would listen. You are a just people, I said, but you unjustly accuse us of being outlaws and "black" Republicans. You say we're sectional because we don't exist in the South. But the truth is, *you* won't let us run candidates there; you've restricted us to the North. You've discarded the old policy of the founders as far as slavery is concerned; you've instituted a new policy for the old; and we resisted, and still resist, your innovation. True, you're divided as a party: some of you desire a congressional slave code for the territories; some want the judiciary to maintain slavery there; and still others (here I made a face) advocate the *gur-reat pur-rinciple* that if one man enslaved another, no third man could object—fantastically called popular sovereignty!

When the great hall rang with cheers and applause, I grew more confident. I began crouching down and rising high up on my toes, as was my style when I felt inspired. "You charge that we stir up insurrection among your slaves," I said, still speaking to southerners. "We deny it; and what is your proof? Harpers Ferry! John Brown!! John Brown was no Republican; and you have failed to implicate a single Republican in his Harpers Ferry enterprise. The charge is simply malicious slander." I paused. "Some of you admit that no Republican designedly aided or encouraged the Harpers Ferry affair; but still insist that our doctrines and declarations necessarily lead to such results. We don't believe it. Republican doctrines and declarations are accompanied with a continual protest against *any interference whatever* with your slaves, or with you about your slaves. Surely, this does not encourage them to revolt. In your political contests among yourselves, each faction charges the other with sympathy with Black Republicanism; and then, to give point to the charge, defines Black Republicanism to simply be insurrection, blood and thunder among the slaves.

"You say you won't abide the election of a Republican President! In that supposed event, you say, you'll destroy the Union; and then, you say, the great crime of having destroyed it will be upon us! That is cool. A highwayman holds a pistol to my ear, and mutters through his teeth, 'Stand and deliver, or I'll kill you, and then you'll be a murderer!'"

Then I addressed a few words to my fellow Republicans. "It is exceedingly desirable that all parts of this great Confederacy shall be at peace, and in harmony, one with another. Let us Republicans do our part to have it so. Even though *much provoked*, let us do *nothing* through passion and ill temper. Even though the southern people will not so much as *listen* to us, let us calmly consider their demands and determine what will satisfy them. Will they be satisfied if the territories be unconditionally surrendered to them? We know they won't. In all their present complaints against us, the *territories* are scarcely mentioned. *Invasions* and *insurrections* are the rage now. Will it satisfy them, if, in the future, we have nothing to do with invasions and insurrections? We know it won't because we know we never had anything to do with invasions and insurrections; and yet this does not exempt us from the *charge* and the *denunciation*.

"The question recurs, what *will* satisfy them? Simply this: We must not only let them alone, but we must, somehow, convince them that we do let them alone. This, we know by experience, is no easy task. We've been so trying to convince them from the very beginning of our organization, but with no success. What, then, will convince them? This, and this only: cease to call slavery *wrong*, and join them in calling it *right*. And this must be done thoroughly—done in *acts* as well as in *word*s. They want us to stop calling slavery wrong and join them, in acts as well as words, in calling it *right*. The whole atmosphere must be disinfected from all taint of opposition to slavery before they'll cease to believe that all their troubles proceed from us."

What, I asked, was their ultimate demand? While they did not yet say so, logic dictated that they would next call for the overthrow of free-state constitutions and for the nationalization of slavery. "Holding, as they do, that slavery is morally right, and socially elevating, they cannot cease to demand full national recognition of it, as a legal right, and social blessing. If slavery is right, all words, acts, laws, and constitutions against it, are themselves wrong, and should be silenced and swept away. All they ask, we could readily grant, if we thought slavery right; all we ask, they could as readily grant, if they thought it wrong. *Their thinking it right, and our thinking it wrong, is the precise fact upon which depends the whole controversy*. Thinking it wrong, as we do, can we yield to them? Can we cast our votes with their view, and against our own? In view of our moral, social, and political responsibilities, can we do this?"

The audience was with me now, clapping and cheering me on. "Let us not," I said, "be slandered from our duty by false accusations against us, nor frightened from it by menaces of destruction to the government nor of dungeons to ourselves. LET US HAVE FAITH THAT RIGHT MAKES MIGHT, AND IN THAT FAITH, LET US, TO THE END, DARE TO DO OUR DUTY AS WE UNDERSTAND IT."

People say that speech made me a viable presidential candidate. Yes, I went on across New England, giving similar addresses to Republican crowds there; but it was the Cooper Union speech, which was widely published and remarked upon, that brought the name of Lincoln to the attention of national party leaders. When I got back home, I found that Illinois Republicans were now lining up behind my candidacy. By April, the state Republican machine under Judd's shrewd leadership was hard at work for me; and Joe Medill of the *Press and Tribune* was over to Washington City, telling important people that I was the only Republican aspirant who could carry the lower North.

"Are you a serious contender?" asked Trumbull from Washington. "The taste *is* in my mouth a little," I confessed. The taste got a lot stronger when word came of the Democratic breakup at Charleston. I had predicted that Judge Douglas could not hold the antagonistic elements of his party together and that another explosion would come upon our adversaries. Now the long-expected split had happened, thanks to irreconcilable differences among the Democrats as to the best *means* of accomplishing a common purpose.

When the Republican state convention met in May, the Republican state organization crushed out a feeble move for Seward and locked up the Illinois delegation for me. As the date for the national convention approached, two old friends and judicial colleagues took over as managers of the Lincoln-for-President boom. One was Judge David Davis, a clean-shaven three-hundred-pounder who had to be transported around the Eighth Circuit by a two-horse rig. The Judge spoke in a loud, rasping voice and ruled over the Eighth "like a potentate of old." The other friend was Leonard Swett, the most famous criminal lawyer in Illinois, a boyish-looking fellow who sported a full beard. He belonged to a jolly set of rollicking young lawyers who mixed law and Latin, water and whiskey, with equal success. But one day the whiskey they drank seemed to be possessed of the very spirit of Jonah. Young Swett got so sick he went out to the hog-pen, leaned over, and began to throw up Jonah. The hogs, thinking it feed time, rushed over and began to squabble over the voided matter. "Don't fight (hic)," said Swett. "There's enough (hic) for all."

I still didn't think I could defeat Seward. Neither did Trumbull off in Washington. But Davis and Swett were more than a little optimistic when we met to plan our convention strategy. "This is the way we'll play it," Davis said. "We'll tell every delegation the plain truth, that Seward can't carry the doubtful states of the lower North. His reputation as a radical and an alleged backer of John Brown will repel the mass of conservative voters there. In short, the Republican ticket will be doomed if he's the nominee." He turned to me. "We'll promote you as the only candidate who can win in November. You have no radical national image, have offended no Republican groups or factions, have no alleged link with John Brown, and have the strongest appeal in the lower North."

"Equally important," said Swett. "You're a deeply principled and dedicated Republican. You proved that to the country at Cooper Union. This is going to be a bitter, abusive campaign. The party can count on you to defend the cause without letting the standard down."

"I hope you'll stress that point first," I said.

In mid-May, Davis, Swett, and a small army of other Lincoln men hurried up to Chicago while I stayed in Springfield, anxiously awaiting news. "There is no way I'm going to win this thing," I told my friends. "If Seward fails to get the nomination on the first ballot, the convention will likely turn to Chase or Bates."

From Lincoln headquarters in Chicago came a steady stream of telegrams. From Davis and Jesse Dubois: "We are quiet but moving heaven and earth. Nothing will beat us but old fogy politicians." From Davis: "Am very hopeful—dont be Excited—nearly dead with fatigue." From a delegate of the Springfield district: "Things are working; keep a good nerve—be not surprised at any result—but I tell you that your chances are not the worst. We have got Seward in the attitude of the representative Republican of the East—you at the West. We are laboring to make you the second choice of all the delegations we can where we cannot make you first choice. Be not too expectant, but rely upon our discretion. Again I say brace your nerves for any result."

Then came a telegram from Dr. Ray of the *Press and Tribune*. "A pledge or two may be necessary when the pinch comes." I'd warned the Lincoln men not to promise Federal appointments to this or that faction, this or that state delegation; I intended to distribute the patronage with a free hand. Suddenly apprehensive that I might be compromised, I wired Davis urgent instructions. "*Make no contracts that will bind me.*" And he made none.

When the balloting began, I steeled myself for another failure. I called at the law office of my old friend, James Conkling, and lay on his sofa with both legs hanging over the end while he expatiated on my probabilities for success. Too anxious to stay there, I went over to my own office and passed time with a couple of law students. Around noon, Eddie Baker, co-editor of the *Illinois State Journal*, burst in with the first ballot results: Seward was first, I was second, and the other candidates were far back in the counting. "Amazing!" I said. Unable to stay put, I went to the *Journal* office and sank into a chair. I was so nervous I felt sick to my stomach.

After a while another telegram arrived. On the second ballot, Seward had picked up eleven delegates, but I'd picked up seventy-nine—including Pennsylvania's forty-eight! I now had three of the critical states and heavy support throughout the lower North. Everybody in the *Journal* office was talking at once. How would Ohio go on the next ballot? Would Seward win back strength in the lower North? The minutes crawled by at glacial speed. Either I was on the verge of an incredible upset, or the bitterest defeat yet.

A messenger rushed into the office and handed me another telegram. I tore it open and felt a flush come over my face; I stared at the telegram, dumbfounded.

"Well," I said finally, "we've got it."

Everybody in the office cheered and shook my hand. Another telegram arrived from Chicago and I read it aloud: "We did it glory to God." Outside, cannon boomed the news, rattling the windows of the *Journal* office. I suddenly remembered Mary, my strongest supporter, who had always insisted that I was going to be President of the United States.

"There's a little woman down at our house would like to hear the news," I said. "I'll go down and tell her."

When I stepped into the street, church bells were tolling and Republicans were dancing and singing in the streets to the boom of the artillery. "Hurrah for Lincoln!" they shouted when they saw me. At home, little Molly had already heard the news and squealed with excitement. For the rest of the day, friends and neighbors came by to offer congratulations. Molly's round, dimpled face was positively radiant. "I'm so *proud* of you," she said, squeezing my hand.

Outside, the celebrations went on into the night. There were fireworks and torch-lit parades. At one point, a huge procession, led by the Young America Band, surrounded our home at Eighth and Jackson. I stood in the glare of torches and declared this not a personal victory, but a victory for the great Republican cause.

"I would invite all of you into the house," I said, "if it was big enough to hold you."

"We'll give you a larger house on the fourth of next March," someone cried.

44. DOUGLAS

The Democratic convention reconvened in June in Baltimore's Front Street Theater. It was an appropriate setting for the drama about to take place. My nomination hinged on which of the southern delegations were seated by the credentials committee—the Charleston seceders or the new delegations pledged to me. Both were present at the convention. If the Charleston seceders were admitted, I would never get the two-thirds vote required for the nomination. Therefore my men pulled every wire, applied every pressure, resorted to every argument, to get the new delegations seated.

I stayed in Washington and followed developments by telegraph and special messenger. While the credentials committee haggled for three days, the convention degenerated into a Goddamned shouting match between Douglas men and southern-rights men. In a typically abusive tirade, Yancey accused northern Democrats of being "corrupt and abolitionized." "They are ostrichlike," he cried; "their heads are buried in the sand of squatter sovereignty, and they don't know their great ugly, ragged abolition body is exposed!" The southerners even called us nigger-lovers! They were deranged, or drunk out of their Goddamned skulls. The *Black Republicans* were the nigger-lovers, not the Douglas Democrats.

The convention appeared to be in imminent danger of breaking up again. If that happened, it would destroy the party. It would expose the country to the perils of sectional strife between the northern and southern partisans of congressional intervention with slavery in the territories. Intervention meant disunion. There was no difference in principle between northern and southern interventionists. The one intervened *for* slavery and the other *against* slavery; but each appealed to the passions and prejudices of his own section against the peace of the whole country and the right of self-government by the people of the territories. I believed, firmly and unequivocally, that only a rigid adherence to congressional *non-intervention* could save the Union.

While I swore never to sacrifice that principle, I gladly offered to sacrifice myself to maintain it: I dispatched an urgent message to my floor manager, Dick Richardson: "If you and my friends who stood by me at Charleston decide that the principle can be preserved and unity and ascendancy of party maintained, and country saved from perils of northern abolitionism and southern disunion, by withdrawing my name and uniting upon some other non-intervention and Union-loving Democrat, I beseech you to pursue that course. The action of the Charleston convention in sustaining me by so large a majority on the platform and designating me as the first choice of the party for the Presidency is all the personal triumph I desire."

The next morning, the credentials committee reported to the raucous assembly inside the theater. The majority report ruled in my favor, admitting two Douglas delegations (Alabama and Louisiana), two secessionist delegations (Texas and Mississippi), one split delegation (Georgia), and certain individual delegates from Delaware and Arkansas, but excluded all the other southern groups. The minority report allowed all the secessionist delegations in. The convention, in near riot, voted on the two reports the next morning, and the pro-Douglas majority report won. There was no doubt now that the convention would be disrupted. This, I thought, was the time for Richardson to read my letter of concession. But there was no word from Richardson. I sent a similar letter to Dean Richmond of the New York delegation: "I beseech you to pursue the course which will save the party and the country. If necessary, withdraw my name and nominate somebody else on the principle of non-intervention. Act boldly for the right."

But Richmond wouldn't read my offer because, as I learned later, Richardson threatened him if he did. "If you slaughter Douglas," Richardson vowed, "we'll slaughter any candidate you put forth."

"Compromise is out of the question," Richmond reported. "We can't arrest a hurricane."

The next night, both the lower South and the upper South stormed out of the convention. The remaining two hundred delegates then nominated me on the first ballot and drafted a platform faithfully embodying the principle of non-intervention. The bolters defiantly met in a nearby hall and nominated John C. Breckinridge of Kentucky on a slave-code platform. The rupture of the party, which I had fought so long and hard to avoid, was now complete and irreparable.

At Douglas headquarters in Washington, my friends and backers celebrated my nomination with whiskey and champagne. But our fury at the southerners knew no bounds. There was a great deal of cursing all around. "What I don't understand," I said, "is the defection of men like Gallatin Brown and Toombs. I can understand shits like Slidell and Jeff Davis. They hate me so much that they would rather destroy the party than let me be its nominee. But Brown and Toombs don't hate me. They once said I was one of America's greatest statesmen. I can't understand why they would forsake the party and the country and go over to the disunionists."

"I think they all believe that popular sovereignty is as dangerous as abolition," someone said.

"How little they know," I said. "If I'm elected, I'll bring peace to the country. No Goddamned abolitionist will be in my Administration, or get a single Federal job from me. I'll bring around me a new set of men and put the government back on the old constitutional track."

A friend said: "A new set of men is the whole point. The southerners have ruled the party for years, and we northern Democrats have followed their lead like country cousins. We've worked our asses off for them. Well, now the northern Democracy is taking over by sheer force of numbers. You and Pugh and Richardson will run the party. And Toombs and Brown can't accept that any more than Davis can. You said yourself: it's rule or ruin with them."

"We may not have a *country* to rule when this is over," I said.

It was going to be a vicious, brutal campaign. Four candidates were now in the field: me, Breckinridge, Lincoln, and John Bell of the new Constitutional Union party, made up of die-hard Know-Nothings and Whigs. Because their platform advocated no political principles except the Constitution and the Union, a lot of people said they were crazy, as cracked as the Liberty Bell they used as their symbol. But I ordered my followers to cultivate good relations with the Bell people, because they were at least *Union* men. I vowed, however, to wage unrelenting warfare against the Black Republicans and the southern disunionists, those Goddamned traitors, and give no quarter to either.

A few days after my nomination, Jefferson Davis called at my house. It took me completely by surprise when he sent in his card. My servant opened the door, and there Davis stood like a bony apparition, staring at me with his one good eye. What appeared to be a gray film now covered the pupil of his blind eye. Striving to be civil, I invited him into the parlor.

"I have a proposition to make," he said, and frowned. His face was ghastly white.

"Go ahead," I said.

"If the Democrats run two candidates," he said, "the Black Republicans will win the election. In that event, the slave states will secede. As you know, I've long advocated secession rather than submit to a Republican takeover. But I also love the old Union and want to save her, if that is possible. I have a plan for a fusion candidate to put up against Lincoln. It calls for you, Breckinridge, and Bell to agree to withdraw and unite behind a compromise candidate like R. M. T. Hunter of Virginia, or Horatio Seymour of New York. I've just seen Bell and Breckinridge, and they like the plan. Breckinridge was all set to reject his nomination because he thought his candidacy was a forlorn hope. But I convinced him that my fusion plan would only work if he accepted. A replacement candidate might be hostile to the idea. So he agreed to run, in a sense, so that he could withdraw. He and Bell authorized me to tell you that they are willing to withdraw if you will, so that our divided forces can unite behind someone more generally acceptable to the country."

This was strange talk from Davis, and I was damned suspicious that it might be a trap. It was all I could do to control my hatred for the Goddamned bastard. "The plan is impractical," I said coldly. "If I withdraw, my friends will go over to Lincoln. I'm in the hands of my friends; they won't accept this proposition."

"Then I've done all I can," he said, rose, and walked out.

Why the Goddamned hell should I withdraw? I asked my aides. It was a matter of honor with me. I had won my nomination fairly, on the basis of the party's time-honored principles. I refused to unite with a bunch of traitors and disunionists. Maybe Breckinridge himself and some of his followers were not for disunion; but every southern disunionist was a Breckinridge man.

Others pressed me to unite with the "vandals," as we called the Breckinridge party, but I answered with a thundering no. "I'm utterly opposed to fusing with any man or any party who'll not enforce the laws, maintain the Constitution, and preserve the Union in all contingencies," I said. "I wish to God Old Hickory was still alive, so that he could hang northern and southern traitors from the same gallows."

"But if you don't fuse with Breckinridge," a fellow Democrat said, "it'll ensure Lincoln's victory."

"Then let it," I snapped. "It will give us the organization in 'sixty-four. I mean to crush out the disunion wing of the party once and for all."

I broke with tradition and took the stump in my own behalf. Yes, I still felt sickly, my throat hurt, my nerves were frayed, I had trouble sleeping. But I couldn't stay at home! The country faced the greatest danger in its history, a violent storm was gathering over the land, and I had to warn the people—had to convince them that I was the only candidate who could save the Union.

I set out across New England and New York state, speaking in one town and city after another. But the Black Republicans were out in force, singing their Goddamned song, "Ain't I glad I joined the Republicans," and I was stunned by the size of their crowds and the support they had in the press. The *New York Times* boldly predicted a Lincoln victory and averred that it was "not unlikely that Mr. Douglas himself fully shares this opinion."

Not yet, I didn't. I hadn't given up all hope. But warding off disunion was more important than my candidacy. After a hurried conference with aides and advisers, I invaded the border South in a furious attempt to rally Union men and stamp out the vandals. "I didn't come here to ask your vote," I told my southern crowds. "I'm not here on an electioneering tour. I'm here to make a plea, an appeal for the invincibility of the Constitution and the Union. There is a mature plan throughout the slave states to break up the Union. Certain southern leaders *desire* the election of Lincoln so as to have an excuse for disunion. But for my apprehension on this subject, I would not have taken the stump."

While I was speaking at Norfolk, Virginia, someone handed me a set of questions from a local editor.

First question: If Lincoln was elected, did I think the South would be justified in seceding from the Union?

"Never on earth," I replied.

Second question: If the South seceded before Lincoln committed an overt act, would I advise forceful resistance against secession?

"I myself would do all in my power to aid the government in maintaining the supremacy of the laws against all resistance to them, come from whatever quarter it might," I said. "I think the President, whoever he may be, should treat all attempts to break up the Union as Old Hickory treated the nullifiers in 1832."

Dubbing my response Douglas's "Norfolk doctrine," the disunionists ranted and raved. They accused Stephen A. Douglas of preaching violence and coercion. They called Stephen A. Douglas a Black Republican ally. I heard that Jefferson Davis himself urged Mississippi to construct two gallows, a "tall" one for Lincoln and a "short" one for the Little Giant. At Raleigh, North Carolina, I answered that Mississippi turd: "I would hang every man higher than Haman who tries to resist by force the execution of any provision of the Constitution our fathers made and bequeathed to us."

Then it was back to New York for a consultation with my vice-presidential nominee, Herschel Johnson, and other party men. The Republicans had just won the Maine and Vermont state elections. There was more talk about a fusion ticket. "No!" I cried. "God-damn it, no! If the withdrawal of my name would defeat Lincoln, I would withdraw it right now. But what other non-intervention northern Democrat is there who can beat Lincoln? If there was one, the Baltimore convention would have nominated him." I was against fusion, I said, all the way from Maine to California.

I headed west to campaign in Iowa and the Great Lakes states. While I was in Iowa, the Republicans swept Pennsylvania, Indiana, and Ohio in the fall state elections. These were all critical states of the lower North.

"That does it," I told my secretary. "Lincoln is the next President. We must try to save the Union. I'll go to the Deep South where the secession spirit is strongest."

45. LINCOLN

"Well," I said, "the Democrats have failed to unite behind a single candidate. And the early state elections in New England and in Pennsylvania, Indiana, and Ohio have surpassed all our expectations. I hesitate to say it, but it really looks as if the government is about to fall into our hands. I see Douglas is on the hustings himself, off in the Deep South now. I'll give him credit: he's got great hardihood, pertinacity, and magnetic power, and he's a loyal Union man. He also has the most audacity in maintaining an untenable position. He's still arguing that slavery can be legally expelled from where it can legally exist. That's as untenable a proposition as you can get, yet he's bamboozled thousands into believing him."

It was a few weeks before election day, and I was sitting in my temporary "shop"—the governor's office on the second floor of the Illinois statehouse. The office was packed with reporters and political emissaries from all over the North. It had been that way since my nomination, and my visitors, day in and day out, bombarded me with questions about my background. "Mr. Lincoln, the public knows little about you. Outside Illinois, you're almost totally unknown. Can you tell us something about yourself we can report to our readers or constituents?" I always directed them to a recently published campaign biography by John Locke Scripps of the Chicago *Press and Tribune*. I asked them to please get my first name right. It was *Abraham*, not Abram, as I was tired of pointing out.

The most persistent questions, however, concerned the election and the state of the country. "Mr. Lincoln, what are your plans? policies? Cabinet choices? Mr. Lincoln, what will you do if you're elected and the slave states secede? Mr. Lincoln, do you think there will be war?" I tell you, these people would try the patience of Job. While I did comment on the election, I refused to address the state of the country or to issue a statement of policy. My position on the great questions of the hour, I said, were already well known. Besides, I added, my enemies would distort and misrepresent anything I said, as they always had.

Since the opening of the campaign, I had stayed put in Springfield, which was the proper thing to do, and let an army of other Republican leaders canvass for the ticket. Mr. Seward apparently harbored no ill will over the loss of the nomination and proved to be an exceptionally loyal party man: he stumped New England and then took off across the more westerly states of the lower North. If we won, I had him pegged for my Cabinet as Secretary of State. Chase, Trumbull, Billy Herndon, Giddings, Lovejoy—all were out there, campaigning hard for the Republican cause.

Springfield was probably typical of how the campaign went in towns and cities across the North. On Springfield's unpaved square, wooden stands hawked fence rails and other election curios. I'd been dubbed the "rail splitter" candidate, on account of the work I'd done with an ax in my early years. Every few nights, young Republican Wide-Awakes, bearing torches and wearing caps and shiny cloth capes, marched through town in zigzag lines that resembled fence rails. There were banquets and barbecues, rallies and parades. At the head of one procession, young Republican men carried a huge ball that read on one side, *The People mourn insulted laws, And curse Steve Douglas as the cause*, and on the other, *Westward the Star of Empire takes its way; We link-on to Lincoln—our fathers were for Clay*. In a flag-draped replica of the Chicago wigwam in which I had been nominated, Republican orators harangued as many as three thousand people at a time. "The Republican party is the party of the future," they cried. "Our motto is Free Soil, free labor, and free men. We mean to contain slavery and provide free homesteads on the frontier, a transcontinental railroad, and Federal subsidies for agricultural colleges." When the speeches were done, all would break out singing the Republican campaign song to the tune of "The Old Gray Mare":

> *Ain't I glad I joined the Republicans,*
> *Joined the Republicans, joined the Republicans,*
> *Ain't I glad I joined the Republicans,*
> *Down in Illinois.*

I've been through a lot of abusive campaigns, but few matched this one for the slinging of mud and much else. Here in Illinois, the Douglas papers belittled me as a party hack, said I'd never done anything in my entire life that entitled me to the Presidency. They said I was illiterate, crude, vulgar, degenerate, and worse, far worse. There were even stories passed around that Lincoln was a bastard, that his real father was Abraham Enloe. That rankled me. The Democrats also resorted to their favorite smear, arguing that Lincoln was a dangerous abolitionist who lusted for Negro equality and race mixing. "That is not so!" I said whenever I heard that reckless lie. "The abolitionists aren't for me. Garrison calls us a 'cowardly party.' Wendell Phillips says Lincoln is 'a huckster in politics.' They have their own organization, the Radical Abolition party, and their own candidate, Gerrit Smith, the backer of John Brown. True, we share a hatred of slavery, but we don't advocate abolition in the southern states as they do. We're pledged to leave slavery alone where it already exists."

A thousand Republicans had said that ten thousand times, but our disclaimers fell on deaf ears down in Dixie. It amazed me that Republicans and southerners spoke the same languge, yet when we promised to "leave slavery alone where it exists," southerners heard abolitionist rantings about invasion and destruction of their "institutions."

I tell you, I couldn't believe the hysteria my candidacy caused down there. My name didn't even appear on the ballot in ten slave states, and my effigy burned in windows and public squares. My law partner, Herndon, with black eyes flashing, brought me the latest issues of the fire-eating Charleston *Mercury* and other southern papers. They called Lincoln a chimpanzee, "a vulgar mobocrat," "a free-soil border ruffian," a "horrid-looking wretch" with "the leanest, lankiest, most ungainly mass of legs and arms and hatchet face ever strung on a human form." Lincoln was a scourge, a partisan of John Brown, a lunatic, "a blood-thirsty tyrant," whose "fiendish" abolitionist spies prowled southern slave quarters, distributing "Lincolnisms" in order to incite the blacks to arson, murder, and rebellion. Mobs and militia units rooted out and lynched northern agents and arrested Negroes who had been heard cheering for Lincoln in the slave quarters. The blacks apparently thought "Black Republican" meant that I was a Negro coming to free them. On platforms draped with state flags, fire-breathing orators damned me as a "sooty" and "scoundrelly" abolitionist who had "nigger" blood and a mulatto running mate, Hannibal Hamlin of Maine. The victory of Lincoln's "Black Republican, free love, free Nigger" party, they warned, would toll the bells of doom for the white man's South. "I shudder to contemplate it!" one man wrote in an Alabama paper. "What social monstrosities, what desolated fields, what civil broils, what robberies, rapes, and murders of the poorer whites by the emancipated blacks would then disfigure the whole fair face of this prosperous, smiling, and happy southern land."

How could they say such things? I just shook my head in disbelief. They seemed to think that Republican armies were going to invade them and free their four million blacks by gunpoint, appoint them to Federal jobs, and let them run loose in a riot of "rapine" and butchery. White orators and editors vowed to destroy the Union before they would let us put the "niggers" on top. "Let the consequences be what they may, whether the Potomac is crimsoned in human gore, and Pennsylvania Avenue is paved ten fathoms deep with mangled bodies," said an Atlanta paper, "the constitutional

South will never submit to such humiliation and degradation as the inauguration of Abraham Lincoln."

These were serious threats, according to a report I got from Republican Frank Blair over in St. Louis. "This glorious Union," he wrote me in October, "will be sundered in consequence of the triumph of our party in the contest so close at hand. The misrepresentations of our enemies have been so persistent and malignant in the South where we have few or no defenders, that we feel sure, judging from our intelligence from that quarter, that there exists there a large and influential class who are even now ready to apply the torch which will light the fires of civil discord."

I discounted such reports. I believed that hotspur editors and politicians and the big slaveowners were responsible for the secession threats and anti-Lincoln, anti-Republican diatribes. The good people of the South themselves had too much good sense and good temper to attempt the ruin of the government. Their love of the Union was too strong to let that happen. At least I so hoped and believed at the time.

Besides, I'd heard it all before, all this talk about disunion and civil war if the southern leaders didn't get their way. I thought it an empty threat and refused to give in to them, abandon the Republican platform, withdraw from the contest, or make any concessions whatever. I remember this one fellow, a Connecticut politician by the name of Sanford, who called on me the day before the election. He brought letters and an urgent plea from a number of New England industrialists who did business with southerners and were terrified of civil war.

"I've come to see if their alarm can be relieved," he said. "I'm interested in manufactures myself, and I can tell you how bad things are in the Northeast. Our trade has fallen off, our workmen are idle, we get no orders from the South, and with the increasing chances of civil war, bankruptcy and ruin stare us in the face."

The man's persistent manner irritated me. So did the insistent tone in the letters from the industrialists, which he demanded that I read.

"They wish you to be conciliatory," Sanford said, "to offer some conservative promise that would reassure southerners who are honestly alarmed."

What a mercenary appeal! "There are no such men," I snapped. "This is the same old trick southerners try to use to break down every northern victory. I'm not going to barter away the moral principle involved in this contest for the commercial gain of a new submission to the South. If I did, I would lose the support of my entire party. I would go to Washington as powerless as a block of buckeye wood."

"But can't you offer honest southern men something?"

"The honest men," I said, getting hotter by the second, "can look at our platform and what I've already said. There they'll find everything I could say now. All I could add would be repetitious. Since I've told them my beliefs and principles ten times already, would they believe an eleventh time?"

"But, sir, the South is making armed preparations!"

"The North doesn't fear invasion from the slave states, nor do we intend to invade them. Never have. They've talked so much about what they plan to do, in the event of a Black Republican victory, they've convinced themselves that northerners have no courage left."

The next day was November sixth, election day. At three that afternoon, I went to the polling place in the courthouse, cut my name from the ballot, and voted a straight Republican ticket. A huge crowd, cheering wildly and throwing their hats in the air, followed me through the hall, up the stairs to the booth, and back down again. It appeared that I would not have another awakened moment to myself for the next four years.

That night, Jesse Dubois and other old friends accompanied me to the telegraph office to monitor the returns. As the superintendent read off the returns from Illinois, I lay on the sofa, as quiet and tranquil as I'd ever been during an election. Only when I carried my own precinct did I show emotion, letting loose with something between a crow and a cheer. Presently, Lyman Trumbull came in and examined the state races through his gold-rimmed spectacles, enough to know that he would be reelected Senator. The telegraph started ticking again. The returns from New England and the Northwest pointed to a Republican sweep of both the upper and lower North.

"If we get New York," Trumbull said, "that settles it."

When the wire from New York ticked in, the superintendent was so excited he couldn't read it clearly.

Jesse Dubois, who'd dozed off, bolt straight up. "How's that?" he asked.

"We've carried New York!" the telegraph man blurted out.

Dubois seized the wire and screaming "spatch! spatch!" ran over to the statehouse where a great Republican crowd was gathered. We could hear them yelling when they got the news.

Around midnight, returns from the slave states started coming in. "Now," I said, "we'll get a few licks back." When the reports became monotonous, I left to attend a victory party in the statehouse arranged by Mary and the other Republican ladies of Springfield. It seemed as though all the Republicans in town were out in the streets, parading arm in arm and shouting at the top of their lungs. Others were on rooftops singing and yelling, "Ain't you glad you joined the Republicans, down in Illinois!"

When I entered the hall where the party was going on, the lady folk crowded around me, their faces lit up with smiles. "How do you do, *Mr. President*," they said, and escorted me to a seat. They made over me to the point of embarrassment, brought me coffee and sandwiches and sang Republican choruses so vigorously that I had to laugh. I spotted Mary across the room—she was giggling and carrying on, flushed with happiness over a victory she had long predicted. She looked at me and silently spoke the words: *I told you.*

46. DOUGLAS

Election day found me down in Mobile, Alabama. I was physically exhausted, my voice reduced to a painful whisper, from the hardest campaigning I'd ever done—three and a half months on the stump in the North, West, and upper and lower South. I spent election night with John Forsyth in his office at the Mobile *Register*, where we kept track of the returns by telegraph. Before the night was over, it was clear that I would come in second behind Lincoln in popular votes, with Breckinridge third and Bell fourth.

"Well, John, I'm beaten," I said hoarsely. "Lincoln will win by a big margin in the Electoral College. Even if Breckinridge, Bell, and I had withdrawn and united behind a single Democratic candidate, Lincoln would still have won a majority of the electoral votes. It looks like he'll carry California and Oregon and every northern state with the probable exception of New Jersey. Richardson refuses to be pessimistic, though. He says we're beaten but not conquered. 'We must raise the standard for Douglas in 'sixty-four,' he says."

But I speak frankly when I tell you I was depressed. It didn't help that Forsyth, my friend and longtime supporter, wanted to call a state convention to deliberate Alabama's course. He had his associate read me an article he had written for his newspaper that called for such a convention.

"The only way to manage the secession current," he said, "is to appear to go with it and then try to control it."

I disagreed. "If you can't prevent a convention from meeting," I said, "you can't hope to control it."

Forsyth, however, insisted on publishing the article. "Frankly," he said, "if the Black Republicans win the election, we must part. And it won't be a peaceful separation. A giant nation can't die without a giant struggle. But that's preferable to four million freed blacks turned loose on us."

With my secretary, Sheridan, I walked back to the hotel in the dark and empty streets. I felt Goddamned hopeless. I was sure there was a conspiracy afoot in the South to break up the Union, and I doubted that it was within my power to frustrate that hellish scheme.

The next day, Adele and I took a steamboat down the Gulf coast to New Orleans. In a rainstorm, I spoke to a large crowd from the steps of the St. Charles Hotel. Adele said my eyes were flashing some of their old fire. But my voice was so hoarse that I had trouble making myself heard. "This storm," I rasped, "reminds us of the storm now threatening our country. But we need not despond. The bright sun will soon chase away those clouds and the patriots of the land will rally as one man, and throttle the enemies of our country."

A few days later, in response to the importuning of ninety-six New Orleans citizens, I issued an urgent statement to the nation. "No man in America regrets the election of Mr. Lincoln more than I do," I said; "none made more strenuous exertions to defeat him; none differ with him more radically and irreconcilably upon all the great issues involved in the contest. No man living is more prepared to resist, by all the legitimate means, the aggressive policy which he and his party are understood to represent. But, while I say this, I am bound to declare my conscientious conviction that the mere election of any man to the Presidency does not of itself furnish just cause for dissolving the Union.

"It is apprehended that the policy of Mr. Lincoln and the principles of his party endanger the peace and safety of the slaveholding states. Is this apprehension well founded? No, it is not. Mr. Lincoln and his party lack the power, even if they had the disposition, to disturb or impair the rights and institutions of the South. They certainly cannot harm the South under existing laws. Will they have the power to repeal or change these laws, or to enact others? It is well known that they will be in a minority in both houses of Congress, with the Supreme Court against them. Hence no bill can pass either house of Congress impairing or disturbing the rights or institutions of the southern people in any manner whatever, unless a portion of the southern senators and representatives absent themselves so as to give an abolition majority in consequence of their absence.

"In short, the President will be utterly powerless to do evil. What good or harm can he do to anybody, except to humble the pride and wound the sensibilities of a large portion of the American people by occupying the chair once filled by Washington, Jefferson, Madison, and Jackson? Four years will soon pass, when the ballot box will furnish a peaceful, legal, and constitutional remedy for the evils and grievances with which the country may be afflicted."

I left the South feeling angry and hurt. The *Little Giant* was the legitimate heir of Washington, Jefferson, Madison, and Jackson; the *Little Giant* should occupy the chair they once filled. It was unthinkable that Lincoln would hold the office of the Presidency in my place; a jewel that was rightfully mine had been stolen from me by the treachery of the southern Democrats, and I cursed those God-damn bastards until tears burned my eyes.

47 . DOUGLASS

I was back in the country in 1860. My youngest daughter had died while I was in England and I had come home in May to be with my family. I did not care if the Virginia slave hounds were still after me because of my association with John Brown; I was prepared to receive them with fists if they came calling at my home in Rochester.

I had watched Lincoln's rise to the Republican party nomination with awe and admiration. I told the readers of my newspaper that he was a man of unblemished private character. He had a cool, well-balanced head; had great firmness of will; was perseveringly industrious; and was one of the most frank, honest men in political life. He was, moreover, a member of the Republican party's most liberal wing, and was fully committed to the denationalization of slavery and the doctrine of the "irrepressible conflict." In his debates with Douglas, Lincoln came fully up to the highest mark of Republicanism. He was a man of will and nerve, I said, and would not back down from his own assertions.

Yet the Republican party as a whole troubled me. It struck me as being opposed to the *political power* of slavery, rather than to slavery itself. At times it seemed both to *hate* and *defend* colored Americans; it could deny us the full joys of citizenship—deny us the right to vote and sit on juries—and yet insist that we were endowed with the inalienable rights of life, liberty, and the pursuit of happiness just like whites. I struggled to understand why this party, which had so much promise, would denigrate and uplift us at the same time.

Through most of the 1860 campaign, I remained loyal to the Radical Abolitionist party and urged my readers to vote for its candidate and my friend, Gerrit Smith. But I had little heart for such a futile gesture—I was a *realist* in political matters—and before the contest was over, I found myself campaigning hard for Mr. Lincoln. And I rejoiced when he won the election. For fifty years, I told my readers, the country had taken the law from the lips of an exacting, haughty, and imperious slave oligarchy. The masters of slaves had been masters of the Republic. But no longer! Lincoln's election had vitiated their authority and broken their power.

48. STOWE

Long before Mr. Lincoln's election, I had turned away from the antislavery cause and drawn into myself because of an unbearable personal loss: my dear son Henry had drowned in the Connecticut River while a student at Dartmouth College. Henry had died without grace; he'd been hurried into eternity without a moment's warning, without preparation, and it almost drove me mad wondering where he was and whether he'd died "unregenerate." I felt cold—weary—dead inside, everything a burden to me; I wanted like the woman in the St. Bernard to lie down with my arms around the wayside cross and sleep away into a brighter day. I couldn't even water the plants in my garden and let them die by inches before my eyes. I was ready to curse God and die.

Then I realized that all my doubting was Satan's work, that he was trying to separate me from the love of Christ. I was finally able to function again when, like my sister Catharine, I rejected the Calvinist tenets of "original sin, conversion, and God's grace." I did so because they denied salvation to children like my dear Henry and added torture to a bereaved mother's grief.

A couple of years later, Mr. Lincoln's election revitalized my antislavery sentiments and caused me to start writing again about slavery, in articles I contributed to the New York religious paper, the *Independent,* now edited by my brother Henry Ward Beecher. What, I asked, had God wrought in Lincoln's victory? This election was like no other one: it turned on a great moral principle—hatred of slavery—and was the first, firm national step taken to arrest a downward course of concession to evil that had been going on ever since the Constitution was adopted.

I reminded my readers what slavery meant: it meant four million men and women whom the southern law, systematically, and with logical accuracy not to be misunderstood, had stripped even of the name of human beings, and declared not persons but things. They could not sue or be sued—they could not buy or sell—they could not own a foot of land—they could not form a legal marriage—they could not own or educate their own childen—their family loves were all accidents of bargain and sale—they could not learn to read or write—they could not raise a hand against the will of any white person who might choose to insult or dishonor them or their wives or children, on pain of death.

Thinking on all this, one could only remember the question of the great Christian abolitionist, Sojourner Truth: "Is God dead?"

49. GARRISON

At first I disparaged Lincoln. "He may stand six feet four inches high," I said, "but he's a mental dwarf." Brother Phillips did me one better, deriding Lincoln as "the slave hound of Illinois" because he supported the hellish fugitive slave law. Whoever returned, or consented to return, a fugitive slave to the clutches of his master was, in the sight of God, an accomplice in man-stealing.

But when I studied Lincoln's speeches, I developed a certain respect for him—nay, an admiration. He was honest and eloquent in his hatred of slavery as *a moral wrong*. And if the division between his party and the South in 1860 related solely to the further *extension* of slavery, it really signified a much deeper stirring in the hearts of the northern people which, in time, must ripen into more decisive action against that accursed institution.

I took immense delight that Lincoln's victory operated upon the whole slaveholding South in a manner indicative of the torments of the damned. The brutal and bloody-minded tyrants, who had so long ruled the country with impunity, were now furiously foaming at the mouth, gnawing their tongues in pain, indulging in the most horrid blasphemies, uttering the wildest threats, and avowing the most treasonable designs. Their passions, "set on fire of hell," led them into every kind of excess, and they were inspired by a demoniacal frenzy. To the South was strikingly applicable, at this hour, the language of the Book of Revelations: "Babylon is fallen, is fallen, and is become the habitation of devils, and the hold of every foul spirit, and a cage of every unclean and hateful bird. Her sins have reached into heaven, and God hath remembered her inequities. . . . Therefore shall her plagues come in one day, death, and mourning, and famine; and she shall be utterly burned with fire."

Never had the truth of the ancient proverb "Whom the gods intend to destroy, they first make mad" been more signally illustrated than in the condition of the southern slaveholders following Lincoln's election. They were insane from their fears, their guilty forebodings, their lust of power and rule, their hatred of free institutions, their consciousness of merited judgments; so that they may be properly classed with the inmates of a lunatic asylum. Their dread of Mr. Lincoln, of his Administration, of the Republican party, demonstrated their insanity. In vain did Mr. Lincoln tell them, "I do not stand pledged to the abolition of slavery where it already exists." They raved just as fiercely as though he were another John Brown, armed for southern invasion and universal emancipation! In vain did the Republican party present but one point of antagonism to slavery—to wit, no more territorial expansion. In vain did that party exhibit the utmost caution not to give offense to any other direction—and make itself hoarse in uttering professions of loyalty to the Constitution and the Union. The South protested that its designs were infernal, and for them there was "sleep no more!" Were not these the signs of a demented people?

Nevertheless, I said in the *Liberator*, there was "method" in their madness. In their wildest paroxysms, they knew precisely how far to proceed. Would they secede from the Union? Would they jump into the Atlantic? Would they conflagrate their own dwellings, cut their own throats, and enable their slaves to rise in successful insurrection? By their bullying and raving, they had many times frightened the North into a base submission to their demands—and they expected to do it again! Would they succeed? The next few months would tell.

PART FOUR

THE STORM HAS BURST UPON US

50. DAVIS

I was at Brierfield when Lincoln won the Presidency. I had, of course, long advocated disunion in case of a Black Republican victory. But now that the fateful day had arrived, I shrank from secession because I was certain it could not be peacefully accomplished. I was haunted by recurring images of civil war, of towns and homesteads in flames across the whole of our land.

A letter came from Robert Barnwell Rhett, Jr., secessionist editor of the Charleston *Mercury*, asking me how Mississippi would react if South Carolina left the Union immediately and separately. I replied that South Carolina ought not to secede alone, but should wait until the other slave states could be brought into cooperation with her. But, I added, if the secession of South Carolina should be met by an attempt to coerce her back into the Union, that act of usurpation, folly, and wickedness would enlist every true southern man for her defense.

South Carolina was in no mood to wait. The state legislature called for a secession convention to convene on December seventeenth, and James Chesnut and James Hammond both resigned their seats in the national Senate. Should Mississippi follow South Carolina's lead? That was the question confronting myself, Governor John Pettus, Gallatin Brown, and the Mississippi congressmen when we met for a two-day conference in the governor's mansion in Jackson.

I urged caution. "I'm opposed to separate and immediate state action," I said. "Secession will likely trigger a war, and gentlemen, we're not prepared for war. Mississippi would be crushed. That is why I think we must move slowly. When eight or ten states are ready to leave, then they should hold secession conventions and all go out together."

Gallatin Brown and Congressman L. Q. C. Lamar agreed with me. But fiery and tempestuous Reuben Davis and two other congressmen favored immediate, separate secession. So did Governor Pettus, a grim, crude planter with a full beard and large ears. Their belligerence took me by surprise. "The time's come for drastic action," Reuben Davis said. "Governor Pettus must convene the legislature so that it can call for a secession convention to meet as soon as possible. This will amount to a declaration of war, but I see no other way."

I pleaded in vain for Pettus to wait for the other states or until Lincoln took office before pushing for a secession convention. Events were moving too fast and too dangerously to suit me. Because I continued to urge caution, the majority grumbled against me, said I was "too slow," said I was behind the general opinion of the state, which favored prompt secession. As we debated, someone handed me a telegram from Washington City urging me to return at once to consult with the President. Before leaving the governor's mansion, I said I would abide by the majority decision in the governor's conference, so that we could present a united front to the people of Mississippi. Brown and Lamar went along as well. Pettus forthwith called the legislature into session; at his urging, it scheduled a convention to meet on January seventh, 1861.

On the train back to Washington, I was certain the state would secede before Lincoln was inaugurated. Varina, who had remained in Washington, greeted me with a warning: "There is a settled gloom hanging over everyone here. Everybody is scared, especially Mr. Buchanan." When I called at the White House, Buchanan seemed to have aged twenty years: his face was furrowed, his body stooped, his hair snow white. Muttering to himself, with his head tilted forward and to one side, he seemed confused, frightened, and desperate.

"South Carolina's forces are encircling the Federal forts in Charleston Harbor," he said, and added that Cass of Michigan, his Secretary of State, wanted to reinforce them. But his southern Cabinet members, Cobb, Thompson, and Floyd, all counseled inaction. So did I.

"Yes, I knew you would," he muttered, avoiding my stare. Then he showed me a rough draft of his message to Congress and solicited my advice. I was glad to read that he appreciated our grievances and that he blamed the crisis entirely on northern antislavery agitation. "Good, good," I said. "That is the correct view of the matter." I suggested a few changes in the message, and the President agreed to make them.

"The President is with us," I reported to my southern colleagues in the Senate. But I had been misled. The final version of his message, which was read to Congress on December third, denied the right of the southern states to secede, arguing that the founders of the general government were not guilty of "the absurdity of providing for its own dissolution." Far worse, Buchanan announced his intention to collect revenues in the slave states regardless of what happened, and he reported that he had ordered the commander of the forts in Charleston Harbor to defend them. I was shocked and furious. Clearly the old imbecile had surrendered to Cass! True, Buchanan did concede that the government had no right to "coerce a state into submission," but I and my southern colleagues were offended by his promise to collect revenue in South Carolina even if she seceded. I was even more offended by Buchanan's denial of a state's constitutional right to leave the Union, and I said so in the Senate. The theory of our Constitution is one of the equality of sovereign states, I pointed out. It was made by the states and for the states. Since the sovereign states had created the Union in the first place, any of them could leave it whenever they considered such action necessary.

Senator Thomas Clingman, a grim-faced North Carolinian, elaborated on our position. "I fully agree with the President that there is no power or right of this government to attempt to coerce a state back into the Union," he said; "but if a state does secede, and thus becomes a foreign state, it seems to me equally clear that you have no right to collect taxes in it. The President says he will collect revenue. I deprecate it. Sir, the current of resistance is running rapidly over the South. If anything can be done to avert the evil, let those who have the power do it."

It was indeed up to the majority section, the aggressor, to avert the storm. "I call upon all men who have in their hearts a love of the Union, and whose service is not merely that of the lip," I said in the Senate, "to look the question calmly but fully in the face, that they may see the true cause of our danger, which I believe to be that a sectional hostility has been substituted for a general fraternity, and thus the government rendered powerless for the ends for which it was instituted. Is there a remedy for the crisis? If so, it should come from those on the other side of the chamber, from the majority section, from the section which has committed the act that now threatens the Union. I call on you, the representatives of that section, here and now, to say so, if your people are not hostile to us and our institutions."

Many southern Senators declared that secession would occur no matter what concessions the North offered. "We've been deeply aggrieved," my Mississippi colleague, Gallatin Brown, raged at the Republicans. "The accumulating wrongs of years have finally culminated in your triumph, in the triumph of principles which, if we submitted to them, would be the deepest degradation that ever befell a free people. We will *not submit*. But do not misunderstand us. We invite no war. All we ask is to be allowed to depart in peace."

Bristling with anger, little Iverson of Georgia took the floor. "Sir, we believe that the only security for the institution to which we attach so much importance is secession and a southern confederacy. We're satisfied that the Black Republicans intend to use Federal power to put down and extinguish the institution of slavery in the southern states. That is my opinion. And it's the opinion of a large majority of the people of Georgia and of the South. We believe that the destruction of slavery is the ultimate aim and design of the Republican party, the abolitionists of the North. We don't intend to stay in this Union until we become so weak that we won't be able to resist when the time comes for resistance. Our true policy is, to go out of this Union now while we have strength to resist any attempt on the part of the Federal Government to coerce us. And I can tell you that South Carolina is not the only state going out. Her destiny is fixed beyond a doubt. She's determined, in the words of Senator Hammond, to go out *high, dry*, and *forever*. South Carolina will resolve herself into a separate, sovereign, and independent state before the ides of January. Florida and Mississippi, whose conventions are soon to meet, will follow the example of South Carolina; and Alabama will go out of the Union on the seventh of January next. Then the Georgia convention follows on the sixteenth of January. Sir, before the fourth of March, five states, if not eight, will certainly be out of the Union and will have formed a constitution and frame of government for themselves.

"It's time to look this thing in the face," he told the Republicans. "Some of you talk about repealing the North's personal liberty laws as a concession to the South. We don't dread your personal liberty laws. What we dread is the existence and action of the public sentiment of the northern states that are opposed to the institution of slavery, and are determined to break it down—to use all the power of the Federal Government, as well as every other power in their hands, to bring about its ultimate and speedy extinction. That's what we apprehend. Sir, we *see* the approaching storm. We're *determined* to seek our own safety and security before it bursts upon us and overwhelms us with its fury. We intend, Mr. President, to go out peaceably if we can, forcibly if we must."

Bluff Ben Wade rose to speak for the Black Republicans. As was his style, he began by telling an obscene joke that I will not repeat. The man sickened me. When the laughter subsided, he said in a sneering voice: "I disavow all intention on the part of the Republican party to harm a hair of your heads anywhere. We hold to no doctrine that can possibly work an inconvenience on you. We've been faithful to the execution of all the laws in which you have any interest. It's not, then, that Mr. Lincoln is expected to do any overt act that would injure you. You won't wait for any. Anticipating that the government *may* work an injury, you say you'll put an end to it. This means that you intend either to *rule* or *ruin* this government. That is what your complaint comes to; nothing else."

Wade's speech darkened our mood. "The schism between the North and South is deeper than hell," Iverson told a group of us. "Look at the spectacle on this floor. There are the Republican Senators on that side. Here are the southern Senators on this side. How much social intercourse is there between us? They sit on their side, silent and gloomy; we sit on ours with knit brows and portentous scowls. In this state of feeling, divided as we are by interest, by a geographical feeling, by everything that makes two people separate and distinct, I ask, why in hell should we remain in the same Union together?"

"The Union was dear to me when it was a Union of fraternal states," I said. "But that Union no longer exists. The abolitionists and Black Republicans have destroyed that Union."

On the evening of December thirteenth, a group of Senators and representatives from nine southern states met in the apartment of Congressman Reuben Davis of Mississippi. Two men—Wigfall of Texas and Pugh of Alabama, I believe—had drawn up a joint address, "To Our Constituents." I well remember the heads nodding around me as the joint address was read aloud. "The argument is exhausted," it said. "In our judgment, the Republicans are resolute in the purpose to grant nothing that will or ought to satisfy the South. We are satisfied that the honor, safety, and independence of the southern people require the organization of a southern confederacy—a result to be obtained only by separate state secession."

A number of Senators and congressmen signed the address that evening. But I hesitated. If secession must come, I still favored all the states going out together. And, to tell the truth, I still held a tiny thread of hope that *my* Union, the Union of fraternal states, might be revived somehow. My colleagues beseeched me to sign the address. "There is no longer any hope of saving the Union," one argued. "We must keep ourselves clean of all compromises," said another. "A show of unity and strength from us will impress northerners who favor coercion." I considered their arguments all night, and the next day decided to sign. In all, thirty of us did so.

It was the most difficult decision I had ever made up to then. Coercion and civil war, I feared, were sure to follow. But I believed that the time had come for me to join the ranks of the immediate and separate secessionists, which included the vast majority of my constituents in Mississippi. The strain of that decision, however, brought on an attack of dyspepsia and facial neuralgia, which left me miserably ill. My face burned as if red-hot knives were lancing it.

A few days later, I saw an editorial in Horace Greeley's New York *Tribune* that gave me a ray of hope. "If the cotton states shall become satisfied that they can do better out of the Union than in it," he wrote, "we insist on letting them go in peace." If only the Black Republicans would do that! I told Varina. It was the *only* way to avoid war.

There were southerners, I admit, who opposed secession. The most prominent was John J. Crittenden of Kentucky, the senior member of the Senate. He kept begging us to find some way to save the Union on honorable terms. "We must find a remedy to do that," he cried. "I'm filled with despair that the Union might be stricken down." A spare, erect old man with thick brows, dark, deep-set eyes, and a weather-beaten face, Crittenden had served off and on in the Senate since 1817, and he beseeched me to help him forge a compromise to ward off secession. I did not see how the Senate could accomplish anything now, not with powerful, irreversible secession movements sweeping the lower South, and I told Crittenden so.

"We have to *try*," he said. "We must *try*. Disunion is the greatest evil that can befall us."

"*Civil war* is the greatest evil that can befall us," I corrected. "And that will come if we're not allowed to depart in peace."

Goaded on by Crittenden and others, the Senate in mid-December voted to create a Committee of Thirteen and charged it with the task of reporting a compromise that would keep the South in the Union. Vice-President Breckinridge asked me to serve, but I declined because I had signed the address "To Our Constituents" and favored disunion. I was even more determined to stay off the committee because Douglas was sure to be on it. The thought of working closely with that fatheaded weasel made my face burn worse than ever. But Breckinridge, who stood six feet two inches in height, with auburn hair and haunted, dark-blue eyes, begged me to reconsider with such deep emotion that I finally relented. But my heart was not in the work. My *heart* was in Mississippi.

Two days later, Breckinridge announced the composition of the Committee of Thirteen. It consisted of eight Democrats—Douglas, William Bigler, and Henry Rice of the North, Crittenden, Lazarus W. Powell, Robert Toombs, R. M. T. Hunter, and myself of the South—and five Republicans led by Seward. That same day, December twentieth, South Carolina seceded from the Union and declared herself a sovereign, independent nation. In Charleston, where the secession convention met, they were dancing in the streets, throwing hats and canes into the air, and firing artillery salutes.

When the Committee of Thirteen convened, Douglas predictably tried to take control. "We must put aside partisan politics," he said in his whiskey-strained voice; "we must devote ourselves to the questions on which the fate of the country is hanging. We must forget past commitments. I'm ready to make any reasonable sacrifice of party tenets to save the country." By that, I suppose, he meant he would sacrifice squatter sovereignty. Why hadn't he put aside that inflammatory doctrine years earlier, when it might have made a difference? Now it was too damned late.

Crittenden, his voice and dark gray eyes radiating sincerity, offered a set of compromise proposals in the form of constitutional amendments. One restored the Missouri Compromise line to all present and future territories, with slavery permitted below the line and excluded above it. Another amendment prohibited Congress from abolishing slavery in Federal forts, arsenals, and other installations in the slave states or in the District of Columbia. And a third forbade any abolition amendment to the Constitution from ever being adopted.

As far as the lower South was concerned, the Crittenden plan was an exercise in futility. South Carolina was already out of the Union; six other states would soon follow; and no compromise measures were going to change that. If there was any purpose to the plan, it was to prevent the secession of the upper South. As we debated the Crittenden measures, only Douglas, Bigler, and Crittenden voiced their support of it.

To no one's surprise, Douglas proposed his own compromise plan. After you boiled out all his vague and clumsy wording, his proposal amounted to yet another version of popular sovereignty. "No adjustment will restore and preserve peace," he said unctuously, "which does not banish the slavery question from Congress and place it beyond the reach of Federal legislation." So much for putting aside old party tenets! This overweening little egotist had a single purpose, and that was to force a party test on the northern Democrats. The Douglas plan, I'm happy to say, received no consideration by the committee whatever.

Toombs and I offered counter proposals, which we knew the Black Republicans and Douglas would repudiate—we wanted to show the South just how intransigent all the Yankees were. Our plan called for constitutional amendments that guaranteed slavery in the territories; prohibited Congress from ever abolishing slavery without the consent of a majority of the slave states; nullified the personal liberty laws; and assured slaveholders the right of transit with their slaves into the free states. As we expected, the Black Republicans rejected the plan out of hand. Douglas, decrying our proposals as "abstract phantoms," refused to vote on them.

That left the Crittenden plan. I moved that no compromise should be recommended to the Senate without the support of a majority of both parties on the committee. The motion carried. I made it plain that I would reject the Crittenden plan if the Republicans did so. The Republicans, however, were reluctant to commit themselves to a vote until they had heard from Lincoln, that blackest of all Republicans.

51. LINCOLN

I wanted no part of the so-called Crittenden compromise and instructed Congressman Elihu Washburne, Senator Trumbull, and other Republicans in Washington to stay clear of it. "Let there be no compromise on the question of *extending* slavery," I told them. "There is no possible compromise upon it, but which puts us under again, and leaves all our work to do over again. The dangerous ground—that into which some of our friends have a hankering to run—is popular sovereignty. Have none of it. The Republican party is not going to become 'a mere sucked egg, all shell and no meat,—the principle all sucked out.'"

The Crittenden plan, I feared, would put the country back on the high road to a slave empire. Whether it was the revival of the Missouri Compromise line or popular sovereignty, it was all the same. "Let either be done," I warned Republicans in Washington, "and immediately filibustering and extending slavery recommences. Within a year, we shall have to take Cuba as a condition upon which the South will stay in the Union. Next it will be Mexico, then Central America. On the territorial question, I am inflexible. On that point hold firm, as with a chain of steel. The tug has to come, and better now, than any time hereafter."

I'll tell you what bothered me: the compromise measures introduced in Congress required the *Republicans* to make all the concessions. Marking time in Springfield, I was in no mood to offer the South anything. It would make me appear as if I repented for the crime of having been elected and was anxious to apologize and beg forgiveness. I had nothing to apologize for: I had won the Presidency in a fair election. If southerners didn't like the verdict of the people, they had a clear recourse: they could try to vote me out in the next election. That was the way our system worked and always had.

Ever since election day, I'd been bombarded with appeals to clarify my position, issue a statement, announce a pacification program, publish my Cabinet choices, make a grand gesture, do *something*. "Like what?" I asked a mob of reporters one day. "What can I do that I haven't already done? Repeat my views on slavery? Why should I do that? All my views are in print. If southerners want to know what I believe, they can read my speeches or study the Republican platform."

"But Republican papers don't circulate in the South," someone said.

"That's the South's fault, not ours," I replied.

In truth, I did not take the secession threat seriously. "It's all humbug," I said. "The southern people love the Union too much to let secession take place. Yes, I'm aware of southern complaints. They're wrong. I'm not hostile to the southern people and neither is Seward or any other Republican. No, I won't make a public statement to 'allay' southern fears. Southern papers and politicians would misrepresent whatever I said. As far as I'm concerned, southern politicians have manufactured this entire crisis just to scare us into making concessions. And we're not going to concede anything. Self-respect demands of me and the party that elected me that when threatened I shall be silent."

But the pressures on me to say something were so great that I decided to make a trial run. I offered our southern adversaries words of reassurance, which Senator Trumbull included in a speech he gave in Springfield in late November. "The states will be left in as complete control of their own affairs and property within their respective limits as they have ever been under any administration. I regard it as extremely fortunate for the peace of the whole country, that this point, upon which the Republicans have been so long, and so persistently misrepresented, is now to be brought to a practical test, and placed beyond the possibility of doubt. Disunionists *per se*, are now in hot haste to get out of the Union, precisely because they perceive they cannot, much longer, maintain apprehension among the southern people that their homes, and firesides, and lives, are to be endangered by the action of the Federal Government. With such 'Now, or never' is the maxim. I'm rather glad of this military preparation in the South. It will enable the people the more easily to suppress any uprisings there." Trumbull, on his own, added that "all true Republicans" now had the chance to demonstrate to the world that they were not "advocates of Negro equality or amalgamation, with which political demagogues have so often charged them."

Just as I expected, the opposition papers called our remarks "a declaration of war" against the slave states! This was just what would happen with any statement I could make. "The South will never understand anything," I lamented, "because it has eyes but does not see, and ears but does not hear." I resolved to make no further public comments about the manufactured crisis until after my inauguration. Until then, it was up to Buchanan to maintain the Union and enforce the laws.

When I read Buchanan's message to Congress, however, I was appalled. "He reiterates most of the southern complaints about us," I told some friends, "and tries to straddle the fence about secession. The South can't secede, he says, but he has no right to stop them. That boils down to capitulation. The right of secession is not a debatable question. The President must *not tolerate* any attempt to dismember the Union. Look at how Jackson handled the nullification crisis in 'thirty-two. He threatened to put an army into South Carolina to collect the revenues and uphold Federal law. That's the way to deal with treason."

On December twentieth, Thurlow Weed, Seward's chief lieutenant, called on me at my house in Springfield. So this was "Lord Thurlow," I thought, the powerful political boss of Albany. He was nearly my height, with a dark, clean-shaven face, big feet and hands like mine, and a powerful frame. He had a warm and gregarious way about him—the first thing he did was offer me a cigar. "Don't smoke," I said, and escorted him into the parlor where we could talk in private. As we did so, I was alert to anything this wily politico might reveal about Seward. My chief concern was whether Seward, the former leader of the party, would heed my wishes.

I had already offered Seward the portfolio of Secretary of State and trusted that he would accept it; Weed hinted that he would. High on my list for other Cabinet posts were Chase of Ohio, Gideon Welles of Connecticut, and Monty Blair of Maryland. I told Weed I aimed as nearly as possible at perfection: any man I appointed must be, as far as possible, like Caesar's wife, pure and above suspicion, of unblemished reputation and undoubted integrity. My Cabinet would be shaped to appease all Republican factions, with an equal balance of easterners and westerners, former Whigs and former Democrats. As we reviewed my list of prospective Cabinet members, Weed, an ex-Whig, complained that former Democrats outnumbered former Whigs by four to three.

"You seem to forget," I said, "that I expect to be there."

Later in the day, we learned that South Carolina's secession convention had just voted unanimously for disunion. The news upset Weed. "Unless you want a war on your hands," he said, "you'd better offer the South a compromise on slavery in the territories. In my opinion, the recent election has made that question obsolete. The South is too weak politically to recover the power they've lost—we've taken it away from them. We can afford to be generous."

This disturbed me. I had to assume it was Seward's position, too. Unless I controlled him and Weed on this territorial business, they would undoubtedly try to sway the Republicans in Congress.

"Yours are not the views of most Republicans," I pointed out.

"No," Weed admitted, "but you've got to realize the magnitude of the crisis we face and offer the South something on the territorial issue."

"I'm not going to offer them anything," I said. "I don't care if there are loud threats and much muttering in the cotton states. I'm unalterably opposed to concessions that would lose us everything we gained by the election. The best way to avoid serious trouble is through wisdom and forbearance."

I wrote down the following resolutions: "That the fugitive slave clause of the Constitution ought to be enforced by a law of Congress; that all state laws in conflict with such law of Congress ought to be repealed; and that the Federal Union must be preserved."

I handed the resolutions to Weed. "I want Seward to introduce these to the Committee of Thirteen," I said. "These constitute the

Republican position. We will not go beyond them. The Crittenden plan also calls for a constitutional amendment guaranteeing slavery in the states. Tell Seward I don't desire any such constitutional amendment myself. But since the question of such an amendment belongs to the American people, I don't feel justified, or inclined, to withhold it from their consideration. I remain committed to the right of each state to control its own domestic institutions."

As he left, Weed promised to do as I directed. That, I told myself, ought to rein in Seward, if reining in he needed.

A couple of days later, I sent Alex Stephens of Georgia a confidential letter marked "*for your own eye only.*" I had served in Congress with that slim, pale-faced, consumptive man, and greatly admired his eloquence. He was a former Whig and, I hoped, still a patriot. "Do the people of the South," I asked, "really entertain fears that a Republican administration would, *directly*, or *indirectly*, interfere with their slaves? If they do, I wish to assure you, as once a friend, and still, I hope, not an enemy, that there is no cause for such fears.

"The South would be in no more danger in this respect, than it was in the days of Washington. I suppose, however, this does not meet the case. You think slavery is *right* and ought to be extended; while we think it is *wrong* and ought to be restricted. That I suppose is the rub. It certainly is the only substantial difference between us."

Stephens replied: "Personally, I am not your enemy, far from it; and however widely we may differ politically, yet I trust we both have an earnest desire to preserve and maintain the Union. When men come under the influence of fanaticism, there is no telling where their impulses or passions may drive them. This is what creates our discontent and apprehensions, not unreasonable when we see such reckless exhibitions of madness as the John Brown raid into Virginia, which has received so much sympathy from many, and no open condemnation from any of the leading members of the dominant party. In addressing you thus, I ask you to do what you can to save our country. A word fitly spoken by you now would be like 'apples of gold in pictures of silver.'"

I thought he was wrong and continued to say nothing. Looking back on things now, I admit that I and most other Republicans badly underestimated the depth of southern discontent. Though letters full of warnings poured in from the slave states, I couldn't believe that the southern people would willingly destroy our experiment in popular government, the beacon of hope for oppressed people the world over. *I* was a native-born southerner, and I *loved* our government; I loved its promise of equal opportunity for all, its central idea of the right to rise. I refused to believe that the majority of southerners felt any differently. "If we pursue a policy of forbearance," I kept telling myself, "southern Unionism will surely assert itself and save the day."

On the day I wrote Stephens, young John G. Nicolay, my personal secretary, handed me a telegraph from the *New York Times* correspondent. The dispatch warned that Buchanan intended to surrender the three Federal forts in Charleston Harbor.

"If that's true," I snapped, "they ought to hang him."

Congressman Washburne had already written me that Winfield Scott, General-in-Chief of the army, felt outraged that the President wouldn't reinforce the forts, as Scott wished him to do. I wrote Washburne to tell General Scott confidentially that I wanted him to be prepared, immediately after my inauguration, to make arrangements at once to hold the forts, or, if they had been surrendered, to take them back again. "That is good ground to live and to die by," I said.

Every mail, and almost every visitor, brought reports of threats on my life, but I tried not to take them seriously. Army officers in Kansas warned that they had evidence of an assassination plot, and General Scott himself wrote that I was in real danger. Horace White, a young reporter for the New York *Herald,* relayed a story that in the St. Charles Hotel in New Orleans a subscription of $40,000 had been gotten up for my assassination. "The gentleman who witnessed this unparliamentary proceeding," said White, "is of unimpeachable character. He represents the state of feeling in Louisiana and Mississippi to be that of pure frenzy. War is deemed a quite probable event."

Then there were the hate letters, most of them from Dixie. I tell you, they were strewn with obscenities. They demanded my immediate execution by the dagger, the gun, the gibbet, the hangman's noose. Some of the letters had accompanying illustrations, which showed Lincoln being drawn and quartered; struck dead by a bolt of lightning; tarred, feathered, and hanged; impaled by the Devil on a three-pronged fork and pitched into the flames of Hell.

No decent man, I said, would write such things. Still, being superstitious, I wondered what to make of the signs. Not just the threats, but the broken panes of glass I found by our front door. What did they portend? One sign in particular troubled me for a time. It happened one day after the election; the news had come in thick and fast all that day, and I was well tired out and went home to rest, lying down on a couch in Mary's sitting room. Opposite where I lay was a bureau with a swinging glass on it. When I looked into that glass, I saw myself reflected nearly at full length. But my face, I noticed, had two separate and distinct images. Startled, I got up and looked in the glass, but the illusion had vanished. I lay down again and saw it a second time, clearer than before. I noticed that one of the faces was paler than the other—a ghostly pale. I got up and the thing disappeared. I went off, and in the excitement of the hour tried to forget about it. But now and then I would remember the ghostly image and feel a little pang, as if something uncomfortable had happened.

A few days later, I tried the experiment again. And sure enough! The ghost came again. I never succeeded in bringing it back after that. I did tell Mary about it and tried industriously to show it to her. I probably shouldn't have done that, because it upset her pretty bad. She thought it was a sign that I was to be elected to a second term of office. The healthy face indicated that I would survive the first four years. But the ghostly pale face, she feared, was an omen that I wouldn't live through the second term. I was skeptical of that view and still am. Since the double image was visible only from a certain angle and position, it can probably be explained by some principle of science.

52. DOUGLAS

When Congress recessed for Christmas, the prospects were gloomy, but I did not yet despair for the Union. I could never acknowledge the right of a state to secede, but in view of impending civil war with our brethren in nearly one half of the states, I would not consider force and war until all efforts at peaceful adjustment had been made and failed. I was fearful, however, that many of the Black Republican leaders *wanted* civil war so that they could have the pretext of saving the Union, which in turn would give them permanent ascendancy in the country.

On the day after Christmas, three commissioners from the so-called Republic of South Carolina arrived in Washington. They had come, they said, to gain formal recognition of their "republic" and to negotiate the surrender of the Federal forts in Charleston Harbor, only one of which, Fort Moultrie, was garrisoned. But on that very day, word came that the garrison commander, Major Robert Anderson, had spiked his guns at Moultrie and moved his troops to a far stronger structure—Fort Sumter out in Charleston Harbor. The southerners were furious and declared that this "sneak" move had "made war inevitable."

Because Buchanan was a Goddamned coward, a tool of Slidell and the southern swine on the Cabinet, Cobb and Floyd, there was a rumor that the President would receive the commissioners and capitulate to their demands. But I didn't think Buchanan would dare do that. "If there is such a rumor afoot," I told a Senate colleague, "it was put afoot by him. He likes to deceive people—he enjoys treachery, enjoys it as other men do a good cigar. He likes to sniff it up, to relish it."

As I expected, Buchanan did rebuff the South Carolinian commissioners, refusing to withdraw the troops or to recognize the "nation" of South Carolina. Several of my friends contended that changes in the Cabinet accounted for Buchanan's uncharacteristic rejection of a southern demand. Southerners Cobb and Floyd had resigned (Floyd was an outrageous thief, his War Department a public scandal), and northern Unionists Jeremy Black, who had replaced Cass at State, and Edwin Stanton, the new Attorney General, had reportedly won Buchanan's ear—and put a spine in his back—in dealing with South Carolina. I didn't care. I still didn't trust that treacherous son of a bitch.

When the Committee of Thirteen reconvened after Christmas, the Republicans were ready for a vote on the Crittenden plan. I pleaded with my fellow Senators to listen to reason and support the plan. "I'm for the Union," I said, "and hence am ready to make any reasonable sacrifice to save it. In my opinion, no adjustment will restore and preserve peace which does not forever banish from Congress the question of slavery in the territories. Crittenden's proposition to extend the Missouri line accomplishes this object, by making a partition in the territories by constitutional amendment. True, it doesn't submit the slavery question to the people, as does my own plan of popular sovereignty and non-intervention, the plan I prefer. But I'll support Crittenden's proposals and won't waste the committee's time asking whether this is consistent with my previous record. The country has no very great interest in my consistency. I'm prepared, gentlemen, to act on this question with reference to the present crisis, as if I'd never given a vote, or uttered a word, or had an opinion on the subject. I hope you'll all do the same."

When Crittenden put his plan to a vote, all five Republicans opposed it, which killed the plan outright, because of our agreement that any plan must have the support of a majority of both parties before it could be recommended to the Senate. Davis and Toombs also voted against the plan because the Republicans had done so. "No human power can save the Union now," Davis sneered, "all the cotton states will go."

The peevish turd enraged me. But I was even more furious at the Black Republicans. "Tell us what you want, what you'll do," I shouted at them. "Don't you see that you and the southern radicals are pushing the country into revolution and war? Offer to compromise, Goddamn it! Our entire system is based on compromise. Don't just sit there in silence!"

Seward finally brought forth a proposal for three constitutional amendments, which I understood were based on instructions from Lincoln. One amendment prohibited Congress from ever abolishing slavery in the states; another granted jury trials to fugitives; and a third urged the repeal of the North's personal liberty laws. I was aghast. "Is that *all*?" I asked. "That's no Goddamn compromise!" The first proposition simply repeated a Republican promise which southerners did not believe would ever be kept. The second proposal was out of the question, and the third was a miserly excuse for a concession. Slavery in the territories—the momentous issue tearing the committee, the Congress, and the country apart—was totally ignored. The Democrats greeted the Republican plan with howls of derision.

As the fateful year drew to a close, the Committee of Thirteen could not agree upon any compromise plan and reported that fact to the Senate. I was so mad at the Goddamned Republicans that I could barely restrain myself. To make matters worse, Ben Wade of Ohio gave an incendiary speech in the Senate that had Democrats of both sections on their feet, cursing and crying out in protest. Wade made no attempt to correct the South's "fatal misapprehension" as to the true purposes of the Black Republican party. He furnished no guarantees, no security against the dangers the South believed to exist, and the existence of which he and his party denied. He stood there on the Senate floor and demanded unconditional submission, threatened war, and talked about armies, navies, and military force for the purpose of preserving the Union. Worse still, he tried to throw the entire responsibility for the present difficulties upon the northern Democracy; he charged *us* with misrepresenting and falsifying the purposes and policy of the Republican party, which thereby deceived the southern people and precipitated the current crisis.

Just after the New Year, 1861, I took the Senate floor to answer Wade and plead for compromise. "Sir, the Senator charges that the northern Democracy has falsified and misrepresented the goals of the Republican party, and that this has deceived the South and caused our present difficulties. I feel called upon to repel the charge. I ask of the Senator, whether it's not the policy of his party to use all the powers of the Federal Government to restrain and cripple the institution of slavery, with a view to its ultimate extinction in all the states? Is it not their policy to exclude slavery from all the territories we now possess or may acquire, so as to surround the slave states with a cordon of abolition states, and thus confine the institution within such narrow limits that, when the number of slaves increases beyond the capacity of the soil to raise food for their subsistence, the institution must end in starvation, colonization, or servile insurrection? Has not the head of their party, in his 'house divided' speech of 'fifty-eight, uttered dangerous and revolutionary opinions? I hope that when their President-elect assumes the high responsibilities which will soon devolve upon him, he'll sink the politician in the statesman, the partisan in the patriot, and regard the obligations he owes to his country as paramount to those he owes to his party.

"Now I hold that the election of any man, no matter who, by the American people, according to the Constitution, furnishes no cause, no justification, for the dissolution of the Union. But we can't close our eyes to the fact that the southern people view the result of just such an election as conclusive evidence that the dominant party of the North is determined to invade their states and destroy their constitutional rights. Believing that their institution of slavery, their hearthstones, and their family altars are to be assailed, at least by indirect means, the southern people are prepared to rush wildly, madly, into revolution, disunion, war, and defy the consequences, rather than to wait for the development of events. It matters not, so far as the peace of the country and the fate of the Union are concerned, whether these fears of the southern people are real or imaginary, so long as they believe them and are determined to act upon them. So I say to the Republicans: is it not a duty you owe to God and your country to relieve their anxiety and remove all causes of discontent?

"Do not misunderstand me. No man will go further than I to maintain the authority of the government, to preserve the Union, to put down rebellion, to suppress insurrection, and to enforce the laws. I agree that the secession of South Carolina is wrong, unlawful, unconstitutional, and criminal. Unquestionably we have the right to use all the power and force necessary to regain possession of that state. Sir, the word government *means* coercion. There can be no government without it. Withdraw the right of coercion, and you dissolve your government. But are we prepared for war? Are we prepared in our hearts for war with our own brethren and kindred? I confess *I'm* not. War means final, irrevocable, eternal separation. I will not advocate coercion and war until every effort at peaceful adjustment has been exhausted.

"In my judgment, no system of compromise can be effectual and permanent which does not banish the slavery question from the halls of Congress and the arena of Federal politics, by unrepealable constitutional amendment. We have one such plan to effect this, the Crittenden plan, for which I voted in the Committee of Thirteen and for which I am prepared to vote again if it's called before this body.

"The principal provision in the Crittenden plan is the reestablishment and extension of the Missouri Compromise line. Yet you Republicans are opposed to this. Why? You have sung paeans enough in its praise, and uttered imprecations and curses enough on my head for its repeal. One would think you would feel justified now, and call it a triumph, by reestablishing that line. I call upon you to give up your party feelings and help me to reestablish and extend that line, as a perpetual bond of peace between the North and the South. Better that all party platforms be scattered to the winds; better that all political organizations be broken up; better that every public man and politician in America be consigned to political martyrdom, than that the Union be destroyed and the country plunged into civil war."

My appeal to reason pleased almost nobody on either side. Most southerners responded with icy silence. And the Black Republicans, one after another, attacked me because they claimed I had attacked them. They even accused me, me of all people, of *vindicating* southern treason. One of the Goddamned bastards, Congressman Washburne I believe it was, said that my speech was "utterly infamous and damnable, the crowning atrocity of Douglas's life."

Within the next week, Mississippi, Florida, and Alabama seceded from the Union. Their Senators, Davis included, stopped attending the Senate—we heard they were preparing their resignations. With the country disintegrating, Congress was deadlocked and paralyzed. Senators entered the chamber wielding revolvers and Bowie knives. Chandler of Michigan, hard-drinking and eternally grim, let it be known that he was exercising and improving his marksmanship in case he had to fight. In the halls and corridors of the Capitol, there was talk of war, war, and nothing but war, and it disgusted and sickened me.

I had a glimmer of hope when Seward, Lincoln's choice for Secretary of State, made something of a conciliatory speech the day after Alabama seceded. Usually he leaned against a column and twirled his watch as he spoke. This time he stood squarely in the aisle between the Republicans and Democrats, and spoke with a dignity uncharacteristic of an irrepressible-conflict Republican.

"I dread, abhor war," he said. "I don't know what the Union would be worth if saved by the use of the sword. Yet, for all this, I don't agree with those who, with a desire to avert that great calamity, advise an unopposed separation." Those were my sentiments exactly. To prevent the defection of any more slave states, he offered a revised version of his compromise plan. In addition to the three propositions he'd presented to the Committee of Thirteen, he called for the admission of Kansas as a free state and the organization of the remaining territories into two new states. One, New Mexico, would be a slave state, the other would be free.

I liked that last proposal, thought it an entering wedge for a workable settlement. But the cotton-state Senators who were still with us angrily dismissed it as too little and far too late. And most Republicans were against it, too. Still, I admired Seward for trying to get beyond party obligations and partisanship, and I invited him to dinner in the Douglas mansion. There was a good deal of drinking, and Seward, happy and a bit unsteady, offered a toast that echoed my own appeal. "Away with all parties," said the New Yorker, "all platforms, all previous committals, and whatever else will stand in the way of saving the American Union."

"Senator," I said, "don't forget in the morning what you've drunk to here, tonight."

In mid-January, with Georgia, Louisiana, and Texas preparing to secede, Crittenden, with my support, brought his compromise plan before the entire Senate. I had hoped that Seward might support it this time. But, on orders from Lincoln most likely, he came out against it, as did the rest of the Black Republicans. Even if the Senate should adopt the plan, they made it clear that they would never let it be implemented. To prevent the plan from even coming to a vote, the Republicans offered a substitute stating that the Crittenden proposals were "dangerous" and "illusory" and that the Constitution required no such amendments to protect the country sufficiently. The Black Republicans carried the substitute because six southern Senators, from Texas, Louisiana, and Georgia, refused to vote.

One of those Senators told me: "We wanted to show our constituents that the Goddamned Republicans are hostile to genuine conciliation."

"Congratulations," I said. "You've just helped those Goddamned Republicans defeat the last hope of compromise."

In the Senate and House alike, all efforts to devise a workable compromise plan with the cotton states came to naught. Their Senators and congressmen were just as much at fault as the Black Republicans. The cotton-state men took the position that the separation of the Union was complete and final and that they would never consent to a reconstruction in any contingency—not even if we furnished them with a blank sheet of paper and allowed them to inscribe their own terms.

I turned my efforts to the eight states of the upper South. If we could find reasonable and satisfactory terms of adjustment with Tennessee, Arkansas, North Carolina, Virginia, and the border slave states, maybe it would create a Union party in the cotton states that would be strong enough at the ballot box to vote the lower South back into the Union. But if the states of the upper South seceded, I feared all was lost.

53. DAVIS

On January ninth, 1861, the day Mississippi seceded, I was on my way to Capitol Hill when I learned that a Federal warship, the *Star of the West*, had attempted to reinforce and provision Fort Sumter in Charleston Harbor, but had been turned back by rebel cannon fire. That ship, I told myself, could only have sailed by order of the President! I reversed my steps and headed straight for the

White House, furious that Buchanan had again ignored my counsel. Ever since the South Carolina commissioners had arrived in Washington and sought negotiations, I had beseeched Buchanan to withdraw the garrison at Fort Sumter and surrender all the Charleston forts as South Carolina demanded. "It's the only way to avoid war," I told the President. "You have the power to prevent it. You *must act*." But the old fool had refused to listen to reason and clung stubbornly to the forts.

Now he had done worse than that: he had given in to the entreaties of General Scott, the head of the army. This stubborn old troglodyte, so fat and infirm he could neither mount his horse nor climb the steps of the Capitol, wanted the forts *reinforced* and let the consequences be damned. I could envision the two of them, goaded on by the northern members of the Cabinet, recklessly conspiring to send that Federal warship to Charleston, heedless of what a mad and provocative act that was.

Once again, upon entering the White House, I pleaded with Buchanan to give up Fort Sumter and avert impending calamity. Once again the old imbecile refused, after his fashion, which is to say that he muttered to himself, nodded and tilted his head as if in agreement, begged leave to say a prayer, and then did nothing at all. Plainly the reins of state were in feeble hands. Had this lame-duck President withdrawn the troops from Sumter, he might have turned away the threatening brow of civil war. Then we would not have stood as we did that January ninth, waiting hourly for what the telegraph might bring, to decide whether we would have peace or war.

The next day, I returned to the Senate and took the floor to explain why Mississippi had seceded. I had not yet resigned from the Senate because I had received no official confirmation of Mississippi's decision to leave the Union. I told my fellow Senators that I blamed much of the current crisis on the bungling President. But most of the blame I reserved for the Black Republicans, whose fanaticism and sectionalism, like the blind giant of old, had seized the pillars of the American temple to tear it down, destroy its inmates, and create from the rubble a *consolidated* government that would be far more fatal to popular liberty than the separation of the states. Hence it remained for us of the South to withdraw and commence the erection of another temple on the same plan on which our fathers had built the original.

I faced the Republican side of the chamber, where the birdlike Seward was twirling his watch; Wade and Chandler were frowning;

and Sumner was wearing his usual fanatical sneer. "We've warned you for many years that you would drive us to this alternative," I told them, "and you would not heed us. You've turned upon our friends in the North who have pointed out the danger of your course, and you've held *them* responsible for the censure you receive from us, as though you've not been the aggressor. Even after forty years of bitter debate, you still ask us *what is the matter*.

"I will tell you *what is the matter*." I was so angry that my lips and hands were trembling. "Your platform on which you elected your presidential candidate denies us equality in the Union. It refuses us equal enjoyment of the territories, even though we've paid equally in their purchase and bled equally in their acquisition in war. Is this how you honor your compact with us? I ask you, do you give us justice; do we enjoy equality? If we're not equals, this is not the Union to which we were pledged; this is not the Constitution you've sworn to maintain; this is not the government we're bound to support. Without equality, we would be degraded to remain in the Union.

"Whose fault is it if the Union be dissolved? Your votes refuse to recognize our domestic institutions which existed before the formation of the Union, our slave property which is guarded by the Constitution. You elect a candidate upon the basis of sectional hostility; one who, in his speeches, now thrown broadcast over the country, made a distinct declaration of war upon our institutions. We care not whether that war be made by armies marching for invasion, or whether it be by proclamation, or whether it be by indirect and covert process. In all three modes, you declare your hostility. The leading members of your party, some of them now before me, made speeches after the election announcing that the Republican triumph signaled the downfall of our domestic institutions! And you dare to ask us, 'What is the matter?'

"When you use figurative language, its harshness indicates the severity of your temper and the bitterness of your hate. When you talk about having your heel on the Slave Power and grinding it into dust; when you talk about the final triumph; when you talk about the extinction of slavery, with which you have nothing to do and about which you know nothing, is this the fraternity, is this the Union, to which we were invited? Yours is not an administration of the government under which we can live in safety. If we submit to you, we would surrender our birthright of freedom and become slaves ourselves.

"I don't care to quote your platform; I don't care to quote the speeches of your President-elect. You know them as I do; and the man who's regarded across the country as the directing intellect of your party, the Senator from New York"—I pointed a trembling finger at Seward—"has indicated, with less harshness of expression than others, but with more of method, the same deadly hostility toward us. We didn't unite with you in order that the powers of the general government should be used to destroy our domestic institutions; and we will not consent to remain united to a government exercised for such a purpose.

"I seek not to exasperate the causes of our difficulty. It is urgent that we understand each other. I thought we had done so. The last canvass expressed the feelings and the opinions of the southern states. The state of Mississippi gave warning and declared her purpose to take counsel with her southern sister states whenever a President should be elected on the basis of sectional hostility to them. With all this warning, you paused not. Such a President has now been elected. The quarrel, then, is not of our making. Our hands are stainless. It is *you* who are the aggressor."

I felt such a riot of emotions that I was near tears. I paused, trying to steady myself. "I've striven . . . I've striven to avert the catastrophe which now impends over the country unsuccessfully; and I regret it. I'm willing, however, to make every effort to limit the catastrophe and salvage peace between us. But if you'll not have it thus—" I paused again. "If in the pride of power, if in contempt of reason and reliance upon force, you say we shall not go, but shall remain as subjects to you, then, gentlemen of the North, *a war is to be inaugurated the like of which men have not seen before.*"

When I finished, I was shaking all over. I loved the old Union of fraternal states, had served it in war and peace for much of my life, and I could scarcely bear the idea that the old Union was destroyed and gone forever. The realization that it *was* gone, and the fear of just such a war as I described, filled me with unutterable grief and prostrated me with a sudden and severe attack of neuralgia. Confined to my chamber for a week, I could not stop shaking. My head was bursting and my face burning with pain.

While I lay confined, Georgia seceded from the Union, the fourth state to go out. That same day, January nineteenth, I received an urgent telegram from Governor Pettus informing me that a copy of Mississippi's secession ordinance was on its way by mail, and informing me that my immediate presence was required in Jackson to organize the state militia into an army. So this was it, I told myself. I took up my pen and with a trembling hand wrote former President Frank Pierce.

> My Dear Friend: I have often and sadly turned my thoughts to you during the troublous times through which we have been passing and now I come to the hard task of announcing to you that the hour is at hand which closes my connection with the United States, for the independence and Union of which my father bled and in the service of which I have sought to emulate the example he set for my guidance. Mississippi not as a matter of choice but of necessity has resolved to enter on the trial of secession. Those who have driven her to this alternative threaten to deprive her of the right to require that her government shall rest on the consent of the governed. In the attempt to avoid the issue which had been joined by the country, the present administration has complicated and precipitated the question. When Lincoln comes in he will have but to continue in the path of his predecessor to inaugurate a civil war and leave a democratic administration responsible for the fact.
>
> I leave immediately for Missi. and know not what may devolve upon me after my return there. Civil war has only horror for me, but whatever circumstances demand shall be met as a duty and I trust be so discharged that you will not be ashamed of our former connection or cease to be a friend. Jeffn. Davis.

On January twenty-first, against the advice of my physician, I rose from my sickbed and with an aching head made my way to the Senate to announce my resignation. Clement Clay of Alabama and three other Deep South Senators intended to resign with me. I was stunned to see so many carriages in the streets leading to the Capitol: word that I would resign and give my last speech to the Senate must have gone abroad. When I entered the chamber, the galleries, even the aisles, were packed with people, including a great many well-dressed southern gentlemen and their fashionable ladies. The chamber buzzed and echoed with voices and scraping noises. I noticed Varina taking a seat in the galleries; she had sent one of our slaves to hold a place for her.

The four other southern Senators spoke first. Then I rose, steadied myself, and waited until there was complete silence.

"I rise, Mr. President, for the purpose of announcing to the Senate that I have satisfactory evidence that the state of Mississippi, by a solemn ordinance of her people, has declared her separation from the United States, and that my functions are terminated here. My physical condition will not permit me to rehearse the reasons for such separation. Suffice it to say that Mississippi has justifiable cause and that I approve of her act. I would, however, say a word to those who have attacked our social institutions by evoking the Declaration of Independence and its phrase 'all men are created equal.' By that Jefferson clearly meant not the equality of the races, but the equality of the men of the political community at that time. The phrase had no reference to Negroes, who were not then regarded as citizens.

"Still, I bear our adversaries no animosity. On the contrary, I wish you well. So, I'm sure, do the people of Mississippi. We hope for peaceful relations with you. But the reverse may bring disaster on every portion of the country; and if you will have it thus, we will invoke the God of our fathers."

I paused, reluctant to close. "I have, Senators, in this hour of our parting, to offer you my apology for any pain which, in the heat of discussion, I have inflicted. I go without memory of any injury received. Mr. President and Senators, having made the announcement which the occasion seemed to me to require, it only remains for me to bid you a final adieu."

The chamber was perfectly silent for a moment, then burst into applause. In the galleries, southern ladies wept and waved handkerchiefs. Many Republicans, however, looked at me in apparent disbelief that the crisis had come to this. I turned and walked out of the chamber with Clay and Fitzpatrick of Alabama, Mallory and Yulee of Florida. The Republicans stared grimly at us as we swept past. I heard later that Ben Wade took the floor and predicted that secession would bring about the thing we most feared. "The first blast of civil war," he cried, "is the death warrant for your institution of slavery." We would see about that, I said.

Varina and I set about packing all our trunks and preparing our three children for the long journey home. There were rumors that the Republicans had demanded my arrest and that of the other "traitor" Senators. "*Let* them arrest me," I said. "Let them put me in chains and throw me in prison. It would be a good way to test the question of the right of a state to secede." All that day I kept hoping they *would* come for me.

But no policemen appeared, and the next morning we left for the

Republic of Mississippi and a new destiny. As the train roared southward, I told Varina that I anticipated a long, bloody, exhausting war and that my property in cotton planting would probably be destroyed.

When we reached Jackson, Governor Pettus and four new brigadiers in the Army of Mississippi escorted me to a nearby boardinghouse, where Pettus appointed me to command the Mississippi army, with a commission as major general. Then we set about dividing the state into military districts and making other military preparations. The major difficulty was the want of serviceable weapons for our troops. Without them, Mississippi was wholly unprepared for the war I feared was coming.

"I've taken steps to procure the necessary weapons," Pettus said. "Seventy-five thousand stands ought to be sufficient."

I disagreed. "We'll need all of that and many more than we can get, I fear."

"General, you overrate the risk," Pettus said.

"I *never* overrate a risk," I said, "and *certainly* not this one."

The conversation turned to the upcoming convention in Montgomery. Called by the seceded states, which now included Louisiana, the convention was scheduled to meet on February fourth to discuss what should be done. It would of course go on to establish a new confederacy and a provisional government.

"The eight states of the upper South," I said, "are crucial for the future of a southern confederacy. If they unite with us, there may be a chance for a peaceful separation. But if the seven cotton states are to maintain their position alone, there will be war."

A message reached me from a Mississippi delegate to the Montgomery convention. Would I accept the post of provisional President if offered? In the midst of our discussions, I scribbled a reply in great haste. "If we have peaceful separation," I said, "the civil branch of the government will be the only field for useful labor. But if we have war, the military branch of the government becomes of paramount importance. With the limited knowledge I now possess, it is not possible to decide what it is best for me to do in relation to the position I should occupy. The post of President of the provisional government is one of great responsibility and difficulty. I have no confidence in my capacity to meet its requirements. I think I could perform the functions of general of the confederacy if the executive did not cripple me in my operations by acts of commission or omission. I would prefer not to have either place, but in this hour of my country's severest trial will accept any place to which my fellow citizens may assign me. You have a mighty work before you."

As Varina and I headed home to Brierfield, I kept telling myself: *I don't want the Presidency. Let them give it to Toombs of Georgia. I'm a warrior now—I'm done with politics.* At Brierfield, along the quiet, majestic Mississippi, I entered upon the most agreeable of all labors to me: planting shrubs and trees and directing the operations of my fields. But the events of the hour—the secession of Texas, the formation of the Confederacy in Montgomery—filled me with foreboding about the reaction in the North. Unable to sleep, I talked all night, keeping poor Varina awake with my insomniac ramblings.

On the afternoon of February tenth—I'll never forget the day—I was helping Varina prepare rose-cuttings in the garden when a messenger rode up at a near gallop, dismounted, and handed me a telegram from the office in Vicksburg. I put my shears down and read the message.

My face must have betrayed my anguish. "What is it?" Varina asked, alarmed. "Has someone died?"

"It's from the convention," I said. "They've elected me provisional President. I'm to go to Montgomery at once."

"You make it sound like a death sentence," she said, and smiled. "I'm so very proud of you."

I was profoundly disappointed. With my West Point background and experience in the Mexican War, I thought myself better adapted to command in the field, and Mississippi had given me the position I preferred to any other—the highest rank in her army. I prayed that the Presidency would be temporary, and I expected soon to be with the Army of Mississippi again.

I summoned my Negroes and gave them a farewell speech. "Serious trouble probably lies ahead," I warned them. The next day, February eleventh, I took a boat upriver to Vicksburg and there caught a train for Jackson and Montgomery.

54. LINCOLN

On the morning of our departure for Washington City—that was February eleventh—a thousand people came to the Great Western Railroad Station to see us off. A cold, drizzling rain fell from low-hanging clouds, but it didn't seem to bother the crowd. I stood in an overheated waiting room shaking hands and saying good-bye to old friends and well-wishers, then went outside to the platform, where a special flag-draped train was waiting. One car was reserved for "the President-elect" (I still wasn't used to that title), another for the press, and a third for local escorts. Seventeen-year-old Robert would ride with me, while Mary and the little fellows, Willie and Tad, would follow on an evening train.

Mary and I'd had a row about our traveling arrangements. Because of all the threats against my life, I didn't want her and the three boys to ride on the same train as I did, because I feared somebody might try to blow it up. Also, it was going to be a grueling journey across much of the North, and I thought to spare Mary and the boys the ordeal. I tried to reason with Mary, pointing out the potential danger, but she stood her ground with her little blue eyes flashing.

"I'm *not* going to take another train," she said. "You're my husband. My place is with you. I'm going to see you to Washington, danger or no danger."

"But, Mother," I said. "Think of the danger—think of the boys."

"We're *coming* with you," she insisted.

We finally struck a compromise in which I did most of the conceding. We would split up the family and take separate trains to Indianapolis. From there we would travel together on a route mapped out by Seward and General Scott. Our itinerary would take us across Ohio, western Pennsylvania, back to Ohio, across New York state, and then down through New Jersey, Pennsylvania a second time, and then to Washington City. The circuitous route was Seward's idea, to expose me to the public and rally Union morale. I felt worn out just thinking about it.

As Robert and I made our way to the car reserved for the President's party, the crowd called for a speech. I hadn't planned to say anything, but the sight of all those folk—friends and neighbors, lawyers, judges, politicians, and their wives—looking expectantly at me in the drizzle, well, I had to say something. I mounted the train's rear platform and told them: "My friends—No one, not in my situation, can appreciate my feeling of sadness at this parting. To this place, and the kindness of these people, I owe everything. Here I've lived a quarter of a century, and have passed from a young to an old man. Here my children have been born, and one is buried. I now leave, not knowing when, or whether ever, I may return. I now leave with a task before me greater than the one that faced Washington. Trusting in Him, who will go with me and remain with you, I bid you an affectionate farewell."

Presently the train lurched forward with clanging bells and headed east in the rain. The inside of my car looked like a small palace, with tassels and scrolls, a thick carpet, heavy furniture, strips of blue silk studded with silver stars draped on the walls below the windows, and Union flags hanging at both ends of the coach. As the train rocked along at thirty miles an hour, the flat brushlands passed in the windows where I sat swapping stories with several old friends. There was square-jawed Norman Judd; rotund Judge Davis; and Ward Hill Lamon, a big, powerful fellow with an unmatched proficiency with the glass. Hill had appointed himself my personal bodyguard and was so loaded down with pistols and knives that he looked like a one-man arsenal. There was also an army escort composed of Colonel Edwin V. "Bull Head" Sumner, Major David Hunter, and Captain John Pope.

Later I sat by myself, staring out the window and mulling over the difficulties and uncertainties that lay ahead. One of my biggest headaches was my Cabinet. I wanted Chase, one of the great architects of the party and an "iron-back" Republican who opposed concessions to the South, to be Treasury Secretary, but he didn't like it that Seward was to be in the Cabinet, since he questioned Seward's integrity and commitment to the party cause. But that was nothing compared to the problem I had with Simon Cameron of Pennsylvania. I'd written him that he would head the War or the Treasury departments, but I'd withdrawn the offer, under great anxiety, because of fearful if unproved accusations that he was corrupt. The trouble was, Pennsylvania, a crucial state, had to have a Cabinet post, and Cameron, a former Democrat and a United States Senator, was the only Pennsylvanian with the right credentials. When I learned that my withdrawal had mortified him, I wrote him a softer letter to replace the offensive one and promised to consult him before I appointed any Pennsylvanian. I tell you, that state gave me more trouble than the balance of the Union, not excepting secession.

Oh, secession was giving me its share of fits, all right. I could hardly bear to think about the wreckage, the seven cotton states having declared themselves out of the Union and, worse yet, having formed a pretended "government" down in Montgomery. I had seen in the papers that Jefferson Davis had been chosen President of the

Confederate States of America, so called. Alex Stephens, despite his assurances to me that we weren't enemies, was to be his Vice-President. It disturbed me no end that Stephens had surrendered to treason. At one of our railroad stops on the way to Indiana, I learned that Davis had left for Montgomery the same day I'd left for Washington. It was a subject of morbid fascination that we were riding trains at the same time, both of us heading into the unknown.

I wondered what he was thinking, whether he wanted peace or war. I kept telling myself there would not, could not, be war . . . Americans weren't the kind of people who would resort to killing one another . . . the southern people would bring the errant states back . . . the crisis would solve itself if left alone . . . the important thing was not to abandon our Republican platform and principles.

On the matter of congressional compromise, I worried that Seward and other Republican conciliators might barter away the party platform, and thus our very reason for existence, in order to keep the upper South in the Union. While I had worked on my Cabinet and started a draft of my Inaugural Address in Springfield, Seward helped a couple of Republican congressmen, Charles Francis Adams and Thomas Corwin, concoct a House compromise plan which they sent out to me by a special messenger. That plan, a sop to the upper South, called for New Mexico Territory, which had already legalized slavery and had a few slaves in it, to be admitted as a slave state. The plan also promised reassurances to the South that the fugitive slave law would be faithfully enforced, and provided for a constitutional amendment guaranteeing slavery in the states where it already existed. As I studied these proposals, I told myself I would rather die than yield the integrity of the government and give the appearance that I was buying the right to take office.

I wrote Seward where I stood. On the territorial question—that is, the question of extending slavery under the national auspices—I remained inflexible. I was opposed to any compromise which assisted or permitted the extension of the institution on soil owned by the nation. I cared but little, however, if there were reassurances about fugitive slaves, slavery in the District of Columbia, the internal slave trade, and whatever sprang of necessity from the fact that the institution existed among us, so long as what was done be comely and not altogether outrageous. Nor did I care much about New Mexico, if further extension were hedged against.

I made it plain that this was absolutely as far as I would go, and that the party had to remain steadfast in its purpose. Anyway, it appeared to me that all compromise efforts were doomed. The Democrats had made it plain that they weren't going to accept the Republican platform on which I had been elected, and we had no intention, if I could help it, of supporting their Crittenden plan with its provision for extending slavery. As it turned out, House Republicans voted down the New Mexico bill, and Senate Republicans, following my instructions, rejected and killed the Crittenden plan.

To find some way out of the impasse, the promoters of compromise—and that included Seward, I learned later—tried another trick while I was still in Springfield. They staged a so-called peace conference in Washington, consisting of delegates from twenty-one of the remaining Union states. Judge Douglas urged me to endorse the enterprise, but I refused—I even objected to Illinois sending delegates. "I'm not going to buy my right to be peacefully inaugurated," I said. "I would rather die first." Nevertheless, the conference had opened a week before I left Springfield and was in session at Willard's Hotel while I rode east on the Presidential train.

The train reached Indianapolis late in the afternoon of February eleventh. There was a huge crowd at the station, a reception committee headed by the governor, and a thirty-four-gun salute whose concussions made our ears ring. The noise and confusion were pretty near unbearable as we made our way to the hotel by carriage or by foot. In all the hubbub, Robert, who carried a little black satchel containing my Inaugural Address (he didn't know it was in there), became separated from us. At the hotel, which was swarming with people, I made my way to my room, only to be called on to give a speech from the balcony. Afterward, I returned to the room and looked for the satchel with my Inaugural Address, but Robert was nowhere to be found. When he was finally located and brought to the room, I was mortified to learn that he didn't have the satchel. With irritating nonchalance, he said he'd given the damned thing to the hotel clerk. My God, I thought, what if reporters got hold of the address and it appeared a week ahead of time in the papers! Without a word to the boy, I flung the door open and strode down to the clerk's desk in the lobby. In the pile of luggage were a number of small black bags like mine. To the amusement of bystanders, the President-elect of the United States took out his key and systematically worked his way through the black bags until he found his own and saw that the Inaugural Address was in it. I took the satchel back to the room and handed it to Robert. "Now, you keep it," I told him. Lamon told me later that he'd never seen me so annoyed, perplexed, and angry. I was sorry it showed; I tried never to show anger toward my boys.

The next day, Mary and the little boys arrived in town, and all of us boarded the Presidential train for the harrowing, two-week journey to Washington. All along the route, knots of rural folk would wave as the train shrieked past. At every stop, crowds would press against the cars, calling for me to speak. At first I tried to say something to every group; but it was clear I couldn't keep that up for two weeks, not with the official speaking schedule I faced. So I adopted the practice of sitting in the coach until the conductor announced our departure; then I would appear on the back platform and bow as the train pulled out.

In the state capitals and the larger cities, there were endless receptions, cannonades, bright banners and flags, and huge, jostling crowds. I shook so many hands that my own became sore and swollen. I gave so many speeches—from a railroad platform, or the steps of a statehouse, or a hotel balcony—that my voice grew hoarse. After a while, I was so worn down I was speaking by rote.

Wherever I appeared, reporters and citizens demanded to know what I intended to do about the secession crisis. I was guarded in my replies, lest I make a commitment I couldn't keep, or say too much and get myself into trouble. I guess some of my remarks sounded pretty trite, but I was tired and as confused as the next fellow when it came to the state of affairs, which I imperfectly understood. I kept saying that there was nothing going wrong, that the North and the South entertained different views upon political questions, but nobody was suffering anything. To overcome the present difficulty, I said, we needed time, patience, and a reliance on that God who had never forsaken this people.

I remember the stop in Pittsburgh because I had to speak outside in a heavy rain to an immense throng of black umbrellas. "There is no crisis except an '*artificial one*' caused by designing politicians," I told the umbrellas. "Even if you take a southern view of the matter, nothing can justify the course they're pursuing. If both sides will only maintain their self-possession, the crisis will clear up."

In Cleveland, our next major stop, I spoke from a hotel balcony in swirling snow and rain to five thousand shivering people in the street below. "Why," I asked, "are southerners so incensed? Have they not all their rights now as they ever had? Do they not have their fugitive slaves returned now as ever? Have they not the same Constitution that they've lived under for seventy odd years? What then is the matter with them? Why all this excitement? Why all these complaints?"

And so it went from one city to the next. I didn't have to save the country, I said; the country would save itself. It was up to the people, not the President, to preserve the Union. Yet, if necessary, I promised to *put my foot down firmly*. But the banalities I kept uttering embarrassed me, and I looked to humor for relief. At one stop, I brought Mary out with me, and we stood side by side, the short, plump First Lady and the tall, gangly President. "This," I said, "is the long and the short of it."

From Cleveland, the train swept around Lake Erie into New York state. We stopped at Westfield long enough for me to seek out an eleven-year-old girl named Grace Bedell, who was responsible for my new look. Before the election, she had written me that my face was too thin and that I would look better with a beard. She pointed to a sensible political reason to grow one: "All the ladies like whiskers and they would tease their husbands to vote for you and then you would be President. My father is going to vote for you and if I was a man I would vote for you too but I will try and get every one to vote for you that I can." After the election, I followed her advice and for the first time in my life grew a beard.

When I spoke from the train at Westfield, I asked if the young lady was present who had advised me to let my whiskers grow. A boy sitting on a post cried out, "there she is, Mr. Lincoln," and pointed to a lovely young girl with black eyes, whose face was turning beet red. I stepped down from the car, made my way through the crowd, and kissed her several times. But that only got me in trouble with the opposition newspapers. While the Union collapses, they said, all Lincoln does is kiss little girls.

55. DAVIS

Because of poor rail connections in the Confederacy, my special train had to travel a circuitous route by way of Chattanooga and Atlanta to reach Montgomery. In my private car, with the southern landscape rolling by, I did as much preliminary work as I could. I needed a chief field commander, and there was one officer in the United States army I wanted above all others who was now stationed in California; I thought he was with us and wrote to him. It was Brevet Brigadier General Albert Sidney Johnston.

In the railroad junctions and towns we passed through in the seceded states, crowds gathered, artillery thundered, troops paraded, and bonfires and torches blazed in my honor. Speaking from the back of my private car, I assured the crowds that France and England would denounce the North's hellish fanaticism and grant us diplomatic recognition. Troubled by the festival atmosphere at these stops, I warned our people that they had better prepare for a long and bloody conflict.

I gave so many speeches that I was hoarse and bone weary by the time we pulled into the station in Montgomery at ten o'clock at night, the sixteenth of February. Another throng of people and more cannon fire greeted me at the station. Tired though I was, I managed a few words: "We have separated from the North *forever*. No compromise—no reconstruction—can now be entertained."

William Yancey, the Alabama secessionist leader, a square-faced man with a bow tie, headed my reception committee and escorted me to the Exchange Hotel, where still another crowd was gathered and clamored for me to speak. I climbed to the balcony with Yancey and we faced the sea of cheering, torch-lit faces below. Yancey introduced me in his sonorous voice. "We have the leader we need now. The man and the hour have met!"

I stepped forward, exuding defiance. "Fellow Citizens and brethren of the Confederate States of America, men of one flesh, one bone, one interest, one purpose, it may be that our career will be ushered in amidst storm and trouble. If war should come, we shall show that southern valor still shines as brightly as in the days of 'seventy-six. Rest assured, that as the sun disperses the clouds, the progress of the southern Confederacy will carry us safely over the sea of troubles."

The Inaugural ceremonies took place just two days later, on a Monday. Just before noon, Alexander Stephens and I climbed into a carriage and joined the Inaugural parade in front of the Exchange Hotel and the public fountain. A band struck up a song specially orchestrated for the occasion, "I Wish I Was in Dixie Land," and the parade moved up Market Street to the white-domed state capitol, which stood atop a hill. Barnwell Rhett introduced me to the provisional Congress, then I took my place on a speaker's stand on the front portico between towering white pillars. There, in brilliant sunlight, I read my Inaugural Address to a large and festive audience:

"Our present political position has been achieved in a manner unprecedented in the history of nations. It illustrates the American idea that governments rest on the consent of the governed, and that it is the right of the people to alter or abolish them at will whenever they become destructive of the ends for which they were established.

"I hope the northern states will let us alone in peace. If, however, passion or lust of dominion should cloud the judgment or inflame the ambition of those states, we must prepare to meet the emergency and maintain, by the final arbitrament of the sword, the position which we have assumed among the nations of the earth. If the North should make war, it must assume the terrible responsibility for doing so. The suffering of millions will bear testimony to the folly and wickedness of our aggressors."

The audience responded with frequent bursts of applause. After I took the oath of office as provisional President, artillery roared and the crowd cheered and cheered. I wrote Varina that upon my weary heart that day was showered smiles, plaudits, and flowers. But beyond them I saw troubles and thorns innumerable.

With the Inaugural ceremony behind me, I set about building a government and a nation. I made Cabinet appointments, set civil and military departments in operation, saw that the Federal installations we'd captured were put in order, and dispatched three commissioners to Europe to secure the recognition of the Confederacy as a nation. Since Britain's manufacturing interests needed our cotton, I was certain that Great Britain would recognize us. I was equally certain that France would follow England's lead. The one obstacle to recognition, I knew, was our institution of slavery. Because the leading European powers tended to oppose it, I instructed the commissioners to ignore the slavery question and stress our right of self-determination. Tell them, I said, that we're breaking away from the Union for the same reason that the colonies broke away from England. That analogy ought to please the English government of Lord Palmerston!

I expected Confederate civilian leaders to honor my policy of playing down the slavery issue. Imagine my chagrin, then, when I read in the papers what Vice-President Stephens said in a rabble-rousing speech in Savannah. "Many governments," he said, "have been founded upon the principle of the subordination and serfdom of certain classes of the *same* race; such were, and are in violation of the laws of nature. Our system commits no such violation of nature's law. With us, all of the white race, however high or low, rich or poor, are equal in the eye of the law. Not so with the Negro. Subordination is his place. He, by nature, or by the curse against Cain, is fitted for that condition which he occupies in our system. Our new government is founded on the opposite idea of the equality of races. Its foundations are laid, its cornerstone rests upon the great truth, that the Negro is not equal to the white man; that slavery—subordination to the superior race—is his natural condition."

That speech infuriated me. Oh, what Stephens said was true, perfectly true, but could anything hurt us more abroad than such impolitic remarks? It was the beginning of a fatal falling out between me and that rebellious and vindictive dwarf, who was hell-bent upon forming his own policies and disputing mine with niggardly deviousness.

Meanwhile Varina and the children had joined me in Montgomery, arriving by steamboat up the Alabama River. No sooner had we reached our rooms at the Exchange Hotel than Mary Boykin Chesnut called to see Varina. She is the wife of my protégé, James Chesnut of South Carolina, who had helped draft South Carolina's ordinance of secession and had come to Montgomery to assist in making our new Confederacy. Only five feet tall, with a pug nose, high cheekbones, and dark, radiant, deep-set eyes, Mary Chesnut is the most garrulous and altogether charming woman I've ever known—aside from Varina, of course. She and Varina got along famously: as they shared the latest news, they held hands and laughed like two schoolgirls.

56. MARY BOYKIN CHESNUT

I told Mrs. Davis I was a *born rebel*, since my father, Stephen Decatur Miller, had been a nullifier and governor of South Carolina during the nullification crisis. But my husband's family, the Chesnuts, swore themselves to the Union party, which rather exasperated my Confederate zeal, as they constantly threw out taunts and sneers against the faith I had adopted. I told Mrs. Davis I felt a nervous dread and horror at breaking with so strong a power as the United States, but I was ready and willing, for South Carolina had been rampant with secession fever for years. Nobody could live in the state unless he was a fire-eater. Come what would, I wanted South Carolinians to stop talking and fight. So I was a seceder, but I dreaded the future. When my husband, James, resigned from the United States Senate and joined us in South Carolina, he announced that there was no hope now and that he was in bitter earnest. I thought him right, but when he sent me back to Mulberry plantation to stay with his aged parents, I felt I was offering up my life on the altar of country.

Mulberry is located northeast of Columbia, near the quiet town of Camden in central South Carolina. The plantation's centerpiece is a proud old three-story mansion, which rises by the shore of the Wateree River, at the end of a line of magnificent old live oaks. During my stay, I liked to sit at the windows of my sleeping apartment, thinking how sad the landscape always looked. The freshet, I noticed, was up on every side. The swollen river came to our very doors. From the windows, I could see the lower limbs of the trees dip mournfully in the water. With so many sheep and cattle gathered at the river, the scene reminded me of Noah's ark. Mulberry, I thought, was not at all like the Chesnut's Sandy Hill plantation, where hot winds blew night and day, and moonlight brought weird sounds of lonely whippoorwills and screech owls.

Old Colonel Chesnut, James's eighty-seven-year-old father, was a kind but opinionated lord of the manor who treated everyone with flamboyant courtesy. He was as absolute a tyrant as the Czar of Russia, or the Sultan of Turkey, but amiable when not crossed, jovial, and courtly in his politeness. What I despised about him was his weakness of the flesh in years gone by—his adulterous frolicking with his slave Rachel, which had produced a brood of little *colored* Chesnuts. The Colonel's poor, suffering, invalid wife had closed her eyes to his indiscretions. She seemed to think the mulatto children at Mulberry had been delivered by the stork.

So dedicated to duty that she spent hours each day making clothes for the slave babies, she saw only good in people, including her old tyrant of a husband. She bore him *fourteen* children and saw ten of them die. The very thought of her fecundity depressed me, for James and I have no children—a lack which the Chesnuts seemed to think owed to some flaw in my character. Every time I came to Mulberry, the Chesnuts *never failed* to make some snide reference to what *I* was unable to bear. I remember one time in particular—I'd had a tooth pulled and was perfectly miserable with pain. Mrs. Chesnut bragged to me, a childless wretch, about her *twenty-seven* grandchildren. Colonel Chesnut said to her, "*You* have not been a useless woman in this world," meaning, of course, that I *had* been useless.

God help me! I thought. No good have I done to myself or anyone else, with the power I boast so much of possessing, the power to make myself loved. Where am I now? Where are my friends? I'm allowed to have none. Why, oh why, am I so cursed?

It gave me such an excruciating headache that I retired to my rooms and took a dose of opium, as was my habit. Opium enabled me to retain every particle of mind or sense or brains I ever had, and quieted my nerves so that I could calmly reason and take rational views of things that were otherwise maddening. In a dreamy state, I thought back over what the Chesnuts had said about children. I should have told them, "Sir, Madam, you did not count *all* your children!"

Imagine how *happy* I was to get away from Mulberry and go to Montgomery with James! We had such an *exciting time* there, receiving or paying calls every day and entertaining almost every night. The hotel's drawing rooms were full of judges, governors, Senators, generals, and congressmen. I had such fun matching wits and exchanging gossip with so many handsome gentlemen, who spoke in the hot, fervid, after-supper southern style. Oh, there was no end of them! Mr. Josselyn, the poet, said I looked younger and better than I had in Washington. I wondered if in the thousand compliments I heard there was one grain of truth. I never was handsome—I wonder what my attraction was, for men did fall in love with me wherever I went; they sent me flowers, invited me to dine, called for tea and conversation. I felt like such a *belle* again.

I was indisposed during Mr. Davis's Inauguration, but I heard how Mrs. Aurelia Fitzpatrick, the second wife of former governor and United States Senator Ben Fitzpatrick of Alabama, made herself conspicuous by sitting among the congressmen—the only woman who did so—and then poking Mr. Davis in the back with her parasol before the assembled multitude to make him speak to her. What a perfectly despicable woman she was, to behave like that.

I noticed how happy Mr. Davis was when Varina and their children arrived in town. I called at once on the Davises in their rooms at the Exchange Hotel. Mr. Davis looked so terribly thin, had sunken eyes, a gaunt face, and trembling, bloodless hands. He wore a trimmed goatee, which he stroked with one hand as he spoke. While he attended to executive business, Varina and I sat by the window and talked for almost two hours.

"Poor Jeffy," she said. "He so dislikes being President. General of all the armies would have suited his temper better."

"Judge Withers—my uncle—says that corruption is the cry," I said. "Everybody wants an office and everybody raises an outcry at the corruption of those who get the offices. Some of the politicians have brought old hatreds and grudges and spites from the old Union. Already they seem willingly to injure our cause to hurt Mr. Davis."

"People are so hard to please," Varina said, and sighed. "But let's not talk about politics. Where are you staying?"

"The Montgomery Hall Hotel," I said. "It's just awful, a din of dirt and horror. The hotel is teeming with politicians—the whole city is. There I go—talking politics again. I'm sorry. Still, isn't it all perfectly exhilarating? To be present at the birth of a nation, I mean. I'm keeping track of everything in a journal—it's a volume bound in red leather. I intend to make it entirely objective. My subjective days are over. I try to write every day, which may be disadvantageous for me, since I now spend my time like a spider spinning my own entrails instead of reading, as my habit was at all spare moments. Oh my, look at the time! I really must go."

"Only if you promise to call every day," Varina said.

I did call almost every day, and we became fast friends. We are so much alike—both of us have strong opinions, like to match wits with gentlemen, and share what might be called an impious sense of humor. And we both have perfectly *humorless* husbands. My James wouldn't know a witticism if it bowed to him and wrote its name across his cheek. He considers himself open, frank, and confiding, but he really hides behind an iron wall. Sometimes I feel that we understand each other a little—then up goes that iron wall once more. Not that for a moment he ever gives you the impression of an insincere or even a cold person—reticent is what he is; like the Indian he is too proud to let the world know how he feels.

A couple of days after Varina's arrival, I saw something that unsettled me. It was a Negro girl being sold at auction on the steps of the public fountain. She was nice-looking, a bright mulatto with a pleasant face, and was magnificently gotten up in silks and satins. She seemed delighted with it all—sometimes ogling the bidders, sometimes looking quite coy and modest, but her mouth never relaxed from its expanded grin of excitement. She was *selling herself*, and I dare say she knew who would buy her. South Carolina slave-holder that I was, my very soul sickened—it was too dreadful. I went into a shop and sat down on a stool. I tried to reason: *this is not*

worse than the willing sale most women make of themselves in mar-
riage, nor can the consequences be worse. The Bible authorizes mar-
riage and slavery—poor women! poor slaves!

So often I wondered if it be a sin to think slavery a curse to any land. "Senator Sumner," I wrote in my journal, "said not one word about this hated institution which is not true. Men and women are punished when their masters and mistresses are brutes and not when they do wrong. We live surrounded by prostitutes. Who thinks any worse of a Negro or mulatto woman for being a thing we can't name? God forgive *us*, but ours is a *monstrous* system and a wrong and an iniquity. Perhaps the rest of the world is as bad. This only I see: like the patriarchs of old our men live all in one house with their wives and their concubines, and the mulattos one sees in every family exactly resemble the white children—and every lady tells you who is the father of all the mulatto children in everybody's household, but those in her own; she seems to think they drop from the clouds. Good women we have—they are, I believe, in conduct the purest women God ever made. Thank God for them—alas for the men! They are no worse than men everywhere, but the lower their mistresses, the more degraded they must be."

I hated slavery because of the hurt it caused my poor country-women. You say there were no more fallen women on a plantation than in London in proportion to numbers; but what say you to this? A magnate who runs a hideous black harem with his lovely white wife, and his beautiful and accomplished daughters, holds his head high and poses as the model of all human virtues to these poor women whom God and the laws have given him. From the height of his awful majesty, he scolds and thunders at them, as if he never did wrong in his life. Fancy such a man finding his daughter reading *Don Juan*. "You with that immoral book!" And he orders her out of his sight. You see, Mrs. Stowe did not hit the *sorest spot*. She made Simon Legree a bachelor.

A few days after the sale of the mulatto girl, we had a scene in the hotel parlor. Mrs. Charles Lewis Scott of Alabama brought up Lincoln. "He is the *cleverest* Yankee type. Awfully ugly—even grotesque in appearance, the kind who are always at corner stores, sitting on boxes, whittling sticks, and telling stories as funny as they are vulgar."

Personally I considered Lincoln an insidious villain, but refrained from saying so in polite company. I said: "Stephen Douglas once told Mr. Chesnut, 'Lincoln is the hardest fellow to handle I have ever encountered yet.'"

Mr. Scott was from California. He said: "Lincoln is an utterly American specimen, coarse, tough, and strong. A good-natured creature."

"As pleasant-tempered as he is clever," Mrs. Scott said sarcastically. "And if this country can be *joked* and *laughed* out of its rights, he is the *kind-hearted* fellow to do it. Now if war pinches the Yankee pocket instead of filling it—"

Here a shrill voice sounded from the next room. "Yankees are no more *mean* and *stingy* than you are. People at the North are as good as people at the South."

The speaker, a northern exile, advanced upon us in great wrath. Mrs. Scott apologized and made some smooth, polite remarks. But the vinegar-faced exile refused to receive any concession. She said: "That comes with a very bad grace after what you were saying."

She harangued us loudly for several minutes. Someone in the other room giggled outright. We were quiet as mice. Nobody wanted to hurt her feelings. She was one against so many. If I were at the North I should expect *them* to belabor us—and should hold my tongue. We separated from the North because of incompatibility of temper. We were *divorced*, North from South, because we *hated* each other so. I just hoped it would be a "séparation à l'agréable," as the French say it, and not a horrid fight for divorce.

This poor exile had already been insulted, she said. To soothe her wounded spirits, she played "Yankee Doodle" on the piano before breakfast. My uncle, Judge Thomas Jefferson Withers, came in and calmly requested her to leave out the Yankee while she played the Doodle. The Yankee end of it was totally out of place here.

One afternoon I spotted Mr. Davis coming out of his office building. I turned and fled up the street. I was a little afraid of him, I guess, he being the President. The next time I visited Varina, he told me: "You ought to be ashamed to fly away at the sound of my footsteps." He said it with such kindness that I *blushed*. Those who criticized Jeff Davis as President—those who said he was cold, peevish, and petulant—did not know how *kind* and *gentlemanly* he could be. After that discussion with him, I never again flew away from the sound of his footsteps.

57. DAVIS

The Chesnuts were often with us in our "executive mansion," a two-story frame residence to which we had moved; it stood on a corner facing the Capitol. James never said much; he seemed content to let his sparkling wife lead the conversation, which she did with fervor. The only flaw Mary Chesnut had was an undue reliance on the morphine bottle. She took morphine, Varina said, to ease her "racking nervous headaches."

A group of us stood on a hotel balcony the day they raised our new Confederate flag to the booming of cannon. The new flag had one white and two red stripes of the same width and a blue union with seven white stars, which we hoped to augment to fifteen if we could induce the remaining slave states to join us. From the outset, the Confederacy pursued negotiations with those states, but one after another they decided against immediate secession. They would wait and see what Lincoln would do after his Inauguration—would wait for "an overt act" against the South.

I had sent three commissioners to Washington to negotiate peace terms with Lincoln, but none of us in Montgomery had any idea how he would treat them. Our friends in Washington reported that Seward, Lincoln's Secretary of State, favored appeasement, and the New York *Tribune* editorialized that "the South has as good a right to secede from the Union as the colonies had to secede from Great Britain." But did Seward and the *Tribune* speak for Lincoln? I thought a good deal about my adversary, wondering what his policy would be. In all candor, I knew almost nothing about the man. I studied press reports of his slow journey to Washington, but could divine nothing of his intentions in his vague, often flippant remarks about the crisis. I wondered if a speech he had given in Congress in 1848 offered any clues. "Any people anywhere," Lincoln had said, "have the *right* to rise up, and shake off the existing government and form a new one that suits them better. This is a most valuable—a most sacred right—a right, which we hope and believe, is to liberate the world. Nor is this right confined to cases in which the whole people of an existing government may choose to exercise it. Any portion of such people that *can*, *may* revolutionize, and make their *own*, of so much of the territory as they inhabit." Those were my own sentiments exactly. The question was: Would Lincoln allow us to shake off the Union government and organize a new one that suited us better? Or would he try to reinforce Fort Sumter—even send down an invading army?

I made it clear that any Federal attempt to reinforce Sumter would lead to war. Though the North outnumbered us, it remained to be seen whether it could outfight us. Still, it troubled me that we were so poorly prepared for war and had little capacity for speedy repair of past neglect. Valor was on our side and the justice of our cause would nerve the arm of our sons to meet the issue of an unequal conflict, but we had to render the inequality as small as it could be made.

As the day of Lincoln's Inauguration approached, I turned to the task of mobilizing and equipping an army.

58 . LINCOLN

It was February nineteenth, I think, when our train reached New York City for a two-day layover. As the presidential party rode through town in an eleven-carriage parade, an estimated 250,000 people crowded the sidewalks and windows of buildings to see the "westerner" and his family. At the Astor House, where we had rooms, I told a crowd that since the presidential election I'd occupied a position of silence, of avoiding public speaking, of avoiding public writing. I'd done so because I thought that this was the proper course for me to take. But when the time did come, I would take the ground I thought was right for the North, for the South, for the East, for the whole country.

Later, in our room, Mary told me she'd overheard people talking about us. "They said we were so *gauche*. They said, 'Did you hear how Lincoln pronounced Inauguration? *Inaugeration*, he called it.' They said we were a disgrace to the nation; said you would dishonor the presidential chair. One man struck a table and cried: 'Well! if nothing more is done, it will help civilize the people of Illinois.'"

"I guess they think we're hicks," I said, which upset Mary no end. "We're *not hicks*," she said with tears in her eyes. "God, I *hate* these New York snobs. Every time I come here to shop, I hear snide remarks about our western manners and accents, and I'm sick of it."

As she carried on, I saw myself as the New Yorkers did, a gauche westerner who referred to the head of a committee as "Mr. Cheerman," scratched his elbow when he laughed, and shook hands as if he were sawing wood. Well, I wasn't going to apologize for who I was.

The next evening, after a whirlwind day of receptions, meetings, and serenades, I attended the opera with Judge Davis and a city alderman. Not knowing any better, I wore black kid gloves instead of white ones and further violated etiquette by hanging my hands, which are pretty big, over the railing of our box. The "snobs" in the audience pointed and sniggered. The next day, when we departed for Trenton and Philadelphia, the hostile New York papers said I had the manners of a gorilla.

At Trenton, I was scheduled to address both houses of the New Jersey legislature. Going over what I might say, I kept thinking about Weems's *Life of Washington,* which I'd read as a boy. I remembered all the accounts there given of the battlefields and struggles for the liberties of the country, and none fixed themselves upon my imagination so deeply as the struggle at Trenton—the crossing of the river; the contest with the Hessians; the great hardships endured at that time.

When we reached Trenton, I told the New Jersey senate about my reading of Weems and said that I had thought then, boy though I was, that there must have been something more than common that those men struggled for. I was exceedingly anxious, I said, to protect that "thing" which they struggled for; that "something" even more than national independence; that "*something*" that held out a great promise to all the people of the world for all time to come.

I was tired and never quite explained what that "something" was. In Philadelphia the next day, Washington's birthday, I clarified what I meant in a few impromptu remarks in Independence Hall, where the Declaration of Independence had been adopted. Speaking with deep emotion, I said that I'd never had a feeling politically that did not spring from the sentiments embodied in that document. "I've often inquired of myself what great principle or idea it was that kept this Confederacy so long together. It was something in that Declaration giving liberty, not alone to the people of this country, but hope to the world for all future time. It was that which gave promise that in due time the weights should be lifted from the shoulders of all men, and that *all* should have an equal chance. This is the sentiment embodied in that Declaration of Independence."

It was that principle, the central idea of the Republic, which was at stake in our present difficulties. "Can this country be saved upon that basis?" I asked. "If it can, I'll consider myself one of the happiest men in the world if I can help to save it. But, if this country can't be saved without giving up that principle," I said and then paused. "I was about to say I would rather be assassinated on this spot than surrender it."

Assassination was on my mind because of something I'd learned the previous night. After our arrival, we'd had dinner and then attended a public reception in the Continental Hotel where we were staying. Near the end of the reception, John Nicolay, my personal secretary, brought a note from Norman Judd saying that he wanted to see me in his room on an urgent matter. I went to Judd's room and found there stout and bearded Allan Pinkerton, head of the Chicago private detective agency.

"He's working for the Philadelphia, Wilmington, & Baltimore Railroad," Judd said. "I want him to tell you what he and the head of the railroad, Mr. Felton, just told me."

"Mr. President," Pinkerton said, speaking with a slight Scottish burr, "my agents and I have uncovered a plot to assassinate you in Baltimore. The attempt will be made while you pass through town to change trains, day after tomorrow. The danger is very real, sir. I'm here to help you and Mr. Judd foil the plan."

"I'm listening," I said.

He and his operatives, he said, had gone to Baltimore to search out suspicious persons. They found the state of feeling there "embittered and poisoned"—the city was crawling with southern secessionists and pro-Confederate thugs and plug-uglies who congregated at Barnum's Hotel. He and his agents had penetrated a circle of rabid secessionists who belonged to a secret military organization, and from them had learned of the plan to assassinate me, the exact time when I expected to go through Baltimore being publicly known. An Italian barber who had once lived in the South, Fernandina, was the leader. He told Pinkerton that my election had enraged southerners, who were justified in resorting to murder to keep me from taking office. As Pinkerton told it, the barber said, "Lincoln will never, never be President. He must die—and die he will. Then all Maryland will be with us, and the South will be forever free."

"How can you be sure this plot will be carried through?" I asked.

"Because, sir, one of my men has penetrated to the very core of the plot and learned how thoroughly the whole thing has been prepared."

"And you trust this detective?"

"I do, Mr. President. He's a former Jesuit priest and a dedicated Unionist. He ingratiated himself with one of the plotters and attended a secret meeting where the conspirators drew ballots to decide who would strike the blow. Captain Fernandina then went over the details of the scheme. The Baltimore chief-of-police, a secessionist, is privy to it; he will deploy only a small force at the Calvert Street Station, where you'll arrive from Harrisburg. A carriage is supposed to take you to Camden Street Station for the change of trains to Washington. At the Calvert Street depot, a vast crowd of secessionists will gather before you arrive, filling the narrow streets and passages. One group will start a fight to distract the policemen, leaving you entirely unprotected and surrounded by a dense, excited, and hostile crowd. As you pass between the narrow vestibule of the station to enter your carriage, the crowd will surround you and the assassins will strike. A fast steamer waiting in Chesapeake Bay will take them south to the Confederacy."

"If all of this is true," I said, "what do you propose to do about it?"

"We propose," Pinkerton said, "to take you on to Washington this very night, on the eleven o'clock train."

"I can't do that," I said. "I promised tomorrow morning to raise the flag over Independence Hall, and after that to visit the legislature at Harrisburg. I intend to keep those engagements."

"Have the public authorities in Baltimore made any arrangements for your reception in that city?" Pinkerton asked.

"None that I know of," I said. "All the other places have sent reception committees ahead to escort me into town, but Baltimore hasn't even extended me an invitation to visit." I thought for a moment. "I tell you what I'll do. If a reception committee from Baltimore comes to Harrisburg, I'll feel safe and go on according to schedule. If there is no such reception committee, I'll put myself in your hands."

I could not believe that there was a plot to assassinate me. Yes, Baltimore was full of secessionists. Yes, some of them had threatened to kill the pro-Union governor, Thomas Hicks, and shoot any northern troops who tried to cross Maryland soil. And yes, I had the utmost confidence in Allan Pinkerton and his men. Even so, I found it hard to believe that a gang of secessionist bullies would try to murder me in a crowded street in broad daylight.

When I made my way back to my room, through crowds of people, I ran into Ward Hill Lamon and young Frederick Seward, who brought a letter from his father, Senator Seward. We went to my room, where I read the letter and an enclosed note from General Scott and a report from an army colonel named Stone. According to Stone, a New York detective on duty in Baltimore believed that I would be assassinated by a band of rowdies on my passage through the city. The risk could be avoided, the colonel said, if I passed through Baltimore by a night train "without previous notice." Seward and Scott both concurred.

The New York detective knew nothing of Pinkerton's movements. Here, then, was corroboration of Pinkerton's story from another source, so I guessed I would have to believe it now. But I hated to admit that we had reached a point in this country where a fairly elected President faced an assassination attempt by his own people. With that weighing on me, I slept little that night. By morning, I thought it prudent to do as Judd and Pinkerton advised and change my plans so that I would pass through Baltimore at a different time from the hour that had been announced. I told Judd of my decision and later informed young Seward so that he could advise his father and General Scott. We all agreed that nobody else was to know except for the railroad and telegraph officials who would help arrange my getaway.

At six thirty that morning, I went to Independence Hall for the flag-raising. It was on that occasion that I said I would rather be assassinated than give up the principle of the right to rise. I should have clarified that statement, pointing out that the principle included *my* right—the right of *anybody*—to rise peacefully and safely to the Presidency. I went on to talk about the state of the country. "There is no need of bloodshed and war. I'm not in favor of such a course, and I may say in advance, there will be no blood shed unless it be forced upon the government. The government will not use force unless force is used against it." Perhaps this was an indiscreet remark, I added, but I'd said nothing but what I was willing to live or die by. Then I raised Old Glory over the hall. It was a new version of the flag, containing a thirty-fourth star for Kansas. It had been admitted as a state in late January, after most of the Deep South congressmen had resigned.

On the train to Harrisburg later that day, Judd outlined a getaway plan he and Pinkerton had worked out during the night with Felton, the president of the railroad, and other officials. "At six this evening you'll slip away from the Jones Hotel in disguise and ride a closed carriage to the depot," Judd said. "Telegraph climbers will cut all telegraph wires from Harrisburg to prevent any messages about you from getting out. A special train will take you to West Philadelphia. There Pinkerton and a railroad superintendent named Kenney will meet you in a carriage and take you to the Philadelphia, Wilmington, & Baltimore Station, where you'll board a sleeping car and stay concealed in a rear berth. On a signal from Kenney to the conductor that you're safely aboard, the night train will pull the sleeping car to Baltimore, and another train will take it to Washington. Tomorrow the Presidential train will proceed to Baltimore as scheduled. I'll be on board with the military escort to protect your family and traveling companions."

I hated the idea of sneaking into Washington in disguise, but decided to run no risk where no risk was required and agreed to Judd's plan. But I insisted on telling Mary about it, as otherwise she would be very much excited by my absence. When I spoke to Mary in our hotel room, she made quite a scene, saying it was her duty—her *right*—to travel with me and stand by my side in case of danger. She couldn't tolerate the idea that I would be taken from her and rushed through a hostile town where violent men were plotting to kill me. It did no good to point out that she could not prevent mischief against me, that her presence would *augment* the risk; she wouldn't listen to reason. Still, there wasn't much she could do: the plan had already been arranged; I had agreed to go ahead without her. Reduced to tears, she insisted that Lamon accompany me because she could count on him to protect me with his life.

On Judd's advice, I also told Judge Davis, Colonel Sumner, and the others in my traveling party. Old Colonel Sumner, white-haired and white-bearded, insisted that it was his duty to accompany me to Washington, saying so in a booming voice that was the source of his nickname, "Old Bull." Judd tried to dissuade him from going along, pointing out that his uniform would attract attention, but Sumner would not be dissuaded.

That night, wearing an old overcoat and carrying a shawl on my arm, I left the hotel in Harrisburg by a back door. Putting on a soft wool hat, I climbed into a closed carriage with Lamon. There were many people about, but nobody recognized me. Lamon was armed with two of everything—revolvers, derringers, and knives. Bull Sumner, who'd followed me out of the hotel, tried to get in the carriage with us, but Judd caught him by the arm and held him back. "Hurry!" Judd told Lamon. We raced to the station, boarded an empty coach pulled by a darkened locomotive, and roared eastward into the night.

When we reached West Philadelphia, Pinkerton and a railroad superintendent were waiting for us in another carriage. They drove us to the Philadelphia, Wilmington, & Baltimore Station just as the train for Baltimore was about to depart. As I leaned on Pinkerton and stooped to disguise my height, we sneaked aboard the rear door of a crowded sleeper—the last car on the train. The interior was lit by candle lamps and heated by a couple of wood stoves. One of Pinkerton's female agents had reserved the four rear berths for "a sick friend" and his traveling companions. I climbed into the one for the sick friend and closed the curtains as the train jerked forward and moved off down the track.

The berth had no bedding beyond a mattress, a blanket, and a pillow. It was so short that I had to double up my legs. Unable to sleep, I lay there listening to the drone of the train. Maybe Judd and Pinkerton were right about Baltimore, but I was not proud of myself for what I was doing. What if something happened to Mary and the boys? I pictured a mob of secessionists beating on the presidential coach and screaming my name . . . a fight with policemen . . . gunshots. I tried to rearrange my legs and sleep, but sleep wouldn't come. It was around three thirty in the morning when the train reached Baltimore. Pinkerton rustled in the dark, then whispered to me: "An officer of the road just entered the car and whispered in my ear, 'All's well,'" meaning we had not been detected. Horses then pulled the sleeping car through the dark, empty streets to the Camden Street Station, where it would be hooked up to a Washington-bound train. We lay there, waiting. I told a couple of jokes under my breath—don't recall what they were now—and then fell silent again. On the platform outside, a very drunk fellow was singing "Dixie." *Ah wish Ah was in Dixie (hick). Hooray! Hooray! In Dixie land (hick) Ah'll take my stand, To live or die in Dixie.*

I whispered: "No doubt there will be a great time in Dixie by and by."

Presently we heard the sounds of engines and shifting cars. It was the Washington-bound train at last. We were soon under way through Baltimore's dark suburbs. The rest of the trip was uneventful—we finally reached Washington just as day was breaking. We could see the uncompleted dome of the Capitol against the fiery streaks of dawn. Scaffolds enfolded the cupola, and cranes stretched over the dome. Stacks of building material surrounded the Capitol and the unfinished Treasury Building. Down on the Potomac, a white shaft of marble rose against the horizon; it was the uncompleted new monument to President Washington.

At the train station, Lamon, Pinkerton, and I joined the crowds of passengers making their way toward the outer door. I still wore the hat and overcoat, with the shawl over my shoulders. Suddenly, someone stepped from behind a pillar and said: "Lincoln, you can't play that on me!" It was Washburne, the Illinois congressman. Pinkerton raised his fist to strike a blow, but I grabbed his arm. "Don't hit him," I said. "It's my friend, Washburne. Don't you know him?"

"How are you, Lincoln?" Washburne asked. He was a gray-haired, broad-shouldered fellow with thin legs and an ample belly. "Seward told me when you would arrive," he said. "He's supposed to be here, too, but I don't see him."

We walked slowly because Washburne had a bad limp. Outside we hailed a hack and headed up Pennsylvania Avenue for Willard's Hotel, where rooms were reserved for us. I hadn't been in Washington for almost twelve years and had forgotten how filthy it was and how foul it smelled. The Mall and side streets off the Avenue were strewn with garbage; we could see pigs rooting about in the filth. The old canal was full of trash, sewage, the carcasses of dead animals, and other putrid waste, which gave off a terrible stench.

At Willard's, a fortresslike structure on the Avenue, I registered at the desk and found an obscene letter awaiting me. "You are nothing but a Goddamn Black nigger," it said. The rest of it was full of unrepeatable obscenities. It was the first of hundreds of hateful letters I would receive in Washington; after a while, I stopped reading the damn things.

Seward joined us for breakfast. Out of breath, he apologized for missing me at the depot. With his beaked nose, protruding ears, thick, grizzly brows, and mussed-up hair, he reminded me of a rare bird chewing on a Havana cigar. He spoke nonstop about Baltimore, insisting that he had "conclusive evidence" of the plot to kill me there and reassuring me—and I needed reassuring—that I could not have passed through the city in any other manner without bloodshed. I was already exhausted—I hadn't slept all night—and found it impossible to keep up with his flood of chatter.

After breakfast, we called on President Buchanan at the White House. Bent, white-haired, and muttering, he seemed old beyond his years. I thought to myself: I'll probably look like that, too, when my turn comes to stand in his place. A little later, I retired to my suite of rooms, but got no rest there owing to a steady stream of visitors.

Late that afternoon, to my great relief, Mary and the boys arrived safely at the hotel. Mary, however, was much shaken and afflicted with headache from their ordeal in Baltimore. The news that I'd gone ahead to Washington "*unseen, unnoticed,* and *unknown*" had reached Baltimore that morning, but most people dismissed it as a hoax. "When the presidential train stopped at Calvert Street Station," Mary said, "a frenzied crowd was waiting for you. It was just terrible. All those menacing faces. They kept screaming, 'Come out, Abe.' 'We'll give you hell, you bloody Black Republican.' When we left the train, the crowd pinned us against the coach and shouted the filthiest obscenities I've ever *heard*. Somehow Mr. Judd, Mr. Davis, and the officers got us away from those shrieking ruffians. The boys and I took a carriage to Camden Station, and the men followed in an omnibus. The streets were just mobbed. I was terrified something would happen. When we reached the station, there must have been ten thousand people! There were loud cheers for Jeff Davis and boos for you. When we boarded the coach, a crowd of men and boys surrounded it, and leered at us, and screamed obscene insults. Oh God my head hurts. I'll never forget any of it."

Neither would I. The whole thing, I said, was a grave mistake. Oh, Lamon and Pinkerton kept insisting on the truth of the assassination plot and the wisdom of the "secret passage." And a Baltimore Unionist wrote me that my course had prevented bloodshed. But it left me with a bad feeling. I still don't think I would have been assassinated had I gone through Baltimore as planned.

Inevitably, the press got hold of the story. A *New York Times* correspondent, I think it was, reported that I'd sneaked into Washington disguised in "a Scotch plaid cap and a very long military cloak," and other papers picked up the story, referring to it as "the flight of Abraham." *Vanity Fair* published a cartoon, "The McLincoln Harrisburg Highland Fling," which showed a scarecrowish Lincoln dancing in Scottish kilts. One paper, I remember, called me "a braying ass" whose "weak, wishy-washy, namby-pamby efforts" had made America "the laughing stock of the whole world." Those words hurt. But I make it a policy of never responding to abusive journalism. It goes with the job.

For the next week, a mob of rabid, persistent office-seekers descended on me in Parlor Number Six, teasing me to near insanity with their demands. It was bad enough in Springfield, but that was child's play compared with the tussle in Washington. I hardly had a chance to eat or sleep. I was fair game for everybody of that hungry lot.

Somehow, in all the hubbub, I managed to complete my Cabinet, although the rival factions hassled me down to the final appointment. Chase would head the Treasury Department, Cameron the War Department, Welles the Navy Department, and Monty Blair the Post Office. All of my chief Republican rivals—strong, intelligent, ambitious men—were in the Cabinet where I could keep an eye on them.

My chief Democratic rival, Judge Douglas, called at Parlor Number Six with the Illinois congressional delegation. At my request, Douglas returned a few days later so that we could talk in private. Gesturing with a cigar, he shook his mammoth head and spoke in a stentorian voice as though he were addressing a huge crowd. He pleaded with me to support the Washington Peace Convention, whose compromise formula now lay before Congress. Like the Crittenden plan, it called for the revival and extension of the Missouri Compromise line, to which I remained categorically opposed, and I told Douglas so.

Douglas scowled. "We both have children," he said. "In God's name, act the patriot and save our children a country to live in."

That, I told him, was exactly what I was trying to do.

"Seward has proposed a national convention," he said. "I hope you'll endorse it." I made a mental note to keep an eye on Seward; he seemed to be making his own promises and assurances, as if he intended to run the government. "As head of the loyal opposition in Congress," Douglas was saying, "I promise you that I will not resort to partisan politics and try to make political capital from any move you make to save the country." He paused, eyeing me. "What will you offer the South? Do you have a compromise plan?"

I was not going to be tricked into a statement before my Inauguration. "The problem is much on my mind," I said. "Thanks for coming by, Douglas." He left grumbling that it was impossible to get me "to a point on the subject."

Delegations from Virginia and the other border states also called at Parlor Number Six. One group came from the Virginia secession convention, which remained in session, refusing to vote for secession or for adjournment until I made my move. The Virginians urged me to give them "a message of peace" to take home with them.

"All I can say," I told them, "is that southerners will be protected in all their rights." They grumbled that this wasn't much, but what else could they expect?

Another border-state delegation, including three Virginians, came from the Peace Convention itself. Sitting in a semicircle around me, they told me what I *must do*. I *must* avoid coercion, *must* withdraw the troops from Fort Sumter, *must* offer satisfactory guarantees to the eight slave states still in the Union. "Mr. Seward," one fellow added, "assures me that within sixty days after you take office, the crisis will be passed, or I can have his head. We want the same assurance from you."

I decided to see if I could bargain with them. "Tell your people that this is what I'll do. I'll support the proposed slave amendment to the Constitution, the so-called Corwin amendment, which is now before the Senate. But I will *not* guarantee slavery in the territories, will *not* betray the party that elected me. You border men say I must not collect revenues in the Deep South and retake the Federal forts and custom houses seized by the secessionists. Why not? How is it coercion to defend the integrity of the government?" Since last December, I had consistently argued that all the forts and other property captured by the rebels must be retaken and Fort Sumter reinforced.

Morehead of Kentucky spoke up. "Sir, Fort Sumter is up to your discretion. You can withdraw the troops if you please. You're the commander-in-chief, and the power belongs to you, either to keep them there or withdraw them. But if you leave them there, you risk starting a deadly and ruinous war."

"That reminds me of a little anecdote from Aesop's Fables," I said. "A lion was once desperately in love with a beautiful lady, and he courted her, and the lady became enamored of him and agreed to marry him, and the old people were asked for their consent. They were afraid of the power of the lion with his long, sharp claws and his tusks, and they said to him, 'We can't object to so respectable a personage as you, but our daughter is frail and delicate, and we hope that you'll submit to having your claws cut off and your tusks drawn, because they might do serious injury to her.' The lion submitted, being very much in love. His claws were cut off and his tusks drawn. Then they took clubs and knocked him on the head." I looked around the group, but not one of them cracked a smile.

"Very interesting," said Morehead, "but not a very comprehensive answer to a very serious question. I appeal to you, put jesting aside and help us avert a calamity."

Rives of Virginia stood up and said in a quavering voice, "I'm a very old man and my heart longs for the salvation of the Union. But

I want you to know, sir, that I agree with every word Mr. Morehead has said about the horrors of civil war. If you resort to coercion, Virginia will leave the Union and join the seceding states. In that event, as much as I've loved the Union, I'll go with Virginia with all my heart and soul."

I rose from my chair and went over to him. "Mr. Rives," I said, "I'll make you an offer. If Virginia will break up its convention, I'll withdraw the troops from Fort Sumter."

"Mr. President," he said, "I have no authority to speak for Virginia. All I can promise, if you withdraw the troops and give us guarantees, is that I'll do all I personally can to promote the Union and restore it to what it was." The other two Virginians said much the same thing. If they had no authority, I thought, then why in hell had they come to see me? We parted with nothing agreed to and nothing solved.

As Inauguration Day approached, I worked on the final draft of my Address in our suite, sitting at a desk with my reading spectacles on. The eight states of the upper South were all waiting to hear what I had to say, and I took great pains to be precise and clear. On March third, a Sunday, I gave the speech to Seward to read, and he advised me to make more concessions to the South. He insisted that I remove one sentence in particular—that I would recapture all the forts and arsenals seized by the rebels. That sentence, he said, would alienate southern Unionists upon whom any pacification program depended. I agreed with him and deleted the offending sentence.

But that was all I would concede. As far as I was concerned, the future of the Union and popular government itself depended on my standing firm. Damn it, I had been freely and fairly elected. I owed it to the party and the people who elected me to preserve the nation and the principle of self-government on which the nation was based. That principle was the right of a free people to choose their leaders and expect the losers to accept the majority decision. If southerners hated me so much, they could vote me out in the next election. But they had no authority under the Constitution to secede from the Union, to break it up, simply because they were unhappy with the results of a presidential election. Some Republicans—Greeley, for one—demanded that I let the seceded states go and good riddance. But if I did that, it would set a catastrophic precedent that any state could leave the Union whenever it liked, without the consent of the Union or any other state.

The argument of secession was nothing but an insidious

debauching of the public mind, an ingenious sophism without legal, logical, or historical defense. The sophism derived its currency from the assumption that there is some omnipotent and sacred supremacy of a *state* over the Union. This is like arguing that the proper place for the big kettle is inside the little kettle. The fact is, when the original states, and every subsequent state, entered the Union, they acknowledged the Constitution of the United States, and the laws and treaties of the United States made in pursuance of the Constitution, *to be the supreme law of the land*. The states have their status *in* the Union, and they have no other legal status. If they break from this, they can only do so against law, and by revolution. The whole principle of secession is one of disintegration, and upon which no government can possibly endure.

There was something else that bothered me. The Declaration of Independence prevents free men from being chained to the conditions of their births. It guarantees us equal opportunity to lift ourselves as far as our talents and hard work can take us. It allowed *me* to climb from humble beginnings to the Presidency. That is the genius of our experiment in popular government. I could not tolerate the thought that the very system that had permitted me to rise to the Presidency was collapsing because I *had done so*—because a disaffected minority could not accept that result. It was a terrible irony that our system, which offers so much of hope in the world, might disintegrate into civil war, into anarchy and chaos, just as its European critics always claimed would happen. Somehow *I* had to hold our system together. Upon *my* shoulders fell that difficult task, and nobody else's.

March fourth, Inauguration Day, dawned with heavy storm clouds hanging over the city. Because of the many assassination threats and a report that rebel troops or rebel sympathizers intended to blow up the speaker's platform during the Inaugural ceremonies, Scott had called out the army to guard the capital. From our rooms, Mary and I could hear the clatter of cavalry and artillery and the tramp of infantry in the streets outside.

At five o'clock that same morning, the final vote on all the compromise measures took place in the Senate. Both the Crittenden plan and the Peace Convention plan, with their provisions for slavery expansion, went down to defeat, as they deserved. Only the projected slavery amendment narrowly passed in the Senate, as it had in the House, over the opposition of more than two-thirds of the Republicans. Personally, I had no objection to the amendment. It was consistent with all we'd ever said about leaving slavery alone where it already existed of necessity.

When the clock struck twelve noon, I stood Mary's inspection. I carried a gold-headed cane and wore a new black suit, shined black boots, and a new stovepipe hat made of silk.

"You look very distinguished, Mr. Lincoln," she said, straightening my cravat. "I'm sure all the young women will want to dance with you at the Inaugural Ball tonight. You know I don't want you to talk to them."

"But Mother," I said, "I have to talk to somebody. I can't stand around like a simpleton and say nothing."

"You know very well, Mr. Lincoln, that I don't approve of your flirtations with silly young women, just as if you're a beardless boy, fresh from school."

I didn't have the time or the inclination to argue with her. In a few minutes, Buchanan called to escort me on the traditional carriage ride to the Capitol. Outside, the sky had cleared and the sun shone brilliantly. We climbed into an open carriage and started up Pennsylvania Avenue in a color-splashed parade that featured horse-drawn floats and strutting military bands. To my annoyance, double files of cavalry rode along both flanks of the carriage and infantry marched in front and behind it. It made me feel like a damned king. Hundreds of people lined the sidewalks and stood at the windows and on the roofs of passing buildings; some were cheering, others were frowning and shouting things I couldn't make out in all the noise. Armed soldiers cordoned off intersections, stood on the sidewalks, peered over the rooftops on both sides of the Avenue. The presence of all these soldiers depressed me. It was further proof that our system was breaking down.

When we reached the Capitol, we could see the silhouettes of soldiers in the windows and on the roofs of adjacent buildings. On a nearby hill stood a line of artillery, whose gunners were ready to rake the streets with cannon fire at the first sign of assassins or rebel troops. Finally, the moment of my Inauguration arrived. I stood at the podium on the Inaugural platform at the Capitol's east wing, facing a vast, sunlit throng. Behind me sat some three hundred dignitaries, including Judge Douglas, who had generously taken my silk hat when I rose to speak and could find no place to put it. He held the hat throughout the proceedings.

I donned my spectacles, unrolled my manuscript, and started reading in a nervous shrill voice. First, I tried to reassure southerners. "Apprehension seems to exist among the people of the southern states, that by the accession of a Republican Administration, their property, and their peace, and personal security, are to be endangered. There's never been any reasonable cause for such apprehension." I quoted from one of my many speeches: "I have no purpose, directly or indirectly, to interfere with the institution of slavery in the states where it exists. I believe I have no lawful right to do so, and I have no inclination to do so." I also quoted from the 1860 Republican platform, which promised to maintain inviolate the power of each state to control its domestic institutions. Moreover, I said, I had no objections to the proposed constitutional amendment that had just passed Congress, to the effect that the Federal Government could never interfere with the domestic institutions of the states, including that of persons held to service.

As I spoke, I heard Judge Douglas muttering "Good" or "That's fair" behind me. I defended the supremacy of Federal authority at some length, directing my remarks in large part at southern Unionists. If they could be rallied to the flag, as Seward kept arguing, maybe they would arrest secession and end the crisis. The Union of states, I contended, was perpetual. No government ever had a provision in its organic law for its own termination, and neither did this one. It followed that no state, upon its own mere motion, could lawfully get out of the Union, and that resistance to Federal authority, within any state, was insurrectionary and revolutionary.

I was warming to my speech now, swinging my arms back and forth and rising up on my feet. "I consider that the Union is *unbroken*," I said, "and that the Constitution expressly enjoins me to execute the laws of the Union in all the states." Yet, I reassured southerners, there needed to be no bloodshed or violence; and there would be none, unless it was forced upon the national authority. The power confided in me would be used to collect the duties and imposts and to hold, occupy, and possess the property and places belonging to the government; by which I specifically meant the two forts still in our possession, Fort Sumter in Charleston Harbor and Fort Pickens in Pensacola Bay. "But beyond what may be necessary for these objects, there will be *no invasion*—no using of force against, or among the people anywhere." I did not, however, specifically rule out the use of force to keep Sumter and Pickens.

And so to my conclusion. "In *your* hands, my dissatisfied fellow countrymen, and not in *mine*, is the momentous issue of civil war," I said. "The government will not assail *you*. You can have no conflict, without being yourselves the aggressors. *You* have no oath registered in Heaven to destroy the government, while *I* shall have the most solemn one to 'preserve, protect, and defend' it.

"I am loth to close. We are not enemies, but friends. We must not be enemies. Though passion may have strained, it must not break our bonds of affection. The mystic chords of memory, stretching from every battlefield, and patriot grave, to every living heart and hearthstone, all over this broad land, will yet swell the chorus of the Union, when again touched, as surely they will be, by the better angels of our nature."

59 . DOUGLAS

As Lincoln spoke that day, I said in an undertone, "Good," "That's so," "No coercion, good," "That's fair, "No backing out there," "That's a good point." When he finished, Chief Justice Taney rose and administered the oath of office. Standing beside Lincoln, whom he detested, Taney looked old and shriveled like a Goddamned corpse. He was what—eighty-four years old? Enormous bags sagged under his eyes. He looked as if he was about to fall asleep on his feet. When he finished swearing Lincoln in, *boom! boom! boom!* went the cannon on the nearby hill, which startled everybody. I handed Lincoln his stovepipe hat and congratulated him. But I would be lying if I said his Inauguration as President didn't bother me. It bothered the Goddamned Hell out of me.

Afterward I told a reporter: "Lincoln doesn't mean coercion. He says nothing about retaking the forts or other Federal property—he's all right." I didn't believe we ought to hold Fort Sumter and Fort Pickens, much less recapture the forts that had already been taken, unless we intended to reduce the seceded states themselves into subjection. I believed that no man could deny that whoever permanently held Charleston and South Carolina was entitled to Fort Sumter. Which meant the Confederacy was entitled to it. We could not deny that there was a southern Confederacy, de facto, in existence, with its capital at Montgomery. We might regret it. *I* regretted it most profoundly; but I couldn't deny the truth of the fact, painful and mortifying as it was. Therefore I favored withdrawing the garrisons at Sumter and Pickens, both of which lay within the Confederacy.

Southerners heard in Lincoln's speech, not conciliation, but a declaration of war. Senator Louis Wigfall of Texas, a loudmouthed fire-eater, declared flatly: "The Inaugural means war." When I had a chance to read Lincoln's address, I hardly knew what he meant. He seemed to offer the South a sword and an olive branch at the same time. Every point in the address was susceptible to a double construction; but I told my friends that I thought, I hoped, he didn't mean coercion. If he tried to retake the forts and custom houses the rebels had seized in the seceded states, it would mean war.

The Inaugural Ball was held the night of March fourth in the Palace of Aladdin behind City Hall. Lincoln invited me to join the presidential party and to escort Mrs. Lincoln. The presidential procession swept into the ballroom at eleven that night, and the band struck up "Hail Columbia" as we marched the length of the hall. Lincoln led the march arm in arm with the mayor while I followed with Mrs. Lincoln on my arm. Dressed in a blue dress and gold necklace and bracelets, she looked radiant, as plump and pretty as I'd ever seen her. I danced the quadrille or square dance of the evening with her, and it reminded me of the times we'd danced together in the old days in Springfield, before either of us had married. As we whirled across the floor, she smiled and laughed like a young girl.

I noticed that Lincoln looked tired and anxious and kept tugging at his white kid gloves. Maybe it had something to do with the letter handed to him when he first entered the hall. As he read it, his face looked stricken, as if he'd been given a death sentence.

60. LINCOLN

The first thing handed to me, after I entered the Inaugural Ball, was a letter from Major Robert Anderson, the commander of the little two-company garrison at Fort Sumter, saying that his provisions would be exhausted before an expedition could be sent to his relief. He would run out of food in six weeks. It was his professional opinion that it would require a force of twenty thousand good and well-disciplined men to hold the fort, and that reinforcements of that number could not be gotten up and sent to him in time. This opinion was concurred in by all the officers of his command, and their memoranda on the subject were made enclosures of Major Anderson's letter.

I was stunned. If what Anderson said was true, it was a calamity. I confronted the officer from the War Department who had brought me the letter. "Anderson is a Kentuckian," I said. "And his wife is from Georgia. Can he be trusted?" The officer assured me of Anderson's loyalty.

The next day, my first on the job, I laid the matter before General Scott, who at once concurred with Major Anderson's opinion. On reflection, however, he consulted with other officers of the army and navy; and at the end of four days came reluctantly, but decidedly, to the same conclusion as before. "We don't have twenty thousand men to send," he said, standing unsteadily before me in full uniform. "We've got just sixteen thousand men in the entire regular army, and most of them are stationed on the frontier. We can't raise a third of the men in several months necessary to give the fort relief. I see no alternative—and the distinguished Chief Engineer concurs—but to surrender the fort and evacuate the troops, if indeed the worn-out garrison be not assaulted and carried within the week."

I tell you, that reply gave me the hypo. I had vowed in my Inaugural Address to hold the forts still in our possession, and people had cheered those remarks. To abandon the fort now would be utterly ruinous. The loyal people of the North—the people who had elected me—would not fully understand the necessity under which it was to be done. It would discourage the friends of the Union, embolden its adversaries, and go far to insure European recognition of the so-called Confederacy. In short, it would be our national destruction consummated. *This*, I told myself, *you cannot allow.*

But the conflicting opinions from my Cabinet and leading men of the military left me nervous and perplexed. We met repeatedly in the executive office, gathered around a big oak table. There was Seward, smoking a Havana cigar and acting serenely confident, as though there were no crisis. There were the other Cabinet secretaries—the acerbic Blair, the intellectual Chase, the quiet Cameron, and the sour-looking Welles, whose long-haired wig and snow-white beard earned him the nickname of Neptune. There was huge General Scott, seventy-five years old, suffering from vertigo and dropsy, his head and hands trembling. To his left and right were assorted other army and naval officers in their glittering uniforms. Finally there was the harried President, running his hand through his hair in great anxiety as the secretaries and military men argued, cursed, and slapped the table.

Seward maintained that the best policy was to evacuate Sumter and hold Fort Pickens, in Pensacola Bay, as a symbol of national authority. That remote area, he pointed out, was far less volatile than Charleston Harbor; therefore a show of Federal strength at the Florida fort could be done without risking a war. I agreed that Fort Pickens ought to be reinforced and held, before starvation was upon the Sumter garrison. Holding Pickens, I said, would be a clear indication of policy and would better enable the country to accept the evacuation of Sumter, if it came to that, as a *military necessity*. Accordingly I ordered a troopship anchored near Pickens to reinforce it without delay.

Which brought us back to Sumter. I asked the group: What about throwing reinforcements in there as well?

"No, no," Seward piped up, "absolutely not. The army thinks this would be disastrous."

The army men did indeed think that. But the navy men considered the danger slight. In the welter of conflicting advice, I tried another approach. What if we sent only a provisioning flotilla? Welles voiced his support for the idea, saying it could be done with a fleet of tugs. Then he changed his mind and favored surrender. Seward insisted emphatically that the garrison be withdrawn. The situation in Charleston, he argued, was fraught with danger, what with batteries dotting the harbor and troops, politicians, and reporters crowding the city. An aggressive move there would almost certainly destroy Unionism in South Carolina and trigger a civil war.

"Surrender Sumter," he said, "and we gain time so that Unionists in all the seceded states can consolidate strength, crush the rebellion, and return their states to the Union."

Blair hotly disagreed with Seward. He turned to me with his narrow eyes on fire. "You've got to be like Andrew Jackson," he said, pounding the table. "Issue a proclamation like he did in the nullification crisis. Threaten to send an army into South Carolina to crush the Goddamned traitors."

I studied Seward, troubled by his cocksure manner—he behaved as if *he* was President and *I* was his adviser. Frankly, I said, I liked the idea of provisioning Sumter without reinforcements. But I wanted the opinion of the Cabinet about that. I asked them: "Assuming it to be possible to provision Fort Sumter now, under the circumstances, is it wise to attempt it?" Only Blair and Chase responded affirmatively. The other secretaries sided with Seward and voted to evacuate.

I hated to give the fort up. Blair was probably right: Jackson would never have done that. So that the facts alone might guide me, I sat down at my desk and wrote out the arguments for withdrawal. To hold the fort would require a large force—Scott estimated at least twenty-five thousand men—and would likely start a bloody conflict. The fort had little military value. If I gave it up, it might remove a source of irritation to the southern people and deprive the secession movement of its most powerful stimulant. It would indicate both an independent and a conservative position on the part of the new Administration, and would gratify and encourage those who were friendly to the Union, yet were reluctant to see extreme measures pursued. And it would confound and embarrass the enemies of the Union both at the North and South who relied on the cry of "coercion" as a means of keeping up the excitement against the Republican party. Finally, the moral advantage to the secessionists of a successful attack would be very great.

Then I summarized the arguments against withdrawal. The fort had become such a powerful symbol that evacuation might demoralize the Republican party and show that this Administration had a want of pluck. Worse, the secessionists might construe evacuation as a victory on their part.

I stared at the arguments. Those for evacuation were persuasive but so were those against it. It was a terrible dilemma. The fate of the Union, of popular government itself, could well hang in the balance. What the hell was I to do? It didn't help that Judge Douglas introduced a resolution in the Senate demanding the withdrawal of the garrison. At the same time, three commissioners from Jefferson Davis arrived in Washington and tried to see me in order to open negotiations—in other words, to demand that I give up the forts or else. I refused to see them under any circumstances; to do so would be tantamount to recognizing the Confederacy. I told Seward not to see them either.

To make matters worse, I was beset daily by swarms of office-seekers insisting on their share of loaves and fishes. The Sumter crisis was bad enough by itself; the demands of the accursed patronage and the unending diplomatic correspondence made the pressure all but unbearable. I felt like a man letting lodgings at one end of his house, while the other end was burning down. I tell you, all the troubles and anxieties of my life couldn't equal those that plagued me during the Sumter nightmare. I didn't think it was possible to survive them.

I ended up postponing a decision. It was now mid-March—four weeks before Sumter ran out of provisions. That was enough time to dispatch a few men to South Carolina on fact-finding missions. I asked General Scott to send down a reliable officer to find out all he could about Anderson and his garrison. Scott chose Gustavus V. Fox, Assistant Navy Secretary and Blair's brother-in-law, who had already expressed his preference for holding Sumter. At the same time, I sent Stephen A. Hurlbut, an old Illinois friend who was born and educated in South Carolina, to talk with rebel leaders in Charleston and report back to me toward the end of March. I asked Hill Lamon to go with him. Once I had their reports, I would decide what to do.

A great many Republicans, meanwhile, accused me of indecisiveness. That attitude was summed up by a *New York Times* headline: WANTED, A POLICY. I'll never forget what the *Times* story said: "It is idle to conceal the fact that the Administration thus far has not met public expectation. It has done nothing toward carrying the country through the tremendous crisis which is so rapidly and so steadily settling down upon us. It allows everything to *drift*. This might be well enough, if the southern states were pursuing the same policy. But while we are idle, they are active. While we leave everything at loose ends, they make everything tight and snug for *the coming storm*. The President must adopt some clear and distinct policy in regard to secession, or the Union will not only be severed, but the country will be disgraced. We are in danger of losing everything—even honor." Every mailbag brought angry letters, impassioned letters, that struck the same tone. In the Senate, Trumbull offered a resolution that it was the *duty* of the President to hold and protect Federal property with all his power.

By the end of March, I had the results of the fact-finding missions before me. Fox reported that Major Anderson could hold out until April fifteenth, but that the Sumter commander was against a relief expedition on the grounds that it would fail. Fox, however, had inspected the fort and the harbor and thought we could successfully put in reinforcements by sea.

I turned to Hurlbut's report of what he'd found in South Carolina. Contrary to what Seward claimed, South Carolinians had "no attachment to the Union," Hurlbut said. In fact, a sizable minority *wanted* a clash with Washington to unite the Confederacy. Unionism appeared to be equally dead everywhere else in the South, which convinced Hurlbut that the seceded states were "irrevocably gone." Nothing would pacify the rebels, he believed, save "unqualified recognition of absolute independence." As for Fort Sumter, it did not matter whether we sent reinforcements, or merely tried to supply it; the rebels would open fire on any Federal ships that appeared there, even a strictly provisioning flotilla. Hurlbut added that we could not avoid conflict merely by abandoning Sumter. If we did that, the rebels would next demand that we surrender Fort Pickens and the Keys of the Gulf. "Nor do I believe that any policy which may be adopted by the government will prevent the possibility of armed collision."

This report was like a slap across the face. It told me that all I had believed and said about the strength of southern Unionism was wrong. The people of the Deep South did *not* love the Union and its system of government as I did. They really *were* traitors. Regardless of what I did about Sumter, a violent showdown with Jefferson Davis and his insurrectionaries could not be avoided. If I evacuated the fort, it would only postpone the conflict. Somewhere, if I hoped to salvage anything of our people's government, our party, and our honor, I had to make a stand.

The next day brought another shock—a memorandum from General Scott urging me to surrender both Sumter and Pickens so as to appease the loyal slave states. I was bitterly disillusioned. Until now, I'd had the greatest confidence in the old general as a military man. But this memorandum was *political* advice—from a native Virginian at that—which strayed far beyond military considerations. After dinner with the Cabinet, I called the secretaries into a separate room. Much agitated, I told them what Scott had advised. Nobody said anything for a moment. Then Blair spoke up, damning Scott for his "political generalship." Welles, too, was upset and glared at Seward, as if to accuse him of engineering Scott's memo. But Seward was noncommittal. What was that bird up to? It appeared to me, too, that something nefarious might be going on.

I instructed the Cabinet to give me another opinion about Sumter tomorrow morning. But when I was alone, I realized that neither Scott nor the Cabinet could make my decision for me. I had to do it myself. I returned to my office and closed the door. By dawn, March twenty-ninth, I'd made up my mind. I summoned the Cabinet and informed them that I would send bread to Major

Anderson, a provisioning fleet, and leave it up to Jefferson Davis whether to start a war or not. Call this a calculated risk, if you like. I couldn't see any other way. That same day I ordered the War and Navy Departments to begin outfitting a relief expedition for Fort Sumter. A few days later, learning that my order to reinforce Pickens had not been executed, I directed that a similar expedition be sent to the Florida fort.

Only Seward and Caleb Smith, head of the Interior Department, opposed my decision on Sumter; the rest of the Cabinet stood with me. On April first, Seward sent me a memorandum of thoughts for my consideration, which tipped his hand. I read it in awe. This was April Fools' Day; was he playing me for the fool? He accused me of lacking a policy either domestic or foreign and proceeded to lay one out. Sumter, he said, must be evacuated. Pickens, however, should be held and a blockade thrown around the Confederacy. At the same time—and my eyebrows went up at this—the government must arouse "a vigorous continental spirit of independence on this conti- nent against European intervention." With the foreign powers mak- ing designs on Mexico, the United States should demand an immedi- ate "explanation." If that explanation was not satisfactory, the country should declare war on England, France, and Spain. What- ever policy was adopted, Seward said, all debate must cease and the policy must be pursued energetically by the President, or by "some member of his Cabinet." Meaning, of course, William H. Seward.

Of all the gall! This conceited little buzzard was offering to take over the Administration. Don't get me wrong: I liked Seward then as I do now; I enjoyed swapping jokes with him, thought him highly intelligent and competent, and wanted to keep him in the Cabinet despite his Machiavellian bent. But it was time to put him in his place. I started to write a blunt reply to his memo, then thought bet- ter of it and summoned him for a private conversation.

"You say we have no policy," I told him. "That is not so. I intend to do what I promised in my Inaugural: to hold, occupy, and possess Forts Sumter and Pickens. You read and you approved of that address, as I recall. Who must frame Administrative policy? Who must carry it out? *I* must do it. What's more, I have no inten- tion of stifling debate. I wish and am entitled to have the advice of the Cabinet."

Seward avoided my stare. "Executive force and vigor are rare qualities," he said sheepishly. "I'm sorry, sir, if my memorandum offended you."

Maybe so, but he wasn't through trying to manipulate me. A few days later, he brought a Virginia Unionist named John B. Baldwin over to talk with me about the Virginia secession convention and Fort Sumter. I told Baldwin that I was anxious for the secession convention to adjourn. But Baldwin insisted that I had to surrender Sumter first. True, I had once offered to give up the fort if the Virginia secession convention would disband. But I made no such offer now because so many Virginia Unionists had come to pledge their loyalty in the past few weeks that I truly believed Virginia would reject secession.

"If you don't evacuate," Baldwin warned, "if a shot is fired, as sure as there is a God in Heaven the thing is gone. Virginia will be out of the Union in forty-eight hours."

"Sir," I retorted, "that is impossible."

On that same day, April fourth, I directed that Gustavus Fox command the Sumter expedition, which was to sail in four or five days. It was to consist of a gunboat, three warships, and a steamer carrying two hundred soldiers and a year's worth of provisions. That same April fourth, I sent word to Major Anderson that a relief flotilla was on its way. Two days later, I dispatched a State Department clerk to South Carolina, with a message informing Governor Pickens that a supply fleet was coming down to provision Sumter. The Union flotilla, the message said, would not open fire, or attempt to throw in troops, unless the rebels resisted the ships or bombarded the fort.

On April ninth, Fox's little fleet set sail for Charleston—minus its flagship, the steamer *Powhatan*, heavily armed with three 8-inch smoothbores and six 32-pounders. By a mix-up of orders, it had gone off with the Pickens expedition instead. Secretary Welles flew into a tirade. He accused Seward of switching the warship in a deliberate attempt to sabotage the Sumter relief effort. But it turned out to be my fault: in all the confusion and tension of the past week, I had signed orders that gave the warship to both flotillas.

On the day Fox sailed, I stood at a rain-spattered White House window, staring at stormy skies. For two days it had rained in torrents, and muddy water ran a foot deep in the streets. *Well, Lincoln, I told myself, this is it. The decision is made. You've taken a stand as you said you would do in your Inaugural. The rebels can have no conflict without being themselves the aggressors. If the rebel batteries open fire, the momentous issue of war is indeed in their hands.*

61. DAVIS

The Lincoln Administration deliberately lied to us, bating us with false promises and pacific pledges all the while it was planning for war. Never in history has a government behaved with such malicious deceit and bad faith. *Washington* was the aggressor, not us, not us! Do you want to hear the truth about the Sumter crisis? I will tell you the truth.

By mid-March, all three of my commissioners had arrived in Washington. These discreet, able, and distinguished Confederates promptly requested an appointment with Lincoln to open negotiations so as to avoid war. Not getting an official response, the commissioners asked Justices Campbell and Nelson of the United States Supreme Court to talk informally with Secretary of State Seward as the commissioners' intermediaries. On March fifteenth, the two men had a long discussion with Seward, which Campbell described to me by letter. Seward said that it was impossible for him or Lincoln to receive the commissioners or even to see them informally, on the grounds that the state of public sentiment in the North would not sustain any recognition of the Confederacy. "The evacuation of Sumter," said Seward, "is as much as the Administration can bear." He assured Judge Campbell that Lincoln would withdraw the garrison immediately. Seward even authorized Judge Campbell to tell me that I would learn by telegraph, within a few days of March fifteenth, "that the order for the evacuation of Sumter had been made." Campbell told Seward that he wanted that pledge put in writing, and Seward obliged him. Campbell was absolutely certain that Seward spoke for Lincoln, and I thought so, too. *He was Lincoln's Secretary of State.* How in God's name could he make such a promise without official approval from above? Believe me, *he had that approval.*

Feeling thus assured, I followed a policy of hopeful waiting. Five days passed, however, and Sumter had not been evacuated. Campbell and Nelson then saw Seward again. "The Secretary was buoyant and sanguine," Campbell reported to me; "he spoke of his ability to carry through his policy with confidence. He accounted for the delay as accidental, and not involving the integrity of his assurances that the evacuation would take place. I have every reason to suppose that the President is advised of them."

At the very moment when Seward was repeating to the Confederate Government, through Judge Campbell, his positive assurance that "the evacuation *would* take place," Mr. Gustavus Fox was on his way to Charleston to obtain information and devise measures by which this promise might be broken. He secured from Governor Pickens permission to visit Fort Sumter in exchange for Fox's pledge that it was for peaceful purposes. As we would soon discover, Fox employed the opportunity afforded by his visit to mature the details of a plan for reinforcing and furnishing supplies to the garrison. He then reported to Washington, his plan was approved by Lincoln, and he was ordered to make arrangements for putting it into execution.

A few days after Fox's visit, another confidential agent from Lincoln arrived in Charleston. This was Mr. Lamon. He informed Governor Pickens that he was there to arrange the withdrawal of the Sumter garrison. After he returned from the fort, he asked the governor if a war vessel would be permitted to remove the troops. Pickens told him firmly that "no war vessel could be allowed to enter the harbor on any terms." Lamon said that Anderson himself preferred "an ordinary steamer," and Pickens gave his permission that the garrison "might be thus removed." Lamon said he hoped to return "in a very few days for that purpose."

Did we not, at this juncture, have every reason to expect evacuation? But April came and the fort remained in Union hands. Again Judge Campbell called on Seward. This time Seward informed him in writing: "The government will not undertake to supply Fort Sumter without giving notice to Governor Pickens." Campbell wrote me: "I know that this came from the President." I was stunned. This was a very material variation from the positive pledge previously given, and reiterated, to the two judges, to Governor Pickens (by Mr. Lamon), and to myself. In my Montgomery office, I asked myself: Have we been lied to? betrayed? Judge Campbell had warned me about Lincoln: "The President is light, inconstant, and variable. His ear is open to every one—and his resolutions are easily bent. His Inaugural is a great stumbling block, for notwithstanding the characteristics I have mentioned, he is conscientious, and tenacious of his word, & easily affected when he supposes *that* will be called into question. His reluctance to abandon the forts is undisguised. I do not doubt that Sumter will be evacuated shortly, without any effort to *supply* it, but in respect to Fort Pickens I do not think there is any settled plan." But he added: "I make these assurances on *my own responsibility*. I have no right to mention any name or to pledge any person."

What was I to make of Judge Campbell's observation? To me, Lincoln was inscrutable, a loose cannon capable of anything—of suddenly surrendering the fort, or just as suddenly committing a rash act. My suspicions leaped to the latter possibility when we received reports from Washington that Union officers were boasting that Sumter would be reinforced and Charleston annihilated! This seemed more than just idle talk. But when Judge Campbell asked Seward if his assurances would be kept, Seward replied in writing: "*Faith as to Sumter fully kept. Wait and see.*"

Such skulduggery! He was lying to us to buy time for hostile preparations. On the very next day, April eighth, Governor Pickens and General Beauregard both received the following message from an official of Lincoln's State Department. They relayed the message to me.

> *I am directed by the President of the United States to notify you to expect an attempt will be made to supply Fort Sumter with provisions only; and that, if such an attempt be not resisted, no effort to throw in men, arms, or ammunition will be made, without further notice, or in case of an attack upon the fort.*

Thus disappeared the last vestige of the plighted faith and pacific pledges of the Federal Government. We of the South had tried honorably to avoid war, had attempted to negotiate, had offered Lincoln an olive branch. What did we get in return? Nothing but lies and perfidy! During all this period of reiterated assurances that the Sumter garrison would be withdrawn, the government of the United States was assiduously engaged in devising means for furnishing supplies and reinforcements to the garrison, with the view of retaining possession of the fort!

I summoned my Cabinet and told them that negotiation was now at an end, that it was time to bombard the fort. Yes, I said, we would be firing the first shot, but that was not our fault. It was *Lincoln* who intended war. He and that lying Seward had drawn the sword, and we were responding to them. *We were defending our honor*.

Toombs, my Secretary of State, disagreed. "Sir," he said to me, "firing on the fort is suicide. It's unnecessary, it puts us in the wrong, it's fatal."

"Sir," I said, "*you* are *wrong*."

On April tenth, I ordered General Beauregard to demand the evacuation of Fort Sumter and, if that was refused, to reduce it with his guns. Beauregard replied: "The demand will be made tomorrow at twelve o'clock." I waited by the telegraph in the war office with my blood up. At last Beauregard's ultimatum and Major Anderson's reply came ticking in. Anderson refused to surrender, but then seemed to hedge: "I will await the first shot, and if you do not batter us to pieces we will be starved out in a few days."

Aha! I thought. Did this not suggest a way to win the fort short of war? If Anderson ran out of food, he would be forced to surrender without our firing a single shell. On my instructions, Secretary of War Walker wired Beauregard: "We do not desire needlessly to bombard Fort Sumter, if Major Anderson will state the time at which, as indicated by him, he will evacuate. You are thus to avoid the effusion of blood. If this or its equivalent be refused, reduce the fort as your judgment decides to be most practicable."

Then all we could do was wait. The hours dragged by. Night came on. In a distracted moment, I thought about the Chesnuts. They had gone to Charleston after the Confederate Congress had adjourned, and James had joined Beauregard's staff as a colonel. Varina missed Mary Chesnut, and so, frankly, did I. My attention turned back to the telegraph, which was ticking off the latest news from Charleston. Colonel Chesnut and Captain Stephen D. Lee, also of Beauregard's staff, had rowed out to Fort Sumter and delivered our last message to Major Anderson. They rowed back to Charleston with his reply: "I will evacuate Fort Sumter by noon on the 15th instant, should I not receive, prior to that time, controlling instructions from my Government, or additional supplies."

This was no good! We knew that the "controlling instructions" had already been issued by Lincoln, and that the "additional supplies" were momentarily expected. That left us no choice. Beauregard had to reduce the fort. I sent him the order forthwith.

62. MARY CHESNUT

The excitement was perfectly unbearable! Ever since we'd arrived in Charleston, the focus of attention was on Fort Sumter. Would the Yankees try to reinforce it? Would they throw in an army? There it stood out in the harbor, unfinished, an inchoate pile of rock with the stars and stripes flying over it, and I told myself, *on that crude structure hangs peace or war*. When we heard that a Federal fleet was on the way, all was stir and confusion at our hotel. My heart beat painfully. Mr. Chesnut went off with Louis Wigfall of Texas, the "stormy petrel" with the scraggly black beard and ferocious eyes. He had also joined Beauregard's staff and was in his glory: he wore a rough-looking uniform, a bandanna about his thick neck, and huge brass spurs. Mrs. Wigfall, the daughter of a wealthy Rhode Island family, retired with me to my room, where she silently wept and we disconsolately discoursed on the horrors of civil war. Then we added what we had a right to fear, the Negroes rising up in the rear while the Yankees attacked in front.

We heard shouts and cannon fire, and I dashed off to find out what was happening. Governor Pickens, they said, had ordered cannon to be fired as a signal to the Seventh Regiment. Soldiers marched and drilled in the streets, and ammunition wagons clattered by.

James returned to our rooms, donned some sort of uniform with sash and sword, and left to demand the surrender of Fort Sumter. There was an undercurrent of intense excitement throughout the city. *Patience, oh my soul*, I told myself, *if Anderson will not surrender tonight, the bombardment begins. Have mercy upon us, Oh Lord!* Mrs. Wigfall could not stand the excitement and called for me constantly. Later, James returned and told me he'd had an "interesting interview" with Major Anderson. An *interesting* interview? How could he use such a mild adjective at a time like this! In his dry, laconic way, James said they had asked President Davis by telegram what answer James was to give Major Anderson.

At eleven that night, April eleventh, James, Stephen Lee, and two other men rowed out to Fort Sumter again, offering Major Anderson the final terms. If he did not surrender the fort, at four A.M.—the orders were—the bombardment was to commence. All the livelong night I tossed and turned in my bed, unable to sleep. I heard the chimes on St. Michael's—counted four and began to hope. Alas! at four thirty I heard the heavy boom of cannon. I sprang out of bed and on my knees, prostrate, I prayed as I'd never prayed before. There was a sound of stirring all over the house—pattering of feet in the corridor—all seemed hurrying one way. I put on my double gown and a shawl and went, too. The way was to the housetop.

We could see the shells bursting like lightning flashes. The concussions of the guns shattered the night. I knew my husband was rowing about in a boat somewhere in that darkened bay. Shells were darting overhead with a shriek and exploding toward the fort. Oh God what if one hit James! Who could tell what each volley accomplished of death and destruction? On the housetop the wind whipped about us and the women were wild. Prayers from them and imprecations from the men, and then a shell would light up the scene. We watched up there and let out a collective *ooh* and *ahh* every time the cannon fired and the delayed reports reached our ears, yet Fort Sumter did not fire a shot in return.

At that very moment, the Federal invasion fleet lay off the mouth of the harbor, prevented from entering by a gale. One warship did try to get in, but our guns wrecked her wheelhouse and drove her away. Proud Carolinians! I cried. You must *conquer* the enemy—he must *not* be permitted to land.

I was so hungry my stomach was in rebellion. I dressed and hurried down to dine with friends. All the talk was about war, war, war. James marched in—I was so happy he was safe that I burst into tears! He looked perfectly handsome in his uniform and red sash. He had no time to eat, though, and rushed off to get an order somewhere.

63. DAVIS

The concussions of our proud guns in Charleston Harbor resounded across the Confederacy. In Montgomery that day, rumors flew that Sumter and Pickens had both surrendered. People cheered, bands played, and the militia marched smartly through the streets.

Though called on to make a public statement, I declined to do so. In my office, I lay on a sofa, smoking a cigar. "Well," I said, "the long-gathering storm has burst upon us. All the fault lies in Washington, with Lincoln's treachery. We've been patient and forbearing here. Nothing was left for us but to forestall their schemes by a bold act. I regret we've come to blows. But as a people we're ready and resolved."

The next day, April thirteenth, came a triumphant wire from Beauregard regarding Fort Sumter. "Quarters all burnt down. White flag up—have sent a boat to receive Surrender." As it turned out, no blood was spilled by our guns save that of a mule. The forbearance of the Confederate Government, under the circumstances, is perhaps unexampled in history. The attempt to represent us as the aggressors in the conflict which ensued is as unfounded as the complaint made by the wolf against the lamb in the familiar fable. He who makes the assault is not necessarily he that strikes the first blow or fires the first gun. To have awaited further strengthening of the enemy position by land and naval forces, with a hostile purpose now declared, for the sake of having them "fire the first gun," would have been as unwise as it would be to hesitate to strike down the arm of the assailant, who levels a deadly weapon at one's breast, until he's actually fired. The disingenuous rant of northern demagogues about "firing on the flag" might seem to rouse the passions of insensate mobs in times of general excitement, but will be impotent in impartial history to relieve the Federal Government from the responsibility of the assault made by sending a hostile fleet against the harbor of Charleston, to cooperate with the menacing garrison of Fort Sumter. After the hostile descent of the fleet, the reduction of Fort Sumter was a measure of defense made absolutely and immediately necessary.

64. LINCOLN

I learned by the Friday morning papers that the rebel batteries were now bombarding Fort Sumter. Standing at a White House window, I thought to myself: *Well, I left the momentous issue of civil war in Davis's hands. Now I have his answer.*

All through Friday and Saturday we were cut off from direct communication with the embattled fort and had no idea what was happening down there beyond what was reported in the Washington papers. On Sunday, April fourteenth, the headlines screamed that Sumter had fallen, that the rebels had allowed Fox to evacuate the garrison. I called the Cabinet together and announced that the enemy, by firing the first shot, had forced on us the decision of immediate dissolution or blood. We all realized it would be a gigantic contest; how many troops would it require? Some of the secretaries thought fifty thousand; but Seward said it ought to be one hundred thousand. We settled on seventy-five thousand. We all agreed that we couldn't await the convening of Congress to devise a war policy—we had to move now to avoid disaster, and trust that Congress would sanction our war measures after the fact.

On April fifteenth, I issued a proclamation calling up seventy-five thousand militia from the states to suppress the rebellion, and I summoned Congress to convene in special session on Independence Day. Just two days later—two days!—the Virginia convention adopted a secession ordinance, which the voters would ratify in May. Virginia Unionists went over to the rebellion, they claimed, because they could not tolerate the specter of Federal troops marching across their soil to suppress the insurrection in the cotton states.

"Those traitors," I said bitterly in the privacy of my office. "How many times have I heard Virginia Unionists, right here in this room, proclaim their loyalty to the flag? I was sure on that basis that Virginia would remain loyal. But when I choose to defend the flag against traitors to the government, these *professed* Union men almost instantly embrace the rebellion and become traitors themselves. The *sons of bitches*. With Virginia on its way out, we may lose the entire upper South. Damn, damn, *damn*. Well, Virginia will be exceedingly sorry for this. I have no choice but to deal with the rebellion where I find it."

65 · DOUGLAS

The firing on Fort Sumter destroyed the hopes of northern Democrats that southern Unionism and the retention of the border South would bring back the errant states. We were enraged by an announcement made by the revolutionary government at Montgomery that the secession flag should be planted upon the walls of the Capitol in Washington, and a proclamation issued by so-called *President* Davis inviting the pirates of the world to prey upon the commerce of the United States. Had I been President, I would have hanged that Goddamn traitor—I would have hanged them *all* within forty-eight hours! Then came the rebels' swaggering boast that war and carnage should be transferred from the cotton fields of the South to the wheat fields and cornfields of the North. These astounding facts furnished conclusive evidence that it was the *fixed purpose* of the secessionists to vanquish the government of our fathers and obliterate the United States from the map of the world.

It became the imperative duty of every Union man, every friend of constitutional liberty, to rally to the support of our common country. The course of Clay and Webster, the two Whig leaders, toward the Democratic Administration of General Jackson in the days of nullification, presented a noble and worthy example of all true patriots. During that crisis, the two great leaders of the opposition sank the partisan in the patriot and rushed to the support of the government, and thus became its ablest and bravest defenders.

Vowing to emulate their example, I rushed to the White House and offered Lincoln my unwavering support. He looked tired and stooped, with huge dark circles under his eyes.

"Glad to see you, Douglas," he said.

"I heartily approve of your proclamation calling up 75,000 militia," I told him. "Except that I would make it 200,000. You don't know the dishonest purposes of those southern men as well as I do."

"You may be right," Lincoln said. "I see that Davis issued a counter proclamation summoning up 32,000 rebel soldiers. I'm going to issue a supplemental call for 42,000 three-year volunteers and increase the size of the regular army to right at 22,000. That'll put an army of 157,000 into the field. That ought to crush out the rebellion soon enough. Come, Douglas, look at this." He directed me to a map of the country hanging on the wall and pointed to strategic points that needed to be strengthened.

"Mr. President," I said. "Let me speak plainly. I remain unalterably opposed to your Administration on its purely political issues. Yet I'm prepared to sustain you in the exercise of all your constitutional functions to preserve the Union, maintain the government, and defend the capital. A firm policy and prompt action are necessary. The capital of our country is in danger, and must be defended at all hazards, and at any expense of men and money. I speak of the present and the future without reference to the past."

He shook my hand, hard. "We need more patriots like you, Douglas," he said as he walked me to the door.

"I deprecate war," I said in parting, "but if it must come, I'm with my country and for my country, under all circumstances and in every contingency."

I told the northern Democrats in Washington: "We must fight for our country and forget all differences. There can be only two parties now—the party of patriots and the party of traitors. We belong to the first."

I soon left for Illinois to address a special session of the legislature and to rally loyal Democrats to the flag. We owed it to ourselves, our children, and our God to protect that flag with our lives.

66. CHESNUT

On the day Sumter surrendered, I saw my husband carried by a mob to tell General Beauregard the news. Later, back at our hotel, Colonel Chesnut, who had taken it all quietly enough—if anything, more unruffled than usual in his serenity—told us how the surrender came about. Wigfall was with them on Morris Island when he saw the fire in the fort; he jumped into a little boat and, with his handkerchief as a white flag, rowed over to Fort Sumter. He went in through a porthole. When Colonel Chesnut arrived shortly after and was received at the regular entrance, Major Anderson told him he'd need to pick his way warily, for the passageway was all mined. As far as I could make out, the fort had surrendered to Wigfall. Our flag was now flying over the fallen bastion, which was smoking from the cannonade. Fire engines had been sent to put out the fire inside the walls.

In the afternoon, Mrs. Preston, Mrs. Joe Heyward, and I drove round the battery in an open carriage. What a scene! The very liveliest crowd I think I ever saw. Everybody talking at once. All eye glasses were still turned on the grim old fort.

Even the staid and severe-of-aspect Thomas Lanier Clingman of North Carolina was here. He'd resigned his seat in the U.S. Senate a couple of weeks earlier. He said that the U.S.A. would now swoop down on us, and that Virginia and North Carolina were arming to come to our rescue. We had burned our bridges, he said, and we were obliged to go on now. He called us a poor little hot-blooded, headlong, rash, and troublesome sister state. But was it not the Yankees who were headlong, rash, and troublesome?

67. DOUGLASS

"God be praised!" I cried when Fort Sumter fell and Lincoln called for troops. The first flash of rebel gunpowder pouring shot and shell upon the starving handful of men at Sumter instantly changed the nation's whole policy. Until then, the ever hopeful North was still dreaming of compromise. The Heavens were black, the thunder rattled, the air was heavy, and vivid lightning flashed all around; but our sages were telling us there would be no rain. But all at once, down came the storm of hail and fire.

Oh was *I* on fire. I was bursting with patriotism. I ran into the streets of Rochester shouting hosannas for the flag. I dashed off editorials in hot haste. During the previous few months there had been such retrograde tendencies: the cry of "down with abolition!" had rung across the North. Shrieking mobs had invaded abolitionist meetings. Black people had seemed more hated and despised than ever.

But now, thanks to the reckless impetuosity of the dealers in the bodies and souls of men, the attack upon Sumter had done much to arrest this retrograde and cowardly movement in the North, and had raised the question as to the wisdom of pampering treason.

I wrote in my newspaper: "On behalf of our enslaved and bleeding brothers and sisters, thank God! The slaveholders themselves have saved the abolition cause from ruin! The government is aroused, the dead North is alive, and its divided people united. Never was a change so sudden, so universal, and so portentous. The whole North, east and west, is in arms. Drums are beating, men are enlisting, companies forming, regiments marching, banners are flying. 'Southern brethren,' 'forbearance,' 'concession,' 'compromise,' 'peace,' and 'reconstruction,' have everywhere been exchanged for sterner watchwords. The cry now is for war, vigorous war, war to the bitter end, and war till the traitors are effectually put down."

68. GARRISON

Realist that I am, I flung aside my doctrines of non-resistance, no-government, and disunion, and threw my full support behind Mr.

Lincoln's efforts to crush the South and save the Union. Yes, yes, I had once damned the Union as an agreement with Hell and a covenant with Death. But I did not know that Hell and Death would secede and make war upon the government! All my sympathies and wishes were with the government and Mr. Lincoln, because they were entirely in the right, and acting strictly in self-defense and for self-preservation. Yes, I said, war would be terrible, but if it ended in the speedy and total abolition of slavery, the fountain-source of all our national difficulties, it would bring with it inconceivable blessings.

I called on all abolitionists to rally behind Mr. Lincoln. "Now that civil war has begun," I told them, "and a whirlwind of violence and excitement is to sweep through the country, every day increasing in intensity until its bloodiest culmination, it is for the abolitionist to 'stand still and see the salvation of God.' It is no time for minute criticism of Lincoln, Republicanism, or even the other parties, now that they are fusing for a death-grapple with the southern slave oligarchy."

69. STOWE

Mr. Lincoln's proclamation threw all Andover into intense excitement. The town's young men organized the Andover Light Infantry and made ready to leave for the warfront as part of a Massachusetts regiment. At the same time, the theology students formed the Havelock Grays, the Phillips Academy boys organized the Phillips Guard, and both units drilled every day. The sounds of their fife and drum, and the steady tramp of their march, were a strange sound in these peaceful shades! On the eve of my fiftieth birthday, the seminary presented the theology company with a flag, and I composed a banner-hymn for the flag-raising over old Phillips Hall. Then the drums of the Andover Light Infantry were heard approaching. The company was coming to salute the flag! The officers of the two student companies escorted the Light Infantry to the esplanade in front of the buildings, where various complimentary military evolutions were executed with great precision, and interspersed with so much cheering.

Then, gathering at the far end of the Common, the Light

Infantry marched in review before the trustees, ministers, professors, and their families. They were singing a new song we had never heard before!

> *John Brown's body lies a-mouldering in the grave,*
> *John Brown's body lies a-mouldering in the grave,*
> *John Brown's body lies a-mouldering in the grave,*
>   *As we go marching on.*
> *Glory, glory, hallelujah!*
> *Glory, glory, hallelujah!*
> *Glory, glory, hallelujah!*
>   *His soul is marching on.*

Afterward, everybody came to the Cabin for coffee and a collation. It was a pretty and animated sight to see the American flag standing in a stack of muskets in the green oval in front of the Stowe Cabin.

"Let us look at this in the face," I said in the *Independent*. "Our sons and brothers whom we are sending off take their lives in their hands, and may never return; but this is a cause to die for—and, thanks be to God, our young men embrace it as a bridge, and are ready to die. When we see the whole-hearted, unselfish devotion of our northern people, we thank God that we have a country. We thank God for mothers that cheer on their sons, for young wives that have said 'go' to their husbands, for widows who have given their only sons. It is our solemn belief that, since the Proclamation of the President, there has been in this country more earnest, unselfish heroism, more high-minded self-devotion, in one week than in years of ordinary life."

Yet I trembled for all of us, for in the gathering fury I saw God's terrible judgment—that this nation, the North as well as the South, must now atone in blood for their complicity in the sin of slavery. The ill-gotten wealth, which had arisen from striking hands with oppression and robbery, would now be paid back in the taxes of war. The blood of the poor slave, that had cried so many years from the ground in vain, would now be answered by the blood of the sons from the best hearthstones through all the free states. The slave mothers whose tears nobody regarded would soon have with them a great company of weepers, North and South.

70. FITZHUGH

I had once opposed secession and civil war, thinking as I did that the North would come to see the wisdom of the master-slave relationship and the serenity of our agrarian way of life based on it, and copy our system. But there was no hope of that with the ascendancy of the Black Republicans and their acolyte, Lincoln, and at Port Royal I urged the South to gather courage from despair and quit the Union. With our blood, we would resist the abolitionist armies and defend the great truth that the Negro was physically, morally, and intellectually a different and inferior being from the white man, and must ever remain so.

The clash of arms between South and North came about in part because the Cavaliers, Jacobites, and Huguenots who settled the South naturally hate, condemn, and despise the Puritans who settled the North. The former are master races, the descendants of Romans. The latter, especially the New England Yankees, are a slave race, the descendants of the Saxon serfs, and are the most cruel, ignorant, fanatical, and cold-blooded of all the types of man.

The southern bolt for independence was a reactionary counter thrust to the excesses of the spirit of the Reformation and the Enlightenment. It was a solemn protest against the doctrines of natural liberty, human equality, and the social contract as taught by Locke, Thomas Jefferson, and the other American sages of 'seventy-six. The Fathers of the Republic most unwisely rested the Republic on such powder-cask abstractions, and the Black Republican party based its entire existence upon such aberrations. To the biggest of those powder-keg abstractions—human equality—Horace Greeley and his Black Republican confreres applied a slow match at Chicago when they nominated Lincoln. This produced, on or about the fourth of March, 'sixty-one, the grandest explosion the world ever witnessed. When the smoke cleared, there stood the new southern nation, slave-based, proudly reactionary, and ruled by a legitimate master class, the crème de la crème of the white race.

The South had suffered from too many years of peace. When nations, communities, sects, or individuals never fight, they take to cheating and become thoroughly contemptible, selfish, and sensual— lose their intellectual and moral natures, assimilate themselves to the lowest order of the brute creation, and grow fat and lazy, like well-fed pigs. All history shows that overpacific individuals, sects, and nations become knavish, cowardly, mean, and contemptible, depraved in morals and in intellect, and, finally, the easy prey of more warlike, virtuous, and intelligent peoples.

War, therefore, would be good for us. It would purify and elevate our natures, draw us closer together, allay domestic strife, banish selfishness, and win for us the respect of foreign nations.

71. DAVIS

You want to know what caused the war? That's not difficult to explain. The *truth* lies in history, and requires a review of our relations with the northern states which were now united in warfare against us. The Federal Constitution, when it was ratified, represented a compact among *independent states*. This fact was placed *beyond any pretense of doubt* when amendments were added to the Constitution reserving to the states all their sovereign rights and powers not expressly delegated to the United States. Strange though it must appear to the impartial observer, these carefully worded clauses proved unavailing to prevent the rise and growth in the northern states of a *political school* which persistently claimed that the government thus formed was *not* a compact among states, but was in effect a *national* government, set up *above* and *over* the states. Long and angry controversies grew out of such claims. And the danger of disunion was enhanced by the fact that the northern population was increasing by immigration and other causes in a greater ratio than the population of the South. As the northern states gained preponderance in the national Congress, self-interest taught their people to advocate their right as a majority to govern the minority *without control*. They listened with churlish impatience to anyone from the minority section who suggested a constitutional impediment to the exercise of their will. So utterly were the principles of the Constitution corrupted in the northern mind that Lincoln, in his first Inaugural Address, asserted as an axiom that *in all cases the majority should govern*. This was the *lamentable* and *fundamental error* on which rested the policy that culminated in Lincoln's declaration of war against the Confederacy.

There existed for nearly half a century another subject of discord, involving interests of such transcendent magnitude as at all times to create the apprehension in the minds of many devoted lovers of the Union that its permanence was impossible. I speak of our institution of slavery. As soon as the so-called free states reached a number sufficient to give their representation a controlling voice in the Congress, a persistent and organized system of hostile measures against the rights of the owners of slaves in the southern states was inaugurated and gradually extended. A continuous series of measures was devised and prosecuted for the purpose of rendering property in slaves insecure. Fanatical organizations, supplied with money by voluntary subscriptions, were assiduously engaged in exciting among the slaves a spirit of discontent and revolt; means were furnished for their escape from their owners, and agents secretly employed to entice them to abscond; the constitutional provision for their rendition to their owners was first evaded, then openly denounced as a violation of conscience and religious duty; men were taught that it was a merit to elude, disobey, and violently oppose the execution of the laws enacted to secure the performance of the promise contained in the constitutional compact; owners of slaves were mobbed and even murdered in open day solely for applying to a magistrate for the arrest of a fugitive slave.

The dogmas of these voluntary organizations soon obtained control of the legislatures of many of the northern states. Emboldened by success, the theater of agitation and aggression against the southern states was transferred to Congress. Senators and representatives were sent to the common councils of the nation whose chief title to distinction consisted in the display of a spirit of ultra fanaticism, and whose business was not "to promote the general welfare or insure domestic tranquillity," but to awaken the bitterest hatred against the citizens of the southern states by violent denunciation of their institutions. The transaction of public affairs was impeded by repeated efforts to usurp powers not delegated by the Constitution, for the purpose of impairing the security of property in slaves and reducing the slaveholding states to a condition of inferiority. Finally, a great northern party was organized for the purpose of obtaining the administration of the government, with the avowed object of using its power for the total exclusion of the slave states from all participation in the benefits of the public domain acquired by all the states in common, whether by conquest or purchase; of surrounding them entirely by states in which slavery should be prohibited; of thus rendering the property in slaves so insecure as to be comparatively worthless, and thereby annihilating property worth thousands of millions of dollars. This great northern party, thus organized, succeeded in electing to the office of the Presidency a man who openly proclaimed his hatred of slavery, who declared that the government could not endure "half slave and half free."

In the meantime, under the mild and genial climate of the southern states and the increasing care and attention for the well-being and comfort of the laboring class, dictated alike by interest and humanity, the African slaves had augmented in number from about six hundred thousand at the time the Constitution was adopted to upward of four million. In moral and social condition they had been elevated from brutal savages into docile, intelligent, and civilized agricultural laborers, and supplied not only with bodily comforts but with careful religious instruction. Under the supervision of a superior race their labor had been so directed as not only to allow a gradual and marked amelioration of their own condition, but to convert hundreds of thousands of square miles of the wilderness into cultivated lands covered with a prosperous people.

With interests of such overwhelming magnitude now imperiled, the people of the southern states were driven by the conduct of the North to the adoption of some course of action to avert the danger which openly menaced them. Faced with the most alarming crisis in their history, the people of the slaveholding states voiced their desires through specially called conventions, which passed ordinances resuming all their rights as sovereign and independent states and dissolved their connection with the northern states of the Old Union. They then proceeded to form a new compact and a new government among themselves.

In sum, we left the Union to free ourselves from the rule of the majority. Submitting to the Lincolnites, the Black Republicans and abolitionists who controlled the North, would put our slavery system at the mercy of an abolitionist majority. This we could not allow.

Our cause, I told the Confederate Congress, was *just* and *holy*. We protested solemnly to all mankind that we desired peace at any sacrifice save that of honor and independence. We sought no conquest, no aggrandizement, no concession of any kind from the states with which we were lately confederated. *All we asked was to be left alone.* But that was not to be, for our hated foe was determined to subjugate us by force of arms. We were just as determined to resist him to the direst extremity, so as to preserve our inherent right to freedom, independence, and self-government.

72. LINCOLN

The vexed slavery question lay at the center of the controversy. One eighth of the nation's whole population were colored slaves who were localized in the South. These slaves constituted a peculiar and powerful interest. All knew that this interest was, somehow, the cause of the war. To strengthen, perpetuate, and extend this interest was the object for which the insurgents would rend the Union, even by war; while the government claimed no right to do more than to restrict the territorial enlargement.

Both parties deprecated war, dreaded it; but one of them would *make* war rather than let the nation survive; and the other would *accept* war rather than let it perish.

More was at stake, however, than the survival of the nation. The contest presented to the whole family of man the question whether a *democracy*—a government of the *people*, by the same *people*—can maintain its territorial integrity against its domestic foes. It presented the question whether discontented individuals can always break up their government, and thus put an end to free government upon the earth. To save popular government, we of the Union had to meet force with force. We had to teach southern traitors the folly of being the beginners of war. We had to show the world that those who could fairly carry an election could also suppress a giant insurrection. We had to show the world that popular government *was* a workable system, that people *could* rule themselves, and that the course of history was *against* the return of class, caste, and despotism.

And the war came.

REFERENCES

The following references indicate the sources on which each monologue is based. In quoting from them, I corrected spelling and capi-
talization for purposes of consistency and in some instances altered
the wording for the sake of clarity. I also deleted repetitious remarks
from many of the Senate speeches. As I said in my prefatory
remarks, I sometimes did what Allan Nevins did in the *Emergence of
Lincoln*: I wove letters, speeches, interviews, and other recorded
utterances into scenes with a little simulated dialogue; these
instances are pointed out in my references. I do not think that using
facts to fashion such scenes violates the truth of history. We can
assume that my speakers told their families, friends, and colleagues
what they stressed in their recorded remarks.

ABBREVIATIONS
(Listed alphabetically by author or title)

HBS SDL	Acquisitions Stowe-Day Library, Hartford, Conn.
ACS	Authors Collection, Sophia Smith Collection, Smith College, Northampton, Mass.
BFS	Beecher Family Papers, Sophia Smith Collection, Smith College
BSR	Beecher-Stowe Papers, Schlesinger Library, Radcliffe College, Cambridge, Mass.
JB ISHL	John Brown Letters, Illinois State Historical Library, Springfield
JB KSHS	John Brown Papers, Kansas State Historical Society, Topeka
JBLC	John Brown Papers, Library of Congress, Washington, D.C.
JBJ OHS	John Brown Jr. Papers, Ohio Historical Society, Columbus
JCCC	John C. Calhoun, *Correspondence of John C. Calhoun* (ed. J. Franklin Jameson, vol. II of the *Annual Report of the American Historical Association, 1899*, Washington, D.C.: Government Printing Office, 1900)

JCCP   John C. Calhoun, *Papers* (ed. Robert L. Meriwether and others, 21 vols., Columbia: University of South Carolina Press, 1959–)

JCC U&L   John C. Calhoun, *Union and Liberty: The Political Philosophy of John C. Calhoun* (ed. Ross M. Lence, Indianapolis: The Liberty Fund, 1992)

JCCW   John C. Calhoun, *Works* (ed. Richard K. Crallé, 6 vols., New York: D. Appleton and Co., 1854–61)

MCCW   Mary Boykin Chesnut, *Mary Chesnut's Civil War* (ed. C. Vann Woodward, New Haven: Yale University Press, 1981)

PMC   Mary Boykin Chesnut, *The Private Mary Chesnut: The Unpublished Civil War Diaries* (ed. C. Vann Woodward and Elisabeth Muhlenfeld, New York: Oxford University Press, 1984)

HCP   Henry Clay, *Papers* (ed. James F. Hopkins and others, 11 vols., Lexington: University Press of Kentucky, 1959–92)

HCW   Henry Clay, *Works* (ed. Calvin Colton, 7 vols., New York: Henry Clay Publishing Co., 1897)

CG   *Congressional Globe*

JD LPS   Jefferson Davis, *Jefferson Davis, Constitutionalist: His Letters, Papers and Speeches* (ed. Dunbar Rowland, 10 vols., Jackson: Mississippi Department of Archives and History, 1923)

JD MP   Jefferson Davis, *The Messages and Papers of Jefferson Davis and the Confederacy* (comp. James D. Richardson, 2 vols., New York: Chelsea House, 1983)

JDP   Jefferson Davis, *Papers* (ed. Haskell M. Monroe, Jr., and others, 8 vols., Baton Rouge: Lousiana State University Press, 1971–)

JD PL   Jefferson Davis, *Private Letters, 1823–1889* (ed. Hudson Strode, New York: Harcourt, Brace, & World, 1966)

VD JD   Varina Davis, *Jefferson Davis, Ex-President of the Confederate States of America: A Memoir* (reprint of 1890 ed., 2 vols., Baltimore: The Nautical & Aviation Publishing Co., 1990)

JD R&F   Jefferson Davis, *The Rise and Fall of the Confederate Government* (2 vols., New York: D. Appleton and Co., 1881)

SADL   Stephen A. Douglas, *Letters* (ed. Robert W. Johannsen, Urbana: University of Illinois Press, 1961)

SADP   Stephen A. Douglas Papers, University of Chicago

FDP   Frederick Douglass, *Papers* (ed. John W. Blassingame, 5 vols., New Haven: Yale University Press, 1979–)

HBS L&L   Annie Fields (ed.), *Life and Letters of Harriet Beecher Stowe* (Boston: Houghton, Mifflin, 1898)

GFS   George Fitzhugh, *Sociology for the South, or the Failure of Free Society* (reprint of 1854 ed., New York: Burt Franklin, Research and Source Work Series #102, 1964)

GFCA   George Fitzhugh, *Cannibals All! or Slaves Without Masters*
             (ed. C. Vann Woodward, Cambridge: Harvard University
             Press, 1960)

FD L&W   Philip S. Foner (ed.), *The Life and Writings of Frederick
             Douglass* (4 vols., New York: International Publishers,
             1950)

WLG Life   Wendell Phillips Garrison and Francis Jackson Garrison,
             William Lloyd Garrison, 1805–1879: The Story of His Life
             (reprint of 1885–89 ed., 4 vols., New York: Negro Universi-
             ties Press, 1969)

WLGP BPL   William Lloyd Garrison Papers, Boston Public Library

WLGL   William Lloyd Garrison, *Letters* (ed. Walter M. Merrill and
             Louis Ruchames, 6 vols., Cambridge: Harvard University
             Press, 1971–81)

GFP SC   Garrison Family Papers, Sophia Smith Collection, Smith Col-
             lege

HL   William H. Herndon and Jesse William Weik, *Herndon's
             Lincoln: The True Story of A Great Life* (Springfield, Ill.:
             The Herndon's Lincoln Publishing Co. [1889])

TJP   Thomas Jefferson, *Papers* (ed. Julian P. Boyd and others, 20
             vols., Princeton: Princeton University Press, 1950–1982)

TJWKS   Thomas Jefferson, *Works* (ed. Paul Leicester Ford, 12 vols.,
             New York and London: G. P. Putnam's Sons, 1904–1905).

TJW   Thomas Jefferson, *Writings* (ed. Paul Leicester Ford, 10
             vols., New York: G. P. Putnam's Sons, 1892–99)

ALCW   Abraham Lincoln, *Collected Works* (ed. Roy P. Basler and
             others, 9 vols., New Brunswick, N.J.: Rutgers University
             Press, 1953–55)

ALCWS   Abraham Lincoln, *Collected Works, Supplement,
             1832–1865* (ed. Roy P. Basler, Westport, Conn.: Greenwood
             Press, 1974)

ALC   Abraham Lincoln, *Conversations with Lincoln* (ed. Charles
             M. Segal, New York: G. P. Putnam's Sons, 1961)

RTLC   Robert Todd Lincoln Collection of the Papers of Abraham
             Lincoln, Library of Congress, Washington, D.C.

JBR   Louis Ruchames (ed.), *A John Brown Reader* (London:
             Abelard-Schuman, 1959)

JB L&L   Franklin B. Sanborn, *Life and Letters of John Brown*
             (Boston: Roberts Brothers, 1885)

FSH   Franklin B. Sanborn Folder, Houghton Library, Harvard
             University, Cambridge, Mass.

HBS Life   Charles Stowe, *The Life of Harriet Beecher Stowe* (Boston:
             Houghton, Mifflin, 1890)

HBSW   Harriet Beecher Stowe, *Writings* (16 vols., Boston:
             Houghton, Mifflin, 1896)

BSC   Boyd B. Stutler Collection of John Brown Papers,
             Charleston, West Virginia

LTP   Lyman Trumbull Papers, Library of Congress

1. **Prologue: Thomas Jefferson.** TJ's poor health: *TJWKS*, 12:164–65; *TJW*, 10: 163; Lester Cappon (ed.), *The Adams-Jefferson Letters* (Chapel Hill: University of North Carolina Press, 1987), 546–47; *TJ, Writings* (comp. Merrill D. Peterson, New York: Library of America, 1984), 1373, 1416. Description of Monticello: George Ticknor, *Life, Letters, and Journals of George Ticknor* (2 vols., Boston: James R. Osgood and Co., 1877), 2: 34–36; Adrienne Koch (ed.), *Jefferson* (Englewood Cliffs: Prentice-Hall, 1971), 95; Paul Wilstach, *Jefferson and Monticello* (New York: Doubleday, Doran & Co., 1939), 107; Alf J. Mapp, Jr., *Thomas Jefferson, Passionate Pilgrim: The Presidency, the Founding of the University, and the Private Battle* (Lanham, N.Y., 1991), 272; Jack McLauglin, *Jefferson and Monticello: The Biography of a Builder* (New York: Henry Holt and Co., 1988), 367. TJ's reaction to the Missouri crisis: *TJWKS*, 12:151, 156–59, 164–65, 179–80, 187–89, 191; *TJW*, 10:156n, 158, 163, 172, 177–78, 181; Cappon, *Adams-Jefferson Letters*, 561, 565. TJ's hatred of slavery: TJ, *Notes on the State of Virginia* (ed. William Peden, Chapel Hill: University of North Carolina Press, 1955), 201; John Chester Miller, *The Wolf By the Ears: Thomas Jefferson and Slavery* (New York: Free Press, 1977), 44–45, 278; *TJP*, 8:184, 258–9, 667–8, 10:18, 17:246. TJ's racial views and plan for gradual emancipation and colonization: TJ, *Notes on the State of Virginia*, 137–84; *TJP*, 2:472, 6:298; Dumas Malone, *Jefferson: The Virginian* (Boston: Little, Brown, 1948), 268. The fate of TJ's plan: *TJP*, 2:472–3, 9:199; Albert Matthews, "Notes on the Proposed Abolition of Slavery in Virginia in 1785," *Publications of the Colonial Society of Massachusetts* (Boston, 1904), 6: 370–380; TJ, *Writings* (Library of America), 44; Malone, 264. TJ's remarks to Démeunier: *TJP*, 10:63. Emancipation left to the young men of Virginia: *TJP*, 8:184, 356–57; Miller, 89–90. TJ's plan to free his own slaves, home to Virginia, daughter's dowry: *TJP*, 14: 492–93, 16: 154, 155n, 189–90; Miller, 102. Smith quotation: ibid., 124. TJ on unwise passions of current generation: *TJWKS*, 12:159, and *TJW*, 10:158. TJ on the ravages of old age, poem: Cappon, *Adams-Jefferson Letters*, 578–79. I also learned much from Peter Wallenstein's provocative "Thomas Jefferson and Antislavery: The Myth Goes on," *Virginia Magazine of History and Biography* (Apr. 1994), 193–228; from Merrill D. Peterson's *Thomas Jefferson and the New Nation* (New York: Oxford University Press, 1970); and from Noble E. Cunningham, Jr.'s *In Pursuit of Reason: The Life of Thomas Jefferson* (Baton Rouge: Louisiana State University Press, 1987).

2. **Henry Clay**. First and second Missouri compromises: *HCP*, 2:766, 776–77, 790, 3:79, 81–82; John Quincy Adams, *Memoirs* (12 vols., Philadelphia: Lippincott, 1874–77), 5:526; Glyndon G. Van Deusen, *The Life of Henry Clay* (Boston: Little, Brown, 1937), 134–47; Merrill D. Peterson, *The Great Triumverate: Webster, Clay, and Calhoun* (New York: Oxford University Press, 1987), 60–63, 381; Glover Moore, *The Missouri Controversy, 1819–1821* (Lexington: University of Kentucky Press, 1953), passim; Robert V. Remini, *Henry Clay: Statesman for the Union* (New York: W. W. Norton, 1991), 178–92. HC's hatred of slavery, Wythe influence: *HCW*, 5:337, 339; Bernard Mayo, *Henry Clay: Spokesman of the New West* (Boston: Houghton, Mifflin, 1937), 29. HC description: Van Deusen, 13, 25. Lexington: J. Winston Coleman, Jr., *The Court-Houses of Lexington* (Lexington, privately printed, 1937), 10–29; George W. Ranck, *History of Lexington, Kentucky* (Cincinnati: Robert Clarke & Co., 1872), 1–5, 25–31, 42–45, 114–17, 205–7; Mayo, 57. HC and gradual emancipation movement: *HCP*, 1:5–8, 9:244; Mayo, 64–69; Van Deusen, 21. Marriage, Ashland, slaves, wealth: *HCP*, 1:402, 526, 628; *HCW*, 4:587, 10:425; Mayo, 194–95, 206–7; Peterson, 372–80; Van Deusen, 137; Remini, 30; Clement Eaton, *Henry Clay and the Art of American Politics* (Boston: Little, Brown, 1957), 62–77. Anne's death: *HCP*, 8:808–9, 813; Remini, 481–82. HC as slaveowner, Black Lottie: *HCP*, 1:370, 2:391–92. HC on African slave trade and domestic slave trade: ibid., 8:85, 140–41. HC and American Colonization Society: *HCW*, 5:329–30; *HCP*, 2:263–64, 276, 384, 420–22, 6:83–94, 8:138–60, 390, 7:601; *Annual Reports of the American Colonization Society, 1st–93rd* (Washington, D.C., 1818–1910).

3. **Nat Turner**. Nat's monologue is based on Thomas R. Gray, *The Confessions of Nat Turner* (Baltimore: Lucas & Deaver, 1831); Southampton County, Virginia, Slave Trial Records, Minute Book of the Southampton County Court (1830–1835), 72–146; [William C. Parker], unsigned communiqué of Sept. 17, 1831, in *Richmond Whig*, Sept. 26, 1831; unsigned letter from Jerusalem, Oct. 3, 1831, in ibid., Nov. 7, 1831; unsigned letter from Southampton County, Nov. 1, 1831, in *Richmond Enquirer*, Nov. 8, 1831; ibid., Nov. 15, 1831; Henry Irving Tragle (ed.), *The Southampton Slave Revolt of 1831: A Compilation of Source Material* (Amherst: University of Massachusetts Press, 1971); William Sidney Drewry, *The Southamp-*

ton Insurrection (reprint of 1900 ed., Murfreesboro, N.C.: Johnson Publishing Co., 1968); F. Roy Johnson, *The Nat Turner Insurrection* (Murfreesboro, N.C.: Johnson Publishing Co., 1966). For a defense of the authenticity of Nat's confession to Gray, see Stephen B. Oates, *The Fires of Jubilee: Nat Turner's Fierce Rebellion* (New York: Harper & Row, 1975), 122–24. The last sentence of the monologue derives from *The Confessions of Nat Turner,* in which Thomas Gray wrote of Nat: "I looked on him and my blood curdled in my veins."

4. **William Lloyd Garrison.** Two valuable collections of WLG's editorials in the *Liberator* are Truman Nelson (ed.), *Documents of Upheaval: Selections from William Lloyd Garrison's The Liberator, 1831–1865* (New York: Hill and Wang, 1966), and William E. Cain, *William Lloyd Garrison and the Fight Against Slavery: Selections from the Liberator* (Boston: Bedford Books of St. Martin's Press, 1995). WLG's poem and caution to slaves: *Liberator,* Jan. 1, 1831, Sept. 1, 1831. Southern press denunciations: see Stephen B. Oates, *The Fires of Jubilee* (New York: Harper & Row, 1975), 134–35; Nelson, 37; Russell B. Nye, *William Lloyd Garrison and the Humanitarian Reformers* (Boston: Little, Brown, 1955), 52–53; Ralph Korngold, *Two Friends of Man* (Boston: Little, Brown, 1950), 55. WLG's response to South, Floyd's demands, police investigation: *Liberator,* Sept. 3 and 24, 1831, Oct. 29, 1831; *WLG Life,* 1:220–21; Korngold, 55; John L. Thomas, *The Liberator: William Lloyd Garrison* (Boston: Little, Brown, 1963), 138; Nye 55. WLG's letter to *Daily National Intelligencer: Liberator,* Oct. 15, 1831; *WLGL,* 1:130–35. Emerson to WLG: quoted in Korngold, 48. WLG background: *WLGL,* 1:3–72; *WLG Life,* 1:21–100; Walter M. Merrill, *Against Wind and Tide: A Biography of William Lloyd Garrison* (Cambridge: Harvard University Press, 1963), 2–83; Thomas, 21–67, 255; Nye, 3–13. WLG and Benjamin Lundy, Baltimore: Nelson, x–xi, 100; *WLGL,* 1:64–65, 75–92; *WLG Life,* 1:88–164; Thomas, 75–76, 92, 97–101, 104–7; Merrill, 26–31; Nye, 23–27. WLG in jail: *WLGL,* 1: 92–106; WLG to Rev. George Shepard, Sept. 13, 1830, GFP SC; *WLG Life,* 1:165–218; Merrill, 35–36. WLG to May: *WLGL,* 1:114–15, 285–86; Korngold, 51–52. WLG v. HC and American Colonization Society: WLG, *Thoughts on African Colonization* (Boston, 1832); *Liberator,* May 28, 1831, Jan. 14, 1832, May 4, 1833, Nov. 9, 1833; *WLGL,* 1:173, 197–98, 253, 447, 453n; Nelson, 58–63, 76; Thomas, 147–54; Merrill, 60–61; Nye 68.

WLG on immediate emancipation: quoted in ibid., 96. WLG and American Anti-Slavery Society, WLG proud of abolitionist success: *WLGL*, 2:2, 199; Nye, 72; *WLG Life*, 1:458–62. WLG on gag rules: WLG to "Esteemed Friend," Mar. 3, 1849, WLGP BPL. WLG and anti-abolitionists: Thomas, 190; *Liberator*, Dec. 12, 1837. WLG, Helen Benson, marriage: *WLGL*, 1:279–80, 291–92, 303–4, 308, 313, 316, 322, 327–28, 330, 339, 358; *WLG Life*, 1:420–28; Merrill, 84–95 (description of Helen p. 84). WLG and Boston mob: *WLGL*, 1:433; *Liberator*, Nov. 17, 1835; also described in *WLG Life*, 1:434–522; Merrill, 101–7; Thomas, 201–4; Korngold, 99–104; Nye, 86–87. WLG v. clergymen, come-outer stance: *WLGL*, 2:178, 281; Nelson, 140; Merrill, 132–33; Thomas, 227–32. Woman question, split in movement: *Liberator*, July 14, 1832, Dec. 15, 1837, Jan. 12, 1838, Sept. 28, 1838, Feb. 28, 1840, May 22, 1840; *WLGL*, 2:199, 273, 298–99, 321–22, 566–67, 608, 611; WLG to Miss Phoebe Jackson, Mar. 3, 1839, WLGP BPL; also described in the biographies cited above. WLG on Lovejoy murder: *Liberator*, Dec. 8, 1837.

5. **John C. Calhoun.** South against colonization: *JCCP*, 8:476, 482–83. Slave unrest, tariff, nullification: *JCCP*, 7:210, 220, 226–27, 10:xlii, 300–301, 405, 415, 442–539, 532, 626, 11:258, 613–49, 12:106, 136; *JCCW*, 6:1–58, 124–43; *JCCC*, 403; Gerald M. Capers, *John C. Calhoun, Opportunist: A Reappraisal* (paperback reprint of 1960 ed., Chicago: Quadrangle, 1969), 73, 101–64; William W. Freehling, *Prelude to Civil War: The Nullification Controversy in South Carolina* (New York: Harper & Row, 1966), 155–292; Peterson, *Great Triumverate*, 154–69, 192–233; Charles M. Wiltse, *John C. Calhoun* (3 vols., New York, reprint of 1944–51 ed., New York: Russell & Russell, 1968), 2:passim. JCC and abolitionist petitions, 1835–36: *JCCP*, 12:xliv,547–55, 197, 13:22–26, 42–43, 73–74, 101–8, 111, 250, 443; *JCCC*, 344–45, 361–62; Margaret L. Coit, *John C. Calhoun, American Portrait* (Boston: Houghton, Mifflin, 1950), 307; Peterson, 258–62; Van Deusen, *Clay*, 316. JCC at Fort Hill 1836: *JCCP*, 11:232, 254, 257, 462, 13: 275; *JCCW*, 4:505–6; Peterson, 403; Capers, 45, 212; Coit, 102, 287–90, 250–52, 383–84, 388, 292. JCC's major speech on abolitionists: *JCCP*, 13:387–96. JCC's return to the Democratic party and JCC resolutions: Capers, 189–98; Wiltse, 369–73; Peterson, 283–88; *JCCP*, 15:273.

6. Clay. HC on abolitionist onslaught: *HCP*, 8:814, 833, 9:56, 64, 246; Van Deusen, *Clay*, 313–14. HC regrets southern defense of slavery: *HCP*, 6:94, 8:789; Peterson, *Great Triumverate*, 285. Abolitionist criticism of HC: *HCP*, 9:223, 246; Peterson, 286, 288–89. As is shown in their monologues, Garrison and Frederick Douglass both called HC a hypocrite. HC v. gradual emancipation in Kentucky: *HCP*, 8:814, 9:223, 224n, 244; Peterson, 287. HC on JCC's resolutions: *HCP*, 9:109, 123–25. HC on political abolitionism: ibid., 9:246. HC's major address on abolitionists: *HCW*, 6:140–59; also see *HCP*, 9:746, 779–81, 852; Peterson, 287. HC's political setbacks and "forever off the public stage": Peterson, 366. I also benefited from Carl Schurz, *Henry Clay* (2 vols., Boston: Houghton, Mifflin, 1887), 2:172–268.

7. Calhoun. England's abolitionist designs and Texas annexation: *JCCP*, 17:354–56, 18:273–78, 19:568–78; *Diplomatic Correspondence of the United States: Inter-American Affairs, 1831–60* (selected by William R. Manning, 12 vols., Washington: Carnegie Endowment for International Peace, 1932–39), 7:252–53; *JCCW*, 5:330–47; *JCCC*, 573–77, 579–80, 592–94, 647–48; Peterson, *Great Triumverate*, 348; Capers, *Calhoun*, 221; John Niven, *John C. Calhoun and the Price of Union* (Baton Rouge: Louisiana State University Press, 1988), 265–82. JCC's concurrent majorities: *JCC U&L*, 3–284; Peterson, 338–39, 411–13. JCC's attack on Jefferson and Declaration: *JCCW*, 1:57–59, 4:507–12; *JCC U&L*, 565–70; Capers, 244. JCC cares "nothing for slavery": Redelia Brisbane, *Albert Brisbane* (reprint of 1893 ed., New York: Burt Franklin, 1969), 221–22; Peterson, 411. I also learned much about Calhoun from Richard Hofstadter, *The American Political Tradition and the Men Who Made It* (New York: Alfred A. Knopf, 1959), 67–91.

8. Garrison. WLG to Brother Quincy, July 18, 1845, GFP SC. Texas annexation and Slave Power conspiracy: *WLGL*, 3:131, 283–84, 290–91, 300, 470; *Liberator*, Oct. 31, 1845, Mar. 7, 1846; *WLG Life*, 3:134–49; Thomas, *The Liberator*, 336–37, 374; Merrill, *Against Wind and Tide*, 210. Proslavery Constitution, "No Union with Slaveholders": *Liberator*, Dec. 29, 1832, Apr. 22, 1842, May 6, 1842, June 10, 1842, Feb. 3, 1843, Mar. 17, 1843, Apr. 3, 24, and 31, 1844, June 7, 1844, Jan. 10, 1845, Mar. 8, 1850; *WLG Life*, 3:88–116; *WLGL*, 3:118; Merrill, 204–7; Korngold, *Two Friends of*

Man, 164–65. Liberty party opposition: Nye, *Garrison*, 145; *WLGL*, 3:245, 248. How disunion would help the slaves: *Liberator*, May 7, 1847; Thomas, 348–49. Disunion a question of morality: quoted in Korngold, 165. WLG on Mexican War: *Liberator*, Dec. 25, 1846, Nov. 10, 1848; *WLGL*, 3:326, 338, 476; Merrill, 211, 214; Thomas, 343. WLG and Frederick Douglass: *WLGL*, 3:506–9, 526–27, 532–33; *FDP*, 2:86, 94–95; *FD L&W*, 1:286, 290; *Liberator*, July 1, 1842, Jan. 15, 1847, Mar. 5, 1847, July 23, 1847; *WLG Life*, 3:188–210; Merrill, 228–42.

9. **Calhoun.** Oregon: *JCCW*, 5:414–57; *JCCP*, 22:xii–xvi, 705–28; *JCCC*, 693–98; Peterson, *Great Triumvirate*, 419–20; Niven, *Calhoun*, 283–300. JCC's opposition to Mexican War: *JCCP*, 21:528–29; *JCCW*, 4:303–27, 338, 396–425; *JCCC*, 687, 690–91, 693–98, 715–16, 734, 738–39, 741–43; Niven, 302–5; Peterson, 422–25, 436; Ernest M. Lander, Jr., *Reluctant Imperialists: Calhoun, the South Carolinians, and the Mexican War* (Baton Rouge: Louisiana State University Press, 1980), 6–7, 8–11, 61–111. Polk description: Charles Sellers, *James K. Polk, Jacksonian, 1795–1843* (Princeton: Princeton University Press, 1957), 366–67. JCC's fears of Wilmot Proviso: *JCCW*, 4:347–48, 385–96; *JCCC*, 731; Wiltse, *Calhoun*, 3:309–10. Oregon bill and JCC's compromise effort: *JCCW*, 4:346–48; *JCC U&W*, 519–20. JCC's resolutions (Calhoun Proviso) and speech: *JCCW*, 4:340–49; *JCC U&L*, 513–21, 526; *JCCC*, 759–60; *TJW*, 10:157; Wiltse, 3:294–307, 351–53; Niven, 306–18; Peterson, 423–28, 443–46, 454; Capers, *Calhoun*, 235–39. Oregon bill, passions high: Capers, 224. Description of Hale: Richard H. Sewell, *John P. Hale and the Politics of Abolition* (Cambridge: Harvard University Press, 1965), 17. Description of Foote: Reuben Davis, *Recollections of Mississippi and Mississippians* (Boston: Houghton, Mifflin, 1889), 101. Jefferson Davis speech: *JDP*, 2:334. JCC's major speech (June 27, 1848): *JCCW*, 4:480–512; *JCC U&L*, 541–70; Wiltse, 3:354; Peterson, 443, 445–46.

10. **Clay.** Laments Mexican War: *HCP*, 10:285, 270, 274, 301; *HCW*, 4:517. HC's sons, Henry Jr.'s death: *HCP*, 9:391–92, 395, 10:208, 215, 220–21, 310, 315, 337, 340–41; *HCW*, 4:539–40; Remini, *Clay*, 558–59, 673–74, 681, 684–85; Peterson, *Great Triumverate*, 375–76. First speech against the war: *HCP*, 10:361–75. Speech to the American Colonization Society: ibid., 10:396–98. HC's popular-

ity: ibid., 10:420–21; Remini, 702. Taylor's nomination: *HCP*, 10:401–2, 435, 478, 489, 494–95, 497, 504, 515, 521; *HCW*, 4:541, 565, 568; Remini, 708. New danger, HC out of retirement: *HCP*, 10:497, 521; Schurz, *Clay*, 2:325–26; Remini, 713. HC's letter on gradual emancipation: *HCP*, 10:574–81, 588, 601–2, 621, 681, 808, 830, 925; *HCW*, 3:346–52; Remini, 717–19.

11. **Garrison.** Illnesses: *WLGL*, 3:550–52, 555–56, 564–69; WLG to Edmund Quincy, Aug. 10, 1848, GFP SC. Birth of Francis Jackson Garrison, Charley Garrison's death: *WLGL*, 3:599, 601, 618–19; Merrill, *Against Wind and Tide*, 251–52. WLG's full letter to Clay is in *WLGL*, 3:608–12. My version of the letter is an abridgement. FD on Clay: *FDP*, 2:206.

12. **Calhoun.** "Abolitionist" attack in House: Wiltse, *Calhoun*, 3:377, 381–82; *JCCW*, 6:295–313. The obscure Whig from Illinois was indeed Abraham Lincoln. Senate caucus, JCC's "Address to the Southern People": *JCCW*, 6:295–313; *JCCC*, 761–62; Peterson, *Great Triumverate*, 447; Wiltse, 3:385–87, 451; *JCCC*, 761; Allan Nevins, *Ordeal of the Union* (2 vols., New York: Charles Scribner's Sons, 1947), 1:326–27. Toombs description: Benjamin Perley Poore, *Reminiscences of Sixty Years in the National Metropolis* (2 vols., Philadelphia: Hubbard Bros., 1886), 1:360; William Y. Thompson, *Robert Toombs of Georgia* (Baton Rouge: Louisiana State University Press, 1966), frontispiece photo and 162. Taylor's inauguration: Wiltse, 3:396; *JCCC*, 765; Niven, *Calhoun*, 337; Capers, *Calhoun*, 244. Fort Hill: *JCCC*, 763–77, 778–80; Wiltse, 3:443–44; Niven, 328, 338; *JCC U&L*, 35–39, 45–49, 275–76.

13. **Clay.** National Hotel, Taylor: *HCP*, 10:632–33, 638; *HCW*, 4:589–90, 591–95; Remini, *Clay*, 723. Senate chamber: Fred J. Maroon and Suzy Maroon, *The United States Capitol* (New York: Stewart, Tabori & Chang, 1993), 109–10; *The Senate Chamber, 1810–1859* (pamphlet put out by the U.S. Senate Commission on Art and Antiquities, Washington, D.C.), 5, 7. Zachary Taylor description: Brainerd Dyer, *Zachary Taylor* (New York: Barnes and Noble, 1946), 184–85, 398. Embattled Congress: *HCP*, 10:639, 635, 642, 653, 658, 661–72, 680–81, 729–30; *HCW*, 4:543, 593, 600, 6:432, 453, 455–57; *JDP*, 4:26–28, 63–70, 77; *JCCW*, 4:498–99; Holman Hamilton, *Prologue to Conflict: The Crisis and*

Compromise of 1850 (reprint of 1964 ed., New York: W. W. Norton, 1966), 33, 43–46; Wiltse, *Calhoun*, 3:449, 461; Remini, 737. Taylor's special message and plan: James D. Richardson (ed.), *A Compilation of the Messages and Papers of the Presidents* (20 vols., New York: Bureau of National Literature [1917]), 5:26–30, 18–19; *HCW*, 4:610, 6:473–78, 475; *HCP*, 10:695, 720; Hamilton, 13–17, 46–47; Wiltse, 3:453; *JCCC*, 778–80; Niven, *Calhoun*, 338, 340. HC matures a plan, sees Webster: *HCW*, 4:600, 601; Van Deusen, *Clay*, 399; Claude M. Fuess, *Daniel Webster* (2 vols., Boston: Little, Brown, 1930), 2:204–5; Frederic Austin Ogg, *Daniel Webster* (Philadelphia: George W. Jacobs & Co., 1914), 413–14 (Webster description). HC's resolutions and speech: *HCP*, 10:655–57, 661–72, 675, 680, 682, 687; *HCW*, 6:394–409, 577, 603; *CG*, 31st Cong., 1 Sess. (1849–50), Appendix, 115–27; Hamilton, 54–68; Remini, 732–40. Sam Houston description: *The Senate Chamber*, 7. HC to his son: *HCW*, 4:603. During the nullification crisis of 1833, HC had peered into the future and grimaced at what he saw. "We want no war," he'd pleaded with his countrymen on that occasion, "above all, no civil war, no family strife. We want no sacked cities, no desolated fields, no smoking ruins, no streams of American blood shed by American arms." Quoted in Peterson, 230; see also Calvin Colton, *Life and Times of Henry Clay* (2 vols., New York: A.S. Barnes & Co., 1846), 2: 232. During the crisis of 1850, HC again peered into the future and again saw "certain and irretrievable destruction" awaiting his country. HC's speech, *CG*, 31st Cong., 1st Sess., Appendix, 115–27.

14. **Calhoun.** *JCCC*, 779–87; *JCCW*, 4:542–73; Wiltse, *Calhoun*, 3:455–68; Niven, *Calhoun*, 339; Hamilton, *Prologue to Conflict*, 71–77; Peterson, *Great Triumverate*, 460–67; Capers, *Calhoun*, 248–52. My version of JCC's speech is an abridgement. JCC's prophecy (mine is not an exact quotation): Virginia Mason, *The Public Life and Diplomatic Correspondence of James Murray Mason* (Roanoke, Va.: The Stone Printing and Manufacturing Co., 1903), 72–73; Capers, 252.

15. **Clay.** JCC's death: *JCCP*, 10:692–93; Coit, *Calhoun*, 512. Omnibus bill: *HCP*, 10:713–18, 723, 760–62, 741; *HCW*, 6:414–18, 427, 431–32, 453, 455–57; Hamilton, *Prologue to Conflict*, 62, 95–155; Remini, *Clay*, 747, 750–52; Van Deusen, *Clay*, 408. Taylor's death:

HCP, 10:767, 771; Hamilton, 106–8; Remini, 752–53. Fillmore description: Charles M. Snyder (ed.), *The Lady and the President: The Letters of Dorothea Dix and Millard Fillmore* (Lexington: University Press of Kentucky, 1975), 17, 27. Collapse of omnibus bill: *HCP*, 10:736; *SADL*, 191–92; Hamilton, 111–12, 114; Remini, 756–57. HC at Newport: *HCP*, 10:792, 794, 800. Compromise of 1850: ibid., 10:803–13, 817, 863, 871, 917, 926–27; *HCW*, 4:612; *SADL*, 192–93; Remini, 758–61, 769; Hamilton, 135–84; Peterson, *Great Triumverate*, 475; *VD JD*, 1:565. HC's last days: *HCP*, 10:942, 946–67; *HCW*, 3:153–54, 4:615, 624–25, 631; Remini, 772–81; Van Deusen, 423–24.

16. **Frederick Douglass.** Resisting the fugitive slave law: FD, *Life and Times of Frederick Douglass* (reprint of revised ed. of 1892, London: Collier-MacMillan: 1962), 279–80; *FD L&W*, 2:43–44; *FDP*, 2:262–90, 303, 391, 422n; Vincent Harding, *There Is a River: The Black Struggle for Freedom in America* (New York: Harcourt Brace Jovanovich, 1981), 159–61; *WLG Life*, 3:365. FD and *Liberator*: FD, *Narrative of the Life of Frederick Douglass: An American Slave* (reprint of 1845 ed., New York: New American Library, 1968), 118; FD, *My Bondage and My Freedom* (reprint of 1855 edition, New York: Arno Press and the *New York Times*, 1969), 354. Slave days: FD, *Narrative*, 49, 57–58, 60, 68–83, 101–13; FD, *Bondage*, 90, 146, 160, 200–249, 341n; FD, *Life and Times*, 48–52, 77, 79, 83–84, 91–93, 96, 112–44, 179–80, 187–201; *FDP*, 1:401–2; Dickson J. Preston, *Young Frederick Douglass: The Maryland Years* (Baltimore: The Johns Hopkins University Press, 1980), 51–54, 67–71, 87, 93, 95–101, 108–56. New Bedford: FD, *Bondage*, 370–72; FD, *Narrative*, 117–18; FD, *Life and Times*, 211–14. Garrisonian: FD, *Life and Times*, 214–19; *FD L&W*, 1:22, 26–27, 33, 50, 59; *FDP*, 1:xxiv–xxx, xxxvii, xlviii, 1–5, 24, 29, 2:6–7, 28–29; FD, *Bondage*, 359, 361–62, 399–400. In England: FD, *Bondage*, 371; *FDP*, 1:liv–lv, 2:19–27, 59; Preston, 173–75; *FD L&W*, 1:72, 76, 87; Nathan Irvin Huggins, *Slave and Citizen: The Life of Frederick Douglass* (Boston: Little, Brown, 1980), 33–35. Homecoming: William S. McFeely, *Frederick Douglass* (New York: W. W. Norton, 1991), 145. *North Star*, Julia Griffiths: *FD L&W*, 1:75–78, 82–83, 284–90, 98, 352, 2:163, 282; David W. Blight, *Frederick Douglass' Civil War: Keeping Faith in Jubilee* (Baton Rouge: Louisiana State University Press, 1989), 19–21; Huggins, 45; Arna

Bontemps, *Free at Last: The Life of Frederick Douglass* (New York: Dodd, Mead & Co., 1971), 184–86, 197, 209; McFeely, 163–65. Assails Clay: *FD L&W*, 1:284–90, 98, 352; also *FDP*, 2:124–25, 149–50, 163, 173, 191–92, 206. John Brown, FD's growing militance: FD, *Life and Times*, 271–75; *FDP*, 2:153, 222; *FD L&W*, 1:359–60, 398–99, 2:49–51; *North Star*, Feb. 11, 1848; Blight, 92–94. Garnet: John Bracey and others (eds.), *Black Nationalism in America* (Indianapolis: Bobbs-Merrill, 1970), 73; Martin B. Pasternak, *Rise Now and Fly to Arms: The Life of Henry Highland Garnet* (New York: Garland Publishing, Inc., 1995), 46. FD urges resistance: *FD L&W*, 2:44; *Frederick Douglass' Paper*, June 9, 1854. Political abolitionist: FD, *Life and Times*, 260–62; *FDP*, 2:337–41, 349–50, 350n, 397n; *FD L&W*, 2:52–53, 155–57, 280; Blight, 31–32. Break with Garrison: *FD L&W*, 2:53–62; *FDP*, 3:14, 16–17, 627–30; *Liberator*, May 23, 1851, Sept. 2, 1853, Nov. 18, 1853, Dec. 2, 6, and 15, 1853; *WLGL*, 4:256n, 391–92; Blight, 20–21 (FD's stress); Benjamin Quarles, "The Break Between Douglass and Garrison," *Journal of Negro History* (Apr. 1938), 144–54; *Frederick Douglass' Paper*, Dec. 9, 1853. Anthony Burns: *FD L&W*, 2:284–89; *New York Times*, June 3, 5–6, 1854.

17. **Harriet Beecher Stowe.** Boston and Brunswick: *HBS Life*, 144; *HBS L&L*, 124; HBS to Sarah Beecher, June 3, 1850, HBS SDL; Forrest Wilson, *Crusader in Crinoline: The Life of Harriet Beecher Stowe* (Philadelphia: J.B. Lippincott, 1941), 242; Catherine Gilbertson, *Harriet Beecher Stowe* (New York: D. Appleton-Century Co., 1937), 127. First and second Charley: E. Bruce Kirkham, *The Building of Uncle Tom's Cabin* (Nashville: University of Tennessee Press, 1977), 111; *HBS L&L*, 118–19, 173; *HBS Life*, 198; Wilson, 233. Fugitive slave law: HBS to Sarah and James Parton [1869], Parton Papers, Sophia Smith Collection, Smith College; HBS to Rev. Dr. Paton, ACS; *HBS L&L*, 145; HBS to Henry Ward Beecher, Feb. 1, 1851, BFS; Kirkham, 66. HBS will write something: *HBS Life*, 145–46; Wilson, 252; HBS to Calvin Stowe, Jan. 27, 1851, HBS SDL. Winter, HWB's visit: *HBS Life*, 133–35, 147; Gilbertson, 130–31; Wilson, 254–55; Milton Rugoff, *The Beechers: An American Family in the Nineteenth Century* (New York: Harper & Row, 1981), 320. HBS on herself, hard Cincinnati years: HBS's autobiographical letter to Mrs. Follen in *HBS Life*, 197–200; ibid., 92–111; HBS to Calvin Stowe, May 8 and 21, 1844, June 22, 1844, July 19,

1844, Aug. 31–Sept. 2, 1844, Jan. 1, 1847, Feb. 20, 1847, BSR; Calvin Stowe to Lyman Beecher, May 6, 1844, ibid.; Calvin Stowe to HBS, Sept. 29, 1844, ibid.; Wilson, 162–234; *HBS L&L*, 86–109; Edward Wagenknecht, *Harriet Beecher Stowe: The Known and the Unknown* (New York: Oxford University Press, 1965), 51, 56, 75, 168; Kirkham, 47–48; Rugoff, 228–49. HBS's book of New England sketches was published under her own name. Joan D. Hedrick, *Harriet Beecher Stowe* (New York: Oxford University Press, 1994), 137, states that this "extraordinary recognition" gave her a "professional identity." Eliza and Underground Railroad: HBS, *Uncle Tom's Cabin* (New York: Penguin Books, 1981), 618; HBS, *The Key to Uncle Tom's Cabin*, in *HBSW*, 2:270–71; *HBS Life*, 93; Kirkham, 28–30, 37, 137; Wilson, 144–47, 193–94; Rugoff, 224–25; *HBS L&L*, 141, 145–46. Weld's book, Charles's story: Kirkham, 102; HBS, *Uncle Tom's Cabin*, 618–19; Wilson, 218. Black women's stories: HBS, *Uncle Tom's Cabin*, 626; *HBSW*, 2:257, 294; *HBS Life*, 200–202; *HBS L&L*, 141–42, 175–76; Kirkham, 115–16, 136–37. HBS and abolitionists: *HBS Life*, 87–88; *HBS L&L*, 96, 142; Kirkham, 56, 173. HBS on Negro character: HBS to HWB, Feb. 1, 1851, BFS; Hedrick, 209. Vision in church: *HBS L&L*, 146–47; Wilson, 256–57; cf. Kirkham, 72–74. Writing *UTC*: *HBSW*, 2:257–64, 257–94; HBS, *Uncle Tom's Cabin*, 618–29; also Ann Douglas's insightful "Introduction," ibid., 7–34; *HBS L&L*, 141–77; *HBS Life*, 150–54; Wilson, 259–78; Rugoff, 150, 321–23; Kirkham, 88–98, 102, 115, 131; Wagenknecht, 6, 182–84; Hedrick, 16 (family myth of HBS's mother as a saint), 213 (Uncle Tom a perfect Christian), 222; HBS to Sir Arthur Helps, Aug. 22, 1852, HBS SDL; John Anthony Scott, *Woman Against Slavery: The Story of Harriet Beecher Stowe* (New York: Thomas Y. Crowell, 1978), 108. *UTC*'s sales and success: Wilson, 279–300; Hedrick, 246. God wrote *UTC*: *HBS L&L*, 148, 163, 169; Wilson, 270, 336. Andover "Cabin": ibid., 294, 300–302, 331–32; *HBS Life*, 185. FD's visit: *FD L&W*, 2:226–36; FD, *Life and Times*, 282–83; *FDP*, 2:448, 448n. FD praised *Uncle Tom's Cabin* in his newspaper (*FD L&W*, 2:226, 227); we can assume that he told HBS much the same during his visit. WLG's visit: HBS's letters in *WLG Life*, 3:363n, 395–401; HBS to WLG, Feb. 18, 1853, HBS SDL; *HBS L&L*, 212–13; *Liberator*, Mar. 26, 1852; Merrill, *Against Wind and Tide*, 265–66. I've used WLG's review in the *Liberator* and HBS's letters to WLG as the basis for the scene describing his visit. We can assume that they talked about the same matters discussed in the documents. HBS as mediator: *FD L&W*, 2:63–64. Southern response to *Uncle Tom's Cabin*: *HBS L&L*, 270–71; Avery O. Craven, *The Growth of Southern Nationalism, 1848–1861* (Baton Rouge: Louisiana State University Press, 1953), 150–57; Douglas's introduction in *UTC*, 14–15; Wilson, 296–98, 332; Scott, 126; Wagenknecht, 105; George C. Rable, *Civil Wars: Women and the Crisis of Southern Nationalism* (Urbana: University of Illinois Press, 1989), 39; Thomas F. Gossett, *Uncle Tom's Cabin and American Culture* (Dallas: Southern Methodist University Press, 1985), 185–211. One "anti-Tom" novel was called *Uncle Robin in His Cabin in Virginia and Tom Without One in Boston*. Mary H. Eastman's was titled *Uncle Tom's Cabin—Aunt Phyllis's Cabin; or, Southern Life as It Is*. HBS and *Key to Uncle Tom's Cabin*: *HBS Life*, 203–4; *HBS L&L*, 177–78.

18. **George Fitzhugh.** Woman's proper place, HBS: *GFS*, 213–16. GF background: Harvey Wish, *George Fitzhugh: Propagandist of the Old South* (reprint of 1943 ed., Gloucester, Mass.: Peter Smith, 1962), 7–20, 72–73; John McCardell, *The Idea of a Southern Nation: Southern Nationalists and Southern Nationalism, 1830–1860* (New York: W. W. Norton, 1979), 86; C. Vann Woodward's Introduction in *GFCA*, xiii–xv. Failure of free society, defense of South and slavery: *GFS*, 11–14, 34–35, 42, 76–77, 133, 144–48, 190–91, 203, 226–71; Wish, 84–88, 106–08. Against Enlightenment, Locke, Jefferson, equality: *GFS*, 175–82; Wish, 94–96, 189–90. Against "Types of Mankind": *GFS*, 95. New Haven lecture: Wish, 129–41; Moncure Conway (ed.), *Addresses and Reprints, 1850–1907* (Boston, 1907), 112–13; GF's letter in Moncure Conway, *Autobiography, Memoirs, and Experiences* (2 vols., Boston: Houghton, Mifflin, 1904), 1:224–25; *GFCA*, 374n. GF's second book: *GFCA*, 15, 17–19, 247; McCardell, 87. GF's southern reputation, "Fitzhughisms": *De Bow's Review*, 22 (1857):543; Muscogee *Herald* as reprinted in *Illinois State Journal*, Aug. 15, 1856; Wish, 197, 209–11. GF and house divided: Richmond *Examiner*, May, 6, 1855; Wish, 152, 170–71, 208–9; Eugene D. Genovese, *The World the Slaveholders Made: Two Essays in Interpretation* (reprint of 1969 ed., New York: Vintage, 1971), 215. GF and WLG: *GFCA*, 102–5, 211, 259; *Liberator*, Nov. 23, 1855, Feb. 22, 1857, Mar. 6 and 13, 1857; Wish, 200–201. GF as South's Sancho Panza: Genovese, 153–54. Invasion of North: quoted in

John Hope Franklin, *The Militant South, 1800–1861* (reprint of 1956 ed., Boston: Beacon Press, 1964), 83.

19. **Stephen A. Douglas.** I owe a great debt to Robert W. Johannsen's scholarly biography of SAD, which not only helped me understand him and the events in which he was the principal player, but showed me where to go for SAD materials. SAD and "Appeal of Independent Democrats": *CG,* 33rd Cong., 1st Sess. (1853–54), 1:281–82; Allan Nevins, *Ordeal,* 2:112–13. SAD's remarks to the son of a friend in Major George Murray McConnell, "Recollections of Stephen A. Douglas," *Transactions of the Illinois Historical Society* (Springfield: Phillips Bros., 1900), 49, and also in Robert W. Johannsen, *Stephen A. Douglas* (New York: Oxford University Press, 1973), 419. SAD background: *SADL,* 3, 9–10, 15, 18n, 23, 25, 29, 55, 57–62, 217; "Reminiscences of Stephen A. Douglas," *Atlantic Monthly* (Aug. 1861), 205–10. Adams, *Memoirs,* 11:510–11, describes a memorable SAD performance in the national House in 1844: SAD "raved out his hour in abusive invectives. . . . His face was convulsed, his gesticulations frantic, and he lashed himself into such a heat that if his body had been made of combustible matter it would have burnt out. In the midst of his roaring, to save himself from choking, he stripped off and cast away his cravat, unbuttoned his waistcoat, and had the air and aspect of a half-naked pugilist." SAD's motives for organizing Nebraska: *SADL,* 268–71, 285–90. Wilmot Proviso: ibid., 182, 191, 241–42, 244n; *CG,* 33rd Cong., 1st Sess., 277–78. Origins of popular sovereignty: Johannsen, 227; Allan Nevins, "The Constitution, Slavery, and the Territories," *The Gaspar G. Bacon Lectures on the Constitution of the United States, 1940–1950* (Boston: Boston University Press, 1953), 97–141. Nevins claims that Congressmen Leake of Virginia and Caleb B. Smith of Indiana first suggested popular sovereignty, in the House in 1846, in response to the Wilmot Proviso, and that Dickinson later applied it to Oregon. Compromise of 1850: *SADL,* 191–94, 207, 242; *CG,* 33rd Cong., 1st Sess., 1:277–79. SAD and Mississippi plantation: *SADL,* 190; see also Johannsen, 211. New Nebraska bill: *SADL,* 271; *New York Times,* Jan. 6, 1854; Johannsen, 407–10; Nevins, *Ordeal,* 2:95. Repeal of Missouri Compromise line, Pierce's support: Nevins, *Ordeal,* 2:95–96; Glyndon G. Van Deusen, *William Henry Seward* (New York: Oxford University Press, 1967), 150–53; Allen Johnson, *Stephen A. Douglas: A Study in American Politics* (New York: Macmillan, 1908), 236–38; Johannsen, 411–15; *JD R&F,* 1:28;

JDP, 5:68n; Hudson Strode, *Jefferson Davis* (3 vols., New York: Harcourt, Brace & World, 1959–64), 1:263–66; Roy F. Nichols, *Franklin Pierce: Young Hickory of the Granite Hills* (2nd, revised ed., Philadelphia: University of Pennsylvania Press, 1969), 320–24; Henry B. Learned, "The Relation of Philip Phillips to the Repeal of the Missouri Compromise of 1854," *Mississippi Valley Historical Review* (Mar., 1922), 303–17. SAD's speech, Jan. 30, 1854, and debates: *CG,* 34th Cong., 1st Sess. (1853–54), 1:275ff., Appendix, 139, 262–70, 325–38, 340, 342, 346–47, 390, 768–71, 783; *SADL,* 283, 285–90; Charles Sumner, *Works* (15 vols., Boston: Lee & Shepard, 1870–83), 3:320, 332; William H. Seward, *Works* (ed. George E. Baker, 5 vols., reprint of 1853–84 ed., New York: AMS Press, 1972), 4:455–79; Frederic Bancroft, *Life of William H. Seward* (2 vols., New York: Harper & Brothers, 1900), 1:357–59; *New York Times,* Jan. 19, 1854; Nevins, 2:114, 135, 143–44, 301; Johnson, 238–56; Johannsen, 423–31; Hans L. Trefousse, *The Radical Republicans: Lincoln's Vanguard for Racial Justice* (New York: Alfred A. Knopf, 1969), 71–74. Description of Toombs: Poore, *Reminiscences,* 1:360; *VD JD,* 1:409–12; photographs in Thompson, *Toombs.* SAD's cursing: New York *Tribune,* Mar. 7, 1854. SAD passed Kansas-Nebraska bill himself: J. Madison Cutts, *A Brief Treatise Upon Constitutional and Party Questions and the History of Political Parties* (New York: D. Appleton and Co., 1866), 122–23; also quoted in Nevins, 2:113; Johannsen, 434. Backlash: *SADL,* 315–20; *New York Times,* June 6 and 7, 1854; Rodman M. Price to SAD, June 9, 1854, SADP; Nevins, 2:128, 333; Johannsen, 445, 450–51; Johnson, 258 (they called him "Judas," "traitor Arnold"); Albert Beveridge, *Abraham Lincoln, 1809–1858* (2 vols., Boston: Houghton, Mifflin, 1928), 2:231. SAD's effigy: George Fort Milton, *The Eve of Conflict: Stephen A. Douglas and the Needless War* (Boston: Houghton, Mifflin, 1934), 175.

20. **Garrison.** Reaction to Kansas-Nebraska Act: *Liberator,* May 26, 1854, June 15, 1855; *WLG Life,* 3:406–11. Steps of Slave Power plot: see *FDP,* 2:548, 468n. FD's criticism of SAD: ibid., 548–57. Stowe's "Appeal": New York *Independent,* Mar. 2, 1854; *HBS L&L,* 210–12. Wendell Phillips's dismay: *WLG Life,* 3:411. WLG's burning of Constitution: *Liberator,* July 7, 1854; Boston *Daily Commonwealth,* July 5, 1854; Boston *Daily Atlas,* July 6, 1854; Nye, *Garrison,* 164; also described in Merrill, *Against Wind and Tide,* 268; Thomas, *Liberator,* 387; Korngold, *Two Friends of Man,* 239.

21. **Abraham Lincoln.** Reaction to Kansas-Nebraska Act: *ALCW*, 2:247–83, 398–410. Hatred of and opposition to slavery: ibid., 1:75, 2:126–32, 320, 385, 494, 3:29. No abolitionist: ibid., 1:272–73, 2:130. Containment, Wilmot man, colonization: ibid., 2:131–32, 235, 238–39, 242–45, 249–50, 252, 255–56, 262–67. From the mid-1850s on, Lincoln argued in speech after speech that containing the spread of slavery would lead to its "ultimate extinction." SAD in Chicago: Chicago *Tribune*, Sept. 2, 1854; *New York Times*, Sept. 6, 1854; "Reminiscences of Stephen A. Douglas," *Atlantic Monthly* (Aug. 1861), 211; Johannsen, *Douglas*, 453–54; *SADL*, 327, 327n, 331; Nevins, *Ordeal*, 2:337–38. AL's illustration as response to SAD: *ALCW*, 2:230. Springfield, AL paced in lobby, said he would answer SAD: Benjamin P. Thomas, *Abraham Lincoln: A Biography* (New York: Alfred A. Knopf, 1952), 148. AL's dress: Beveridge, *Lincoln,* 2:243. AL description: *HL*, 405–6 passim; J. G. Randall, *Mr. Lincoln* (ed. Richard N. Current, New York: Dodd, Mead & Co., 1957), 29–30; *ALCW*, 3:512. "Peoria Speech": ibid., 247–83. Failed try for the Senate: Elihu Washburne to AL, Nov. 14, 1854, RTLC; *ALCW*, 2:288, 296–306; *ALCWS*, 65, 66–67; Beveridge, *Lincoln*, 2:274–90; also described in Thomas, 153–54, and Don E. Fehrenbacher, *Prelude to Greatness: Lincoln in the 1850's* (Stanford: Stanford University Press, 1962), 38–39. Ready to fuse: *ALCW*, 2:316–17. Letter to Speed: ibid., 2:320–23. AL reacts to Fitzhugh: Wish, *Fitzhugh*, 152–55; David Donald, *Lincoln's Herndon* (New York: Alfred A. Knopf, 1948), 93, 128–29; Herndon to Trumbull, Feb. 15, 1856, LTP; Beveridge, 2:436–39; *ALCW*, 2:222–23, 318, 353. AL didn't know that Fitzhugh had authored the unsigned articles in the Richmond *Examiner*. Bloomington: *ALCW*, 2:340–41; *HL*, 383–85; Elwell Crissey, *Lincoln's Lost Speech* (New York: Hawthorn Books, 1967), 117–221, 297 (description of Wentworth); Fehrenbacher, 44–47; Beveridge, 2:361–80.

22. **John Brown.** To Kansas: *JB L&L*, 563; John Brown Jr. to JB, June 29, 1854, FSH. Fear of and dependence on God: Notes for a sermon in JB's handwriting, BSC; JB to Frederick Douglass, Jan. 9, 1854, *Frederick Douglass' Paper*, Jan. 27, 1854. Brown's letters and other recorded utterances in the 1830s, 1840s, and 1850s rang with statements about his fear and dependence on God. See, for example, Stephen B. Oates, *To Purge This Land with Blood* (New

York: Harper & Row, 1970), 15, 22, 30–31, 50, 77–78, 81, and *JBR*, 48, 50, 52, 57, 67, 79–80, 82. Slave boy episode: John Brown to Henry L. Stearns, June 15, 1857, BSC; Oates, 30–31. Northern indifference: *JBR*, 61–64; JB to FD, Jan. 9, 1854, *Frederick Douglass' Paper*, Jan. 27, 1854. JB's oath: *JBR*, 181. JB and FD: FD, *Life and Times*, 273–75. League of Gileadites: *JBR*, 76–78; *JB L&L*, 132. JB's love for blacks: Oates, 32–33, 62–63. JB's reasons for going to Kansas: ibid., 82–93. John Jr. on conditions in Kansas: John Jr. to his father, May 20, 1855, Fernand Julius Dreer Papers, Historical Society of Pennsylvania, Philadelphia; JB to Mary Brown, Oct. 13, 1855, JB KSHS; *JBR*, 89–90; Oates, 97–103. God raised JB to "break the jaws of the wicked": Sarah Everett to a relative, Dec. 31, 1859, John Everett Papers, Kansas State Historical Society. Wakarusa War and aftermath: JB's letter in *JBR*, 90–92. Winter, new and shocking outrages: JB to Mary Brown, Feb. 1, 1856, JB KSHS; Oswald Garrison Villard, *John Brown, 1800–1859: A Biography Fifty Years After* (reprint of 1910 ed., New York: Alfred A. Knopf, 1943), 129; "Howard Report," *U.S. House Committee Reports* (1855–56), 2:981ff.; Oates, 112–14. Pierce, Federal troops, Giddings: *JB L&L*, 223; JB to Giddings, Feb. 20, 1856, Villard, 131; Giddings to JB, Mar. 17, 1856, JB KSHS; Richard D. Webb, *Life and Letters of John Brown* (London: Smith Elder & Co., 1861), 420. Settlers' meeting: Oates, 118–19. Pottawatomie Rifles: John Brown Jr. to Friend Louisa, Mar. 29, 1856, BSC; Oates, 117–18. Proslavery court, proslavery men on the Pottawatomie, Georgia company: ibid., 119–24; Villard, 155; James C. Malin, *John Brown and the Legend of Fifty-Six* (reprint of 1942 ed., New York: Haskell House Publishers, 1971), 540–56. The Pottawatomie massacre: Hanway's reminiscences in Malin, 328–30; JB to Mary Brown and children, June 24, 1856, JB ISHL; Hanway to James Redpath, Mar. 12, 1860, James Hanway Papers, Kansas State Historical Society; Salmon Brown, "John Brown and Sons in Kansas Territory," *Indiana Magazine of History* (June 1935), 142–50; Salmon's statement, BSC; Salmon's remarks in *JB L&L*, 268; Townsley's "Confession," *Lawrence Daily Journal*, Dec. 10, 1879; affidavits of Mahala and John Doyle and Louisa Jane Wilkinson, *U.S. House Committee Reports* (1855–56), 2:1175, 1179–81; Oates, 125–31, 133–37, 384–85; Villard, 148–88. Jason lacked guts, JB's mind roaring with Scripture, and JB's remark "Nits grow to lice": Leonard Ehrlich, *God's Angry*

Man (New York: Simon and Schuster, 1932), 22, 8, 10, 3. JB learned of fate of Jason and JB Jr. from a *New York Times* piece sent from home: *New York Times*, June 2 and 7, 1856; William Hutchinson ("Randolph") to ibid., June 23, 1856, clipping in Hutchinson Scrapbook, Kansas State Historical Society; JB notes for lectures [circa 1857], JB KSHS. Black Jack: JB to wife and children, June 24 and 26, 1856, JB ISHL; Oates, 151–55. Black Jack: Oates, 149, 151–59. Like David of old: JB to wife and children, June 24 and 26, 1856, JB ISHL. Osawatomie, carrying the war into Africa: Oates, 167–71; Villard, 245–46, 248. Called out of Egypt: Ehrlich, 105.

23. **Douglas.** SAD blamed free-state revolutionists for Kansas troubles: SAD's report, Mar. 12, 1856, *Senate Reports*, 34th Cong., 1st Sess., No. 34, 1–61; SAD's report, June 30, 1856, ibid., No. 198, 1–10; SAD's report, Aug. 11, 1856, ibid., 1–16; *CG*, 34th Cong., 1st Sess. (1855–56), 1:638–58, Appendix, 280–89; *SADL*, 355, 356, 358; Nevins, *Ordeal*, 2:420–23; Johannsen, *Douglas*, 492. Sumner's "Crime Against Kansas," SAD's response: Sumner, *Works*, 4:125–256; *CG*, 34th Cong., 1st Sess., Appendix, 544–47; Nevins, 2:438–43. "That damn fool": Milton, *Eve of Conflict*, 233; also in Johannsen, 503. Beating of Sumner: *SADL*, 364–65; New York *Herald*, May 23, 1856; Johnson, *Douglas*, 296–98; Nevins, 2:444–45; David Donald, *Charles Sumner and the Coming of the Civil War* (New York: Alfred A. Knopf, 1967), 293–97. Election of 1856: *SADL*, 343, 361–62, 368, 371; Nevins, 2:458–59, 511–14; Johannsen, 521–23, 537; Milton, 239. Adele Cutts: Sister Marie Perpetua Hayes, "Adele Cutts, Second Wife of Stephen A. Douglas," *Catholic Historical Review* (June 1945), 181–85; *SADL*, 399–400; Johannsen, 541–42; Milton, 255–58, 277, 287. Description of Adele: Henry Villard, *Memoirs* (2 vols., Boston: Houghton, Mifflin, 1904), 1:92. Buchanan description: Irving Vassell to Uncle Stephen Barton, Mar. 23, 1857, Clara Barton Papers, Henry E. Huntington Library; Elbert B. Smith, *The Presidency of James Buchanan* (Lawrence: University Press of Kansas, 1975), 12; photograph in Philip Shriver Klein, *President James Buchanan: A Biography* (University Park: Pennsylvania State University Press, 1962), 12. SAD's visit with Buchanan, the President's southern views: based on James Buchanan, *Works* (ed. John Bassett Moore, 12 vols., reprint of 1908–11 ed., New York: Antiquarian Press, 1960), 10:84, 88, 96, 100, 106–7; *SADL*, 372; Nevins, 2:513–14;

Johannsen, 546, 550–51; Allan Nevins, *The Emergence of Lincoln* (2 vols., New York: Charles Scribner's Sons, 1950), 1:73–74, 88. Buchanan talked on several occasions, most notably in his Inaugural Address, about the Kansas troubles and the need to adopt the southern view of the territorial question; we may assume that he also expressed his opinions to SAD. See Buchanan, *Works*, 10:106–7. SAD on Jesse Bright: Nevins, *Emergence*, 1:73–74. Dred Scott decision: ibid., 91–100, 141; Don E. Fehrenbacher, *The Dred Scott Case: Its Significance in American Law and Politics* (New York: Oxford University Press, 1978), 335–414. Lecompton, SAD and free-state Kansans: Johannsen, 560; Nevins, *Emergence*, 1:69–70, 143; *SADL*, 386–89; Milton, 264–65; Samuel J. Mills to SAD, Feb. 22, 1856, and James Shields to SAD, Mar. 6, 1856, SADP. SAD and Charles E. Stuart: Stuart to SAD, Mar. 29, 1857, ibid. Walker's visit, SAD's remarks to Walker: Nevins, *Emergence*, 1:146; *SADL*, 386–87. SAD's Springfield speech: *New York Times*, June 23, 1857; Johannsen, 567–72; Beveridge, *Lincoln*, 2:501–7.

24. **Lincoln.** Dred Scott decision: Beveridge, *Lincoln*, 2:494–98, 509; Donald, *Lincoln's Herndon*, 100–107; Nevins, *Emergence*, 1:98. AL and Mary: this scene is based on the historical record, including AL's and Mary's recorded utterances on different occasions. I do not think I have violated history by depicting, from Lincoln's view, how they related to one another. Though AL was "a shut-mouthed man" about his personal affairs, I believe he would have described Mary and their marriage as I have simulated it. He would not, however, have revealed any details about their spats. As for the Lincoln marriage, the current trend among certain male Lincoln scholars is to bash Mary as an ill-tempered shrew and a terrible wife to Lincoln, which was Herndon's highly prejudiced view (see *HL*, 295–96, 424–28, 432–34, and discussion of Herndon's relationship with Mary in Justin G. Turner and Linda Levitt Turner, *Mary Todd Lincoln: Her Life and Letters* [New York: Alfred A. Knopf, 1972], 33–34, and Stephen B. Oates, *With Malice Toward None: A Life of Abraham Lincoln* [New York: HarperPerennial, 1994], 74–75). I do not subscribe to the malicious view of Mary. Lincoln's domestic affairs and his boys: Oates, 64–66, 73–74, 93, 98–99, 135 passim; Oates, *Abraham Lincoln: The Man Behind the Myths* (New York: Harper & Row, 1984), 42–45; Turners, 3–62; Ruth Painter Randall, *Mary Lincoln: Biography of a Marriage* (Boston: Little, Brown, 1953), 75ff.; Carl Sandburg and Paul M. Angle, *Mary Lincoln, Wife*

and Widow (New York: Harcourt, Brace and Co., 1932), 63–78.
Mary's belief that AL would be President: Villard, *Memoirs*, 1:96;
Henry Villard, *Lincoln on the Eve of '61* (New York: Alfred A.
Knopf, 1941), 6. AL's speech on Dred Scott decision: *ALCW*,
2:398–410.

25. **Brown.** Brown-Garrison debate: "They discussed peace and non-
    resistance together, Brown quoting the Old Testament against Gar-
    rison's citations from the New, and Parker from time to time inject-
    ing a bit of Lexington into the controversy, which attracted a small
    group of interested listeners." *WLG Life*, 3:487–88. Since the views
    of Brown and Garrison are fully documented in my text and refer-
    ences, I have simulated what they surely said to one another on this
    historic occasion. For JB's militancy, see Oates, *Purge*, 185–273; *JB
    L&L*, 131. Sanborn, Higginson, and Massachusetts Kansas Com-
    mittee: Oates, 181–99; *JB L&L*, 332ff.; Thomas Wentworth Hig-
    ginson, *Letters and Journals, 1846–1906* (ed. Mary Thacher Hig-
    ginson, Boston: Houghton, Mifflin, 1921), 77; Tilden G. Edelstein,
    Strange Enthusiasm: A Life of Thomas Wentworth Higginson
    (New Haven: Yale University Press, 1968), 196, 203–4. Scene with
    Blair: Oates, 199–200; Nevins, *Emergence*, 2:15–16. Hugh Forbes:
    Oates, 200–214, 217–18; Villard, *Brown*, 285ff. Scene on Kansas
    prairie: Oates, 219–21; Nevins, 2:17–18.

26. **Douglas.** SAD's reaction to Lecompton: *SADL*, 403–9. SAD and
    Walker: ibid., 386–87; Milton, *Eve of Conflict*, 270; Nevins, *Emer-
    gence*, 1:252, 267–68; George W. Brown, *Reminiscences of Gov.
    R. J. Walker* (Rockford, Ill.: published by author, 1902), 18–155.
    "I made Mr. James Buchanan": Milton, 273; Nevins, 1:250. SAD
    and Buchanan: reported in Chicago *Times*, Nov. 20 and 21, 1857;
    also Johnson, *Douglas*, 328; Milton, 273–74; Nevins, 1:252–53;
    SADL, 405. Renovations to Capitol: William C. Allen, *The Dome
    of the United States Capitol: An Architectural History* (Washing-
    ton: U.S. Government Printing Office, 1992), 30–59; I. T. Frary,
    They Built the Capitol (Richmond: Garrett and Massie, 1940),
    179ff.; Glenn Brown, *History of the United States Capitol* (2 vols.,
    Washington: U.S. Government Printing Office, 1901–3), 2: 122–31;
    George C. Hazelton, Jr., *The National Capitol, Its Architecture,
    Art and History* (New York, 1897), 51ff.; *CG*, 35th Cong., 1st
    Sess. (1857–58), 3:2588–89; Benjamin Brown French, *Witness to*

the Young Republic: A Yankee's Journal, 1828–1870 (Hanover: University Press of New England, 1989), 288. Buchanan's message: Buchanan, *Works*, 10:145–51. SAD's reply: *CG*, 35th Cong., 1st Sess., 1:5, 15–18, 48–50, 117–140ff.; Milton, 279, 285; Johannsen, *Douglas*, 589–93. SAD's meeting with congressional Republicans: Nevins, 1:261–63; Milton, 281–84. Buchanan's "incoherent tirade" against SAD: *Washington Union* quoted in *New York Times*, Jan. 30 and Feb. 1, 1858. Schuyler Colfax description: Noah Brooks, *Washington, D.C., in Lincoln's Time* (ed. Herbert Mitgang, Chicago: Quadrangle Books, 1971), 30–31. SAD's war against the Administration: Nevins, 1:259–69. Lecompton defeated: *SADL*, 408–9; James W. Sheahan, *Life of Stephen A. Douglas* (New York, Harper & Brothers, 1860), 333. Buchanan's special message, debates, Lecompton: Buchanan, *Works*, 10:179–92, 200–202; *SADL*, 413–18; *CG*, 35th Cong., 1st Sess., 1:523–619, 960–62, 1002–6, 2:194–201, 1025–35, 1060–1101, 1111–65, Appendix, 193–201; *New York Weekly Tribune*, Feb. 13, 1859; Sheahan, 328–53; Milton, 290–91; Edward A. Pollard, *Life of Jefferson Davis* (reprint of 1869 ed., Freeport, New York: Books for Libraries Press, 1969), 38–40; Johnson, 341; Nevins, 1:270–96; Johannsen, 595–613.

27. **Jefferson Davis** JD's illness, Seward: *VD JD*, 1:575–83; Strode, *Davis*, 1:301–4; William C. Davis, *Jefferson Davis, The Man and the Hour* (New York: HarperCollins, 1991), 261–63. JD on SAD: Strode, 1:301. Buchanan, English bill: Strode, 1:300; Davis, *Davis*, 262; *JDP*, 6:220, 222–23, 229; *CG*, 35th Cong., 1st Sess. (1857–58), 1:618. Brierfield, slaveowning: *VD JD*, 1:171–80; *JDP*, 2:245n, 4:364, 5:212–13; Strode, 1:112–22, 237–38, 240; Clement Eaton, *Jefferson Davis* (New York: Free Press, 1977), 37–41. JD's defense of slavery: *JDP*, 3:354–56, 361–63, 367, 369, 6:147, 158; *JD LPS*, 3:315–32; Strode, 1:311. Death of Sarah Taylor Davis: Strode, 1:104–6. Marriage to Varina: *VD JD*, 1:187–206, 538; *JDP*, 2:12–21, 53n–54n, 127–28, 173, 238n, 543; *JD PL*, 71; Strode 1:111, 126–38; Davis, *Davis*, 95–99. Mexican War, marital strain, back to Senate: *JDP*, 2:641; Strode, 1:157–90; Davis, *Davis*, 131–70; *VD JD*, 1:361; *JDP*, 5:212–13. JD v. Foote: ibid., 4:135–36, 207, 220, 231–32, 244, 249n, 396; *VD JD*, 1:469–70; Strode, 1:235–37. Back to the Senate after Pierce term ended: *JDP*, 6:161. JD on territorial question, against squatter sovereignty: *JDP*,

3:332–59, 4:49, 78, 5:141–42, 6:vi–ix, 134, 137–59, 229; Eaton, 73–74. "How *far* are you to push us?": *CG*, 35th Cong., 1st Sess., 1:618–19. Black Republicans: *JDP*, 5:141–42, 6:vi, ix, 228; *JD LPS*, 3:339–60, 4:63–64, 86–87, 339; Davis, *Davis*, 257.

28. **Lincoln.** Lecompton, SAD's break with Buchanan: *ALCW*, 2:427, 429, 430, 457. Herndon and Greeley: *HL*, 391–96. AL warns Republicans against SAD: *ALCW*, 2:444, 446–51. Illinois Republicans rallied behind AL: Trumbull to AL, Jan. 3, 1858, RTLC; Horace White, *The Life of Lyman Trumbull* (Boston: Houghton, Mifflin, 1913), 87; Herndon to Trumbull, Apr. 12 and 28, 1858, LTP; Beveridge, *Lincoln*, 2:544–63; Fehrenbacher, *Prelude to Greatness*, 61–64; Milton, *Eve of Conflict*, 297–98; *ALCW*, 2:443. AL and Slave Power conspiracy: *ALCW*, 2:341, 448–54, 3:53–54; Beveridge, 2:564. AL's "house divided" speech: *ALCW*, 2:461–69; *HL*, 397–400.

29. **Brown.** Peterboro: Franklin B. Sanborn, *Recollections of Seventy Years* (2 vols., Boston: Gorham Press, 1909), 1:145–48; *JB L&L*, 438–40; Ralph V. Harlow, *Gerrit Smith, Philanthropist and Reformer* (New York: Henry Holt and Co., 1939), 405–6, 345–50; Salmon Brown's statement in Villard, *Brown*, 56; JB to Sanborn, Feb. 24, 1858, JBJ OHS; Oates, *Purge*, 203, 229–32, 399. Secret Six: ibid., 232–40; Jeffery Rossbach, *Ambivalent Conspirators: John Brown, the Secret Six, and a Theory of Slave Violence* (Philadelphia: University of Pennsylvania Press, 1982), 90–159. JB and black leaders: Benjamin Quarles, *Allies for Freedom: Blacks and John Brown* (New York: Oxford University Press, 1974), 39–43; Pasternak, *Rise Now and Fly to Arms*, 94; Oates, 232–33, 240–42. JB and Harriet Tubman: JB to John Brown Jr., Apr. 8, 1858, BSC; Earl Conrad, *Harriet Tubman, Negro Soldier and Abolitionist* (New York: International Publishers, 1942), 33; Sarah H. Bradford, *Harriet Tubman: The Moses of Her People* (reprint of 1886 ed., New York: Corinth Books, 1961), 115. Chatham convention: Oates, 243–47, 400; Quarles, 42–51; Nevins, *Emergence of Lincoln*, 2:19–20; *JBR*, 111–14. Thorns in JB's path, Forbes's defection: Loguen to Brown, May 6, 1858, JB KSHS; *JB L&L*, 456; Oates, 248–51; Rossbach, 160–81. JB's great mission, interview with New York *Tribune* correspondent: William A. Phillips, "Three Interviews with Old John Brown," *Atlantic Monthly* (Dec. 1879),

743–44; William Hutchinson to his wife, Jan. 1859, *Publications of the Kansas State Historical Society* (Topeka, 1901–2), 7: 398–99; Villard, *Brown*, 373.

30. **Douglas.** SAD's reaction to Lincoln's "house divided" speech: Paul M. Angle (ed.), *Created Equal? The Complete Lincoln-Douglas Debates of 1858* (Chicago: University of Chicago Press, 1958), 18; New York *Tribune*, June 24, 1858; Beveridge, *Lincoln*, 2:585–89; Johannsen, *Douglas*, 634. SAD on AL: John W. Forney, *Anecdotes of Public Men* (2 vols., New York: Harper & Brothers, 1881), 2:179. Buchanan's opposition to SAD: *SADL*, 413, 418; Milton, *Eve of Conflict*, 301–4; Johannsen, 636. Buchanan's offer of reconciliation: Milton, 309. Chicago, SAD's speech: Angle, 9–24; *New York Times*, July 12, 1858; Milton, 311–14; Johannsen, 641–44. Buchanan v. SAD again: John P. Heiss (editor of the *Washington States*) to SAD, July 15, 1858, SADP; Johannsen, 645–47; Milton, 327–28.

31. **Lincoln.** On SAD's Chicago speech: *ALCW*, 2:502. AL's Chicago speech: ibid., 484–85; Chicago *Press and Tribune*, June 12, 1858; *New York Times*, July 12, 1858; Beveridge, *Lincoln*, 2:608. AL followed SAD to Springfield: Earl Schenck Miers and others (eds.), *Lincoln Day by Day: A Chronology, 1809–1865* (3 vols. in one, Dayton, Ohio: Morningside, 1991), 2:221; *ALCW*, 2:504; Milton, *Eve of Conflict*, 320–22, 322n; Johannsen, *Douglas*, 655, 660; Henry C. Whitney, *Life on the Circuit with Lincoln* (Boston: Estes & Lauriat, 1892), 540. SAD's Springfield speech: Angle, *Created Equal?*, 50–63. AL's Springfield speech: *ALCW*, 2:504–21. Debate agreement: ibid., 522, 528–30; SAD to AL, July 24, 1858, RTLC; Fehrenbacher, *Prelude to Greatness*, 99–100. AL's strategy v. SAD: *ALCW*, 2:530, 3:22–23.

32. **Douglas.** Reluctance to debate: Frank E. Stevens, "Life of Stephen A. Douglas," *Journal of the Illinois Historical Society* (1924), 553; Milton, *Eve of Conflict*, 329. SAD's "staying power": Carl Schurz, *Reminiscences* (3 vols., Garden City, N.Y.: Doubleday, 1908), 2:94. Total speeches, travel: Milton, 316. Trumbull's speech, SAD's reply, Lamphier's research: Chicago *Press and Tribune*, Aug. 8, 1858; *SADL*, 426; Milton, 334–36. Ottawa: Chicago *Press and Tribune*, Aug. 26, 1858; Schurz, *Reminiscences*, 2:92; Angle, *Cre-*

ated Equal?, 102–3; Harold Holzer, *The Lincoln-Douglas Debates: The First Complete, Unexpurgated Text* (New York: Harper-Collins, 1993), 40–44. SAD's opening at Ottawa: *ALCW*, 3:1–12; cf. Holzer, 45–58. AL's gait: Francis Fisher Browne, *The Every-Day Life of Abraham Lincoln* (reprint of 1887 ed., Lincoln: University of Nebraska Press, 1995), 205. AL dazed and confused: Milton, 339; Holzer, 42 ("not a young man"). AL's style of speaking: *HL*, 405–8; Villard, *Memoirs*, 1:93; Schurz, *Reminiscences* 2:93. AL's reply: *ALCW*, 3:12–30; cf. Holzer, 59–77; Milton, 339. SAD's rejoinder: *ALCW*, 30–37; cf. Holzer, 78–85. AL carried off platform: Villard, *Memoirs*, 1:93; *ALCW*, 3:133.

33. **Lincoln.** Dangerous SAD: *ALCW*, 3:37; *HL*, 404–5. AL's new strategy: AL to Ebeneezer Peck and Norman B. Judd, Aug. 23, 1858, RTLC; Medill to AL [Aug. 27, 1858], ibid.; Fehrenbacher, *Prelude to Greatness*, 125–27; *ALCWS*, 84. Freeport: Angle, *Created Equal?*, 138–39; Holzer, *Lincoln-Douglas Debates*, 86–90; *Illinois State Journal*, Aug. 30, 1858. Description of Medill: John Tebbel, *An American Dynasty: The Story of the McCormicks, Medills and Pattersons* (Garden City, N.Y.: Doubleday, 1947), 3. SAD's "plantation outfit": Holzer, 88; Milton, *Eve of Conflict*, 342–43; Johannsen, *Douglas*, 660. Freeport debate: *ALCW*, 3:39–76; cf. Holzer, 91–133; *Illinois State Journal*, Aug. 30, 1858. SAD description: Schurz, *Reminiscences*, 2:95. AL's notes for mode of attack: *ALCW*, 3:97–99, 101, 128–31.

34. **Douglas.** Hellhounds: *SADL*, 427; Milton, *Eve of Conflict*, 345–47. SAD's private car: ibid., 320; Johannsen, *Douglas*, 655, 661. Jonesboro debate: Angle, *Created Equal?* 189; *ALCW*, 3:102–44; cf. Holzer, *Lincoln-Douglas Debates*, 140–84. Train ride north: We may assume that, for the pleasure of his guests, SAD discussed the debate in typical SAD style.

35. **Lincoln.** Charleston: Chicago *Press and Tribune*, Sept. 21, 1858; Angle, *Created Equal?*, 232–33; Holzer, *Lincoln-Douglas Debates*, 186; *ALCW*, 3:29, 38. Charleston debate: ibid., 145–201; cf. Holzer, 189–233. Horizontal wrinkle between SAD's eyes: Schurz, *Reminiscences*, 2:95. AL's fragments on SAD and proslavery assault on Declaration: *ALCW*, 3:204–5. Galesburg debate: ibid., 207–44; cf. Holzer, 238–76. Quincy debate: *ALCW*, 245–83; cf. Holzer, 281–320.

36. **Douglas.** Conspiracy, AL's inconsistency: *ALCW*, 3:159–65, 171–72, 176, 212–16; Holzer, *Lincoln-Douglas Debates*, 243–47. At Alton: Holzer, 322; Milton, *Eve of Conflict,* 350. SAD's speech: *ALCW*, 284–97; cf. Holzer, 325–39.

37. **Lincoln.** At Alton: Angle, *Created Equal?*, 361; Holzer, *Lincoln-Douglas Debates*, 321–22; Miers, *Lincoln Day by Day*, 2:232; Villard, *Memoirs*, 1:96. Press abuse: William E. Baringer, *Lincoln's Rise to Power* (Boston: Little, Brown, 1937), 23, 37; Herbert Mitgang, *Abraham Lincoln: A Press Portrait* (Chicago: Quadrangle Books, 1971), 118–21. AL's reply to SAD: *ALCW*, 3:312–16; cf. Holzer, 252–68. AL's worries about fraudulent votes: *ALCW*, 3:330. Election results: Holzer, 371–73; Angle, xxix–xxx. Democrats rejoiced: Johannsen, *Douglas*, 679; Milton, *Eve of Conflict,* 352. Lincoln in defeat: David Davis to AL, Nov. 7, 1858, RTLC; Chicago *Press and Tribune*, Nov. 20, 1858; Paul M. Angle (ed.), *Abraham Lincoln, by Some Men Who Knew Him* (reprint of 1950 ed., Freeport, N.Y.: Books for Libraries Press, 1969), 50; *ALCW*, 3:339, 340; Browne, *Every-Day Life of Lincoln*, 307. Lincoln felt like the boy who stubbed his toe: P. M. Zall, *Abe Lincoln Laughing: Humorous Anecdotes from Original Sources by and about Abraham Lincoln* (Berkeley: University of California Press, 1982), 22.

38. **Davis.** Assails SAD and Freeport doctrine: *JD LPS*, 3:344–45; *JDP*, 6:vii, 588, 604, 661; *CG*, 36th Cong., 1st Sess. (1859–60), 379. Seward's irrepressible conflict speech: Seward, *Works*, 4:289–302. JD's reaction: *JD LPS*, 3:339–60, 4:63, 86–87; Strode, *Davis,* 1:313–14, 339; *JDP*, 6:228, 587. JD's farewell speech at Vicksburg: *JDP*, 6:228. Clement Clay and Buchanan on SAD: Johannsen, *Douglas*, 685, 687; Milton, *Eve of Conflict,* 357. Description of Clay: Ruth Ketring Nuerenberger, *The Clays of Alabama: A Planter-Lawyer-Politician Family* (Lexington: University of Kentucky Press, 1958), 120, 176–77, 218. Description of Slidell: Murat Halstead, *Three Against Lincoln: Murat Halstead Reports the Caucuses of 1860* (ed. William B. Hesseltine, Baton Rouge: Louisiana University Press, 1960), 3, 10. Ouster of SAD: New York *Tribune*, Dec. 10, 1858; New York *Weekly Tribune*, Dec. 18, 1858; *New York Times*, Dec. 9, 1858; *The Independent* (New York), Dec. 9, 1858. Description of Albert Gallatin Brown: James Byrne Ranck, *Albert Gallatin Brown, Radical Southern Nationalist* (New York:

D. Appleton-Century Co., 1937), 16. Brown's proposal of congressional intervention to protect slavery: Nevins, *Emergence of Lincoln*, 1:416. JD's response: *JDP*, 6:254. Cuba, Central America: *CG*, 35th Cong., 2nd Sess. (1858–59), 2:1187; Nevins, 1:449; *JDP*, 6:607, 628; *JD LPS*, 4:79. New Senate chamber: French, *Witness to the Young Republic*, 305; Poore, *Reminiscences*, 486; Robert C. Byrd, *The Senate, 1789–1989: Addresses on the History of the United States Senate* (Washington: U.S. Government Printing Office, 1988), 1:216; Frary, *They Built the Capitol*, 183. SAD a "calumniator," the "King of thugs": Nevins, 1:420, 451. Debates on Federal slave code: *CG*, 35th Cong., 2nd Sess., 2:1242–72; *JD LPS*, 3:573–74; Johannsen, 693–96; Milton, 366–69, 371. Brierfield, Varina: *JDP*, 6:244, 247, 251; Davis, *Davis*, 272. Varina told her mother that JD had "a perfect right to name the child." We may assume that she said the same thing to JD. JD description: Halstead, 121. Eye surgery: Davis, *Davis*, 273. Maryland sojourn, return to Mississippi: *JDP*, 6:251; *JD LPS*, 4:86–87.

39. **Brown.** Missouri raid, price on Buchanan's head: Oates, *Purge*, 261–62, 267; Cleveland *Plain Dealer*, Mar. 22 and 30, 1859; J. W. Schuckers, "Old John Brown," Cleveland *Leader*, Apr. 29, 1894. In Boston: Oates, 269–72; Villard, *John Brown*, 396–97; *JB L&L*, 523; JB to his wife and children, May 12, 1859, Byron Reed Collection, Omaha Public Library; Sanborn to Higginson, June 4, 1859, Higginson Papers, Boston Public Library. Maryland farmhouse: Oates, 274–83. Meeting with FD: FD, *Life and Times*, 317–20; *FD L&W*, 2:89–90; Quarles, *Allies for Freedom*, 77–79. See ibid., 63–84, for why northern blacks did not join JB in the numbers he expected. JB's expectations at Harpers Ferry, JB orders his men there: JB, "VINDICATION OF THE INVASION," in *New York Times*, Oct. 22, 1859; Osborn P. Anderson, *A Voice from Harpers Ferry* (Boston, printed by the author, 1861), 27–32; Owen's statement in Sanborn, *Recollections*, 1:183; Oates, 288–89. The raid: testimony of eyewitnesses in "Mason Report," *U.S. Senate Committee Reports*, 1859–60, 2:22ff.; Anderson, 32–62; Ehrlich, *God's Angry Man*, 299–305 (for quotation "Tell Kagi to stand firm"); Oates, 290–306; Villard, 426–64; Jean Libby, *Black Voices from Harpers Ferry* (Palo Alto, Cal.: published by the author, 1979), 96–172; Quarles, 92–108; Douglas Southall Freeman, *R.E. Lee, A Biography* (4 vols., New York: Charles Scribner's Sons,

1934), 1:397–400. JB's interrogation: New York *Herald*, Oct. 21, 1859; Sanborn, *Life and Letters*, 562–59; *JBR*, 118–27. Wise on JB's sanity: Wise to the superintendent of the state lunatic asylum, Nov. 10, 1859, JBLC. For a discussion of the question of JB's insanity, see Oates, 329–34, 411–12. JB wants to hang: ibid., 335; JB to "Dear Brother" Jeremiah, Nov. 12, 1859, *Lawrence Republican*, Dec. 8, 1859; JB's prison letters in *JBR*, 127–59. We may assume that the jailer, John Avis, who admired JB, spoke with him often, and treated him with kindness, told him what "a hell of a ruckus" the raid had caused. For the North's and South's response, see Oates, 310–24, 337; Nevins, *Emergence*, 2:98–131; Richard Scheidenhelm (ed.), *The Response to John Brown* (Belmont, Cal.: Wadsworth Publishing Co., 1972). According to Quarles, 116, a group of New York City blacks thought the raid "signalled the coming of the irrepressible conflict." Nightly fires: ibid., 108, 116; Libby, 175, 177. The hymn quoted in the text is "Blow ye the trumpet, Blow," JB's favorite. JB expected God to give him "mighty and soul-satisfying rewards" at Harpers Ferry: JB to Sanborn, Feb. 24, 1858, JBJ OHS.

40. **Douglass.** Escape to Canada: FD *L&W*, 2:90–93, 461–63, 487. FD's letter to Rochester *Democrat and American*: ibid., 460–63. FD defends violence against slavery: ibid., 460. WLG endorses JB· *Liberator*, Dec. 16, 1859. A tyrant's only penetrable point: FD *L&W*, 2:487.

41. **Davis.** JD's belief in a conspiracy: *CG*, 36th Cong., 1st Sess. (1859–60), 1:62; *JD LPS*, 4:108. Southern senators at White House: this scene is based upon what the President and the Senators said about Brown and Harpers Ferry in their writings and speeches. We may assume that they expressed their views in their discussions with one another. See Buchanan, *Works*, 10:339–41, and Buchanan as quoted in *VD JD*, 1:644–47; *CG*, 36th Cong., 1st Sess., 1:9–10, 15, 33–34, 62, 98–99, 121–22, 128; *JD LPS*, 4:162. Reward of $50,000 for Seward: Van Deusen, *Seward*, 215. Hinton Rowan Helper, *The Impending Crisis of the South: How to Meet It*, published in 1857: Nevins, *Emergence*,1:210–17, 2:117; David Potter, *The Impending Crisis, 1848–1861* (New York: Harper & Row, 1976), 386–87; Iverson in *CG*, 36th Cong., 1st Sess., 1:15; *VD JD*, 1:648–50. JB's carpetbag allegedly contained an SAD let-

ter: Milton, *Eve of Conflict,* 396. Southern states mobilized: Nevins, 2:85, 122; Oates, *Purge,*321; Clarence Phillips Denman, *The Secession Movement in Alabama* (reprint of 1933 ed., Freeport, N.Y.: Books for Libraries Press, 1971), 76–79. Debates over Senate investigating committee: *CG,* 36th Cong., 1st Sess., 1:5–145; *JDP,* 6:619–21. Ben Wade description: H. L. Trefousse, *Benjamin Franklin Wade: Radical Republican from Ohio* (New York: Twayne Publishers, 1963), 116–19, 180. The committee's investigations: *CG,* 36th Cong., 1st Sess., 150–51; "Mason Report," *U.S. Senate Committee Reports,* 1859–60, 2:1–25; *JD LPS,* 4:1ff.; Villard, *John Brown,* 533–35, 580. Seward description: Halstead, *Three Against Lincoln,* 119–20. Seward's "conciliatory" speech: *CG,* 36th Cong., 1st Sess., 1:911–14; Seward, *Works,* 4:619–43. Wilson's speech: *JD LPS,* 4:159, 161–62; *CG,* 36th Cong., 1st Sess., 1:568–72, also 1:127–28. Capitol's violent atmosphere, fight over Speaker: Nevins, 2:116–30. JD's majority report on JB: *U.S. Senate Committee Reports,* 1859–60, 2:1–19; *JDP,* 6:267–68, 620–21; *JD R&F,* 1:41. Harpers Ferry united the South against Black Republicans: Oates, 320–24; *JD LPS,* 4:118–19. Pierce for president: *JDP,* 6:271. SAD's *Harper's* article: *CG,* 36th Cong., 1st Sess., 1:382. SAD took his seat in Senate on Dec. 27, 1859. JD-SAD greeting: given how much they hated each other, they doubtlessly greeted one another with ill-disguised animosity. JD at this time did indeed look like a corpse, and SAD's face showed the strain he'd been under. His wife, Adele, had been extremely sick, and SAD had remained constantly at her side. SAD had also carried on a grueling "pamphlet war" against Attorney General Jeremiah Black over SAD's *Harper's* article (*SADL,* 476–79; Johannsen, *Douglas,* 711–16). SAD on Harpers Ferry: *CG,* 36th Cong., 1st Sess., 1:551–54. Gallatin Brown's warning to SAD: Nevins, 2:175–76. Brown's and JD's resolutions: *CG,* 36th Cong., 1st Sess., 1:494, 592, 837; *JD LPS,* 4:370, *JDP,* 6:x, 272n, 273–74. Democratic caucus: *JDP,* 6:275n–276n; *CG,* 36th Cong., 1st Sess., 1:935; Johannsen, 731. Nevins, 2:179, calls JD's resolutions "a grim sectional manifesto." John A. McClerndon saw them for what they were: "The *platform* movement in the Senate is designed to break down Douglas" (Johannsen, 731). Johannsen and other sources agree that the resolutions were a southern "ultimatum" to the Democratic convention: ibid.; *JDP,* 6:276n, 295n; *JD LPS,* 4:196. SAD a "grog-drinking demagogue": *JDP,* 6:661.

42. Douglas. On JD and Senate caucus: *CG*, 36th Cong., 1st Sess. (1859–60), 2:312; Milton, *Eve of Conflict*, 411. SAD's political machine and southern support: Johannsen, *Douglas*, 734, 740–41; John Forsyth to SAD, Apr. 5, 1860, SADP; Halstead, *Three Against Lincoln*, 9; Milton, 412, 421; Nevins, *Emergence of Lincoln*, 2:202. SAD's health and aggressive strategy to gain the nomination: Nevins, 2:209, 213; Milton, 421; New York *Tribune*, Apr. 13, 1860. Description of Richard Richardson: Halstead, *Three Against Lincoln*, 13, 22. SAD's political team in Charleston: Johannsen, 748; Halstead, 7, 17. Charleston convention: Halstead, 18–110; Charles E. Stuart to SAD, Apr. 24, 1860, and C. P. Culver to SAD, Apr. 28, 1860, SADP; Nevins, 2:216–28; Johannsen, 749–60; Milton, 429–49. SAD's response to Charleston: Edgar Eugene Robinson (ed.), "The Day Journal of Milton S. Latham, January 1 to May 6, 1860," *Quarterly of the California Historical Society* (Mar. 1932), 18; Halstead, 119. Richardson and SAD men confer with SAD: this scene is based on Halstead, 101; Johannsen, 760; Nevins, 2:264; Milton, 450–51. We may assume that SAD and his managers discussed political strategy, the Charleston rupture, the Republican convention, JD, and the upcoming Baltimore convention. Alexander Stephens feared civil war: Milton, 468; Nevins, 2:262. SAD's health: Johannsen, 766–67; Nevins, 2:209. JD's speech on JD resolutions: *CG*, 36th Cong., 1st Sess., 3:1938–42, 1970–71. SAD's reply: ibid., Appendix, 301–16. JD's reply to SAD: ibid., 3:2143–51; *JD R&F*, 1:46; Milton, 452, 453. SAD's response to JD: *CG*, 36th Cong., 1st Sess., 3:2151–55; Milton, 453–54. SAD's article: SAD, "The Dividing Line Between Federal and Local Authority: Popular Sovereignty in the Territories," *Harper's Magazine* (Sept. 1859), 521–37. SAD in bed, warning from Richardson: Richardson to SAD, May 17 and 22, 1860, SADP; Johannsen, 766–67; Milton, 454. SAD on AL's nomination: based on quotations in James Ford Rhodes, *History of the United States from the Compromise of 1850* (7 vols., New York: Harper & Brothers, 1893–1906), 2:428; Johannsen, 761.

43. Lincoln. Scene with Jesse Fell: Fell's statement in Osborn H. Oldroyd (ed.), *The Lincoln Memorial: Album Immortelles* (Springfield, Ill.: Lincoln Publishing Co., 1890), 473–76. AL not fit for Presidency: *ALCW*, 3:395, 505. AL's arduous speaking campaign: ibid., 3:368–69, 375–76, 380, 387–88, 390–91. AL's defense of free-wage system: ibid., 3:462–63, 477–81; *ALCWS*, 43–45. SAD the most dangerous enemy: *ALCW*, 3:345, 368–69, 394–95, 397–98. SAD's article, AL's research: SAD, "The Dividing Line Between Federal and Local Authority," *Harper's Magazine* (Sept. 1859), 521–33; *ALCW*, 3:522–34; Milton, *Eve of Conflict*, 387–89; Johannsen, *Douglas*, 706–12. Medill's advice to AL: letter of Sept. 10, 1859, RTLC. Columbus and Cincinnati: *ALCW*, 3:400–425, 438–63; Baringer, *Lincoln's Rise to Power*, 96–108. JB and Harpers Ferry: Chicago *Press and Tribune*, Oct. 19–21, 1859; *ALCW*, 3:496–503; Baringer, 113–26. AL's pre-convention moves: Fehrenbacher, *Prelude to Greatness*, 145, 194; *ALCW*, 3:505; AL's "Autobiography" for Fell in ibid., 511–12; *HL*, 452–53; Baringer, 131–32, 141–51; Orville H. Browning, *Diary* (ed. Theodore Calvin Pease and James G. Randall, 2 vols., Springfield, Ill.: Illinois State Historical Library, 1925–33), 1:395, 407, 409; Donald, *Lincoln's Herndon*, 131–37; AL's letter to Judd in *ALCW*, 3:517; Chicago *Press and Tribune*, Feb. 16 and 24, 1860; Judd to AL, Feb. 27, 1860, RTLC; Willard L. King, *Lincoln's Manager: David Davis* (Cambridge: Harvard University Press, 1960), 127–33. Cooper Union address and influence: *HL*, 453–545, 454n–455n; *ALCW*, 3:494, 522–50; Browne, *Every-Day Life of Lincoln*, 312–18; Baringer, 148, 153–64; Reinhard H. Luthin, *The Real Abraham Lincoln* (Englewood Cliffs, N.J.: Prentice-Hall, 1960), 209; Thomas, *Lincoln*, 202–5; Fehrenbacher, 153–54. AL's new $100 suit: Miers, *Lincoln Day By Day*, 2:271. Trouble with AL's collar: *HL*, 454n–455n. AL as serious contender: *ALCW*, 4:34, 36, 45–46, 47. Description of Judge Davis: Ward Hill Lamon, *Recollections of Abraham Lincoln, 1847–1865* (ed. Dorothy Lamon Teillard, reprint of expanded second ed. of 1911, Lincoln: University of Nebraska Press, 1994), 18–19; John J. Duff, *A. Lincoln, Prairie Lawyer* (New York: Rinehart & Co., 1960), 87, 188. Description of Swett, Lincoln's joke: ibid., 63; Zall, *Abe Lincoln Laughing*, 62. Convention strategy, AL with Davis and Swett: I have taken the liberty of casting into dialogue what the sources state about AL's convention strategy. See King, 133–36; Baringer, 172–76, 187, 193–219; Swett in Oldroyd, 70–71. Chicago convention, AL in Springfield: Davis and Dubois to AL, May 15, 1860, and Davis to AL, May 17, 1860, RTLC; Nathan Knapp to AL as quoted in Baringer, 231; *ALCW*, 4:50; *HL*, 461–63; King, 138; Baringer, 289–90, 305; Paul M. Angle, *"Here I Have Lived": A History of Lincoln's Springfield, 1821–1865* (reprint of 1935 ed., Chicago:

Abraham Lincoln Book Shop, 1971), 236; telegrams to AL in David C. Mearns, *The Lincoln Papers* (Garden City, N.Y.: Doubleday, 1948), 237; New York *Tribune*, May 25, 1860; *Illinois State Journal*, May 19, 1860; Browne, 339–42; Luthin, 219; Thomas, 213–14; Randall, *Mary Lincoln*, 179; Miers, *Lincoln Day by Day*, 2:280; AL's response to serenade, *ALCW*, 4:50. AL's managers made no binding deals: *ALCWS*, 147; King, 137–38.

44. **Douglas.** Baltimore convention a shouting match: Halstead, *Three Against Lincoln*, 221; Nevins, *Emergence of Lincoln*, 2:269. SAD on northern and southern interventionists: *SADL*, 492, 495. SAD's letter to Richardson: ibid., 492; Johannsen, *Douglas*, 770. Report of credentials committee, southern bolt: Halstead, 210–79; John J. Seibels to SAD, June 25, 1860, SADP; Johannsen, 769–72; Milton, *Eve of Conflict*, 473–79. Scene at SAD HQ: based on quotations in Milton, 479; Johannsen, 794. Good relations with Constitutional Union party, no quarter to Republicans: *SADL*, 498. JD's visit, withdrawal plan: *JD R&F*, 1:52; *VD JD*, 1:685; Strode, *Davis*, 1:138; Davis, *Davis*, 283. SAD on the stump, North and border South: *SADL*, 497–99; Henry Wilson, *History of the Rise and Fall of the Slave Power in America* (3 vols., Boston: J. R. Osgood & Co., 1872–77), 2:699; David R. Barbee and Milledge L. Bonham, Jr. (eds.), "The Montgomery Address of Stephen A. Douglas," *Journal of Southern History* (Nov. 1939), 551; Johnson, *Douglas*, 431–34; Johannsen, 778–98; Milton, 485–96; Nevins, 2:290–98. "Lincoln is the next President": Sheridan letter in Wilson, *History of the Rise and Fall of the Slave Power*, 2:700; Johnson, 437.

45. **Lincoln.** Remarks on campaign and on SAD: *ALCW*, 4:82, 90, 91, 126–27, also 123–24; Ohio State Republican Central Committee to AL, Oct. 17, 1860, RTLC. AL with reporters and visitors: we can assume that AL told them what he told others in his correspondence. See *ALCW*, 4:56–57, 68, 71, 82, 90, 91, 95. Election campaign in Springfield: Angle, *"Here I Have Lived,"* 242–46; *ALCW*, 4:91–92. Abusive campaign, Lincoln assailed by Democrats North and South: Oates, *Malice*, 185–89; Potter, *Impending Crisis*, 434–41; Richard N. Current, *The Lincoln Nobody Knows* (New York: McGraw-Hill, 1958), 28–29; Michael Davis, *The Image of Lincoln in the South* (Knoxville: University of Tennessee Press, 1971), 3–23, 272–73; Steven E. Channing, *Crisis of Fear: Secession in South Carolina* (New

York: Simon and Schuster, 1970), 229–39; Nevins, *Emergence of Lincoln*, 2:287–98, 306–9; Donald E. Reynolds, *Editors Make War: Southern Newspapers in the Secession Crisis* (Nashville: Vanderbilt University Press, 1970), 55–58, 116–17, 124–26; J. G. Randall, *Lincoln the President* (4 vols., New York: Dodd, Mead, 1945–55), 1:186–92; George S. Bryan, *The Great American Myth* (New York: Carrick & Evans, 1940), 390; *Southern Advocate*, Dec. 12, 1860; Atlanta *Southern Confederacy* as quoted in *New York Times*, Aug. 7, 1860. These were serious threats: Frank Blair and others to AL, Oct. 31, 1860, RTLC. AL on the threats: *ALCW*, 4:95. Sanford's interview: *ALC*, 35–37. Election day: New York *Tribune*, Nov. 7, 8, 10, and 12, 1860; Mitgang, *Press Portrait*, 212–18; *Illinois State Journal*, Nov. 7, 1860; Angle, "*Here I Have Lived*," 251–53; Harry E. Pratt, *Concerning Mr. Lincoln* (Springfield: Abraham Lincoln Association, 1944), 27–29; William E. Baringer, *A House Dividing: Lincoln as President Elect* (Springfield: Abraham Lincoln Association, 1945), 4–7; Luthin, *Real Lincoln*, 237; Thomas, *Lincoln*, 225; *ALC*, 37–38; Randall, *Mary Lincoln*, 186–90.

46. **Douglas.** In Forsyth's office: Sheridan letter in Wilson, *History of the Rise and Fall of the Slave Power*, 2:700; *Illinois State Register*, Nov. 22, 1860, quoting Forsyth's Mobile *Register*; Johnson, *Douglas*, 439; Milton, *Eve of Conflict*, 500; Johannsen, *Douglas*, 803. Forsyth for secession: Forsyth to SAD, Dec. 12, 1860, SADP; also quoted in Johannsen, 808. We can assume that Forsyth told SAD in person that the South must separate if AL won. SAD in New Orleans: *New York Times*, Nov. 15, 1860; Johannsen, 806; *SADL*, 499–502.

47. **Douglass.** Home from England: *FD L&W*, 2:95. On Republicans: ibid., 484, 494–97, 527–28; Blight, *Douglass' Civil War*, 53, 56–57, 60; Benjamin Quarles, *Frederick Douglass* (reprint of 1948 ed., New York: Atheneum, 1968), 162–63.

48. **Stowe.** Henry Stowe's death: *HBS L&L*, 243–45, 248, 253; *HBS Life*, 340–41; Wagenknecht, *Stowe*, 165, 199–201; Hedrick, *Stowe*, 277–80. Lincoln's election: *Independent*, Nov. 15, Dec. 20, 1860.

49. **Garrison.** On AL: *Liberator*, Sept. 7, Nov. 9, 1860; Thomas, *Liberator*, 399; *WLG Life*, 3:494–505; Nye, *Garrison*, 168–69; Merrill,

Against Wind and Tide, 273. AL's victory: *Liberator*, Nov. 16, 1860 (printed in Cain [ed.], *Garrison and the Fight Against Slavery: Selections from the Liberator*, 162–63).

50. **Davis.** Rhett's letter: *JDP*, 6:369. Governor's conference: *JD R&F*, 1:58; *JDP*, 370n–71n; Strode, *Davis*, 1:363; Davis, *Davis*, 287. Description of Pettus: John K. Bettersworth, *Confederate Mississippi: the People and Policies of a Cotton State in Wartime* (Baton Rouge: Louisiana State University Press, 1943), 46–47; William Howard Russell, *My Diary North and South* (ed. Fletcher Pratt, New York: Harper & Brothers, 1954), 299. Varina's greeting: *JDP*, 6:371–72. JD and Buchanan: *JD R&F*, 1:58–59; *JDP*, 6:376n; Strode, 1:364–65. Buchanan's message: Buchanan, *Works*, 11:7–26. JD's response: *CG*, 36th Cong., 2nd Sess. (1860–61), 1:30. Clingman's response: ibid., 3–5. JD's speech: ibid., 28, 30; also in *JD LPS*, 4:544–45. Iverson's speech: *CG*, 36th Cong., 2nd Sess., 1:11–12. Wade's speech: ibid., 102. Iverson's observations: ibid., 12; Nevins, *Emergence*, 2:385 ("deeper than hell"). The fraternal Union was dear to JD: *CG*, 36th Cong., 2nd Sess., 1:30. Southern address "To Our Constituents": *JDP*, 6:377, 377n–378n; Strode, 1:368–69; Davis, *Davis*, 19–20. Crittenden urges compromise, description: Mrs. Chapman Coleman (ed.), *The Life of John J. Crittenden, with Selections from His Correspondence and Speeches* (2 vols., Philadelphia: J.B. Lippincott & Co., 1873), 1:153–54, 333; Albert D. Kirwan, *John J. Crittenden: The Struggle for the Union* (Lexington: University of Kentucky Press, 1962), 15. JD on Committee of Thirteen: *JDP*, 6:378n; Strode, 1:369; *CG*, 36th Cong., 2nd Sess., 1:19ff., 243. Breckinridge description: William C. Davis, *Breckinridge: Statesman, Soldier, Symbol* (Baton Rouge: Louisiana State University Press, 1974), 88, 96, 305. SAD urges compromise: *SADL*, 505; Johannsen, *Douglas*, 813. Crittenden plan, SAD's compromise plan, Toombs and Davis plans: Strode, 1:369, 378; Nevins, *Emergence*, 2:392; *CG*, 36th Cong., 2nd Sess., 1:41; *SADL*, 505; David M. Potter, *Lincoln and His Party in the Secession Crisis* (New Haven: Yale University Press, 1942), 171–72; Johannsen, 816–17.

51. **Lincoln.** No compromise on territorial issue: *ALCW*, 4:149–50, 151–54, 183. Appeals to AL to do something: Joshua Speed to AL, Nov. 14, 1860, William Cullen Bryant to AL, Nov. 10, 1861, Horace Greeley to AL, Dec. 22, 1860, and numerous other letters

to AL, RTLC; Baringer, *House Dividing*, 234–47. About 150 people called on AL each day at the statehouse (ibid., 28). AL's response to appeals: John G. Nicolay's notes in Helen Nicolay, *Lincoln's Secretary: A Biography of John G. Nicolay* (New York: Longman's, Green and Co., 1949), 54; *ALC*, 44–43; Webster to Sherman, Nov. 15, 1860, Sherman Papers, Library of Congress; *ALCW*, 4:130, 132–33, 138–40; New York *Tribune*, Nov. 20, 1860; *ALC*, 42–45; Villard, *Memoirs*, 1:145–46; Baringer, 49, 52–55. AL's trial run: *ALCW*, 4:141–42, 146; *Illinois State Journal*, Nov. 21, 1860; Villard, *Lincoln on the Eve*, 34. AL on Buchanan: John G. Nicolay and John Hay, *Abraham Lincoln* (10 vols., New York: Century Co., 1890), 3:248; Nicolay, *Lincoln's Secretary*, 55; *ALC*, 43. Weed's visit: Thurlow Weed, *Autobiography* (reprint of 1883 ed., New York: Da Capo Press, 1970), 605–14; *ALC*, 54–61; *ALCW*, 4:156–57, 157n, 158. AL to Alexander Stephens: ibid., 160, 160n. Letters full of warning poured in: William C. Smedes to Henry J. Raymond (forwarded to AL), Dec. 8, 1860, and many similar letters in RTLC. The Federal forts at Charleston: Nicolay memorandum, Dec. 22, 1860, John G. Nicolay Papers, Library of Congress; *ALC*, 61–62; *ALCW*, 4:157–59. Hate mail: New York *Tribune*, Nov. 20, 1860; *Illinois State Journal*, Nov. 24, 1860; Randall, *Mary Lincoln*, 190; Mearns, *Lincoln Papers*, 296, 336, 402–12; *ALC*, 43; telegram to AL, Nov. 8, 1860, and numerous other missives in RTLC. AL's looking-glass image: Brooks, *Washington, D.C., in Lincoln's Time*, 198–200; Lamon, *Recollections of Lincoln*, 112–13. See Fehrenbacher's analysis of this incident in John L. Thomas (ed.), *Abraham Lincoln and the American Political Tradition* (Amherst: University of Massachusetts Press, 1986), 33–35. Death was certainly on AL's mind. At a Republican rally in Springfield, he said that he would "be dead and gone" by the next presidential election (*ALCW*, 4:91).

52. **Douglas.** SAD did not yet despair: *SADL*, 504, 505. SAD on Buchanan: Milton, *Eve of Conflict*, 513. Buchanan's Cabinet changes and policy on Charleston forts: Nevins, *Emergence*, 2:363–79; Potter, *Impending Crisis*, 537–42. SAD's compromise efforts, anger at Republicans: *JD R&F*, 1:69; *CG*, 36th Cong., 2nd Sess. (1860–61), 1:41; Johannsen, *Douglas*, 818; Strode, *Davis*, 1:378; SAD's letters in *SADL*, 504–5. We may assume that SAD repeated to the Republicans the views and principles stressed in his

letters. JD quotation ("no human power"): James M. McPherson, *Battle Cry of Freedom: The Civil War Era* (New York: Oxford University Press, 1988), 254. Seward's plan: *CG*, 36th Cong., 2nd Sess., 1:343–44; Seward, *Works*, 4:670–78; Bancroft, *Seward*, 2:91–122; Van Deusen, *Seward*, 240–43; Milton, 525–26. Failure of Committee of Thirteen: *JD R&F*, 1:199; Johannsen, 818; Nevins, 2:396–97. SAD's reaction to Wade's speech, SAD's own speech: *CG*, 36th Cong., 2nd Sess., Appendix, 35–42. Senate reaction to SAD's speech: ibid., 42ff.; Washburne to AL, Jan. 7, 1861, RTLC; Johannsen, 820–22. Senators armed, Chandler's exercises: Stephen W. Sears (ed.), *The Civil War: The Best of American Heritage* (New York: American Heritage Press, 1991), 107. Seward's speech: *CG*, 36th Cong., 2nd Sess., 1:341–44. SAD liked the speech: Milton, 532; Johannsen, 824. Seward at SAD dinner party: Daniel B. Carroll, *Henri Mercier and the American Civil War* (Princeton: Princeton University Press, 1971), 34–36; Burton J. Hendrick, *Lincoln's War Cabinet* (Boston: Little, Brown, 1946), 148. Failure of Crittenden plan in Senate: ibid., 826; Nevins, 2:402; *JD R&F*, 1:199. SAD's hopes on upper South: *SADL*, 511–12.

53. **Davis.** *Star of the West*, JD's appeal to Buchanan: Strode, *Davis*, 1:380; *JD LPS*, 4:580–81. JD's speech (Jan. 10, 1861): ibid., 5:1–35. JD's illness: ibid., 36; *VD JD*, 1:696; Strode, 1:384. Word of Mississippi's secession, JD to Pierce: *JDP*, 7:16–18; *JD LPS*, 5:37–39; Strode, 1:384–85. JD's speech announcing resignation: *JD LPS*, 5:40–45; *JDP*, 7:18–22; *VD JD*, 1:696–97. Wade's remark ("death warrant"): Trefousse, *Wade*, 181. Rumors of JD's arrest, journey home: Strode, 1:393–96; *VD JD*, 2:5–6, 11; *JDP*, 7:27n. JD with Pettus: *JD R&F*, 1:226–27; Strode, 1:397; *VD JD*, 2:7–8. Message from Mississippi delegate: *JD R&F*, 1:237; *JDP*, 7:27–28. JD at Brierfield: *JDP*, 7:35, 37n; *JD R&F*, 230; *VD JD*, 1:474, 2:10–12, 18–19.

54. **Lincoln.** AL's departure: Lamon, *Recollections*, 30–32; Helen Nicolay, *Lincoln's Secretary*, 61; Browne, *Every-Day Life of Lincoln*, 378–80; Randall, *Mary Lincoln*, 195, 199; Villard, *Lincoln on the Eve*, 53, 66–72, 74; Angle, *"Here I Have Lived,"* 260–61; *ALCW*, 4:190. Inside of Lincoln's coach: Randall, 202. Cameron problem: *ALCW*, 4:165–67, 169–70, 174, 179–80; W. C. Bryant to AL, Jan. 4, 1861, Trumbull to AL, Dec. 30, 1861, and Jan. 20, 1861,

RTLC; Herndon to Trumbull, Jan. 27, 1861, LTP; White, *Trumbull*, 146; Randall, *Lincoln the President*, 1:264; Luthin, *Real Lincoln*, 248. AL and secession: *ALCW*, 4:192ff. AL's letter to Seward: ibid., 183, also 172, 175–76; Potter, *Lincoln and His Party*, 170–87, 247–314; Van Deusen, *Seward*, 248–49; Herndon to Trumbull, Jan. 27, 1861, LTP. Indianapolis: Villard, 75–80; Baringer, *House*, 270–72. Robert's loss of AL's satchel: Nicolay, 65. Lamon, 35–36, claims that the incident occurred at Harrisburg. From Indianapolis to Westfield, New York: Nicolay, *Lincoln's Secretary*, 66; *ALCW*, 4:129–30, 197–219, 219n; Villard, 80–87; Miers, *Lincoln Day by Day*, 3:12–16; Baringer, 273–80.

55. **Davis.** En route to Montgomery: *JD R&F*, 1:230–31; *JDP*, 7:43–45; *JD LPS*, 47; Strode, *Davis*, 1:406; Davis, *Davis*, 305–6. Montgomery depot, Exchange Hotel: *JD LPS*, 4:48. Inaugural parade: Strode, 1:410–11; Davis, 307. JD's Inaugural Address: *JD LPS*, 5:49–54; *JDP*, 7:46–50. JD's diplomacy, deemphasizes slavery, Stephens's cornerstone speech: Strode, 2:14–16, 24; *JDP*, 7:84; Russell, *Diary*, 94; Davis, 305, 319; William C. Davis, "*A Government of Our Own": The Making of the Confederacy* (New York: Free Press, 1994), 408; McPherson, *Battle Cry*, 310–12; Thomas E. Schott, *Alexander H. Stephens of Georgia: A Biography* (Baton Rouge: Louisiana State University Press, 1988), 334–35. Varina and the children in Montgomery: *VD JD*, 2:34–35; Strode, 1:425. Mary Chesnut: *MCCW*, 13; Elisabeth Muhlenfeld, *Mary Boykin Chesnut: A Biography* (Baton Rouge: Louisiana State University Press, 1981), 53, 74 (photograph of Mary), 102, 98.

56. **Mary Boykin Chesnut.** Born secessionist: *PMC*, 4–5. MC recorded her views in her diary before she called on Varina; we can assume that garrulous Mary expressed her views to the Confederate First Lady. Mulberry description: *MCCW*, 250, 256. This is a description of Mulberry in Nov. and Dec. 1861; we may assume that it looked the same to MC a year earlier. Old Colonel Chesnut and wife: *MCCW*, xxxiv–xxxv, 29, 31, 72; Muhlenfeld, *Mary Chesnut*, 47–48. Childless MC, opium: *PMC*, 41, 44–45; Muhlenfeld, 62. MC in Montgomery: *MCCW*, 8–19, 21, 31; *PMC*, 10–17; Muhlenfeld, 102. JD description: Russell, *Diary*, 93; Halstead, *Three Against Lincoln*, 121; J. B. Jones, *A Rebel War Clerk's Diary* (2 vols., new and enlarged ed., New York: Old Hickory Bookshop,

1935), 1:36. MC with Varina: *MCCW*, 13, 31; *PMC*, 3, 10–17, 31, 33–34; Muhlenfeld, 98. "We discussed the world," MC wrote. While neither MD nor Varina recorded what they talked about specifically, we can assume that MC covered the subjects stressed in her diary, and that Varina shared her concerns about JD. Sale of mulatto girl: *PMC*, 21; *MCCW*, 15; Russell, 90, described the place where the auctions occurred. MC on evils of slave system: *MCCW*, 30, 31; *PMC*, 42; Mary Boykin Chesnut, *A Diary from Dixie* (ed. Ben Ames Williams, reprint of 1905 ed., Boston: Houghton, Mifflin, 1949), 21–22, 122. Hotel parlor scene, discussion of AL: *MCCW*, 25; *PMC*, 36. JD urges her not to run from him: *MCCW*, 17; *PMC*, 23.

57. **Davis.** Executive mansion: *VD JD*, 2:37; Davis, *Davis*, 313. MC's morphine habit: *PMC*, 4. New flag: *VD JD*, 2:36; Strode, *Davis*, 1:425. JD studied AL: Strode, 1:417, 419; *ALCW*, 1:438; New York *Tribune*, Feb. 23, 1861. JD and forts, deplored Confederacy's unpreparedness: *JD LPS*, 5:61; *JDP*, 7:55, 84.

58. **Lincoln.** New York City: *Lincoln Day by Day*, 3:18–19; *ALCW*, 4:200, 230–31; Randall, *Mary Lincoln*, 204–7; New York *Herald*, Feb. 21, 1861; *New York Times*, Feb. 21, 1861; Thomas, *Lincoln*, 241. AL's manner of laughing: Horace H. Furness, *Letters* (2 vols., Boston: Houghton, Mifflin, 1922), 1:126; Villard, *Memoirs*, 1:143. Herman Melville said that AL shook hands "like a man sawing wood at so much per cord" (Melville, *Letters of Herman Melville* [ed. Merrell R. Davis and William H. Gilman, New Haven: Yale University Press, 1960], 209–10). AL at Trenton: *ALCW*, 4:235–36. AL at Independence Hall, Philadelphia: ibid., 240. Baltimore plot, AL's secret ride, AL's arrival in Washington: AL's account in Benson J. Lossing, *The Pictorial Field Book of the Civil War* (3 vols., Hartford: T. Belknap, 1874–81), 1:279–80; Norma B. Cuthbert (ed.), *Lincoln and the Baltimore Plot, 1861: From Pinkerton Records and Related Papers* (San Marino, Cal.: Huntington Library, 1949), xv–xvi, 1–123; Lamon, *Recollections*, 38–45; Seward to AL, Feb. 21, 1861, General Scott's note to Seward, same date, Stone's report, Feb. 21, 1861, RTLC; Frederick W. Seward, *Reminiscences of a War-Time Statesman and Diplomat, 1830–1915* (New York: G. P. Putnam's Sons, 1916), 134–39; Allan Pinkerton, *The Spy of the Rebellion* (reprint of 1883 ed., Lincoln:

University of Nebraska Press, 1989), 49–99; Elihu Washburne in Allen Thorndike Rice (ed.), *Reminiscences of Abraham Lincoln by Distinguished Men of His Time* (reprint of 1888 ed., New York: Haskell House, 1971), 39; Barringer, *House Dividing*, 292–96; Randall, *Mary Lincoln*, 205–8; Bryan, *Great American Myth*, 24–48; Carl Sandburg, *Abraham Lincoln: The War Years* (4 vols., New York: Harcourt, Brace, & World, 1939), 1:68–77. Sandburg also includes simulated dialogue between AL and Pinkerton. Description of Elihu Washburne: Gaillard Hunt, *Israel, Elihu and Cadwallader Washburne: A Chapter in American Biography* (New York: Macmillan, 1925), 165–66, 192, 194. Description of Washington: Russell, *My Diary*, 17–18, 195; Brooks, *Washington, D.C., in Lincoln's Time*, 13, 20, 46; Bryan, 3–12, 51. AL at Willard's, Seward: Cuthbert, 16–17, 82–83; Lamon, 46–47; Russell, 19. Hate letter to AL: A. G. Frick [?] to AL, Feb. 14, 1861, Chicago Historical Society (Randall, *Mary Lincoln*, 207). Mary's ordeal: Cuthbert, 134–35; Sandburg, 1:81. AL on secret ride: Lamon, 46–47; Sandburg, 1:81; William L. Schley to AL, Feb. 23, 1861, RTLC; Cuthbert, 149. Press reaction to secret ride: R. Gerald McMurtry, "Scotch Cap and Military Cloak a Fabrication," *Lincoln Lore* (Oct. 1956); Luthin, *Real Lincoln*, 256–57; *ALC*, 81; Sandburg, 1:78–84; also Russell, 26. Office-seekers: Villard, 1:156; Nicolay and Hay, *Lincoln*, 3:370; Randall, *Lincoln the President*, 1:291. SAD's visit with AL: *New York Times*, Feb. 28, 1861; *National Intelligencer*, Mar. 1, 1861; Miers, 3:21–23; Johannsen, *Douglas*, 841–42. Virginia and other border-state delegations with AL: John Hay, *Lincoln and the Civil War in the Diaries and Letters of John Hay* (selected by Tyler Dennett, reprint of 1939 ed., Westport, Conn.: Negro Universities Press, 1972), 30; Charles S. Morehead's eyewitness account in *ALC*, 85–90; J. P. Usher in Rice, 80–81; Potter, *Lincoln and His Party*, 353–54; Baringer, *House Dividing*, 315–18, 321, 329. AL's Inaugural Address completed: *ALCW*, 4:249–62; Potter, 327–28. AL on secession: *ALCW*, 4:154, 421–40; Nicolay and Hay, *Lincoln*, 3:248; Zall, *Abe Lincoln Laughing*, 55–56; Nicolay, *Lincoln's Secretary*, 54–55; Current, *Lincoln Nobody Knows*, 100–103. L. Pierce Clark, *Abraham Lincoln, A Psycho-Biography* (New York: Charles Scribner's Sons, 1933), quotes Lincoln in a frontispiece: "I had my ambitions— yes—as every American boy worth his salt has. And I dared to dream this vision of the White House,—I the humblest of the humble, born in a lowly pioneer's cabin in the woods of Kentucky. My dream came true, and where is its glory? Ashes and blood. I . . . have lived with aching heart through it all and envied the dead their rest on the battlefields." Inauguration: *New York Times*, Mar. 5, 1861; Bryan, 53–55; Miers, 3:24–26; Randall, *Mary Lincoln*, 208–9; AL–Mary Lincoln dialogue in Elizabeth Keckley, *Behind the Scenes: Thirty Years a Slave and Four Years in the White House* (New York: Arno Press and the New York Times, 1968), 124–25; Nicolay, *Lincoln's Secretary*, 71–73; Browne, *Every-Day Life of Lincoln*, 402–8; R. Gerald McMurtry, "The Inauguration of Abraham Lincoln," *Lincoln Lore* (Jan. 1952); Poore, *Reminiscences*, 2:69; New York *Herald*, Mar. 5, 1861; *New York Times*, Mar. 5, 1861; New York *Tribune*, Mar. 5 and 6, 1861; Lamon, 53–55; Thomas, *Lincoln*, 245. SAD at AL's Inauguration: "Reminiscences of Stephen A. Douglas," *Atlantic Monthly* (Aug. 1861), 212; Allan Nevins, "He Did Hold Lincoln's Hat," *American Heritage* (Feb. 1959), 98–99; Benjamin Perley Poore in Rice, 225–26. AL's Inaugural Address, *ALCW*, 4:262–71.

59. **Douglas.** AL's Inauguration: "Reminiscences of Stephen A. Douglas," *Atlantic Monthly* (Aug. 1861), 212; *New York Times*, Mar. 5 and 7, 1861; Johannsen, *Douglas*, 844; Milton, *Eve of Conflict*, 547; Nicolay, *Lincoln's Secretary*, 73. Southern reaction: Alvy L. King, *Louis T. Wigfall, Southern Fire-eater* (Baton Rouge: Louisiana State University Press, 1970), 111; Reynolds, *Editors Make War*, 190–95; Mitgang, *Lincoln, A Press Portrait*, 242–44. Inaugural Ball: "Reminiscences of Stephen A. Douglas," 212; Margaret Leech, *Reveille in Washington, 1860–1865* (New York: Harper & Brothers, 1941), 46; Miers, *Lincoln Day by Day*, 3:26; also Milton, 548; Randall, *Mary Lincoln*, 209–10.

60. **Lincoln.** Anderson's letter: Miers, *Lincoln Day by Day*, 3:26; Anderson's report and Joseph Holt and Winfield Scott to Lincoln, Mar. 5, 1861, and Scott to Lincoln, Mar. 11, 1861, RTLC. I am greatly indebted to Richard N. Current's excellent study, *Lincoln and the First Shot* (New York: J. B. Lippincott, 1963), 43 passim. My account also draws generally from Van Deusen, *Seward*, 276–85; Potter, *Lincoln and His Party*, 337–66; Potter, *Impending Crisis*, 570–83; John Niven, *Gideon Welles, Lincoln's Secretary of the Navy* (New York: Oxford University Press, 1973), 325–30; Kenneth M. Stampp, *And the War Came: The North and the Secession Crisis* (reprint of 1950

ed., Chicago: University of Chicago Press, 1964), 263–86; Allan Nevins, *The War for the Union* (4 vols., New York: Charles Scribner's Sons, 1959–71), 1:39–66; Randall, *Lincoln the President*, 1:311–50; Seward, *Reminiscences*, 145–50. Specific documentation for Sumter crisis: Gideon Welles, *Diary* (ed. John T. Morse, 3 vols., Boston: Houghton, Mifflin, 1909–11), 1:13–15; replies of Cabinet members to AL's interrogatory in RTLC; AL's memorandum on Sumter, *ALCW*, 4:288–90; "loaves and fishes" in Luthin, *Real Lincoln*, 288; "man letting lodgings" in Nicolay and Hay, *Lincoln*, 4:69, also 44; AL's troubles and anxieties in Browning, *Diary*, 1:476; *ALC*, 43–61; Villard, *Memoirs*, 1:159; *New York Times*, Apr. 3, 1861; Gideon Welles, *Lincoln and Seward* (reprint of 1874 ed., Freeport, N.Y.: Books for Libraries Press, 1969), 64–65; Seward's Apr. 1 memorandum to AL in RTLC; AL's reply, *ALCW*, 4:316–17, also 424–25, on Pickens; Seward on AL as "the best of us" in Thomas, *Lincoln*, 254; AL's meeting with Baldwin in *ALC*, 102–7. Weather in Washington Apr. 7 and 8, 1861: Russell, *My Diary*, 41.

61. **Davis.** Sumter crisis: *JD R&F*, 1:265–92; *JDP*, 7:88, 101; *JD LPS*, 5:67–68n, 71–75, 82, 98; *JD MP*, 1:60, 63–82; *ALCW*, 4:425; Davis, *Davis*, 322–24; Strode, *Davis*, 2:31–43.

62. **Chesnut.** *PMC*, 55–60; *MCCW*, 40–46; *JD R&F*, 2:292; MC, *Diary from Dixie*, 31–34. Description of Wigfall: Eric H. Walers, *The Fire-Eaters* (Baton Rouge: Louisiana State University Press, 1992), 160.

63. **Davis.** *JD R&F*, 2:289–92; *JDP*, 7:102; Davis, *Davis*, 324–25.

64. **Lincoln.** *ALCW*, 4:331–32, 425–28; Nicolay and Hay, *Lincoln*, 4:70–78; Seward, *Reminiscences*, 152; Union men of Virginia convention to AL, Mar. 10, 1861, RTLC; Welles, *Diary*, 1:39; Potter, *Lincoln and His Party*, 373–74. When angry, as he was when Virginia seceded, or even when telling a story, AL could utter an expletive like son of a bitch, damn, or hell. See, for example, Hay, *Diary*, 17–18, 111–12; Carl Sandburg, *Abraham Lincoln: The Prairie Years* (2 vols., New York: Harcourt, Brace, & World, 1926).

65. **Douglas.** Sumter and rebels: *SADL*, 512–13. SAD would hang them all: "Reminiscences of Stephen A. Douglas," *Atlantic*

Monthly (Aug. 1861), 212. With AL: *SADL*, 509–10; *ALC*, 110–11; *CG*, 36th Cong., 2nd Sess. (1860–61), 2:1438; "Reminiscences of Stephen A. Douglas," 212; Randall, *Lincoln*, 1:376–78; Johannsen, *Douglas*, 859–60; Luthin, *Real Lincoln*, 278; also Welles, *Diary*, 1:32–34. Only two parties now: Forney, *Anecdotes*, 1:224; Johnson, *Douglas*, 478.

66. **Chesnut.** *PMC*, 60–61; *MCCW*, 49–50; Muhlenfeld, *Mary Chesnut*, 107.

67. **Douglass.** *FD L&W*, 3:89–92; *FDP*, 3:424, 487.

68. **Garrison.** WLG to T. B. Drew, Apr. 25, 1861, WLG BPL; *WLGL*, 4:2–3, 17, 19, 28n; *Liberator*, May 3, 1861; *WLG Life*, 3:508, 4:10, 17–19, 20–21, 25–27, 30–31; Merrill, *Against Wind and Tide*, 278; James M. McPherson, *The Struggle for Equality: Abolitionists and the Negro in the Civil War and Reconstruction* (Princeton: Princeton University Press, 1964), 52, 55.

69. **Stowe.** Andover's excitement, student drills, "John Brown's Body": *Independent*, June 13, 1861; Wilson, *Crusader in Crinoline*, 469–70; Rugoff, *The Beechers*, 352. "Let us look at this in the face": *Independent*, Apr. 25, 1861. God's judgment, great company of weepers: *HBS L&L*, 258; *HBS Life*, 363.

70. **Fitzhugh.** GF for disunion: Ulrich Bonnell Phillips, *The Course of the South to Secession: An Interpretation* (ed. E. Merton Coulter, reprint of 1939 ed., New York: Hill and Wang, 1964), 160. Negro inferiority: GF, "The Black and White Races of Men," *De Bow's Review*, 30 (1861):446–56; McCardell, *The Idea of a Southern Nation*, 89–90; Wish, *Fitzhugh*, 298–99. The clash of arms: GF, "The Message, the Constitution, and the Times," *De Bow's Review*, 30 (1861):156–67; Wish, 300–302. Good of war: GF, "The Uses and Morality of War and Peace," *De Bow's Review* (new series), 1 (1866): 75–77; Wish, 310–11.

71. **Davis.** JD's review of the causes of the war: Message to Congress, Apr. 29, 1861, in *JD LPS*, 5:67–85; also in *JD MP*, 1:63–82. "We seceded to rid ourselves of the rule of the majority," JD said in

1864. See Alan T. Noland, *Lee Considered: General Robert E. Lee and Civil War History* (Chapel Hill: University of North Carolina Press, 1991), 45. The Richmond *Dispatch*, Mar. 23, 1863, elaborated on JD's point: "Adhering to the North . . . puts our slave system at the mercy of an abolitionist majority."

72. **Lincoln.** Based on AL's Second Inaugural, Mar. 4, 1865, AL's message to Congress, July 4, 1861, *ALCW*, 8:332, 4:426, 438–40; AL's remarks in Hay, *Diary*, 19–20.

ACKNOWLEDGMENTS

I am most grateful to the editors of the published papers, collected works, writings, diaries, or reminiscences of my speakers, which are listed in my references. Without these massive and meticulously assembled works, my book could not have been written. I am indebted, too, to the many biographers of my speakers and to numerous other specialists for breaking the ground ahead of me and showing me where to go. My debt to these distinguished scholars is indicated in my references.

Anne-Marie Taylor, my talented research assistant, not only helped immensely in the research stages of the project, but also read the manuscript and offered cogent and constructive criticism, which I appreciate. My enduring thanks to my other assistants, Liang He, Lisa May, Susanna Yurich, and James Leach, for performing their labors with alacrity and skill. Professor Emeritus Robert E. Taylor and Olga Taylor also read the manuscript and gave me helpful suggestions and ardent support when I most needed it. William C. Davis took time from his many writing projects to read the manuscript and offered constructive criticism and pointed out several embarrassing slips. Linda Davis, my friend and fellow biographer, perused part of the manuscript and understood perfectly what I was attempting to do, and I am grateful for her encouragement. Members of the Amherst Creative Biography Group—Dr. Sandra Katz, Dr. William Kimbrel, Elizabeth Lloyd-Kimbrel, Dr. Ann Meeropol, Helen Sheehy, and Dr. Harriet Sigerman, accomplished biographers all—heard segments of the work during our monthly meetings and proferred invaluable advice on structure, content, and technique. A special group—the University of Massachusetts Boston alumni, novelist

Mary McGarry Morris, Dr. Bruce Laurie, chairman, and Dr. Neal Shipley, associate chairman, of the History Department of the University of Massachusetts, Amherst, and many of my former students—also heard a segment of the book read at a public lecture sponsored by the alumni association, and I appreciate their enthusiastic response to my innovative approach. My agent, Gerard McCauley, and my longtime editor at HarperCollins, M. S. "Buz" Wyeth, gave unstinting support and encouragement through the many years it has taken to prepare this volume.

I owe a special debt to Davis Grubb, whose novel *The Voices of Glory* served as a model of how to tell a story through various first-person narrators. Michael Shaara's *The Killer Angels*, the best novel ever written about the Civil War, and Leonard Ehrlich's *God's Angry Man*, the best novel ever written about John Brown, were also sources of inspiration. To the staff of the library of the University of Massachusetts, Amherst, I offer my sincere appreciation for the professional services they rendered. My thanks, too, to the officers and staffs of all the repositories listed at the beginning of my references, for their professional help and courtesies.

INDEX